Individuals, Families, and the New Era of Genetics

A Norton Professional Book

Individuals, Families,
AND THE
New Era of Genetics

BIOPSYCHOSOCIAL PERSPECTIVES

Edited by
Suzanne M. Miller, Ph.D.
Susan H. McDaniel, Ph.D.
John S. Rolland, M.D.
Suzanne L. Feetham, Ph.D., R.N.

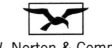

W.W. Norton & Company
New York • London

Production Manager: Jean Blackburn, Bytheway Publishing Services, Norwich, NY
Manufacturing by Courier Westford, Westford, MA

Library of Congress Cataloging-in-Publication Data

Individuals, families, and the new era of genetics : biopsychosocial perspectives / edited by Suzanne Miller . . . [et al.].
    p. cm.
"A Norton professional book."
Includes bibliographical references and index.
ISBN-13: 978-0-393-70374-0
ISBN-10: 0-393-70374-6
    1. Medical genetics—Social aspects.   2. Medical genetics—Psychological aspects.   3. Genetic disorders—Social aspects.   4. Genetic disorders—Psychological aspects.   5. Family—Health and hygiene.   I. Miller, Suzanne M. (Suzanne Melanie), 1951–

RB155.I525 2006
616'.042—dc22   2006040144

W. W. Norton & Company, Inc., 500 Fifth Avenue, New York, N.Y. 10110
www.wwnorton.com

W. W. Norton & Company Ltd., Castle House, 75/76 Wells St.,
London W1T 3QT

1 3 5 7 9 0 8 6 4 2

*To the patients and families who have taught us through
their stories and experiences.*

Contents

III. Applications to Specific Genetic Conditions

IV. Ethical, Legal, Policy, and Professional Issues

Contributors

LOUISE ACHESON, M.D., M.S.
Professor
Case Western Reserve University
Cleveland, OH

M. DOMINIQUE ASHEN, PH.D., CRNP
Nurse Practitioner
Ciccarone Center for the Prevention
  of Heart Disease
Johns Hopkins University
Baltimore, MD

LINDA HAMMER BURNS, PH.D.
Assistant Professor
Director of Counseling Services
University of Minnesota Medical
  School
Minneapolis, MN

JOANNE S. BUZAGLO, PH.D.
Associate Director, Psychosocial and
  Behavioral Medicine Program
Fox Chase Cancer Center
Philadelphia, PA

CAROLYN CONSTANTIN, PH.D., R.N.C.
Independent Contractor, Booz Allen
  Hamilton
Division of Human Development
  and Disabilities
Center for Birth Defects and Devel-
  opmental Disabilities
Centers for Disease Control and
  Prevention
Atlanta, GA

LISA S. COX, PH.D.
Research Assistant Professor,
  Preventive Medicine and
  Public Health
University of Kansas Medical Center
Kansas City, KS

MARY B. DALY, M.D.
Senior Vice President for Population
  Science
Fox Chase Cancer Center
Philadelphia, PA

SUZANNE L. FEETHAM, PH.D.,
  R.N., FAAN
Professor, School of Nursing, Univer-
  sity of Maryland
Professor, College of Nursing,
  University of Wisconsin
  Milwaukee
Adjunct Professor
University of Pennsylvania School of
  Nursing
Philadelphia, PA

LINDA FLEISHER, M.P.H.
Program Director, Health Communi-
  cations and Public Health
Fox Chase Cancer Center
Philadelphia, PA

NORMAN FOST, M.D., M.P.H.
Professor, Pediatrics and Bioethics
University of Wisconsin Hospital
Madison, WI

ANDREW K. GODWIN, PH.D.
Director of Clinical Molecular
  Genetics Laboratory
Director of the Biosample
  Repository
Fox Chase Cancer Center
Philadelphia, PA

KAREN HURLEY, PH.D.
Clinical Assistant Psychologist
Memorial Sloan-Kettering Cancer
  Center
New York, NY

SUZANNE BENNETT JOHNSON, PH.D.
Professor and Chair, Medical
  Humanities and Social Sciences
Florida State University College of
  Medicine
Tallahassee, FL

SUSAN H. MCDANIEL, PH.D.
Professor of Psychiatry and Family
  Medicine
Director, Family Programs and the
  Wynne Center for Family
  Research, Psychiatry Associate
  Chair, Family Medicine
University of Rochester School of
  Medicine and Dentistry
Rochester, NY

JEAN MCEWEN, J.D., PH.D.
Program Director
Ethical, Legal and Social Implications
  Program
National Human Genome Research
  Institute
National Institutes of Health
Bethesda, MD

NEAL J. MEROPOL, M.D.
Senior Member, Divisions of Medical
  Science and Population Science
Director, Gastrointestinal Cancer
  Program

Director, Gastrointestinal Tumor Risk
  Assessment Program
Fox Chase Cancer Center
Philadelphia, PA

SUZANNE M. MILLER, PH.D.
Senior Member, Population Science
  Division
Director, Psychosocial and Behavioral
  Medicine Program
Fox Chase Cancer Center
Philadelphia, PA

KELLY ORMOND, M.S., CGC
Associate Professor and Director,
  Graduate Program in Genetic
  Counseling
Northwestern University
Chicago, IL

JUNE PETERS, M.S., CGC
Genetic Counselor
Clinical Genetics Branch
National Cancer Institute
Rockville, MD

DAVID REISS, PH.D.
Professor of Psychiatry
George Washington University
  Medical Center
Washington, DC

JOHN S. ROLLAND, M.D.
Professor of Psychiatry
Co-Director, Center for Family
  Health
University of Chicago Pritzker
  School of Medicine
Chicago, IL

LAINIE FRIEDMAN ROSS, M.D., PH.D.
Associate Director
MacLean Center for Clinical Medical
  Ethics
University of Chicago
Chicago, IL

LISA R. RUBIN, PH.D.
Research Fellow
Memorial Sloan-Kettering Cancer
    Center
New York, NY

JOHN SCARPATO, M.A.
Behavioral Scientist
Fox Chase Cancer Center
Philadelphia, PA

KERRY A. SHERMAN, PH.D.
Lecturer, Division of Linguistics and
    Psychology
Macquarie University
Sydney, Australia

HETAL R. SHETH, M.S., M.G.C.
Genetic Counselor
Fox Chase Cancer Center
Philadelphia, PA

PETER G. SHIELDS, M.D.
Professor of Medicine and
    Oncology
Associate Director for Cancer
    Control and Population Sciences
Director, Cancer Genetics and
    Epidemiology
Lombardi Cancer Center
Georgetown University Medical
    Center
Washington, DC

SUSAN SOBEL, M.S.W.
Associate Professor
Psychiatry
University of Vermont College of
    Medicine
Burlington, VT

ERICA L. SPOTTS, PH.D.
Assistant Research Professor
George Washington University
    Medical Center
Washington, DC

LAURA STANTON, PH.D.
Co-Director of Continuing Education
HealthForumOnline
Jenkintown, PA

BETH J. STEARMAN, M.P.H.
Project Manager
Fox Chase Cancer Center
Philadelphia, PA

KENNETH P. TERCYAK, PH.D.
Assistant Professor
Georgetown University School of
    Medicine
Washington, DC

ELIZABETH J. THOMSON, D.N.Sc.,
    R.N., CGC, FAAN
Program Director, Ethical, Legal, and
    Social Implications Research
National Human Genome Research
    Institute
National Institutes of Health
Bethesda, MD

PEKKA TIENARI, M.D.
Professor
University of Oulu
Oulu, Finland

AUDREY TLUCZEK, PH.D., R.N.
Assistant Professor, School of
    Nursing
Affiliate Assistant Professor, Depart-
    ment of Psychiatry
School of Medicine and Public
    Health
University of Wisconsin
Madison, WI

HILARY TOWERS, PH.D.
Center for Family Research
Department of Psychiatry and
    Behavioral Science
The George Washington University
Washington, DC

KARL-ERIK WAHLBERG, PH.D.
Professor
University of Oulu
Oulu, Finland

DAVID WEINBERG, M.D., M.SC.
Associate Professor
Temple University Medical
   School
Director of Gastroenterology
Fox Chase Cancer Center
Philadelphia, PA

JANET K. WILLIAMS, PH.D., R.N.,
   PNP, CGC, FAAN
Kelting Professor of Nursing
Co-Director of Post-Doctoral Training
   in Clinical Genetics Research
The University of Iowa
Iowa City, IA

LYMAN C. WYNNE, M.D., PH.D.
Professor Emeritus of Psychiatry
University of Rochester
Pittsford, NY

Foreword

GENETIC SCIENCE HAS TRAVELED A REMARKABLE PATH, FROM THE 1866 publication by Gregor Mendel describing the laws of heredity, to the 1900 rediscovery of Mendel's theories, the April 1953 report by Crick and Watson on the structure and function of DNA, and finally to the April 2003 reporting on the completion of the Human Genome Project (HGP) by the International Human Genome Sequencing Consortium. At the time, some claimed that this accomplishment was the end of an era. But the completion of the HGP was actually just the beginning of the genome era. The completion of a high-quality, comprehensive sequence of the human genome, at the fiftieth anniversary of the discovery of the double-helical structure of DNA, serves as a foundation for further research and clinical applications. As a result, genomics has now become a central discipline of current and future biomedical and biopsychosocial research.

Since the completion of the HGP, several other important genomic research projects have been completed or are now underway. They include: the cataloging of common variations in human DNA (i.e., more than 10 million single-nucleotide polymorphisms, called SNPs) and their arrangement in chromosomal "neighborhoods" by the International HapMap project. The information resulting from the HGP and these other projects is now being used to establish connections between particular genetic variations and common human diseases. Contributing to these rapid scientific advances is the continuing commitment by genome scientists to global accessibility to genomic information by placing a wide variety of genome databases on public Web sites.

As a result of all of these activities, we are now beginning to unravel the specifics about how genes play a role in disease susceptibility and resistance; prognosis and progression, and responses to illness and its treatments. Building on these new approaches, it is likely that the major genetic risk factors for common diseases like diabetes, cancer, heart disease, hypertension, bipolar illness, asthma, Alzheimer disease, osteoporosis, and many other diseases will be identified by 2010. These discoveries will move us from conceptualizing disease based on symptoms and signs to consideration of the underlying molecular mechanisms of the disease. In some instances, clinical opportunities are already becoming available for gene-based asymptomatic or presymptomatic prediction of risk for illness or adverse drug response, and those applications will rapidly expand in the next few years as knowledge increases. For health care and public health professionals, an understanding of genetic and genomic technologies and information will become ever more essential, as this knowledge will increase the ability to identify those who may be at risk to develop disease, provide opportunities for interventions to reduce risk, offer improved treatments, and help to ameliorate the ill effects of diseases in individuals, families, or populations.

The advances in our understanding of genetics and genomics cannot, however, take away from the importance of studying health and disease in the context of individuals, families, communities, and society as a whole. This book provides a comprehensive framework for the analysis of the many implications of the new era of genetics and genomics for individuals and the entire family. Authored by experts across many health and social science disciplines, this book serves to organize thinking about genetics and genomics for clinical practice, research, education, public health, and policy.

In the past, biomedical technologies have sometimes raced ahead of the understanding of core biopsychosocial issues that face individuals, families, and society. To address this gap, the HGP made a significant commitment to study the potential ethical, legal, and social implications (ELSI) that would likely accompany the development of genetic and genomic technologies and information. Among the principles defined by the ELSI program are the following:

1. Ensure that obtaining genetic and genomic information is voluntary and accessible to those who desire it
2. Ensure that genomic information is properly considered in the context of other health and disease risk factors
3. Ensure that individuals and families receive a thorough explanation of this information to increase understanding and retention of the information
4. Ensure that genetic and genomic information can be kept private and protected so that it can be used appropriately to maximize benefits and minimize harm

Researchers in genomics and genetics must provide reliable data and rigorous approaches to inform practice, education, and policy. This research must include both basic investigations that develop conceptual tools, and more applied translational projects that use these tools to explore and define appropriate clinical applications, together with public-policy options that incorporate diverse points of view. To achieve the vision of genomics for biology, health, and society will require interdisciplinary research with basic scientists, clinicians, and social scientists. The era of genomics will thus reach its potential best in an environment where traditional boundaries become ever more porous.

This book offers a comprehensive review of possible clinical and research approaches across the spectrum of genetic disorders over the life cycle, including recent psychosocial research with specific disease populations. It strives to demonstrate the integration of the advances in genetics and genomics with the perspectives of individuals and families. Understanding the interactions of genes with genes, genes with the environment, and all in the context of individuals and families will be essential; that way individuals, families, and society can achieve the potential benefits and avoid the potential harms of the genomic era. The National Human Genome Research Institute will continue to engage scientists, clinicians and the public in order to meet the challenges and capitalize on the benefits of the genomic era. This book will assist in moving this field of knowledge forward. It has far-reaching implications for research, clinical practice, and basic and continuing education for all health care and mental health professionals.

Francis S. Collins, M.D., Ph.D.
Director, National Human Genome Research Institute
National Institutes of Health
U.S. Department of Health and Human Services

Preface

WITH THE MAPPING OF THE HUMAN GENOME, THERE IS INCREASING scientific knowledge that is rapidly expanding our understanding of the mechanisms, treatment, and prevention of disease. Along with this knowledge comes the expectation that health care professionals will integrate the new understanding into their practices and be able to address its effects on individuals and their families. Genetic screening and testing for inherited disease susceptibility, based on the recent identification of major genes, will soon be available on a large scale. Indeed, genomic research has made it possible to identify individuals at risk for disease and to diagnose and treat disease in ways that were inconceivable until quite recently.

The purpose of this volume, *Individuals, Families, and the New Era of Genetics: Biopsychosocial Perspectives*, is to bring together state-of-the-science information on the psychosocial and family aspects of genetics and genomics. This volume is unique in drawing together individual and family dynamic perspectives into an integrative approach. The book addresses the theoretical, methodological, and clinical aspects of the new era of genomics in a comprehensive, unifying single volume. The goal is to enable researchers and health and mental health professionals to incorporate genetic and genomic issues into their empirical studies, treatment modalities, and training. This knowledge is important to facilitate research and clinical applications in areas such as patient decision making, quality of life, behavior change, and family communication.

Typically, research into the psychosocial impact of genetic screening and testing on the individual is conducted parallel to—and separate from—research on family effects, failing to consider that they are interdependent. Also, the research has focused on what is seen as genetic disease when, in fact, the mapping of the human genome has brought increased understanding that almost all diseases and conditions have a genetic component. Therefore, all health care and public health professionals need to be able to shift their perspectives on research and practice. This volume guides the reader in the integration of this wider perspective of genetics and genomics into practice, research, and education, while weaving together the complementary approaches of the individual and family to create a unified perspective on the topic areas.

In attempting to define the territory, we strike a balance between a broad-brush approach—providing an overview of the larger conceptual, empirical, and training issues involved—and a more fine-grained clinical and culturally sensitive approach to the issues relevant to the new era of genetics and genomics. The goal is to provide the beginning of a prototype to prepare health care, mental health, and public health professionals for a future in which the genetic and psychosocial aspects of almost every medical condition will be a basic component in the detection, management, and understanding of disease risk and the promotion of health.

As editors, we represent several key areas in the psychosocial and family approaches to the new era of genetics and genomics (e.g., psychiatry, psychology, family medicine, family nursing, and family therapy), spanning the research, clinical, and training domains of these fields. As such, we bring together the multidisciplinary linkages required for the informative study and management of the individual and family issues that arise from—and in turn impact—the new era of genetics and genomics. This type of collaboration is crucial for the development of a cohesive field that not only is biologically sophisticated, research based, and clinically relevant, but that interweaves medical, individual, and family approaches together. It should also be noted that the four coeditors contributed equally to the conceptualization and integration of this volume, drawing on their specialized expertise and experience in the field.

At the individual level, we explore the implications of the fact that there are often no clear, objective, immediate health benefits of knowing one's genetic risk; that is, there may be no "right" recommendation for treatment or prevention. Decades of research and theorizing have shown that humans are not purely rational in how they process and respond to information about their health risks and challenges, especially when the information is emotionally threatening and the stakes are personal and entail significant challenges for individuals and their families. Hence, decisions about potential health risks and options need to take in-depth account of the psychosocial consequences for a given individual. Yet most researchers and clinicians are not well prepared to help people deal with such decisions, which until recently have been little more than a theoretical possibility. This volume explores the role of individual processing of genetic risk information and feedback and the implications for how to help people calculate and weigh the costs and benefits of different courses of action for themselves and their families.

While genetic scientists have been working to map the human genome and understand genetic relationships, social scientists have been working to understand not only individual patterns of response, but also family relationships. We apply family systems theories—in conjunction with individual approaches to health beliefs and behaviors—to comprehensively conceptualize the experience of patients with a genetic condition. Patients do not just experience the biological outcomes of genetic mutations; they also respond with distinctive thoughts, feelings, and interactions with family members as they move through stages of information processing, decision making, and management of genetic conditions and genomic information. This volume also addresses the ongoing complex challenges for families and individual members as they live with genetic risk information over the life course. Family systems theory, family consultation, and cognitive-behavioral approaches to coping with illness—and the threat of illness—are core elements of a comprehensive approach to the discovery and management of genetic disorders and conditions.

Finally, we explore the provocative legal, ethical, and policy aspects of genomic science. The application of this new knowledge requires decisions for which there are limited precedents. Genetic and genomic discoveries have preceded the basic scientific knowledge needed for systematic clinical applications by many years. This time lag creates an interim phase in which detection of genetic abnormalities and genetically related conditions is possible, understanding is limited, and prevention-based treatment is, as yet, largely unavailable—a period in which the consequences, from the individual to the societal level, are potentially deleterious. In this book, the authors delineate a conceptual infrastructure that can be applied to guide the study and counseling of individuals and their families, so they may reap the greatest benefit from the current state of genetic and genomic technology.

Today's health care consumer has access to information from a variety of sources, including the Internet. It is from these various information sources that families often form their questions and opinions about genetic conditions. In addition to this information (and misinformation), health and mental health professionals must understand the psychosocial dimensions of the experience, including how to deal with uncertainty (whether through denial and avoidance or information seeking and treatment), disclosure (who has the right to know and who does not), meaning (what the individual and family members make of the illness and their treatment options), management (whether all affected family members follow the same treatment protocol), and planning (what can be done regarding prevention or how to cope with a shortened life span). Issues about genetic conditions occur within a context of the family culture and the characteristic approaches of the family members to previous (sometimes identical) illnesses. Illnesses occur as part of a tapestry of ongoing relationships, simultaneously coloring and being colored by the strengths and difficulties inherent in all family relationships.

All health and mental health professionals and students now need a basic literacy in genetics and genomics and must be able to apply this knowledge to their research and practice. While genetic and genomic discoveries are becoming a reality that will define a new set of options and contingencies for future generations, the majority of health professionals still lack the ability to interpret the science of the gene discoveries. Fewer still are prepared to address the potential psychosocial effects of the information on individuals and families. Even when health professionals are aware of the content of information that needs to be conveyed to individuals and their families, they often fail to recognize the individual, family life cycle, and social constraints that affect the processing of such information.

We have organized the material into four main sections. Part I addresses the issue of why it is necessary to study genetics and genomics, and explores how the genetics paradigm has shifted our understanding of the diagnosis, treatment, and prevention of all diseases and conditions. We also put forth an innovative model to help interpret psychosocial research and guide clinical practice in this area. In Part II, we present individual and family models and innovations related to genetics and genomics and consider such themes as individual differences in cognitive-affective processing, family systems concepts, the impact of genetic risk-related anticipatory loss over the life course, the role of psychosocial interventions, and the nature of behavioral genetics. Part III focuses on applications of the individual and family approaches to specific genetic conditions, including neurodegenerative genetic conditions; cystic fibrosis; breast, colorectal, and lung cancer susceptibility; prenatal testing; type 1 diabetes; inherited cardiovascular disease; and schizophrenia spectrum disorders.

In Part IV, we address many of the ethical, legal, policy, and professional issues related to genetic testing, reproductive genetics, and genetics and genomics with children and families. We also present a proposal for the optimal collaborative genetic health care team, to assess and care for persons with genetic risk and genetic conditions.

There have been significant advances in the study and practice of genetics and genomics, even during the process of preparing this book. It is now a truism that the discoveries in genomics have moved us from a conceptualization of disease in terms of symptoms and systems, to a conceptualization based on underlying genetic mechanisms. These advances have added to our knowledge of heredity and complex diseases. The goal of this book is not only to create a prototype for continued systematic and comprehensive study of the psychosocial and family implications of the discoveries of the Human Genome Project and other genomic research. Progress toward full realization of the potential benefits of genomics, as well as success in avoiding its potential harm, is a complex challenge that will require the consideration of a number of factors, as outlined in the book. Central to this mission is the political and social will to support the science, as well as to educate professionals and the public and clinicians so that we are better prepared for the translation of genomic advances into practical benefits at the clinical, community, and public health levels.

Francis Collins, M.D., Ph.D., Director of the NIH National Human Genome Research Institute (2006), projected the likely beneficial outcomes of genomics circa 2015 for an individual and family if the translation of basic science efforts from bench to bedside proceeds in an enlightened fashion. The potential beneficial outcomes are likely to unfold if, among other developments: (1) clinicians use validated family history tools to identify risk, even for those in the first decades of life; (2) genomic technologies, such as genome sequencing, are used to inform risk assessment efforts to identify the most appropriate and targeted therapies; (3) clinicians understand the types of psychological factors that facilitate or undermine the processing of, and adaptive response to, personalized risk feedback; and (4) clinicians apply the principles of the family perspective (both biological and social) to engage family members in understanding and communicating risk and treatment information.

For clinicians to be positioned for the genomic era, we must continue to build on and refine our existing models, so that we develop a truly interdisciplinary approach whereby psychosocial research is conducted in tandem with genomic research. Additional research is desperately needed to refine our knowledge of the complex relationships among social, behavioral, environmental, and biological variables, at both the individual and family levels. This research needs to be longitudinal and involve diverse cohorts, and must examine gene–environment interactions, as well as gene–gene interactions. An example of one potential outcome of such research would be a greater understanding of the determinants, correlates, and consequences of the responses of individuals, families, and the public to rapidly changing genetic and genomic information. Models are also needed to facilitate the prompt translation of science into clinical practice, along with timely education of practitioners and the public. The development of such models requires building on our knowledge from population-based public health research, as well as on our studies of individuals and families, as described in this volume. The challenges faced by researchers are no less daunting for the clinician or educator. Innovative, interdisciplinary approaches will be needed to advance the application of the science to this endeavor. We intend this book to serve as an important beginning step in this process.

We would like to gratefully acknowledge the contributions of a number of people to this project. First and foremost, we thank Deborah Malmud at Norton for her foresight in soliciting this volume and for her continued support and guidance at all phases of the process. We also thank Michael McGandy at Norton, who has been there to provide ongoing direction and input. In our own institutions, we want to thank our outstanding administrative support staff, notably Margaret Atchison and Mary Anne Ryan at Fox Chase Cancer Center as well as Jeanne Klee at the University of Rochester. Thanks to our dear friends and colleagues who reviewed chapters for us and provided helpful critiques and support while writing this book: Paul Benacerraf, Betsy Bove, Joanne Buzaglo, Eric Coine, Tom Campbell, Yeates Conwell, Mary Daly, Michael Diefenbach, Linda Fleisher, Frank V. deGruy, Scotty Hargrove, Jeri Hepworth, Amy Lazev, Stephen LaMonica, Howard and Elaine Leventhal, Alan Lorenz, Neal Meropol, Tom O'Connor, Hong Nguyen, June Peters, Mary Ropka, Pagona Roussi, Peter Rowley, David Siegel, Jenny Speice, Elizabeth Thomson, Froma Walsh, David Weinberg, Janet Williams, and Catharine Wang. Suzanne Miller would like to especially express her gratitude to Robert C. Young, President of Fox Chase Cancer Center, for his vision, leadership, and wisdom in recognizing and highlighting the need to study and respond to the psychosocial implications of emerging technology in genetics and genomic medicine. In addition, Susan McDaniel would like to honor the memory of University of Rochester geneticist Peter Rowley, who died in March 2006. Dr. Rowley was a pioneer in genetics research, recognized the importance of psychosocial factors, and provided valuable critiques of concepts and chapters in the book.

On the home front, we are indebted to our life partners (Michael Lewis, David Siegel, Froma Walsh, and Terry Feetham) and children (Nicolas Miller Benacerraf, Natasha Miller Benacerraf; Tania, Marc, and Andrea Benacerraf; Hanna Lynn McDaniel Siegel, Marisa Jane McDaniel Siegel; and Claire Whitney) for believing in this book and for showing us the importance of understanding how the family contextualizes and enriches the individual.

REFERENCE

Collins, F. (2006, February). *Genomics and risk assessment.* Paper presented at the ninth annual meeting of the National Coalition for Health Professional Education in Genetics, Bethesda, MD.

PART I

AN INTRODUCTION TO THE NEW ERA OF GENETICS

Chapter 1

Keeping the Individual
and Family in Focus

Suzanne L. Feetham and Elizabeth J. Thomson

HISTORICALLY, THE STUDY OF HUMAN GENETICS WAS CONDUCTED BY A small number of scientists and health professionals who specialized in studying and caring for individuals and families who were known or believed to have one of the rare, inherited, "genetic disorders." In recent years, however, this has changed dramatically. As our understanding of the human genome has increased, so too has our understanding that genes play a role in virtually all human diseases, from relatively rare Mendelian disorders such as Huntington disease, cystic fibrosis, and sickle-cell disease, to complex common diseases such as cardiovascular disease, cancer, and diabetes. In fact, we are now beginning to understand that genes have a role not only in the cause of disease, but also in disease susceptibility and resistance, prognosis and progression, and responses to illness and its treatments. The completion of the human genome project (HGP, the mapping and sequencing of all human genes) in April 2003 and the analysis of these data and other genomic research are the underlying reasons for our rapidly increasing understanding of the relationships of health, disease, and the environment (Collins, Green, Guttmacher, & Guyer, 2003). The year 2003 was an important marker for the beginning of the genomic era and the trajectory of discovery with direct application of genetic and genomic

Sections adapted with permission of Blackwell Publishing from Feetham, S., Thomson, E. J., & Hinshaw, A. S. (2005). Genomics for health and society: A framework for nursing leadership. *Journal of Nursing Scholarship, 37*(2), 102–110.

technologies and information to personal health care and public health. The role of these technologies is expected to increase exponentially through the coming decades. To put these achievements in context, the knowledge about genomics has been said to be to this century what the knowledge of infectious disease was to the last.

For health care and public health professionals, an understanding of genetics and genomics is essential, as this knowledge will increase the ability to determine the risk of disease susceptibility beyond what is known from the traditional risk factors, improve early detection of illness or even risk of illness, and predict with more certainty prognosis, progression, and responses to treatment. The molecular characterization of diseases learned through genetic and genomic discoveries may result in early and more effective diagnosis and treatment, and decreased effects of complex diseases (Frazier, Johnson, & Sparks, 2005).

In this chapter, a summary of the advances in understanding of genetic and genomic research are described with an interpretation for individuals, families, health, and society. The burgeoning science from the HGP and other genetic and genomic research are analyzed in the context of individuals and their families and the constructs of the interdependence of individuals and their families, including family functioning, structure, and boundaries. Attention is given to an individual lens and a family systems lens to demonstrate how they can strengthen interventions with individuals and their families. Using these lenses, the unique challenges of genetics and genomic information for individuals and families are described to guide care by health care and public health professionals. The need to use individual and family systems lenses for research, practice, education, and health and social policy is described. In this chapter, concepts related to individuals and families with genetics and genomics are defined and analyzed as foundational for this book. Genomics is redefining the continuum of health and illness and is informing our understanding of disorders traditionally considered genetic, as well as some that were rarely or never considered to be genetic. Issues in genetic testing technologies and the increasing availability of genetic information in health and non-health-related settings are also discussed.

In all aspects of basic and applied research, the new era of genetics, genomics, and health care has arrived. It is important that health care and public health professionals, as well as social and behavioral scientists, have the knowledge and skills to interpret this burgeoning science to ensure the potential benefits for individuals, families, and society. This book provides direction for integrating the perspectives of individuals and families for scientists and health care and public health professionals in the era of genetics and genomics.

BIOLOGICAL CONTEXT FOR THE NEW ERA
OF GENETICS AND GENOMICS

The term *genomics* was first used in 1987 (McKusick & Ruddle, 1987). Previously, the term *genetics* had been used in the study of individual genes and their impact on relatively rare single-gene disorders. *Genomics* was meant to reflect the study of all of the genes in the human genome together, including their interactions with each other, the environment, and other psychosocial and cultural factors. Without consideration of the interdependence of these interactions, there is the risk of a failure to fully understand, appreciate, and interpret the genome and its functions. The concept of genomics is important to understand as it guides clinicians, educators, and researchers to recognize that this is a new way of thinking about the mechanisms of health and disease, its potential treatments and cures.

The HGP was initiated in 1990, and sequencing of the human genome was completed in less than the stated goal of 15 years due to the commitment of numerous scientists from around the world According to the International Human Genome Sequencing Consortium (Lander et al., 2001), the HGP was primarily accomplished by 20 research centers from six countries with political support, in the form of funding, from the governments in these countries. The contribution of international collaboration to the rapid completion and success of the HGP cannot be overstated. In the United States, the lead agencies for the HGP were the Department of Energy, the National Institutes of Health, National Human Genome Research Institute (Collins et al., 2003; Collins & McKusick, 2001).

The hereditary material deoxyribonucleic acid (DNA) is found in virtually every cell in the human body. DNA consists of four bases, A (adenine), T (thymine), G (guanine), and C (cytosine) repeated in various sequences 3.1 billion times. These bases pair up with each other, A with T and C with G, to form the human genome. The entire human genome now appears to have somewhere between 20,000 and 25,000 genes, far fewer than previously believed (Lander et al., 2001). In addition, the concept that one gene produces one protein has also been rejected. Scientists now believe, through a process called alternative splicing, the 25,000 or so genes in humans produce somewhere around 100,000 proteins (Graveley, 2001), far more than the number seen in other organisms. To advance science and the integration of the discoveries to practice, the entire DNA sequence of a human is now publicly available for anyone to use and can be accessed at the National Institutes of Health Web site at www.ncbi.nlm.nih.gov/genome/guide/human/.

While it is known that the genome of any two individuals is 99.9% the same, it is also the case that there are about 1 in 1,000 base pairs or 3 million base pair differences between individuals. Once the HGP was nearing completion, research efforts were undertaken to discover common DNA variations called single-nucleotide polymorphisms (SNPs). It was believed that the identification and cataloguing of these SNPs would be necessary in order to begin to more fully understand the genetic contribution to many human diseases. The number of SNPs in the human genome turned out to be very large (10 million common SNPs and about another 10 million rarer SNPs; see www.ncbi.nlm.nih.gov/projects/SNP/snp_summary.cgi) and it became clear that studying them on an individual basis would be extremely challenging. Thus, a research project is currently underway, the International HapMap Project, aimed at discovering common patterns of DNA sequence variation in the human genome, so that sequence variation can be studied in a more organized and "data-reduced" fashion. It is by studying these patterned variations that many of the associations with common diseases will be discovered (International HapMap Consortium, 2003).

ANTICIPATED BENEFITS OF THE NEW ERA OF GENETICS AND GENOMICS

The completion of the HGP marked the beginning of a new era of genetics and genomics. Health care and public health professionals need knowledge of genetics and genomics to ensure that the potential benefits of this era are maximized and potential risks are minimized.

The anticipated benefits of genetic and genomic advances for health and health care include improved diagnosis of disease, earlier detection of genetic predispositions to disease, and the development of drugs, other treatments, and one day hopefully cures, based on a person's entire genotype and considered in the context of the environment and other factors. This will move the design of treatments to attacking the underlying causes of the disease rather than merely trying to ameliorate outward signs and symptoms. This will also result in more effective and rational pharmaceutical approaches (pharmacogenomics) with personalized or customized medications based on individual genetic profiles. The results of genetic and genomic research will also advance our ability to evaluate health risks of individuals and families. For example, recent reports on risk of cardiovascular disease indicate that in individuals with a family history of cardiovascular risk, the individual's risk is more strongly linked to that of a sibling than to that of the parents (Nasir et al., 2004). A history of premature coronary atherosclerosis in any first-degree relative may reflect a genetic predisposition via a complex interaction of multiple genes with environmental factors or environmental factors operating on a susceptible genetic background (Frazier et al., 2005; see Chapter 15).

The high public visibility of the HGP and other genetic and genomic research has resulted in some expectation by the public for rapid progress from gene discovery to treatment. Review of the genetic literature demonstrates that a decade or more may pass between the discovery of a gene and a treatment (Collins & Guttmacher, 2001; Collins et al. 2003; Feetham, 1999; Feetham, Thomson, & Hinshaw, 2005). Individuals and families will need additional psychosocial support and understanding during the interim phase between gene discovery regarding mechanisms of a disease and when effective prevention and treatment options become available (see Chapters 6 and 9). As new discoveries are made through genetic and genomic research, the risk information available to individuals and families may change.

For example, multigenerational research on families with different penetrance of the *BRCA1* gene has shown a change in risk. Initial studies showed an 85% risk of developing breast cancer by age 70, but the estimated risk fell to 50% in later studies (McKiernan-Leo et al., 2004; Struewing et al., 1997). For other conditions such as familial hypertrophic cardiomyopathy, with the identification of new mutations, we now understand that the risk of sudden cardiac death and age at death varies by the mutation (see Chapter 15). This changing information requires health care professionals to stay current and recognize that individual family members may have different levels of interest in learning the new information and may have outdated information regarding level of risk and prevention or treatment options.

Beyond human health, the U.S. Department of Energy (2005) describes anticipated benefits from the genomic era across several areas of science, including molecular medicine, microbial genomics, bioarchaeology, anthropology, and human migration, forensics, agriculture, and bioprocessing.

It is anticipated that the advances in genomics of animals and plants have the potential to address the problems of world hunger and pandemics of disease such as malaria (World Health Organization, 2002). In microbial genomics, the advances will result in more rapid detection and treatment of pathogens (disease-causing microbes), the development of new energy sources, increased ability to monitor the environment to detect pollutants, safe cleaning of toxic wastes, and advances in protection from biological and chemical warfare.

In bioarchaeology, anthropology, and human migration, there is now a greater ability to study evolution through germline mutations in lineages, study the migration of different population groups based on maternal inheritance, and also study mutations on the Y chromosome to trace lineage and migration of males. Studies in these areas will allow the comparison of mutations resulting from breakpoints based on the ages of populations and historical events (U.S. Department of Energy, 2005). The science of forensics has been enhanced by the understanding of DNA. DNA has been used to identify crime and victims of catastrophe, and establish paternity, parentage in general, and other familial relationships.

INDIVIDUALS, FAMILIES, AND THE NEW ERA OF GENETICS AND GENOMICS

Traditionally, the health care system is structured toward, and health care professionals' education focuses on, the individual. Health care systems are designed to address individuals. For example, the Institute of Medicine (2001) does not identify family-centered care as one of the six aims of quality health care. Consistent with this, the research and literature of the responses to genetic information, including genetic testing, have tended to focus on individuals (Chapple, Campion, & May, 1997; Chapple & May, 1996; Croyle & Lerman, 1999), yet the scholarship of Thorne and Robinson (1988, 1989) and others has reported that the expectation of families is a health system that identifies the family as the center for care. Also, Weihs, Fisher, and Baird (2001), in their Institute of Medicine–commissioned report, summarized the growing body of research regarding the impact of serious illness on families across the life cycle and the relationship of family dynamics to illness behavior, adherence, and disease course. In spite of this important scholarship, individuals and their families still must advocate with health care professionals to receive the family-centered collaborative care they expect and want from the health care system (Campbell, 2003; see Chapter 20).

The genetic and genomic era requires a practice lens that maintains the perspective of the individual within the context of the family and at times the community (Daly et al., 1999, 2001; Reiss, 1995; Sze & Prakash, 2004). Genetic and genomic information has always been important within families. For example, biological family members have many genes in common (50% are shared between any two first-degree relatives—parents and their children and among siblings). Family members also share common environments and cultures. However, the genetic family ties exist only with the biological family members, while the environment and culture are shared among biological family members and social families that result from marriage, adoption, or other life events. A challenge for health care professionals is that with individuals' increased knowledge of, and providers' emphasis on, genetics and genomics, family structures, interactions, and reactions may be affected. Multigenerational themes and family response patterns typically impact individual family members in distinctive ways, including even those family members separated emotionally or geographically from their families.

The scholarship of health professionals whose research and practice have used the perspective of the individual has tended to be parallel, rather than convergent, with those applying a family lens. One key purpose of this book is to provide an integration of the individual and family perspectives in the era of genetics and genomics. This chapter begins the dialogue by reviewing how both research and practice related to individuals and the genetic and genomic era (Miller & Roussi, 2005; Miller et al., 2004; Chapter 3) can and should inform those who apply the family lens. This convergence of knowledge is required to achieve the potential benefits of the genomic era and also address its associated risks. This book provides the conceptual basis, as well as the empirical focus, for the complementary meshing of the two perspectives within the genetic and genomic context. The work of Schumm and colleagues, while reported as a framework for the statistical analysis of family data, can facilitate understanding of the interdependence of the individual and family perspectives (Schumm, Barnes, Bollman, Jurich, & Milliken, 1984). This work demonstrates the complexity of the processes and factors affecting individuals' and their family's decisions about, and responses to, genetic information. Families and individual members mutually influence each other. Impacting on each family is the perspective and coping dynamics of each individual member (Miller, Shoda, & Hurley, 1996); the shared or common perspective of the family system; and the perspectives within sets of relationships such as between parents, parent and child, and among siblings. The individual and shared experiences among family members, such as dyads, and the common factors across all family members are interactive and to some degree additive (Schumm et al., 1985). The responses of the individual or family system derive from these perspectives. Whether practice or research focuses on the individual or the family, there is interplay of varying experiences across different family relationships that enter most interactions. Fortunately, in the last decade conceptual and methodological approaches have evolved to enable individual and family researchers to analytically combine consideration of measures at the individual, subgroup (dyads and triads), and family system levels.

The Individual Lens

In Chapter 3, the authors describe the research that, over the past decades, has proposed and evaluated the conceptual and methodological approaches to person-centered research. As evidenced by the research findings and clinical information reported in Chapter 3, factors affecting an individual are as complex as those affecting families. Understanding the interaction among and across these individual difference factors is essential to the formulation and selection of appropriate interventions by health care professionals (Miller et al., 2005; Miller & Roussi, 2005). The questions examined in research on individuals are often different from those examined in research on families and can inform the clinical practice and research of those applying the family lens. For example, person-centered researchers have identified the influence that numeracy (the individual's facility with numbers) can have on the communication of genetic information. Risk of disease, penetrance, mutation prevalence, inheritance patterns, and risk reduction achieved by preventive measures are all typically expressed numerically, and thus lack of numerical understanding may substantially affect interpretation of genetic information (Lipkus, Samsa, & Rimer, 2001). Considering the numeracy differences among family members may improve the dissemination of information. Research on individuals' beliefs and expectations also adds important knowledge for practice in the genomic era (Miller et al., 1999; Miller & Diefenbach, 1998; Miller & Schnoll, 2000; Shoda, Mischel, & Miller, 1998).

In Chapter 3, Hurley and colleagues describe the cognitive-social health information processing (C-SHIP) model (Miller et al., 1996). This model, which employs variables examined in theories within health psychology, has moved the research from the examination of linear paths between predictors and outcomes to research which suggests that these variables form a dynamic network in which the strength and direction of the connections vary from person to person, as well as within individuals across different genetic situations. The variables within the individual network interact both with each other and with characteristics of the genetic challenge. The framework of the person-centered research described in Chapter 3 provides typologies of behavior that translate into clinical practice for health professionals in the genomic era (Diefenbach & Hamrick, 2003; Diefenbach, Schnoll, Miller, & Brower, 2000; Fang, Miller, Daly, & Hurley, 2002; Miller, Fang, Diefenbach, & Bales, 2001; Miller et al., 1999).

The Family Lens

While person-centered research and practice contributes to quality care, the benefits and potential of the discoveries from research in the new genetic and genomic era can be enhanced through the application of a family lens. In the diagnosis and treatment of genetically influenced conditions, health care and public health professionals need guidance to refocus their lens from the biological family to the persons who meet the family functions of the individuals in their care (Chapple & May, 1996; Feetham, 1999; Rolland & Williams, 2005). This focus on the biological relationship can result in little attempt to engage other persons of significance to the proband (person of genetic interest) beyond the biological family members and may result in missing key relationships, particularly spouses or partners, that may influence the individual's response to genetic and genomic information, or their response to illness (Kessler, 1993). As with the individual perspective, a family systems lens integrates the social and psychological information with biological and physical information (Campbell, 2003; Campbell & Patterson, 1995; Hilscher, Bartley, & Zarski, 2005; Rolland, 1994).

A key tenet of a family systems theory is that major life challenges and crises impact the entire family unit, and in turn, core family processes mediate coping and adaptation of the family unit and each individual member. A family systems approach attends to core aspects of family functioning, such as communication processes, problem solving, structure, rules and boundaries, multigenerational patterns and themes, and belief systems when interpreting genomic information for the health of individuals and their families (see Chapters 2 and 4). A family systems lens enables health care professionals to retain a focus on the individual while recognizing their relationships with family, friends, and their extended environment including their community and the health care system. Clarifying patterns of responses, relationships, and networks increases the potential to identify interventions for more beneficial responses to genetic information, and choices for diagnosis, prevention, and treatment. With a family lens, a focus of care is on how familial factors influence and are influenced by the processing of genetic and genomic information. The integration of a family approach in the care of individuals provides health care and public health professionals with the perspective that the family is central in the interpretation of genetics and genomics (Feetham, 1999; Hilscher et al., 2005; Reiss, 1995; Rolland & Williams, 2005; see Chapters 2 and 5).

More recently, genetic researchers and other scholars have addressed the importance of genetic information in the context of the family (Croyle & Lerman, 1999; Feetham, 1999, 2000; Gallo, Angst, Knafl,

Hadley, & Smith, 2005; Rolland & Williams, 2005; Van Riper & Gallo, 2005; see Chapter 2). For example, in a study of 212 men and women tested for a *BRCA1* mutation, Smith, West, Croyle, and Botkin (1999) concluded that the familial context in which genetic testing is conducted may be important for understanding how individuals react to their own test results. The purpose of this book is to analyze a variety of genetic conditions through the perspectives of the individual and the family to demonstrate approaches for health care and public health professionals to enable them to have a reference point in the genomic era to respond to the complexity of the interdependence of individuals and families.

Family Concepts Affecting the Response to Genetic and Genomic Information by Individuals and Families

An understanding of basic concepts of family systems can enhance the health care and public health professionals' understanding of genetic and genomic information in a family context. For example, family structure can affect the response of individuals and families to genetic information and the interpretation of this information. In Figure 1.1, Family A chose not to have genetic testing even though the mother and daughter had been diagnosed and treated for early-onset breast cancer. Their decision was based on the fact that there were no other immediate family members who might benefit from this information. For Family B, where a mother and daughter had also been diagnosed and treated for early-onset breast cancer, the daughter chose to have genetic testing to inform other family members about their risk and the possibility of surveillance for other family members.

Family members' multigenerational experience and perception of family functioning during previous illness can also influence the decision to have genetic testing. In Family C (Figure 1.2), the daughter chose to have genetic testing due to her concern for the response of the family to the diagnosis, use of the information for treatment, and the death of two family members. In contrast, in Family D, the second daughter diagnosed with early-onset breast cancer chose not to have genetic testing, as she and other family members perceived they had functioned well through the diagnosis and treatment of breast cancer in three family members across two generations.

The Place of Family History in the Genomic Era

The family history is a shared record of health and disease among family members and reflects the complex interactions between genomic

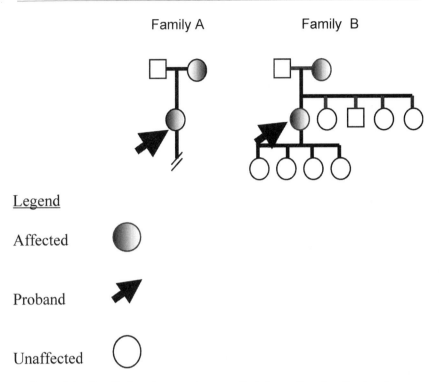

Figure 1.1   Family lens interpreting genetic information; family structure.

information and the environment, which both influence health and disease. That a family history of disease informs one's health risk is now accepted but not consistently applied in practice (U.S. Department of Health and Human Services, 2005). The work of Lynch and colleagues (Douglas et al., 2005; Lynch et al., 2000; Lynch et al., 1990; Lynch & Lynch, 1979) using multigenerational family histories was instrumental in the identification of the risk within families for colorectal cancer. It preceded the identification of one of the genes (*MSH2*) for hereditary nonpolyposis colorectal cancer (HNPCC), the *MSH2* gene. HNPCC, also known as Lynch syndrome, is caused by mutations in the mismatch repair genes and confers a high risk of colorectal, endometrial, and other cancers. HNPCC is the most common form of hereditary colorectal cancer, accounting for 2–7% of all colorectal cancer cases. The advances in genetic testing for persons with a family history of inherited colon cancer tremendously improves the opportunity for cancer surveillance and prevention strategies that can have a major impact on at-risk family members. Comprehensive counseling and education

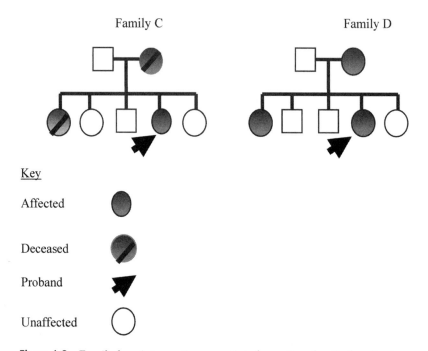

Figure 1.2   Family lens interpreting genetic information; family functioning.

about Lynch syndrome's natural history, an individual's own heredi-tary cancer risk, family members' possible risks, opportunities for sur-veillance and prevention, and potential outcomes and responses of individuals and the family are essential prior to, during, and after test-ing (Lynch et al., 2000; Lynch & Lynch, 2000; Tercyak et al., 2001).

Family history can help predict risk for such varied health conditions as heart disease, colorectal cancer, breast cancer, ovarian cancer, osteo-porosis, asthma, type 2 diabetes, and suicide. Health care professionals have known for a long time that common diseases such as heart dis-ease, cancer, and diabetes, and even rare diseases such as hemophilia, cystic fibrosis, and sickle-cell anemia, can run in families. If one genera-tion of a family has high blood pressure, it is not unusual for the next generation to have similarly high blood pressure. Persons tracing the illnesses of parents, grandparents, and other blood relatives can help health professionals identify the disorders for which someone may be at risk and take preventive action to protect the health of the individual and other family members. However, many people are unaware of their relatives' health histories. In addition, many health care professionals underutilize this information in advising patients on how to maintain good health. In this era of genomics, although we will gain important new genomic tools for risk assessment, family history will always remain a low-cost, effective, and relevant risk assessment tool.

A question for health professionals and the public is whether people care about family history. In a survey of 1,000 individuals, 96% reported that in thinking of their own health, knowledge of family health history was very or somewhat important (Parade/Research America, 2004). Similarly, in a survey of over 4,000 individuals, 97% thought that knowledge of family health history was important, but only 30% had actually ever collected health information from relatives to develop a family health history ($N = 4,345$; Centers for Disease Control and Prevention, 2004).

If family history is so useful, why don't health professionals use it consistently? Work through the National Human Genome Research Institute Ethical, Legal and Social Implications Program has shown that clinicians underestimate the utility of the family history. Better teaching and more pervasive role modeling of effective use of the family history is required. Health professionals typically believe that there is not enough time to obtain, organize, and analyze family history information.

The Family History Initiative, started in 2004, is a creative approach to family history that demands less time from health care professionals. This effort by the U.S. Department of Health and Human Services (2005) is being led by the Office of the U.S. Surgeon General. The goals of the Family History Initiative national public health campaign include focusing attention on the importance of family health history by encouraging all families to learn more about their family health history, increasing the public's awareness of the importance of family history in health; giving the public tools to gather, understand, evaluate, and use family history to improve their health; and increasing genomics and health literacy. For health care professionals, the goals are to give them tools to gather, evaluate, and use family history information; communicate with their patients about family history; increase genomics and health literacy; and prepare both the public and their health professionals for the coming era in which genomics will be an integral part of regular health care (Guttmacher, Collins, & Carmona, 2004). Today the family health history is used as a surrogate for an individual's genetic makeup. In the future, the family history will be used in conjunction with genetic testing to predict disease risk, prognosis, and response to therapy.

Interpreting family histories can be complicated by many factors, including small families, incomplete or erroneous family histories, and variable penetrance and the current lack of understanding of the multiple genes involved in most complex conditions such as diabetes and cardiovascular diseases. Family risk is often cited in terms of the absolute number of affected relatives with a disease, when (particularly in larger families) the ratio of affected to nonaffected relatives may be a more telling statistic. Interpreting statistics and risk factors are no easy tasks under any circumstances, much less one as potentially significant as genetic testing (Guttmacher, Collins, & Carmona, 2004).

Application of the family lens when obtaining a family health history includes taking a family genogram with the family pedigree (see Chapter 4). An understanding of the patterns of family relationships and communication including vulnerabilities and sources of resilience, as identified through a genogram, enables the health care professional to interpret genetic information in the context of family dynamics and guide family members to anticipate potential responses to genetic information. Family relationships can be affected by genetic information. Knowing there is a genetically influenced condition in a family can change the perception of multigenerational family stories to more definitive information on risk. Obtaining a multigenerational family history may require reaching out to extended family members. The knowledge of patterns of family relationships, family rules for information dissemination, family boundaries, and the expectations of individuals and families for information is critical for health care professionals to provide anticipatory care to individuals and families considering whether to pursue their genetic information.

CHANGING PARADIGMS FOR INDIVIDUALS AND FAMILIES

Genomics and Conceptualization of Health and Illness

Some researchers report that the findings from genomic research and advances in genomic technologies and information obtained through genetic testing require a reframing of how we think of the continuum of health and illness, and even the concept of disease (Feetham, Thomson, & Hinshaw, 2005; Guttmacher et al., 2004; Rolland & Williams, 2005; Varmus, 2002; see Chapter 2). Childs (2003) contended that, as the understanding of genomics increases, so too will the understanding of the mechanisms of disease, which will contribute to more targeted and individualized care. Zerhouni (2004) stated that the application of new genetic and genomic knowledge creates a central challenge for medicine and for health care to evolve from the model of intervention after disease or loss of function to more predictive models of interventions before the onset of disease or loss of function. Also, the way in which diseases are categorized and ultimately how they are treated and managed will change. No longer named by their symptoms (such as asthma), diseases will be more specifically identified by their genetic and environmental causes, leading to more focused treatments (Guttmacher, 2002; Guttmacher & Collins, 2002; Khoury, Burke, & Thomson, 2000).

As the knowledge of the mechanisms of diseases increases, individuals and families will be faced with reframing their concepts and experience with diagnosis, treatment, and prevention to include the term *genetically influenced disorders*. The boundary between health and chronic illness may become blurred (Rolland & Williams, 2005; see Chapter 2). For individuals and their families choosing to obtain genetic information, the findings may result in the need to extend the concept of time phases after disease onset (Rolland, 1994) to include nonsymptomatic genomic illness time phases. This begins with an awareness phase (Rolland, 1999; Rolland & Williams, 2005; Sobel & Cowan, 2003; Street & Soldan, 1998), which refers to the time before a statistical risk is known or acknowledged, or before the availability or the consideration of genetic testing. Then individuals and families can enter a phase of active consideration of testing (crisis phase I) and test/posttesting (crisis phase II). Subsequently, individuals and families enter the long-term adaptation phase, which may extend for decades until the onset of the disease, as is seen in Huntington disease, or it may extend throughout the remainder of individual's life if the genetic risk does not result in the expression of the disease, as can be seen in iron overload, cardiomyopathy, or even breast, ovarian, or colon cancer (Rolland, 1999; Rolland & Williams, 2005; see Chapter 2). Knowledge of the risk state may require interventions for individuals and families to respond to the increased awareness of risk, the newly gained genetic risk information, or even the earliest (previously denied or unobserved) occurrence of symptoms. Family members may need to begin to deal with anticipatory loss, accept increased surveillance, adhere to changes in health behaviors, or accept interventions that may potentially delay the onset or progression of the disease (Rolland & Williams, 2005; see Chapters 2 and 5).

Because of our improved understanding of the human genome, we have gained many insights into what was considered traditional thinking about genetics and its contribution to disease. The following sections discuss some of these new understandings and challenges of our new understandings.

Whatever Happened to Simple Genetic Disorders?

Cystic fibrosis (CF) has been described as one of those "simple genetic disorders." However, as details have been learned about the genetic contribution to CF, the less simple it seems. The gene associated with CF (cystic fibrosis transmembrane conductance regulator, *CFTR*) was first reported in 1989. It was identified on chromosome number 7 and found to be about 250,000 DNA base pairs in length. At the time, a single mutation, a three-base-pair deletion (deltaF508), was found to account for about half of the people in the United States with CF. Also, at the time, it was believed that another few mutations in the gene might be discovered and the genetics of this so-called simple Mendelian disorder would be known.

More than a decade later, more than a thousand mutations have been described in the *CFTR* gene and these mutations still account for only about 90% of classical CF in the United States. A genetic test for CF mutations has been developed and is beginning to be widely used for preconception risk assessment and prenatal and postnatal diagnostic testing. As the test has been used in a much more diverse population, many unexpected findings have occurred. First, not all people with classical CF have been found to have mutations in *CFTR*. Second, people with the same *CFTR* mutations can have quite different courses of disease (variable expression), even when they are in the same family. Thus, making prognostic assertions based on genotype is extremely flawed. Third, the frequency of CF mutations varies substantially from one population group to another (Ashkenazi Jewish, 1 in 29; European white, 1 in 29; Hispanic American, 1 in 46; African American, 1 in 65; Asian, 1 in 90 (American College of Obstetrics and Gynecology, 2001; Gene Tests, 2006). This results in variable testing sensitivity, specificity, and predictive value of the genetic test. Fourth, not all people who have two mutations in their *CFTR* gene have classical CF. There have been relatively healthy individuals who have been found to have two CF mutations, including males whose only health problem has been infertility, due to congenital absence of the vas deferens (see Chapter 9).

As more genes are being discovered and genetic tests are provided to large and diverse populations, similar unexpected findings continue to occur. Thus, what was once believed to be a simple genetic disorder of autosomal recessive inheritance three or four decades ago is now understood to be more complex, requiring a more sophisticated knowledge and expertise for interpretation. In addition to its complexity has come a greater understanding of the molecular biology, biological functioning, and possible targets for therapeutic interventions for this disease.

Penetrance: Genetic Effects, Environmental Effects, and Family Differences

The concept of penetrance—the chance that a person who has altered genes will have or develop the disease—is often a moving target. For decades, it was believed that in Mendelian disorders, someone who inherited the relevant gene alteration would one day, ultimately, develop the disease, if he or she lived long enough. This has turned out to be the case only in some disorders. For example, in Huntington disease, the penetrance is almost always 100%; that is, someone who gets the mutation will express the disease. In contrast, it has been quite surprising to learn that someone who gets a double dose of *HFE* mutations has an extremely low risk of developing the full set of signs and symptoms observed in hereditary hemochromatosis (some suggest less than 1%; Beutler, Felitti, Koziol, Ho, & Gelbart (2002); Waalen, Felitti, Gelbart, Ho, & Beutler, 2002).

As is often the case, early gene discovery studies take place in so-called high-risk families, in which multiple family members in multiple generations are affected with the disease under study. Enlisting the participation of members of these families can make the discovery of the gene and its mutations somewhat more straightforward. However, as a result of this selection bias, the estimation of the penetrance of the mutation provided by the results of the initial studies is often higher than those seen in subsequent studies, in which lower-risk families and members of the general population participate. Unfortunately, the later publications often receive less media attention, and knowledge about penetrance can remain faulty for many years (Feetham, 1999; Feetham et al., 2005).

This phenomenon occurred in the discovery and description of breast and ovarian cancer genes, *BRCA1* and *BRCA2*, for which early studies cited a penetrance of 85–90%, with later studies describing a 27–55% penetrance (McKiernan-Leo et al., 2004; Satagopen et al., 2001; Struewing et al., 1997; Wacholder et al., 1998). These studies reported the significance of family history in addition to the presence of a mutation when determining risk and the age-specific penetrance (Antoniou et al., 2003; Chatterjee et al., 2001; Satagopan et al., 2001; see Chapter 10). Meta-analysis across 22 *BRCA1* or *BRCA2* breast and ovarian cancer risk studies, unselected for family history, adds to the understanding of risk and demonstrates the complexity of interpreting risk status and changing information on penetrance (Antoniou et al., 2003).

It is important for health care professionals and the public to understand that risk information may change over time and that the reports of penetrance based on the results of early studies announcing a gene discovery may be different and higher than those found in subsequent studies. Family history may partially inform the risk of penetrance, but health care professionals must continue to monitor the scientific literature to provide the most accurate and up-to-date information to patients and their families.

One Genetic Health Policy May
Not Work for All Families

Another challenge has been associated with attempts to develop health policies related to genetics and genomics for an extremely diverse population, such as that found in the United States. Scientists and clinicians sometimes turn to research results and policy recommendations from countries outside the United States in developing policy recommendations. And this is to be commended. However, while such recommendations may be important to consider in the development of policies for this country, it is also important to keep in mind that policies from countries with extremely homogeneous populations may or may not serve well as guidance for the U.S. population, which is extremely diverse.

In the case of hereditary hemochromatosis, an inherited form of iron overload, the mutations in *HFE* genes were first discovered in patients who were quite severely affected with iron overload and their families. Those early studies indicated that *HFE* mutations accounted for most cases of iron overload in the United States. Once the *HFE* mutations were discovered, there were immediate calls for genotypic screening of the entire U.S. population. The reasons given were that this was a very common mutation (1 in 10 whites had been found to have a single mutation, and about 1 in 400 were homozygous for two mutations— which should have made it one of the most common genetic disorders in the United States). Since the disorder was thought to be so common and to lead to very serious complex diseases (diabetes, heart disease, cirrhosis of the liver, liver cancer, arthritis, and impotence), and the treatment and prevention interventions inexpensive and easy (regular phlebotomy), it seemed that it could become the poster disease for genetic testing. However, further studies (Cogswell et al., 2003; Waalen et al., 2002) of this condition have yielded information that has challenged the above assumptions in many ways.

Large follow-up studies revealed that, in addition to the fact that penetrance rates were far lower than predicted by the early studies conducted in iron overload patients and their families, the prevalence of the *HFE* mutation, C282Y, was very different among various populations (whites, 1 in 10; Hispanic Americans, 1 in 30; African Americans, 1 in 50; and Asians, 1 in 1,000). Such findings caused some concern that many people would be labeled as having hemochromatosis because of their mutation status, when they might never become ill. Such a label could potentially have devastating effects, such as causing loss of health or life insurability due to stigmatization and discrimination, altered family relations, or psychiatric morbidity, such as increased anxiety and depression. Further, the idea of the genotypic screening of an entire population, in which the sensitivity and specificity of the test was diminished and large segments of the population were not likely to benefit, resulted in the moderation of enthusiasm by some for genotypic screening for this disorder in the U.S. population (McLaren et al., 2003; for further discussion of these issues, see Chapters 18 and 19).

Genetic Testing: Advantages and Challenges

Genetic testing in the United States started in the late 1950s as an experimental laboratory test, done as often on research animals as on humans. At that time, cytogenetic testing was a blunt instrument that could detect the presence or absence of a whole chromosome, as in Down syndrome (trisomy 21) and Turner syndrome (45, X0). In the 1970s, as a result of new staining technologies, cytogenetic testing could identify smaller and smaller deletions or additions of partial chromosomes, such as those seen in cri du chat syndrome (a deletion in the short arm of chromosome 5) or Prader-Willi syndrome (a deletion in the long arm of chromosome 15). The 1980s brought new recombinant DNA technologies, which were used for genetic tests called genetic linkage studies. Genetic linkage studies allowed researchers and clinicians to begin to track disease-causing mutations that were closely linked to known genetic markers.

The 1990s resulted in far more sophisticated genetic testing technologies that allowed for very specific genetic mutations to be discovered (individual or multiple base pair deletions, additions, substitutions, inversions, and insertions associated with diseases such as breast, ovarian, and colon cancer, Alzheimer disease, and also multiple DNA repeat sequences of base pairs such as those seen in Huntington disease, spinal muscular atrophy, and fragile X syndrome). Today, genetic tests are available for more than 1,000 genetic disorders. Tests are used for preconception, prenatal, and newborn screening, predispositional and presymptomatic testing, diagnostic confirmation, prognostic information, and also in choosing the optimal therapeutic alternative, as in pharmacogenomic testing (Burke, 2002; Patenaude, Guttmacher, & Collins, 2002).

Many of these tests are imperfect. They sometimes come to market before their analytic validity, clinical validity, and clinical utility have been well established. Further, sensitivity, specificity, and predictive value may remain uncertain. Thus, it is critical that health professionals be aware of both the promises and pitfalls of undergoing genetic testing. This will allow them to assist individuals and their families in deciding whether they wish to undertake genetic testing. Health professionals need to understand that sometimes these tests will not tell them what they want to know. For example, if a mutation for colon cancer is known in a family, it can be fairly straightforward to test other family members to see if they have the mutation or not. However, if there is a family whose family history reveals an inherited form of colon cancer with no known mutation, a negative test may mean very little. It may mean that they have an inherited form of colon cancer in which the genetic contribution remains unknown.

A second issue is whether genetic testing is useful, if no treatment to reduce risk is available. Many people believe that knowledge is powerful and in general a good thing to have. Others believe that if there is no prevention to reduce risk or treatment to improve outcome, there is no point in having this knowledge. The latter belief has been observed in Huntington disease families. Before a direct genetic test for Huntington disease was available, surveys suggested that 75 to 79% of people at risk would have testing when it became available (Kessler, Field, Worth, & Mosbarger, 1987; Schoenfeld, Myers, Berkman, & Clark, 1984). Since the test became available about 10 years ago, only 3% of those at 50% risk have undergone testing (personal communication with Ira Shoulson, Huntington Disease Study Group, March 21, 2006).

Pharmacogenomic testing will likely become a common genetic test in the not-too-distant future. The reasons why individuals respond differently to the same drug are being identified through pharmacogenetics. It has become clear that some drugs are more or less effective in certain individuals. In addition, adverse reactions to drugs have become one of the leading causes of morbidity and mortality in the developed world (Lazarou, Pomeranz, & Corey, 1998; Prows & Prows, 2004). As pharmacogenomic tests become available to identify those individuals who will be more or less likely to be responsive to a certain drug treatment and, perhaps more important, to identify those who are at increased risk for an adverse or toxic reaction to certain pharmaceuticals, these tests will soon become routine or certainly commonplace in the delivery of health care.

For example, the beta-2-adrenergic receptor gene is the target of medicines often used in the treatment of asthma. One study showed a relationship between genotype in the beta-2-adrenergic receptor gene and the therapeutic response to albuterol in children with asthma. The response range was 10% for children with two glycine amino acids

(GlyGly) for position 16 in the gene, 25% for children with one arginine and one glycine amino acid (ArgGly) in the gene, and 60% in children with two arginine mutations (ArgArg; Martinez, Graves, Baldini, Solomone, & Erickson, 1997). Thus, this study showed that the effectiveness of albuterol appeared to be highest in children with the Arg-Arg genotype. However, a subsequent study by Palmer, Silverman, Weiss, and Drazen (2002) showed that the children with the ArgArg genotype also had a significant decrease in response to the drug with repeated use, whereas those with GlyGly had no decrease in effectiveness with repeated use over time. Later studies have applied this genomic knowledge to the understanding of the mechanisms of asthma and to identifying children at risk for asthma (Tantisira et al., 2004; Turner et al., 2004).

While application of genetic testing for response to albuterol is not common practice at this time, it is expected that findings such as these will drive the increased use of pharmacogenomic testing. It is expected that the choice and dose of therapeutic agents for common diseases such as deep vein thrombosis, cancer, diabetes, and heart disease will likely be made after this type of pharmacogenomic testing.

Genetic Exceptionalism

There are aspects of the integration of genetics and genomics into health care that have been identified by some scholars and researchers as unique compared to the knowledge of other scientific, medical, and clinical information. It is important for health care professionals to know of these discussions in order to be well positioned for the translation of the science to practice. The concept of genetic exceptionalism suggests that genetic information is inherently different, powerful, and unique such that it should receive special consideration and be handled separately and perhaps differently from other information obtained about an individual or their family members (Goston & Hodge, 1999; Green & Botkin, 2003; Ross, 2000, 2001; Suter, 2001; see Chapters 18 and 19).

A number of factors support this perspective. Genetic information is a unique identifier and is specific to an individual (except for identical twins). Unlike blood pressure, hemoglobin, and kidney function tests, it does not vary or change each time it is measured. Genetic information is heritable, shared through generations, and because of this has relevance not only to the individual but to family members, including both ancestors and descendants. Because of the individual yet intergenerational nature of genetic information, the interpretation and dissemination of this information within a family can have psychological and social implications for the whole family (Feetham, 1999; Rolland, 1999; Rolland & Williams, 2005; Ross, 2001; Slaughter, 1998; Suter, 2001). It can serve to relieve or heighten anxiety and alter family relationships positively or negatively (Rolland, 1999). Genetic information can be obtained to identify a risk state or be predictive of future disease and may be used to encourage persons to alter health behaviors to attempt to reduce personal risk. At the same time, it has the potential to be used to stigmatize and discriminate against certain individuals, families, or groups.

Some indicate that most of the characteristics of genetic information are also true for other medical information such as the presence of mental illness, sexually transmitted disease, or HIV status (Ross, 2001; Suter, 2001; National Institutes of Health-Department of Energy Working Group, 1993). While this may turn out to be the case, there is not yet sufficient evidence to know how genetic information will be used. Because the word *genetics* has been used synonymously with *fate*, many believe that genomics needs to be treated as unique and exceptional for a period of time until public and professional education can deconstruct these old and imprecise meanings. Thus, early in the genomic era, until knowledge is more pervasive and applies to everyone, the issue of genetic exceptionalism is relevant and should be kept under consideration. Concerns about genetic exceptionalism, however, may prove to be transitory and only an interim issue of concern (Feetham et al. 2005).

Family Diversity and the Genomic Era

Determining who a family includes is increasingly complex, given both the growing recognition of multiple family forms in today's society and the advances in reproductive technology in recent decades. Any working definition of *family* in genetics and genomics needs to embrace both factors. Is the "real" family the individuals who carry out the functions of family life? How does the view of family include the biological father and any other children conceived from his sperm? In the context of genetic risk assessment and testing, biological factors are paramount. Yet the lived experience of coping and adaptation to genetic knowledge and risk exists in the functional family unit. Demographic trends document the increasing diversity and complexity of family forms, and that the intact biological nuclear family is no longer the norm for most families and individuals (Coontz, 1992, 1995; Pinsof, 2002; Walsh, 2003, 2006). This dovetails with Edwards's (1991) contention that the increase in families with structures based on known multiple biological linkages supports the rethinking of the traditional model of nuclear biological families. This highlights the central importance of a broader and inclusive definition of family in clinical and research models as we enter the era of genetics and genomics.

Assistive reproductive technologies have moved beyond persons with infertility problems to persons with a history of genetic diseases, gay and lesbian couples, single women, and persons deferring pregnancies beyond the years of typical childbearing. While the prevalence of the application of these technologies remains small in proportion to total births, it has increased substantially since the first birth following in vitro fertilization in 1978. Leahy (2005) reported on the search of a single mother for the biological father (sperm donor) for her two children. This search resulted in a visit with the biological father, who is also the sperm donor to other women and the father to numerous other children, who may or may not want to have contact with their biologically related siblings. Sensitivity to individual and family boundaries and communication processes will increasingly become an important component in dealing with families in which children were conceived by gamete donation.

As new genetic technologies are developing, it is becoming increasingly easy to determine biological parentage. Home testing kits are already available and are being used in some families to confirm parentage. These same technologies are making it more feasible to identify sperm or gamete donors. Disclosure of family and health information about the sperm or gamete donor is recommended in order to provide more information for the family health (genetic) history for the child. However, some note such disclosure is not always necessary. One reason is that more genetic and other health screening is carried out in most donor programs than in the general population. Therefore, if testing is carried out thoroughly as recommended, the incidence of unknown major genetic defects could be lower than that observed in the general population. It is also expected that within the next decade, health and genetic profiles for individuals by using DNA chips may provide more reliable genetic information than a multigenerational family history (Patrizio, Mastroianni, & Mastroianni, 2001). For many families where donor gametes are used, the child is the genetic or biological child of one of the parents who will raise the child, therefore providing continuing access to the family history (McGee, Brakman, & Gurmankin, 2001).

Disclosure of information about donors (including their identity) is required in some countries (Gottlieb, Lalos, & Lindblad, 2000; Weber, 2000). Such identification may result in a reduction in the number of gamete donors willing to participate and a substantial increase in the waiting time for gametes. While some individuals may be willing to make such a donation anonymously or identified, others may only be willing to do so anonymously. At this time, the genetic and genomic technologies may be considered to be ahead of the social, legislative, and family responses to the complex issues raised by gamete donors. This gap between technologies and social and family responses reinforces the need for health care professionals to not only understand the advancing science but also be able to interpret these advances in the context of individuals, families, ethical dilemmas, social policies, and legal parameters (see Part IV).

Continuing Process of Interpreting Genetic Information

Genetic information is personal and is viewed by many as potentially powerful. It is information that many prefer to keep private, and yet in this day and age it will become increasingly difficult to protect personal genetic information. Genetic information has familial implications and can sometimes result in the disclosure of unintended information, such as misattributed paternity. At this time, there is a significant risk that genetic information may be misinterpreted, especially since we are only beginning to learn the meaning of this information. Furthermore, this information could potentially be used to inappropriately label or stigmatize individuals or groups and to discriminate against individuals, families, or groups (Jeffery, 1999; Martindale, 2001; Ross, 2000).

Understanding the meaning and interpretation of this information is critical (Feetham, 1999; Varmus, 2002; see Chapters 2 and 19). Of particular importance for health care and public health professionals is to understand the limitations of genetic information. Genetic information is not deterministic; that is, having a genetic mutation does not predict with certainty that a disease is present or that it will develop in the future. Furthermore, the absence of an identifiable genetic mutation does not mean that an individual has no mutation or no risk to develop a disease (a concept that is particularly difficult for people to understand). Health care professionals can ensure that genetic information is always interpreted and used in the context of what is known about the individual, the family, and their sociocultural perspective. Only then will this information be likely to benefit and not harm individuals and families.

As noted, family rules and boundaries, influenced by culture, multigenerational values, norms, and experiences with the health care system, will also affect the responses of individual family members and the family system to genetic information (Rolland, 1994; Rolland & Williams, 2005; see Chapter 5). The interpretation of genetic information by a family member is also affected by the number of relationships among family members, which is determined by the number of family members (Bodin, 1990). The paucity of attention to family systems and family relationships in the collection and dissemination of genetic information places family members and families at increased risk for altered relationships. The need to apply the individual and family perspectives in genetics and genomics will only increase.

THE FUTURE FOR INDIVIDUALS
AND FAMILIES

In 1999, Collins and Jegalian (1999) suggested that by the year 2010, predictive genetic testing for susceptibility for up to 20 common conditions such as diabetes and hypertension may be available. Health professionals will need to integrate research on genetics and genomics, family and health promotion and risk reduction into their practice for the best health outcomes for individuals and their families. An analysis of concepts of individuals, families, and the importance of a family systems lens has been presented as an introduction to this volume. We have emphasized that quality care for individuals and families in the era of genomics requires an integration of individual and family concepts.

The public expects that health care and public health professionals know the current information on genetics and genomics and can interpret this information to the public and that they recognize the implications of this information for individuals and their families. Because of attention to genomic discoveries in the public media, some of the public may be ahead of health professionals in interpreting the significance of the genomic era to their health. Web sites enable the public to gain rapid access to information. Health professionals can guide individuals and families to credible and current Web sites such as Genetic Resources on the Web (GROW) and the National Institutes of Health (Hesse et al., 2005; National Coalition for Health Professional Education in Genetics, 2000; see Chapter 10).

Chapter 2 bridges the biological and psychosocial worlds of genetics and genomics. It addresses the psychosocial challenges of genomic conditions for patients and their families to help organize this biopsychosocial landscape for clinical practice and research. It describes the innovative family systems genetic illness (FSGI) model to organize the increasing and complex array of genomic conditions (Rolland & Williams, 2005). This conceptual model expands the definition of disease to include the time prior to clinical diagnosis and the potential influences of genetic information on the individual and family system. Based on key characteristics, it groups useful clusters of disorders with similar patterns of psychosocial demands over the nonsymptomatic phases before and after genetic testing. The FSGI model is designed to be flexible and responsive to future discoveries in genomic research. This model can guide both clinical and research endeavors and facilitates dynamic, open communication among health care disciplines and with consumers. Its utility is discussed for research, preventive screening, family assessment, treatment planning, and service delivery in a wide range of health care settings. Part II (Chapters 3 through 7) provides current thinking about individual and family models of genetics and genomics and considers such themes as individual differences in cognitive-affective processing, family systems concepts, the role of anticipatory loss, the impact of psychosocial interventions, and behavioral genetics.

REFERENCES

American College of Obstetrics and Gynecology. (2001). *Preconception and prenatal carrier screening for cystic fibrosis.* Washington, DC: Author.

Antoniou, A., Pharoah, P. D. P., Narod, S., Risch, H. A., Eyfjord, J. E., Hopper, J. L., et al. (2003). Average risks of breast and ovarian cancer associated with *BRCA1* or *BRCA2* mutations detected in case series unselected for family history: A combined analysis of 22 studies. *American Journal of Human Genetics, 72*(5), 1117–1130.

Beutler, E., Felitti, B., Koziol, J., Ho, N., & Gelbart, T. (2002). Penetrance of the 845G→A (*C282Y*) *HFE* hereditary haemochromatosis mutation in the USA. *Lancet, 359,* 211–218.

Bodin, A. M. (1990). Coming of age in the new world of family systems. In F. W. Kaslow (Ed.), *Voices in family psychology* (Vol. 1, pp. 48–68). Newbury Park, CA: Sage.

Burke, W. (2002). Genetic testing. *New England Journal of Medicine, 347*(23), 1867–1875.

Campbell, T. L. (2003). The effectiveness of family interventions for physical disorders. *Journal of Marital and Family Therapy, 29*(2), 263–281.

Campbell, T. L., & Patterson, J. M. (1995). The effectiveness of family interventions in the treatment of physical illness. *Journal of Marital and Family Therapy, 21*(4), 545–583.

Centers for Disease Control and Prevention. (2004). Awareness of family health history as a risk factor for disease, United States, 2004. *MMWR, 53,* 1044–1047.

Chapple, A., Campion, P., & May, C. (1997). Clinical terminology: Anxiety and confusion amongst families undergoing genetic counseling. *Patient Education and Counseling, 32,* 1–2, 81–91.

Chapple, A., & May, C. (1996). Genetic knowledge and family relationships: Two case studies. *Health and Social Care in the Community, 4*(3), 166–171.

Chatterjee, N., Shih, J., Hartge, P., Brody, L., Tucker, M., & Wacholder, S. (2001). Association and aggregation analysis using kin-cohort designs with applications to genotype and family history data from the Washington Ashkenazi Study. *Genetic Epidemiology, 21*(2), 123–138.

Childs, B. (2003). Genomics, proteomics, and genetics in medicine. *Advances in Pediatrics, 50*, 39–58.

Cogswell, M., Gallagher, M., Steinberg, K., Caudill, S., Looker, A., Bowman, B., et al. (2003). HFE genotype and transferring saturation in the United States. *Genetics in Medicine, 5*(4), 304–310.

Collins, F. S., Green, E., Guttmacher, A. E., & Guyer, M. S. (2003). A vision for the future of genomic research. *Nature, 422*, 835–847.

Collins, F. S., & Guttmacher, A. E. (2001). Genetics moves into the medical mainstream. *Journal of the American Medical Association, 286*(18), 2322–2324.

Collins, F. S., & Jegalian, K. G. (1999). Deciphering the code of life. *Scientific American, 281*(6), 86–91.

Collins, F. S., & McKusick, V. A. (2001). Implications of the Human Genome Project for medical science. *Journal of the American Medical Association, 285*(5), 540–544.

Coontz, S. (1992). *The way we never were: American families and the nostalgia trap.* New York: Basic Books.

Coontz, S. (1995). The way we weren't: The myth and reality of the "traditional" family. *National Forum, 75*(3), 11–14.

Croyle, R. T., & Lerman, C. (1999). Risk communication in genetic testing for cancer susceptibility. *Journal of the National Cancer Institute Monographs, 25*, 59–66.

Daly, M., Barsevick, A., Miller, S. M., Rogatko, A., Buckman, R., Costalas, J., et al. (2001). Communicating genetic test results to the family: A six-step skills-building strategy. *Family and Community Health, 24*, 13–26.

Daly, M., Farmer, J., Harrop-Stein, C., Montgomery, S., Itzen, M., Wagner Costalas, J., et al. (1999). Exploring family relationships in cancer risk using the genogram. *Cancer Epidemiology, Biomarkers and Prevention, 8*, 393–398.

Diefenbach, M. A., & Hamrick, N. (2003). Self-regulation and genetic testing: Theory, practical considerations, and interventions. In L. D. Cameron & H. Leventhal (Eds.), *The self-regulation of health and illness behavior* (pp. 314–331). London: Routledge.

Diefenbach, M. A., Schnoll, R. A., Miller, S. M., & Brower, L. (2000). Genetic testing for prostate cancer: Willingness and predictors of interest. *Cancer Practice, 8*, 1–5.

Edwards, J. N. (1991). New conceptions: Biosocial innovations and the family. *Journal of Marriage and the Family, 53*, 349–360.

Fang, C. F., Miller, S. M., Daly, M., & Hurley, K. (2002). The influence of attentional style and risk perceptions on intentions to undergo prophylactic oophorectomy among FDRs. *Psychology and Health, 17*, 365–376.

Feetham, S. L. (1999). Families and the genetic revolution: Implications for primary care, education, research and policy. *Families, Systems and Health,* *17*(1), 27–43.

Feetham, S. L. (2000). Editorial: Genetics and nursing research. Opportunities and challenges. *Research in Nursing and Health, 23*(4), 257–259.

Feetham, S., Thomson, E. J., & Hinshaw, A. S. (2005). Genomics for health and society: A framework for nursing leadership. *Journal of Nursing Scholarship, 37*(2), 102–110.

Frazier, L., Johnson, R. L., & Sparks, E. (2005). Genomics and cardiovascular disease. *Journal of Nursing Scholarship, 37*(4), 315–321.

Gallo, A. M., Angst, D., Knafl, K. A., Hadley, E., & Smith, C. (2005). Parents sharing information with their children about genetic conditions. *Journal of Pediatric Health Care, 19*(5), 267–275.

Gene Tests. (2006). http://www.geneclinics.org/

Gostin, L. O., & Hodge, J. G. (1999, Fall). Genetic privacy and the law: An end to genetics exceptionalism. *Jurimetrics,* 21–58.

Gottlieb, C., Lalos, O., & Lindblad, F. (2000). Disclosure of donor insemination to the child: The impact of Swedish legislation on couple's attitudes. *Human Reproduction, 15*(10), 2052–2056.

Graveley, B. (2001). Alternative splicing: Increased diversity in the proteomic world. *Trends in Genetics, 17,* 100–107.

Green, M. J., & Botkin, J. R. (2003). "Genetic exceptionalism" in medicine: Clarifying the differences between genetic and nongenetic tests. *Annals of Internal Medicine, 138*(7), 571–575.

Guttmacher, A. E. (2002). *Putting genetics into clinical practice: Current and future.* Paper presented at the 15th Annual International Society of Nurses in Genetics Conference, Baltimore MD.

Guttmacher, A. E., & Collins, F. S. (2002). Genomic medicine: A primer. *New England Journal of Medicine, 347,* 1512–1520.

Guttmacher, A. E., Collins, F. S., & Carmona, R. H. (2004). The family history: More important than ever. *New England Journal of Medicine, 351*(22), 2333–2336.

Hesse, B. W., Nelson, D. E., Kreps, G. L., Croyle, R. T., Arora, N. K., Rimer, B. K., et al. (2005). Trust and sources of health information: The impact of the Internet and its implications for health care providers: Findings from the first Health Information National Trends Survey. *Archives of Internal Medicine, 165*(22), 2618–2624.

Hilscher, R. L., Bartley, A. G., & Zarski, J. J. (2005). A heart does not beat alone: Cornary heart disease through a family systems lens. *Families, Systems, & Health. 23*(2), 220–235.

Institute of Medicine. (2001). *Crossing the quality chasm: A new health system for the 21st century.* Washington, DC: National Academy Press.

International HapMap Consortium. (2003). The International Hapmap project. *Nature, 426*(18), 789–796.

Jeffery, N. (1999, February 5). A change in policy: Genetic testing threatens to fundamentally alter the whole notion of insurance. *Wall Street Journal,* p. R15.

Kessler, S. (1993). Forgotten person in the Huntington disease family. *American Journal of Medical Genetics*, 48, 145–150.

Kessler, S., Field, T., Worth, L., & Mosbarger, H. (1987). Attitudes of persons at risk for Huntington disease toward predictive testing. *American Journal of Medical Genetics, 26*(2), 259–270.

Khoury, M. J., Burke, W., & Thomson, E. J. (2000). A framework for the integration of human genetics into public health practice. In M. J. Khoury, W. Burke, & E. J. Thomson (Eds.), *Genetics and public health in the 21st century* (pp. 3–23). New York: Oxford University Press.

Lander, E. S., Linton, L. M., Birren, B., Nusbaum, C., Zody, M. C., Baldwin, J., et al. (2001). Initial sequencing and analysis of the human genome. *Nature, 409*, 860–921.

Lazarou, J., Pomeranz, B., & Corey, P. (1998). Incidence of adverse drug reactions in hospitalized patients: A meta-analysis of prospective studies. *Journal of the American Medical Association, 279*, 1200–1205.

Leahy, M. (2005, June 19). Family vacation. *Washington Post Magazine*, 12–19, 26–31.

Lipkus, A. H., Samsa, G., & Rimer, B. K. (2001) General performance on a numeracy scale among highly educated samples. *Medical Decision Making, 21*(1), 37–44.

Lynch, H. T., Brand, R. E., Lynch, J. F., Fusaro, R. M., Smyrk, T. C., Goggins, M., et al. (2000). Genetic counseling and testing for germline p16 mutations in two pancreatic cancer-prone families. *Gastroenterology, 119*(6), 1756–1760.

Lynch, H. T., Bronson, E. K., Strayhorn, P. C., Smyrk, T. C., Lynch, J. F., & Ploetner, E. J. (1990). Genetic diagnosis of Lynch syndrome II in an extended colorectal cancer-prone family. *Cancer, 66*(10), 2233–2238.

Lynch, H. T., & Lynch, P. M. (1979). The cancer-family syndrome: A pragmatic basis for syndrome identification. *Diseases of the Colon and Rectum, 22*(2), 106–110.

Lynch, H. T., & Lynch, J. (2000). Lynch syndrome: Genetics, natural history, genetic counseling, and prevention. *Journal of Clinical Oncology, 18*(21 Suppl.), 19S–31S.

Martindale, D. (2001). Genetic discrimination: Pink slips in your genes. *Scientific American, 284*(1), 19–20.

Martinez, F., Graves, P., Balding, M., Solomon, S., & Erickson, R. (1997). Association between genetic polymorphisms of the beta 2-adrenoceptor and the response to ablution in children with and without a history of wheezing. *Journal of Clinical Investigation, 100*, 3184–3188.

McGee, G., Brakman, S. V., & Gurmankin, A. D. (2001). Gamete donation and anonymity: Disclosure to children conceived with donor gametes should not be optional. *Human Reproduction, 16*(10), 2033–2036.

McKiernan-Leo, A., Beseecher, B. B., Hadley, D. W., Case, R. G., Giambarresi, T. R., Johnson, E., et al. (2004). BRCA1/2 testing in hereditary breast and ovarian cancer families: Effectiveness of problem-solving training as a counseling intervention. *American Journal of Medical Genetics A, 130*(3), 221–227.

McKusick, V., & Ruddle, F. (1987). A new discipline, a new name, a new journal. *Genomics, 1*, 1–2.

McLaren, C., Barton, J., Adams, P., Harris, E., Acton, R., Press, N., et al. (2003). Hemochromatosis and iron overload screening (HEIRS) study design for an evaluation of 100,000 primary care-based adults. *American Journal of the Medical Sciences, 325*(2), 53–62.

Miller, S. M., Bowen, D. J., Campbell, M. K., Diefenbach, M. A., Gritz, E. R., Jacobsen, P. B., et al. (2004). Current research promises and challenges in behavioral oncology: Report from the American Society of Preventive Oncology Annual Meeting. *Cancer Epidemiology, Biomarkers and Prevention, 13,* 171–180.

Miller, S. M., Buzaglo, J. S., Simms, S., Green, V. A., Bales, C., Mangan, C. E., et al. (1999). Monitoring styles in women at risk for cervical cancer: Implications for the framing of health-relevant messages. *Annals of Behavioral Medicine, 21,* 91–99.

Miller, S. M., & Diefenbach, M. A. (1998). The Cognitive-Social Health Information-Processing (C-SHIP) model: A theoretical framework for research in behavioral oncology. In D. S. Krantz & A. Baum (Eds.), *Technology and methods in behavioral medicine* (pp. 219–244). Mahwah, NJ: Erlbaum.

Miller, S. M., Fang, C. Y., Diefenbach, M. A., & Bales, C. (2001). Tailoring psychosocial interventions to the individual's health information processing style: The influence of monitoring versus blunting in cancer risk and disease. In A. Baum & B. Andersen (Eds.), *Psychosocial interventions in cancer* (pp. 343–362). Washington, DC: American Psychological Association.

Miller, S. M., Fleisher, L., Roussi, P., Buzaglo, J. S., Schnoll, R. A., Slater, E., et al. (2005). Facilitating informed decision making about breast cancer risk and genetic counseling among women calling the NCI's Cancer Information Service. *Journal of Health Communication, 10,* 119–136.

Miller, S. M., & Roussi, P. (2005). Psychosocial factors involved in genetic testing decisions and behaviors. *Hellenic Journal of Psychology, 2*(2), 135–158.

Miller, S. M., & Schnoll, R. A. (2000). When seeing is feeling: A cognitive-emotional approach to coping with health stress. In M. Lewis & J. Haviland (Eds.), *Handbook of emotion* (pp. 538–557). New York: Guilford.

Miller, S. M., Shoda, Y., & Hurley, K. (1996). Applying cognitive-social theory to health-protective behavior: Breast self-examination in cancer screening. *Psychological Bulletin, 119,* 70–94.

Nasir, K., Michos, E. D., Rumberger, J. A., Braunstein, J. B., Post, W. S., Budoff, M. J., et al. (2004). Coronary artery calcification and family history of premature coronary heart disease: Sibling history is more strongly associated than parental history. *Circulation, 110*(15), 2150–2156.

National Coalition for Health Professional Education in Genetics. (2000). Core competencies in genetics essential for all health-care professionals. Retrieved from http://www.nchpeg.org/news box/corecompetencies.html

National Institutes of Health–Department of Energy Working Group on Ethical, Legal and Social Implications of Human Genome Research. (1993). *Genetic information and health insurance report of the task force on genetic information and insurance.* Retrieved from http://www.genome.gov/10001750

Palmer, L., Silverman, E., Weiss, S., & Drazen, J. (2002). Pharmacogenetics of asthma. *American Journal of Respiratory Critical Care in Medicine, 165,* 861–866.

Parade/Research America. (2004). Genetics and personalized medicine, http://www.researchamerica.org/polldata/2004/paradepracticalguide04.pdf

Patenaude, A. F., Guttmacher, A., & Collins, F. (2002). Genetic testing and psychology: New roles, new responsibilities. *American Psychologist, 57*(4), 271–282.

Patrizio, P., Mastroianni, A. C., & Mastroianni, L. (2001). Disclosure to children conceived with donor gamete should be optional. *Human Reproduction, 16*(10), 2036–2038.

Pinsof, W. M. (2002). The death of "till death us do part": The transformation of pair-bonding in the 20th century. *Family Process, 41*, 135–157.

Prows, C. A., & Prows, D. R. (2004). Medication selection by genotype. *American Journal of Nursing, 104*(5), 60–70.

Reiss, D. (1995). Genetics influence on family systems: Implications for development. *Journal of Marriage and the Family, 57*, 543–560.

Rolland, J. S. (1994). *Families, illness, and disability: An integrative treatment model.* New York: Basic Books.

Rolland, J. S. (1999). Families and genetic fate: A millennial challenge. *Families, Systems and Health, 17*(1), 123–133.

Rolland, J. S., & Williams, J. K. (2005). Toward a biopsychosocial model for 21st-century genetics. *Family Process, 44*(1), 3–24.

Ross, L. F. (2000). Genetic testing of adolescents: Is it in their best interest? *Archives of Pediatrics and Adolescent Medicine, 154*, 850–851.

Ross, L. F. (2001). Genetic exceptionalism vs. paradigm shift: Lessons from HIV. *Journal of Law, Medicine, and Ethics, 29*(2), 149–151.

Rusnak, J., Kisabeth, R., Herbert, D., & McNeil, D. (2001). Pharmacogenetics: A clinician's primer on emerging technologies for improving patient care. *Mayo Clinical Practice, 76*, 299–309.

Satagopan, J. M., Offit, K., Foulkes, W., Robson, M. E., Wacholder, S., Eng, C. M., et al. (2001). The lifetime risks of breast cancer in Ashkenazi Jewish carriers of BRCA1 and BRCA2 mutations. *Cancer, Epidemiological Biomarkers, and Prevention, 10*(5), 467–473.

Schoenfeld, M., Myers, R. H., Berkman, B., & Clark, E. (1984). Potential impact of a predictive test on the gene frequency of Huntington disease. *American Journal of Medical Genetics, 18*(3), 423–429.

Schumm, W. R., Barnes, H. L., Bollman, S. R., Jurich, J. P., & Milliken G. A. (1985). Approaches to statistical analysis of family data. *Home Economics Research Journal, 14*(1), 112–122.

Shoda, Y., Mischel, W., Miller, S. M., Diefenbach, M. A., Daly, M., & Engstrom, P. (1998). Psychological interventions and genetic testing: Facilitating informed decisions about BRCA1/2 cancer susceptibility. *Journal of Clinical Psychology in Medical Settings, 5*, 3–17.

Slaughter, L. (1998). Genetic information must remain private to prevent discrimination, spur research. *Genetic Testing, 2*, 1.

Smith, K. R., West, J. A., Croyle, R. T., & Botkin, J. R. (1999). Familial context of genetic testing for cancer susceptibility: Moderating effect of siblings' test results on psychological distress one to two weeks after BRCA1 mutation testing. *Cancer Epidemiology, Biomarkers and Prevention, 8*(4), 385–392.

Sobel, S., & Cowan, C. B. (2003). Ambiguous loss and disenfranchised grief: The impact of DNA predictive testing on the family as a system. *Family Process, 42*(1), 47–57.

Street, E., & Soldan, J. (1998). A conceptual framework for the psychosocial issues faced by families with genetic conditions. *Families, Systems and Health, 16*(3), 217–233.

Struewing, J. P., Hartge, P., Wacholder, S., Baker, S. M., Berlin, M., McAdams, M., et al. (1997). The risk of cancer associated with specific mutations of BRCA1 and BRCA2 among Ashkenazi Jews. *New England Journal of Medicine, 336*(20), 1401–1408.

Suter, S. M. (2001). The allure and peril of genetics exceptionalism: Do we need special genetics legislation? *Washington University Law Quarterly, 79*(3), 669–748.

Sze, J., & Prakash, S. (2004). Human genetics, environment, and communities of color: Ethical and social implications. *Environmental Health Perspectives, 112*(6), 740–745.

Tantisira, K., Klimecki, W. T., Lazarus, R., Palmer, L. J., Raby, B. A., Kwiatkowski, D. J., et al. (2004). Toll-like receptor 6 gene (TLR6): Single-nucleotide polymorphism frequencies and preliminary association with the diagnosis of asthma. *Genes and Immunity, 5*(5), 343.

Tercyak, K. P., Hughes, C., Main, D., Snyder, C., Lynch, J. F., Lynch, H. T., et al. (2001). Parental communication of BRCA1/2 genetic test results to children. *Patient Education and Counseling, 42*(3), 213–224.

Thorne, S. E., & Robinson, C. A. (1988). Health care relationships: The chronic illness perspective. *Research in Nursing and Health, 11*, 292–300.

Thorne, S. E., & Robinson, C. A. (1989). Guarded alliance: Health care relationships in chronic illness. *Image: Journal of Nursing Scholarship, 23*(3), 153–156.

Turner, S. W., Khoo, S. K., Laing, I. A., Palmer, L. J., Gibson, N. A., Rye, P., et al. (2004). Beta2 adrenoceptor Arg16Gly polymorphism, airway responsiveness, lung function and asthma in infants and children. *Clinical and Experimental Allergy, 34*(7), 1043–1048.

U.S. Department of Energy, Office of Science. (2005). Potential benefits of human genome project research. Retrieved from http://www.ornl.gov/sci/techresources/Human_Genome/project/benefits.shtml

U.S. Department of Health and Human Services. (2005). U.S. Surgeon General's Family History Initiative, http://www.hhs.gov/familyhistory/

Van Riper, M., & Gallo, A. (2005). Families, health and genomics. In D. R. Crane & E. S. Mitchell (Eds.), *Handbook of families and health: Interdisciplinary perspectives* (pp. 195–218). Newbury Park, CA: Sage Publications.

Varmus, H. (2002). Getting ready for gene based medicine. *New England Journal of Medicine, 347*(19), 1526–1527.

Waalen, J., Felitti, V., Gelbart, T., Ho, N. J., & Beutler, E. (2002). Penetrance of hemochromatosis. *Blood Cells, Molecules, and Disease, 29*(3), 418–432.

Wacholder, S., Hartge, P., Struewing, J. P., Pee, D., McAdams, M., Brody, L., et al. (1998). The kin-cohort study for estimating penetrance. *American Journal of Epidemiology, 148*(7), 623–630.

Walsh, F. (2003). Changing families in a changing world. In F. Walsh (Ed.), *Normal family processes: Growing diversity and complexity* (3rd ed., pp. 3–26). New York: Guilford.

Walsh, F. (2006). *Strengthening family resilience* (2nd ed.). New York: Guilford.

Weber, W. (2000). Dutch sperm donors will remain anonymous for another 2 years. *Lancet, 355,* 1249.

Weihs, K., Fisher, L., & Baird, M. (2001). Families, health, and behavior. *Families, Systems, and Health, 20*(1), 7–46.

World Health Organization. (2002). *Genomics and world health: Report of the Advisory Committee on Health Research.* Geneva, Switzerland: Author.

Zerhouni, E. (2004). Foreword. In A. E. Guttmacher, F. S. Collins, & J. M. Drazen (Eds.), *Articles from the New England Journal of Medicine: Genomic medicine* (p. x). Baltimore: Johns Hopkins University Press.

Chapter 2

Toward a Psychosocial Model for the New Era of Genetics

John S. Rolland and Janet K. Williams

INTRODUCTION

ILLNESS, DISABILITY, AND DEATH ARE UNIVERSAL EXPERIENCES IN FAMI-lies. Chronic and life-threatening diseases confront all of us with some of life's greatest challenges. The impact of a diagnosis of cancer or daily living with a serious disability reverberates throughout the family system, leaving no one untouched. The quality of life deteriorates for some families and family members, whereas others are resilient and thrive.

Genomic research continues to inform our understanding of the mechanisms of disease for diagnosis, treatment, and prevention. As a result, families and individual members will increasingly come to understand many of their diseases as "genetically influenced" or disorders with a genetic component, which means conditions for which a person has genetic factors that increase the likelihood of developing a particular disorder. The boundary between health and chronic illness will be increasingly blurred by the designation of "genetically at-risk." With the understanding that genetic factors alone seldom determine disease, genomic research will help clarify interactions with risks such as lifestyle and other environmental factors. How will this information alter the processes needed for successful coping and adaptation? How can we best organize this increasingly complex biopsychosocial

This chapter is a revised and expanded version of Rolland, J. S., & Williams, J. K. (2005). Toward a biopsychosocial model for 21st century genetics. *Family Process*, 44(1), 3–24.

landscape to facilitate clinical and research endeavors? This chapter provides a framework to move us in that direction.

There is a clear need for a conceptual model that describes genomic conditions in psychosocial terms and provides a guide useful to both clinical practice and research, one that facilitates dynamic, open communication among health professional disciplines and with health care consumers. We need a comprehensive way to organize our thinking about all the complex interactions between (1) the genetic factors placing individuals at risk for a disorder, (2) the significant family and social network, and (3) the professionals involved in providing care. This model needs to accommodate the changing landscape of interactions between these parts of the system over both the nonsymptomatic and symptomatic phases of a disease with a genetic component and the changing seasons of the individual and family life cycles. Also, it should facilitate thinking about the interface of genetically influenced disorders with important larger systems (e.g., health care, community, religious, education, workplace).

The primary aim of this chapter is to provide a family systems genetic illness (FSGI) model that helps address these needs. This chapter describes a framework to organize genomic diseases based on key characteristics that define useful clusters or types of disorders with similar patterns of psychosocial demands over time. This framework builds on the Family Systems Illness (FSI) Model (Rolland, 1984, 1987a, 1987b, 1990, 1994a, 1998, 2003). As background, we first provide a brief summary of this model and, more specifically, a part of the model—a psychosocial typology and time phase schema, originally developed for chronic disorders from the time of clinical onset. The original typology includes any disorder with a genetic component, from the time after clinical onset of symptoms.

The main section presents a new typology and time phase framework that is tailored to the expanding and evolving world of genomic health, where complex interactions of genetic and environmental factors will be associated with common chronic conditions. The concluding sections provide clinical and research applications, and demonstrate how the original typology and time phases can be used together sequentially with this new framework tailored to genomics.

THE NEED FOR A MODEL

To think in a truly interactive or systemic manner about the interface of genomic diseases and families or individual members, one needs a way to describe the myriad biological disorders in both biomedical and psychosocial terms. Conditions such as genetically influenced cancers or heart disease need to be given a psychosocial meaning that patients and their families can use to guide and empower them in their journey of living with such disorders.

There have been two major impediments to progress in this area. First, insufficient attention has been given to the areas of diversity and commonality inherent in different chronic disorders. Second, the qualitative and quantitative differences in how various diseases manifest over the course of an illness have been glossed over. Disorders need to be conceptualized in a way that organizes similarities and differences over the disease course so that the type and degree of demands relevant to psychosocial research and clinical practice are highlighted in a useful way. Further, this framework needs to be flexible and responsive to the rapid changes in our understanding of health and disease brought on by the study of genomics. We need to consider the future trend, where disease nosology will increasingly reflect causes (e.g., specific genetic mutations in diabetes) rather than traditional symptom clustering.

The great variability of chronic diseases and their changing nature over time have presented an enormous challenge to psychosocial investigators who have attempted to identify the most salient psychosocial variables relevant to the course of an illness or to treatment adherence. When focusing on psychosocial implications, difficulty begins if social scientists and clinicians use only a traditional disease classification based purely on biological criteria clustered to establish a medical diagnosis and treatment plan, rather than one that incorporates the psychosocial demands on patients and their families, and the increasing evidence for complex gene-environmental interactions.

Historically, this specific biomedical orientation has tended to polarize clinicians' and researchers' views of the relationship between psychosocial factors and physical illness. Knowledge is sought either in each specific disease or in "illness" as a general, quasi-metaphorical concept. In the former, clinical wisdom or research findings are not generalized. Researchers continue to study each illness within a narrow focus without highlighting general aspects of adaptation common across illnesses. At the other end of the continuum, findings regarding a particular condition are indiscriminately generalized to all diseases. Both extremes hamper clinical practice. Much of the clinical literature addresses a particular disease or disability. The problem is that insights about a particular disorder can be applied either too narrowly or too inclusively to conditions with markedly different psychosocial demands over time. For example, experience with one kind of disease, such as aggressive forms of cancer that require an intensive focus on separation and loss, may be transferred in an oversimplified way to a different kind of condition, such as disabling arthritis, where problem solving and redefining family roles predominate.

The dimension of time has been neglected. We need a framework that integrates illness into a schema that attends to the past, present, and future. Generally, the literature has focused on a specific phase of what can be referred to as the *illness life course* (e.g., disease onset, long-haul chronic phase, terminal phase, or bereavement). A schema that considers the unfolding of illness-related developmental tasks over the entire course of a disorder is essential (Rolland, 1984, 1987, 1994). When we also consider predictive and presymptomatic testing,[1] this needs to include the nonsymptomatic period of living with knowledge about genetic risk. Moreover, if developmental issues are addressed, they tend to be restricted to one person, usually the patient. It is vital to consider the different impact over time on the person with the disorder, other family members, caregivers, and various relationships. Also, the specific impact differs depending on when a disorder occurs in a family's and in each member's individual development.

With the advent of the era of genomic health, attention to the dimension of time is more critical than ever. An inevitable consequence of genetic advances is that families and individual members will move through the life cycle with increasing information available regarding genetically influenced risk for traits (e.g., hearing loss), specific illnesses (e.g., Parkinson disease, schizophrenia), or a constellation of conditions (e.g., cardiovascular and autoimmune disorders). The identification of alterations in specific chromosomes, genes, or gene products through genetic testing can yield information for several purposes, including prenatal diagnosis, newborn screening, carrier testing, diagnosis/ prognosis of a person with a genetic disorder, presymptomatic and predictive testing (Secretary's Advisory Committee on Genetic Testing, 2000), and, increasingly, medication selection.

The very existence of these genetic tests provides families and individuals with the possibility of learning more about a degree of risk and, in some circumstances, an expected disease. This possibility will affect the individual psyche, specific relationships, family identity, and collective constructions of reality. How individuals, families, and society (through prescriptive policies) relate to this possibility will significantly affect individual and family development. The possibility to obtain genetic information about rapidly increasing numbers of health conditions potentially affects all phases of the life cycle. These phases include forming a committed relationship, contemplating starting a family, work life and retirement, and health from conception to death of each individual. We need a way to organize meaningfully the biopsychosocial experience of this expanding knowledge over the individual and family life cycles.

In sum, the diverse and complex breadth of chronic disorders presents a vast range of symptoms and trajectories, accompanied by varied psychosocial demands for different kinds of disorders over their course. Although there have been elegant descriptions of the physical demands of particular conditions, such descriptions need to be melded into a developmental systemic framework that bridges the biomedical and psychosocial worlds and addresses the pattern of illness demands over time in terms that are useful to clinicians, researchers, patients, and families.

FAMILY SYSTEMS ILLNESS MODEL

The FSI model (Rolland, 1984, 1987a, 1987b, 1990, 1994a, 1998, 2003) provides a framework for psychoeducation, assessment, and intervention with families dealing with the full spectrum of chronic illness and disability over the life span. The model is based on a strength-oriented perspective viewing family relationships as a potential resource and emphasizing the possibilities for growth, not just their liabilities and risks (Walsh, 2003, 2006). It emphasizes the goodness of fit between the psychosocial demands of the disorder over time and the strengths and vulnerabilities of each family. It offers a central reference point for a broad range of clinical services and interventions.

The model addresses three dimensions: (1) "psychosocial types" of illness and disability, (2) major developmental phases in their natural history; and (3) key family system variables (Figure 2.1). It attends to the expected psychosocial demands of an illness through its various phases in relation to family systems dynamics. It emphasizes the interface of the illness with individual and family development; the family's multigenerational history of coping with illness, loss, and other adversity; and family belief systems (Figure 2.2). These include influences of culture, ethnicity, spirituality, and gender. Particularly important are beliefs concerning the meaning of genetic information to family members; the cause or inheritance of an illness; and mastery and acceptance of a future risk that may be beyond control.

A Systemic Orientation

This model is grounded in systems theory. A basic premise in a systemic view is that stressful crises and persistent challenges have an impact on the whole family, and in turn, key family processes mediate the coping and adaptation of all family members and the family unit (Walsh, 2003). The family is conceptualized as an open system that functions in relation to its broader sociocultural context and evolves

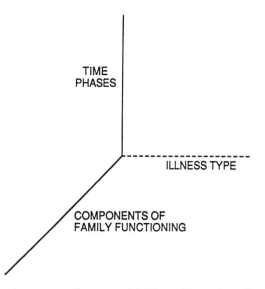

Figure 2.1 Family systems illness model: Three dimensions. Excerpted from: Rolland, J. S. (1987). Chronic illness and the life cycle: A conceptual framework. *Family Process, 26*(2), 203–221.

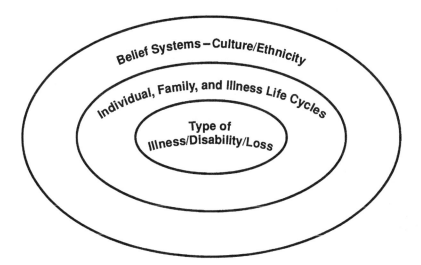

Figure 2.2 Family systems illness model. From: Rolland, J. S. (1994). *Families, illness and disability: An integrative treatment model.* New York: Basic Books.

over the life cycle. Foremost, family systems theory emphasizes *interaction* and *context*. The concept of interaction encompasses not just the interaction among family members, but also that between the family and other systems (e.g., school, work, religious). Individual behavior is viewed within the context in which it occurs. Problems, events, and processes are evaluated in both social and developmental contexts rather than in isolation. From a biopsychosocial perspective, interaction involves the interplay between the multiple recursive influences of biological, psychological, social, and environmental factors (Engel, 1977). Not only does an illness affect the family, but family coping and adaptation can adversely or positively influence disease course and treatment adherence. Also, transactions occur in relation to time, specifically, how multigenerational and life cycle influences affect current functioning. In essence, function and dysfunction, or normality versus pathology, are defined relative to the evolving fit over time among the individual and family, their social context, and the psychosocial demands of the situation—here a genomic health problem or risk. Family or relationship processes are emphasized as much as, if not more than, the content of a problem (e.g., treatment noncompliance). In this sense, changing the interactions among family members in relation to a patient's treatment noncompliance is often considered a better way to produce individual change.

Original Post–Clinical Onset Typology and Time Phases Framework

Typology

The original classification schema was developed to provide a better link between the biological and psychosocial worlds, clarifying the relationship between chronic illness after clinical onset and the family experience (Rolland, 1984, 1987a, 1994a). Chronic conditions can be grouped by key biological similarities and differences that pose distinct psychosocial demands for the patient and family. This typology defines meaningful and useful categories with similar psychosocial demands for a wide array of chronic illnesses affecting individuals across the life span. Illness patterning can vary in terms of *onset* (acute vs. gradual), *course* (progressive vs. constant vs. relapsing), *outcome* (fatal vs. shortened life span or possible sudden death vs. no effect on longevity), *incapacitation* (none vs. mild vs. moderate vs. severe). The level of uncertainty concerning an illness's trajectory overlies the other four variables.

Combining these variables generates a typology that clusters illnesses according to similarities and differences in biological patterns that pose differing psychosocial demands. Each type of condition with its pattern of practical and emotional demands can then be considered in relation to the style, strengths, and vulnerabilities of the family unit and each member (Table 2.1).

Time Phases of Illness

The concept of time phases provides a way for clinicians and families to think longitudinally about the course of an illness and to understand chronic illness as an ongoing process with normative landmarks, transitions, and changing demands. The core psychosocial themes in the natural history of chronic disorders can be described in relation to three major phases: *crisis, chronic,* and *terminal.* Each phase poses salient psychosocial challenges, each requiring particular family strengths or changes for adaptation.

For instance, the crisis phase involves the initial period of socialization to chronic illness. Family developmental tasks include creating a meaning for the disorder that preserves a sense of mastery, grieving the loss of the preillness family identity (this process varies depending on a family's multigenerational experience with a particular condition), undergoing short-term crisis reorganization, and developing family flexibility in the face of uncertainty and possible threatened loss. Also, families must gradually begin to accept the permanence of the condition, begin to redefine their concept of normality, learn to live with illness-related symptoms and treatments, and forge an ongoing relationship with health professionals and institutional settings. The chronic phase, whether long or short, is the "long haul" or living day to day with chronic illness. In this phase, families must pace themselves to avoid burnout, manage relationship imbalances (as in caregiving), and juggle the competing needs and priorities of all family members. They must find ways to preserve or redefine individual and family developmental goals within the constraints of the illness, as well as sustain intimacy in the face of threatened loss. Some diseases have a potential terminal phase, when issues related to death and dying predominate. The terminal phase can provide precious time together to acknowledge the impending loss, to deal with unfinished business, to say goodbyes, and to begin the process of family reorganization.

The psychosocial demands of any condition can be thought about in relation to each time phase of the disorder. The key processes in family functioning, such as belief systems, organizational patterns, and communication processes (see Chapter 4), can be evaluated as they fit the evolving situation. This framework can guide periodic family consultations, or "psychosocial checkups," as salient issues and

Table 2.1 Categorization of Chronic Illnesses by Psychosocial Type

		INCAPACITATING		NONINCAPACITATING	
		ACUTE	GRADUAL	ACUTE	GRADUAL
FATAL	Progressive		Lung cancer with CNS metastases Bone marrow failure Amyotrophic lateral sclerosis	Acute leukemia Pancreatic cancer Metastatic breast cancer Malignant melanoma Lung cancer Liver cancer	Cystic fibrosis*
	Relapsing			Incurable cancers in remission	
SHORTENED LIFE SPAN / POSSIBLY FATAL	Progressive		HIV Emphysema Alzheimer disease Multi-infarct dementia Multiple sclerosis (late) Chronic alcoholism Huntington's chorea Scleroderma		Juvenile diabetes* Malignant hypertension Insulin-dependent adult-onset diabetes
	Relapsing	Angina	Early multiple sclerosis Episodic alcoholism	Sickle-cell disease* Hemophilia*	Systemic lupus erythematosis*
	Constant	Stroke Moderate/severe myocardial infarction	PKU and other congenital errors of metabolism	Mild myocardial infarction Cardiac arrhythmia	Hemodialysis-treated renal failure Hodgkin disease

NONFATAL				
Progressive		Parkinson disease Rheumatoid arthritis Osteoarthritis		Noninsulin-dependent adult-onset diabetes
Relapsing	Lumbosacral disc disorder		Kidney stones Gout Migraine Seasonal allergy Asthma Epilepsy	Peptic ulcer Ulcerative colitis Chronic bronchitis Irritable bowel syndrome Psoriasis
Constant	Congenital malformations Spinal cord injury Acute blindness Acute deafness Survived severe trauma & burns Posthypoxic syndrome	Nonprogressive mental retardation Cerebral palsy	Benign arrhythmia Congenital heart disease	Malabsorption syndromes Hyper/hypothyroidism Pernicious anemia Controlled hypertension Controlled glaucoma

* = Early

Note. From Rolland, J. S. (1984). Toward a psychosocial typology of chronic and life-threatening illness. *Family Systems Medicine*, 2, 245–262. Reprinted with permission of Family Process Inc.

priorities surface and change over time. It also informs evaluation of general functioning and illness-specific individual and family dynamics.

FSGI MODEL: PSYCHOSOCIAL TYPOLOGY
AND TIME PHASES OF GENOMIC
DISORDERS

Any typology is a subjectively constructed map for orienting one to a territory (Bateson, 1972, 1979). The purpose of this typology is to create clinically useful categories for a wide array of genetic conditions that affect individuals and families across the life span. This typology is not designed for traditional medical treatment or prognostic purposes, but for examining the relationship between family or individual dynamics and disorders with genetic components.

Rather than being applied in a strictly literal way, this typology offers a way of thinking about the pattern of expectable psychosocial demands of different kinds of genomic disorders. It is intended for conditions for which genetic alterations contribute to the cause of a disease and for which predictive, presymptomatic, or carrier testing is, or may become, available. This is important because the study of genomics will ultimately change the way illnesses are conceptualized, treated, perhaps named, and potentially prevented. The typology is designed with the understanding that it is very likely that many diseases will potentially be reclassified into a new molecular taxonomy of illness based on systematic molecular analysis and characterization (e.g., somatic mutations, gene expression, protein expression, and modification; Collins, Green, Guttmacher, & Guyer, 2003). The reclassification of certain types of cancer (Golub, 2001; Golub et al., 1999) and neuromuscular diseases (Wagner, 2002) provide early examples on this frontier. Finally, because our ability to foresee the limits of testing is still in its infancy, this schema is offered with the understanding that testing cannot and may never be able to identify all genetic risk. Although this discussion uses categorical distinctions, its broader purpose is to describe and organize the inherent complexity of the genetic landscape in a manner that is useful to both clinical and research endeavors and has important implications for health care policy.

This typology, depicted in Table 2.2 conceptualizes broad distinctions in the pattern of (1) likelihood of developing a condition based on genetic mutations, (2) overall clinical severity, (3) timing of clinical onset in the life cycle, and (4) whether effective treatment interventions exist that can alter clinical onset or progression. The variables chosen

Table 2.2 Psychosocial Typology of Genomic Disorders

Timing of Clinical Onset

Treatment Can Alter Onset or Progression	Clinical Severity	CHILD/ADOLESCENT 0–20 YES	CHILD/ADOLESCENT 0–20 NO	EARLY/MID ADULTHOOD CHILD REARING 20–60 YES	EARLY/MID ADULTHOOD CHILD REARING 20–60 NO	LATER LIFE >60 YES	LATER LIFE >60 NO
High	High	Hemophilia	Tay-Sachs disease		Huntington disease Alzheimer disease (early onset)		
	Low	Hemophilia					
Variable	High			Breast cancer (HBOC linked) Hemochromatosis		Breast cancer (HBOC linked)	
	Low			Hemochromatosis			
Lower	High						Alzheimer disease (APOE e4 allele linked)
	Low						

(Likelihood of Development)

Note. From Rolland, J. S., & Williams, J. K. (2005). Toward a biopsychosocial model for 21st century genetics. *Family Process, 44*(1), 3–24.

are hypothesized to be the most psychosocially significant for a wide range of genomic disorders. Also, they were selected because they strongly influence the nature of the developmental tasks associated with each nonsymptomatic and post–clinical onset time phase of illness. For example, the level of risk for clinical onset significantly affects the quality of the psychosocial developmental tasks normally associated with the nonsymptomatic phases (described later). Also, the interaction and complementarity of these variables are clinically important. This categorization of genomic disorders is fluid, especially with regard to the emerging options for treatment and the detection of clinical symptoms.

The typology includes disorders in which individuals can be carriers of a genetic mutation related to a specific disease, such as cystic fibrosis (CF). Individuals who have carrier status may have no risk of the disease themselves. But from a broader family system and multigenerational perspective, the risk of CF exists for offspring of persons who are carriers of specific mutations in the CF gene. For instance, consider if someone unaware of being a carrier of a CF mutation were to marry another unaware CF mutation carrier and have a child with diagnosed symptomatic CF. This diagnosis would put both family systems on alert that individuals in their respective families may carry the CF mutation and that risk exists for symptomatic disease in their children. The initial diagnosis of CF means the same experience could happen to anyone else in these two families who might be a silent carrier. The carriers or potential carriers of the CF mutation bear the psychosocial burden related to CF—not for their personal risk of symptomatic disease but for their children, particularly when considering forming a committed relationship and family planning.

To limit the number of variables in this model, timing of at-risk testing in the life cycle was not included as a core variable and is beyond the scope of this chapter. Yet this is both a crucial issue psychosocially and one that is the subject of significant ethical, legal, and policy controversy (see Chapters 17–19). In particular, prenatal diagnosis and carrier testing warrant special consideration because available testing is rapidly growing for a broad range of conditions, and because of highly complex and controversial issues related to carrier testing in minor-age children, elective pregnancy termination, the medical usefulness of testing, and who has final decision-making authority.

Although each typology variable is actually a continuum, it is described here in a categorical manner by the selection of key anchor points along the continuum. In reality, much finer distinctions exist. Consider these anchor points as useful markers to clarify the many shades of gray. The typology can provide a useful way to both organize and highlight complexity for the worlds of clinical practice and research. It is designed to be adaptable to the specific priorities of varied clinical contexts as well as the particular aims of different research studies. Also, it is designed to be fluid and responsive to the evolution of genetic knowledge about causes and treatment of disease. In this sense, it provides a picture of where we are early in the 21st century. Over time, it can provide a sequential picture of how the landscape of genomic health evolves. For instance, the development of preventive measures and effective treatment for Alzheimer disease would move this disease to a different category in the typology.

Psychosocial Typology of
Genomic Illness: Components

Likelihood of Developing a Condition Based on Genetic Mutations

Genomic conditions can be grouped in terms of (1) a high likelihood, based on a high level of penetrance of a genetic mutation; (2) a variable likelihood, reflecting complex multiple genes and gene-environment interactions; and (3) a low likelihood, based on complex genes and environmental interactions. *Penetrance* means the proportion of individuals with the gene mutation who will manifest a particular illness associated with that mutation. Genetic testing is used to identify the presence or absence of mutations in a specific gene or genes. Testing is intended to clarify the fundamental uncertainty of whether a person has a specific genetic mutation. After testing, if the test yields informative results, uncertainty remains about the likelihood that a genomic condition will actually develop and the severity of the health problem.

Variability of expression refers to the range and degree of severity of a genetic disorder. This variable in the typology addresses the likelihood of development, meaning clinical onset. It also refers explicitly to the degree of knowledge about risk that can be clarified for a particular condition through current testing. This variable is meant to be flexible to accommodate ongoing scientific discoveries. This means both the multiple mutations and genes that may be involved in various disorders with the recognition that environmental factors will be increasingly identified that interact with gene mutations and increase the likelihood of symptomatic expression of a disorder. Traditional autosomal dominant inherited conditions with mutations that have a high penetrance, such as Huntington disease, are at one end of the continuum in the high-likelihood category. When the gene mutation is in the high penetrance range, the patient and family members must absorb the certainty that the disease will occur (Sobel & Cowan, 2000). Many recent discoveries in genomic health are currently in the variable range, referring to more common-complex or multifactorial disorders, such as many forms of cancer that are determined by the interaction of multiple genes and environmental factors. Variable-likelihood diseases also include some single-gene disorders that involve significant gene-environment interactions. This category is illustrated in families where individuals have a mutation in a gene for breast and ovarian cancer, but they may or may not develop these diseases (Burke, Pinsky, & Press, 2001). Hemochromatosis is an example of a single-gene disorder in which mutations in the gene may present a variable but lower likelihood of development in people under the age of 50 (Cogswell et al., 2003).

The current understanding of the inheritance patterns for Alzheimer disease is typical of how a disease previously thought of as one now might be divided into separate disease subtypes based on different genetic mutation causes. This nomenclature for Alzheimer disease is likely to evolve as new discoveries further clarify the interaction of genetic and environmental causal aspects of this condition. Two categories of genetic mutations have been identified so far that increase the relative risk of this condition. One group of rare mutations in *presenilin-1, presenilin-2,* or in the beta-amyloid precursor protein genes is familial with an autosomal dominant pattern of inheritance and high penetrance. These mutations are a significant cause of early-onset Alzheimer disease before age 60. However, they account for less than 1% of all cases of Alzheimer disease (Campion et al., 1999; Roses, 1998). In contrast, a more common mutation, the *APOE e4* allele, one variant of the gene that encodes for apolipoprotein E, is present in over 25% of the U.S. population (Nussbaum & Ellis, 2003). For individuals carrying this allele, the risk of Alzheimer disease in their mid-70s increases from 3% in the general population to 8% (Kuusisto et al., 1994; Roses, 1998).

Because of these genetic advances, Alzheimer disease has evolved currently into subpopulations that reflect different levels of risk correlated with different mutations. Those individuals with Alzheimer disease who have mutations in genes associated with early-onset Alzheimer disease have a genetically influenced form of the disease, in which the mutations are highly penetrant and with onset before age 60. Psychosocially, those families who know they carry the *presenilin* or beta-amyloid mutations may live with concerns about likely clinical onset and loss from Alzheimer disease that will begin much earlier in the life cycle, perhaps interfering with prime career and child rearing years. Others with later-onset Alzheimer disease may have a form of the disease with some genetic components. However, in some cases, Alzheimer disease is related to mutations that are common but much less penetrant. Finally, we have all the other individuals who develop Alzheimer disease, for whom the causes are beyond our current knowledge. Over time, with further advances in genomic health, we may be able to identify individuals in this last category who have gene mutations and environmental risk factors that increase the likelihood of developing the disease.

A highly penetrant genetic mutation presents a qualitatively different form of stressor to family members than one with lower penetrance. The kind of posttesting uncertainty is vastly different. With highly penetrant mutations, because of the increased odds of disease onset, families may be more likely to prepare for what lies ahead, though uncertainty remains regarding specifics of the disease expression, such as the age of onset and presenting symptoms. Yet the increased odds of the condition occurring can for some individuals and families be psychologically disabling in terms of life cycle planning and general hopefulness about the future (Brouwer-Dudokdewit et al., 2002; Decruyenaere et al., 2005). With lower-penetrance mutations, living with more ongoing uncertainty about whether the disorder will occur becomes a salient adaptational challenge (see also Chapter 5).

Overall Clinical Severity

The variable of overall clinical severity essentially collapses four of the variables in the original psychosocial typology—disease onset, course, outcome, and disability—into one that can be categorized as either high or low severity of clinical symptoms. Overall, it is intended to convey the expected degree of disease burden for patients and their families. When considered with the likelihood of development variable, this category refines the practical and emotional meaning for those who are also living with the strain of whether or when a disease will occur. For instance, if the gene mutation is in the highly penetrant range, for example, in Huntington disease, the disorder is inevitable; it is also progressive, highly disabling, and fatal. The disease course, including increasing dementia, is fairly predictable and has a severe disease burden. In contrast, increased genetic risk for hereditary breast and ovarian cancer is much more uncertain in terms of whether cancer will occur and the trajectory or disease burden if it does. For some, living with such ambiguities can be extremely psychosocially taxing (Boss, 1999; Rolland, 1990, 2004). Research with highly penetrant, progressive, and fatal conditions like Huntington disease has shown that for the subgroup that pursues presymptomatic testing, life can be more psychosocially manageable regardless of test results (Wiggins et al., 1992). It is unclear whether the same will be true for populations at heightened risk for conditions like colon cancer, where if it does occur, overall clinical prognosis is more variable. Also, there is evidence that testing negative (normal) for a known mutation for a disease with high penetrance and disease burden can be highly psychosocially distressing, when individuals had planned their lives in a more restrictive way assuming they had the mutation (Sobel & Cowan, 2003; Williams, Schutte, Evers, & Holkup, 2000).

Timing of Clinical Onset in the Life Cycle

The timing of onset of a disorder in the individual and family life cycles has profound implications. In this framework of genomic diseases, we describe three time periods of typical onset: those that begin in childhood and adolescence (0–20 years old) (e.g., most cases of cystic fibrosis, asthma, Tay-Sachs disease); those that begin in early-middle adulthood/child rearing years (20–60 years old) (e.g., Huntington disease, breast and ovarian cancer in which a mutation in the *BRCA1* or *BRCA2* gene is identified); and those that begin in later life (60-plus years old) (e.g., most forms of Alzheimer disease). Each of these categories is chosen to correspond roughly to typical phases of both the individual and family life cycles, while recognizing the increasingly varied and expanded life course of individuals and families (Carter & McGoldrick, 1999; Levinson, 1986; Walsh, 2003). In using the FSGI model, it is important to be mindful that the intact biological nuclear family is no longer typical of most individuals and families. Demographic trends show the increased diversity and complexity of family forms and challenges. Also, there has been a shift toward later marriage and child rearing (Pinsof, 2002; Walsh, 2003), meaning that a growing number of women and men are raising children in their 50s and 60s. Key factors include the increase in divorce and remarriage, advances in reproductive technology, gay and lesbian couples having children, and single parents raising children.

Both individual and family life cycle models delineate specific developmental tasks for each phase. By considering the timing of clinical onset in relation to those developmental phases, we can appreciate the major life cycle tasks that will be immediately challenged, as well as future developmental tasks that may be most affected. This can help health professionals and families focus more precisely on advance planning given the vicissitudes of the particular genomic condition. Disorders that occur earlier in the life cycle tend to be the most psychosocially taxing. For instance, disorders that strike a parent during the early-middle adulthood child rearing phase are most disruptive to parenting and overall family stability (Altschuler & McFadyen, 1999; Patterson, 1988). They are likely to affect key family developmental tasks including adjusting the couple relationship with child rearing, financial, and house-hold demands, and realignment of relationships with extended family and grandparenting roles (Carter & McGoldrick, 1999). If testing reveals that a genetically influenced form of breast cancer, or a disorder due to a highly penetrant mutation in a single gene, such as Huntington disease, could manifest itself during this phase, planning for a flexible family structure and roles can facilitate healthy coping and adaptation.

Prevention and Treatment

Conditions can be categorized according to whether or not effective treatment interventions exist to alter clinical onset or progression. Huntington disease exemplifies an illness where, currently, treatment does not prevent clinical onset or halt progression. The medical prog-nosis is poor. Those who have the gene mutation in the fully penetrant range will get the disease, and it is fatal. By contrast, those who carry a gene mutation in the BRCA1 or BRCA2 gene have an increased risk for a type of cancer with early detection methods that may improve prog-nosis (e.g., increased mammographic surveillance), options to decrease the risk of clinical onset (e.g., preventive chemotherapy, bilateral mas-tectomy), and a variety of treatment strategies if breast or ovarian can-cer is later diagnosed (Wooster & Weber, 2003). Regarding risk for familial breast cancer, Patenaude, Guttmacher, and Collins (2002) pointed out, "Genetic and genomic developments may also divide women at risk into two groups: those for whom new drugs offer prom-ise of prevention and those who are not genetically suited to the drugs who may be advised to consider prophylactic surgery, with its atten-dant emotional costs" (p. 273). In terms of the FSGI model, this means that some conditions, like genetically influenced breast cancer, may in-volve more than one type: those that are more highly responsive to preventive treatment and those that are less responsive.

A Psychosocial Typology Matrix

By combining the likelihood of development of a condition based on genetic mutations (high, variable, or low), overall clinical severity (high or low), timing of symptomatic onset in the life cycle (childhood–adolescence, 0–20; early-middle adulthood/child rearing phase, 20–60; later life, 60-plus), and whether there exists effective treatment to alter clinical onset or progression (possible or not), we generate a typology with 36 potential psychosocial types of genomic disorders (see Table 2.2). Each type of condition has a distinct pattern of psychosocial demand based on its inherent biological and environmental responsive features.

To fit the priorities of a clinician or researcher, the number of potential types can be adapted. They can be increased by adding variables, such as timing of testing in the life cycle. Or they can be reduced by combining or eliminating certain variables. This would depend on the relative need for specificity in a particular situation. For instance, conditions for which treatment or prevention exists could be studied in relation to the likelihood of development and severity regardless of when clinical onset occurs in the life cycle.

Extending the Concept of Illness Phases

With predictive, presymptomatic, or carrier genetic testing, we expand our thinking about the phases of chronic disorders (Rolland, 1999; Street & Soldan, 1998) to include the time before a disease with a genetic component appears clinically. Like the crisis, chronic, and terminal phases after clinical manifestation of an illness, it is useful to conceptualize phases before the clinical onset of genetically influenced disease. These are the nonsymptomatic phases of (1) awareness, (2) crisis I pretesting, (3) crisis II test/posttesting, and (4) long-term adaptation (Figure 2.3). These nonsymptomatic phases are distinguished by questions of living with uncertainty. Fundamental issues include the potential amount of genetic knowledge medically available, decisions about how much of that information family members choose to access (Street & Soldan, 1998), and living with the psychosocial impact of those choices.

Nonsymptomatic Phases of Genomic Disorders

Awareness Phase

The nonsymptomatic awareness phase begins with some knowledge of possible genetic risk, but before active consideration or availability of genetic testing. For one family, because of a strong multigenerational history of ataxia, there already existed strong beliefs about vulnerability for an unnamed neurological disease that family members linked primarily with physical resemblance to the affected side of the family. This belief was most evident for one daughter and son who resembled their father and his Northern European ethnicity. Based on the belief that this neurological condition "ran in the family," even before the development of predictive testing, this family had experienced a long-term multigenerational undercurrent of anticipatory loss (the experience of living with the possibility or inevitability of future loss; Rolland, 1990, 1994a, 2004; see Chapter 5). Similar dynamics operate for families with known genetic conditions for which

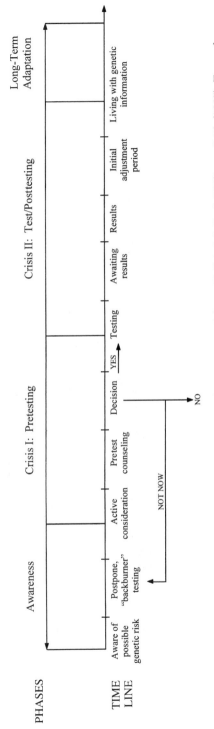

Figure 2.3 Nonsymptomatic time phases of genomic disorders. Excerpted from: Rolland, J. S., & Williams, J. K. (2005). Toward a biopsychosocial model for 21st century genetics. *Family Process, 44*(1), 3–24.

carrier testing may be available, such as hemophilia, where the continuation of an illness in the family system is expected even though the family is uncertain which members will develop it. For example, consider a family in which a son has hemophilia inherited through his mother, who was a carrier of the specific mutation. In this instance, his sister is not at personal risk for the disease. However, she is at 50% risk of being a carrier like her mother. If she is a carrier, any sons she might bear would be at 50% risk of having hemophilia. While aware of this possibility, her engagement in active consideration of carrier testing may remain dormant until adulthood, the time of marriage, or when she actively considers having children of her own.

Some family members in these situations experience life as the "worried well." This phenomenon is prevalent as part of the AIDS epidemic, where some at-risk individuals live in fear, or even a sense of inevitability, that they will eventually become HIV positive. Yet many choose not to get tested to know their HIV status. In some families, the multigenerational experience of illness may seem genetically unremarkable (e.g., they are unaware of genetic risks, do not note illness patterns, or attribute diseases in the family to other causes). These families have not been sensitized to life with genetic risk information and all of its psychosocial ramifications. They may not experience anticipatory loss or concern about lurking genetically influenced conditions, and so may have the sharpest emotional transition as new genetic tests become available for a range of common conditions.

Crisis Phase I: Pretesting

This crisis phase encompasses the period of active consideration of testing, including an understanding of any relevant genetic knowledge as well as the psychosocial ramifications for self and family of pursuing testing. It continues through the period of decision making about whether to get tested. There are a number of key developmental challenges in this phase. One core task is to consider the impact that the decision to pursue genetic testing might have on various family members as well as family dynamics that might affect adjustment. As a family member learns about a genomic condition, that person will need to consider who else in the family may be at risk, who to inform about testing, and with whom to communicate the results. Also, that person will need to consider who to include in decision making about whether to test. In some cases, this would be the spouse or partner, and in others, parents, children, and siblings may also be involved. To address these complex issues effectively, it is most helpful if those considering testing can view the challenge of genetic knowledge as a challenge shared among family members. The emotional intensity of these issues is heavily influenced by the psychosocial characteristics of the specific condition, meaning its likelihood of occurrence, the predicted course and severity, the timing of clinical onset in the life cycle, and whether effective treatments exist that can prevent clinical onset or alter progression. Gaining a psychosocial understanding of the disorder in practical, emotional, and longitudinal terms helps guide a family through this process.

For newly understood illnesses, the nonsymptomatic crisis phase begins for many families when a genetic test becomes available or when a primary care provider suggests consideration. For others who are aware of an existing genetic test, it may begin as they reach a milestone or major transition in the individual or family life cycle resulting in an active desire to consider being tested (e.g., relationship commitment). For instance, some women decide to be tested for the breast-ovarian cancer genes when they reach an age that coincides with the age when another blood relative—a mother, aunt, or older sister—was diagnosed with breast or ovarian cancer. They believe they are in effect entering a period of heightened danger. For other women, this phase may begin when they contemplate starting a family and worry about passing on genetic vulnerability to their children, or when another family member pursues testing and learns that a genomic condition exists in the family.

The intensity of this decision-making process is greatly increased by the type of disease. Jane, a 25-year-old married woman, is a potential carrier of a specific highly penetrant mutation in the dystrophin gene causing Duchenne muscular dystrophy. Since her severely affected brother, Tim, tested positive for the highly penetrant mutation, her issues are analogous to the sister in the earlier example with a brother with hemophilia. Jane entered the nonsymptomatic crisis phase when she and her husband wanted to begin a family. Duchenne muscular dystrophy in her family is caused by a specific mutation that is highly penetrant, has a childhood onset, cannot be prevented except by prenatal diagnosis and elective pregnancy termination, and is generally severe and life shortening. The main difference with Jane's counterpart considering testing for the hemophilia mutation is that the treatment for hemophilia is very effective, potentially decreasing the psychosocial load in the pretesting phase.

This decision-making process may not be a one-time event; some individuals consider and postpone the decision more than once. One 26-year-old married woman with a strong family history of early breast cancer, and a sister who had tested positive for *BRCA1*, considered predictive testing at age 20 and again at 24 before getting married. On both occasions, although anxious about her future risk, she deferred testing after pretesting counseling. However, as she and her husband began to discuss starting a family, her risk of developing a major, potentially life-threatening cancer while raising children and the potential future risk to the next generation tipped the balance. Consultations at that time with the couple led to a decision to proceed with testing.

Frequently, as this vignette illustrates, active entry into a decision regarding testing coincides with major transitions in the individual and family life cycle (e.g., relationship commitment, family planning). Each encounter with the decision-making process may be fraught with intense emotions that can ripple throughout the nuclear and extended family system. When the first family member broaches the testing question, a larger question is at stake: Is this a disease with genetic components and therefore part of our family unit? If so, how would this information affect how we see ourselves as a family (e.g., flawed, stigmatized, special, resilient in the face of adversity)? The intensity of reactions will be influenced by the psychosocial type of the specific condition (Table 2.2). Also, cultural values and attributions of meaning can strongly influence the experience of this phase (see Chapter 6).

Crisis Phase II: Testing and Posttesting

Phase II includes the testing and the early posttest period. Whether family members test positive or negative, either outcome can precipitate a crisis period of reevaluation and incorporation of this knowledge into one's personal and family life.

As with the crisis phase of an illness onset, families must meet certain developmental challenges. These include (1) acknowledging and accepting the "permanence" of the genetic knowledge and its implications, (2) grieving losses or changes in the personal or family identity, (3) creating meaning about the genetic information that preserves a family's sense of mastery and competency, and (4) developing family flexibility in the face of future uncertainty and loss to maximize preservation of key life cycle goals. One family learned that two of five young adult siblings were highly likely to develop spinocerebellar ataxia, an inherited progressive neurological disorder that results in severe muscle incoordination and weakness, including speech and swallowing difficulties. This family was encouraged to have future-oriented discussions about caregiving, role shifts, and financial support when the disease would become disabling for each affected sibling (Taswell & Sholtes, 1999). This exchange exemplified open communication and proactive envisioning of future roles in the face of loss. This type of caregiving-oriented planning can be particularly difficult for family members, such as siblings, who are in early and middle adult phases of the life cycle. Such commitments may need to be revisited and altered depending on the inevitable uncertainties as each sibling's life course and nuclear family unfolds. In these situations, it is important for siblings to consider as an ongoing process the impact of these caregiving decisions, as well as issues of disability and a shortened life span with their partners, each other, and extended kin.

Genetic testing can clarify distinctions between family members regarding predisposition to a variety of serious illnesses. This can have major psychosocial import, as Patenaude et al. (2002) stated: "In some families in which breast and ovarian cancer has occurred with higher than expected frequency, all the female blood relatives in the family may have considered themselves at high, if not certain, risk of developing these cancers. Genetic testing, if undertaken, may now divide the family into those truly at increased risk and those without the BRCA1/2 mutation who are only at the population risk of approximately 10%" (p. 273). Also, it is important to consider the implications of testing results for at-risk family members who defer testing or decide not to be tested. Once a mutation (e.g., BRCA1/2) is identified in a family, those who decide not to be tested still live with a heightened awareness of genetic risk that can affect well-being, especially when addressing significant life cycle decisions, such as starting a family. In addition, relationship realignments can occur among those who test positive or negative, and defer or decide against testing (see Chapter 5). These divisions in the family can have enormous impact on family processes and need to be understood in relation to preexisting functional and dysfunctional family dynamics (see Chapters 4 and 6).

The type of genetic disorder will profoundly affect a family's experience of this phase. Among the most difficult for families are diseases for which no preventive steps or effective treatments are possible, the onset is usually inevitable, and the outcome is grim (e.g., spinocerebellar ataxia, Huntington disease). Sustaining a functional balance between hope and despair is much more challenging for conditions that are currently beyond medical control. Also, there is evidence that, with these types of conditions (progressive, disabling, fatal), a much higher proportion of at-risk families will decline predictive or presymptomatic testing (Babul et al., 1993; Quaid & Morris, 1993), preferring uncertainty, which allows for hope, over the risk of bad news that would bring despair.

Families may be uninformed regarding advances in preventive medical surveillance and lifestyle options that can affect disease onset or outcome. Outdated information or a lack of basic information might contribute to misinformed testing decisions and concerns, especially in families with a multigenerational history of diseases such as breast, ovarian, or colon cancer, where relatives in the past had a relentless course with a fatal outcome, leaving a legacy of hopelessness about these conditions (Reibstein, 2004). Thus, it is important to gather multi-generational information that includes extended family, and for primary care providers to have the most up-to-date information about genomic conditions.

The FSI model distinguishes acute from gradual clinical onset conditions. Some families live in the shadow of concern for many years and mentally rehearse the possibility of developing genomic disorders that "run in" families. This pattern is more akin to that of a gradual-onset disease in the sense of family members having extended time to adapt gradually to the prospect of an illness before the testing phase. Currently, most genetic testing is being made available to high-risk families with extensive histories of diseases like breast cancer. As future testing becomes more widely available for a broad range of illnesses, we may see more people being screened for conditions that have identifiable genetic risk factors. Without careful education in the informed consent process, individuals and their families may be shocked by unexpected positive test results. Family-centered psychoeducation, before and after genetic testing, is a vital approach to mitigating this situation. This means providing information about useful coping and adaptational skills tailored to (1) the psychosocial demands on families of a particular genomic disorder over time, (2) living with specific genetic risk information, and (3) the fit between these psychosocial demands and the strengths and vulnerabilities of each family.

A major difference between the crisis phase with genetic testing and that of a symptomatic illness is the degree of involvement of the health care system. With active disease, an initial period of treatment is typical, providing families with contact and support. In most cases with genetic testing, posttesting contact with the health care system may be minimal or periodic (e.g., more frequent mammograms or colonoscopies). This may also be the experience for families of persons for whom early signs of the disease, such as Huntington disease, may be difficult to recognize or manage (Williams, Schutte, Holkup, Evers, & Muilenburg, 2000). Yet the psychosocial impact may be enormous and individuals and families may benefit from more ongoing or periodic emotional support, timed with difficult transitions. This situation is at odds with the current design of our health care system, where if psychosocial care is provided, it tends to occur around clinically symptomatic health crises.

Long-Term Adaptation Phase

The long-term adaptation phase is the time span between positive genetic testing results and the phase in which the condition manifests. This phase may be short or extend decades or even the rest of a person's life if the genetically influenced illness never emerges analogous to the long haul of living with active disease, although here it involves living with known genetic risk. Families and each member need to maximize their autonomy in the face of possible or inevitable loss. Minimizing relationship skews between the genetically affected and unaffected members is another key developmental challenge (Rolland, 1994b). Resilience can be forged when the experience of genetic knowledge heightens their appreciation of life and relationships, puts problems and priorities into perspective, and fosters meaning and purpose that transcend suffering and loss (Walsh, 2006). The ability of family members to live as fully as possible, given heightened genetic risk, is a major challenge of this phase (Rolland, 2004; see Chapter 5). Several keys to families' maintaining mastery include the following:

1. Acknowledging the possibility or inevitability of future loss; over time, families need to find a balance between open communication that facilitates proactive planning and the need to keep threatened illness in perspective and live a healthy life for as long as possible
2. Remaining mindful of the possible impact of living with genetic knowledge on current and future phases of the family and individual members' development; this consciousness can help build flexibility into family life cycle planning that realistically conserves and adjusts major goals
3. Sustaining hope and finding meaning that transcends the eventual biological outcome
4. Remaining current regarding new information about genetic risk and advances in preventive or symptomatic treatment

Table 2.3 provides a synopsis of the key individual and family developmental tasks associated with each of the nonsymptomatic phases.

Transition Periods

Critical transition periods link these nonsymptomatic time phases. Several authors (Carter & McGoldrick, 1999; Levinson, 1986; Meleis, Sawyer, Eun-Ok, Messais, & Schumacher, 2000) have clarified the importance of transition periods in the family and individual adult life

Table 2.3 Nonsymptomatic Time Phases of Genomic Disorders: Developmental Challenges

Awareness phase (begins with awareness of possible genetic risk)
1. Establish initial communication in family regarding illness and genetics.
2. Seek basic information regarding genetics of specific illness from primary care provider.
3. Consider whether individual family members could pursue genetic testing (e.g., rules for need for family consensus or individual autonomy).
4. Cope and adapt to concerns about conditions where no genetic testing yet exists.

Crisis phase I: pretesting
1. Consider how decision might impact different nuclear and extended family members.
2. Gain understanding of genetics of illness.
3. Gain psychosocial understanding of the illness in
    a. Practical and emotional terms.
    b. Longitudinal and developmental terms.
4. Gain appreciation of developmental perspective (individual, family, illness development).
5. View challenge of genetic knowledge as a shared one in "we" terms.
6. Consider who in family may be at risk and whom to inform (inclusion, privacy).
7. Consider whom to include in decision making about whether to test (e.g., spouse/partner).
8. Explore beliefs and meaning of genetics (e.g., blame, stigma, fate, special).
9. Make decision about testing: yes, no, defer.

Crisis phase II: testing and posttesting
1. Crisis coping and adaptation.
2. Accept permanence of genetic testing knowledge.
3. Maximize preservation of family identity before genetic knowledge.
4. Create meaning that promotes personal and family mastery.
5. Acknowledge possibilities of loss related to genetic risk while sustaining hope.
6. Develop flexibility in the face of uncertainty.
7. Consider implications of testing results for family members who test normal and at-risk members who have not been tested.
8. Establish functional collaborative relationships with health care providers.
9. Adapt to any preventive treatments and health care settings.

Long-term adaptation phase (if results positive)
1. Maximize autonomy and connectedness for all family members within scope of genetic knowledge.
2. Minimize relationship skews.
3. Mindfulness of possible impact on current and future phases of family and individual life cycles.
4. Live with anticipatory loss and uncertainty.
5. Balance open communication (vs. avoidance, denial) and proactive planning with need to live a "normal" life, keeping threatened illness in perspective.
6. Maintain up-to-date genetic and medically relevant information.

Note. From Rolland, J. S., & Williams, J. K. (2005). Toward a biopsychosocial model for 21st century genetics. *Family Process, 44*(1), 3–24.

cycles. Transitions, such as before and after testing, are times when family members consider the fit of their life structure, plans, and dreams in the face of developmental challenges in the next phase. Unfinished business from the previous phase can complicate or block movement forward. Adaptative strategies in one phase may be maladaptive for another and require change (Penn, 1983). For example, it is useful for a family to pull together in the crisis period around genetic risk testing, but overattentiveness can stifle the pursuit of normative developmental goals in the nonsymptomatic long-term adaptation phase.

CLINICAL AND SERVICE DELIVERY IMPLICATIONS

Using the FSGI and FSI Models Together

The FSGI model offers a typology and nonsymptomatic time phase schema for genomic conditions, intended to be used sequentially with the previously developed FSI model, designed for illnesses after they become clinically apparent. The nonsymptomatic phases flow naturally into those phases after clinical onset (crisis, chronic, and terminal phases; Figure 2.4). At the time of clinical onset, the overall clinical severity variable in the genomic disorders typology can then be separated into its key components: type of onset, course, outcome, incapacitation, and level of uncertainty. Together the new FSGI and original FSI models enable conceptualization of a condition with a genetic component through the individual and family life cycle.

As an example, consider a family. The father, Jim, age 50, was the first family member diagnosed with Huntington disease, with onset at age 40. His son, Sam, and a daughter, Sarah, were in their early teens at his diagnosis. This condition falls into the category of high likelihood of development of clinical manifestations, high severity, onset in early-middle adulthood, and no effective treatment to prevent onset or alter progression. These characteristics will heavily influence family members' psychosocial challenges and experience of the nonsymptomatic phases. All potentially at-risk family members are in a nonsymptomatic awareness phase until they actively consider testing, for instance, when Sam reaches adulthood. At this point, Sam enters the crisis I pretesting phase. He may proceed with testing, or he may defer testing (returning to the awareness phase) and reconsider it actively at another developmental transition (e.g., at the time of marriage or family planning). Once Sam decides to go ahead with testing, he enters the crisis II test/posttest phase, which continues through the waiting period, testing results, and initial period of adaptation to the news—in

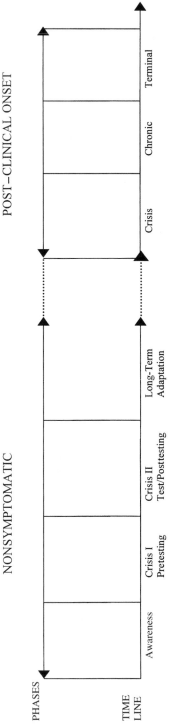

Figure 2.4 Time phases of genomic disorders. Excerpted from: Rolland, J. S., & Williams J. K. (2005). Toward a biopsychosocial model for 21st century genetics. *Family Process, 44*(1), 3–24.

this case, that he carries the mutation. He now enters a nonsympto-matic long-term adaptation phase that lasts until clinical symptoms emerge. Then the FSI post–clinical onset typology tracks the course of the illness. In this case, Huntington disease falls into the category of gradual clinical onset, progressive course, fatal outcome, and highly disabling. This reality will influence the nature of the challenges facing Sam, his partner, and any children they have as they now go through the phases following clinical onset: crisis, chronic, and terminal. It is important to recognize that, while responding to the illness and care-giving challenges presented by a family member's active disease phases, other family members may cope simultaneously with chal-lenges of their own nonsymptomatic phases. For instance, the daugh-ter, Sarah (who deferred testing), may assume responsibilities for her father and her brother while coping with her own fears of developing the disease (see Chapter 5).

Clinical Implications

This typological model provides a framework for assessment and clin-ical intervention by facilitating an understanding of genomic diseases in psychosocial terms. The typology variables—likelihood of develop-ment of a condition based on genetic mutations, overall clinical sever-ity, timing of symptomatic onset in the life cycle, and whether effective treatment interventions exist to prevent clinical onset or alter progression—provide markers that focus a clinical assessment and in-tervention. For instance, Huntington disease, which has a devastating course and fatal outcome, can strike an at-risk parent during child rear-ing. For offspring aware that Huntington disease runs in the family, is-sues of testing, future caregiving, and loss can surface strongly at the time of courtship, commitment, and contemplating starting a family. Preventive consultations to help the at-risk person and couple early on can facilitate highly emotionally charged but important communi-cation, decision making, and contingency planning. It is critical to in-quire about the partner's understanding of Huntington disease and his or her multigenerational experience with illness and loss, particu-larly any similar conditions. Professional support will be much more difficult in situations where family members attempt to maintain se-crecy about the presence of conditions like Huntington disease (see Chapter 6).

The concept of time phases provides a way to think longitudinally and appreciate genetic conditions as an ongoing process with land-marks, transition points, and changing demands. A timeline for ge-nomic disorders delineates non- and postsymptomatic psychosocial phases of the disorder, each phase with its own unique developmental challenges. It is important for family members to address phase-related tasks within the time frame of each successive developmental phase of the illness. Clinicians can help family members acquire a common understanding of the practical and emotional demands of living with a condition over time in the nonsymptomatic crisis phase. This facilitates more focused communication about how to cope and adapt to challenges related to the future risk of the specific condition. Clinicians can assess strengths and vulnerabilities in relation to the present and future phases of the genomic illness. A timeline can reveal clustering of stressors or concurrence of nonsymptomatic time phase transitions with other symptoms in the family, such as a child's behavior or emotional problems (e.g., anxiety, depression). Symptoms may be an expression of concern about an at-risk member, as the following case illustrates.

Phong, age 8, from a traditional first-generation Vietnamese family, was experiencing anxiety and declining school grades. Her maternal grandmother had recently died of breast cancer and her maternal aunt currently had breast cancer. She revealed to her pediatrician her secret fears about her mother's risk of getting breast cancer. Family communication of these issues was constrained by cultural norms and beliefs that discussion of risk could harm at-risk family members. Further, they believed that genetic risk meant inevitable disease and preferred to leave matters up to fate. A culturally sensitive collaborative intervention included the pediatrician, a genetic counselor, and a family therapist. Sessions with the genetic counselor provided accurate information about the BRCA1/2 mutations, early detection, and preventive steps that could alter the course of breast or ovarian cancer. Genetic testing was recommended for the mother. In this crisis testing phase, the family therapist explored the parents' concerns and clarified that living with increased genetic risk would not inevitably lead to cancer. The mother decided to have genetic testing, learning she was BRCA1 positive. Posttesting consultations with the family therapist facilitated more open communication among family members regarding threatened loss of the aunt and now the mother, and the recent loss of the grandmother. With the mother's positive results, they also faced the possible genetic risk to Phong and, with the help of a genetic counselor, decided to defer decision making for her testing until late adolescence. The family faced both posttesting crisis phase challenges for the mother and awareness phase issues for Phong.

The framework helps to clarify treatment planning. Goal setting is guided by awareness of the components of family functioning (see Chapter 4) most relevant to particular types and phases of a genomic condition. Sharing this information with family members and deciding on specific goals provides a better sense of control and realistic hope. Such knowledge also alerts families to warning signs of distress, such as persistent symptoms of anxiety, depression, or relational conflict or distancing when individual or family consultation would be helpful. This knowledge also can guide families in seeking mental health services at appropriate times for brief, goal-oriented consultation or therapy.

We strongly recommend a collaborative psychosocial-biomedical team approach that provides longitudinal family-centered care to prevent genetically tested individuals and families from becoming isolated with their potential suffering (McDaniel, Campbell, Hepworth, & Lorenz, 2005; Seaburn, Gunn, Mauksh, Gawinski, & Lorenz, 1996). Just as all mental health professionals need some basic understanding of genetics and genetic testing, all health professionals need education regarding the common psychosocial strains and dilemmas over time for individuals and families entering the genetic testing process. The FSGI model helps counteract the excessive compartmentalizing of "biomedical" health and "psychosocial" mental health disciplines—a key to facilitating effective collaboration.

Service Delivery Applications

In terms of the organization of services, the FSGI model suggests the value of periodic assessment and reevaluation of individuals, couples, and families in relation to both the nonsymptomatic and symptomatic phases of a condition. This underscores the importance of including a mental health professional as part of the genetic health care team. The time phases and transition points can inform the timing of psychosocial consultations. Strengths and weaknesses in various components of family functioning can be addressed as relevant to the psychosocial type and phase of the condition. Scheduling timely, preventive "psychosocial checkups" with a primary care clinician or family therapist is welcomed, when family members learn the usefulness of preparing for future challenges. For example, consider a family where the most common form of hereditary colorectal cancer, hereditary nonpolyposis colorectal cancer, is carried on the father's side and where he is known to have the mutation (Lynch & Chapelle, 2003). The father, age 40, has been receiving screening colonoscopies for over ten years. With adolescents, the family physician suggests a consultation with the parents regarding the usefulness and timing of genetic testing for their 16- and 17-year-old sons, who are approaching early adulthood, when screening colonoscopies would begin for those carrying the mutation.

Follow-up consultations with a medical family therapist, family physician, and genetic specialist working collaboratively facilitate family communication, while respecting each son's autonomy concerning whether and when to seek genetic testing (McDaniel, Campbell, Hepworth, & Lorenz, 2005).

This typology can facilitate the development of various preventively oriented psychoeducational or support groups for patients and their families (Anderson, Reiss, & Hogarty, 1986; Gonzales & Steinglass, 2002; McFarlane, 2002; Rolland, 1994a; Steinglass, 1998; see Chapter 6). For instance, groups can be designed to meet the needs of patients and families dealing with highly penetrant mutations and high clinical severity conditions in the pretesting, posttesting, and long-term non-symptomatic adaptation phase; those with clinical onset during the child rearing years of early-mid adulthood (ages 20–60); and those with lower penetrance mutations that can result in conditions with onset during later life (age 60-plus). Such groupings are especially useful when there are not enough families involved with any particular disorder to form a specific group (e.g., rare disorder, rural setting). Thinking about group-oriented services in terms of the clusters of psychosocial demands of genomic conditions helps overcome such obstacles while preserving the group's thematic coherence. These services can relieve feelings of isolation expressed by some family members after genetic testing has been completed. New models of involving families with supports in the health care system are needed for persons in the non-symptomatic long-term adaptation phase.

Also, designing brief psychoeducational modules, timed for critical phases of particular types of diseases, helps families to accept and digest manageable portions of a long-term coping process (Rolland, 1994a). Each module can be tailored to a particular nonsymptomatic or clinical phase of the illness and target relevant family skills. Such an educational approach provides a cost-effective means of prevention, reaching families at high risk for maladaptation.

RESEARCH IMPLICATIONS

The FSGI model has several important research implications. Cognizance of the different time phases is important for study design and sample selection in an assessment or intervention study (nonsymptomatic: awareness, crisis pre- and posttesting, and long-term adaptation; or post–clinical onset: crisis, chronic, and terminal). Unreliable or confounded results are likely if studies differ in their timing, or if subjects within a study are in different phases. Knowledge of the different time phases can inform the spacing of intervals in multiple observation and follow-up evaluation.

The typology can facilitate research designed to sort out the relative importance of different psychosocial variables across a spectrum of genomic diseases. This approach posits that conditions grouped within the same category have qualitatively and quantitatively the highest congruence of psychosocial demands on the family unit and each member. Disorders within a particular category can be considered crudely matched as to the likelihood of clinical manifestation of genetic mutations, overall clinical severity, timing of symptomatic onset in the life cycle, and whether effective treatment interventions exist to prevent symptomatic onset or alter clinical progression. Because each of these variables exists on a continuum, the degree of homogeneity of study cases can be fine tuned according to the aims of the research.

For example, one could study a subset of people with a specific genetic risk for Parkinson or Alzheimer disease, where the alpha-synuclein and presenilin-1, presenilin-2, or beta-amyloid precursor protein mutations are present (Campion et al., 1999; Duvoisin, 1996; Polymeropoulos et al., 1997). Both disease populations are characterized by subpopulations in which cases are due to several genetic mutations with high likelihood of manifestation, high clinical severity, mid- or later-life onset, and a clinical onset that is not preventable. This design might allow significant generalizations for that cluster or psychosocial type of disease.

The typology also facilitates isolation of a critical variable of genomic disorders for more intensive study. For instance, one might ask: How important is family adaptability for genetically influenced conditions that have high versus low penetrance genetic mutations in the posttesting, nonsymptomatic phase? A comparison could be made between two conditions where the likelihood of clinical onset is related to high- and low-penetrance mutations, respectively, but that are matched for the other typology variables. For example, Huntington disease and a subset of Alzheimer disease, those with the *APOE e4* allele, could be compared. The diseases are roughly matched in clinical severity (regarding major cognitive impairment) and current lack of effective treatment to prevent clinical onset and progression; and both generally occur at midlife or later. At the same time, they are typologically distinct. The Huntington disease mutation is in a single gene and may be in a highly penetrant range. The *APOE e4* allele variant confers a very modest added risk of Alzheimer disease. For individuals who have tested positive, the person with the Huntington disease gene mutation lives with knowledge of certain onset at midlife of a devastating disease, while the counterpart with the *APOE e4* allele lives with a relatively mild increased risk of Alzheimer disease, even though the disease burden, if it occurs, is similar.

The model simplifies the design of studies intended to explore the interactional effects of the typology's variables. As an extension of the hypothetical study just described, by using a 2×2 design, one could investigate how conditions with high versus low likelihood of development interact with conditions that manifest during early-mid adulthood (child rearing years) versus later adulthood (postlaunching).

Overall, the FSGI typology and time phase matrix provide a framework to generate and test hypotheses about the relationship of various components of family or individual functioning to disease adaptation for different genomic illness types and phases. For instance, if we operationalize the typology, time phases, and components of family functioning (e.g., cohesion, problem solving) as three distinct variables then three kinds of prototypical comparisons can be generated holding any two variables constant. This would facilitate the following inquiry:

1. Given illness type X in the testing and posttesting phase, how does the level of family cohesion affect family adaptation to genetic information?
2. Given illness type X with high family cohesion, how are coping and adaptation affected longitudinally in each of the nonsymptomatic time phases?
3. How does high family cohesion in the testing/posttesting phase affect adaptation to different types of genetically influenced conditions?

This framework can be useful for meta-analysis of previous study data. Stratification of data according to time phases and typology may lead to new insights and more succinct hypotheses. Definitions of independent and dependent variables, along with what to control, will be clarified. When used in conjunction with well-researched models of individual (Miller & Diefenbach, 1998; Miller & Schnoll, 2000) and family functioning (see Chapter 1; Feetham & Meister, 1999), components of the typology and time phases clarify what to control in a study design, helping advance psychosocial research in genomic health.

Finally, serious mental conditions such as schizophrenia, bipolar disorder, and autism are currently understood as having genetic components (McGuffin, Owen, & Gottesman, 2002; Plomin, Defries, McClearn, & McGuffin, 2000; Reiss, Neierhiser, Hetherington, & Plomin, 2000; see Chapter 8). In coming years, behavioral genetic research will better clarify specific genetic mutations, their degree of risk, and interactions with psychosocial factors that can heighten or decrease bi-ological risk and influence the course of the illness. Recent research suggests that family interaction can be an important protective factor counterbalancing genetic risk related to mental health conditions (Reiss et al., 2000; Tienari et al., 2004). This kind of complex family in-teraction is probably not limited to psychiatric disorders, and may well operate in common physical disorders that include genetic factors as causes. This underscores the vital importance of family-based biopsy-chosocial research in genomics.

CONCLUSION

The ability to identify genetic factors that increase the likelihood that individuals, their siblings, and their offspring will develop a gene-tically influenced disease has created new and potentially difficult challenges for families. Prior definitions of health and illness are no longer sufficient when one considers the opportunity to learn informa-tion about the possibility of future development of disease through ge-netic testing. Knowledge of future disease risk must be managed within a context of family relationships, cultural beliefs, resources, and the wider health care and societal communities. This chapter presents the FSGI model as a conceptual framework to organize the expanding and complex landscape of conditions with genetic components based on key characteristics grouping useful clusters of disorders with simi-lar psychosocial demands over the nonsymptomatic phases before and after genetic testing. This model provides a mechanism for considering an expanded definition of disease that includes the time prior to clini-cal diagnosis, as well as the potential influences of genetic information on individuals and families across the life cycle. The model can use-fully guide both clinical practice and research endeavors in the rapidly developing universe of genomic health.

NOTE

1. When genetic tests are used to identify the high likelihood that a healthy person will develop an inherited disease (e.g., Huntington disease), the test is termed a *presymptomatic genetic test*. For some inherited disorders, a genetic test will identify genetic susceptibility through identification of genetic factors that increase the likelihood that the person with a family history of the disorder will develop the disease (e.g., familial breast and ovarian cancer). This is termed *predictive testing*. When tests are used to identify if a person has a mutation in

one copy of a gene for a recessive condition (e.g., cystic fibrosis, Duchenne muscular dystrophy), it is termed *carrier testing*. In most cases, carriers do not have symptoms of the disease but have a 50% chance of passing the gene with the mutation on to their children (Secretary's Advisory Committee on Genetic Testing, 2000).

REFERENCES

Altschuler, J., & McFadyen, A. (Eds.). (1999). Parental illness [Special issue]. *Journal of Family Therapy, 21*(3).

Anderson, C., Reiss, D., & Hogarty, G. (1986). *Schizophrenia and the family.* New York: Guilford.

Babul, R., Adam, S., Kremer, B., Dufrasne, S., Wiggins, S., Huggins, M., et al. (1993). Attitudes toward direct predictive testing for the Huntington's disease gene: Relevance for other adult-onset diseases. *Journal of the American Medical Association, 270,* 2321–2325.

Bateson, G. (1972). *Steps to an ecology of mind.* New York: W.W. Norton.

Bateson, G. (1979). *Mind and nature: A necessary unity.* New York: Dutton.

Boss, P. (1999). *Ambiguous loss: Learning to live with unresolved grief.* Boston: Harvard University Press.

Brouwer-Dudokdewit, A. C., Savenije, A., Zoeteweij, M., Maat-Kievit, A., & Tibben, A. (2002). A hereditary disorder in the family and the family life cycle: Huntington disease as a paradigm. *Family Process, 41,* 677–692.

Burke, W., Pinsky, L., & Press, N. (2001). Categorizing genetic tests to identify their ethical, legal, and social implications. *American Journal of Medical Genetics, 106,* 233–240.

Campion, D., Dumanchin, C., Hannequin, D., Dubois, B., Belliard, S., Puel M., et al. (1999). Early-onset Alzheimer autosomal dominant disease: Prevalence, genetic heterogeneity, and mutation spectrum. *American Journal of Human Genetics, 65,* 664–670.

Carter, E. A., & McGoldrick, M. (Eds.) (1999). *The evolving family life cycle: Individual, family, and social perspectives* (3rd ed.). New York: Allyn and Bacon.

Cogswell, M., Gallagher, M., Steinberg, K., Caudill, S., Looker, A., Bowman, B., et al. (2003). HFE genotype and transferring saturation in the United States. *Genetics in Medicine, 5*(4), 304–310.

Collins, F. S., Green, E., Guttmacher, A. E., & Guyer, M. S. (2003). A vision for the future of genomic research. *Nature, 422,* 835–847.

Decruyenaere, M., Evers-Kiebooms, G., Boogaerts, A., Demyttenaere, K., Dom, R., & Fryns, J. (2005). Partners of mutation-carriers for Huntington's disease: Forgotten persons? *European Journal of Human Genetics, 13,*1005–1085.

Duvoisin, R. C. (1996). Recent advances in the genetics of Parkinson's disease. *Advances in Neurology, 69,* 33–40.

Engel, G. L. (1977). The need for a new medical model: A challenge for biomedicine. *Science, 196,* 129–136.

Feetham, S. L., & Meister, S. B. (1999). Nursing research of families: State of the science and correspondence with policy. In A. S. Hinshaw, S. Feetham, & J. Shaver (Eds.), *Handbook of Clinical Nursing Research* (pp. 251–272) Thousand Oaks, CA: Sage.

Golub, T. R. (2001). Genomic approaches to the pathogenesis of hematologic malignancy. *Current Opinions in Hematology, 8,* 252–261.

Golub, T. R., Slonim, D. K., Tamayo, P., Huard, C., Gaasenbeek, M., Mesirov, J. P., et al. (1999). Molecular classification of cancer: Class discovery and class prediction by gene expression monitoring. *Science, 286,* 531–537.

Gonzalez, S., & Steinglass, P. (2002). Application of multifamily groups in chronic medical disorders. In W. F. McFarlane (Ed.), *Multifamily groups in the treatment of severe psychiatric disorders* (pp. 315–341). New York: Guilford.

Kuusisto, J., Koivisto, K., Kervinen, K., Mykkanen, L., Helkala E. L., Vanhanen M., et al. (1994). Association of apolipoprotein E phenotypes with late onset Alzheimer's disease: Population based study. *British Medical Journal, 309*: 636–638.

Levinson, D. J. (1986). A conception of adult development. *American Psychologist, 41,* 3–13.

Lynch, H. T., & de la Chapelle, A. (2003). Genomic medicine: Hereditary colorectal cancer. *New England Journal of Medicine, 348,* 919–932.

McDaniel, S., Campbell, T., Hepworth, J., & Lorenz, A. (2005). *Family-oriented primary care: A manual for medical providers* (2nd ed.). New York: Springer-Verlag.

McFarlane, W. F. (Ed.) (2002). *Multifamily groups in the treatment of severe psychiatric disorders.* New York: Guilford.

McGuffin, P., Owen, M. J., & Gottesman, I. (2002). *Psychiatric genetics and genomics.* Oxford, UK: Oxford University Press.

Meleis, A. I., Sawyer, L. M., Eun-Ok, I., Messais, D. K. G., & Schumacher, K. (2000). Experiencing transitions: An emerging middle-range theory. *Advances in Nursing Science, 23*(1), 12–28.

Miller, S. M., & Diefenbach, M. (1998). The Cognitive-Social Health Information Processing (C-SHIP) Model: A theoretical framework for research in behavioral oncology. In D. S. Krantz & A. Baum (Eds.), *Technology and methods in behavioral medicine* (pp. 219–244). Mahwah, NJ: Lawrence Erlbaum.

Miller, S. M., & Schnoll, R. A. (2000). When seeing is feeling: A cognitive-emotional approach to coping with health stress. In M. Lewis & J. Haviland (Eds.), *Handbook of emotion* (pp. 538–557). New York: Plenum.

Nussbaum, R. L., & Ellis, C. E. (2003). Genomic medicine: Alzheimer's disease and Parkinson's disease. *New England Journal of Medicine, 348,* 1356–1364.

Quaid, K., & Morris, M. (1993). Reluctance to undergo predictive testing by those at risk for Huntington's disease. *American Journal of Medical Genetics, 45,* 41–45.

Patenaude, A. F., Guttmacher, A., & Collins, F. (2002). Genetic testing and psychology: New roles, new responsibilities. *American Psychologist, 57*(4), 271–282.

Patterson, J. M. (1988). Chronic illness in children and the impact on families. In C. S. Chilman, E. W. Nunnally, & F. M. Cox (Eds.), *Chronic illness and disability: Families in trouble series* (vol. 2, pp. 69–107). Newbury Park, CA: Sage.

Penn, P. (1983). Coalitions and binding interactions in families with chronic illness. *Family Systems Medicine, 1*(2), 16–25.

Pinsof, W. M. (2002). The death of "Till death us do part": The transformation of pair-bonding in the 20th century. *Family Process, 41*, 135–157.

Plomin, R., Defries, J. C., McClearn, G. E., & McGuffin, F. (2000). *Behavioral genetics.* London: WH Freeman.

Polymeropoulos, M. H., Lavedan, C., Leroy, E., et al. (1997). Mutation in the alpha-synuclein gene identified in families with Parkinson's disease. *Science, 276*, 2045–2047.

Reibstein, J. (2004). Staying alive: My family inheritance of breast cancer. In F. Walsh & M. McGoldrick (Eds.), *Living beyond loss: Death in the family* (2nd ed., pp. 406–413). New York: Norton.

Reiss, D., Neierhiser, J., Hetherington, M., & Plomin, R. (2000). *The relationship code: Deciphering genetic and social influence on adolescent development.* Boston: Harvard University Press.

Rolland, J. S. (1984). Toward a psychosocial typology of chronic and life-threatening illness. *Family Systems Medicine, 2*, 245–263.

Rolland, J. S. (1987a). Chronic illness and the life cycle: A conceptual framework. *Family Process, 26*(2), 203–221.

Rolland, J. S. (1987b). Family illness paradigms: Evolution and significance. *Family Systems Medicine, 5*(4), 467–486.

Rolland, J. S. (1990). Anticipatory loss: A family systems developmental framework. *Family Process, 29*(3), 229–244.

Rolland, J. S. (1994a). *Families, illness, and disability: An integrative treatment model.* New York: Basic Books.

Rolland, J. S. (1994b). In sickness and in health: The impact of illness on couples' relationships. *Journal of Marital and Family Therapy, 20*(4), 327–349.

Rolland, J. S. (1998). Beliefs and collaboration: Evolution over time. *Families, Systems and Health, 16*(1), 7–25.

Rolland, J. S. (1999). Families and genetic fate: A millennial challenge. *Families, Systems and Health, 17*(1), 123–133.

Rolland, J. S. (2003). Mastering family challenges in serious illness and disability. In F. Walsh (Ed.), *Normal family processes* (3rd ed., pp. 460–489). New York: Guilford.

Rolland, J. S. (2004). Helping families with anticipatory loss and terminal illness. In F. Walsh & M. McGoldrick (Eds.), *Living beyond loss: Death in the family* (2nd ed., pp. 213–237). New York: Norton.

Rolland, J. S., & Williams, J. K. (2005). Toward a biopsychosocial model for 21st century genetics. *Family Process, 44*(1), 3–24.

Roses, A. D. (1994). Apolipoprotein E alleles as risk factors in Alzheimer's disease. *Annual Review of Medicine, 47*, 387–400.

Roses, A. D. (1998). Alzheimer's disease: A model of gene mutations and susceptibility polymorphisms for complex psychiatric diseases. *American Journal of Medical Genetics, 81*, 49–57.

Seaburn, D., Gunn, W., Mauksh, L., Gawinski, A., & Lorenz, A. (Eds.) (1996). *Models of collaboration: A guide for mental health professionals working with physicians and health care providers.* New York: Basic Books.

Secretary's Advisory Committee on Genetic Testing. (2000). *A public consultation of oversight of genetic tests.* National Institutes of Health. Bethesda, MD, January 31. Available: http://www4od.nih.gov/oba/sacgt.html

Sobel, S., & Cowan, D. B. (2000). Impact of genetic testing for Huntington's disease on the family system. *American Journal of Medical Genetics, 90*(1), 49–59.

Sobel, S., & Cowan, C. B. (2003). Ambiguous loss and disenfranchised grief: The impact of DNA predictive testing on the family as a system. *Family Process, 42*(1), 47–59.

Steinglass, P. (1998). Multiple family discussion groups for patients with chronic medical illness. *Families, Systems, and Health, 16*(1/2), 55–71.

Street, E., & Soldan, J. (1998). A conceptual framework for the psychosocial issues faced by families with genetic conditions. *Families, Systems and Health, 16*(3), 217–233.

Taswell, H., & Sholtes, S. (1999). Predictive genetic testing: A story of one family. *Families, Systems and Health, 17*(1), 111–123.

Tienari, P., Wynne, L. C., Sorri, A., Lahti, I., Laksy, K., Moring, J., et al. (2004). Genotype-environment interaction in schizophrenia-spectrum disorder: Long-term follow-up study of Finnish adoptees. *British Journal of Psychiatry, 184*(3), 216–222.

Wagner, K. R. (2002). Genetic disease of muscle. *Neurological Clinics, 20*, 645–678.

Walsh, F. (2003). Changing families in a changing world. In F. Walsh (Ed.), *Normal family processes: Growing diversity and complexity* (3rd ed., pp. 3–26). New York: Guilford.

Walsh, F. (2006). *Strengthening family resilience* (2nd ed.). New York: Guilford.

Wiggins, S., Whyte, P., Huggins, M., Adam, S., Theilman, J., Bloch, M., et al. (1992). The psychological consequences of predictive testing for Huntington's disease. *New England Journal of Medicine, 327*, 1401–1405.

Williams, J. K., Schutte, D. L., Evers, C., & Holkup, P. A. (2000). Redefinition: Coping with normal results from predictive gene testing for neurodegenerative disorders. *Research in Nursing and Health, 23*, 260–269.

Williams, J. K., Schutte, D. L., Holkup, P. A., Evers, C., & Muilenburg, A. (2000). Psychosocial impact of predictive testing for Huntington disease on support persons. *American Journal of Medical Genetics (Neuropsychiatric Genetics), 96*, 353–359.

Wooster, R., & Weber, B. L. (2003). Genomic medicine: Breast and ovarian cancer. *New England Journal of Medicine, 348*, 2339–2347.

PART II

INDIVIDUAL AND FAMILY
MODELS OF GENETICS

Chapter 3

The Individual Facing Genetic Issues

Information Processing, Decision Making, Perception, and Health-Protective Behaviors

*Karen Hurley, Suzanne M. Miller, Lisa R. Rubin,
and David Weinberg*

THE GENOMIC REVOLUTION HAS EXPONENTIALLY INCREASED THE amount of information available to individuals regarding threats to their health. From its roots in prenatal testing, genetic testing is currently or will soon be available for a variety of pediatric- and adult-onset disorders (Ackerman, 2005; Efferth & Volm, 2005; League & Hooper, 2005; Liljestrom et al., 2005; Garber & Offit, 2005; Tan, Chan, Chan, & George, 2005; Zoller & Cox, 2005). The number of conditions and disorders subject to genetic testing is expanding rapidly. Hence, genetic risk information, once only relevant mainly to specific ethnic groups and members of families subject to relatively rare disorders, is becoming relevant to more and more of the general population (Khoury, McCabe, & McCabe, 2003). The exciting promise of the genomic era is that learning one's genetic information can allow one to take steps to mitigate, avert, or at least anticipate and plan for potential health threats, in the absence of disease in the present. Genetic information can also inform treatment after onset of disease. Genetic information can thus afford a sense of control, inform prevention and treatment efforts, support health behavior change, and contribute to emotional adjustment. As genetic knowledge and options continue to expand, and as this feedback becomes increasingly available to the wider public, it is crucial that we understand how individuals process this information; that is, how they comprehend, interpret, and incorporate it into their health care decisions and into their lives.

Information processing at its simplest level literally refers to the brain's structural capacity to carry out cognitive operations (Marois & Ivanoff, 2005). Functions such as attention and memory are bounded by factors that restrict, distort, or other otherwise modify incoming information. At a more abstract level, information processing follows a computational metaphor (Miller, 2003) in which information is incorporated into algorithms of beliefs to yield optimized health decisions and behaviors (Montgomery, 2004). In the medicolegal realm, the accepted (and the most familiar) standard for information processing is informed consent. Informed consent is typically seen as a social-contractual task, in which information is transferred from one individual to another without alteration. The assumption here is that individuals can assume responsibility for their care and can make rational choices based on objective calculations of the costs and benefits of a particular medical intervention (Kegley, 2002).

The genetic counseling field has followed an expanded version of the informed consent model, in which patients are guided in a nondirective fashion to consider the benefits, limitations, and drawbacks of genetic testing (Fine, 1993). The fact that transmission of genetic information takes place in a counseling setting itself implies a shift away from informed consent as a legal transaction to more of a patient-centered approach. This assumption takes the focus beyond the immediate testing decision to risk management and treatment options after testing and, importantly, to the psychological impact of these decisions. The genetic counseling literature, particularly in the areas of prenatal testing, Huntington disease, and cancer predisposition, is rich with descriptive themes of identity, guilt, distress, family communication, and treatment choices. All of these themes suggest that information processing is done with the "heart" as well as the "head" and point to the centrality of health behaviors and psychological adjustment as endpoints having equal weight with objective knowledge of health facts (Patenaude, 2005).

Accumulating research has shown that people vary widely in their responses to genetic information, with key variables such as distress levels and perceived risk showing large individual differences (Gurmankin, Baron, & Armstrong, 2004; Lerman, Croyle, Tercyak, & Hamann, 2002). In order to capture the highly personal nature of genetic feedback information and the implications of this feedback for major decisions, life plans, and concepts of the self, the clinical descriptive approach—which captures the richness of individual experience—needs to be integrated with empirical methods that seek to establish lawful relations between constructs. The purpose of this chapter is to examine the nature of the information-processing task and to systematically delineate the psychological operations that underlie the individual processing of genetic information.

IMPLICATIONS OF GENETIC AND GENOMIC INFORMATION FOR THE INDIVIDUAL'S DECISIONS AND HEALTH BEHAVIORS

The sheer quantity of information associated with a hereditary disorder presents a major challenge to individuals attempting to learn about potential threats to their health. Genetic information, depending on the particular health condition, incorporates patterns of inheritance, the likelihood of disease, risk management and treatment options, and the potential impact of these options on quality of life. Eventually, as people become eligible for testing for more than one kind of condition, they will be faced with balancing information and choices regarding multiple health threats. The information load posed by genomics bears not only on the individual but on the health professional, requiring a new knowledge base, placing demands on the limited time available during an office visit, and imposing a new level of decision making, often in the absence of illness. Patients rely heavily on their health care providers to communicate reliable, up-to-date information regarding health care issues, including information about genetic testing for risk assessment and treatment planning. However, available evidence indicates that many health care providers are neither comfortable providing such information nor adequately conversant with it, due in part to the rapid advances in genetics and genomics (Baars, Henneman, & Ten Kate, 2005; Burke, 2004). In fact, providers may in some cases not understand the indications for genetic testing. They also do not correctly interpret genetic testing results. Consequently, they may be conveying inaccurate and potentially harmful information concerning this topic to their patients (Giardiello et al., 1997).

Interest in genetic testing by the general public is high, at least in the abstract (Press, Yasui, Reynolds, Durfy, & Burke, 2001; Sanderson, Wardle, Jarvis, & Humphries, 2004), which means that more people will be seeking information than can be served by health care professionals who have an adequate knowledge base from which to interpret requests for information (Suther & Goodson, 2003). Thus, understanding information processing is an important part of facing the genomic era in terms of meeting the standards of informed consent, interpreting genetic information, offering psychosocial support to those who need it, and providing screening and treatment services to those who choose to take action based on their genetic information.

The decision to learn one's genetic information is not merely a single decision about whether to obtain a genetic test, but rather is a series of decisions about how to manage one's genetic risk (Schwartz, Peshkin, Tercyak, Taylor, & Valdimarsdottir, 2005). For example, a woman who learns that her unborn child is at risk for cystic fibrosis then faces the decision whether to continue her pregnancy. Similarly, a man who learns that his newly diagnosed stage I colon cancer is due to an *MLH1* mutation must then decide whether to have his disease treated with limited surgical resection or removal of the entire colon. Each genetic risk management decision, like the decision to undergo genetic testing, has its own set of pros and cons to be weighed. Depending on the complexity of the particular genetic condition and the number of genetic risk management decisions involved, the amount of information to be mastered multiplies rapidly and can become overwhelming.

The person who engages in testing is the same person who engages in risk management, and thus these outcomes are interrelated, although they are often studied separately (McAllister, 2002). For example, expectancies about what one might do with genetic information shape the choice about whether or not to obtain genetic testing, and thus become part of the pros and cons of testing. When risk management options have extreme consequences, such as pregnancy termination or prophylactic surgery, the pros and cons of an option are likely to be considered up front in the decision about whether or not to test (e.g., "If I'm not willing to terminate a pregnancy, there's no point in knowing if my child is at risk"). In this sense, a commitment to know can be a commitment to decide. Furthermore, the values, affects, and beliefs that led to the decision to go through with testing then go on to influence health protective behaviors (screening, prevention) that follow testing (McAllister, 2003). In the following sections, we consider the types of risk feedback and management options that are presented to individuals in pregnancy and childbearing, disease screening, prevention, adjustment, risk behavior reduction, and treatment.

Pregnancy and Childbearing

Up until the mid-1990s, the most common use of genetic testing was in the prenatal setting (Schneider & Kalkbrenner, 1998). Tests for disorders associated with severe disability and mortality in childhood—such as Tay-Sachs disease, beta-thalassemia, and cystic fibrosis—confronted parents with difficult decisions about whether or not to continue pregnancy if the fetus was shown to be affected (Saxton et al., 1991). Prospective parents could also take risk information into account in determining whether or not to even attempt pregnancy in the first place or to continue childbearing. Counseling models took root because genetic information often poses wrenching decisions for individuals and their families, including giving up cherished hopes for a healthy family, guilt about burdening a child with illness, or assuming the responsibility for possibly passing on a disease-predisposing gene if one decided to go ahead with pregnancy, despite the element of chance in inheritance (Weil, 2000).

Decisions about pregnancy and childbearing by individuals who are mutation carriers are influenced by several key factors: whether an inherited disorder is caused by dominant or recessive genes, whether the disorder manifests in childhood or adulthood, and the penetrance of the genotype (the likelihood that a person who carries a deleterious mutation associated with a particular disease will go on to develop the disorder). In the case of recessive disorders (in which a copy of a deleterious gene must be inherited from both parents), the chances are one in four that a child will inherit a disease-causing genotype; the consequences are typically early, inevitable, and severe. By contrast, with diseases caused by autosomal dominant mutations (in which only one copy is needed from one parent), the chances that a child will inherit a disease-causing genotype are increased to one in two, the flip of a coin. Further, the health consequences are more often delayed until adulthood, as in Huntington disease or most cancers. In the latter situation, the implications for pregnancy are less clear, and uptake of prenatal genetic testing for adult-onset disorders is typically much lower than for recessive, childhood-onset disorders (Lerman et al., 2002).

Carriers of deleterious mutations for adult-onset disorders also face a decision about whether or not to become parents, given the possibility that they may become ill or even die before their children reach adulthood (Smith, Ellington, Chan, Croyle, & Botkin, 2004). The choice is most poignant for carriers of highly penetrant mutations that manifest as incurable disease, such as Huntington. Parents often express concern that their children will experience the same suffering that they themselves have endured (such as a breast cancer survivor whose disease was due to a BRCA1 mutation, and who fears passing on the same fate to a daughter). Parents may also express hope that by the time their children reach the age when they are at greatest risk for the onset of disease, new prevention and treatment options will be available.

Emerging reproductive technology is creating a whole new set of options, including preimplantation testing (genetic testing of embryos prior to implantation in the uterus; Simpson, Carson, & Cisneros, 2005), human leucocyte antigen typing of unaffected embryos to facilitate stem cell transplants for siblings affected by inherited hematologic disorders (Kuliev, Rechitsky, Tur-Kaspa, & Verlinsky, 2005), and freezing of fertilized embryos prior to prophylactic oophorectomy for women at risk for ovarian cancer due to *BRCA1/2* or hereditary nonpolyposis colorectal cancer–related mutations. These options, particularly the latter, may be especially challenging for younger women who either do not have a partner, are not yet fully committed to their current partner, or otherwise feel pressured to think about childbearing before they are ready.

Screening

Genetic testing results can lead to specific ongoing screening recommendations to manage risk for disease (Green & Botkin, 2003). Indeed, one of the potential advantages of genetic testing is that it can identify high-risk, asymptomatic individuals who would benefit from disease screening tests that are not usually carried out at a population level. Genetic testing can also identify those individuals who have not inherited a disease-predisposing mutation and therefore are not in need of intensive surveillance. Decisions to pursue screening for disease based on genetic risk information revolve around such factors as the recommended frequency of screening, the efficacy of the screening test in detecting disease, the invasiveness of the screening procedure, and the availability of treatment if disease is detected.

For example, in the case of hereditary hemochromatosis, homozygous carriers of *C282Y* HFE mutations are at increased risk for iron overload (excessive iron storage), which potentially can lead to such complications as cirrhosis, diabetes, cardiomyopathy, and arthritis (Franchini, 2006). Screening of individuals with hereditary hemochromatosis consists of conducting blood tests for transferrin saturation and serum ferratin levels that are highly sensitive in detecting iron overload (Bacon, 2006). Recent evidence suggests that hereditary hemochromatosis has very low clinical penetrance (i.e., the probability that a carrier will develop genetically predisposed disease is low; Waalen, Nordestgaard, & Beutler, 2005). Nonetheless, it is still current clinical practice to recommend that individuals with hereditary hemochromatosis who have iron overload undergo therapeutic phlebotomy, which is effective in preventing liver damage (Bacon, 2006). Although population genetic screening for hereditary hemochromatosis is not currently recommended (Qaseem et al., 2005), genetic testing has been offered to first-degree relatives of carriers; among newly identified carriers who learn that they are at increased risk for iron overload, acceptance of disease screening for elevated iron levels is extremely high (McCune et al., 2003). Indeed, for first-degree relatives of hereditary hemochromatosis patients, some physicians now order genetic testing and blood screening tests for iron overload at the same time (Bacon, 2006), making adherence to disease screening after genetic testing for hereditary hemochromatosis almost a moot concept (except for younger homozygous carriers with normal iron stores who may still be at risk for iron overload later in life; Waalen et al., 2005).

A different type of disease screening is that undertaken in *BRCA1/2* carriers for the early detection of ovarian cancer. In this case, screening is conducted every 6 months and consists of transvaginal ultrasound and the CA-125 blood test (Burke et al., 1997). The tests show only limited specificity and sensitivity and rates of both false positive results and missed malignancies are high (Hakama et al., 1996; Jacobs et al., 1999; see also Chapter 10). Uptake of ovarian cancer screening is relatively low, with many high-risk women opting for risk-reducing oophorectomy instead, despite the effects of surgical menopause (Schwartz et al., 2003). Results of a recent longitudinal study show that emotional functioning in women undergoing ovarian screening declines over time (Kauff et al., 2005). This is likely due to the impact of repeated, frequent exposure to the possibility that one may receive an abnormal result (requiring surgical biopsy) at any point or be diagnosed with a dreaded illness.

Prevention

For certain inherited disorders, preventive measures are available to mitigate or avert morbidity and mortality. These include phlebotomy (hereditary hemochromatosis), low-protein diet (phenylketonuria), implantable defibrillators (ventricular arrhythmias), chemoprevention (cancer), and prophylactic surgery (cancer). These preventive options vary widely in terms of their invasiveness, behavioral requirements, impact on quality of life, and effectiveness. When the preventive measure is highly effective and imposes minimal burden, the decisional load is minimal and uptake is high (Evans, Skrzynia, & Burke, 2001). For example, in hereditary hemochromatosis, where phlebotomy is highly effective in protecting organs from iron damage if started early, uptake of preventive treatment typically exceeds 90% (Hicken, Calhoun, Barton, & Tucker, 2004). In this case, the main potential barrier is a specific phobia of blood or needles (Page, 1994).

In other cases, at-risk individuals do not avail themselves of effective preventive measures. For example, prophylactic bilateral mastectomy reduces the risk of breast cancer by 90% in *BRCA1/2* mutation carriers; yet uptake rates by unaffected women in the United States have been shown to range from 0% to 15% (although rates in Europe are approximately 50%; Wainberg & Husted, 2004). For many women, the risk-reducing benefits of mastectomy are outweighed by a variety of factors, including the risks associated with major surgery, change in body appearance, decreased sexual functioning, interference with breast-feeding, and the availability of relatively effective screening for early detection (Karp, Brown, Sullivan, & Massie, 1999; Press et al., 2005). Decisions about risk-reducing surgery are especially complex, requiring mastery of technical medical jargon in the context of highly emotionally charged material, over and above the decision to seek genetic testing.

An exception is when penetrance nears 100%, as in familial adenomatous polyposis (FAP) or multiple endocrine neoplasia syndrome (MEN1/2), where the virtual inevitability of cancer makes surgical intervention a necessary standard of care rather than an option (Herrera, 1990; Wells et al., 1994). Interestingly, for both of these syndromes, risk management begins in childhood (FAP in mid to late adolescence and in MEN as early as 5 years old), requiring the parent to make the decision for the child and to support the child in understanding the necessity of the surgery and in adapting to any sequelae (see Chapter 11).

In contrast to conditions that can be prevented (e.g., prophylactic surgery for cancer) or controlled (e.g., phlebotomy for hereditary hemochromatosis), those that require ongoing adherence pose special challenges. A prime example is phenylketonuria, a recessive genetic disorder in which homozygous carriers are not able to metabolize phenylalanine, an essential amino acid. Children born with this condition must follow a strict diet and avoid foods high in phenylalanine in order to avert cognitive deficits (Wappner, Cho, Kronmal, Schuett, & Seashore, 1999). Because dietary restrictions must be initiated at birth, children may increasingly chafe at the restrictions that single them out from their peers, without having the maturity to fully understand the potentially grave implications of nonadherence (Hobbs, Perrin, & Ireys, 1985). Perhaps not surprisingly, adherence to the prescribed diet has been shown to fall off dramatically in adolescence and early adulthood (Walter & White, 2004). Even among adults, ongoing adherence to risk-reducing regimens can be challenging. In a sample of 336 adults with a familial history of hypercholesterolemia, 63% failed to take their risk-reducing statin medication at least some of the time (Senior, Marteau, & Weinman, 2004).

Risk Behavior Reduction

In certain cases, genes do not so much confer a direct risk for disease as they do an increased propensity to develop disease when a carrier is exposed to a particular environmental agent. One potential advantage of such gene-environment interactions is that carriers of a susceptibility gene have the possibility of modifying their behavior by limiting their exposure to the environmental agent and thereby reduce their chance of being affected by disease (Imumorin et al., 2005; see also Chapter 12). For example, several studies have indicated that the GSTM1 gene encodes an enzyme that detoxifies a number of the environmental carcinogens found in cigarette smoke; individuals who lack this enzyme and who are smokers are more likely to develop lung cancer than those are not smokers, or who are smokers but who have the enzyme (Bartsch, Rojas, Nair, Nair, & Alexandrov, 1999; McWilliams, Sanderson, Harris, Richert-Boe, & Henner, 1995).

Lerman et al. (1997) conducted a three-arm comparison of 427 smokers, in which individuals were randomized to receive either: (1) quit-smoking counseling; (2) quit-smoking counseling plus exposure to biomarker feedback about carbon monoxide in exhaled breath; or (3) quit-smoking counseling, exposure to biomarker feedback, and feedback about genetic susceptibility to lung cancer. Counseling, combined with exposure to biomarker feedback and feedback about genetic susceptibility to lung cancer, increased perceptions of risk and quitting benefits, compared to counseling alone or counseling plus exposure to biomarker feedback. However, there were no differences in actual smoking behavior at the 2-month follow-up between treatment groups (McBride et al., 2002; see also Audrain et al., 1997).

Subsequent research has found that smokers who are at higher genetic risk for lung cancer based on genetic susceptibility testing (GSTMI testing) are more likely to inaccurately recall whether the result revealed they had the GSTMI enzyme than smokers who are at lower genetic risk (Lipkus, McBride, Pollak, Lyna, & Bepler, 2004). Moreover, those at higher risk are more likely to misinterpret their likelihood of developing lung cancer than are lower-risk individuals. These findings suggest that certain smokers may engage in a kind of defensive processing style, perhaps as a means to distance themselves from threatening health information (Lipkus et al., 2004). Although some subsequent studies have failed to find an interaction effect between GSTM1 status and smoking on lung cancer susceptibility (e.g., Benhamou et al., 2002), the personalized feedback results discussed above provide a template for understanding the complex ways in which individuals process, and respond to, information about gene-environment interactions.

Adjustment to Unmodifiable Risk

Perhaps the most overwhelming information to receive is knowledge of a risk that is likely to occur but cannot be changed. Conditions in this category include Huntington disease, Alzheimer disease, and Li-Fraumeni syndrome, which predisposes children and young adults to cancers that are not readily detectable by screening (e.g., sarcomas, brain tumors). Uptake of genetic testing for these conditions is typically lower than for genetic tests for modifiable risk (Lerman et al., 2002), and raises questions about the purpose of learning one's genotype when no prevention or treatment options are available (Evans et al., 2001). This may be particularly salient for individuals at risk for Huntington disease, which carries a greater than 90% penetrance rate for mutation carriers. Uptake rates of testing range from 5% to 20% for this disease (Evers-Kiebooms, Welkenhuysen, Clases, Decruyenaere, & Denayer, 2000; see Chapter 8). Relief from uncertainty, informing one's children of their risk, and life planning (e.g., making reproductive decisions, settling employment and financial matters) are reasons individuals give for taking the test (Evers-Kiebooms & Decruyenaere, 1998).

In one study, individuals who chose to test for Huntington disease were more likely to overestimate their risk than untested individuals; however, the groups did not differ significantly in their anxiety or their coping strategies (Decruyenaere et al., 1997). On the other hand, Codori, Hanson, and Brandt (1994) found that individuals choosing not to be tested anticipated having problems coping with the information. Women are more likely than men to choose testing (Creighton et al., 2003; Taylor, 1994), with some suggestion that these effects may be related to gender differences in perceived ability to cope with the results of predictive testing (Taylor, 2005).

In contrast to Huntington disease, the penetrance rate of the *APOE* genotype for Alzheimer disease is less well understood, which increases the uncertainty of whether or not disease will occur and makes planning more difficult (Evans et al., 1997). A study examined two groups of individuals with a family history of Alzheimer disease: those who were self-referred and those who were participating in Alzheimer research registries (Roberts et al., 2004). Self-referred patients were more likely to pursue testing (64%) than registry participants (24%), as were college-educated individuals and those under the age of 60. In a qualitative study of 60 individuals participating in the first clinical trial to offer genetic susceptibility testing to adult offspring of individuals with Alzheimer disease, hopes of preventing Alzheimer's, future planning, and a need to know were the primary reasons for testing, despite the fact that these needs were not likely to be satisfied, given the uncertain, probabilistic nature of genetic information about this disease (Hurley et al., 2005). Clearly, more research is needed to understand how individuals process their testing results in these types of uncertain situations, and how they perceive the psychological risks and benefits of testing.

Treatment

As polymorphisms associated with increased or decreased efficacy of particular drugs are discovered, genetic information is beginning to be integrated into medical treatment for disease. While the possibility of gene therapy and genetically tailored medicine has been highly publicized (e.g., Belkin, 2005), the psychosocial impact of these potential treatments has not yet been investigated (Rogausch, Prause, Schallenbert, Brockmoller, & Himmel, 2006). For example, it is unclear how individuals will react to the information that there is a drug available to treat their disease, but that the medication only works for some patients, particularly if they fall into the group that is unlikely to be successfully treated. Pharmacogenetic testing during the time of illness may be a particularly acute form of information overload, because the person is already struggling with the stress of diagnosis, interference from symptoms (e.g., pain that interferes with concentration), and the need to make other treatment decisions, such as what type of surgery to have, or whether or not to undergo chemotherapy.

Timing of the test, relative to an individual's diagnosis and need to make treatment decisions, is also a consideration. Recently there has been interest in peridiagnostic genetic testing for women with a new breast cancer diagnosis, in order to make decisions about prophylactic mastectomy of the unaffected breast. A study found that genetic test results significantly impact patients' decision making regarding prophylactic mastectomy. When newly diagnosed breast cancer patients were offered the option of genetic testing with rapid turnaround (1 to 3 weeks), 48% of mutation carriers and 24% of patients with uninformative results opted for bilateral mastectomy as their surgical treatment (Schwartz, Lerman, et al., 2004). In contrast, published reports show much lower rates of uptake for prophylactic mastectomy when genetic testing is performed either before cancer has been detected or after treatment has been completed. Further, in the Schwartz, Lerman, et al.

(2004) study, 23% of the 194 patients gave a blood sample for genetic testing but proceeded with treatment before receiving their test results. Even as laboratory techniques shorten the turnaround time for test results (Ardern-Jones, Kenen, & Eeles, 2005), patients may cut short their decision process due to anxiety or a perceived need to take immediate action (Donaghy, 2003).

One focus group study conducted with clinicians about their opinions about human epidermal growth factor receptor-2 (HER2) testing may foreshadow some of the psychological issues that are likely to arise with the increasing availability of genetic testing (Hedgecoe, 2005). Overexpression of the HER2 is associated with poor prognosis among female patients with breast cancer. Women who test positive for HER2 overexpression are candidates for herceptin, a treatment that can inhibit tumor cell growth. The clinicians in the focus group study talked about the roller coaster of hope that occurred when patients were informed about HER2 testing. Even though HER2-positive tumors are thought to be more aggressive, patients wanted to be eligible to receive herceptin, since they valued it as "the latest drug." The clinicians noted that, paradoxically, some patients were disappointed at being HER2 negative because it meant that they did not have access to herceptin. Clinicians were also mixed as to whether they saw informed consent as even necessary or desirable.

Summary

Processing of risk management options related to genetic information appears to be influenced along a number of key dimensions, such as penetrance of the genotype, efficacy of the particular risk management option, availability of alternate strategies, typical age at onset of disease, and perceived impact on psychological well-being and quality of life. In general, risk management options that are efficacious, require relatively little of the person, and have minimal impact on quality of life are most likely to be adopted. However, these factors do not exert their influence uniformly across persons. Individuals vary widely in how they understand the options presented to them, how they interpret their options and how they feel about them, the values that lead them to weight some aspects of their options as more important than others, and the skills they bring to bear in carrying out their decisions. In the next section, we review the person variables that influence the processing of genetic and risk management information.

PERSONAL FACTORS THAT INFLUENCE
PROCESSING OF GENETIC AND GENOMIC
INFORMATION

Genetic information differs fundamentally from other forms of medical information in that it originates from the very source of our individuality. Disease shifts subtly from being something that happens to us to something that is *of* us, unfolding from within based on a code we have not hitherto been privy to, simultaneously invoking a sense of family legacy and a forbidden glimpse into the future (Shoda et al., 1998). This profoundly individual sense of meaning, coupled with the unprecedented array of medical decisions and the complexity of the information itself, ensures that people will make widely different choices for many different reasons.

In the past 10 years, several researchers have proposed person-centered frameworks that specifically tackle the issue of how to capture individual differences empirically (Miller, Shoda, & Hurley, 1996; Muthen & Muthen, 2000; Rapkin & Dumont, 2000; Rapkin & Luke, 1993). A unifying theme in these approaches is the identification of relatively homogenous groups of individuals within a larger heterogenous sample. Thus, the focus is on developing profiles or typologies of persons who share certain characteristics and who may benefit from specific types of interventions. These person-centered frameworks do not merely propose variables to be studied but also incorporate methodologies that aim to recover important individual differences that are lost using standard statistical techniques.

The cognitive-social health information processing (C-SHIP) model (Miller & Schnoll, 2000; Miller, Shoda, et al., 1996) provides a theoretical framework for unifying the principles that guide the application of behavioral science to decisions and behaviors relevant to genetic information (Miller & Diefenbach, 1998; Miller, Mischel, O'Leary, & Mills, 1996). The C-SHIP model identifies five cognitive-affective central elements, which have had a long-standing tradition in health behavior theories, communication theories, and self-regulation research (see Table 3.1). These central elements consist of: (1) risk-relevant interpretations and constructs; (2) risk-relevant affective and emotional states; (3) health-relevant goals and values; (4) beliefs and expectations about risk management and disease outcomes, as well as beliefs about one's own self-efficacy; and (5) self-regulatory competencies and skills for decision making and for generating and maintaining goal-oriented health-protective behaviors.

Many of the cognitive-affective elements listed above overlap with prevailing theories in the health psychology literature (such as the

Table 3.1 Central Theoretical Elements of Common Health Behavior Theories Relevant for Health Threat Processing, Decision Making, Adaptation, and Execution of Health Behaviors

Risk-Relevant Interpretations and Constructs

Constructs for encoding of self and situations with regard to health and wellness, health risks and vulnerabilities, and illness and disease (e.g., knowledge levels, numeracy, genetic risk perceptions)

Risk-Relevant Affective and Emotional States

Affective and emotional states activated in health information processing (e.g., intrusive and avoidant thinking; anxiety, depression, and anger; shame and guilt; regret; positive affect)

Health-Relevant Goals and Values

Desired and valued health outcomes and states; includes the subjective importance of health-related values and goals (e.g., importance of maintaining one's body image) for health-relevant life projects (e.g., intentions for dieting and exercising regularly) as well as one's values related to self core constructs (e.g., self-concept)

Beliefs and Expectations About Risk Management, Disease Outcomes, and Self-Efficacy

Specific beliefs and expectancies activated in health information processing; includes expectancies about both outcomes (e.g., beliefs about the efficacy of different prevention, screening, risk reduction, treatment, and management options) and self-efficacy expectancies (e.g., for effectively executing desired decisions and behaviors)

Self-Regulatory Competencies and Skills for Decision Making and for Generating and Maintaining Goal-Oriented Health-Protective Behaviors

Available strategies for dealing with specific barriers to health-protective decisions and for construction and maintenance of health-protective behaviors; includes self-regulatory strategies and behavioral scripts (e.g., planning and anxiety management) for obtaining desired information and for executing decisions in the short term (e.g., about one's risk management options) and for implementing, maintaining, and adhering to health-protective behavioral plans and life projects in the long term (e.g., strategies for adherence to posttreatment surveillance regimens)

Note. From "Applying Cognitive-Social Theory to Health-Protective Behavior: Breast Self-Examination in Cancer Screening," by S. M. Miller, Y. Shoda, and K. Hurley, 1996, *Psychological Bulletin, 119,* p. 73. Copyright 1996 by the American Psychological Association. Adapted with permission.

health belief model and the theory of planned behavior). A key feature of the C-SHIP model is that the level of analysis is how these cognitive-affective units interact within a given person compared to other persons, rather than how isolated variables exert independent influence on outcomes. Key concepts from these models, including perceived risk, perceived severity, self-efficacy, response efficacy, and perceived benefits and barriers, have all been demonstrated to influence the uptake of genetic testing, decisions about risk management strategies, and coping with results. Through investigation of these variables, researchers have attempted to specify the psychological components involved in the overall task of information processing. Relationships between these variables and genetic information outcomes have been most thoroughly explored in the realm of cancer genetic testing, and therefore many of the examples presented come from that literature. In the following sections, we review some of the main cognitive-affective variables that have been studied in relation to genetic and genomic information processing.

Risk-Relevant Interpretations and Encodings

Knowledge of Genetic Concepts

In a series of qualitative interviews, Lanie et al. (2004) demonstrated that many adults do not have a clear understanding of basic concepts related to genetics. For example, almost 50% of participants believed that genes are located in one specific part of the body, such as in one's sperm or eggs, brain, heart, or bloodstream. Participants were unaware that their knowledge was faulty or incomplete, suggesting that these misconceptions could lead to distorted understanding of new information. People also seemed to have difficulty distinguishing between inherited tendencies (genotype) and observable traits (phenotype). Misunderstanding of this distinction may cause particular confusion for mutations with incomplete penetrance, such as BRCA1/2 mutations, which cause some individuals to mistakenly believe that they will definitely get cancer (Bowman, 2000).

Another belief encountered fairly often in the literature is that genetic characteristics are coinherited. For example, some people believe that cancer predisposition mutations are sex-linked, although the major adult-onset autosomal dominant ones are not. Other people erroneously believe that if they have physical characteristics similar to a relative, then they are likely to have the same carrier status as that relative. While certain syndromes do in fact have characteristic phenotypic features (e.g., the presence of café au lait spots in neurofibromatosis), most observable features are not indicative of carrier status. However, challenging these beliefs may not be as important as addressing the meaning of these beliefs for the person and the family. For example, if a genetics-related belief serves a particular function (makes one feel safe, gives one a sense of control, or alleviates guilt), then it is important to offer an alternative way of maintaining the belief (Diefenbach & Hamrick, 2003; see also Chapter 6).

Other studies have painted a more sanguine picture of knowledge levels. Of a sample contacted through random digit dialing, 50% were able to answer at least 5 out of 6 true-false questions correctly, and the average number of correct answers was 4.3 (Rose, Peters, Shea, & Armstrong, 2005). Those with greater knowledge of genetic cancer risk were more likely to endorse the benefits of genetic testing, but were also more likely to endorse health insurance discrimination as a drawback. Jallinoja and Aro (2000) found that those with higher levels of knowledge were more likely to endorse both more positive and more negative attitudes toward genetic testing. Given that individuals who know more appear to appreciate the limitations as well as the benefits of testing, their decisions should be more balanced and informed, which is a major goal of genetic counseling.

Numeracy

A number of researchers have shown that many people lack basic facility with numbers, such as understanding percentiles and proportions (Schwartz, McDowell, & Yueh, 2004; Schwartz, Woloshin, Black, & Welch, 1997; Woloshin, Schwartz, Moncur, Gabriel, & Tosteson, 2001). This presents a major roadblock for the transmission of genetic information. Risk of disease, penetrance, mutation prevalence, inheritance patterns, and risk reduction achieved by preventive measures are all typically expressed numerically, and these concepts are important to decision making about genetic conditions. Even among a highly educated sample (88% had at least some college), participants have difficulty processing numerical risk information (Lipkus, Samsa, & Rimer, 2001). For example, 20% could not tell that 1 in 10 represented a greater risk for disease than 1 in 100.

Patients with low levels of numeracy are also less consistent in their use of percentage and frequency scales to estimate personal risk of breast cancer, calling into question the accuracy of these assessments (Schapira, Davids, McAuliffe, & Nattinger, 2004). Gurmankin et al. (2004) compared three formats for presenting risk data: verbal only, verbal plus likelihood as a percentage, and verbal plus likelihood as a fraction. Each of the three formats yielded a high degree of variability in subjective risk estimates, with the numeric formats yielding only slightly more accurate estimates. Individuals were more likely to overestimate risk when they believed that the physician had minimized the risk to reduce their worry, when they demonstrated a lower level of numeracy, or when they reported a higher level of worry. Thus, presentation format influences the processing of risk information, and interacts with the individual's affects and beliefs.

Some patients misunderstand the nature of chance, because objective facts about the random nature of inheritance conflict with affectively charged beliefs. For example, one individual expressed the belief that he would test positive for a hereditary nonpolyposis colorectal cancer–related mutation because "no one in my family has escaped this yet" (McAllister, 2003). In this case, the belief that the family collectively is "unlucky" overshadows the fact that each family member independently faces a 50-50 chance of being a carrier. Further, the belief that the family's fate is shared may result in confusion or guilt in a member who tests negative (Diefenbach & Hamrick, 2003).

Pretest Awareness

Research on responses to receipt of genetic information often do not take into sufficient account the fact that most people are not tabula rasa when it comes to genetic information (D'Agincourt-Canning, 2005). Prior to counseling about a specific genetic condition by a trained professional, a person may have heard about genetic information from a wide variety of sources, including family members, news articles, the Internet, and nonspecialist health care providers. Information acquired in this manner may be neither complete nor accurate. However, this information may nonetheless become entrenched as lay beliefs that influence how information from a genetic health provider is received (Diefenbach & Hamrick, 2003).

Genetic syndromes also vary in the extent to which they presage their existence within a given family. In the case of recessive disorders, where neither parent may know they are a carrier, there may be no warning at all. For members of ethnic groups in which certain genetic diseases are more prevalent, awareness of risk may be at the community level but not at the individual or family level. For adult-onset inherited disorders, such as Huntington disease or cancer, awareness of genetic information may become salient as one recalls the suffering and loss of affected relatives (Weil, 2000). For example, the experience of having lost a mother to breast cancer at a young age can represent a vivid, highly personal example to a woman that outweighs abstract medical information, such as a discussion of incomplete penetrance of cancer-predisposing mutations or advances in treatment of breast cancer (D'Agincourt-Canning, 2005). Personal experiences with loss thus lay the foundation for activating core constructs about one's risk, as well as one's beliefs about the world as a safe or threatening place, increasing the complexity of processing genetic information.

Perceived Risk

Probably the most extensively researched person variable in relation to genetic information is perceived risk. This construct is central to most influential theories of health behavior change (e.g., the health belief model) as a key factor that motivates individuals to take action to protect themselves against threats to their health, whether it be to obtain a vaccine, undergo cancer screening, or quit smoking (Harrison, Mullen, & Green, 1992; Janz & Becker, 1984; Van der Pligt, 1998). The probabilistic nature of genetic information, conveyed in terms of risks, leads naturally into a consideration of how those risks are subjectively understood. Across numerous studies, perceived risk has been shown to have a modest but significant positive correlation with the uptake of genetic testing and the adoption of risk management strategies (Lerman et al., 2002).

More generally, individuals who are given a risk estimate of being affected by a genetic disorder by a health care practitioner often either over- or underestimate their personal risk, and much emphasis has been placed on improving the accuracy of patients' subjective risk estimates (Braithwaite, Emery, Walter, Prevost, & Sutton, 2004; Hallowell & Richards, 1997). For example, women at familial risk for breast and ovarian cancer have been found to overestimate their risk of developing cancer, and these estimates are impervious to personalized familial risk counseling and receipt of a genetic test result (Bish et al., 2002; Schwartz et al., 2002). However, this finding is not uniform across conditions or diseases; receiving a negative genetic test result has been shown to be effective in lowering perceived risk of being affected by Alzheimer disease, as well as in reducing worry about developing the disease (LaRusse et al., 2005).

Several qualitative studies have attempted to address the question of why perceived risk estimates are so resistant to correction. For example, some individuals dichotomize objective risk information into all or nothing, or 0% chance versus 100% chance; such a person who chose 100% on a continuous scale assessing perceived risk would be considered an overestimator (Lippman-Hand & Fraser, 1979). A health care provider who has just presented a risk estimate based on incomplete penetrance (e.g., 30–50% risk of breast cancer for *BRCA1/2* mutation carriers), may regard such either-or thinking as simplistic.

However, this heuristic (i.e., all-or-none thinking) may have a specific utility in that it helps individuals to visualize the two main possible extreme outcomes; this visualization can enable them to prepare for the possible outcomes (Lippman-Hand & Fraser, 1979; Miller, Roussi, Altman, Helm, & Steinberg, 1994).

In a related vein, some individuals with a family history of colon cancer choose to believe themselves to be mutation carriers, most probably as a coping strategy to prepare themselves for the worst (McAllister, 2003). For these individuals, believing that the worst possible outcome will occur, termed *defensive pessimism*, can be an effective strategy for coping with uncertainty, since it psychologically prepares the individual to deal with the worst-case scenario (Norem & Cantor, 1986). In experimental laboratory studies, individuals who receive counseling that encourages them to think positively about a feared event, and therefore does not take into account their need to maintain a defensive pessimistic stance, show poorer adjustment after they are subsequently exposed to a stressful task (Norem & Illingworth, 1993). Thus, a health care provider who attempts to correct a patient's beliefs, without at the same time understanding the meaning of a belief or the role that it plays in a patient's coping repertoire, may actually undermine a patient's adjustment and decision making, as well as the provider's ability to establish rapport with the patient.

These data point to potential individual difference variables that may need to be taken into account when developing family interventions: family members who diverge in terms of such factors as their levels of knowledge, numeracy, and defensive pessimism styles may manifest conflicting dynamics and may require more individually tailored types of counseling interventions (Miller, Fang, Diefenbach, & Bales, 2001; Miller et al., 2004; Miller, Shoda, et al., 1996; Shoda et al., 1998).

Risk-Relevant Affective and Emotional States

Genetic risk information entails thinking about the possibility of disease or even death to oneself or to a close relative. Such information thus poses the challenge of maintaining enough of a focus on threat to make decisions or take action without experiencing excessive distress (Miller, Shoda, et al., 1996). Assessing levels of distress in individuals undergoing genetic counseling has been a major research priority, due to concerns that genetic risk information is stressful and might therefore cause severe depression, anxiety, or even suicidal behaviors (Horowitz, Sundin, Zanko, & Lauer, 2001; Lerman et al., 1996).

The literature to date suggests that, on average, most people are able to cope with genetic risk testing information with minimal distress

(Claes et al., 2005; Coyne & Palmer, 2005; Molinuevo et al., 2005; Patch, Roderick, & Rosenberg, 2005). However, a subset of people experience heightened distress, most notably in the form of intrusive thoughts about their risk (i.e., they dwell on it, have recurrent thoughts about it, think about it when they don't mean to, etc.; Horowitz, 1986). In these cases, there is concern that distress can have a negative impact on information processing by making it difficult for the individual to accurately process incoming feedback (Ubel, 2005). Distressed individuals recall less from their genetic counseling session than nondistressed individuals do (Valdimarsdottir et al., 2005) and are more likely to selectively attend to the threatening aspects of the information presented (Erblich et al., 2003).

Levels of distress about genetic risk also appear to influence decisions about whether or not to undergo genetic testing and to adopt risk management strategies (Lerman et al., 2002). Some studies show that intrusive thoughts or worry about risk are associated with an increased likelihood of uptake of genetic testing, indicating that greater perceived threats to the self activate the uptake of actions that might have a health-protective quality (Armstrong, Micco, Carney, Stopfer, & Putt, 2005). However, the relation between distress levels and testing decisions has been shown to be more complex in other research. While moderate levels of intrusive ideation promote the uptake of testing for some women at risk of breast cancer, those at the highest levels of distress are actually more likely than other women to decline testing (Valdimarsdottir et al., 2005; see also Coyne, Kruus, Racioppo, Calzone, & Armstrong, 2003).

Among African American women, those who choose to undergo genetic counseling have higher levels of intrusive ideation than those who do not accept counseling, suggesting that distress initially serves to motivate protective actions (Thompson et al., 2002). Ultimately, however, counselees who opt not to test have higher levels of intrusive thoughts than those who accept testing, suggesting that the role of affect in decision making may change over the course of the testing experience.

In some cases, individuals avoid getting tested because they fear they will not be emotionally equipped to handle the results (Hicken et al., 2004) and thus do not afford themselves the potential benefits of genetic testing. Further, some people who decline counseling and testing experience higher levels of distress over time (Lerman et al., 1998). It may therefore be worthwhile to provide interventions that facilitate "pre-living" of the posttesting experience, so that individuals can strategically anticipate and plan for how they will feel, make more informed decisions, and better prepare themselves for the consequences of the decisions that they make (Miller et al., 2005; Shoda et al., 1998).

As an example, in one study, patients undergoing genetic testing for Huntington disease all showed a decrease in anxiety and depression in the first year after testing (Decruyenaere et al., 2003). However, those who indicated that they wanted testing in order to reduce feelings of uncertainty, but could not articulate any specific plans for how to use their genetic test results, showed an increase in anxiety and depression between the first and fifth years, returning to the higher levels of distress that they reported at pretest baseline. Those with specific plans, on the other hand, maintained lower levels of anxiety and depression over the entire 5-year follow-up period. Thus, by talking openly with individuals about how they expect to feel about learning their genetic risk information, and by helping them to clarify their reasons for testing and to formulate specific action plans, distress may be reduced over the long term. Similar studies are needed with a spectrum of genomic conditions that vary in terms of such parameters as penetrance, severity of illness, and whether effective prevention and treatment options exist (see Chapter 2).

Distress in the genetic testing context is often heightened when individuals have closely experienced the effects of familial risk, including witnessing disease or deterioration and death in a family member or members. Women at familial risk for breast cancer who were their mother's caretaker during their mother's battle with breast cancer are more likely to have higher levels of intrusive thoughts about their own risk (Erblich, Bovbjerg, & Valdimarsdottir, 2000). These multigenerational family experiences create powerful schemata that profoundly influence how genetic risk information is received, as well as how subsequent risk management decisions are made. Because affect is not well integrated into most of the prevailing theoretical models, studies in this area have tended to emphasize the rational aspects of genetic information processing (e.g., the role of the "accuracy" of perceived risk estimates in genetic testing decisions) without a corresponding understanding of how affect interacts with other psychological constructs, such as knowledge and risk perceptions, to influence decisions (Miller, Fang, Manne, Engstrom, & Daly, 1999; Schwartz et al., 2005). Unfortunately, the more personal and emotionally laden themes often described in the genetic counseling literature and in qualitative studies (Appleton, Fry, Rees, Rush, & Cull, 2000; DiProspero et al., 2001; Pasacreta, 1999) have largely not been captured in empirical behavioral studies, and this needs to be a focus of future research.

Goals and Values: Self-Concept

Learning whether one carries a genetic mutation, particularly one that does not immediately or with certainty express phenotypically as disease, can provoke a kind of identity crisis about the self, in terms of whether one is sick or well (Weil, 2000). Some individuals cannot process the apparent contradiction that they require medical intervention (e.g., screening, surgery) when they are at present disease free. For others, whose sense of self may have been shaped by an acute awareness of their increased hereditary risk, learning that they are not mutation carriers can be confusing and disorienting. For example, one young woman had lost her mother and several aunts to Huntington disease. She fully expected to contract and die from the disease herself. Yet, while she had expressed clear ideas about her future if she tested positive for the Huntington mutation, upon testing negative, she exclaimed, "the one constant thing in my life has now been taken away" (Tassicker, 2005, p. 102). Thus, it is important to understand how the perception of risk for a hereditary illness affects one's sense of self in terms of health and illness, and how genetic testing information may disrupt ongoing life values and goals.

Beliefs and Expectations: Perceived Control

The availability of genetic information forces a series of choices, to know or not to know, to act or not to act, an existential challenge to commit to a course of action that can seem quite lonely. Patients vary in the extent to which they fully accept responsibility for deciding whether or not to learn about their genetic risk (Geller, Strauss, Bernhardt, & Holtzman, 1997). Differences have been noted in many medical contexts in the extent to which the individual wants to make a decision versus being told what to do by the health care professional (Say, Murtagh, & Thomson, 2006). People may also attempt to draw on input from others, for example, asking their physician, "What would you do in my place?" Patients differ in the extent to which they have been exposed to the opinions of health care professionals and in their inclination to follow those opinions. Giving control to a health care professional in a specific situation has itself been framed as a decision (Shiloh, 1996). This relinquishing may take place when the patient has decided that the provider has a better chance of minimizing threat than the patient does (Miller, 1980). The patient may also wish to avoid self-blame or regret.

Research has shown, however, that patients are more likely to experience regret when they undertake a procedure because a doctor told them to, rather than for their own reasons. For example, in a large-scale study of long-term satisfaction and psychosocial functioning among 609 women who had elected to undergo prophylactic mastectomy, patients who cited physician's advice as their primary reason for undergoing surgery were more likely to be dissatisfied with the procedure (Frost et al., 2000). Moreover, among the relatively small number of women who reported regret about bilateral prophylactic mastectomy (21 out of 307 participants), 19 reported that discussion about this surgery was initiated by their physician (Borgen et al., 1998). These results were confirmed and elaborated on through an in-depth qualitative study of these women (Payne, Biggs, Tran, Borgen, & Massie, 2000).

Cognitive-Affective Processing Styles: High Versus Low Monitoring

The C-SHIP model posits that the cognitive-affective variables described above form a dynamic network in which the strength and direction of the connections among perceptual, expectancy, and emotional factors vary from person to person, as well as within the same individual across different situations. In this manner, the C-SHIP model accounts for the possibility of variation between individuals (e.g., anxiety may activate a decision to test in one individual but decrease the likelihood of the same decision in another individual). The model also allows for variation within individuals across situations (e.g., anxiety may increase the likelihood of adherence to some cancer screening recommendations where there are effective early treatment options available, but decrease the likelihood of adherence to cancer screening recommendations where there are no effective early treatment options).

The C-SHIP model makes a key distinction between high and low monitoring attentional styles (Miller, 1995). High monitors tend to focus excessively on health threats and have a preference for extensive health-related information. In contrast, low monitors tend to minimize and divert from health-related threats. In addition, high monitors characteristically display greater knowledge about health threats than low monitors and tend to be less satisfied with the amount and definitiveness of health information available to them. Thus, high and low monitors exhibit distinctively different cognitive-emotional response patterns when confronted with health-related threats. An example of such differences occurs when high and low monitors face the possibility of testing positive for a *BRCA1/2* genetic mutation. High monitors typically display a greater heightening of both risk perceptions and risk-related distress than low monitors, but also greater vigilance for, and attentiveness to, information about potential health prevention and management strategy options (Miller et al., 1999, 2001).

High and low monitoring styles tend to be relatively stable individual tendencies, with important implications for how individuals process health information. These attentional styles may be particularly relevant for individuals at hereditary risk for life-threatening illnesses, as these individuals must make decisions about whether or not to seek out further information about their risk through genetic testing, and must manage illness fears and anxieties on a potentially long-term basis.

Tercyak et al. (2001) examined relationships between coping style and psychological distress among women at increased risk for breast or ovarian cancer seeking genetic testing. Higher monitoring was associated with increased anxiety while anticipating testing results, whereas mutation status was significantly related to anxiety after receiving results. Hence, immediately after receiving test results, distress related to learning that one is a *BRCA1/2* mutation carrier appears likely to provoke anxiety, independent of attentional style. Thus, it is more important to examine the interaction between monitoring style, feedback status, and temporal factors.

Shiloh, Ben-Sinai, and Keinan (1999) used an experimental paradigm to examine the influence of coping style on interest in predictive genetic testing under conditions of varied certainty (certainty of developing a hypothetical condition vs. increased risk for a hypothetical condition) and varied controllability (surveillance and treatment can stop progression vs. no available medical treatments). Under conditions of high certainty and low control, high monitors were more interested than low monitors in testing. While both high and low monitors preferred tests that provide good treatment options for prevention and disease control, only high monitors preferred tests that provide certainty alone, suggesting different informational needs among high and low monitors. Similarly, Culler et al. (2002) found that monitoring style predicted interest in genetic testing for prostate cancer susceptibility among age-diverse men in urology clinic waiting rooms. Monitoring was also associated with an overestimation of risk status. Taken together, these studies suggest that high monitors will be more likely to seek out genetic testing information, but may also experience more distress while awaiting their test results (Wardle, 1995). Further research is necessary to determine how coping style affects distress levels, subsequent decision making, and health behaviors over time, particularly among mutation carriers and individuals with different types of genomic conditions or disorders.

MESSAGE FEATURES THAT INFLUENCE PROCESSING OF GENETIC AND GENOMIC INFORMATION

In a development that parallels health psychology models, cognitive psychology researchers have generated a sophisticated body of empirical laboratory studies investigating the cognitive processes and contextual issues that affect medical decision making, particularly in the area of risk and probability. Kahneman and Tversky's seminal work in cognitive heuristics and biases (Kahneman, Slovic, & Tversky, 1982; Kahneman & Tversky, 2000) has spawned an impressive literature, demonstrating that variations in the presentation of information affect decisions, independent of the factual content of the message. Even relatively simple features of information provision (e.g., number of options, order of presentation) have been found to influence decisional outcomes (Chapman & Elstein, 2000). For example, when asking people to make a choice between two options, A and B, adding a third choice, C, can actually increase the likelihood of choosing one of the first two options (Redelmeier & Shafir, 1995). Cumulatively, this work suggests the presence of cognitive heuristics or "editorial shortcuts" that people typically use when processing information. These findings have important implications for how individuals process genetic and genomic information, which have just begun to be explored (e.g., Welkenhuysen, Evers-Kiebooms, & d'Ydewalle, 2001).

In one particularly well-developed line of cognitive psychology research, prospect theory proposes that, under conditions of uncertainty, the framing of health communications in terms of potential gains (i.e., positive consequences of engaging in a health behavior) or potential losses (i.e., negative consequences that can result from not engaging in a health behavior) impacts on health behaviors. In general, gain-framed messages are more effective in promoting prevention behaviors, such as sunscreen use (Rothman, Salovey, Antone, Keough, & Martin, 1993), whereas loss-framed messages more effectively promote detection behaviors, such as breast self-examination (Meyerowitz & Chaiken, 1987) and mammography (Banks et al., 1995). Consistent with these results, Welkenhuysen and colleagues (2001) found a framing effect regarding genetic testing for cystic fibrosis. The loss frame (chances of having a child born with the disease) was related to greater interest in obtaining prenatal diagnosis than the gain frame (chances of having a healthy child), but only when risk information was expressed verbally (e.g., a moderate chance of having a cystic fibrosis child) rather than numerically (e.g., a 25% chance).

Thus, framing interacts with other presentation effects. Further, framing interacts with cognitive-affective processing style. For example, individuals with a high monitoring style—who are highly attentive to the negative implications of not performing health-protective behaviors—show better decisional and behavioral outcomes when health risk information is framed in a less negative fashion that focuses them on the benefits of engaging in various health behaviors (Miller et al., 1999; Williams-Piehota, Pizarro, Schneider, Mowad, & Salovey,

2005). These findings underscore the fact that one size does not fit all, and that further research is needed to understand how individual differences affect how people respond to different information presentation formats.

CONCLUSION

In order to fully realize the potential benefits of the genomics revolution in medicine, it is important to incorporate a person-centered clinical and research agenda that systematically and comprehensively addresses the factors that influence how individuals process genetic information. Traditional paradigms for health behavior research, based on rationalist value-expectancy theories, provide some key insights into individual information processing in this most personal of domains. Genetic information processing consists of a complex interplay between the genetic and genomic challenge, cognitive-affective reactions, and the way in which information messages are presented. In addition, health decisions and behaviors relevant to genetics are not isolated entities, but rather entail an interrelated chain of events as people cope with the lifelong task of living with an inherited disease (or susceptibility to disease). There is currently a large, uncharted area between large-scale studies that describe linear group trends but which do not translate well to the individual level, and qualitative studies that capture the intricacies of individual experience but that do not generalize well to evidence-based guidelines for clinical health care settings. Using person-centered approaches, such as the C-SHIP model, individual differences can be studied systematically, without sacrificing either scientific rigor or the rich level of detail that clinicians can achieve in working with patients.

As an example of this type of person-centered, quantitative research, Hurley et al. (2003) used the C-SHIP model to conduct a study of 212 women undergoing genetic counseling and testing for breast or ovarian cancer risk. Three different types were identified. The disengaged type uniformly rated all pros and cons of prophylactic mastectomy as having little weight in their decision about whether or not to undergo surgery. Disengaged types reported low levels of general and cancer-specific distress, as well as low perceived risk of cancer, and were less likely to have undergone mammography screening in the past year. When discussing genetic information with a disengaged type, it may be important for the health care provider to focus communication on developing a personal risk management program and on exploring motivation for undergoing genetic counseling.

The risk-focused group gave high ratings to the pros related to risk reduction afforded by prophylactic mastectomy and to their physician's recommendation for surgery, but low ratings to all other pros and cons of the procedure. The risk-focused types did not appear globally distressed, although they did report elevated levels of intrusive thoughts about their cancer risk. Because individuals in this subtype focused more on the pros of surgery, it would be important to explore whether they are aware of the potential drawbacks and have given them full consideration. Since physician recommendation was one of the three most highly ranked pros in this group, it would also be important to confirm that they were choosing prophylactic surgery for their own reasons, and not just because the doctor advised them to.

Last, the ambivalent group consisted of individuals who gave high ratings to both the pros and cons of prophylactic mastectomy. Ambivalent types showed high levels of global distress and intrusive thoughts about their cancer risk. They were also less likely to have had a mammogram in the year prior to genetic counseling, and may be at risk for continued nonadherence to screening, as well as delays in deciding whether or not to undergo prophylactic surgery (Peshkin et al., 2002; Tiller et al., 2002). Counseling sessions with these individuals may tend to be longer and characterized by discussions of opposing considerations. In this situation, rather than getting caught up in an endlessly looping discussions of pros and cons, it may be better to focus directly on the patient's level of anxiety and distress. With these individuals, health care providers can emphasize the importance of selecting a risk-reducing regimen and encourage them to adhere to health care recommendations while making up their minds about testing and risk management. These patients may also benefit from referral for supportive psychological services, such as assistance in decision making and anxiety reduction.

The approach described above illustrates how theory-driven research on the ways in which different types of people process genetic information can generate guidelines for health care providers to deliver personalized risk information in a way that facilitates optimal decision making and long-term psychological adjustment. Results of person-centered research can also be incorporated into standardized, evidence-based patient decision aids that are used as an adjunct to counseling approaches (e.g., O'Connor, Graham, & Visser, 2005; O'Connor, Legare, & Stacey, 2003; Schwartz et al., 2005). Taken together, these strategies can be used to enhance the provision of objective knowledge of a particular risk condition and the risks and benefits of available treatments, as well as to address personal values and the individual's desired degree of decisional involvement. Future directions for research include conducting studies on different typologies of persons that are based on a broader range of cognitive-affective factors, investigating whether the effects of the features of the information presented vary with patient type, exploring how person type affects family communication about genetic risk, and examining how these types vary in their medical decision making and other health risk–related behaviors within the larger sociocultural context. The ultimate goal is to help individuals fully absorb genetic risk information, which can seem to them by turns frustratingly uncertain, inaccessibly technical, and even ominously threatening, and to process it in a way that empowers them to make positive, well-informed decisions about protecting their health.

Acknowledgments: This work was supported in part by National Cancer Institute Grants R01 CA104979, P30 CA006927, RO3 CA106012-01; National Human Genome Institute Grant R01 HG01766; Department of Defense Grants DAMD17-01-1-0238, DAMD17-02-1-0382, and W81XWH-06-1-0099; American Cancer Society Grant TURSG-02-227-01-PBP; and PA Department of Health Grant SAP#4100026777. We are indebted to John Scarpato, Margaret Atchison, Sabrina Jhanwar, Winton Wedderburn, and Stephen LaMonica for their technical assistance; we also acknowledge the resources and services of the Fox Chase Behavioral Research Core Facility, including the contributions of Pagona Roussi, Mary Ropka, and Catharine Wang.

REFERENCES

Ackerman, M. (2005). Genetic testing for risk stratification in hypertrophic cardiomyopathy and long QT syndrome: Fact or fiction? *Current Opinion in Cardiology, 20,* 175–181.

Appleton, S., Fry, A., Rees, G., Rush, R., & Cull, A. (2000). Psychosocial effects of living with an increased risk of breast cancer: An exploratory study using telephone focus groups. *Psycho-oncology, 9*(6), 511–521.

Ardern-Jones, A., Kenen, R., & Eeles, R. (2005). Too much, too soon? Patients and health professionals' views concerning the impact of genetic testing at the time of breast cancer diagnosis in women under the age of 40. *European Journal of Cancer Care, 14,* 272–281.

Armstrong, K., Micco, E., Carney, A., Stopfer, J., & Putt, M. (2005). Racial differences in the use of BRCA1/2 testing among women with a family history of breast or ovarian cancer. *Journal of the American Medical Association, 293,* 1783–1785.

Audrain, J., Boyd, N. R., Roth, J., Main, D., Caporaso, N. E., & Lerman, C. (1997). Genetic susceptibility testing in smoking-cessation treatment: One-year outcomes of a randomized trial. *Addictive Behaviors, 22,* 741–751.

Baars, M. J., Henneman, L., & Ten Kate, L. P. (2005). Deficiency of knowledge of genetics and genetic tests among general practitioners, gynecologists, and pediatricians: A global problem. *Genetic Medicine, 7*, 605–610.

Bacon, B. (2006). Hereditary hemochromatosis. In B. Bacon, A. M. DiBiscegie, & J. G. O'Grady (Eds.), *Comprehensive clinical hepatology* (2nd ed., pp. 341–349). St. Louis, MO: Elsevier Mosby.

Banks, S. M., Salovey, P., Greener, S., Rothman, A. J., Moyer, A., Beauvais, J., et al. (1995). The effects of message framing on mammography utilization. *Health Psychology, 14*, 178–184.

Bartsch, H., Rojas, M., Nair, U., Nair, J., & Alexandrov, K. (1999). Genetic cancer susceptibility and DNA adducts: Studies in smokers, tobacco chewers, and coke oven workers. *Cancer Detection and Prevention, 23*(6), 445–453.

Belkin, L. (2005, November 6). A doctor for the future. *New York Times.* Retrieved January 9, 2006, from http://www.nytimes.com

Benhamou, S., Lee, W. J., Alexandrie, A. K., Boffetta, P., Bouchardy, C., Butkiewicz, D., et al. (2002). Meta- and pooled analyses of the effects of glutathione s-transferase m1 polymorphisms and smoking on lung cancer risk. *Carcinogenesis, 23*(8), 1343–1350.

Bish, A., Sutton, S., Jacobs, C., Levene, S., Ramirez, A., & Hodgson, S. (2002). Changes in psychological distress after cancer genetic counseling: A comparison of affected and unaffected women. *British Journal of Cancer, 86*(1), 43–50.

Borgen, P. I., Hill, A. D., Tran, K. N., Van Zee, K. J., Massie, M. J., Payne, D., et al. (1998). Patient regrets after bilateral prophylactic mastectomy. *Annals of Surgical Oncology, 5*, 603–606.

Bowman, J. E. (2000). Technical, genetic, and ethical issues in screening and testing of African-Americans for hemochromatosis. *Genetic Testing, 4*, 207–211.

Braithwaite, D., Emery, J., Walter, F., Prevost, A. T., & Sutton, S. (2004). Psychological impact of genetic counseling for familial cancer: A systematic review and meta-analysis. *Journal of the National Cancer Institute, 96*(2), 122–133.

Burke, W. (2004). Genetic testing in primary care. *Annual Review of Genomics and Human Genetics, 5*, 1–14.

Burke, W., Daly, M., Garber, J., Botkin, J., Kahn, M., Lynch, P., et al. (1997). Recommendations for follow-up care of individuals with an inherited predisposition to cancer. II. BRCA1 and BRCA2. *Journal of the American Medical Association, 277*, 997–1003.

Chapman, G. B., & Elstein, A. (2000). Cognitive processes and biases in medical decision making. In G. Chapman & E. Sonnenberg (Eds.), *Decision making in health care: Theory, psychology, and applications* (pp. 183–220). New York: Cambridge University Press.

Claes, E., Evers-Kiebooms, G., Denayer, L., Decruyenaere, M., Boogaerts, A., Philippe, K., et al. (2005). Predictive genetic testing for hereditary breast and ovarian cancer: Psychological distress and illness representations 1 year following disclosure. *Journal of Genetic Counseling, 14*(5), 349–363.

Codori, A. M., Hanson, R., & Brandt, J. (1994). Self-selection in predictive testing for Huntington's disease. *American Journal of Medical Genetics, 54,* 167–173.

Coyne, J., Kruus, L., Racioppo, M., Calzone, K., & Armstrong, K. (2003). What do ratings of cancer-specific distress mean among women at high risk of breast and ovarian cancer? *American Journal of Medical Genetics, 116,* 222–228.

Coyne, J. C., & Palmer, S. C. (2005). National Comorbidity Survey data concerning cancer and depression lack credibility. *Psychotherapy and Psychosomatics, 74*(4), 260–261.

Creighton, S., Almqvist, E. W., MacGregor, D., Fernandez, B., Hogg, H., Beis, J., et al. (2003). Predictive, pre-natal and diagnostic genetic testing for Huntington's disease: The experience in Canada from 1987 to 2000. *Clinical Genetics, 63,* 462–475.

Culler, D. D., Silberg, J., Vanner-Nicely, L., Ware, J. L., Jackson-Cook, C., & Bodurtha, J. (2002). Factors influencing men's interest in gene testing for prostate cancer susceptibility. *Journal of Genetic Counseling, 11,* 383–398.

D'Agincourt-Canning, L. (2005). The effect of experiential knowledge on construction of risk perception in hereditary breast/ovarian cancer. *Journal of Genetic Counseling, 14,* 55–69.

Decruyenaere, M., Evers-Kiebooms, G., Boogaerts, A., Cloostermans, T., Cassiman, J. J., Demyttenaere, K., et al. (1997). Non-participation in predictive testing for Huntington's disease: Individual decision-making, personality and avoidant behavior in the family. *European Journal of Human Genetics, 5,* 351–363.

Decruyenaere, M., Evers-Kiebooms, G., Cloostermans, T., Boogaerts, A., Demyttenaere, K., Dom, R., et al. (2003). Psychological distress in the 5-year period after predictive testing for Huntington's disease. *European Journal of Human Genetics, 11,* 30–38.

Diefenbach, M. A., & Hamrick, N. (2003). Self-regulation and genetic testing: Theory, practical considerations, and interventions. In L. D. Cameron & H. Leventhal (Eds.), *The self-regulation of health and illness behavior* (pp. 314–331). London: Routledge.

DiProspero, L. S., Seminsky, M., Honeyford, J., Doan, B., Franssen, E., Meschino, W., et al. (2001). Psychosocial issues following a positive result of genetic testing for BRCA1 and BRCA2 mutations: Findings from a focus group and a needs-assessment survey. *Canadian Medical Association Journal, 164*(7), 1005–1009.

Donaghy, K. B. (2003). Fostering sound medical treatment decision making. *Annals of the American Psychotherapy Association, 6,* 6–13.

Efferth, T., & Volm, M. (2005). Pharmacogenetics for individualized cancer chemotherapy. *Pharmacology and Therapeutics, 107,* 155–176.

Erblich, J., Bovbjerg, D. H., & Valdimarsdottir, H. B. (2000). Looking forward and back: Distress among women at familial risk for breast cancer. *Annals of Behavioral Medicine, 22*(1), 53–59.

Erblich, J., Montgomery, G. H., Valdimarsdottir, H. B., Cloitre, M., & Bovbjerg, D. H. (2003). Biased cognitive processing of cancer-related information among women with family histories of breast cancer: Evidence from a cancer Stroop task. *Health Psychology, 22,* 235–244.

Evans, D., Beckett, L., Field, T., Feng, L., Albert, M., Bennett, D., et al. (1997). Apolipoprotein E epsilon 4 and incidence of Alzheimer disease in a community population of older persons. *Journal of the American Medical Association, 277*, 822–824.

Evans, J., Skrzynia, C., & Burke, W. (2001). The complexities of predictive genetic testing. *British Medical Journal, 322*, 1052–1056.

Evers-Kiebooms, G., & Decruyenaere, M. (1998). Predictive genetic testing for Huntington's disease: A challenge for persons at risk and for professionals. *Patient Education and Counseling, 35*, 15–26.

Evers-Kiebooms, G., Welkenhuysen, M., Clases, E., Decruyenaere, M., & Denayer, L. (2000). The psychological complexity of predictive testing for late onset neurogenetic diseases and hereditary cancers: Implications for multidisciplinary counseling and for genetic education. *Social Science and Medicine, 51*, 831–841.

Fine, B. (1993). The evolution of nondirectiveness in genetic counseling and implications of the human genome project. In D. Bartels, B. LeRoy, & A. Caplan (Eds.), *Prescribing our future: Ethical challenges in genetic counseling* (pp. 107–117). New York: Aldine de Gruyter.

Franchini, M. (2006). Hereditary iron overload: Update on pathophysiology, diagnosis, and treatment. *American Journal of Hematology, 81*, 202–209.

Frost, M. H., Schaid, D. J., Sellers, T. A., Slezak, J. M., Arnold, P. G., Woods, J. E., et al. (2000). Long-term satisfaction and psychological and social function following bilateral prophylactic mastectomy. *Journal of the American Medical Association, 284*, 319–324.

Garber, J. E., & Offit, K. (2005). Hereditary cancer predisposition syndromes. *Journal of Clinical Oncology, 23*, 276–292.

Geller, G., Strauss, M., Bernhardt, B., & Holtzman, N. (1997). "Decoding" informed consent: Insights from women regarding breast cancer susceptibility testing. *Hastings Center Report, 27*, 28–33.

Giardiello, F. M., Brensinger, J. D., Petersen, G. M., Luce, M. C., Hylind, L. M., Bacon, J. A., et al. (1997). The use and interpretation of commercial APC gene testing for familial adenomatous polyposis. *New England Journal of Medicine, 336*, 823–827.

Green, M. J., & Botkin, J. R. (2003). "Genetic exceptionalism" in medicine: Clarifying the differences between genetic and nongenetic tests. *Annals of Internal Medicine, 138*, 571–575.

Gurmankin, A., Baron, J., & Armstrong, K. (2004). Intended message versus message received in hypothetical physician risk communications: Exploring the gap. *Risk Analysis, 24*, 1337–1347.

Hakama, M., Stenman, U., Knekt, P., Jarvisalo, J., Hakulinen, T., Maatela, J., et al. (1996). CA 125 as a screening test for ovarian cancer. *Journal of Medical Screening, 3*, 40–42.

Hallowell, N., & Richards, M. (1997). Understanding life's lottery. *Journal of Health Psychology, 2*, 31–43.

Harrison, J., Mullen, P., & Green, L. (1992). A meta-analysis of studies of the health belief model with adults. *Health Education Research, 7*, 107–116.

Hedgecoe, A. (2005). "At the point at which you can do something about it, then it becomes more relevant": Informed consent in the pharmacogenetic clinic. *Social Science Medicine, 61,* 1201–1210.

Herrera, L. (1990). *Familial adenomatous polyposis.* New York: Alan R. Liss.

Hicken, B., Calhoun, D., Barton, J., & Tucker, D. (2004). Attitudes about and psychosocial outcomes of HFE genotyping for hemochromatosis. *Genetic Testing, 8,* 90–97.

Hobbs, N., Perrin, J., & Ireys, H. (1985). *Chronically ill children and their families.* San Francisco: Jossey-Boss.

Horowitz, M. (1986). Stress response syndromes: A review of posttraumatic and adjustment disorders. *Hospital and Community Psychiatry, 37,* 241–249.

Horowitz, M., Sundin, E., Zanko, A., & Lauer, R. (2001). Coping with grim news from genetic tests. *Psychosomatics, 42*(2), 100–105.

Hurley, A. C., Harvey, F. R., Roberts, J. S., Wilson-Chase, C., Lloyd, S., Prest, J., et al. (2005). Genetic susceptibility for Alzheimer's disease: Why did adult offspring seek testing? *American Journal of Alzheimer's Disease and Other Dementias, 20,* 374–381.

Hurley, K., Valdimarsdottir, H., Brown, K., Rispoli, J., Jandorf, L., Kaufman, E., et al. (2003, March). *Influence of decision types on distress and adherence in BRCA1/2 testing.* Paper presented at the Society of Behavioral Medicine Twenty-Third Annual Scientific Sessions, Salt Lake City, UT.

Imumorin, I., Dong, Y., Zhu, H., Poole, J., Harshfield, G., Treiber, F., & Snieder, H. (2005). A gene-environment interaction model of stress-induced hypertension. *Cardiovascular Toxicology, 5,* 109–132.

Jacobs, I., Skates, S., MacDonald, N., Menon, U., Rosenthal, A., Woolas, R., et al. (1999). Screening for ovarian cancer: A pilot randomized controlled trial. *Lancet, 353,* 1207–1210.

Jallinoja, P., & Aro, A. R. (2000). Does knowledge make a difference? The association between knowledge about genes and attitudes toward gene tests. *Journal of Health Communication, 5,* 29–39.

Janz, N., & Becker, M. (1984). The health belief model: A decade later. *Health Education Quarterly, 11,* 1–47.

Kahneman, D., Slovic, P., & Tversky, A. (1982). *Judgment under uncertainty: Heuristics and biases.* New York: Cambridge University Press.

Kahneman, D., & Tversky, A. (2000). *Choices, values, and frames.* New York: Cambridge University Press.

Karp, J., Brown, K., Sullivan, M., & Massie, M. (1999). The prophylactic mastectomy dilemma: A support group for women at high genetic risk for breast cancer. *Journal of Genetic Counseling, 8,* 163–173.

Kauff, N. D., Hurley, K. E., Hensley, M. L., Robson, M. E., Lev, G., Goldfrank, D., et al. (2005). Ovarian carcinoma screening in women at intermediate risk: Impact on quality of life and need for invasive follow-up. *Cancer, 104*(2), 314–320.

Kegley, J. (2002). Genetics decision-making: A template for problems with informed consent. *Medicine and Law, 21,* 459–471.

Khoury, M., McCabe, L., & McCabe, E. (2003). Population screening in the age of genomic medicine. *New England Journal of Medicine, 348,* 50–58.

Kuliev, A., Rechitsky, S., Tur-Kaspa, I., & Verlinsky, Y. (2005). Preimplantation genetics: Improving access to stem cell therapy. *Annals of the New York Academy of Science, 1054*, 223–227.

Lanie, A. D., Jayartne, T. E., Sheldon, J. P., Kardia, S. L., Anderson, E. S., Feldbaum, M., et al. (2004). Exploring the public understanding of basic genetic concepts. *Journal of Genetic Counseling, 13*, 305–320.

LaRusse, S., Roberts, J. S., Marteau, T. M., Katzen, H., Linnenbringer, E. L., Barber, M., et al. (2005). Genetic susceptibility testing versus family history-based risk assessment: Impact on perceived risk of Alzheimer disease. *Genetics in Medicine, 7*(1), 48–53.

League, S., & Hooper, W. C. (2005). Molecular diagnostics of inherited thrombosis. *Clinical Laboratory Science, 18*, 271–279.

Lerman, C., Croyle, R., Tercyak, K., & Hamann, H. (2002). Genetic testing: Psychological aspects and implications. *Journal of Consulting and Clinical Psychology, 70*, 784–797.

Lerman, C., Gold, K., Audrain, J., Lin, T. H., Boyd, N., Orleans, C. T., et al. (1997). Incorporating biomarkers of exposure and genetic susceptibility into smoking cessation treatment: Effects on smoking-related cognitions, emotions, and behavior change. *Health Psychology, 16*, 87–99.

Lerman, C., Hughes, C., Lemon, S. J., Main, D., Snyder, C., Durham, C., et al. (1998). What you don't know can hurt you: Adverse psychologic effects in members of BRCA1-linked and BRCA2-linked families who decline genetic testing. *Journal of Clinical Oncology, 16*(5), 1650–1654.

Lerman, C., Narod, S., Schulman, K., Hughes, C., Gomez-Caminero, A., Bonney, G., et al. (1996). BRCA1 testing in families with hereditary breast-ovarian cancer. A prospective study of patient decision making and outcomes. *Journal of the American Medical Association, 275*, 1885–1892.

Liljestrom, B., Aktan-Collan, K., Isomaa, B., Sarelin, L., Uutela, A., Groop, L., et al. (2005). Genetic testing for maturity onset diabetes of the young: Uptake, attitudes and comparison with hereditary non-polyposis colorectal cancer. *Diabetologia, 48*, 242–250.

Lipkus, I. M., McBride, C. M., Pollak, K. I., Lyna, P., & Bepler, G. (2004). Interpretation of genetic risk feedback among African American smokers with low socioeconomic status. *Health Psychology, 23*, 178–188.

Lipkus, I. M., Samsa, G., & Rimer, B. K. (2001). General performance of a risk numeracy scale among highly educated samples. *Medical Decision-Making, 21*, 34–77.

Lippman-Hand, A., & Fraser, F. C. (1979). Genetic counseling: Provision and reception of information. *American Journal of Medical Genetics, 3*, 113–127.

Marois, R., & Ivanoff, J. (2005). Capacity limits of information processing in the brain. *Trends in Cognitive Sciences, 9*, 296–305.

McAllister, M. (2002). Predictive genetic testing and beyond: A theory of engagement. *Journal of Health Psychology, 7*, 491–508.

McAllister, M. (2003). Personal theories of inheritance, coping strategies, risk perception and engagement in hereditary non-polyposis colon cancer families offered genetic testing. *Clinical Genetics, 64*, 179–189.

McBride, C. M., Bepler, G., Lipkus, I. M., Lyna, P., Samsa, G., Albright, J., et al. (2002). Incorporating genetic susceptibility feedback into a smoking cessation program for African-American smokers with low income. *Cancer Epidemiology, Biomarkers and Prevention, 11*, 521–528.

McCune, C., Ravine, D., Worwood, M., Jackson, H., Evans, H., & Hutton, D. (2003). Screening for hereditary haemochromatosis within families and beyond. *Lancet, 362*, 1897–1898.

McWilliams, J. E., Sanderson, B. J., Harris, E. L., Richert-Boe, K. E., & Henner, W. D. (1995). Glutathione S-transferase M1 (GSTM1) deficiency and lung cancer risk. *Cancer Epidemiology, Biomarkers and Prevention, 4*, 589–594.

Meyerowitz, B. E., & Chaiken, S. (1987). The effect of message framing on breast self-examination attitudes, intentions, and behavior. *Journal of Personality and Social Psychology, 52*, 500–510.

Miller, G. (2003). The cognitive revolution: A historical perspective. *Trends in Cognitive Sciences, 7*, 141–144.

Miller, S. M. (1980). Why having control reduces stress: If I can stop the roller coaster, I don't want to get off? In J. Garber & M. Seligman (Eds.), *Human helplessness: Theory and applications* (pp. 71–95). New York: Academic Press.

Miller, S. M. (1995). Monitoring versus blunting styles of coping with cancer influence the information patients want and need about their disease. *Cancer, 76*, 167–222.

Miller, S. M., Bowen, D. J., Campbell, M. K., Diefenbach, M. A., Gritz, E. R., Jacobsen, P. B., et al. (2004). Current research promises and challenges in behavioral oncology: Report from the American Society of Preventive Oncology Annual Meeting. *Cancer Epidemiology, Biomarkers and Prevention, 13*, 171–180.

Miller, S. M., & Diefenbach, M. A. (1998). The Cognitive-Social Health Information-Processing (C-SHIP) model: A theoretical framework for research in behavioral oncology. In D. S. Krantz & A. Baum (Eds.), *Technology and methods in behavioral medicine* (pp. 219–244). Mahwah, NJ: Erlbaum.

Miller, S. M., Fang, C. Y., Diefenbach, M. A., & Bales, C. (2001). Tailoring psychosocial interventions to the individual's health information processing style: The influence of monitoring versus blunting in cancer risk and disease. In A. Baum & B. Andersen (Eds.), *Psychosocial interventions in cancer* (pp. 343–362). Washington, DC: American Psychological Association.

Miller, S. M., Fang, C. Y., Manne, S. L., Engstrom, P. F., & Daly, M. B. (1999). Decision making about prophylactic oophorectomy among at-risk women: Psychological influences and implications. *Gynecologic Oncology, 75*(3), 406–412.

Miller, S. M., Mischel, W., O'Leary, A., & Mills, M. (1996). From human papilloma virus (HPV) to cervical cancer: Psychosocial processes in infection, detection, and control. *Annals of Behavioral Medicine, 18*(4), 219–228.

Miller, S. M., Roussi, P., Altman, D., Helm, W., & Steinberg, A. (1994). Effects of coping style on psychological reactions of low-income, minority women to colposcopy. *Journal of Reproductive Medicine, 39*(9), 711–718.

Miller, S. M., Roussi, P., Daly, M. B., Buzaglo, J. S., Sherman, K., Godwin, A. K., et al. (2005). Enhanced counseling for women undergoing BRCA1/2 testing: Impact on subsequent decision making about risk reduction behaviors. *Health Education and Behavior, 32*(5), 654–667.

Miller, S. M., & Schnoll, R. A. (2000). When seeing is feeling: A cognitive-emotional approach to coping with health stress. In M. Lewis & J. Haviland (Eds.), *Handbook of emotion* (pp. 538–557). New York: Plenum Press.

Miller, S. M., Shoda, Y., & Hurley, K. (1996). Applying cognitive-social theory to health-protective behavior: Breast self-examination in cancer screening. *Psychological Bulletin, 119*, 70–94.

Molinuevo, J. L., Pintor, L., Peri, J. M., Lleo, A., Oliva, R., Marcos, T., et al. (2005). Emotional reactions to predictive testing in Alzheimer's disease and other inherited dementias. *American Journal of Alzheimer's Disease and Other Dementias, 20*(4), 233–238.

Montgomery, G. (2004). Cognitive factors in health psychology and behavioral medicine. *Journal of Clinical Psychology, 60*, 405–413.

Muthen, B., & Muthen, L. K. (2000). Integrating person-centered and variable-centered analyses: Growth mixture modeling with latent trajectory classes. *Alcoholism, Clinical and Experimental Research, 24*, 882–891.

Norem, J. K., & Cantor, N. (1986). Defensive pessimism: Harnessing anxiety as motivation. *Journal of Personality and Social Psychology, 51*, 1208–1217.

Norem, J. K., & Illingworth, K. S. S. (1993). Strategy-dependent effects of reflecting on self and tasks: Some implications of optimism and defensive pessimism. *Journal of Personality and Social Psychology, 65*(4), 822–835.

O'Connor, A. M., Graham, I. D., & Visser, A. (2005). Implementing shared decision making in diverse healthcare systems: The role of patient decision aids. *Patient Education and Counseling, 57*, 247–249.

O'Connor, A. M., Legare, F., & Stacey, D. (2003). Risk communication in practice: The contribution of decision aids. *British Medical Journal, 327*, 736–740.

Page, A. (1994). Blood-injury phobia. *Clinical Psychology Review, 14*, 443–461.

Pasacreta, J. V. (1999). Psychosocial issues associated with increased breast and ovarian cancer risk: Findings from focus groups. *Archives of Psychiatric Nursing, 13*(3), 127–136.

Patch, C., Roderick, P., & Rosenberg, W. (2005). Comparison of genotypic and phenotypic strategies for population screening in hemochromatosis: Assessment of anxiety, depression, and perception of health. *Molecular Genetic Medicine, 7*(8), 550–556.

Patenaude, A. F. (2005). *Genetic testing for cancer: Psychological approaches to helping patients and families*. Washington, DC: American Psychological Association.

Payne, D. K., Biggs, C., Tran, K. N., Borgen, P. I., & Massie, M. J. (2000). Women's regrets after bilateral prophylactic mastectomy. *Annals of Surgical Oncology, 7*, 150–154.

Peshkin, B. N., Schwartz, M. D., Isaacs, C., Hughes, C., Main, D., & Lerman, C. (2002). Utilization of breast cancer screening in a clinically based sample of women after BRCA1/2 testing. *Cancer Epidemiology, Biomarkers and Prevention, 11*, 1115–1118.

Press, N., Reynolds, S., Pinsky, L., Murthy, V., Leo, M., & Burke, W. (2005). That's like chopping off a finger because you're afraid it might get broken: Disease and illness in women's views of prophylactic mastectomy. *Social Science and Medicine, 61,* 1106–1117.

Press, N., Yasui, Y., Reynolds, S., Durfy, S., & Burke, W. (2001). Women's interest in breast cancer susceptibility may be based on unrealistic expectations. *American Journal of Medical Genetics, 99,* 99–110.

Qaseem, A., Aronson, M., Fitterman, N., Snow, V., Weiss, K., Owens, D., et al. (2005). Screening for hereditary hemochromatosis: A clinical practice guideline from the American College of Physicians. *Annals of Internal Medicine, 143,* 517–521.

Rapkin, B., & Luke, D. (1993). Cluster analysis in community research: Epistemology and practice. *American Journal of Community Psychology, 21,* 247–277.

Rapkin, B. D., & Dumont, K. A. (2000). Methods for identifying and assessing groups in health behavioral research. *Addiction, 3,* S395–S417.

Redelmeier, D., & Shafir, E. (1995). Medical decision making in situations that offer multiple alternatives. *Journal of the American Medical Association, 273,* 302–305.

Roberts, J. S., Barber, M., Brown, T. M., Cupples, L. A., Farrer, L. A., LaRusse, S. A., et al. (2004). Who seeks genetic susceptibility testing for Alzheimer's disease? Findings from a multisite, randomized clinical trial. *Genetics in Medicine, 6,* 197–203.

Rogausch, A., Prause, D., Schallenberg A., Brockmoller, J., & Himmel, W. (2006). Patients' and physicians' perspectives on pharmacogenetic testing. *Pharmacogenomics, 7,* 49–59.

Rose, A. L., Peters, N., Shea, J. A., & Armstrong, K. (2005). Attitudes and misconceptions about predictive genetic testing for cancer risk. *Community Genetics, 8,* 145–151.

Rothman, A. J., Salovey, P., Antone, C., Keough, K., & Martin, C. (1993). The influence of message framing on health behavior. *Journal of Experimental Social Psychology, 29,* 408–433.

Sanderson, S. C., Wardle, J., Jarvis, M. J., & Humphries, S. E. (2004). Public interest in genetic testing for susceptibility to heart disease and cancer: A population-based survey in the UK. *Preventive Medicine, 39,* 458–464.

Saxton, M., Anderson, B., Blatt, R., Ayers, K., Finnegan, J., Thayer, B., et al. (1991). Prenatal diagnosis and pregnancy options. *Genetic Resource, 6,* 31–42.

Say, R., Murtagh, M., & Thomson, R. (2006). Patients' preference for involvement in medical decision making: A narrative review. *Patient Education and Counseling, 60,* 102–114.

Schapira, M. M., Davids, S. L., McAuliffe, T. L., & Nattinger, A. B. (2004). Agreement between scales in the measurement of breast cancer risk perceptions. *Risk Analysis, 24,* 665–673.

Schneider, K., & Kalkbrenner, K. (1998). Professional status survey 1998. *Perspectives in Genetic Counseling, 20,* S1–S8.

Schwartz, K. R., Peshkin, B. N., Tercyak, K. P., Taylor, K. L., & Valdimarsdottir, H. (2005). Decision making and decision support for hereditary breast-ovarian cancer susceptibility. *Health Psychology, 24,* S78–S84.

Schwartz, L., McDowell, J., & Yueh, B. (2004). Numeracy and the shortcomings of utility assessment in head and neck cancer patients. *Head and Neck, 26,* 401–407.

Schwartz, L., Woloshin, S., Black, W., & Welch, H. (1997). The role of numeracy in understanding the benefit of screening mammography. *Annals of Internal Medicine, 127,* 966–972.

Schwartz, M. D., Kaufman, E., Peshkin, B. N., Isaacs, C., Hughes, C., DeMarco, T., et al. (2003). Bilateral prophylactic oophorectomy and ovarian cancer screening following BRCA1/BRCA2 mutation testing. *Journal of Clinical Oncology, 21,* 4034–4041.

Schwartz, M. D., Lerman, C., Brogan, B., Peshkin, B. N., Hughes Halbert, C., DeMarco, T., et al. (2004). Impact of *BRCA1/BRCA2* counseling and testing on newly diagnosed breast cancer patients. *Journal of Clinical Oncology, 22,* 1823–1829.

Schwartz, M. D., Peshkin, B. N., Hughes, C., Main, D., Isaacs, C., & Lerman, C. (2002). Impact of BRCA1/BRCA2 mutation testing on psychologic distress in a clinic-based sample. *Journal of Clinical Oncology, 20,* 514–520.

Senior, V., Marteau, T. M., & Weinman, J. (2004). Self-reported adherence to cholesterol-lowering medication in patients with familial hypercholesterolaemia: The role of illness perceptions. *Cardiovascular Drugs and Therapy, 18*(6), 475–481.

Shiloh, S. (1996). Decision-making in the context of genetic risk. In T. Marteau & M. Richards (Eds.), *The Troubled Helix: Social and psychological implications of the new human genetics* (pp. 84–103). Cambridge, UK: Cambridge University Press.

Shiloh, S., Ben-Sinai, R., & Keinan, G. (1999). Effects of controllability, predictability, and information-seeking style on interest in predictive genetic testing. *Personality and Social Psychology Bulletin, 25,* 1187–1195.

Shoda, Y., Mischel, W., Miller, S. M., Diefenbach, M., Daly, M., & Engstrom, P. (1998). Psychological interventions and genetic testing: Facilitating informed decisions about BRCA1/2 cancer susceptibility. *Journal of Clinical Psychology in Medical Settings, 5,* 3–17.

Simpson, J., Carson, S., & Cisneros, P. (2005). Preimplantation genetic diagnosis (PGD) for heritable neoplasia. *JNCI Monographs, 34,* 87–90.

Smith, K., Ellington, L., Chan, A., Croyle, R., & Botkin, J. (2004). Fertility intentions following testing for a BRCA1 mutation. *Cancer Epidemiology, Biomarkers, and Prevention, 13,* 733–740.

Suther, S., & Goodson, P. (2003). Barriers to the provision of genetic services by primary care physicians: A systematic review of the literature. *Genetics in Medicine, 5,* 63–65.

Tan, P. H., Chan, C. L., Chan, C., & George, A. J. (2005). The evolving role of gene-based treatment in surgery. *British Journal of Surgery, 92,* 1466–1480.

Tassicker, R. J. (2005). Psychodynamic theory and counseling in predictive testing for Huntington's disease. *Journal of Genetic Counseling, 14,* 99–107.

Taylor, S. (2005). Gender differences in attitudes among those at risk for Huntington's disease. *Genetic Testing, 9,* 152–157.

Taylor, S. D. (1994). Demand for predictive genetic testing for Huntington's disease in Australia, 1987 to 1993. *Medical Journal of Australia, 161*, 354–355.

Tercyak, K. P., Lerman, C., Peshkin, B. N., Hughes, C., Main, D., Isaacs, C., et al. (2001). Effects of coping style and BRCA1 and BRCA2 test results on anxiety among women participating in genetic counseling and testing for breast and ovarian cancer risk. *Health Psychology, 20*, 217–222.

Thompson, H., Valdimarsdottir, H., Duteau-Buck, C., Guevarra, J., Bovbjerg, D., Richmond-Avellaneda, C., et al. (2002). Psychosocial predictors of BRCA counseling and testing decisions among urban African-American women. *Cancer Epidemiology, Biomarkers, and Prevention, 11*, 1579–1585.

Tiller, K., Meiser, B., Butow, P., Clifton, M., Thewes, B., Friedlander, M., et al. (2002). Psychological impact of prophylactic oophorectomy in women at increased risk of developing ovarian cancer: A prospective study. *Gynecologic Oncology, 86*(2), 212–219.

Ubel, P. A. (2005). Emotions, decisions, and the limits of rationality: Symposium introduction. *Medical Decision Making, 25*(1), 95–96.

Valdimarsdottir, H., Brown, K., Erblich, J., Hurley, K., Thompson, H., & Bovbjerg, D. (2005, June). *Patients' emotional distress reduces the effectiveness of genetic counseling for breast cancer susceptibility.* Poster session presented at Ninth International Meeting on the Psychosocial Aspects of Genetic Testing for Hereditary Cancer, Philadelphia, PA.

Van der Pligt, J. (1998). Perceived risk and vulnerability as predictors of precautionary behaviour. *British Journal of Health Psychology, 3*, 1–14.

Waalen, J., Nordestgaard, B., & Beutler, E. (2005). The penetrance of hereditary hemochromatosis. *Best Practice and Research Clinical Haematology, 18*, 203–220.

Wainberg, S., & Husted, J. (2004). Utilization of screening and preventive surgery among unaffected carriers of a BRCA1 or BRCA2 mutation. *Cancer Epidemiology, Biomarkers and Prevention, 13*, 1989–1995.

Walter, J. H., & White, F. J. (2004). Blood phenylalanine control in adolescents with phenylketonuria. *International Journal of Adolescent Medicine and Health, 16*, 41–45.

Wappner, R., Cho, S., Kronmal, R., Schuett, V., & Seashore, M. (1999). Management of phenylketonuria for optimal outcome: A review of guidelines for phenylketonuria management and a report of surveys of parents, patients, and clinic directors. *Pediatrics, 104*, 68–73.

Wardle, J. (1995). Women at risk of ovarian cancer. *Journal of the National Cancer Institute Monograph, 17*, 81–85.

Weil, J. (2000). *Psychosocial genetic counseling.* New York: Oxford University Press.

Welkenhuysen, M., Evers-Kiebooms, G., & d'Ydewalle, G. (2001). The language of uncertainty in genetic risk communication: Framing and verbal versus numerical information. *Patient Education and Counseling, 43*, 179–187.

Wells, S., Chi, D., Toshima, K., Dehner, L., Coffin, C., Dowton, S., et al. (1994). Predictive DNA testing and prophylactic thyroidectomy in patients at risk for multiple endocrine neoplasia type 2A. *Annals of Surgery, 220*, 237–247.

Williams-Piehota, P., Pizarro, J., Schneider, T., Mowad, L., & Salovey, P. (2005). Matching health messages to information-processing styles III: Monitor-blunter coping styles and mammography utilization. *Health Psychology, 24*(1), 58–67.

Woloshin, S., Schwartz, L., Moncur, M., Gabriel S., & Tosteson, A. (2001). Assessing values for health: Numeracy matters. *Medical Decision Making, 21,* 382–390.

Zoller, H., & Cox, T. M. (2005). Hemochromatosis: Genetic testing and clinical practice. *Clinical Gastroenterology and Hepatology, 3,* 945–958.

Chapter 4

"It Runs in the Family"

Family Systems Concepts and Genetically Linked Disorders

Susan H. McDaniel, John S. Rolland,
Suzanne L. Feetham, and Suzanne M. Miller

ALL ILLNESS IS BIOPSYCHOSOCIAL IN NATURE (ENGEL, 1977). ALL ILLNESS is influenced by and influences the patient's natural support system, which we will call "the family" (Campbell, 2003; McDaniel, Campbell, Hepworth, & Lorenz, 2005; McDaniel, Hepworth, & Doherty, 1992). As more and more becomes known about the genetic components of disease, the family becomes a multifaceted crucible of biological and psychosocial connection. The new scientific reality regarding genetics has profound ramifications for individual psychology and interpersonal relationships. Illness is typically viewed in Western society as an individual event. Yet even in our autonomy-sensitive culture, genetic screening and testing have powerful personal implications for all those in the family who are biologically related. Conditions now known to have important genetic links are no longer experienced solely as individual events. While both the genetic link and the individual's lived experience affect the family, it is also true that the family affects the individual's interpretation and response to health information, including genetic information (see Chapters 7 and 16 for further discussion of the effect of relationships on the expression of genotypes).

All individuals in families must work to achieve a balance between self-care and caring for others. Whether patient or caregiver, individuals need both a strong sense of *agency*, or self-efficacy, and a strong sense of *communion*, or family connection, to achieve a healthy response to stress (Bakan, 1969; McDaniel et al., 1992), such as that experienced with the diagnosis of a genetic disorder. Too much focus on the individual's needs to the exclusion of relationships ("unmitigated agency") or too much focus on others to the exclusion of self-care ("unmitigated communion") can lead to negative health outcomes (Helgeson, 1994). Both extremes, excluding family members or denying one's own needs, can occur as people use old patterns of behavior to cope with new genetic information. It is the balance between the two that makes for healthy individual and family functioning.

Discovering new genetic information can have a range of effects on individuals and families. It can crystalize, define, clarify, or amplify family stories about illness, early loss, etiology, and risk. It can intensify or calm individual and family anxieties about disease; it can activate family strengths or catalyze dysfunctional family interactions. Given this complex interweaving of biology and interpersonal interaction across generations, we offer this chapter as a primer on family systems theory—a framework to understand family dynamics that can be stimulated when confronting the diagnosis and treatment of genetically linked illness, approaching a decision about genetic testing, or planning for future childbearing.

THE "FAMILY" AND FAMILY SYSTEMS THEORY

Family systems theory is an outgrowth of general systems theory that evolved in the beginning of the 20th century (von Bertalanffy, 1950; Wynne, 2003). This theory posited the invisible connections and responsivity that explain the behavior of electrons as well as planets. Family systems theory applies these ideas to natural support systems and asserts that human behavior is influenced by significant others in one's environment or history. A simple example is the adolescent who cannot act in a rebellious manner unless there is some authority to rebel against, someone telling that adolescent what to do. To understand the experience of coping with genetic disorders, it is useful to understand basic concepts of family systems theory (Bowen, 1978; McDaniel et al., 2005; Rolland, 1994).

The term *family* has meanings ranging from a narrow definition of genetic continuity to a functional definition proposed for primary care: "family is any group of people related either biologically, emotionally, or legally" (McDaniel et al., 2005). When it comes to genetic screening and testing, of course the biological connection comes to the foreground. When it comes to the personal and interpersonal experience of potential or actual genetic disorders, however, it is "significant others" rather than just biological others that help to give meaning to the experience. A health professional needs to determine both the biological and the functional family of the patient and understand the genetic risk as well as the psychological and interpersonal risk associated with any genetic information. The functional family may include members of the household as well as extended family (including noncustodial parents after separation or divorce) and key others (such as close friends and professional caregivers).

The Pedigree and the Genogram

The genetic pedigree has long been the vehicle for health professionals to record three generations of family history about illness morbidity and mortality across family members. The pedigree carries particular importance for geneticists and genetics counselors in genetic risk analysis and identifying the expression of genetic conditions. The genogram is a tool used in family therapy to organize biological, psychological, and interpersonal information about a family (McGoldrick, Gerson, & Shellenberger, 1999). It allows the clinician or researcher to depict information about patterns of health and illness across generations, emotional connections among household members as well as with deceased and geographically removed members, and dates that reveal life cycle transitions (such as marriage), in order for the patient, family, and professional to understand the patient's larger context and the family's beliefs and mythologies about illness. Genogram information may be added to the genetic analysis of a pedigree to provide a comprehensive, biopsychosocial view of a patient. See Figure 4.1 for an example of a simple four-generation genogram used by both a geneticist and a family therapist to help Joe, who is contemplating testing for Huntington disease (the appendix at the end of this chapter provides a summary of standard genogram and pedigree symbols). Several genetic specialists have adapted the genogram for use in identifying who should receive information about genetic risk and how that information might be communicated based on the history of family relationships and their responses to past crises (Daly et al., 1999; Eunpu, 1997). The Colored Eco-Genetic Relationship Map (Kenen & Peters, 2001; Peters et al., 2005) is especially useful in that it asks the patient to add genetic risk-relevant psychosocial information to the genogram with colors and symbols (rather than the relationship lines of the traditional genogram) to denote relationships that provide instrumental, emotional, or informational support; family members who act as disseminators of cancer genetics information; and those that block this information.

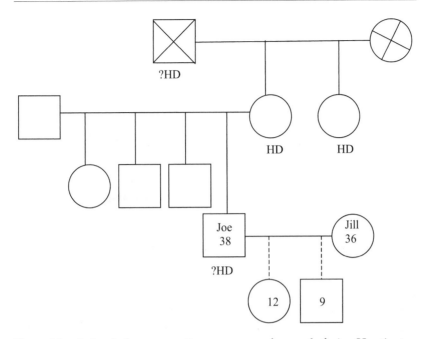

Figure 4.1 A simple four-generation genogram of a couple facing Huntington disease.

While these tools are important components of genetic risk assessment and family relationships, they also act as psychosocial interventions to increase self-awareness and prompt the patient to consider how to communicate genetic information and the likely impact it will have on various family members.

Illness, or the threat of illness, is a major stressor that occurs in a family that already has its own culture of coping—with well-established rules, a history of managing success and loss, and patterns of dealing with risk and resilience, challenge and change. The response of individuals and their families to the genetic components of illness can be understood by assessing family functioning in several domains: family organization, family communication processes, transgenerational patterns of coping, and family life cycle challenges. (Family beliefs, also an important domain of assessment, are discussed in Chapter 6.)

FAMILY ORGANIZATION

Families are organized with spoken and unspoken rules that maintain a stable system by prescribing and limiting members' behavior (Walsh,

2003). As a group, families vary in their adaptability, cohesion, structure, and role flexibility.

Adaptability

One of the most important aspects of family functioning relevant to understanding response to genetic disorders is adaptability. Families vary in their ability to adapt—from chaotic to flexible to rigid (Olson, Russell, & Sprenkle, 1989). Adaptability is tested at points of developmental change and also at any time of crisis. Crises often occur when a genetic test becomes available for an illness that runs in a family, when a person or family member receives a genetic testing result, or when an illness moves from a nonsymptomatic to a symptomatic phase of a disorder. Learning about genetic susceptibility can be a challenge to an individual or family's previously "healthy" identity, resulting in a review of one's goals, relationships, and priorities. Relationships can be strengthened or stressed as people struggle to accommodate new information.

The ability of a family to share tasks and shift roles to meet the changing needs of its members has to be balanced by the need for stability, enduring values, and predictable rules for behavior. Family adaptability can be problematic if the family is either too rigid or too chaotic in its response to needed change (Olson et al., 1989). For example, some families with rigid rules have difficulty moving from the crisis-oriented roles and responses of the acute phase of an individual's illness to the more day-to-day patterns focused on multiple individuals' needs that are important in the chronic phase. These families can become stuck or frozen in the developmental issues that faced individuals when the illness crisis first struck the family (Penn, 1983). Caregiving that was necessary soon after surgery, for example, may be infantilizing several weeks later. Chaotic families, on the other hand, have too little organization and often too few resources. They are so chaotically organized that, for example, they may be unlikely to retain an invitation or attend an informational session after one of their family members is confirmed to have a particular genetic disorder. Healthy families are able to be flexible in response to the changing demands of an illness or disability, while still tending to the developmental needs of family members.

Cohesion

Another primary organizing principle of family functioning involves cohesion, or closeness versus distance. Families vary in their preferred styles of interaction, with some communicating in depth several times a day, for example, while others speak superficially to each other once a month. Culture also influences what is expected in terms of cohesion, so that, for example, many Italian families have a high degree of cohesion and communion whereas British families may expect more distance and individual agency in their style of relating as a family.

Genetic screening and testing, and caring for individuals with genetic conditions, can challenge a family's ability to work together.

A family doctor convened a meeting with the English American family of a woman with early-onset Alzheimer disease. This was a family with a long history of valuing independence. The adult children of the patient lived within a 15-mile radius of their parents, but the children spoke to their parents by phone about once a month, and saw them two to three times a year. The family members clearly loved each other and enjoyed spending time together. The amount of contact represented the level of communication and cohesiveness that was expected. However, the father, the husband of the patient, was beginning to burn out because of the toll caregiving and monitoring was taking on him. Worried, the family doctor called a family meeting to ask the adult children to reorganize and help their father with the caregiving tasks that he knew would grow in the coming year. With quarterly meetings and support from health professionals, the family was able to reorganize to meet the needs of this progressive illness that required a higher degree of closeness and coordination than had been true for the years since the children left home. During the quarterly family meetings, the children also began to gather information about the possible genetic nature of their mother's illness.

Family Rules and Hierarchy

Family rules and recurring patterns of relationships provide some predictability for how family members act (Walsh, 2003); they determine how a family conducts its business of promoting the well-being of its members, especially the young and the ill or disabled. Family structure is an organizing principle for these rules, helping to distribute the instrumental and emotional tasks of family caregiving. Hierarchy reflects how power and authority are managed within a family (Simon, Stierlin, & Wynne, 1985). Family structure typically organizes the roles of family members by age and developmental issue, so that older members nurture the growth of younger members until such time that older members become ill, symptomatic, or disabled and require caregiving themselves. The goal is for each family member to retain some sense of agency. Although significant cultural variation exists, family hierarchy—typically with grandparents at the top, parents in the middle, and children at the bottom—is defined by boundaries between the generations. Illness, or threatened illness, can challenge the rules, the hierarchy, and the family roles when members can no longer play their usual parts.

Boundaries

Boundaries define individuals as well as subgroups in the family, such as the couple, the sibling subgroup, the grandparents, and so on (McDaniel et al., 2005; Minuchin, 1974). They occur and should be considered at different levels, including interpersonal, generational, and family-community. In many Western societies, an effective parental/ marital dyad is a strong alliance or partnership between the adults, which provides leadership for the nuclear family. (In some parts of the world, and in some Western subcultures, grandparents are the undisputed leaders of extended families; the important alliances occur between them and the parents regarding child rearing.) This parental alliance is especially important when the family faces a crisis, such as the new diagnosis of an illness or genetic information. Research has documented that negative aspects of marital functioning have indirect influences on health outcomes of the couple through depression and health habits, and direct influences on cardiovascular, endocrine, immune, neurosensory, and other physiological mechanisms (Kiecolt-Glaser & Newton, 2001). In addition, the primary adult partnership has a direct effect on the experience and health of a child, either positive or negative.

Whether by choice or through death or divorce, a single parent may partner with a close friend or a grandparent so that family tasks are distributed effectively. In less healthy situations, a boundary problem may occur through an *intergenerational coalition*, an unhealthy two-against-one situation in which, for example, a grandmother and a grandchild side against a mother who insists her child make up his schoolwork after having a vaso-occlusive sickle-cell crisis. The coalition in this situation, where the grandmother feels that the mother is pushing the child too hard too soon, can undermine the mother's ability to effectively parent and the child's ability to heal and resume growing. The solution in these situations lies in dismantling the coalitions and helping the adults to form an alliance that is in the best interest of the child.

Family Roles

When a couple's relationship is stressed, for instance with an ill child, one partner may be strict or authoritarian and the other may compensate and be too lenient with the child. Or one may be overresponsible in response to the other being distant and underresponsible, a dynamic that can lead to caregiver burnout in the overresponsible partner. These roles can be either complementary and functional or, if polarized, produce additional problems as a family struggles to face an illness threat or crisis.

In addition to assuming roles in the primary partnership of a nuclear family, family members often take up specific roles, such as the caregiver or nurturer, the breadwinner, the problem solver, the good child, or the "black sheep" or scapegoat. These roles are determined by history and temperament, and are complementary. No family has all black sheep in the child subsystem. Rather, one child is typically seen as the troublemaker and the focus of attention when the family is under stress. In one family with the hereditary nonpolyposis colon cancer mutation, 7-year-old Charles's school behavior always seemed to get worse when his mother planned to get her regular colonoscopy screening. Charles's parents focused on trying to shape his behavior and were distracted from worrying about the test. It took several years before they discovered the pattern. Scapegoating is a process that can hide problems that occur in other family members. Healthy family functioning occurs when roles can be shared or shifted over time so that no one person carries all the responsibility for nurturing, for example (Geller, Doksum, Bernhardt, & Metz, 1999). When roles become rigid, such as when a child in the black sheep role receives no recognition for good behavior, then behavioral, interpersonal, or psychophysiological symptoms may occur.

The role of parentified child occurs when a child is pulled up into the adult generation to perform parenting tasks because of a vacuum in the parenting subsystem due to parental absence, distance, dysfunction, or disability. This role is commonly the oldest child, often female, of a single parent, who helps to raise her younger siblings. When the family has to care for a member with a chronic or disabling condition, this child's service may be very important. It can be unavoidable, normative, and functional. Unfortunately, some parentified children perform these tasks at the cost of meeting their own developmental challenges. They may "miss their childhood" because of all their responsibilities, a problem that has ramifications when they reach adulthood.

Family roles that are especially relevant for an illness or the threat of an illness include family health expert, caregiver, and patient. The family health expert (often the mother or grandmother in a family) is the most important person, after the patient, for health professionals to identify, develop a relationship with, and communicate with (Fanos, 1997). If the family health expert is not included in the assessment or counseling process and disagrees with the health professional's diagnosis or plan, the result may be that the patient does not comply with the professional's recommendations. Including the family health expert's spouse or partner can help to prevent caregiver burnout, as well as to provide a more comprehensive assessment of the family. In an illness crisis, the roles of caregiver and patient are complicated when they are thrust upon family members who do not typically play those roles. For example, if the family nurturer is diagnosed with breast cancer and is temporarily no longer able to care for the family, the breadwinner, parentified child, or grandmother must pick up these tasks.

When undergoing genetic testing, families may have firm beliefs about who will test positive and who will test negative based on family roles (see Chapter 6). When the caregiver, for example, tests positive, and the vulnerable, sickly family member tests negative, family flexibility and resilience are challenged. Returning to the family described in Figure 4.1:

Joe learned in the last two years that his mother and his aunt have Huntington disease, and that his grandfather likely died of the illness. Until this news, Joe and Jill had a marriage that respected traditional gender roles. Joe was the breadwinner, supporting the family through his business, which required frequent travel. Jill stayed home to raise their daughters, now ages 12 and 9. She was the nurturer and also the worrier of the family, monitoring everyone for any symptoms or problems that needed her care. The couple had a strong alliance and were devoted to each other. However, when they learned of the threatening genetic condition in Joe's family, they were frightened, felt protective of each other, and stopped the open communication that had been the hallmark of their relationship.

Jill went back to work, saying the girls no longer needed her full-time. However, the most prominent reason that went unexpressed was her feeling that she needed to develop employable skills in case Joe got sick and could no longer support the family. At times, Jill lay in bed and worried about the future. The couple developed problems in their sex life. In an individual session prior to family therapy, Jill confessed that she no longer saw her husband as the strong man he used to be. Rather she saw him now as vulnerable and potentially disabled.

Joe, for his part, immersed himself in his work, trying not to think about the future or his risk for the debilitating illness. He became more and more distant. Given the vacuum that occurred in this marital dyad under stress, Jill turned more and more to their 12-year-old daughter, going to the movies with her and talking with her as if she were an adult. While the older girl became parentified, the 9-year-old began to develop behavior problems in school. When the family entered family therapy, the younger daughter was the scapegoat, the problem they all worried about. However, in the background, the shadow of Huntington disease was clearly influencing family dynamics and family roles in a way that was problematic for all family members.

Treatment included information about Huntington disease, genetic testing, marital and parenting sessions to strengthen the adult partnership, sibling sessions for the girls to strengthen their relationship, and attention to the youngest daughter's problems at school. The family structure had to shift, strengthening the boundaries around the couple and the siblings and increasing role flexibility, in order to tolerate the uncertainty and accommodate the threat of this illness. The couple remained in monthly treatment for several years, improving their communication and their ability to deal with stress, before they chose to have Joe tested. He tested negative.

Gender

Gender plays a significant part in role socialization regarding illness (McDaniel & Cole-Kelly, 2003). Typically, men are taught that being sick is not masculine; rather men learn to be strong, productive, and instrumental (stereotypically high on agency and low on communion). While these attributes can be very useful with the pragmatic tasks of caring for those who are ill, none are qualities that are traditionally part of the patient role. Women are often encouraged to be passive, receptive, and emotional, which are attributes consistent with the patient role (high on communion and low on agency). In general, women are more likely to acknowledge illness; adult women go to the doctor at a much higher frequency than do adult men (Commonwealth Fund, 2000). Women tend to be the primary caregivers of children and older adults with acute and chronic illness. Illness, or threatened illness, can provoke internal and interpersonal conflict about these roles for men and women.

A Latino man who was the patriarch of his family refused to allow his physician to tell his family that he was entering the terminal phase of his struggle with colon cancer. Though hospitalized and quite ill, he said that his family relied on him and that he was not ready to turn over decision making for the family until his condition deteriorated more. In addition, the news that this illness may have been transferred to his children weighed very heavily on his mind. Eventually, it became obvious that this man was dying. For several days, his wife had difficulty functioning as she tried to absorb the news of her husband's terminal diagnosis and the possibility of the children being at increased risk. Fortunately the father had time in the subsequent 2 weeks to talk with her and to meet regularly with his older son to discuss family business. They discussed the possibility of genetic screening, and the father urged his son to request testing so that he could take any preventive measures that might be recommended. Soon after this talk, the patriarch gathered his family together, with his physician, and told them of his prognosis, his desire for the children to take care of their mother, for the family to seek more information about the illness and their individual risk, and his intention to leave his son in charge. Soon thereafter, the son was tested as well as his siblings. The family pulled together and began to educate themselves about this illness. The father died 1 month later.

In this situation, the physician's and the patient's timetable did not match, but the process worked in the end. In other situations, families can become quite disorganized and stressed because they are unable to shift roles in time to successfully respond to an illness crisis. Medical family therapy, whether consultation or longer-term counseling, can be quite useful in these situations, to help individuals achieve both agency and communion, and to help a family reorganize its structure, grieve its losses, and transform individual roles to meet a new reality (McDaniel et al., 1992; see Chapter 6).

Monitoring and Blunting Coping Styles

Coping styles can affect family roles when facing genetic conditions. As mentioned in Chapter 3, some people use monitoring behavior to cope with illness. They scan for and amplify threatening cues and respond to the anxiety of a new diagnosis or new health information by gathering further information, with a danger of becoming overwhelmed. Family members, especially those not genetically linked, can be useful in gathering and recording information to help their loved one understand a new diagnosis or genetic mutation. Family members or friends can also provide the support that helps their monitoring loved one to be soothed and calmed in the face of stress. People who use blunting behaviors, on the other hand, distract from or avoid threatening cues in response to stress. They focus on moving on with life. Family members can play complementary roles with blunting individuals by helping them to confront their denial and supporting them to receive the screening, testing, or treatment that is needed.

Jeanine exemplifies the blunter style of coping. She was convinced that since she did not look like her mother, she was unlikely to have an inherited genetic predisposition toward breast cancer. As a result, she was disinclined to perform any increased surveillance activities; she felt she was too young to worry about mammograms or breast self-exams. A consultation session with Jeanine and her sister, who was more of a monitor, helped to make conversation about their increased risk, and what to do about it, part of their relationship. Delaying any decision about testing, they decided to go together for early baseline mammograms and to check in with each other to encourage regular breast self-exams.

FAMILY COMMUNICATION PROCESS

News about genetic conditions or genetic risk carries important meaning for the individual who has the first screening, testing, or treatment, and for the family to whom that person is related. Patterns of family communication or communion, before and after a diagnosis, can take on enormous importance, as one person's results have implications for other family members. The pedigree or genogram facilitates identifying the family rules and boundaries that will affect the individual's process of decision making and communication of results. Communication can be described as open versus secretive, emotional versus instrumental, and collaborative versus authoritarian. Coaching an individual is helpful when planning communication with family members about a new diagnosis or positive genetic test (Daly et al., 2001). These behavioral skills may be most useful if the premorbid patterns of family communication are well understood. Baseline patterns are challenged when the content of the communications is stressful.

Disengaged Versus Enmeshed Communication Styles

Some families are characterized by a *disengaged* pattern of communication. Like the family facing Alzheimer disease earlier in this chapter, there may be considerable affection among family members but their style of communicating is minimal and infrequent. Cultural factors play a role in preferred styles of communication. White Protestant families, for example, sometimes tend toward disengaged styles of communication, as in the next example.

Tricia was a 29-year-old German American woman who worked as a junior high school math teacher and attended the Lutheran church. Her church community was supportive when she experienced her first episode of breast cancer at 28, soon after the birth of her first child, a daughter. The illness was very disturbing to Tricia and her husband, but even more disturbing to them was the news that she tested positive for the BRCA1 genetic mutation, because this meant that she might have passed the gene along to her daughter. Tricia responded to the genetic stress by withdrawing into her nuclear family. She said she and her husband decided to take a year to absorb what this meant to them before informing her extended family. About 8 months later, Tricia's first cousin also received a diagnosis of breast cancer. At this time, Tricia told her cousin that she had tested positive for the BRCA1 mutation. Her cousin was furious, believing that if she had known this information perhaps she would have seen her doctor, prevented the cancer, or caught it earlier. Tricia was floored at this response; she had only done what seemed best in caring for herself, but now her family was angry. Her individual coping style (to keep tight boundaries) violated a family rule (to look out for one another). Tricia wrote a long letter detailing the results of her tests, copied the letter, and sent it to everyone in any way related. The experience shook her, and made her question her preferred private style of coping. In this situation, what she had experienced as helpful introspection, others experienced as dangerous disengagement, a lack of communion, neglecting her responsibility to the rest of the family.

At the other end of the coping continuum are families who often have an *enmeshed* style of family communication. These families typically go to the doctor together, speak over or for each other when interviewed, and communicate details about an illness or health problem to other family members as soon as an event happens. Geography is not a factor here. Family members can live across the globe and, especially now with electronic communication, be well informed almost immediately about each other's lives. Families who are more disengaged can live down the street and have very little communication. Again, cultural factors are important in establishing a style of intrafamily contact. While there is wide cultural variation, some Italian families, for example, tend toward expressive and frequent communication.

Some 37 members of a multigenerational Italian family, the Riones, attended a psychoeducational session about the hereditary nonpolyposis colon cancer (HNPCC) prevalent in their family. The session was conducted by an interdisciplinary team, including a geneticist, a genetics counselor, and two family therapists. The 8 children in the adult generation of this family had been traumatized by their father's untimely death 50 years ago, at age 34 from colon cancer, and by the abusive men who followed him as partners for their mother (see Figure 4.2). When the children of the original father began to be diagnosed with colon cancer it stimulated memories of the original trauma, but the cohesion and closeness in the family also resulted in enormous resilience in the face of stress. They developed humorous hospital rituals (such as putting collages of family members' colon X-rays on the walls) and supportive ways of coping, as one after another was treated for the disease. When genetic testing became available, however, the family's communication pattern began to break down under the stress involved with testing the next generation. A pattern of withholding information and intense verbal fighting began. The family was unable to break this enmeshed pattern without professional help. They entered

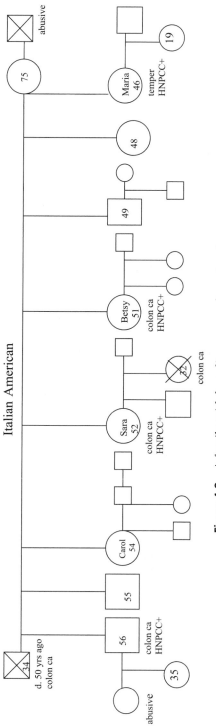

Figure 4.2 A family with hereditary nonpolyposis colon cancer.

medical family therapy and were seen as individuals, subgroups, and extended family until the disagreements were resolved, the boundaries reestablished, and the healthy communication patterns redeveloped.

Triangulation

Triangulation is the process of diffusing anxiety or conflict between two people by talking about a third. (A common example of this is gossip.) In families, members may form coalitions (see the preceding section, Family Organization) and avoid resolving problems by persistently talking about their frustrations to anyone other than the offending party. Triangulation prevents direct resolution of problems by diverting communication to a third party.

When Sara had surgery for her colon cancer, she wanted her sister, Betsy, to care for her, relegating her mother to occasional visits to bring her renowned soup. Instead her mother came for several hours a day. Rather than talking to her mother directly about how she could help in her recovery, Sara complained at least twice a day to Betsy about their mother's long visits. Betsy eventually suggested to their mother that Sara needed her to make shorter visits. Her mother got angry, saying Betsy did not understand what Sara needed like a mother did. The message was not clearly communicated until, in a family therapy session conducted by phone, Sara herself requested that her mother bring soup and stay for an hour over lunchtime each day.

Family Secrets

Family secrets are another form of communication (or lack thereof) that can result in triangulation or coalitions and complicate clear, healthy, direct communication about illness or illness risk. It is useful to distinguish between information that is private (and really does not affect other members) and information that is secret (and has a direct effect but is not shared). Genetic disorders can reveal secrets about paternity, as well as mutation status or illness prognosis.

The youngest child in the Rione family, Maria, had the longest history of behavior problems. She believed that her father was her mother's second husband and that she was not at risk for the HNPCC mutation like her older siblings. However, Betsy confided to the genetics counselor that some of the older siblings strongly suspected that Maria was their father's child. They believed she was conceived before their father's death but that their mother told everyone that she was the child of her second husband to consolidate the relationship that started soon after she became a widow. What Mrs. Rione believed to be private information turned out to be important to Maria's genetic risk (as well as to her emotional well-being).

Family Problem Solving

When secrets are exposed, family members may feel betrayed and conflict may tumble out into the open. Family problem-solving and conflict resolution are important skills that are tested at this point in an illness crisis. Well-functioning families have both agency and communion; they are able to work together to manage the instrumental tasks of caring for an ill family member and process the difficult emotions that may be associated with illness (Epstein, Bishop, Ryan, Miller, & Keitner, 2003; McDaniel, Hepworth, & Doherty, 1997). Epstein and colleagues identified seven sequential steps in problem solving:

1. Identify the problem.
2. Communicate with the appropriate people about it.
3. Develop possible solutions.
4. Decide on one alternative.
5. Carry it out.
6. Monitor to ensure it happens.
7. Evaluate its effectiveness.

Families can falter at any one of these steps. Or they may be very effective in managing the pragmatic, instrumental aspects of caregiving, and quite frozen around communicating about the emotional aspects of illness or risk assessment. Illness or increased risk for illness can stimulate difficult emotions about threatened loss that are sometimes expressed as sadness or depression, other times as anger and interpersonal conflict.

The Riones were an expressive family who prided themselves on their open communication style and ability to solve most any problem. Even so, Maria was known to have a temper, much like the father she only recently came to know was hers biologically. Communication about cancer happening among this sibling group seemed to be direct and clear. However, when testing became possible, suddenly conflict in the family increased, especially about issues of secrecy versus privacy.

Maria tested positive for HNPCC after her mother told her that her biological father was the same man as her siblings'. The family had another meeting with their family therapy/genetics health professional team to discuss testing for the next generation, who ranged in age from 19 to 35. After the geneticist gave them the information about risk and testing, the family was not able to come to any mutual decisions about testing. Some wanted to have the test;

others were undecided. Then they began to argue about how they would inform each other of testing and test results. Some wanted the issue to be private–to have the test on their own time and reveal the results in their own time. Others felt that was artificial and wanted it to be acceptable to ask each other what was going on about testing the children. The family got into an intense struggle about decision making, problem solving, and the rules of communication. They agreed the testing decisions would be made individually and in small groups, and decided to focus on family communication. That issue took several meetings to resolve, with some hurt feelings along the way. Ultimately they agreed that each person's style may be different, so they could not decide on one way of handling communication or problem solving that would work for everyone but rather had to consider the desires of the particular person with whom they were talking. The only blanket rule they agreed to was to forbid illness or testing discussions at family holiday or birthday celebrations.

ILLNESS THROUGH TIME: TRANSGENERATIONAL PATTERNS OF COPING ACROSS THE LIFE CYCLE

Family illness histories provide a blueprint for coping across time with genetic disorders (McDaniel et al., 1992; Rolland, 1994; see Chapter 5). In addition to understanding the current family organization and patterns of communication, it is important to trace these issues across at least three generations with the use of the pedigree or genogram. It is also critical to record the family experience with resilience and strength, as well as their experience with difficulty. ("My mother survived and eventually thrived after her own father's early death. I admire that in her," said one of the Rione sons.) Some work hard to improve on the problematic aspects of their history of coping with illness. ("I am not going to deny my illness, like my father did," said one of the Rione daughters.) Others reenact patterns of coping without being aware of the repetition. *Family projection process* is the transmission of unresolved conflicts, issues, roles, and tasks from one generation to another (Bowen, 1978; McDaniel et al., 2005). Becoming aware of family themes (such as alcohol abuse as a response to early loss) is an important part of the psychosocial assessment that can be recorded with people facing new genetic information or newly diagnosed genetic conditions.

Bob learned that he had myotonic dystrophy—a single-gene, dominant disorder—when he was 45, after having his four children. His mother had a late-onset, mild case of the illness, but his brother developed serious symptoms by the time he was 50. Bob first developed muscle weakness in his hands at 45. His illness progressed over the first year such that his wife, Jenny, felt he needed to use a wheelchair and quit driving. Focused on functioning in spite of the illness, Bob refused both, saying he was perfectly capable of walking and driving. The couple got into such a struggle about this that they separated for several months, attended marital therapy, and eventually reconciled after renegotiating the conditions under which Bob would drive and Jenny would care for him. (For example, Jenny would help Bob use the walker as long as he attended his physicians' appointments and took care of himself in other ways.)

During this period, Bob and Jenny's adult children met with the neurologist to discuss the possibility of testing for the genetic mutation. Two of the children, the females, immediately went for testing. The two males, however, stated that they were not interested in finding out. "We'll find out if we have symptoms." Clearly these children took after their father's blunting approach to illness concerns. Whether or not they inherited his disease remains to be seen. The family benefits from the value they place on functioning in spite of the disorder. However, those who have not been tested are not available for early medical intervention.

Family Life Cycle Challenges

All family interactions occur against a backdrop of life cycle developmental stages, from infancy to old age. Families face predictable developmental challenges (Carter & McGoldrick, 1999) moving from one life stage to the next. For example, all families of adolescents have to reorganize to provide more space for young persons to make decisions and learn to care for themselves. Symptoms or conflict occur if, for example, parents continue to provide the structure needed by an 8-year-old when their child is 14. It is always useful to understand the developmental challenges facing the family and assess the individual and family for how they are managing what is necessary for growth at their particular stage of the life cycle.

Acute stressors are those unexpected difficulties that can occur for individuals and families at any point in the lifespan. Illness is an acute stressor. The interaction of acute stressors and life cycle challenges can produce difficulties, as well as unexpected growth, for families. Illnesses that require considerable caregiving are experienced and managed differently when the family is in a developmental stage, such as childbearing, with tasks that naturally pull the family together. When illness or disability occurs during stages when the family members are naturally more independent, such as adolescence, families sometimes struggle. New-onset juvenile diabetes in an adolescent can be enormously challenging because these teens are in the stage where they do not want parents telling them what to do or monitoring their behavior. Chapter 5 describes family life cycle issues in detail, and examines the effect of developmental challenges on issues common to genetic conditions such as uncertainty and threatened loss.

APPENDIX

Standard Symbols for Genograms

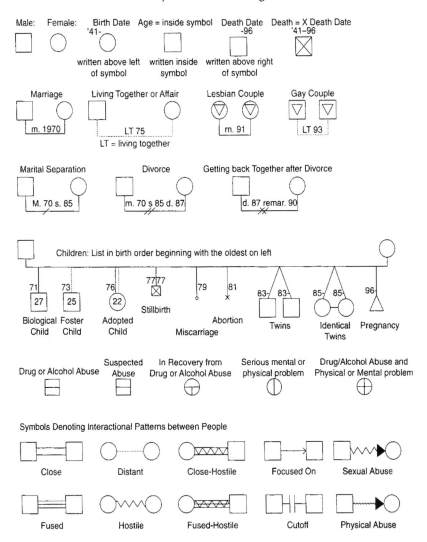

Source: McGoldrick, M., Gerson, R., & Shellenberger, S. (1999). Genograms: Assessment and intervention (2nd ed.). New York: Norton. Reprinted with permission.

REFERENCES

Bakan, D. (1969). *The duality of human existence.* Chicago: Rand McNally.

Bertalanffy, L. (1950). An outline of general systems theory. *British Journal for Philosophy of Science, 1,* 134–150.

Bowen, M. (1978). *Family therapy in clinical practice.* New York: Aronson.

Campbell, T. L. (2003). The effectiveness of family interventions for physical disorders. *Journal of Marital and Family Therapy, 29,* 263–282.

Carter, E., & McGoldrick, M. (1999). *The expanded family life cycle* (3rd ed.). New York: Allyn and Bacon.

Commonwealth Fund. (2000). Many men dangerously out of touch with health care system. *The Commonwealth Fund 1998 survey of men's and women's health.* New York: Commonwealth Fund.

Daly, M. B., Barsevick, A., Miller, S. M., Buckman, R., Costalas, J., Montgomery, S., et al. (2001). Communicating genetic test results to the family: A six-step skills-building strategy. *Family and Community Health, 24,* 13–27.

Daly, M., Farmer, J., Harrop-Stein, C., Montgomery, S., Itzen, M., Costalas, J. W., et al. (1999). Exploring family relationships in cancer risk counseling using the genogram. *Cancer Epidemiology Biomarkers and Prevention, 8,* 393–398.

Engel, G. (1977). The need for a new medical model: A challenge for biomedicine. *Science, 196,* 129–136.

Epstein, N., Bishop, D., Ryan, C., Miller, I., & Keitner, G. (2003). The McMaster model: A view of healthy family functioning. In F. Walsh (Ed.), *Normal family processes* (3rd ed., pp. 581–608). New York: Norton.

Eunpu, D. L. (1997). Systemically-based psychotherapeutic techniques in genetic counseling. *Journal of Genetic Counseling, 6,* 1–20.

Fanos, J. (1997). Developmental tasks of childhood and adolescence: Implications for genetic testing. *American Journal of Medical Genetics, 71,* 22–28.

Geller, G., Doksum, Y., Bernhardt, B., & Metz, S. (1999). Participation in breast cancer susceptibility testing protocols: The influence of recruitment source, altruism, and family involvement on women's decisions. *Cancer Epidemiology, 8,* 377–385.

Helgeson, V. S. (1994). Relation of agency and communion to well-being: Evidence and potential explanations. *Psychological Bulletin, 116,* 412–428.

Kenen, R., & Peters, J. A. (2001). The Colored Eco-Genetic Relationship Map (CEGRM): A conceptual approach and potential tool for genetic cancer risk counseling research. *Journal of Genetic Counseling, 10,* 289–310.

Kiecolt-Glaser, J. K., & Newton, T. L. (2001). Marriage and health: His and hers. *Psychological Bulletin, 127,* 472–503.

McDaniel, S. H., Campbell, T. L., Hepworth, J., & Lorenz, A. (2005). *Family-oriented primary care* (2nd ed.). New York: Springer-Verlag.

McDaniel, S. H., & Cole-Kelly, K. (2003). Gender, couples, and illness: A feminist analysis of medical family therapy. In T. Goodrich & L. Silverstein (Eds.), *Feminist family therapy* (pp. 267–280). Washington, DC: American Psychological Association.

McDaniel, S. H., Hepworth, J., & Doherty, W. (1992). *Medical family therapy: A biopsychosocial approach to families with health problems.* New York: Basic Books.

McDaniel, S. H., Hepworth, J., & Doherty, W. (1997). *The shared experience of illness: Stories of patients, families, and their therapists.* New York: Basic Books.

McGoldrick, M., Gerson, R., & Shellenberger, S. (1999). *Genograms: Assessment and intervention* (2nd ed.). New York: Norton.

Minuchin, S. (1974). *Families and family therapy.* Cambridge, MA: Harvard University Press.

Olson, D., Russell, C., & Sprenkle, D. (1989). *Circumplex model: Systemic assessment and treatment of families.* New York: Haworth.

Penn, P. (1983). Coalitions and binding interactions in families with chronic illness. *Family Systems Medicine,* 1(2), 16–25.

Peters, J., Kenen, R., Giusti, R., Loud, J., et al. (2004). An explanatory study of the feasibility and utility of the Colored Ec-Genetic Relational Map (CE-GRM) in women at high genetic risk of developing breast cancer. *American Journal of Medical Genetics, 130A,* 258–264.

Rolland, J. (1994). *Families, illness and disability.* New York: Basic Books.

Simon, F., Stierlin, H., & Wynne, L. C. (1985). *The language of family therapy: A systemic vocabulary and sourcebook.* New York: Family Process Press.

Walsh, F. (2003). *Normal family processes* (3rd ed.). New York: Guilford.

Wynne, L. C. (2003). Systems theory and the biopsychosocial model. In R. Frankel, T. Quill, & S. McDaniel (Eds.), *The biopsychosocial approach: Past, present and future* (pp. 219–230). Rochester, NY: University of Rochester Press.

Chapter 5

Living With Anticipatory Loss in the New Era of Genetics

A Life Cycle Perspective

John S. Rolland

THE EMERGING FIELD OF GENOMIC HEALTH PRESENTS NEW CHALLENGES for living with uncertainty and threatened loss. Relatively little attention has been given to the process of anticipating future loss and how experience with protracted threatened loss evolves with nonsymptomatic and symptomatic illness and individual and family development. Acquiring and living with genetic information will increasingly become part of the fabric of our personal and family lives. It will expand the meaning of threatened loss to include not only our nuclear but also our extended families and future generations. And it will increasingly impact present and future life cycle planning.

Living with uncertainty or the anticipation of future illness can be challenging and painful for individuals and families. Genetic risk information often imposes complex psychosocial tasks. Families need to sustain the vital attachment and involvement of a person who may develop a serious disorder, while striving to maintain family integrity by building flexibility into life cycle planning.

This chapter presents a developmental systemic framework to address the experience of acquiring and living with genomic information.[1] This can help clarify how the meaning of possible loss evolves over time with changing life cycle demands (Rolland, 1994a, 2004). This discussion focuses specifically on the phases of traditional genetic and multifactorial or genetically influenced disorders before clinical onset (see Chapter 2). The experience of threatened loss after a condition becomes symptomatic is described elsewhere (Rolland, 1990, 1994a, 2004). The first section provides an overview of concepts to understand anticipatory loss in relation to the Family Systems Genomic Illness (FSGI) Model (see Chapter 2; Rolland & Williams, 2005) and individual and family life cycles. These concepts provide a foundation for the rest of the chapter to discuss common issues related to anticipatory loss over time.

THE CONCEPT OF ANTICIPATORY LOSS

Anticipatory loss refers to the experience of living with possible, probable, or inevitable future loss. It is meant to encompass both uncertainty and threatened loss. As distinct from the concept of *anticipatory grief*, which refers more narrowly to the terminal phase of an illness (Rando, 2000), *anticipatory loss* refers to the experience of living with uncertainty and in the face of illness, disability, and death over the life span (Rolland, 1990, 2004). Myriad feelings and interactions associated with anticipatory loss can complicate all aspects of individual and family life.

This discussion is based on a systemic approach to anticipatory loss, attending to the impact of a family member's genetic risk information on the family as a functional unit, with far-reaching effects for every member and all other relationships. Also, like discussion of the experience of illness, death, and loss (Walsh & McGoldrick, 2004), this discussion is based on the awareness that there are many effective coping strategies to deal with anticipatory loss, grounded in diverse cultural norms. Further, research by Wortman and Silver (1989) suggests a broad range of individual normative grief reactions over time and casts doubt on traditional progressive stage theories of loss (Kübler-Ross, 1969). Rather, there are many facets of mourning, such as shock, anger, and sadness that reverberate to varying degrees and can be reactivated at nodal points such as anniversaries and developmental milestones (Walsh & McGoldrick, 2004).

THE DIMENSION OF TIME

The dimension of time is a central consideration when living with both the possibility and reality of genetic knowledge. Coping and adaptation to such knowledge is an ongoing process that evolves over the life cycle. The evolving challenges, demands, and goals of various life cycle phases influence and are influenced by the experience of living with genetic information. Moreover, families' prior experiences with uncertainty, threatened loss, and illness influence how they approach these issues.

The family unit and each member must attend to both present and future challenges. They need to master the practical and emotional tasks related to genetic information in the present. At the same time, they need proactively to chart a course to deal with the complexities and uncertainties of a particular disorder in a largely unknown future. To achieve this requires understanding the intertwining of three evolutionary threads: (1) the individual and (2) family life cycles, and their relationship to (3) the nonsymptomatic and symptomatic developmental phases of a genomic disorder. To think systemically about the interface of these three developmental lines, we need a common language and set of concepts that can be applied to each and yet permits consideration of all three simultaneously.

Two steps are necessary to lay the foundation for such a model. First, we need a language to characterize genomic disorders in psychosocial and longitudinal terms. The FSGI framework (Rolland & Williams, 2005), described in Chapter 2, offers such a language. It conceptualizes the relationship between the nonsymptomatic time phases and various psychosocial types of genomic conditions. This model organizes both traditional single-gene and multifactorial or genetically influenced conditions based on key characteristics in order to define useful clusters or types of conditions with similar patterns of psychosocial demands over time. The model highlights four key characteristics: (1) degree of likelihood of development of a condition based on genetic mutations, (2) expectable clinical severity, (3) timing of expected onset in the life cycle, and (4) whether there exist effective treatment interventions to modify symptomatic onset and clinical progression.

Just as we can describe crisis, chronic, and terminal phases after clinical onset of an illness (Rolland, 1984, 1994a), it is useful to conceptualize nonsymptomatic phases: (1) awareness; (2) crisis I pretesting; (3) crisis II test/posttesting; and (4) long-term adaptation before clinical onset of a genomic disease (Rolland & Williams, 2005; Chapter 2; see Figure 2.3, p. 55). Each nonsymptomatic phase is distinguished by developmental challenges related to living with anticipatory loss (see Table 2.3, p. 62). In this chapter, this framework is used to inform how different disorders and nonsymptomatic phases might interact with individual and family development in shaping the experience of anticipatory loss.

Second, it is essential to consider how genetic risk is woven into the fabric of both individual and family life over time. This involves: (1) the person tested and at risk; (2) the family system response and impact on family functioning; and (3) the ripple effect for all other family members and their relationships. Families need to consider implications for siblings and children who are at genetic risk as well as those who are not affected. The particular impact on individual members will depend on such factors as their phase of development at the time of testing (or other nonsymptomatic time phase), their core commitments at that time, and the phase in the family life cycle. The family life cycle phase will significantly shape—and be shaped by—each family member's personal development. This is vividly demonstrated when we consider the impact of presymptomatic testing for Huntington disease on a couple's relationship and on each partner's subsequent individual development. The relationship skews that often emerge between partners highlight the necessity of using both an individual and relational lens across the family life cycle (Rolland, 1994b).

INTERFACE OF GENOMIC ILLNESS AND INDIVIDUAL AND FAMILY LIFE CYCLES

A multigenerational life cycle lens is essential to construct a normative framework for living with anticipatory loss. It offers a wide-angle view to help understand the ongoing interaction of past, present, and future.

Life cycle is a core conceptual framework for both family and individual development. Traditional life cycle frameworks assumed a "normal" sequence and unfolding of the life course (Erikson, 1959; Levinson, 1986). *Life structure* refers to the core elements (e.g., work, child rearing, leisure, caregiving) of an individual or family's life at any point in time. More recent theory and research have recognized the growing diversity of individual and family development and of larger cultural, socioeconomic, gender, and ethnic influences (Carter & McGoldrick, 1999). Family structures have also become more varied and complex over the life course (Walsh, 2003), complicating adaptation to genomic disorders and their risk. For instance, Joe, a divorced man with a genetic mutation that could have devastating consequences for offspring, is relieved that children from that marriage are not affected. Upon remarriage to Jill, a younger woman with no children, he learns that she is strongly invested in having a family together, while he is reluctant to tempt fate again, leading to marital conflict.

Developmental Phases

Genomic disorders and individual and family development all have in common the progression of phases, each presenting distinct challenges.

Levinson's (1986) theory of individual development posits the ongoing alternation of life structure-building and maintaining (stable) periods and life structure-changing (transitional) periods linking developmental phases (Figure 5.1). In a building and maintaining period, the primary goal is to form a life structure and enrich life within it based on the key choices an individual or family made in the preceding transition period. These plans may be significantly altered by genetic knowledge. Transition periods can be the most vulnerable because previous individual, family, and illness-related life structures are reappraised in the face of new developmental challenges that may require major change.

Carter and McGoldrick (1999) delineated six phases of the family life cycle when marker events (e.g., marriage, birth of first child, last

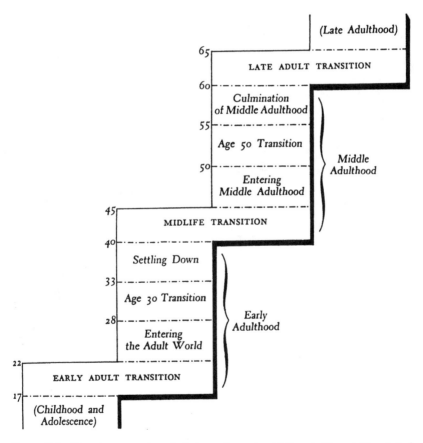

Figure 5.1 Developmental periods in early and middle adulthood. Reprinted by permission from Levinson, D. J. (1978). *The Seasons of a Man's Life.* New York: Knopf, 57.

Table 5.1 The Stages of the Family Life Cycle

FAMILY LIFE CYCLE STAGE	EMOTIONAL PROCESS OF TRANSITION: KEY PRINCIPLES	SECOND-ORDER CHANGES IN FAMILY STATUS REQUIRED TO PROCEED DEVELOPMENTALLY
Leaving home: single young adults	Accepting emotional and financial responsibility for self	a. Differentiation of self in relation to family of origin b. Development of intimate peer relationships c. Establishment of self in respect to work and financial independence
The joining of families through marriage: the new couple	Commitment to new system	a. Formation of marital system b. Realignment of relationships with extended families and friends to include spouse
Families with young children	Accepting new members into the system	a. Adjusting marital system to make space for children b. Joining in child rearing, financial, and household tasks c. Realignment of relationships with extended family to include parenting and grandparenting roles
Families with adolescents	Increasing flexibility of family boundaries to permit children's independence and grandparents' frailties	a. Shifting of parent/child relationships to permit adolescent to move into and out of system b. Refocus on midlife marital and career issues c. Beginning shift toward caring for older generation

Launching children and moving on	Accepting a multitude of exits from and entries into the family system	a. Renegotiation of marital system as a dyad a. Development of adult-to-adult relationships between grown children and their parents c. Realignment of relationships to include in-laws and grandchildren d. Dealing with disabilities and death of parents (grandparents)
Families in later life	Accepting the shifting generational roles	a. Maintaining own and/or couple functioning and interests in face of physiological decline: exploration of new familial and social role options b. Support for more central role of middle generation c. Making room in the system for the wisdom and experience of the elderly, supporting the older generation without overfunctioning for them d. Dealing with loss of spouse, siblings, and other peers and preparation for death

Note. Excerpted from Carter, B., & McGoldrick, M. (Eds.). (1999). *The expanded family life cycle: Individual, family, and social perspectives* (3rd ed.). Boston: Allyn & Bacon.

child leaving home) herald the transition from one phase to the next. These phases include: (1) single young adults; (2) the joining of families through marriage or partnership (the couple); (3) families with young children; (4) families with adolescents; (5) launching children and moving on; and (6) families in later life. Each phase involves key emotional processes of transition and major changes in family structure and relationships required to proceed developmentally (see Table 5.1). Increasingly, many families undergo additional transitions with separation or divorce, single parenting, and remarriage/stepfamily adaptation.

These concepts can provide a foundation for understanding the experience of living with genetic risk. Individual development involves alternating transition and life structure building and maintaining periods. These particular periods occur in relation to the phases of the family life cycle. For instance, older adolescents may be in transition to early adulthood, making initial plans and decisions as they begin adult life. At the same time, a family in the phase of launching children must alter household structure, roles, and focus from raising children. Both parents may be in their own midlife transitions, considering personal and shared goals for their next life phase. Caregiving for elders also complicates this picture.

It is important to consider how the interaction of these challenges fits with the nonsymptomatic phases of a genomic disorder. Consider a family that carries the *BRCA1* mutation and is launching young adults. The mother, who has already tested positive for *BRCA1* and has been in the phase of living with genetic knowledge, is approaching an age of greater risk for onset of breast and ovarian cancer. Heightened fears might affect how she and her husband plan for the next phase of their lives. For children in late adolescence, concerns about their mother's high risk for cancer would influence their planning (e.g., staying close to home in case they are needed to help support their parents). A son and daughter may have been made aware of the potential risk for themselves, but up to now did not actively consider predictive testing. They have both been in the nonsymptomatic awareness phase. Now, as they enter adulthood, concerns about personal vulnerability for the mutation may become more activated, as each is thinking more seriously about future plans such as marriage and having children. They may defer active consideration of testing, remaining for now in an awareness phase. Or one or both might enter a pretesting crisis phase and actively explore whether to proceed with genetic testing and face implications of a positive result for couple and parenting options. Ongoing provider and family awareness should include this kind of developmental interaction to guide timing and content of discussions.

MULTIGENERATIONAL LEGACIES

A family's current response to illness or genetic risk cannot be adequately comprehended apart from its history (Boszormenyi-Nagy & Spark, 1973; Bowen, 1978; Byng-Hall, 1996; Carter & McGoldrick, 1999; Framo, 1992; Walsh & McGoldrick, 2004). How families and individual members cope and adapt to anticipatory loss varies depending on each family's multigenerational experience with actual and threatened loss.

Multigenerational Assessment

Clinicians can use historical questioning and can construct a genogram and timeline to track key events and transitions (McGoldrick, Gerson, & Schellenberger, 1999). This helps them gain an understanding of a family's organizational shifts and coping strategies in response to past stressors, specifically to past illnesses or living with threatened loss. Such inquiry helps explain and predict the family's current meaning making, coping, and adaptation. A multigenerational assessment helps to clarify areas of strength and vulnerability. It also identifies high-risk families burdened by past unresolved issues and dysfunctional patterns that make it difficult to absorb the challenges presented by a serious genomic disorder. For example, one family was shattered by a history of relationship cutoffs and unresolved conflict that began when the paternal grandfather had Alzheimer disease.

An illness-oriented genogram focuses on how a family managed past stressors and tracks the evolution of family adaptation over time. The health care provider explores how a family organized as an evolving system around prior experiences with illness or disability, anticipatory loss, death and dying, and unexpected crises. For instance, a past death may leave catastrophic fears that any life-threatening condition will invariably be fatal. It is important to bring to light areas of consensus and "learned differences" (Penn, 1983) that are sources of cohesion and conflict. Patterns of coping, replications, discontinuities, shifts in relationships (e.g., alliances, triangles, cutoffs), and sense of competence are noted. These patterns are transmitted across generations as family belief systems including pride or shame, myths, taboos, and gendered or catastrophic expectations (Seaburn, Lorenz, & Kaplan, 1992; Walsh & McGoldrick, 2004). For instance, how families have managed caregiving challenges is important. When a female child is traditionally designated the caregiver, she can become overburdened and resentful of siblings, whereas collaborative efforts shared among siblings ease the burden and strengthen their bonds. Also, it is useful to inquire about other forms of loss (e.g., divorce, migration), crisis (e.g., job loss, assault, major disaster), and protracted adversity (e.g., poverty, racism, war, political oppression). These experiences can heighten risk but may also offer models for resilience and effective coping skills in the face of a serious health problem (Walsh, 2006).

Multigenerational information can help clarify how different families or family members may hear the same discussion with health professionals through very distinct historical, ethnic, or cultural filters (see Chapter 6). Beliefs about the likelihood and timing of a future illness can strongly influence the relationship rules established in the face of genetic risk. It is very useful to ask each family member to discuss hopes and fears about the anticipated course and outcome. Differences based on multigenerational experiences can contribute to conflict and dysfunctional patterns with health care providers or within the family. In one family, a 30-year-old woman with a family history of breast cancer was tested for the *BRCA1/BRCA2* genetic mutations. She tested normal and was reassured by her primary care physician. Despite this, her husband was terrified that she would die an untimely death from breast cancer. His mother had died from malignant melanoma a year after being reassured by her physician that her tumor was "benign." His traumatic experience, unknown to the physician, led him to distrust the test results and to live in fear of his wife's death. Also, his wife had been unaware of the misdiagnosis of his mother's illness, limiting her understanding of his terror. This vignette illustrates not only the importance of multigenerational information of other key family members, but also how past illness experience can influence the meaning of predictive testing results. Knowledge of the husband's experience in pretesting assessment could inform brief counseling to avert a posttesting individual and marital crisis.

Outdated Medical Information

Multigenerational inquiry can uncover outdated medical information that may influence family members' current expectations. For instance, in one family the paternal grandfather had died from colon cancer that was only diagnosed in an advanced stage. From that experience, the family had a fatalistic view regarding any form of cancer, but in particular colon cancer, which ran in the family. During routine inquiry regarding family history of illness, primary care health professionals can elicit these kinds of illness legacies. Awareness of these legacies can inform discussion of current strategies concerning predictive testing and prevention.

Families that lack adequate health care are particularly disadvantaged. They may be unaware of predictive testing for hereditary forms of illness, such as colorectal cancer, and lack access to early and regular colonoscopic screening to diagnose and successfully treat precancerous polyps and early stages of colon cancer.

Diseases With Known Manifestations and Multigenerational History

The previous example highlights how legacies or stories of a specific condition are often passed down through the generations. They commonly provide basic scripts for the affected and unaffected family members (Byng-Hall, 1996, 2004). Themes of both suffering and resilience—how to live well with a disorder—are important (Walsh, 2006). The emotional intensity often is highest for at-risk members when they have directly known and witnessed another family member's experience of living with uncertainty or a particular disease. Some may have been in a caregiver role to a family member with the same condition they are at risk of having. It is very valuable to inquire about these kinds of prior exposure or sensitization, as they often contain the essence of meaning about the genomic condition and its role in the family identity (Reiss, 1981; Rolland, 1994a). It is vital to elicit areas of strength as well as vulnerability. In one family, a history of 10 years of grueling caregiving for a family member who was reduced to a childlike state and did not recognize loved ones left a legacy of dread of dementia. One son stated, "If I'm ever disabled like my dad, I'd rather be dead." This contrasts with a son in another family who said, "Even when my father had Alzheimer's, he still was loving and seemed to enjoy being with family. It's inspiring and helps me appreciate that even if I get Alzheimer's, I will have something to live for."

COMMUNICATION

With anticipatory loss, families need to find a balance between open communication regarding genetic risk to facilitate proactive planning with the need to keep a threatened illness in perspective to live a healthy life for as long as possible. Timely, sensitive, open, direct communication about a range of issues is essential to living well. Increased disclosure may be necessary if others are directly affected or at risk. Identifying and normalizing difficult feelings, establishing clear boundaries, and minimizing relationship skews all require effective communication. Illness and risk-related communication is commonly blocked by tentativeness in exploring new territory and concerns about hurting one's partner, children, or other family members (Imber-Black, 1995).

Fears may exist that a relationship will not survive open dialogue. Clinicians can coach parents on when and how to share information with a spouse, children, or frail elders. It is useful to inquire about topics related to anticipatory loss. If such topics are off limits, why? Examples include future caregiving and financial planning and when to discuss genetic risk with children or adolescents. Under what circumstances would they be important to discuss? Clinicians can help family members decide about the conditions under which further family discussion would be useful, and who would be appropriate to include.

Health professionals can promote functional or dysfunctional communication. Providers' sensitive but open encouragement of discussion of issues related to anticipatory loss is an excellent model for families. For instance, inviting and encouraging inclusion of a spouse in critical pre- and posttesting conversations can serve as an empowering model for couples to help prevent marginalization of spouses/partners. It is important to help a couple define genetic testing as a shared challenge, rather than the sole problem of the one being tested, which skews all significant family interactions. As a result, negotiating power and control can become increasingly dysfunctional, with resentments, guilt, distancing, and erosion of intimacy.

ISSUES RELATED TO PSYCHOSOCIAL TYPE
OF GENOMIC DISORDER

A family's experience of anticipatory loss varies with the kind of genetic or genetically influenced disorder, its psychosocial and physical demands over time, and the degree of uncertainty about prognosis. The variables in the typology of genomic disorders can affect the degree and nature of anticipatory loss (see Chapter 2). For instance, genetic disorders with a high likelihood of development, high severity, early onset in the life cycle, and no effective treatment available to alter onset or progression will often be the most difficult (e.g., Duchenne muscular dystrophy). On the other end of the continuum, disorders with a genetic component that occur in later life, with low or variable likelihood of expression, lower severity, and greater response to treatment interventions are likely to be less disruptive. For instance, with variable-likelihood, early-life-onset disorders, the uncertainty related to a specific genetic mutation could easily interfere with career, marriage, or family planning. Later-onset conditions will affect planning for retirement years, the experience of grandparenthood, or the necessity for the well spouse to continue working for insurance coverage and overall financial survival.

Increasingly, discoveries in genomic health are for common conditions, like cardiovascular disease, that have complex multiple gene and environmental interactions (multifactorial) that are not yet well understood. An important research question is how individuals and families will fare over the life cycle with anticipatory loss for most common disorders with a quite variable likelihood of development (e.g., *BRCA1* or *BRCA2* mutation-related breast and ovarian cancer). How emotionally taxing is the high level of ongoing uncertainty in the face of known increased risk? Greater uncertainty regarding the occurrence, timing, and severity of a disease can make life cycle planning arduous as more ongoing contingency plans might be needed. With Huntington disease, the trajectory is clearer. Knowledge that a disease with a predictable course will very likely occur at a certain point in the life cycle reduces the uncertainty factor. This can facilitate aspects of future planning.

It is important to assess anxieties about future *disability* and *suffering* as distinct from *death*, since patients and families often express their greatest fears about helplessness, loss of control, and uncontrollable pain and suffering. For some, providing accurate information regarding effective treatment options and pain control can be very beneficial even in a nonsymptomatic phase either before or after genetic testing.

EVOLUTION OF EXPERIENCE OF
ANTICIPATORY LOSS THROUGH
NONSYMPTOMATIC PHASES

As the nature of anticipatory loss shifts over the course of nonsymptomatic and symptomatic phases (Rolland, 1990, 1994a; Chapter 2), it is essential to distinguish family members' expectation of inevitable loss from their earlier awareness of the risk. One example would be the difference before and after presymptomatic testing for Huntington disease. In the pretesting phases, Huntington disease is a 50% risk for children of an affected parent. After testing, those who are positive for the Huntington mutation now live with the knowledge that they face the nearly inevitable onset of a progressive, fatal condition in midlife (age 40–60).

In the context of genetic testing, it is useful to distinguish different kinds of anticipatory loss that correspond to the nonsymptomatic time phases. First, before anyone in a family undergoes genetic testing, there may be uncertainty regarding whether a specific genetic mutation is carried in a family at all. Second, before testing, there is uncertainty whether a particular family member carries a mutation that confers added risk. Third, after testing, individuals and families live in a "long-term adaptation phase" of anticipatory loss regarding if and when a condition will occur and who else in the family might have the mutation. Last, after clinical onset, anticipatory loss concerns the course and outcome of the condition (Rolland, 1994a, 2004).

Awareness Phase

This phase begins with awareness of possible genetic risk. It refers to life before the active consideration or the availability of genetic testing. Genetic information transforms the experience of anticipatory loss for all family members. In many families, multigenerational stories evolve about a condition that runs in the family. With predictive, presymptomatic, and carrier testing, these family stories collide with high-technology medicine, often clarifying both a diagnosis and its inheritance pattern. In one family, a history of "increasing incoordination" now has a fancy name, spinocerebellar ataxia. Someone who has the genetic mutation will get the disease. That person has a good idea of when in the life cycle it will strike and, based on advances in DNA analysis, a good prediction of how severe it will be. Each family member now knows there is a way to help clarify uncertainty. Previously, outcome was linked to chance or beliefs regarding who will and will not get the condition (see next section). Now, with new technology, living with uncertainty is transformed to include the process of deciding whether and when one may want to help clarify individual risk.

For disorders like Huntington disease, for which no treatment currently exists to alter onset or progression, the decision is between different ways of living with anticipatory loss—either informed by predictive testing or without it. The anticipation of disease or death is a universal experience. But knowing one will very likely develop Huntington disease at midlife clarifies the likely form of illness and death and the approximate timing of onset within a 15-year span. Analogous to the varied responses to clarify prognosis after onset of a serious illness, for some people, acquiring this knowledge is emotionally debilitating. For others, it can help focus priorities and life planning, enhancing a sense of control (Babul et al., 1993; Wiggins et al., 1992). For disorders where the likelihood of development is highly variable and effective prevention and treatment exists (e.g., genetically influenced heart disease), the trajectory is very uncertain, both in terms of disease onset and outcome. For these kinds of conditions, the experience of uncertainty is quite different. For some, the idea of identifying any mutation can be disabling emotionally. For others, preventive steps, when available, may help foster a sense of mastery in meeting a biological challenge.

In some families, when multigenerational experience of illness seems genetically unremarkable to the family (e.g., they are unaware of genetic risks, do not note illness patterns, or attribute diseases in the family to other causes), they do not experience anticipatory loss or concern about lurking genetic or genetically influenced conditions. Such families may have the sharpest emotional transition as new genetic tests become available for a range of common conditions.

Crisis Phase I: Pretesting

Phase I encompasses the period of active consideration of testing through the period of decision making about whether to get tested. A rapidly expanding literature addresses the process of decision making about whether to proceed with prenatal, carrier, and predictive testing (Lerman, Croyle, Tercyak, & Hamann, 2002). Several psychosocial factors have been consistently linked to interest in genetic testing, especially increased perception of personal risk, a high need to clarify uncertainty (Braithwaite, Sutton, & Steggles, 2002), increased worry and distress about a disease, and anticipation of a positive impact of genetic testing. Perception of risk and risk communication are core processes correlated with this decision (Cappelli et al., 2001; Croyle & Lerman, 1999; Jacobson, Valdimarsdottir, Brown, & Offit, 1997; Miller, 1995; Patenaude et al., 1996; Scott, 2000; see Chapter 3). Findings suggest that perception of risk has a higher correlation with interest in testing than actual risk status when there is a family history for a genomic condition. In terms of follow-through on testing, cancer gene testing has been substantially higher than testing for Huntington disease (Bowen, Patenaude, & Vernon, 1999; Quaid & Morris, 1993). Some suggest that this is related to disease severity and the lack of effective medical intervention to modify onset or progression with Huntington disease.

Preselection of Those Likely to Have a Mutation or Not

Often in families with known genomic disorders, family members will engage in a preselection process that identifies those members who they believe will likely inherit the disorder and those that will be spared. Most typically, this is based on physical resemblance to an affected member (e.g., an affected parent) or gender (Kessler & Bloch, 1989). This preselection process and, often, denial of symptoms in family members presumed to be normal are prime ways that families cope with uncertainty and threatened loss. But there can be a cost. For instance, for those believed to be spared the *BRCA1/BRCA2* mutations for breast and ovarian cancer, there is the risk of deciding not to be tested and neglecting regular preventive care—a high-risk bet if wrong, and breast cancer is found at an advanced stage.

Preselection beliefs about being either positive or negative for a particular mutation often organize life choices and future planning in major ways that may not have been openly discussed among family members. In the pretesting phase, providers can inquire about preselection through a life cycle lens: "Are there ways you and your family have already organized your lives in relation to beliefs about your genetic risk?" "What will be the possible implications for you and your family members' lives if you get expected or unexpected test results?"

Crisis Phase II: Testing/Posttesting

Phase II includes the testing and early posttest period. A body of research reports short-term psychological reactions to genetic testing (Chapman & Burn, 1999; Codori, Petersen, Boyd, Brandt, & Giardiello, 1996; Croyle, Smith, Botkin, Baty, & Nash, 1997; Lerman & Croyle, 1996; Lerman et al., 1996, 1998; Lim et al., 2004; Marteau & Croyle, 1998; Quaid & Wesson, 1995; Sobel & Cowan, 2000, 2003; Tibben, Timman, Banninck, & Duivenvoorden, 1997) or anticipated reactions (Williams, Schutte, Evers, & Forucci, 1999). In general, data support a decrease in stress-related symptoms for those who test negative, while those who test positive tend to show little change on average. Research is needed to study subgroups that may show distinct patterns. More important, we need longitudinal research of the longer-term family impact with a range of genomic diseases.

Immediately after receiving genetic test results, it can be difficult to separate emotions related to living with uncertainty and threatened loss from concerns about future symptomatic disease. This is most likely for a disorder where having the specific mutation confers a high likelihood of developing the disease, symptoms are severe, treatments that can modify onset or progression do not exist, and onset is before late adulthood. As one woman lamented on learning about her sister's positive testing for Huntington disease, "You look at my sister. She's no different than 5 minutes before, and all of a sudden she's dying. I guess we all started grieving immediately. It was like living the next 15 years in those 5 minutes" (Chapter 8). These kinds of grief reactions are normative. Learning of added risk is a real loss, meaning family members relinquish hope for a life without added risk for a particular disease. They must now accept the permanency of that fact. In the posttesting period, one of the key developmental challenges is coping and adaptation to this real ongoing stressor. Also, resilient adjustment to a future threat is fostered by minimizing redefinition of the affected family member as "different," "ill," or actively dying (see later section Resilience in the Face of Anticipatory Loss).

Unexpected Test Results

The preselection process can be a risk for those who eventually pursue genetic testing and unexpectedly test positive or negative for a specific mutation. A person who expected to have a specific genetic mutation may experience loss and grief for opportunities not taken when learning of normal testing results. In one case, a son who assumed that he would develop his father's progressive degenerative neurological disease at midlife tailored his life choices in early adulthood to accommodate this expectation. He married a woman whom he privately loved as a good friend but was not romantically in love with, and whom he felt would be a good caregiver when he eventually would become ill and disabled. Further, he had a vasectomy. This was to ensure that this genetically influenced disease would not be passed on to the next generation and because he thought he would not get through child rearing years without disease onset, disability, or death—causing caregiving burden and limitation as an adequate parent. Finally, he abandoned his ambition to pursue a career in medicine because of the lengthy training period and instead chose a more modest career path as a computer technician. As specific testing became available when he was 35, he tested normal for the mutation. In the aftermath, he became extremely depressed, feeling he had needlessly sacrificed passionate love, having children, and becoming a physician. His depression and a serious marital crisis led to referral to a family therapist. A life cycle–attuned and family-oriented intervention when this man was an adolescent or young adult might have helped avert this kind of outcome. Asking adolescents or young adults about their future dreams and how fears regarding any familial illnesses impact their life planning allows open discussion of the pros and cons of building life goals in relation to perceived or actual risk.

Sometimes the preselection process goes in the other direction. For example, Mary, a 27-year-old woman married for 2 years, was referred a month after testing positive for *BRCA1*. Her family history was significant in that a maternal aunt had recently died at age 49 of breast cancer and her own mother had been diagnosed with in-situ breast cancer a year earlier, electing a bilateral mastectomy. Mary's 25-year-old sister, Jane, strongly resembled their mother, while Mary was strikingly similar to her hardy father both physically and in personality. Also, Mary had always been the protector of her younger, somewhat physically frail sister. Mary and her husband had discussed testing before marriage, but they decided to defer what they saw as low risk until they wanted to start a family and then revisit the earlier decision. When Jane became engaged, she and her fiancé decided to pursue testing. Mary then decided to be tested at the same time to be supportive to her sister, whom she assumed would be *BRCA1* positive. The testing results were the opposite. Mary was positive and Jane negative. Mary was devastated, feeling completely unprepared not only to find that she carried the *BRCA1* mutation, but also that her sister did not. Not only were the genetic testing results a shock, but for the first time Mary was in the unfamiliar position of needing and receiving support from Jane, who was unaccustomed to being the giver of support. This unexpected testing outcome started a process of reshaping the dynamics in their relationship. Mary and Jane began to rebalance their previously skewed relationship to be more mutually supportive. In the process, they redefined competence in a more flexible way to include life challenges, areas of strength, and vulnerability. They shared the grief of Mary's high risk for breast cancer and discussed ways Jane could assist emotionally and pragmatically if and when Mary developed cancer. Both became stronger and more resilient individuals.

Normal Tests and Altered Bond to At-Risk Group

Genetic testing creates three distinct subgroups: (1) those that test positive for the specific mutation, (2) those that test negative, and (3) those that have yet to be tested and remain potentially at risk. Those that test positive often remain psychologically linked to those who remain potentially at risk. Both groups live with anticipatory loss, but with different degrees of knowledge. Those with normal test results get good news but can experience a change in their tie to those family members who remain at risk. This differentiation might lead to a realignment of family relationships, where some members become increasingly bonded by their common threat or sense of entering the world of chronic illness. Some relationships may distance because of the distinction between the worlds of waiting for illness and those without genetic risk. In other cases, a family member with normal test results may have a strong bond with the member testing positive and must now live in fear of loss of that relationship. A well sibling with only one sister or brother or who raised younger siblings in a parental role may experience particularly strong fear. For couples, differences in health risk commonly lead to skewed relationship dynamics, where one spouse/partner develops a major health problem and the other is expected to assume a caregiver role (Rolland, 1994b). Optimal prevention includes pretesting consultations that educate family members about these challenges as well as the usefulness of ongoing open dialogue and periodic follow-up consultations.

Posttesting Long-Term Adaptation Phase

Families are strongly impacted by questions of both if and when a condition will occur. At the time of testing, most disorders are uncertain on both counts. The questions concern the degree of uncertainty and when anticipatory loss will become salient. Some conditions can be expected to occur within a certain period of the life cycle. For instance, BRCA1/BRCA2-related breast and ovarian cancer usually occurs from early adulthood onward. If so, increased anxieties about threatened loss might surface as individuals and families approach the specific life cycle phase of heightened danger of clinical onset, or a life cycle transition, such as family planning, when threatened loss becomes more relevant. For others it might occur as they approach the age at which a family member developed the specific condition (e.g., when a woman's mother developed breast cancer), underscoring the importance of noting on a genogram the age of illness onset for family members. Prevention-oriented individual and family consultations are valuable at any of these transitions.

Vigilance in Looking for First Signs

Looking for the first sign of a genomic disorder has similarities to vigilance for a recurrence of cancer, when the loss of the first remission may shatter a family's hope for a cure, bringing their worst fears to the surface. Analogously, for multifactorial, genetically influenced conditions where the likelihood of occurrence is variable, the first sign would mean the loss of hope of not getting the disorder at all. For conditions like Huntington disease, looking for the first sign is not a question of if but when. Here, surveillance for a first sign may be more about the individual and family transitioning into the world of active disease with high severity, major caregiving needs, and a fatal outcome. Some individuals and families will tend to minimize possible first signs of disease. It is important to distinguish those in denial from those who are preoccupied with anticipatory loss and fears regarding the next phase.

Premature distancing can occur during this long-term adaptation phase as a way to avoid future psychological pain and loss. Family members may distance emotionally to defend themselves from anticipated loss of the affected member or fear of the strains of the caregiver role. Family members may be torn between their wishes to sustain intimacy and their need to prepare to let go emotionally of a member they expect to develop a progressive condition that involves dementia or extensive suffering. While all relationships are predicated on the existential dilemma of choosing intimacy in the face of eventual separation and loss, disorders with high severity and associated with highly penetrant mutations often intensifies the experience of anticipatory loss.

With conditions that involve cognitive impairment, the experience of anticipatory loss is compounded further with fears regarding loss of the person psychologically before death and loss of the relationship with that person (Boss, 1999). Often, this form of suffering and loss is more emotionally taxing than the thought of the person's eventual death from the disease. The progressive loss of intimacy is especially painful for a couple and family.

Fears about genetic susceptibility, especially for those posttesting with known mutations, can continue throughout life. Every ambiguous symptom and appointment with the physician brings apprehension. One woman, age 55, had a strong family history of colon cancer and had tested positive for the specific high-risk mutation. Regular screening colonoscopies over the years had revealed benign polyps, but no cancer. Despite the length of time without getting colon cancer, she revealed, "Whenever I get a pain in my body, not just my abdomen, my first thought is that I finally got cancer and it will now kill me." Since this is a normative experience, preventive psychoeducation in the early posttesting period can be very helpful to families.

Vigilance for first signs of a condition is particularly difficult when they might include common normative experiences of aging, such as memory lapses. Clinicians can help families keep functional awareness without disabling hypervigilance for the onset of conditions like Alzheimer disease. Individuals with a blunting style of coping with perceived risk (e.g., minimizing symptoms) can tend to be less vigilant in an emotionally adaptive way when living with increased genetic risk (Miller, 1995; Miller & Diefenbach, 1998; see Chapter 3). A monitoring style is more useful in situations where early detection and treatment intervention might affect the course and outcome of a genomic disorder. Often, different family members or two spouses fill these roles in a complementary manner. These normative differences in style and role functions can become polarized and conflictual in the context of uncertainty where the stakes are very high and at significant medical or life cycle junctures, as in the following case.

Joan and Bill sought a couple's consultation with a family therapist for increasing marital discord. Joan had tested positive for *BRCA1* several years earlier. Her blunting style led her to minimize any symptoms (e.g., lumpiness) in her breasts, while her husband, Bill, with a more monitoring style, would become very anxious about her minimizing concern over possibly significant symptoms. At times when his wife was due for her annual mammogram, her laissez-faire style of scheduling the exam conflicted sharply with his insistence on prompt and timely appointments. He felt she was being irresponsible and insensitive to him. She felt he was both morbidly obsessed with disease and death, and overinvolved in trying to be in control of her body. This led to escalating conflict in a vicious cycle. The more she told him to leave her alone, the more his hypervigilant anxious behavior escalated, and in turn the more she dug in her heels. This relational impasse was complicated by the fact that, when Bill was a teenager, his own mother died of colon cancer that was discovered in an advanced inoperable stage.

In situations like that of Joan and Bill, of living with anticipatory loss, interventions that help family members balance both monitoring and blunting positions can diminish stylistic differences that become dysfunctionally skewed and polarized. At the same time, it is helpful to coach family members to better accept a reasonable level of normative differences. Also, it is very useful to educate the family to distinguish important warning signs from insignificant ones. Inquiry about prior sensitization or trauma regarding loss (like Bill's mother) in a spouse's multigenerational history is essential and can help facilitate an empathic awareness rather than reactive anger.

It is very helpful to educate family members about expectable times and life cycle transitions when anticipatory loss will likely be more activated. Besides annual checkups, this might include consultations timed with major life cycle transitions, such as (1) planning to have children, (2) launching children, (3) retirement, (4) diagnosis of cancer or another serious illness in immediate or extended families or friends, and (5) the genetic testing phase of another family member. Helping families live more fully in the present can help offset regrets and unfulfilled wishes later on (see later section, Resilience in the Face of Anticipatory Loss). As we identify more of the lifestyle and environmental factors involved in gene mutation expression, we will increasingly be able to offer individuals and families actions they can take to assert some control over disease onset or course.

Anticipating Future Caregiving Expectations and the Life Cycle

It is important to inquire about expectations and traditions regarding caregiving. In some families and cultures, there may be explicit expectations that unaffected siblings (usually sisters and daughters) will provide caregiving for affected ones. These traditions offer scripts (Byng-Hall, 1996) that guide family members through unfamiliar times and can help foster a sense of control that helps allay anxieties about genetic risk. Yet rigid gender role scripts can overburden women, lead to resentments, and leave men out. Promoting family discussion provides an opportunity to reconsider gendered role expectations so they are flexible and fairly balanced among siblings as a collaborative team. This is particularly relevant for more severe conditions, such as Alzheimer disease, that currently lack treatments that can modify disease onset or progression. Also, a number of differences between the current and earlier generations may significantly alter the realistic feasibility of using an old script.

Furthermore, any commitments at one point in time need to be periodically revisited in the context of changing life cycle demands and general life circumstances. Again, transitions in the nonsymptomatic and symptomatic phases of a genomic condition, or in individual or family development, are natural nodal points to revisit prior decisions. The following case illustrates this point.

One family learned that the father's long-standing progressive and severely disabling ataxia was caused by an autosomal dominant inherited mutation, spinocerebellar ataxia 1. The father's condition, with increasingly severe muscle incoordination and weakness, had begun at age 40. After the father tested positive, his four adult children, who were in their 20s and early 30s, decided to pursue predictive testing. Test results revealed that two of the four siblings were highly likely to develop spinocerebellar ataxia. Subsequently, they had future-oriented discussions, where the two unaffected siblings decided to provide caregiving and financial support when the disease would become disabling for the affected siblings (Taswell & Sholtes, 1999). This exemplified open communication and proactively envisioning future roles in the face of anticipated loss. This type of long-range caregiving-oriented planning is particularly difficult when family members, such as siblings, are in early stages of the family life cycle. Initial caregiving and financial commitments may need to be revisited and altered later given the normative uncertainties as the life course of each sibling unfolds. In these situations, it is particularly important for siblings to consider the impact of these caregiving decisions, as well as issues of disability and a shortened life span with their partners, each other, and extended kin as an ongoing process. The risk of couple dysfunction can be considerably diminished by inclusion of these nonbiological family members in these discussions from the beginning (Kessler, 1993).

Grief Over Possible Loss of Future Hopes and Dreams

Mutations like presenilin-1 or presenilin-2 for early onset Alzheimer disease or those causing Huntington disease are highly penetrant and cause severe disease that typically occurs at midlife. Also, no effective treatments are currently available to alter onset or progression. The affected individual faces severe cognitive impairment and a shortened life span. The anticipated loss of future life phase hopes and dreams, such as golden years of retirement involving companionship and grandparenthood, can be extremely painful. As the previous case highlights, family members can be helped to place a greater emphasis on enhancing the quality of relationships in the present and near future. Also, building flexibility and acceptable alternatives into future goals helps buffer aspects of life beyond personal control.

Learning that a genetic mutation exists in a family can foster a somewhat unique form of anticipatory loss that extends into future generations. In essence, it can involve the loss of a common dream or unconditional universal hope that the children will have a better life than the parents' generation. A family must grapple with the fact that some of their own children will be at risk for a specific condition. This seems particularly likely with mutations that cause severe illness with currently limited preventive options, such as Parkinson's disease or Huntington disease. As an antidote, it is especially important to help families sustain hope for future medical advances that may help prevent clinical onset or progression. Also, families' process of making meaning from genetic knowledge and in the face of possible loss that preserves their sense of value and competence is vital (see Chapter 6; Wright, Watson, & Bell, 1996).

Survivor Guilt and Altruistic Intentions

The stress of living with anticipatory loss can be emotionally exhausting and lead to feelings of ambivalence. The emotional state of living in limbo, anticipating the worst, can be fraught with enormous guilt and shame. Some family members' feelings may even shift from a fear to an ambivalent secret wish for the disorder to occur. This is especially true when waiting for the onset of inevitable and devastating conditions, such as Huntington disease. Because families seldom discuss these issues, clinicians need to acknowledge normative ambivalence arising from an extended period of living with anticipatory loss and be aware that preexisting conflicts in family relationships may become heightened. Ambivalent thoughts and feelings, frequently shame based, often remain underground. Later, if a condition enters a clinical phase and progresses to death, they can contribute to survivor guilt and complicated grief reactions. Family members not at risk might express thoughts such as, "How can I enjoy life and my own good health, when she will likely get breast cancer and maybe die from it?" They may conduct their lives in self-defeating ways or even become preoccupied with their own health concerns. Some, consciously or unconsciously, may even take risks that undermine their own health. Psychoeducational family interventions that explore and normalize these complex emotions related to threatened loss can help prevent cycles of blame, shame, and guilt. Also, it is useful to address the normative skews that develop between those that test negative versus those who test positive and those who are untested and remain at risk.

For those who test normal, survivor guilt can be channeled in positive ways through altruistic intentions (Williams, Schutte, Evers, & Holkup, 2000). In one family, two sisters tested positive for *BRCA1*, learning they were at high risk for breast or ovarian cancer. A third sister, who tested normal, became involved as a volunteer in Y-Me, a national breast cancer organization that provides public education, advocacy, and peer counseling for those affected or at high risk. This gave her a sense of purpose that helped offset her feelings of being the lucky one.

ADDITIONAL INDIVIDUAL
AND FAMILY LIFE CYCLE ISSUES

It is important to consider how future life cycle plans might be impacted by anticipatory loss. A primary developmental task is to flexibly accommodate the anticipation of a possible or inevitable future disorder and untimely death (Rolland, 1990, 1994a).

Increasingly, predictive testing may occur at earlier life cycle phases, many years before a disease would most likely occur. This can make the immediate testing and posttesting adjustment period far removed in time from future life cycle transitions that may be impacted by testing results. Heightened concerns regarding future loss may become more remote to health care professionals and other family members. Presentation with anxiety, depression, or psychosomatic complaints in a primary care setting may not get linked to anticipatory loss related to genetic testing many years earlier. In the posttesting period, individual and family psychoeducation should address how life cycle nodal points can heighten concerns about loss. It is useful for primary health care professionals to inquire about life cycle transitions expected over the next 3–5 years. This provides an opportunity to explore how specific genetic knowledge might affect major upcoming life cycle decisions in the near or distant future. Collaboration and prevention-oriented consultations with a mental health professional are often useful at these life cycle junctures.

With genomic disorders, an overarching goal is to deal with the developmental challenges over the course of the nonsymptomatic time phases without family members entirely sacrificing their own or the family's development. In one first generation Italian American family, the father tested positive for a mutation that confers high risk for early onset of heart disease. As part of discussion after testing, the family was helped to dialogue about cultural norms that typically would designate the oldest daughter as the future caregiver. An agreement to share any future caregiving among siblings and extended family helped protect the oldest daughter, age 18, from assuming the sole responsibility. This preserved her dreams of going away to college and pursuing a career. As this vignette illustrates, at major life cycle junctures it is important to reevaluate whose life plans might need to be altered or sacrificed. In this way, clinicians can anticipate life cycle nodal points related to "autonomy within" versus "subjugation to" anticipatory loss.

Life Cycle Transition Periods

Life cycle transitions pose nodal points of strain when feelings of anticipatory loss that family members thought were worked through may resurface. Developmental transitions heighten awareness of anticipatory loss, since they involve beginnings and endings (e.g., births, young adults launching, retirement, divorce, and death). Commonly, preoccupations about death, life's limits, and anticipation of separation and loss surface at such times. The experience of genetic risk is superimposed onto normative individual and family life cycle transitions.

As the previous example illustrates, transitions are critical junctures to examine issues of anticipatory loss and weigh them in light of other developmental considerations. Open discussion and shared decision making help prevent later blame-guilt cycles if disease onset and loss occur. Upcoming developmental challenges may need to accommodate anticipatory loss. At each transition, intense grieving may occur over opportunities and experiences that were anticipated but may need to be altered or given up by choice (e.g., decision to have children). Clinicians can be helpful by inquiring about possible loss (e.g., disease onset) in relationship to future life phases. This includes exploring options to both build flexibility into life cycle plans (e.g., adoption as an alternative) and to consider contingency plans that affirm human resiliency should genetic risk turn into symptomatic disease.

In health care, biologically meaningful transitions such as disease onset, flare-up, or progression are noted, with an expectation that the patient and family might experience a period of crisis. It is more complex to make a connection with genetic risk when an individual family member or the family unit is in emotional crisis and the situation is biologically stable and no symptomatic disease exists. This is typical at times of transition in the individual or family life cycle, when life cycle planning may be affected by the presence of anticipatory loss. Health care professionals' mindfulness and inquiry about these more hidden transitions are especially important. Also, increased use of a collaborative psychosocial-biomedical team approach that provides longitudinal family-centered care can help prevent genetically tested individuals and families from becoming isolated and suffering at these key nodal points (McDaniel, Campbell, Hepworth, & Lorenz, 2005; Peters, Djurdjinovic, & Baker, 1999; Seaburn, Gunn, Mauksh, Gawinski, & Lorenz, 1996).

Multigenerational Nodal Life Cycle Events

It is common for the experience of anticipatory loss to intensify as an individual approaches the age when a parent got ill or died from a disease suspected to be familial (e.g., heart disease). The experience may be even more intense for individuals living with genetic knowledge who are reaching the age when disease onset is more likely to occur. They are entering a heightened danger period. For conditions like Huntington disease, where testing is presymptomatic, the individual and family may have had more time to prepare for an inevitable disorder.

Courtship and Early Marriage

Communication about genetic risk can be complex for a young couple or family at early life cycle transitions. Often, these challenges are experienced as "premature" by comparison with most age peers. During courtship and early marriage, the partner at potential genetic risk may feel vulnerable to rejection as potentially defective. This can lead to either overemphasizing the risk in order to test the other partner or minimizing risk and its potential impact on their lives. The unaffected partner may minimize concerns out of a lack of real-life exposure to the specific disease (e.g., Parkinson disease), a desire to preserve a glossy picture of courtship and marriage, a wish to not express any ambivalence, or a shame-based fear of seeming weak. During this time, a couple might need to consider such issues as whether and when to pursue testing.

Having Children

Another common nodal point for couples occurs with decisions about having biological children (Rolland, 1994a, 1994b). Important considerations include whether to have children (or consider adoption), decisions about prenatal testing, beliefs about terminating a pregnancy of a genetically affected fetus, possible onset and progression of a disease during child rearing, and potential shifting roles in the face of loss (Brouwer-Dudokdewit, Savenije, Zoeteweij, Maat-Kievit, & Tibben, 2002). When an individual or couple considers starting a family, the time frame shifts from day-to-day living to roughly a 20-year plan. Essentially, they are building a life structure that is tailored to raising a family. The experience of future risk complicates this type of longer-range planning, especially with a disorder that typically begins during this child rearing period (roughly age 20–60), such as Huntington disease, *BRCA1/BRCA2*-linked breast cancer, or early-onset Alzheimer's disease. Huntington disease would be particularly problematic as it poses intense caregiving burdens on top of child rearing demands. Genetic risks must be considered for both the at-risk parent and the unborn children. Some basic fears include the following:

- Genetic transmission to children
- Anticipation of loss of a "dream child" who may develop the genomic disorder at some point in his or her life
- Anticipation of illness onset in the at-risk parent and complications that interfere with effective parenting
- Fears that the ill parent might not survive to rear children to adulthood
- Associated financial and psychosocial burdens for the well partner

At-Risk Children and Adolescents

Witnessing a parent's disease unfold can affect any phase of child and adolescent development. For example, consider a family in the child-launching phase when the father has a serious heart attack linked to a familial form of cardiovascular disease (e.g., familial hypercholesterolemia). The threat of his further disability or death may influence young adults in transition to alter life decisions in ways that compromise personal strivings. In these circumstances, it is important both to explore the interplay of personal developmental plans with expectations for family loyalty and to be aware of important differences across cultures.

Also, when children or adolescents are potentially at risk of having the same mutation as a parent, their transition to early adulthood would normatively uncover concerns about their own vulnerability. As this example illustrates, the timing of a parent's disease onset or progression at this transition might further heighten their experience of vulnerability. This might propel some adolescents to actively consider predictive testing, and others to avoid it out of intense fear. When facing their own fears about personal genetic risk, adolescents and young adults may become emotionally stuck. They can feel blocked when personal dreams for adulthood conflict with uncertainty and fears of untimely disease. This can manifest in a number of ways, including substance abuse, depression, anxiety, oppositional behavior, distancing, or intensified conflict with family members. The following case highlights a few of the complex themes when at-risk children witness a specific kind of genetic disorder unfolding for a parent and how that experience can impact the individual and family life cycle.

In the Ruiz family, the mother, Carla, has polycystic kidney disease (PKD). PKD is inherited as an autosomal dominant disorder, affecting 50% of children of an affected parent. It is a progressive condition characterized most commonly by ever-enlarging cysts on the kidney, ultimately leading to renal failure and the need for dialysis or a kidney transplant. Hypertension, heart valve abnormalities, and cerebral aneurysms are also a risk. Often it remains clinically silent until an advanced stage. Carla learned of her disease at age 32, when her two sons were ages 5 and 7. Because she knew her sons were at risk, she always tried to shield them from her disease complications, which included dialysis (and later a kidney transplant), beginning when her sons were in their early teens. Carla and her husband, Jose, have had a good marriage in spite of the challenges. Because lifestyle adjustments can alter the course of PKD, both sons were offered presymptomatic testing at age 16. Both sons have witnessed some of the serious complications of PKD. Juan, the older son, chose to proceed with testing, finding out he was indeed positive for the PKD mutation. Arturo adamantly refused testing and distanced from the family. Arturo, now 25, has suffered from depression, lives alone, and moves from job to job. Despite family members' concern, he continues to deny that the risk of PKD matters to him. Juan is married. Because of the risk to offspring, he and his wife have adopted two children. Like his mother, he optimistically pursues his career, marriage, and raising children in spite of the challenges. He believes that both his mother and his parents' relationship inspired him in the "art of the possible." For him, this means accepting what he cannot control and seizing opportunities to make the most of possible options (Walsh, 2006).

Individual treatment for Arturo combined with family consultations gradually addressed the meaning of his potential risk for PKD, his fears, and how his life became stuck in the wake of refusing genetic testing. When Arturo was 16, at the time testing was initially suggested, a family-centered biopsychosocial consultation was not offered. In hindsight, Arturo's difficulties could have been averted by a mixture of family and individual consultations for him and Juan that included education about the disease and its psychosocial implications over time, particularly concerns about loss, and the specific issues for an adolescent in transition to early adulthood.

RESILIENCE IN THE FACE OF
ANTICIPATORY LOSS

Overemphasis on anticipatory loss can itself become emotionally disabling if it is not counterbalanced by ways to harness the experience to enhance the quality of life. Clinicians can be very helpful by assisting families to achieve a healthy balance. For illnesses with long-range risks, families can maintain mastery in the face of uncertainty by: (1) acknowledging the possibility of future loss; (2) sustaining hope; (3) building flexibility into family life cycle planning that realistically conserves and adjusts major goals (e.g., child rearing); and (4) creating meaning that preserves a sense of mastery and competence regardless of the eventual outcome.

Most of us cannot tolerate an unrelenting encounter with threatened loss. There is a need for mental and physical respite. Taylor (1989) has described the normal, healthy need for positive illusions and their importance in successful coping and adaptation. The healthy use of minimization or selective focus on the positive, as well as timely doses of humor, should be distinguished from pathological denial.

In situations of anticipatory loss, we must be cautious about judging the relative usefulness of positive illusions or minimization versus direct confrontation with and acceptance of painful realities. Often both are needed, and clinicians must support both the usefulness of exaggerated hope and the importance of proceeding with genetic testing when preventive action or medical treatment can affect disease onset or progression.

The ability of family members to live as fully as possible, given the heightened uncertainties or certainties of genetic risk, is a major challenge. Genetic testing provides an opportunity to confront catastrophic fears about loss. This can lead family members to develop a better appreciation of loved ones and a sharpened perspective on life that clarifies priorities. Seizing opportunities can replace procrastination for the right moment or passive waiting for losses to occur. Threatened loss, by emphasizing life's fragility and preciousness, provides families with an opportunity to heal unresolved issues and develop more immediate, caring relationships. In the more resilient families, individual members may well find that the experience of genetic knowledge heightens their sense of being alive, the preciousness of life and relationships, a perspective on problems, an appreciation for daily events, and a hopeful attitude for a meaningful life that can transcend suffering and loss.

Finally, many families emphasize plans far in the future. Anticipatory loss provides an opportunity for individuals and family members to strike a healthier balance between longer-range life plans and those with more immediacy that are less dependent on the vicissitudes of uncertainty.

ISSUES FOR CLINICIANS

Clinicians working with anticipatory loss need to consider their own experiences and feelings about loss (McDaniel, Hepworth, & Doherty, 1997; Rolland, 1994a, 1994b). Our own family history with threatened or actual loss, health beliefs, and current life cycle stage will influence our ability to work effectively with families living with anticipatory loss.

Fears about our own vulnerability are easily triggered when working with families coping with genetic risk, especially if the patient and family are at the same life stage as the clinician. Self-awareness is particularly important if one has a similar disorder or is at high risk of illnesses involving loss (e.g., strong family history of cancer or heart disease). Because these situations are so compelling, clinicians who work with a family for an extended period tend to align their hopes and beliefs with those of the family. We must be cautious of excessive optimism, forgetting that loss is really possible, likely, or inevitable. Our own unresolved issues related to actual or threatened losses and fears about our own mortality can lead us to distance emotionally, avoid important, often painful discussions related to anticipatory loss, or become overinvolved with a particular family. As we come to accept the limits of our ability to control the uncontrollable and work through unresolved personal losses, we can work more sensitively with the dilemmas facing the individuals and families we serve.

CONCLUSION

This chapter has presented a family systems developmental framework to help organize thinking about anticipatory loss with genomic disorders. The FSGI model provides a conceptual base for discussing the ongoing interaction of the nonsymptomatic phases of genetic and genomic conditions with family and individual members' life cycle development. This framework offers a theoretical foundation for clinical practice and research. Research is needed to study a broad diversity of families facing different types of genomic disorders that may show distinct patterns of coping and adaptation. More important, we need longitudinal, ethnographic, and culturally sensitive research on the longer-term family impact with a range of genetic and genomic disorders.

NOTE

1. Genomics refers to both traditional single-gene genetic conditions and multifactorial or genetically influenced disorders, where multiple genes and gene-environment interactions determine whether a disorder occurs.

REFERENCES

Babul, R., Adam, S., Kremer, B., Dufrasne, S., Wiggins, S., Huggins, M., et al. (1993). Attitudes toward direct predictive testing for the Huntington's disease gene: Relevance for other adult-onset diseases. *Journal of the American Medical Association, 270,* 2321–2325.

Boss, P. (1999). *Ambiguous loss: Learning to live with unresolved grief.* Boston: Harvard University Press.

Boszormenyi-Nagy, I., & Spark, G. (1973). *Invisible loyalties: Reciprocity in intergenerational family therapy.* New York: Harper and Row. Bowen, D. J., Patenaude, A. F., & Vernon, S. W. (1999). Psychological issues in cancer genetics: From the laboratory to the public. *Cancer Epidemiology, Biomarkers, & Prevention, 8,* 326–328.

Bowen, M. (1978). *Family therapy in clinical practice.* New York: Jason Aronson.

Braithwaite, D., Sutton, S., & Steggles, N. (2002). Intention to participate in predictive genetic testing for hereditary cancer: The role of attitude toward uncertainty. *Psychology and Health, 17*(6), 761–772.

Brouwer-Dudokdewit, A. C., Savenije, A., Zoeteweij, M., Maat-Kievit, A., & Tibben, A. (2002). A hereditary disorder in the family and the family life cycle: Huntington disease as a paradigm. *Family Process, 41*(4), 677–692.

Byng-Hall, J. (1996). *Rewriting family scripts.* New York: Guilford.

Byng-Hall, J. (2004). Family scripts and loss. In F. Walsh & M. McGoldrick (Eds.). *Living beyond loss: Death in the family* (2nd ed., pp. 85–98). New York: Norton.

Cappelli, M., Surh, L., Walker, M., Korneluk, Y., Humphreys, L., Verma, S., et al. (2001). Psychological and social predictors of decisions about genetic testing for breast cancer in high-risk women. *Psychology Health and Medicine, 6*(3), 321–333.

Carter, E. A., & McGoldrick, M. (Eds.) (1999). *The evolving family life cycle: Individual, family, and social perspectives* (3rd ed.). New York: Allyn and Bacon.

Chapman, P., & Burn, J. (1999). Genetic predictive bowel cancer predisposition: The impact on the individual. *Cytogenetics and Cell Genetics, 86,* 118–124.

Codori, A. M., Petersen, G. M., Boyd, P. A., Brandt, J., & Giardiello, F. M. (196). Genetic testing for cancer in children: Short-term psychological effect. *Archives of Pediatric and Adolescent Medicine, 150,* 1131–1138.

Croyle, R. T., & Lerman, C. (1999). Risk communication in genetic testing for cancer susceptibility. *Journal of the National Cancer Institute Monographs, 25,* 59–66.

Croyle, R., Smith, K., Botkin, J., Baty, B., & Nash, J. (1997). Psychological responses to BRCA1 mutation testing: Preliminary findings. *Health Psychology, 16,* 63–72.

Erikson, E. (1959). Identity and the life cycle. *Psychological Issues, 1*, 1–171.

Framo, J. L. (1992). *Family -of-origin therapy: An intergenerational approach*. New York: Brunner/Mazel.

Imber-Black, E. (1995). *Secrets in families and family therapy*. New York: Norton.

Jacobsen, P., Valdimarsdottir, H., Brown, K., & Offit, K. (1997). Decision-making about genetic testing among women at familial risk for breast cancer. *Psychosomatic Medicine, 59*(5), 459–466.

Kessler, S. (1993). Forgotten person in the Huntington disease family. *American Journal of Medical Genetics, 48*, 145–150.

Kessler, S., & Bloch, M. (1989). Social system responses to Huntington disease. *Family Process, 28*, 59–68.

Kubler-Ross, E. (1969). *On death and dying*. New York: Macmillan.

Lerman, C., & Croyle, R. T. (1996). Emotional and behavioral responses to genetic testing for susceptibility to cancer. *Oncology, 10*(2), 191–195.

Lerman, C., Croyle, R., Tercyak, K., & Hamann, H. (2002). Genetic testing: Psychological aspects and limitations. *Journal of Consulting and Clinical Psychology, 70*(3), 784–797.

Lerman, C., Hughes, C., Lemon, S., Durham, C., Narod, S., & Lynch, H. (1998). What you don't know can hurt you: Adverse psychologic effects in members of BRCA1-linked and BRCA2-linked families who decline genetic testing. *Journal of Clinical Oncology, 16*, 1650–1654.

Lerman, C., Narod, S., Schulman, K., Hughes, C., Gomez-Caminero, A., Bonney, G., et al. (1996). BRCA1 testing in families with hereditary breast-ovarian cancer: A prospective study of patient decision making and outcomes. *Journal of the American Medical Association, 275*(24), 1885–1892.

Levinson, D. J. (1986). A conception of adult development. *American Psychologist, 41*, 3–13.

Lim, J., Macluran, M., Price, M., Bennett, B., Butow, P., & the kConFab Psychosocial Group. (2004). Short and long-term impact of receiving genetic mutation results in women at increased risk for hereditary breast cancer. *Journal of Genetic Counseling, 13*(2), 115–124.

Marteau, T. M., & Croyle, R. (1998). Psychological responses to genetic testing. *British Medical Journal, 316*, 693–696.

McDaniel, S., Campbell, T., Hepworth, J., & Lorenz, A. (2005). *Family-oriented primary care: A manual for medical providers* (2nd ed.). New York: Springer-Verlag.

McDaniel, S., Hepworth, J., & Doherty, W. (Eds.) (1997). *The shared experience of illness: Stories of patients, families, and their therapists*. New York: Basic Books.

McGoldrick, M., Gerson, R., & Schellenberger, S. (1999). *Genograms: Assessment and Intervention* (2nd ed). New York: Norton.

Miller, S. (1995). Monitoring and blunting styles of coping with cancer influence the information patients want and need about their disease: Implications for cancer screening and management. *Cancer, 76*, 167–177.

Miller, S., & Diefenbach, M. (1998). The Cognitive-Social Health Information Processing (C-SHIP) model: A theoretical framework for research in behavioral oncology. In D. S. Krantz & A. Baum (Eds.), *Technology and methods in behavioral medicine* (pp. 219–244). Mahwah, NJ: Lawrence Erlbaum.

Patenaude, A., Schneider, K., Keiffer, S., Calzone, K., Stopfer, J., Basili, L., et al. (1996). Acceptance of invitations for p53 and BRCA1 predispositional testing: Factors influencing potential utilization of cancer genetic testing. *Psycho-Oncology, 53*(3), 241–250.

Penn, P. (1983). Coalitions and binding interactions in families with chronic illness. *Family Systems Medicine, 1*(2), 16–25.

Peters, J., Djurdjinovic, L., & Baker, D. (1999). The genetic self: The human genome project, genetic counseling, and family therapy. *Families, Systems, and Health, 17*(1), 5–25.

Quaid, K., & Morris, M. (1993). Reluctance to undergo predictive testing by those at risk for Huntington's disease. *American Journal of Medical Genetics, 45*, 41–45.

Quaid, K. A., & Wesson, M. K. (1995) Exploration of the effects of predictive testing for Huntington disease on intimate relaitonships. *American Journal of Medical Genetics, 57*(1), 46–51.

Rando, T A. (Ed.). (2000). *Clinical dimensions of anticipatory mourning: Theory and practice in working with the dying, their loved ones, and their caregivers.* Champaign, IL: Research Press.

Reiss, D. (1981). *The family's construction of reality.* Cambridge, MA: Harvard University Press.

Rolland, J. S. (1984). Toward a psychosocial typology of chronic and life-threatening illness. *Family Systems Medicine, 2*, 245–263.

Rolland, J. S. (1987). Chronic illness and the life cycle: A conceptual framework. *Family Process, 26*(2), 203–221.

Rolland, J. S. (1990). Anticipatory loss: A family systems developmental framework. *Family Process, 29*(3), 229–244.

Rolland, J. S. (1994a). *Families, illness, and disability: An integrative treatment model.* New York: Basic Books.

Rolland, J. S. (1994b). In sickness and in health: The impact of illness on couples' relationships. *Journal of Marital and Family Therapy, 20*(4), 327–349.

Rolland, J. S. (1999). Families and genetic fate: A millennial challenge. *Families, Systems and Health, 17*(1), 123–133.

Rolland, J. S. (2004). Helping families with anticipatory loss and terminal illness. In F. Walsh & M. McGoldrick (Eds.), *Living beyond loss: Death in the family* (2nd ed., pp. 213–237). New York: Norton.

Rolland, J. S., & Williams, J. K. (2005). Toward a biopsychosocial model for 21st century genetics. *Family Process, 44*(1), 3–24.

Seaburn, D., Gunn, W., Mauksh, L., Gawinski, A., & Lorenz, A. (Eds.) (1996). *Models of collaboration: A guide for mental health professionals working with physicians and health care providers.* New York: Basic Books.

Seaburn, D., Lorenz, A., & Kaplan, D. (1992). The transgenerational development of chronic illness meanings. *Family Systems Medicine, 10*(4), 385–395.

Scott, R. J. (2000). Anticipating response to predictive genetic testing for Alzheimer's disease: A survey of first-degree relatives. *Gerontologist, 40*(1), 43–52.

Sobel, S., & Cowan, D. B. (2000). Impact of genetic testing for Huntington's disease on the family system. *American Journal of Medical Genetics, 90*(1), 49–59.

Sobel, S., & Cowan, C. B. (2003). Ambiguous loss and disenfranchised grief: The impact of DNA predictive testing on the family as a system. *Family Process, 42*(1), 47–59.

Taswell, H., & Sholtes, S. (1999). Predictive genetic testing: A story of one family. *Families, Systems and Health, 17*(1), 111–123.

Taylor, S. (1989). *Positive illusions: Creative self-deception and the healthy mind.* New York: Basic Books.

Tibben, A., Timman, R., Banninck, E., & Duivenvoorden, H. (1997). Three-year follow-up after presymptomatic testing for Huntington's disease in tested individuals and partners. *Health Psychology, 16*, 20–35.

Walsh, F. (2003). Changing families in a changing world. In F. Walsh (Ed.), *Normal family processes: Growing diversity and complexity* (3rd ed., pp. 3–26). New York: Guilford.

Walsh, F. (2006). *Strengthening family resilience* (2nd ed.). New York: Guilford.

Walsh, F., & McGoldrick, M. (Eds.) (2004). *Living beyond loss: Death in the family* (2nd ed.). New York: Norton.

Wiggins, S., Whyte, P., Huggins, M., Adam, S., Theilman, J., Bloch, M., et al. (1992). The psychological consequences of predictive testing for Huntington's disease. *New England Journal of Medicine, 327*(20), 1401–1405.

Williams, J. K., Schutte, D. L., Evers, C. A., & Forucci, C. (1999). Adults seeking presymptomatic testing for Huntington Disease. *Image: Journal of Nursing Scholarship, 31*(2), 109–113.

Williams, J. K., Schutte, D. L., Evers, C., & Holkup, P. A. (2000). Redefinition: Coping with normal results from predictive gene testing for neurodegenerative disorders. *Research in Nursing and Health, 23*, 260–269.

Wortman, C., & Silver, R. (1989). The myths of coping with loss. *Journal of Consulting and Clinical Psychology, 57*, 349–357.

Wright, L. M., Watson, W. L., & Bell, J. M. (1996). *Beliefs: The heart of healing in families and illness.* New York: Basic Books.

Chapter 6

Psychosocial Interventions for Patients and Families Coping With Genetic Conditions

Susan H. McDaniel, John S. Rolland,
Suzanne L. Feetham, and Suzanne M. Miller

IN PREVIOUS CHAPTERS, WE HAVE DOCUMENTED THE PERSONAL AND INterpersonal challenges faced by individuals and their families as they learn, or seek to learn, about genetic conditions and understand genetic risk in their families. The new frontier in psychosocial genomic medicine is what to do about it: how to facilitate informed decision making; support family strengths; prevent depression, anxiety, and destructive family conflict; and support people, their families, and their genetic health care teams with sensitivity to the multicultural contexts within which we live. While some intervention research has been published, especially with individual patients, this area is new and requires innovation and demonstration projects that will inform systematic studies of patients and families. In this chapter, we report on what is known from research and from our own clinical work.

The experience of facing a genetic risk or condition is like facing a shifting landscape because information about genetic conditions is rapidly changing as scientists learn more and more about the human genome, mechanisms of disease, and interactions with the environment. Any psychosocial intervention, therefore, must be flexible and able to accommodate changes in knowledge that affect testing, diagnosis, and treatment of genetic conditions. In addition, psychosocial interventions must be sensitive to the psychosocial demands of a particular condition and the time phase of the experience for the patient and family—from the developing awareness that may come from history taking at a visit to the primary care clinician or other family members' illness experiences, to decision making about testing, responding to the results and deciding about disclosure, coping with the illness or threat of illness as an individual, and coping with its meaning to other family members and its potential meaning for future generations (see Chapters 2 and 5). Our clinical models also need to be sensitive to ethnocultural and racial differences among and within families. Much work is needed to take into consideration all these factors and develop interventions that meet the varying needs of patients and their families.

We begin this chapter with a discussion of health beliefs and cultural issues that inform all patient and family responses to health threats and illness. With that as a backdrop, we then turn to different psychosocial interventions for people with genetic concerns: individual and family consultations, psychoeducational groups, family therapy, couples therapy, and individual psychotherapy. Case examples are drawn from actual clinical experience.[1]

GENETIC HEALTH BELIEFS

An individual's genetic health beliefs are based on a past history of personal and family illness, family stories, cultural beliefs and values, and any understanding of genetic transmission. These health beliefs inform care seeking, decision making, requests and responses to testing, and many other aspects of managing genetic conditions.

Each of us individually, and as part of our family and other systems (e.g., religious, community, larger society), develops a belief system or philosophy that shapes our patterns of behavior toward the common challenges of life. Beliefs provide coherence to life, facilitating continuity between the past, present, and future (Antonovsky & Sourani, 1988; Reiss, 1981). They serve as a cognitive map, guiding decisions and action: they offer a way to approach new and ambiguous situations such as genetic testing and living with genetic knowledge about future disease risk. Depending on which system we are addressing, beliefs can be labeled as values, culture, religion, or worldview, from an individual or family paradigm. With advances in genetics and genomics, it is vital that clinicians appreciate the contribution and interaction of personal, family, and ethnocultural beliefs.

In the context of genetic knowledge, how do individuals and families create meaning that preserves or enhances their sense of competence and promotes a meaningful existence? This is a primary developmental challenge, similar in many ways to living with actual illness (Kleinman, 1988; Rolland, 1994a, 1998; Taylor, 1983; Wright, Watson, & Bell, 1996, Wynne, Shields, & Sirkin, 1992). Since illness is often experienced as a betrayal of our fundamental trust in our bodies and belief in our invulnerability (Kleinman,1988), creating an empowering narrative can be a formidable task. Health beliefs help us grapple with the existential dilemmas related to our fear of death, our tendency to deny death, and our attempts to reassert control when suffering and loss occur.

Inquiry into patient and family beliefs is perhaps the most powerful foundation of collaboration among individuals, families, and health professionals (Wright et al., 1996). Beliefs are the fiber that weaves a resilient collaborative relationship. For example, there is growing research evidence that family members' distress about cancer can be more closely associated with perceived risk or appraisals of seriousness than objective characteristics of the disease (Miller & Diefenbach, 1998; see also Chapter 3).

Our society is becoming increasingly "geneticized." Research advances on the human genome, rapidly increasing diagnostic genetic technology, and society's and the media's fascination with the hopes and fears of this technology, have stimulated discussions about the relative importance of nature versus nurture in disease and human behavior. Many perceive this discourse as dominated by culturally ingrained meanings about genetics that are connected to fate and stigma, despite the increasingly strong evidence that a variety of factors interact with genetic risk to cause disease. Health professionals need to help families deconstruct old deterministic beliefs, such as "genetics equal fate." With new discoveries occurring weekly in genetics and genomics, knowledge of risk for some families with some illnesses can lead to risk reduction or prevention (Feetham, Thomson, & Hinshaw, 2005).

Differences in cultural background and orientation are powerful factors affecting the personal and family experience of genetic knowledge. A multidimensional definition of culture is "those sets of shared world views, meanings and adaptive behaviors derived from simultaneous membership and participation in a multiplicity of contexts, such as rural, urban or suburban setting, language, age, gender, cohort, family configuration, race, ethnicity, religion, nationality, socioeconomic status, employment, education, occupation, sexual orientation, political ideology, migration and stage of acculturation" (Falicov, 1995, p. 375). Effectively and sensitively addressing issues such as ingrained meanings of the word *genetics* requires carefully avoiding a one-size-fits-all approach. Strategies to design and disseminate educational information must appreciate all these aspects of multicultural diversity.

Specific Health Beliefs

During initial consultations, it is useful for clinicians to inquire about key beliefs that shape the individual's and family's narratives and coping strategies. Multicultural issues overlie these specific beliefs and need to be considered in guiding dialogue. This includes tracking beliefs about the following:

1. Normality
2. Mind-body relationship, control, and mastery
3. The meaning of *genetics* as well as types of illnesses (e.g., life-threatening) or specific diseases, such as hereditary breast and ovarian cancer
4. What can cause a genetic disorder and what can influence its prevention, course, and outcome (e.g., a birth defect as punishment for previous wrongdoing)
5. Illness and loss through the generations that have shaped a family's health beliefs
6. Anticipated nodal points in the nonsymptomatic phases of individual and family life cycles when health beliefs will be strained or need to shift (see Chapter 2)

It is important for a clinician to assess the consistency of health beliefs within the family and its various subsystems (e.g., spouse, parental, extended family), as well as between the family and the professional health care system (Rolland, 1994a).

Multicultural Beliefs and Different Types of Genetic Conditions

Ethnicity, race, and religion strongly influence family beliefs concerning health and illness (Fisher, 1996; McGoldrick, Giordano, & Garcia-Preto, 2005; Walsh, 1999). Significant ethnic differences regarding health beliefs typically emerge at the time of a major health crisis, such as genetic testing. Health professionals need to be mindful of the belief systems of various ethnic, racial, and religious groups in their community, particularly as these translate into different behavioral patterns (Greb, 1998; Wang, 2001). This is especially true for minority groups (e.g., African American, Asian, Hispanic) that experience discrimination or marginalization from prevailing white Anglo culture.

Enormous cultural variation exists in how different kinds of genetic disorders are perceived. For instance, cultures that place a high premium on cognitive abilities and intellectual achievement may show greater anxiety with genetically determined or influenced conditions, such as Alzheimer disease or forms of mental retardation. In more rural or agricultural regions, physical labor and participation in social and family life are more important, so physical limitations may be a greater concern than mild or moderate mental retardation (Hauck & Knoki-Wilson, 1996).

Cultural norms vary as to the kind and degree of open communication about genetic risk: (1) between the health care professional and the patient and family; (2) within the nuclear family; (3) within the extended family; and (4) within the wider community. For example, many Middle Eastern cultures believe that only God knows how bad a prognosis is. Therefore, to give up hope or convey hopelessness would mean to doubt God's power to help (Lipson & Meleis, 1983). To deliver a bad medical prognosis, such as with predictive testing for Huntington disease, could be considered tactless and potentially unforgivable, since it could bring disaster to the patient. In Latino culture, Penchaszadeh (2001) pointed to the fact that many emphasize optimism in future health outcomes and use folk beliefs and religious faith for reassurance. For some, this optimism can result in reducing, in a relative sense, the significance of genetic risk information in reproductive decision making.

In certain cultures, for instance, many Asian, Middle Eastern, and Muslim ones, sharing family history is not considered appropriate behavior (Daneshpour, 1998; Wang & Marsh, 1992). In such cultures, personal and family problems are carefully withheld from anyone outside the family, since shame and mistrust are associated with revealing relevant information, even to health care providers. Seeking complete family and medical history information could be seen as an inappropriate intrusion and as an attempt to make a family responsible for an illness. Also, in addition to shame, a genetic condition could seriously affect the ability of any offspring to marry. In these circumstances, a family's reluctance to convey crucial medical information can easily be misinterpreted by the clinician as noncompliance. The family may feel they are in a significant bind because at the same time, a cultural value is to revere health care professionals, such as physicians or genetic counselors, as experts who should be obeyed. In these circumstances, collaborative conversation and decision making are culturally dissonant, and sharing family illness history may conflict directly with a fear of shaming one's ancestors.

Tremendous cultural variation exists as to who should or should not be included in decision making regarding genetic testing (e.g., extended family, friends, professionals). In many Asian cultures, personal autonomy is subordinate to the primacy of the family unit (collective family responsibility). From this perspective, genetic counseling meetings need to be directed to the family rather than an individual potentially at-risk member. Further, seeking help outside the family (including from health care professionals) is seen as publicly shameful. These beliefs are seen as protecting the family unit from detrimental decisions or actions that may be interpreted as bringing shame on the entire family and ancestors. These beliefs can be serious obstacles to utilizing genetic services (Sue & Sue, 1990; Wang, 2001; Wang & Marsh, 1992).

Ethnocultural influences on personal and family beliefs regarding the explanation of health and illness are particularly important. In the face of illness or genetic risk information, all of us wonder, "Why me?" "Why us?" and "Why now?" (Lowery, Jacobsen, & McCauley, 1987; Taylor, 1983; Thompson & Kyle, 2000). Humans invariably construct an explanation or story that helps organize our experience. Even in the context of genetic testing, tremendous uncertainties persist about the relative importance of myriad factors, leaving individuals and families to make idiosyncratic attributions about what caused the genetic risk (Lewis & Daltroy, 1990). It is important to ask each family member for his or her explanation. Responses will generally reflect a combination of medical information, family mythology, and cultural or religious beliefs. For instance, Mittman, Crombleholme, Green, and Golbus (1998) found among recent immigrants of both Asian Pacific and Hispanic origins a cultural belief in the "evil eye" and eating of specific foods as explanations of birth defects. Also, there is a belief among some Asian Pacific people that blood and other body fluids carry the essence of life and must be conserved. This belief can foster resistance to amniocentesis and diagnostic tests that require blood samples. Further, a lack of familiarity with Western medicine may lead to misunderstanding or disbelief that prenatal tests can predict the future child's health or development (Mittman, 1988).

Cultural or religious beliefs can influence diagnostic and intervention options. In Islamic teachings, prenatal diagnosis is okay and pregnancy termination is permitted until 120 days, because it is believed that until that time the soul has not emerged (Swinford & El-Fouly, 1987). Also, birth control is permitted to prevent genetic conditions, but artificial insemination and ovum donation are not culturally acceptable.

Racial differences in the interest in and uptake of genetic testing have been documented in a number of areas, including *BRCA1/2* testing (Armstrong, Micco, Carney, Stopfer, & Putt, 2005; Hughes et al., 1997; Lerman et al., 1999) and amniocentesis testing (Saucier et al., 2005). Racial disparities in genetic testing are also due, in part, to factors such as socioeconomic status, objective risk, risk perceptions and attitudes, and physician recommendations (Armstrong et al., 2005). However, culture-specific beliefs and attitudes also appear to play a role in the uptake of genetic testing. For example, in a recent study, white women were more likely to attribute the cause of breast cancer to genetic and environmental factors, whereas African American women were more likely to attribute breast cancer to causes such as a blow to the breast and personal behaviors (Kwate, Thompson, Valdimarsdottir, & Bovbjerg, 2005). African Americans are also less likely to endorse the health benefits of testing, less likely to believe that testing could provide reassurance, more likely to believe that cancer genetic tests would be anxiety provoking, and more likely to express concern about the government's use of genetic testing information (Armstrong et al., 2005; Peters, Rose, & Armstrong, 2004).

Genetic diseases are not distributed equally among ethnic groups. Therefore, certain diseases can become associated with specific groups due to increased prevalence. This association, in turn, can increase an ethnic group's risk of stigma and discrimination. Stigma has long been an issue in the Ashkenazi Jewish population, where genetic diseases are more prevalent. The increased prevalence of genetic disease may also interact with isolation and discrimination against Jewish culture. While the focus on prenatal and breast and ovarian cancer testing in the Jewish community may thus facilitate awareness and medical management, it may also foster discrimination and stigmatization (Bowen, Singal, Eng, Crystal, & Burke, 2003).

Clinicians need to be mindful of ethnocultural and racial differences that exist between themselves, the individual, and the family as a necessary step to forging a workable and enduring alliance (Seaburn, Gunn, Mauksch, Gawinski, & Lorenz, 1996). When clinicians disregard these issues, families may wall themselves off from health providers and available community resources—a major cause of noncompliance and treatment failure. A strong relationship with primary care clinicians is particularly important for genetic conditions where prevention is possible (e.g., regular mammography for hereditary breast and ovarian cancer; screening colonoscopy for hereditary forms of colon cancer).

PSYCHOSOCIAL INTERVENTIONS

Family health psychologist Anne Kazak (2005) proposed a general model of prevention, drawing from her work with children with cancer and their families. This model assumes that all illness and trauma have psychosocial consequences. Applying the model to genetic conditions (Figure 6.1), at the universal level, all patients and families undergoing

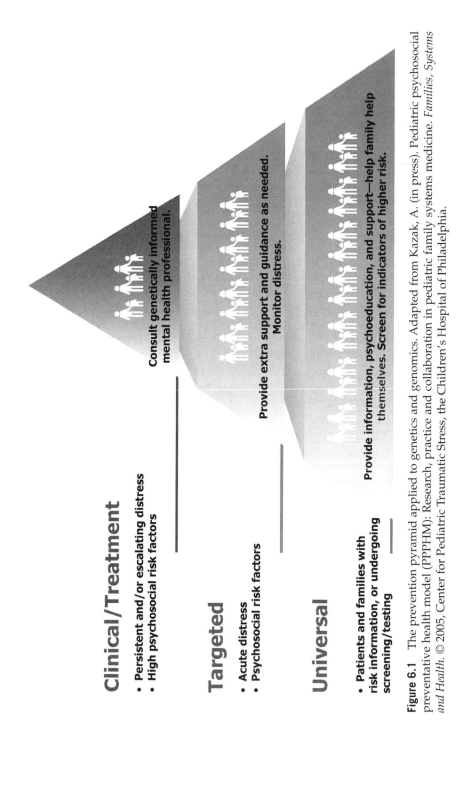

Clinical/Treatment

- Persistent and/or escalating distress
- High psychosocial risk factors

Consult genetically informed mental health professional.

Targeted

- Acute distress
- Psychosocial risk factors

Provide extra support and guidance as needed. Monitor distress.

Universal

- Patients and families with risk information, or undergoing screening/testing

Provide information, psychoeducation, and support—help family help themselves. Screen for indicators of higher risk.

Figure 6.1 The prevention pyramid applied to genetics and genomics. Adapted from Kazak, A. (in press). Pediatric psychosocial preventative health model (PPPHM): Research, practice and collaboration in pediatric family systems medicine. *Families, Systems and Health.* © 2005, Center for Pediatric Traumatic Stress, the Children's Hospital of Philadelphia.

genetic screening or testing and living with risk information benefit from general support, including psychoeducation about common emotional reactions to illness or stress. This support and information can be provided by a primary care clinician or genetic specialists. Patients and family members at this stage also need to be screened for indicators of higher psychosocial risk—depression, anxiety, and interpersonal conflict. This screening can occur through family-centered consultations that assess individual and relational functioning and with screening instruments such as the PHQ9, a validated nine-item instrument used to screen for depression in primary care. Moving up the pyramid, targeted patients and families are those in acute distress or who have a few psychosocial risk factors, but whose symptoms are not severe. Those patients and families need extra support and guidance from their health professionals. They also need to be monitored for ongoing distress so they can be referred to a family therapist or other mental health professional if needed. Finally, at the top of the pyramid are patients and families with persistent and serious distress, who are at most psychosocial risk because of significant history of mental disorder, family dysfunction, or substance abuse, who require specialist mental health intervention. These patients have persistent distress or risk factors and require psychosocial support or mental health treatment from professionals who are trained and sensitive to issues related to genetic conditions.

Referral to a family therapist or other mental health professional is a special skill. If hurried or awkward, the patient may feel dismissed or burdened by yet another problem: "I may have a genetic condition, and now you think I'm crazy too?" The key to overcoming resistance and making a successful referral is to be patient and family centered, refer for what concerns the patient, couple, or family the most, and express strong confidence in the competence of the mental health professional as part of the health care team:

You told me how hard it is right now to decide whether or not you want to be tested for the breast cancer mutation before you become pregnant. The information you received in genetic counseling was very helpful. Since it has been a couple of months and you are distressed at not being able to make a decision, I'd suggest you see Dr. McDaniel, the psychologist on our genetic team. We work closely together; she sees our patients and their families who are trying to decide about testing. Many who have found her very helpful started in exactly the same spot you find yourself.

In addition, it is crucial to consider any cultural or religious beliefs regarding the meaning of genetic testing or the inclusion of a mental health professional that might interfere with such a referral. All referrals for psychosocial intervention require collaboration with the rest of the health care team for effective, integrated care of the patient and family (see Chapter 20).

Once a need is identified, a variety of psychosocial interventions can be useful for patients and families struggling with genetic risk or genomic information—from genetic counseling and individual or family group psychoeducation to individual, couples, and family consultation, brief intervention, or psychotherapy. Techniques may range from cognitive-behavioral to psychodynamic or systemic, but an overall family orientation is useful because of the familial nature of the condition. Psychosocial consultation may occur at different times during the course of the genetic condition—from individual and family consultations and psychoeducation for help with decision making about testing to individual, couple, family, or group therapies for help with the psychosocial challenges that occur at different nonsymptomatic and post-clinical-onset phases over the course of the illness and at transitions in the individual and family life cycle (see Chapter 5). Often interventions are relatively brief, but sometimes consultation about a genetic condition opens up previously unresolved issues that then become the focus of longer-term psychotherapy.

Family Consultation

Having all relevant family members at initial and periodic consultations over time allows the health or mental health professional to assess the impact of the genetic condition on the family and its members, without having to hear one person's version in isolation (see Chapter 3 for relevant family systems concepts in this assessment).

The family systems genetic illness framework described in Chapter 2 provides a guide to assessment and clinical intervention by facilitating an understanding of genetic disorders in psychosocial terms. Key variables—likelihood of development of a condition based on genetic mutations, overall clinical severity, timing of symptom onset in the life cycle, and whether effective treatment interventions exist that can prevent clinical onset or alter progression—provide markers that focus a clinical assessment and intervention.

The concept of time phases described in Chapter 2 provides a way to think longitudinally and view genetic conditions as an ongoing process with landmarks, transition points, and changing demands. The timeline for genomic disorders delineates non- and postsymptomatic psychosocial phases of the disorder, each phase with its own unique developmental tasks. In an initial consultation during the nonsymptomatic crisis phase, family members can acquire a common understanding of the practical and emotional demands of living with a condition over time. This consultation helps create a foundation for more focused communication about ways to cope and adapt to challenges related to the future risk of the specific condition. Clinicians can assess family strengths and vulnerabilities in relation to both present and future expectable phases of the genetic illness. A timeline can reveal clustering of stressors or concurrence of nonsymptomatic time phase transitions with other symptoms in the family, such as a child's behavior or emotional problems, which may be an expression of concern about an at-risk member.

Goal setting is guided by awareness of the components of family functioning most relevant to particular types and phases of a particular genetic condition. Sharing this information with family members and deciding on specific goals fosters a better sense of control and realistic hope. Such knowledge also alerts families to warning signs of distress, such as symptoms of anxiety, depression, or relational conflict or distancing when individual or family consultation would be helpful. This information can guide families in seeking mental health services at appropriate times for brief, goal-oriented consultations or therapy. It also can guide timing of preventive "psychosocial checkups" with a primary care clinician or family therapist.

Psychoeducation

Psychoeducation is part of any good psychotherapy. However, it is especially important for patients and families responding to genetic information. This psychoeducation may occur as part of an individual session with a primary care clinician, a genetic counselor, or a psychotherapist. It may also be part of an individual or multifamily group intervention. Below we discuss genetic risk counseling, group psychoeducation, family psychoeducation, and multifamily discussion groups.

Genetic Risk Counseling

The purpose of genetic risk counseling is to facilitate decision making over the course of genetic risk assessment and testing, by providing information about genetic risk (often in group format) along with individualized counseling that documents the individual's personal pedigree profile and discusses the implications of the pedigree for genetic testing options and subsequent decision making about risk management. The underlying goals are to facilitate knowledge, address uncertainty, encourage the weighing of the pros and cons of different options, and maximize adjustment. However, given the highly personal nature of the information provided, the impact and interpretation of the information, along with the subsequent quality of the decision, are often enhanced when the process is individualized and tailored to the individual's or family's cultural, cognitive, social, and affective profile (Miller et al., 2004; Miller, Roussi, et al., 2005; see Chapters 3 and 10).

Evidence on efforts to enhance the efficacy of psychoeducational approaches, such as genetic risk counseling, are beginning to emerge. Adjunctive interventions, such as tailored print materials (see Skinner, Campbell, Curry, Rimer, & Prochaska, 1999) and CD-ROM computer programs (Green et al., 2004; Wang, Gonzalez, Milliron, Strecher, & Merajver, 2005), offer promising approaches. These types of materials and programs have been found useful in supplementing genetic risk counseling, by preparing individuals for genetic risk assessment services (Miller, Fleisher, et al., 2005) and by facilitating decisional processing about genetic risk assessment and testing (Wang et al., 2005). When individuals have access to these informational and decisional aids, it also allows more time for clinicians to spend on the psychological concerns and familial issues of clients.

Group Psychoeducation

Psychoeducation can occur in individual or family groups as well. Speice, McDaniel, Rowley, and Loader (2002) described an innovative 6-week psychoeducational group for women who tested positive for the breast cancer mutations BRCA1/2. The group was composed of nine white women, including two sisters and one woman and her niece. They ranged in age from 32 to 60. Six already had survived cancer. The women requested an individual, rather than couples or family, group. Many had never met anyone who also tested positive, and they wanted to focus on the unique problems of women who have tested positive for one of these mutations. The format of the group was similar to that of psychoeducational groups described for patients with other chronic illness (Anderson, Reiss, & Hogarty, 1986; Gonzales & Steinglass, 2002; McFarlane, 2002; Rolland, 1994a; Steinglass, 1998). In the first 15 minutes of each group, the geneticist and genetic counselor answered the women's questions and communicated any new information about the gene, the disease, or its treatment. The genetic specialists then left, and the next 75 minutes were facilitated by two family therapists. The sessions were organized around topics developed by the women themselves in the first session, which included these:

1. Family reactions to testing (partners, children, and extended families)
2. Disclosure—who in the family is also at risk, and who to tell and when
3. Confidentiality with insurers and the workplace
4. Their own emotional reactions and coping strategies
5. Body image
6. Relationships with health professionals

The sessions were emotionally intense. The women were initially hesitant, but then quickly bonded with each other as they discovered their shared experiences living with a lifetime of increased risk for breast cancer. Some said they felt understood for the first time. Many powerful issues surfaced, such as spouses who distanced, or children who became angry at their own potential vulnerability. One woman was quite distressed at the conflict and cutoff that occurred when, after her urging, her adult son tested positive for both the *BRCA1* and *BRCA2* gene mutations. Her son's wife said, "Now when I look at my daughters I see death on their faces. I'm angry at what you've done to our future." Most of the women in the group had taken prophylactic measures, such as preventive mastectomies, that they believed would prolong their lives because they knew they had the mutation. The woman whose son quit talking to her said, "I'm glad I had the testing because it's that information that is keeping me alive. For me, it's been very important, but now I feel guilty that I pushed so hard with my children." The group allowed a place to discuss these difficulties and receive helpful consultation and support from women who shared the experience of testing positive and from therapists who could normalize emotional responses and provide psychotherapy referrals for those who experienced persistent distress (such as the woman described above).

Family Psychoeducation

Family psychoeducation can be very useful for couples and nuclear or extended families that must confront decisions about testing and the ramifications of genetic risk and genetically influenced illness in multiple family members. As with group psychoeducation, collaboration among genetic specialists, family therapists, and primary care clinicians is very useful.

For example, two medical family therapists joined together with a geneticist and a genetic counselor to offer what started as one 90-minute, extended family psychoeducational session for an Italian American family in which one member, Carol, a 54-year-old married woman with two children, tested positive for the hereditary nonpolyposis colon cancer (HNPCC) genetic mutation (see Figure 4.2, p. 131). With 8 siblings in the proband's generation, 37 family members came to this session, ranging from her niece, age 19, to her mother, age 75. The group also included partners who were not themselves genetically at risk but shared the psychosocial risk with their partners and their children.

The session began with a slide presentation and lecture from the geneticist about HNPCC and its characteristics. The genetic counselor then talked about genetic testing for this mutation, what it involved, and what they could expect. The family asked many questions.

After about 45 minutes, the family therapists turned the discussion to how the family members felt about what they had heard. The family then told stories about their experiences with cancer, including how they predicted (before testing) who would get cancer. One superstition was that it would hit every other sibling in the proband's generation. Another was that family members with a crooked pinky finger would have the illness. The laughter was frequent, sometimes anxious, and often indicative of healthy coping with a very difficult family health history. Preliminary discussion about testing revealed the range of responses, from a commitment to intensive surveillance without testing to a commitment to testing immediately. This range gave the family therapist an opportunity to talk about different coping styles and the importance of respecting the fact that different family members would go about making the decision about testing in different ways.

Discussion in the last part of the session focused on communication, setting rules in the family about whether and how often to inquire about testing among each other. The session ended with a request for future sessions, as the family moved through the testing process and beyond. Several years later, family members continued to meet quarterly. At a talk delivered to primary care physicians, Carol stated, "I can't tell you how important having these sessions is. We still have family meetings. Nobody lacks for something to say. They are critical because things change."

Multifamily Discussion Groups

Time-limited (4–6 session) multifamily discussion groups for patients and families can help families adjust to illness issues and uncertainty, as well as providing counsel and support from people who share the testing or illness experience (Anderson et al., 1986; Gonzales & Steinglass, 2002; McFarlane, 2002; Rolland, 1994a; Steinglass, 1998). These services can relieve feelings of isolation expressed by some family members after genetic testing has been completed. When desirable and feasible, groups can be based on cultural or ethnic background.

These groups can be disease specific or they can be tailored to a cluster of genetic conditions with similar psychosocial demands in order to maintain thematic coherence (see Chapter 2). For instance, groups can be designed to meet the needs of patients and families dealing with highly penetrant mutations and conditions with high clinical severity; those with clinical onset during the child rearing years of early to mid adulthood (20–60); and those with onset during later life (60 and up). Such groupings are useful when there are not enough families involved with any particular disorder to form a specific group (e.g., rare disorder or a rural setting).

Designing brief psychoeducational modules, timed for critical phases of genetic diseases, helps families to accept and digest manageable portions of a long-term coping process (Rolland, 1994a). Each module can be tailored to a particular nonsymptomatic or clinical phase of the illness and target relevant family skills. This educational approach provides a cost-effective means of prevention, reaching families at high risk for maladaptation.

Family Therapy

Family therapy is important when members of a family share a common concern about testing or the impact of the illness on the family. As mentioned earlier, many kinds of psychotherapy benefit from beginning with a family consultation, no matter what kind of therapy is chosen in the end.

For example, in one family four adult children came in with their parents, concerned about the diminishing quality of their parents' marriage (McDaniel, Johnson, & Sears, 2004). Bob and Jenny had been married for 20 years and already had their children when Bob's brother was diagnosed with a single-gene disorder, myotonic dystrophy, which in its classic form is characterized by muscle weakness and wasting, myotonia, cataracts, and often by cardiac conduction abnormalities. It can occur at any age and is extremely variable in degree of severity and may result in a shortened life span. Bob became so anxious about his brother's illness that he went to see a psychologist about his anxiety. The psychologist suggested that he go ahead with testing. Bob tested positive. It was 5 years after the testing before he began to have symptoms. The family consultation session occurred 6 years after his first symptoms, when Bob was becoming increasingly disabled, having difficulty walking or driving. Jenny was enraged that Bob could no longer take care of her in the way they were accustomed to before his illness.

The adult children came to the initial consultation with their parents, complaining about their parents' uncharacteristic high-decibel fighting.

During the session, the couple revealed that Jenny had been physically abusive to Bob five times during the past year, in the middle of the night when Bob was helpless in bed. Both were distraught about the violence and the conflict. Having their children at the session was important, as it allowed the family to plan for Bob and Jenny to live separately for some period of time, to work on their reactions to the disease and its effect on their relationship. In addition to the focus on partner violence, much of the family therapy focused on testing and adjustment for the adult children, who carried a 50-50 risk of having the genetic mutation. Jenny, in particular, worried about the two children who tested positive but were not yet symptomatic. It was important for all family members to share feelings and provide mutual support regarding the strains of living with future illness, in this case for a genetic condition that has an inevitable onset and progressive severity, and is possibly life shortening (see Chapter 5).

Couples Therapy

As illustrated above, responding to information about the risk for, as well as the reality of, a genetic condition can be a serious stressor in a couple's relationship. The threat of an illness, or the illness itself, can disrupt the dreams, expectations, and basic relationship understandings or contract between spouses or partners.

This disruption happened with Bob and Jenny, erupting some years after testing and the onset of symptoms. The more disabled Bob became, the more angry Jenny became. After the initial family consultation focused on a safety plan, couples therapy began in earnest during the separation to understand the history of the couple's relationship, their multigenerational experience of illness, the history of Bob's illness and each partner's response, and the ways in which their anger over the illness became directed at each other. Much of the anger covered up the couple's fears regarding Bob's continuing disease progression and limited future and the inevitable increasing need for Jenny's caregiving.

Twenty sessions over the course of a year helped the couple to renegotiate and rebalance their relationship to include Bob's illness and disability without it defining their marriage. When they moved back in together, each agreed to have nurse's aides come in to help with some of Bob's daily needs, lessening the caretaking pressure on Jenny. Once Jenny's anger subsided, she became quite sad about Bob's decreased functioning. She also worried about their two children who had tested positive for the mutation but were not yet symptomatic. The couple then went to a support group, which helped them to identify some creative devices and ideas that helped them remain involved in their church and their social network. At termination of treatment, the couple was determined not to allow the strains of the genetic condition to determine the quality of their marriage again.

This couples therapy included discussion of the inevitable relationship skews that occur when one member of a couple has a chronic illness (Rolland, 1994b). If the problem is defined as the exclusive domain of the ill or at-risk partner, then serious imbalances with power and control often develop, leading to dysfunctional resentments, guilt, distancing, and general erosion of intimacy. Bob and Jenny were helped to see the challenges of chronic illness as shared ones, such that the ill spouse carries the disease-related biological burden and the well spouse more of the caregiving burden. Also, their relationship crisis provided an opportunity to explore cultural, ethnic, and gender-based beliefs regarding illness. For instance, typically women carry greater societal expectations regarding caregiving. This was particularly salient for both Bob and Jenny, who grew up in first-generation Irish-American families, where wives and daughters were expected to provide caregiving. Jenny came from a family where she saw her mother tend to her father's chronic respiratory condition while never asking anything in return. She and her sisters were instructed not to bother their father with their needs. For Jenny, powerful multigenerational beliefs and scripts dictated extremely skewed gender-based role relations of a daughter and wife, with the burdens of a caregiver and well spouse not acknowledged. Both Bob and Jenny were helped to reevaluate these beliefs in the context of a very disabling, progressive disease that would require shared responsibility among a team of caregivers and in terms of evolving gender norms in society. This case also highlights the importance of preventive family-centered psychoeducation and consultation when facing a genetic condition, particularly early on during the testing and posttesting phases. In hindsight, early education about the physical and emotional demands of myotonic dystrophy over time may have provided the family and couple a psychosocial map for the experience of illness that could have averted some of their dysfunction and suffering.

Decision making about genetic testing can be another time when couples consultation or brief therapy may be very useful, because of the importance of the decision and the results to both members of the couple and because of the potential for both support and conflict during this time.

Joe and Jill, ages 38 and 36, from German and Irish backgrounds, respectively, came to couples therapy, referred by their family physician, because Joe's mother and aunt had been diagnosed with Huntington disease in the last several years (see Figure 4.1, p. 121). Both Joe and Jill were nervous that Joe had the mutation, but both said they were unclear whether they were "ready" for Joe to be tested (McDaniel, 2005b). Joe was somewhat depressed about the prospect of having such a tragic illness; Jill was frightened. Both said they believed they had a reasonably healthy marriage, but felt they needed to shore up their communication skills before dealing directly with the stress of testing. The only prior strain on their marriage had been during a period of years when they pursued treatment for infertility, finally adopting two children. Ironically, this prior source of stress now seemed to them a true blessing, in that they did not have to worry about passing on any Huntington disease genes. A year of couples therapy focused on their family illness histories (Jill's mother was diagnosed with Alzheimer disease during this time), communication, conflict resolution, and protecting and enhancing their relationship while tending to their parents' illnesses and parenting their children. Given that they both had family histories of dementing illness, it was important to explore specific fears, contingency planning, and sources of resilience in the face of possible cognitive impairment. At the end of this time, the couple took a year off therapy, delaying any testing, just to enjoy themselves.

Individual Psychotherapy

Individual psychotherapy can be a useful extension of genetic counseling, an important feature of decision making and managing the patient's reactions to test results, or an important adjunct to couples or family work. The patient always benefits from a family orientation but may benefit from cognitive-behavioral or other individual psychotherapy treatments as well.

For example, Jill asked for some individual sessions during her couples work with Joe. Joe decided to see a social worker to talk through his reactions to his mother's illness and his own decision regarding testing. Both members of the couple agreed that it would be efficient and acceptable for Jill to work with Dr. McDaniel and collaborate with Joe's therapist to inform the couples work. Jill's sessions were infrequent and family systems oriented while focusing on managing her fears regarding the testing and how much she should plan on being a single parent. While she spoke to Joe about these issues, she felt that extensive conversation would be hurtful to him. Joe used a blunting coping style in dealing with health information (see Chapter 3), while Jill exhibited much monitoring behavior with regard to her husband. She described waking up at night because of Joe's twitching in bed and not being able to go back to sleep for fear these were the first signs of Huntington disease. Even when their physician reassured her that nighttime twitches were not typical early warning signs, she remained fearful. Individual sessions with Jill focused on increasing her contact with her own family and coping with her mother's progressive dementia, consultation with her physician about her own risk for Alzheimer's, then her sense of confidence about taking care of herself (whether Joe became ill or not), and her connection to Joe during this time of uncertainty. Jill had a large extended family that lived in the same community. Her cultural values facilitated discussion of ways that her extended family, particularly siblings and cousins, could share in caregiving needs for her mother. Interestingly, a year after Joe and Jill each took a break from individual and couples therapy, they called to say that they decided to have Joe tested, and he tested negative. They were both relieved and pleased that they had done needed work on themselves and their relationship, regardless of his mutation status.

At major points of developmental transition such as marriage or a decision about having children, the issue of knowing one's family history and consideration of genetic testing may come to the foreground (see Chapter 5).

Sharon, a 26-year-old African American with a family history of breast cancer, came to individual therapy as she became more seriously involved in a relationship with Walter, who lived several states away (McDaniel, 2005a, 2005b). She had been to genetic counseling twice—once several years before, just after her mother died at age 42 of breast cancer (at the urging of her primary care doctor), and another time more recently when considering marriage. After her second round of genetic counseling, Sharon became depressed and mired in the decision-making process. Individual therapy focused on grief and loss in relationship to her mother's death. She worked with her father and sister to have a memorial service on the anniversary of her mother's death. With regard to considering testing, she spoke to her boyfriend and contacted her mother's sister, who survived breast cancer in her 30s, to discuss the situation. Sharon's own sister, Charlene, was involved in their mother's memorial service, but would not discuss testing. "Why would you want to know?" she said. Not only did Charlene use blunting behavior to cope, but growing up in a poor segregated neighborhood and as a service worker in a hotel, she was sensitized to racial discrimination and fearful that genetic risk information would compound this lifelong problem and jeopardize her employment and insurability. This contrasted with Sharon's monitoring style and greater security as an upwardly mobile computer programmer. It was important to discuss the pros and cons of testing in the context of each one's experience with poverty, lack of access to adequate health care growing up, and racial discrimination.

Often individual psychotherapy may be mixed with couples or family work.

In this case, at the end of her individual grief work and now engaged to be married, Sharon came in to therapy with her fiancé for a couples consultation.

Sharon decided not to be tested until after they had children. "I know it's irrational. I don't think the test results would affect our decision to have children, and I'd rather not know until after they're born." Walter felt the decision should be Sharon's, but said he was happy with this approach. Growing up in poverty, he learned resilient values from his family that led him to believe, "Together we'll deal with whatever comes in the future." With this decision made, the couple focused on Sharon's reluctance to do monthly breast self-exams and mammography. They worked out a system in which Walter playfully reminded her on a monthly basis, and rewarded her with a small, affectionate gift once the surveillance task was accomplished. "It's an investment in our family," he said.

Just as couples work can be helpful to individual therapy, so individual therapy can be a useful addition to large family meetings or family therapy. We return now to the case involving the HNPCC genetic mutation.

Carol and one of her sisters, Betsy, came for individual therapy for several years, in addition to the large family meetings related to HNPCC. In addition to focusing on how to handle family conflict over testing and communication, Carol described the importance of having a place to work on regulation of her emotional response to testing, her illness experiences, and especially to the heartbreak of having both her children test positive as well: "There are so many emotions and most of them I think of as bad, but they bubble like a stew—one is there one day and the next day is a different one, and you keep going between all of these. . . . It is devastating at times. . . . So, where there got to be a settling point for me is the counseling sessions. They are a great help to me in working on this with my family."

CONCLUSION

Research is needed on the family management of genetic information, which will then inform treatment research. A variety of psychosocial interventions, delivered by different kinds of health professionals, are potentially available for patients and families facing genetic conditions. An appreciation of individual and family beliefs, ethnicity, culture, race, and socioeconomic class issues is essential. Treatments need to be collaborative, coordinated, and integrated by having a systemic perspective. To deliver the care, primary care and mental health professionals must receive training about the psychosocial issues involved in consulting for or treating patients and their families facing genetic conditions. Family strengths and resiliency must be underscored, and community and professional resources described.

As Carol said in her talk, "Give us resources. Know what support groups are available. Know what counseling is available—counselors that treat and understand heritable diseases. We don't want to go to a counselor who is going to start with your first memory at 2 or 3 years old. We need them to focus on the present, because we are in crisis and we need people who understand that."

NOTE

1. We have camouflaged the identity of the people in the situations, to protect their confidentiality. These patients did give permission for their situations to be reported, in hopes that health professionals will provide better and more comprehensive care as they learn about the emotional and interpersonal dilemmas that their patients experience.

REFERENCES

Anderson, C., Reiss, D., & Hogarty, G. (1986). *Schizophrenia and the family*. New York: Guilford.

Antonovsky, A., & Sourani, T. (1988). Family sense of coherence and family adaptation. *Journal of Marriage and the Family, 50*, 79–92.

Armstrong, K., Micco, E., Carney, A., Stopfer, J., & Putt, M. (2005). Racial differences in the use of BRCA1/2 testing among women with a family history of breast or ovarian cancer. *Journal of the American Medical Association, 293*, 1729–1736.

Bowen, D. J., Singal, R., Eng, E., Crystal, S., & Burke, W. (2003). Jewish identity and intentions to obtain breast cancer sceening. *Cultural Identity and Ethnic Minority Psychology, 9*(1), 79–87.

Daneshpour, M. (1998). Muslim families and family therapy. *Journal of Marital and Family Therapy, 24*, 355–390.

Falicov, C. (1995). Training to think culturally: A multidimensional comparative framework. *Family Process, 34*, 373–388.

Feetham, S., Thomson, E. J., & Hinshaw, A. S. (2005) Genomics for health and society: A framework for nursing leadership. *Journal of Nursing Scholarship, 37*(2), 102–110.

Fisher, N. L. (Ed.). (1996). *Cultural and ethnic diversity: A guide for genetic professionals*. Baltimore: Johns Hopkins University Press.

Gonzalez, S., & Steinglass, P. (2002). Application of multifamily groups in chronic medical disorders. In W. F. McFarlane (Ed.), *Multifamily groups in the treatment of severe psychiatric disorders* (pp. 315–340). New York: Guilford.

Greb, A. (1998). Multiculturalism and the practice of genetic counseling. In D. Baker, J. Schuette, & W. Uhlman (Eds.), *A guide to genetic counseling* (pp. 171–198). New York: Wiley-Liss.

Green, M. J., Peterson S. K., Baker, M. W., Harper, G. R., Friedman, L. C., Rubin-stein, et al. (2004). Effect of a computer-based decision aid on knowledge, perceptions, and intentions about genetic testing for breast cancer suscep-tibility: A randomized controlled trial. *Journal of the American Medical Asso-ciation, 292*, 442–452.

Hauck, L., & Knoki-Wilson, U. M. (1996). Culture of Native Americans of the Southwest. In N. L. Fisher (Ed.), *Cultural and ethnic diversity: A guide for gene-tic professionals* (pp. 60–85). Baltimore, MD: Johns Hopkins University Press.

Hughes, C., Gomez-Caminero, A., Benkendorf, J., Kerner, J., Isaacs, C., Barter, J., et al. (1997). Ethnic differences in knowledge and attitudes about BRCA1 testing in women at increased risk. *Patient Education Counseling, 32*, 51–62.

Kazak, A. (2005). Evidence-based interventions for survivors of childhood can-cer and their families. *Journal of Pediatric Psychology, 30*(1), 29–39.

Kazak, A. (in press). Pediatric psychosocial preventative health model (PPPHM): Research, practice and collaboration in pediatric family systems medicine. *Families, Systems and Health.*

Kleinman, A. (1988). *The illness narratives: Suffering, healing, and the human con-dition.* New York: Basic Books.

Kwate, N. O., Thompson, H. S., Valdimarsdottir, H. B., & Bovbjerg, D. H. (2005). Brief report: Etiological attributions for breast cancer among healthy African American and European American women. *Psychooncol-ogy, 14*(5), 421–425.

Lerman, C., Hughes, C., Benkendorf, J. L., Biesecker, B., Kerner, J., Willison, J., et al. (1999). Racial differences in testing motivation and psychological dis-tress following retest education for BRCA1 gene testing. *Cancer Epidemiol-ogy, Biomarkers and Prevention, 8*, 361–367.

Lewis, F. M., & Daltroy, L. (1990). How causal explanations influence health be-havior: Attribution theory. In K. Glanz & F. M. Lewis (Eds.), *Health behavior and health education: Theory, research, and practice* (pp. 92–114). San Fran-cisco: Jossey-Bass.

Lipson, J. G., & Meleis, A. I. (1983). Issues of health care of Middle Eastern pa-tients. *Western Journal of Medicine, 139*, 854–861.

Lowery, B. J., Jacobsen, B. S., & McCauley, K. (1987). On the prevalence of causal search in illness situations. *Nursing Research, 36*(2), 88–93.

McDaniel, S. H. (2005a). Does DNA determine destiny? A role for medical fam-ily therapy with genetic screening for breast cancer and other genetic ill-nesses. In R. Crane (Ed.), *Families and health: Interdisciplinary perspectives* (pp. 396–406). Thousand Oaks, CA: Sage.

McDaniel, S. H. (2005b). The psychotherapy of genetics. *Family Process, 44*, 25–44.

McDaniel, S. H., Johnson, S. B., & Sears, S. (2004). Psychologists promote biopsychosocial health in families. In N. Johnson, C. Goodheart, R. Rozen-sky, & R. Hammond (Eds.), *Psychology builds a healthy world* (pp. 49–75). Washington, DC: American Psychological Association.

McFarlane, W. F. (Ed.). (2002). *Multifamily groups in the treatment of severe psychi-atric disorders.* New York: Guilford.

McGoldrick, M., Giordano, J., & Garcia-Preto, N. (2005). *Ethnicity and family therapy* (3rd ed.). New York: Guilford.

Miller, S. M., Bowen, D. J., Campbell, M. K., Diefenbach, M. A., Gritz, E. R., Jacobsen, P. B., et al. (2004). Current research promises and challenges in behavioral oncology: Report from the American Society of Preventive Oncology annual meeting. *Cancer Epidemiology, Biomarkers and Prevention, 13*, 171–180.

Miller, S. M., & Diefenbach, M. (1998). The cognitive-social health information processing (C-SHIP) model: A theoretical framework for research in behavioral oncology. In D. S. Krantz & A. Baum (Eds.), *Technology and methods in behavioral medicine* (pp. 219–244). Mahwah, NJ: Erlbaum.

Miller, S. M., Fleisher, L., Roussi, P., Buzaglo, J. S., Schnoll, R. A., Slater, E., et al. (2005). Facilitating informed decision making about breast cancer risk and genetic counseling among women calling the NCI's Cancer Information Service. *Journal of Health Communication, 10*, 119–136.

Miller, S. M., Roussi, P., Daly, M. B., Buzaglo, J. S., Sherman, K. A., Godwin, A. K., et al. (2005). Enhanced counseling for women undergoing BRCA1/2 testing: Impact on subsequent decision making about risk prevention behaviors. *Health Education and Behavior, 32*(5), 654–667.

Mittman, I. (1988). Conflict between ancient culture and modern technology. *Perspectives in Genetic Counseling, 10*, 3–4.

Mittman, I., Crombleholme, W. R., Green, J. R., & Golbus, M. S. (1998). Reproductive genetic counseling to Asian Pacific and Latin American immigrants. *Journal of Genetic Counseling, 7*, 49–70.

Penchaszadeh, V. (2001). Genetic counseling issues in Latinos. *Genetic Testing, 5*(3), 193–200.

Peters, N., Rose, A., & Armstrong, K. (2004). The association between race and attitudes about predictive genetic testing. *Cancer Epidemiology, and Biomarkers Prevention, 13*(3), 361–365.

Reiss, D. (1981). *The family's construction of reality.* Cambridge, MA: Harvard University Press.

Rolland, J. S. (1994a). *Families, illness, and disability: An integrative treatment model.* New York: Basic Books.

Rolland, J. S. (1994b). In sickness and in health: The impact of illness on couples' relationships. *Journal of Marital and Family Therapy, 20*(4), 327–349.

Rolland, J. S. (1998). Beliefs and collaboration in illness: Evolution over time. *Families, Systems and Health, 16*(1/2), 7–27.

Saucier, J. B., Johnston, D., Wicklund, C. A., Robbins-Furman, P., Hecht, J. T., & Monga, M. (2005). Racial-ethnic differences in genetic amniocentesis uptake. *Journal of Genetic Counseling, 14*(3), 189–195.

Seaburn, D., Gunn, W., Mauksch, L., Gawinski, A., & Lorenz, A. (Eds.). (1996). *Models of collaboration: A guide for mental health professionals working with physicians and health care providers.* New York: Basic Books.

Skinner, C., Campbell, M., Curry, S., Rimer, B., & Prochaska, J. (1999). How effective are tailored print communications? *Annals of Behavioral Medicine, 21*, 290–298.

Speice, J., McDaniel, S. H., Rowley, P., & Loader, S. (2002). Family-oriented psychoeducation group for women found to have a BRCA mutation. *Clinical Genetics, 62,* 121–127.

Steinglass, P. (1998). Multiple family discussion groups for patients with chronic medical illness. *Families, Systems, and Health, 16*(1/2), 55–71.

Sue, D. W., & Sue, D. (1990). *Counseling the culturally different: Theory and practice* (2nd ed.). New York: Wiley.

Swinford, A. E., & El-Fouly, M. H. (1987). Islamic religion and culture: Principles and implications for genetic counseling. *Birth Defects Original Article Series, 23,* 253–257.

Taylor, S. (1983). Adjustment to threatening events: A theory of cognitive adaptation. *American Psychologist, 38*(11), 1161–1173.

Thompson, S., & Kyle, D. (2000). The role of perceived control in coping with the losses associated with chronic illness. In J. Harvey & E. Miller (Eds.), *Loss and trauma: General and close relationship perspectives* (pp. 131–145). Philadelphia: Brunner-Routledge.

Walsh, F. (Ed.). (1999). *Spiritual resources in family therapy.* New York: Guilford.

Wang, C., Gonzalez, R., Milliron, K. J., Strecher, V. J., & Merajver, S. D. (2005). A randomized controlled trial of two strategies to facilitate the education and counseling process. *American Journal of Medical Genetics, 134A,* 66–73.

Wang, V. O. (2001). Multicultural genetic counseling: Then, now and in the 21st century. *American Journal of Medical Genetics, 106,* 208–215.

Wang, V. O., & Marsh, F. H. (1992). Ethical principles and cultural integrity in health care delivery: Asian ethnocultural perspectives in genetic services. *Journal of Genetic Counseling, 1*(1), 81–92.

Wright, L. M., Watson, W. L., & Bell, J. M. (1996). *Beliefs: The heart of healing in families and illness.* New York: Basic Books.

Wynne, L., Shields, C., & Sirkin, M. (1992). Illness, family theory, and family therapy: I. Conceptual issues. *Family Process, 31,* 3–18.

Chapter 7

Behavior Genetics, Families, and Mental Health

Erica L. Spotts, Hilary Towers, and David Reiss

BEHAVIOR GENETIC RESEARCH EMPLOYS METHODS THAT CAN ENLIGHTEN the medical field in terms of both research and clinical practice. In this chapter, behavior genetic studies are used to show how behavior genetics can aid in explaining etiologies of behaviors and health issues. Theories and assumptions of different types of genetically informed studies are discussed. More specific ways in which genetically informative studies can enlighten us about the etiology of disorder, associations between relationships and disorder, and various other qualities of relationships and disorder, such as extreme ranges of symptoms, gender differences, and comorbidity are examined. Gene-environment correlations and interactions are also crucial for the understanding of development. Finally, the role of behavior genetics in treatment, intervention and prevention is discussed.

OVERVIEW OF BEHAVIOR GENETICS

Quantitative genetic theory, the more general theory on which behavior genetics rests, seeks to explain sources of individual differences within a population. For example, clinicians may be interested in individual differences in risk for depression or differences in personality features such as sociability or schizoid traits. The simplest form of this theory is that these individual differences result from environmental and genetic influences that combine in an additive way. Additivity is the simple addition of genetic and environmental effects based on how much of each is present. The simple theory does not assume that genetics and environment may combine in ways that are more complex. Individual differences, or statistically speaking, variance, can be partitioned into genetic and environmental portions, expressed in the formula $P = G + E$, where P is the phenotypic variance, G is the genetic portion of the variance, and E is the environmental portion of variance. Quantitative genetic theory further distinguishes environmental variation as either shared or nonshared. Shared environmental variation is a function of all those nongenetic factors that serve to make family members similar: for example, the common effect of neighborhood on all family members. Nonshared environmental variation encompasses those nongenetic aspects of the environment that serve to make family members different and include measurement error. An example of possible nonshared environmental influence would be when a mother consistently treats one child differently than the other.

A more complex form of quantitative genetic theory acknowledges that genetic and environmental influences could also combine in a nonadditive way. One example would be when genetic influences on depression are expressed in adverse family environments where there is marital strife and economic stress, but not in favorable ones. This phenomenon is known as genotype × environment ($G \times E$) interaction.

Quantitative genetic models assume five basic propositions: (1) Genetic differences among individuals in a defined population will influence behavioral differences among them. (2) Nongenetic (environmental) differences will also influence individual differences. (3) If genetic differences are important to the expression of a trait, similarity between members of a family should vary according to the degree of genetic relatedness between these members. For example, monozygotic (MZ) twins come from the same fertilized egg and therefore share the same genes, or are genetically identical. Adopted unrelated siblings have different biological parents and therefore are genetically unrelated (Plomin, DeFries, McClearn, & Rutter, 1997). (4) If shared environmental factors, or those factors that serve to make siblings similar, influence a certain trait, phenotypic similarity will be greater for relatives living together than for relatives living apart. For example, if shared environment within a family contributed to personality differences of children from different families, we would expect that MZ twins living together would be more similar to each other than those reared apart. (5) Finally, variation due to the nonshared environment is indicated by uniformly low similarity between siblings of all types.

Behavior genetic studies attempt to tease apart genetic and environmental influences on traits and behaviors. As we will explain, these studies can also investigate the relationship between two or more measures of behavior (e.g., depression and anxiety). These studies can estimate whether the observed association between these measures is due to common genetic or common environmental influences. Both types of studies use samples that include individuals of varying degrees of genetic relatedness. There are several kinds of genetically informed designs: the family design, the adoption design, and the twin design. Family designs rely on varying degrees of genetic relatedness of family members. For example, full siblings share an average of 50% of the same genes, whereas cousins share an average of 25% of the same genes. Therefore, if siblings show a higher similarity for a trait than cousins do, it can be inferred that this is due to genetic influence. However, as will be discussed, siblings and cousins may differ in their environmental similarity. Thus, caution is warranted in making inferences about genetic influences from this kind of comparison.

Adoption studies provide a unique way of disentangling genetic and environmental effects by using two different "types" of parents, so to speak. The biological parents of the adopted-away child serve as a marker of genetic influence, while the adoptive parents serve as a marker of environmental influences. Any correlation between the adopted child and the biological parents for a given trait is assumed to be due to genetic influences since the biological parent has had little if any contact with the child. Conversely, any association between the adoptive parent and the adopted child suggests an environmental contribution to the parent-child resemblance. For example, if schizoid personality traits were largely heritable, we would expect to see similarities between birth parents and adopted children, but no similarity between adopting parents and adopted children. There are several potential problems with adoption designs. First, any postnatal similarity between the biological mother and the adopted-away child might be due to in utero environmental conditions. Evidence for this possibility is inconclusive, as early studies provide reassuring data on this point (Kety, 1987), while more recent preliminary data suggest that maternal characteristics may be transmitted to offspring by the intrauterine route (Niederhofer & Reiter, 2000). Another important issue is that of selective placement, or placing the adoptive child in an environment similar to the environment of his or her biological parents. This can be assessed directly in studies that have information on both the biological and adoptive parents. If found, selective placement should be taken into account when interpreting genetic and environmental estimates.

Twin studies compare the resemblance of MZ and dizygotic (DZ) twins. MZ twins share 100% of their genes. DZ twins are similar to full siblings in that they come from two fertilized eggs and therefore share, on average, 50% of the same genes that account for differences among individuals. By comparing these two types of twins, estimates of genetic and environmental influences can be obtained. If genetic influences are at work, it is expected that the correlation between the twins will be higher for more genetically related siblings (MZ) than for less genetically related siblings (DZ). An estimate of genetic influence is referred to as a heritability estimate. If variation in a characteristic is influenced mainly by the shared environment, the correlations are expected to be the same for all twin types regardless of their genetic relatedness. Nonshared environmental influences are indicated in cases where MZ twin resemblances are not equal to 1. An example comes from a behavior genetic analysis of marital quality (Spotts, Neiderhiser, Towers, et al., 2004). The MZ correlation for total dyadic marital satisfaction was .32, much less than unity. As a result, 66 percent of the variance of this measure of marital satisfaction could be attributed to nonshared environmental factors. Analyses employing twin studies assume that environmental influences operate similarly across twin types. If this assumption is violated and environmental factors are more influential on MZ rather than DZ twins, estimates of genetic influences would be inflated. However, in most cases this assumption is upheld (Bouchard & Propping, 1993; Nettema, Neale, & Kendler, 1995), though there may be some forms of psychopathology that are exceptions (e.g., bulimia, smoking initiation; Kendler & Gardner, 1998).

Estimates of genetic and environmental influences from twin studies also assume no assortative mating for the parents of twins or for the twins themselves if they are adults. If present, assortative mating, or choosing one's mate for nonrandom reasons, can have serious implications for the findings of behavior genetic studies. For example, if schizoid men feel comfortable only with schizoid women, and are unlikely to marry women with other personality types, estimates of genetic influence on schizoid qualities in children will be distorted. Usually, assortative mating is discussed in relation to how assortative mating of parents influences estimates obtained from their twin children. In such a case, it will inflate correlations between DZ twins while having no effect on MZ twins (MZ twins cannot become more genetically similar). Because DZ twins appear more similar, the heritability estimates will be deflated. Fortunately, correlations between spouses are usually relatively low: less than .30 for height and weight (Price & Vandenberg, 1980) and .10–.20 for personality characteristics (Vandenberg, 1972). Spouse correlations for factors such as education are higher ($r = .60$; Jensen, 1978). Assortative mating can also affect estimates obtained from the data of spouses, for example when one is looking at genetic influences on wife and husband reports of marital quality. If spouse selection is based upon genetically influenced traits, then the spouses of MZ twins should be more similar to each other than the spouses of DZ twins. As a result, MZ correlations would increase relative to DZ correlations for measures of spousal and dyadic characteristics. This would inflate heritability estimates and decrease nonshared environment estimates. If spouses choose mates based on environmentally influenced characteristics, then environmental estimates would be inflated with a consequent decrease in genetic effects. Research on the similarity of mate selection has shown that MZ twins do not seem to select more similar mates than do DZ twins, so it is unlikely that assortative mating will factor into analyses of dyadic constructs (Lykken & Tellegen, 1993).

The applications of behavioral genetic findings are extensive. In general it is important to examine the sources of genetic and environmental variation in specific characteristics. In the case of medical and psychological disorders, such analyses increase knowledge of their etiology. Shared environmental influences indicate environmental factors shared between the siblings—perhaps a shared rearing environment, or ongoing contact between the siblings—that are influential to a particular disorder. Behavioral genetic studies can put long-held assumptions to more stringent tests. For example, it has long been assumed that severe depression in a mother may disrupt her relationships with her children and, as a result, the children themselves become more likely to develop psychiatric disorders (Marchand & Hock, 1998; Radke-Yarrow, Cummings, Kuczynski, & Chapman, 1985; Simons, Lin, Gordon, Conger, & Lorenz, 1999; Whitbeck et al., 1992). However, the predominant environmental influence on depression is nonshared or sibling specific (Kendler, Neale, Kessler, Heath, & Eaves, 1993). A genetically informed finding of this kind requires a major change in the theory of simple effects of maternal depression. Nonshared environmental influences would suggest experiences that are unique to each sibling and result in dissimilar outcomes. Genetically informed research can also help to better inform our understanding of how relationships are associated with adjustment. For example, we can examine the genetic and environmental mechanisms underlying the links between depression and marital quality.

NATURE OF DISORDERS

Genetically informed research can play a crucial role, along with other methods, in elucidating the etiologies of behavioral problems and psychiatric disorders. Often, genetically informed data provides an important contribution to developing an etiological theory. It can indicate the broad domains in which more specific etiological mechanisms might be delineated.

Preliminary Weighting of Genetic and Environmental Influences

The first step in conducting genetically informed analyses is to identify portions of genetic and environmental influences accounting for differences among individuals on a particular behavior or trait. For example, the Virginia Twin Study of Adolescent Behavioral Development reported the main genetic and environmental effects on a range of behavioral disorders, including attention deficit/hyperactivity disorder, conduct disorder, and depression (Eaves et al., 1997) as the beginning of an exploration of the etiology of juvenile psychopathology. Indeed, in order to construct accurate etiological theories, it is important to know whether serious psychological disorders run in families because of environmental factors or genetic factors.

Analyses of this type have been useful in reexamining environmental influences that seem to play a major role in the evolution of psychopathology. For example, quality of parenting had typically been considered an environmental construct. However, twin studies have found substantial genetic influences on measures of parenting, as first reported by Rowe (1981, 1983). Rowe found evidence of genetic influences for parental warmth and shared environmental influences for parental control. Nonshared environmental factors also accounted for approximately half of the variance in the twins' perceptions of parental warmth and control. These findings have been replicated in child (Braungart, 1994), adolescent (Elkins, McGue, & Iacono, 1997; Goodman & Stevenson, 1989), and adult (Plomin, DeFries, & Fulker, 1988) samples. Other close relationships constituting the family environment have also been examined. For example, findings from a study of Swedish twin women and their families suggested that genetic influences are present for wife and husband reports of marital quality, though environmental influences do play a predominant role (Spotts, Neiderhiser, Towers, et al., 2004). Other studies have indicated that other "environmental" constructs like social support (Bergeman, Plomin, Pedersen, McClearn, & Nesselroade, 1990; Kessler, Kendler, Heath, Neale, & Eaves, 1994) and controllable life events (Plomin, Lichtenstein, Pedersen, McClearn, & Nesselroade, 1990) are in part genetically influenced. The most likely explanation for these findings is that a heritable trait, such as temperament or personality, influences the seemingly environmental phenomenon. For example, a child who is genetically predisposed to be passive and cooperative will elicit very different responses from his or her parents than a child who is inherently more aggressive. A similar pattern seems to occur in marriages, where the genetically influenced characteristics of one spouse affect the tone of the marriage to the extent that the other spouse's perceptions of the marriage are influenced (Spotts et al., 2005; Spotts, Neiderhiser, Towers, et al., 2004). As is explained below, these findings suggest that observed associations between environmental measures and psychopathology might be due, in part, to genetic influences that are common to both and cannot be explained by environmental mechanisms alone.

These simple analyses have also suggested the source of the environmental variation. As described earlier, genetically informed studies can identify two types of environmental variation: shared and nonshared. Shared environmental variation is attributable to all those nongenetic influences that serve to make siblings similar to each other. Nonshared environmental variation results from those influences that serve to make siblings different from each other. Traditionally, family studies have assessed only one sibling in a family because it was assumed that parental influences on each child would have similar effects. However, findings from behavior genetic studies have suggested otherwise. For example, when parents are asked about the extent to which they monitor their children, they report that they monitor both of their children similarly, but children report that their parents treat them quite differently (Reiss, Neiderhiser, Hetherington, & Plomin, 2000). As might be expected, the role of each type of environment is complex. For example, in family systems that include adolescents, shared environmental variation in sibling relationships is greater than in parent-child relationships, where nonshared environmental variation is greatest (Reiss et al., 2000). These genetically informed results draw attention to the symmetrical nature of sibling relationships. For example, anger and aggression by one sibling is highly likely to evoke anger and aggression from the other sibling. In this sense, the sibling environment of each is comparable or "shared." In contrast, parent-child relationships are responsive not only to the unique features of the child but also to the parents' own developmental history. Reciprocal relationships between spouses or between a parent and a sibling pair are unlikely to influence parenting. If these factors were important, then genetically informed studies of parenting would show more shared environmental influences. Many earlier studies reported that when variation in a particular construct was found to be the result of environmental factors, it was often of the nonshared variety (Plomin & Daniels, 1987). However, findings of more recent studies using more reliable measures have identified a number of constructs for which shared environmental variation is prominent as well (Reiss et al., 2000). What numerous findings of primarily nonshared environmental variation suggest is that the experiences most important to development are those that make siblings different. It is quite clear that two children in the same family do not necessarily develop similarly.

Findings of nonshared environment emphasize the importance of different experiences, which could be of several types: actual differential parenting from one's parents, perceived differential parenting, and relationships outside of the family of origin (e.g., peers, school, marriage). As children age, they become more independent and are likely to seek out their own experiences, which in turn are influential to their development. Studies showing increases over time in nonshared environmental variation in broad constructs such as personality and IQ lend support to this hypothesis (McCartney, Harris, & Bernieri, 1990). In addition, forthcoming results from analyses from the Twin Moms project (Reiss et al., 2001a, 2001b) reveal that one source of nonshared environmental variation in adult adjustment may well be the atmosphere created by the current family unit, or family environment (Towers, 2005). In these analyses, nonshared environmental variation in women's marital satisfaction was influenced by family cohesion and family conflict. While most studies assessing the link between family environment and environment have used retrospective self-reports of family of origin, this study indexed the family environment using a composite of reports of the women, their husbands, and their adolescent children. As such, this appears to be the first report to suggest that one aspect of the environment that may cause adult siblings to differ in terms of their marital satisfaction is differences that exist in their current family life.

Understanding Associations Among Variables

Results of analyses on single constructs are interesting in their own right, but they have led to more questions and complex analyses. Many "environmental" factors (that may be genetically influenced) have been phenotypically linked with various measures of adjustment. In terms of the etiology of a disease, one might wonder if there is an underlying genetic liability for these associations. Extending the simple model to more complex cases allows for an examination of just such a question by examining the covariance between two or more constructs.

Extensive research has been conducted on how environmental factors might influence and moderate various forms of adjustment and psychopathology. It is beyond the scope of this chapter to do a thorough review here. However, a common example would be that harsh and punitive parenting influences antisocial behavior in children (Patterson, DeBaryshe, & Ramsey, 1989). As detailed above, findings from genetically informed analyses of seemingly environmental measures call into question a purely environmental explanation, whether the trait being examined is normal or psychopathological in nature. As these analyses evolved, the logical next step was to see how associations between constructs were influenced genetically and environmentally. In this manner, we can get a better handle on how particular risk or protective factors might interact to lead to a particular outcome.

The idea that environmental constructs might influence illnesses by way of genetic mechanisms may at first seem paradoxical. However, as described previously in this chapter, constructs that have been traditionally thought of as environmental, such as life events and the quality of parenting, have been found to be influenced genetically. It is also well known that various forms of mental and physical illness have some degree of genetic origin. If both the environmental construct and the adjustment construct are genetically influenced to some degree, and are also correlated, then it is possible that the association will reflect genetic influences that are common to both. While there has been extensive use of this technique, only a few examples are mentioned here.

To return to the example of parenting and child behavior, genetically informed research has shown that associations between the quality of parenting and child outcome are not environmentally linked to the extent previously assumed. Rather, when such an association is found, the primary contributing factors are genetic influences, though there are some contributing environmental factors as well (Reiss et al., 2000). For example, nearly half of the associations between mother positivity and her children's sociability and autonomy are explained by the child's genetic influences (Reiss et al., 2000). These findings can be explained in two ways. Genetically influenced behaviors of the child may be eliciting a particular kind of parenting. It is also possible that the parent and child share genes that lead to positive parenting in the parent and positive behavior in the child.

The presence of good social support has long been associated with reduced rates of psychopathology. A study of Swedish twins who were either reared together or reared apart showed that the link between social support and depressive symptoms was influenced by genetic and nonshared environmental factors (Bergeman, Plomin, Pedersen, & McClearn, 1991). Further exploration of this association indicated that in many cases, the genetic and environmental factors that influence levels of support also have direct effects on depression during times of high stress, suggesting that environmental interpretations of the associations between social support and depressive symptoms may in fact be inaccurate (Kessler, Kendler, Heath, Neale, & Eaves, 1992).

Are Extreme Cases Variants of Normal Variability?

An important question for models of etiology concerns to what extent psychopathology is "merely the quantitative extreme of genetic and environmental factors operating dimensionally throughout the full range of normal variation in a population" (Deater-Deckard, Reiss, Hetherington, & Plomin, 1997, p. 515). In other words, are clinical levels of a disorder simply the upper end of a continuum of a cluster of behaviors, or are clinical levels indicative of a disorder that is etiologically distinct from what is considered to be the normal distribution of behaviors? For example, is mental retardation a quantitative extreme of normal IQ variation, or is it a distinct syndrome? Another often-debated example is whether Asperger's syndrome (Frith, 1991) is a disorder unto itself or is a high-functioning form of autism. Examples could be drawn from nearly every diagnosable form of disorder, particularly from psychopathology.

A quantitative genetic technique known as DF extremes analyses (DeFries & Fulker, 1985, 1988; DF comes from the names of the two authors) is useful in this regard. Simplistically, a DF analysis compares estimates of genetic and environmental influences from an extreme (i.e., clinical) group of a particular disorder with estimates from a group within a normal (i.e., nonclinical) range. Similarities in estimates between the two groups would suggest that the cluster of symptoms constitutes a continuum of symptoms ranging from mild to severe, rather than an etiologically distinct disorder. While not extensively used, several studies have utilized this technique on a variety of subjects.

Deater-Deckard and colleagues (1997) used these techniques to examine selected and unselected samples of internalizing and externalizing behaviors in an adolescent sample. For both types of behaviors, no significant differences in estimates between the selected and unselected portions of the sample were found. This implies that, at least for adolescents, the presentation of extreme behaviors is not a distinct disorder, but rather a higher concentration, so to speak, of symptoms that are present in the normal range of behaviors.

Rende, Plomin, Reiss, and Hetherington (1993) examined depressive symptomatology in adolescence and obtained findings suggesting differences between normal and extreme groups. While there was no significant difference in estimates of genetic influence for the two groups, there were significant differences in estimates of shared environmental variation. Shared environmental variation was present for the extreme group but was not found for the normal group. This suggests that there are environmental factors shared by adolescent siblings that play a role in the presentation of higher levels of depressive symptoms that do not play a role in the presentation of lower levels. In other words, experiences common to siblings in the same family played an etiological role in severe depressive disorder, but these same experiences had no role or were not present in the families of those with milder forms.

A study was conducted to examine whether specific language impairment in 2-year-olds is a distinct clinical syndrome, or if it is the low end of a continuum of language learning (Dale et al., 1998). The extreme group of the lowest 5% of the distribution on productive vocabulary was compared with the rest of the distribution. Findings suggested that heritabilities were significantly higher for the extreme group than for the total sample and that estimates of shared environmental influences were higher for the total sample than for the extreme group. These findings strongly suggest that severe language impairment, at least in young children, is etiologically distinct from milder forms of linguistic difficulties.

Another way to address the question of the continuity of symptoms is to use what is called a multiple threshold model (Neale & Cardon, 1992). This technique is similar conceptually to DF analysis in that it examines whether clinical levels of a disorder lie on the same continuum as nonclinical levels by estimating genetic and environmental influences on different levels of disorder classification. However, this model is able to accommodate more levels of classification than a DF analysis. For example, Kendler, Gardner, and Prescott (2001) divided panic disorder into three categories: Individuals either could be unaffected, could have reported the occurrence of a panic attack, or could have received a diagnosis of a broad to intermediate panic disorder. The best-fitting model suggested that these diagnostic dimensions were part of the same continuum of disorder.

It is clear that, at present, there is support for both models of liability. Findings like those of Deater-Deckard and Kendler lend support to the idea of a continuum of behaviors rather than etiologically and diagnostically distinct categories. On the other hand, the findings of Dale and of Rende show that in some cases extremes of behavior and disorder may stem from different sources than do behaviors in the normal range. It is likely that continued use of this method will yield results that vary not only by diagnostic method, but also by demographic characteristics (e.g., age, sex), all the while adding to our understanding of the boundaries between normal and clinical.

Gender Differences

Research exploring differences in genetic and environmental influences by gender is just beginning, mostly because such large sample sizes are required to ensure adequate power to detect sex differences. But why look at sex differences in the first place? First, there are often differences in rates of disorders between the sexes. For example, clinical and non-clinical depression is at least twice as common in females as it is in males (Kessler, McGonagle, et al., 1994), and other disorders, such as autism, are more prevalent in males (Burd, Fisher, & Kerbeshian, 1987). Some of the discrepancy in rates between the sexes may result from so-cially influenced differences. For example, the importance of social rela-tionships is emphasized differently for boys and girls; therefore relationships become more salient for females (Nolen-Hoeksema, 2000). As a result, relationship problems tend to have a greater impact on the mental health of women than on that of men. Sex differences might also be accounted for through genetic explanations that can be tested using genetically informed samples. Second, even if rates of a disorder are similar for males and females, the risk factors and processes underlying the disorder may differ by gender. Uncovering such differences could be helpful for prevention and treatment purposes.

In most cases, estimates of genetic and environmental estimates for rates of disorder do not seem to differ by gender. A study of mecha-nisms underlying a broad range of behavioral problems in juveniles found little evidence for differences in genetic and environmental con-tributions, with the exception of separation anxiety, which evidenced a higher genetic contribution for girls (Eaves et al., 1997). Differing rates of alcoholism for males and females, even across different definitions, were not explained by differing genetic influences (Prescott, Aggen, & Kendler, 1999), as was also the case with various definitions of panic disorder (Kendler, Gardner, et al., 2001). Several studies have exam-ined sex differences in major depression (MD) and depressive symp-toms with mixed results. Most studies show that genetic influences on depression do not differ by sex (e.g., Kendler & Prescott, 1999). How-ever, two studies have been unable to distinguish between models al-lowing for different genetic influences for men and women and models that set genetic effects equal (Bierut et al., 1999; Jansson et al., in press), leaving this question unresolved.

Gender differences in estimates of genetic and environmental influ-ences do seem to be relevant for the risk of different disorders. A por-tion of the risk factors for MD in adults were not shared by men and women (Kendler & Prescott, 1999). In other words, some of the genetic influence on risk for MD was different for men and women. A similar pattern of results was obtained for a range of definitions of alcoholism, where some sources of genetic influence overlapped for men and women, leaving some unique genetic influences operating separately by sex (Prescott et al., 1999). Unlike depression, genetic risk factors for panic disorder symptoms did not seem to differ for males and females (Kendler, Gardner, et al., 2001). Studies like these, then, can not only further understanding of the processes underlying disease, but can also enable further understanding of how diseases manifest differentially in males and females. Future research on the nature of the genetic factors that are different for males and females can only enhance our understanding of the origins and course of disease and aid in developing appropriate preventions and treatment.

Comorbidity

The co-occurrence, or comorbidity, of psychological disorders is seen more often than not (Kessler et al., 1996). Much research has already investigated the origins of comorbidity and it has been fairly well established that it is not due to artifacts caused by chance, help-seeking tendencies, or population sampling characteristics (Wittchen, 1996). Some overlap might be caused by redundant diagnostic criteria, but there is likely to be true overlap in disorders. A behavior genetic examination of the comorbidity of disorders can further examine why disorders co-occur and sharpens questions in the development of an etiologic model. For example, are two co-occurring disorders really two distinct disorders or are they part of a spectrum of disorders? Should a particular illness be considered differently when occurring alone and when co-occurring with another disorder? Nearly 75% of those who had been diagnosed with a lifetime prevalence of MD had also been diagnosed with another disorder at some point (Kessler et al., 1996). Do these people have the same kind of depression as those individuals who have never had another diagnosis? In fact, an important determinant of the severity of MD is whether or not the individual has been previously diagnosed with any other disorder or not, with prior diagnoses being associated with increased persistence and severity (Kessler et al., 1996). By examining the genetic and environmental influences on the covariation of two or more conditions, we can see if they are related and why. Genetic influences on the association would imply an underlying genetic predisposition to each disorder. Either the same genetic influences cause both disorders, or there is an underlying diathesis which, when triggered, can lead to either one disorder or the other, or both simultaneously. Environmental contributions to the covariance would suggest environmental causes for the overlap of both disorders.

The example of MD and generalized anxiety disorder (GAD) can be used to illustrate this technique. There has been some speculation that clinical depression and anxiety may be two sides of the same coin and, with an incidence of comorbidity of 58% between MD and anxiety disorders (Kessler et al., 1996), this speculation is not unwarranted. When lifetime risk for MD and GAD in women was examined, the genetic correlation between the two could not be distinguished from unity (Kendler, Neale, Kessler, Heath, & Eaves, 1992). In other words, all of the genetic factors that played a role in the lifetime prevalence for MD also played a role in the lifetime prevalence for GAD; there were no genetic influences acting independently on either disorder. On the other hand, the same study found that nonshared environmental factors had both common and unique influence on the lifetime prevalence of both disorders. These findings were replicated on data of one-year prevalence, rather than lifetime prevalence (Kendler, 1996). Taken together, these findings suggest that genetic influences are quite nonspecific in their effects on MD and GAD. It also suggests that in terms of genetic etiology, the two disorders are not distinguishable. It seems that environmental factors may, in large part, determine whether the disorder manifests itself as anxiety or depression. It should be reiterated, however, that these studies were conducted in women only. Processes may be different for men.

Of particular interest is a comparison of these studies on MD and GAD with another study using the same sample to examine the comorbidity of lifetime histories of a range of disorders including MD, GAD, phobias, panic disorder, alcoholism, and bulimia (Kendler, Walters, et al., 1995). Findings from this study strongly suggest that genetic and environmental influences on anxiety disorders are not homogenous. Phobia, panic disorder, and bulimia were linked by common genetic influences, while MD and GAD were linked to each other by a separate set of genetic influences. The only nonshared environmental influences that jointly influenced disorders were found for MD and GAD; disorder-specific nonshared environmental influences accounted for the remaining nonshared environmental variance.

How does this research provide new insight on comorbidity? First, these studies inform us whether two particular disorders co-occur by chance or not. One would not expect this degree of overlapping genetic influences if the co-occurrence was by chance. Second, research such as this might reopen the debate about the nosology of disorders. Phenotypic research has already led to speculation on the classification of MD versus GAD. The results of these genetically informed studies of women only serve to further question diagnostic specificity, since all genetic influences contributed to the two disorders and a large portion of the nonshared environmental influences were also common to both disorders, making it clear that underlying mechanisms of both disorders are quite similar. At the least, MD and GAD might be considered as part of a spectrum of closely intertwined disorders. This research also emphasizes the specificity of other disorders by distinguishing between the cluster of disorders including MD and GAD, and another cluster that included panic disorder, phobia, and bulimia. Future research should address distinctions between individuals with pure, or noncomorbid, disorder and individuals with comorbid disorders, to address the question of whether or not these are manifestations of the same disease or are, in fact, separate disorders.

Genetic and Environmental Influences Over Time

From a developmental and clinical standpoint, it is of interest to examine processes over time. Some risk factors may be important early in the course of an illness, whereas others may play a more prominent role later in the development of psychopathology. We can now ask and answer questions about changes in genetic and environmental influences at different points along the course of development. Are the same genetic and environmental risk factors present throughout life or throughout the course of a disorder? One might expect stability or change at particular times during the life course. For example, during a developmentally fluid time such as adolescence, one might expect that there would be a relatively large amount of genetic change that would coincide with the physical and emotional changes occurring at that time. At other points in time, such as midlife, one might expect either relatively stable development (at least less chaotic than adolescence) or changes in development as the result of environmental changes (e.g., relocation, childbearing). As is also the case with phenotypic research, genetically informed longitudinal studies are somewhat harder to come by because of the cost and effort required. Nonetheless, headway is being made.

Adolescence is typically characterized as a period of change. The Nonshared Environment in Adolescent Development project (NEAD; Reiss et al., 2000) examined such changes at two points during adolescence, with a third wave of data collection now completed (Neiderhiser, 2002). In brief, genetic influences were most important to the stability of adolescent adjustment measures such as antisocial behavior and depression, while genetic and, to a lesser extent, nonshared environmental factors influenced change over time in these adjustment measures. In other words, adjustment during adolescence is marked by a period of changes in the expression of genetic and nonshared environmental influences. Relationships during adolescence exhibit a different pattern of stability and change. Genetic influences are important for stability in parenting over time, particularly for negative parenting. These findings suggest that parents are consistently responding to stable genetically influenced characteristics of their children. Shared environmental influences are also important for parenting stability, especially of positive parenting, suggesting a stable family tone. Other studies employing more complex modeling have examined more time points over the course of adolescence. Simplex modeling allows one to examine not only the genetic and environmental influences that are constant throughout the course of development, but also allows one to estimate the genetic and environmental "innovations" that occur at each new time of measurement. For example, Australian researchers examined personality traits longitudinally at ages 12, 14, and 16 (Gillespie, Evans, & Martin, 2001). They found that for personality characteristics as measured by the Eysenck Personality Questionnaire, not only did the same genetic influences operate on personality throughout this time span, but there were also new genetic influences occurring at the ages of 12 and 14. A different picture emerged for nonshared environmental influences in that different environmental factors were salient at different ages rather than being constant. Analyses such as these help to clarify the role of genetically controlled changes in development while also describing how environmental factors also play a role.

When examining the course of a particular disorder, one typically is concerned with onsets, remissions, and any change in severity over time. Genetically informed research is just beginning to address these issues. It seems likely that depressive symptoms in adulthood are partially the result of enduring, heritable characteristics of temperament (Kendler et al., 1994), but this is not to say that there are not vulnerabilities and risk factors that also play an important role in the onset of depression. Identifying vulnerabilities to particular disorders is important for prevention efforts. Kendler has found that almost all of the association between neuroticism (emotional instability and vulnerability to stress) and MD is due to genetic factors in a sample of adult twin women (Roberts & Kendler, 1999). Additionally, the genetic contributions to neuroticism account for almost half of the variance of MD. What this implies is that the genetic vulnerability for MD may be manifested largely as a personality characteristic. This is an important step on the way to identifying risk factors for various forms of psychopathology. Other research on vulnerabilities suggests that genetic factors may play a role in the risk of onset of major depressive disorder by increasing an individual's sensitivity to the depressogenic effect of stressful life events (Kendler, Kessler, et al., 1995). There is an interaction between genetic risk for MD and the way that stressful life events are associated with MD (Kendler, Thornton, & Gardner, 2001). For those with low genetic risk, there is a decline in the association between stressful life events and the risk for depression as the number of depressive episodes increases, suggesting that over time, smaller amounts of environmental stress are required to predict the onset of a depressive episode. This is not the case for those at high risk for depression. For them, environmental stressors do not seem to be as important in triggering an episode; the genetic risk is sufficient.

In short, research seems to be suggesting that genetic influences are important to both creating a sensitivity to the environment and influencing exposure to the environment (Kendler, 1998). Of course, much more research needs to be done to more completely specify the pathways leading to the onset of a disorder, as well as predictors of severity and relapse.

Interplay of Genes and Environment

Thus far we have discussed the main effects of genetic and environmental influences. But might not genetic and environmental factors interact with each other to create outcomes? In fact they do. Two ways that this might occur are discussed in this section: gene-environment (GE) interaction and GE correlation.

GE interactions refer to the sensitivity of one's genotype to the environment, such that genetic propensities might be modified by environmental circumstances. The problem with assessing GE interaction in humans has been, and remains, the necessity of isolating a group of individuals with a genetic propensity toward a particular behavior, some of whom have experienced a certain type of environment, others of whom have not. In animal experiments, researchers can breed strains of animals that are uniform for the genes that influence particular behaviors. Samples of these strains can by randomly assigned to different environments. Sometimes two different strains are assigned so that each strain experiences the same favorable and unfavorable environment, a process called cross-fostering. This design can only be roughly approximated in humans. In fact, some of the most useful information obtained concerning the potential relevance of early rearing environment to gene expression has come from rearing experiments using nonhuman primates (Suomi, 2000). This is because, in addition to the ethical issue cited above, most Old World monkeys (e.g., rhesus) and chimps share between 90 and 99% of their genes with human beings, depending on the species. This means that while the analogy is not perfect, animal models of the mechanisms underlying biological/gene-behavioral links constitute an indispensable part of human research—including research aimed at illuminating family processes.

A series of animal studies shows biological evidence of strong associations between serotonergic functioning and highly aggressive behavior of a group of preadolescent rhesus monkeys (Champoux, Higley, & Suomi, 1997; Mehlman et al., 1994). Low levels of a particular serotonin metabolite (5-HIAA) in the cerebrospinal fluid (CSF) of these monkeys are highly predictive of certain patterns of extremely aggressive and often deadly behaviors (Mehlman et al., 1994). Furthermore, individual differences in rhesus monkey levels of 5-HIAA are genetically influenced (Higley et al., 1993). Research suggests an identical biological mechanism that may account for acts of aggression in human children and adults (Brown, Linnoila, & Goodwin, 1990; Kruesi, 1989; Kruesi et al., 1990; Linnoila et al., 1983; Mann, Arango, & Underwood, 1990).

What is most interesting is the moderating effect of early family rearing environment on this well-documented association between rhesus monkeys' genetic propensity toward low CSF 5-HIAA levels and their aggressive behaviors (Bennett et al., 1998). The development of a secure attachment pattern with the mother is a critical factor in determining the expression of a monkey's genetic risk toward aggression. For instance, having a short version of a transporter gene implicated in serotonergic activity led to adverse outcomes (e.g., depressed serotonergic functioning, increased alcohol consumption) for those monkeys reared by their peers, while being raised by their mothers seemed to serve as a buffer against these negative effects among monkeys with the same short version of the gene. In other words, the early rearing environment (family environment, if you will) moderates the effects of this transporter gene. These findings suggest, among other things, a more complex role of the early family environment in the biological and genetic processes involved in human functioning than is commonly admitted. As has been stated by a prominent researcher in reference to the above findings, "It is hard to imagine that the situation would be any less complex for humans" (Suomi, 2000, p. 253). The analogy, again, is not perfect—rarely do we come across a child raised by his or her peers. The point is that having a genetic propensity toward a particular behavior does not mean that expression of that behavior is necessary—the environment can moderate the effects of genes. Knowledge of an individual's genotype (a not-too-distant prospect), combined with early intervention at the level of the family environment, may well prove to be a critical combination. However, it should also be emphasized that knowing a person's genotype in no way allows us to know the person's outcome.

While animal experiments are certainly better suited to assess specific GE interactions, numerous human studies have demonstrated the usefulness of adoption and twin designs for uncovering GE interactions among humans (Bohmen, 1996; Cadoret et al., 1996; Tienari et al., 1994; Tsuang, Stone, & Faraone, 2001). Many focus on psychiatric illnesses like schizophrenia (Tienari et al., 1994; Tsuang et al., 2001; see Chapter 16, this volume) or antisocial personality disorder (Bohmen, 1996). The basic premise of most of these studies is that children adopted at a young age into a new environment, or home, come with a genetic history (usually indexed via the psychiatric status of their biological parent). If the environment is capable of either constraining or modifying one's genetic tendencies, then it would be expected that the developmental trajectories of individuals with the same genetic propensities (toward antisocial behavior, for example) differ as a function of whether they are placed in a supportive or a disruptive adoptive home. For example, depression spectrum disease is a form of MD characterized by families in which male relatives are alcoholics and female family members are depressed (Winokur, 1991). Several recent adoption studies have reported an interaction between women's genetic risk for alcoholism (defined by alcoholism in a biological parent) and an adverse environmental event, such as the adoptive family's low socioeconomic rural status, or pathology (Cadoret, 1995; Cadoret et al., 1996), in the onset of MD in adulthood. In other words, these studies suggest that adult women with a genetic predisposition to alcoholism who become depressed are those women who were placed, as infants, in adoptive homes characterized by environmental stress of some kind. Women with the same genetic risk who were placed in a home with few stresses simply do not express that genetic inclination to be severely depressed.

There are other examples of moderating effects in human samples. Turkheimer, Haley, Waldron, D'Onofrio, and Gottesman (2003) addressed the apparent paradox of previous findings from studies of IQ that (a) variability in twin and adoption studies has not been found to be attributed to shared environment and (b) intentional or incidental amelioration of impoverished environments (assumed to be a shared environment effect) appears to have a great effect. Their analyses showed that the heritability of IQ in children varied by socioeconomic status, specifically that heritability was higher in middle-class families than it was in more impoverished families. Therefore, environmental changes for lower-class children will have a more marked effect than might changes in environments for less impoverished children. Similar studies support these findings (Purcell, 2001; Rowe, Jacobson, & Van den Oord, 1999). Jenkins, Rasbash, and O'Connor (2000) also dealt with the common finding of little shared environmental influence, but in a different way, by examining whether shared environmental factors moderated nonshared environmental effects. The extent to which parents parented each of their children differently, either positively or negatively, varied as a function of socioeconomic status and marital dissatisfaction for children aged 4 to 11 years. Heath, Eaves, and Martin (1998) examined the heritability of depression as a function of marital status in a sample of women. They found that married women have a lower genetic liability for depression than nonmarried women (Heath et al., 1998). Caspi and colleagues (2002) have extended examinations of genetic influences to include specific genetic markers, with fruitful results. Research has shown that the *MAOA* gene moderates the effects of child abuse on later childhood externalizing behavior. In another prospective study, this group found that a functional polymorphism in the promoter region of the serotonin transporter (5-HTT) gene moderated the influence of stressful life events on depression (Caspi et al., 2003). This last finding has been replicated a number of times (Grabe, et al., 2005; Kaufman et al., 2004; Kendler, Kuhn, Vittum, Prescott, & Riley, 2005).

GE correlations are also an important way to think about how genes and the environment might work together. A GE correlation is simply a correlation between a genotype and the environment to which the genotype is exposed. There are three ways that a genotype and an environment can be correlated: passively, evocatively, and actively (Plomin, DeFries, & Loehlin, 1977; Scarr & McCartney, 1983). Passive GE correlation refers to the transmission of both genes and environment from parents to their children. For example, parents who are very warm and outgoing may not only pass on those genetically influenced tendencies but may also provide an environment that fosters warm, outgoing behavior in the child. Evocative GE correlation refers to environments that are evoked by the child's genotype. To again use the example of warm and outgoing behavior, a child who exhibits these characteristics will tend to elicit pleasant responses from others. Finally, active GE correlation occurs when children actively select environments that are correlated with their genotype. A warm and outgoing child will most likely seek out other children who are also warm, rather than children who tend toward more negative behaviors. Although evocative and active GE correlations are distinct conceptually, they are difficult to disentangle empirically. Scarr (Scarr, 1992; Scarr & McCartney, 1983) has delineated a developmental theory incorporating passive, evocative, and active GE correlations. This theory predicts that passive GE correlation would be more apparent in infancy than in later childhood and adolescence. While infants are able to elicit some environmental responses, for the most part they must make do with the environment provided by their caregivers. As children develop cognitively and physically throughout childhood and adolescence, they are increasingly able to act upon the environment and seek out environments that suit them. At this point, evocative and active GE correlations would predominate over passive GE correlations.

GE correlations might account for change over time. Previous examinations of this topic have found some support for this theory, in that reactive and evocative correlations appeared only in later childhood and not in infancy; only passive effects were present in infancy (Plomin & DeFries, 1985; Plomin et al., 1988). Evocative GE correlations in the Colorado Adoption Project (CAP) have also been found for externalizing behaviors from ages 7 to 12 (O'Connor, Deater-Deckard, Fulker, Rutter, & Plomin, 1998). In contrast to Scarr's theory, passive effects do not seem to decrease over the course of childhood, at least in the CAP sample (Hershberger, 1994). An examination of GE correlations from ages 1 through 12 yielded little support for Scarr's theory, though the presence of GE correlations did vary by the construct examined (Spotts & Neiderhiser, 2003).

What is most important to take away from the literature on moderating effects of environment on genes is that genes and genetic influences are not deterministic and do not seal one's fate. If anything, this research provides hope of finding ways to moderate the genetic effects of many disorders as a therapeutic intervention. Ironically, the first available techniques for moderating genetic influences may be drawn from the field of family therapy, not gene therapy.

INTERVENTION, PREVENTION, AND TREATMENT

It is all well and good that the genetic and environmental influences on particular phenotypes can be estimated. But how is this helpful? Silberg and Rutter (2002) have discussed the implications of nature-nurture interplay, specifically as to how this interplay relates to the risks encountered by children who are exposed to depressed parents. Some of the implications that are drawn are relevant to psychopathology in general and are worth highlighting here. The first is that genetic mediation accounts for some of the risks to children associated with parental psychopathology. In other words, children may be more at risk for developing psychopathology if they have parents with a disorder because the parents transmit some of their genes to their child. The second implication is that the findings of GE correlations and interactions emphasize the importance of indirect genetic effects. Genetic influences may make it more likely for an individual to be exposed to high-risk environments or to be more sensitive to such environments. Such findings imply that genetic effects are open to environmental manipulation. This point is particularly important to remember when every day the popular media reports that another gene has been found for one disorder or another. What is often forgotten is not only that these genes account for a small portion of the variance of any given phenotype, but they can also be moderated by environmental effects, so having a gene is not equivalent to having the disease.

Third, many genetic effects seem to operate through personality characteristics of one kind or another. For example, genetic influences on marital quality are accounted for by optimistic and aggressive aspects of personality (Spotts et al., 2005), and neuroticism accounts for approximately half of the variance in MD (Roberts & Kendler, 1999). While this was not extensively discussed in this chapter, it is an important point for consideration. In nongenetic studies, childhood personality characteristics are phenotypically associated with outcomes in adulthood (Caspi, 1987) and have been implicated in a wide range of other health-related issues. More genetically informed research should be conducted to better understand the mechanisms underlying the role of temperament and personality in human well-being. A fourth point is that genetic studies have been very informative in providing rigorous testing of environmental assumptions and mediation, as discussed in the first section of the chapter. The implication is that genetic studies can aid us in beginning to sort out true environmental risks from those that are, in fact, genetic risks, thus helping to inform the effectiveness of prevention and intervention.

A fifth implication is that one cannot assume that psychopathological risks to children associated with one disorder are not derived from an associated comorbid disorder. In other words, one cannot assume that the alleviation of the symptoms of the primary disorder in the parent will remove all risk factors for the child. More specific genetically informed research will enable more precise specification of the origins of risk, thereby improving chances of effective prevention and intervention.

Finally, in conjunction with the fifth point, we need to question how we intervene with individuals at risk. A child with a depressed mother is at risk in several ways. Not only has the child potentially inherited genetic predispositions to depression or other disorders, but the child is also situated in a risky environment as the result of the mother's psychopathology (a GE correlation). Not only should prevention and intervention be conducted at the level of the child but perhaps intervention should also take place higher in the family by also intervening at the level of the parent to alleviate as much risk as possible. To effectively do this, more research is needed to further define how genes and environment correlate and interact to create risky environments.

The discussion presented by Silberg and Rutter (2002) emphasizes the importance of considering the whole—the person, his genes, his environment, and the general milieu that results from the cumulative effects of each of these domains. This kind of comprehensive approach, of course, makes research not only more challenging but also rife with possibilities. This chapter, for example, has alluded to familiar findings that interpersonal relationships are important correlates of psychopathology. However, genetic research has questioned whether the mechanisms accounting for these associations are purely psychosocial. This new research must more completely address the issue of how interpersonal relationships and adjustment are associated. For example, there may be an underlying genetic liability that causes both dysfunctional relationship quality and poor mental health. There may be a third, undisclosed, factor that influences both relationship quality and mental health, creating the semblance of a causal association. Other research might address the question of extremes in relationships. It will be interesting to investigate the etiology of particularly poor relationships.

Genetic studies can enlighten us about the etiology of particularly poor relationships and whether they are at the severe end of a continuum of relationship quality, or if they are substantively different from "normal" relationships. These studies will also be able to identify whether pathways between relationships and adjustment differ for extreme relationships and relationships within the normal range. Over 10 years ago, the NEAD study began to explore the associations between parent-child, sibling, and marital relationships and adjustment in a sample of adolescents. Later, the Twin Moms study (Reiss et al., 2001a, 2001b) continued where NEAD left off by examining parenting, marital quality, and adjustment in a sample of adult women and their families. Recent analyses using the Twin Moms sample examined associations between marital quality, social support, and depressive symptoms in adult women (Spotts, Neiderhiser, Ganiban, et al., 2004). Findings indicated marital quality and social support explained similar portions of depressive symptom variance, while social support accounted for variance beyond that accounted for by marital quality. Associations between interpersonal variables and mental health were accounted for largely by nonshared environmental influences, though genetic factors played a modest role, particularly in independent associations between social support and depressive symptoms. What should be emphasized is that marital quality was linked to depressive symptoms primarily through nonshared environmental factors, while social support was linked to depressive symptoms primarily through genetic factors. These findings emphasize the specificity of different aspects of relationships on outcomes. Future analyses stemming from this research will examine these interpersonal factors as they are associated with other forms of female adjustment in an effort to better understand how relationships and adjustment are linked.

This chapter was intended to briefly discuss how behavior genetic research can inform the health community. Clearly, genetically informed analyses are crucial for a complete understanding of disorder in humans. Future research using such techniques can only allow health professionals to better serve their clients and communities.

REFERENCES

Bennett, A. J., Lesch, K. P., Heils, A., Long, J., Lorenz, J., Shoaf, S. E., et al. (1998). Serotonin transporter gene variation, strain, and early rearing environment affect CSF 5-HIAA concentrations in rhesus monkeys (Macaca mulatta). *American Journal of Primatology, 45,* 168–169.

Bergeman, C. S., Plomin, R., Pedersen, N. L., & McClearn, G. E. (1991). Genetic mediation of the relationship between social support and psychological well-being. *Psychology and Aging, 6*(4), 640–646.

Bergeman, C. S., Plomin, R., Pedersen, N. L., McClearn, G. E., & Nesselroade, J. R. (1990). Genetic and environmental influences on social support: The Swedish adoption/twin study of aging: SATSA. *Journal of Gerontology: Psychological Science, 45*(3), 101–106.

Bierut, L. J., Heath, A. C., Bucholz, K. K., Dinwiddie, S. H., Madden, P. A. F., Statham, D. J., et al. (1999). Major depressive disorder in a community-based twin sample: Are there different genetic and environmental contributions for men and women? *Archives of General Psychiatry, 56,* 557–563.

Bohmen, M. (1996). Predispositions to criminality: Swedish adoption studies in retrospect. In G. R. Bock & J. A. Goode (Eds.), *Genetics of criminal and antisocial behavior, CIBA Foundation Symposium 194* (pp. 99–114). Chichester, UK: Wiley.

Bouchard, T. J., & Propping, P. (1993). *Twins as tools of behavioral genetics.* New York: Wiley.

Braungart, J. M. (1994). Genetic influence on "environmental" measures. In J. C. DeFries, R. Plomin, & D. W. Fulker (Eds.), *Nature and nurture during middle childhood* (pp. 233–248). Cambridge: Blackwell.

Brown, G. L., Linnoila, M., & Goodwin, F. K. (1990). Clinical assessment of human aggression and impulsivity in relation to biochemical measures. In H. M. Van Praag, R. Plutchik, & A. Apter (Eds.), *Violence and suicidality: Perspectives in clinical and psychobiological research* (pp. 184–217). New York: Brunner/Mazel.

Burd, I., Fisher, W., & Kerbeshian, J. (1987). A prevalence study of pervasive developmental disorder in North Dakota. *Journal of the American Academy of Child and Adolescent Psychiatry, 26,* 700–703.

Cadoret, R. J. (1995). Familial transmission of psychiatric disorders associated with alcoholism. In H. Begleiter (Ed.), *Alcohol and alcoholism* (pp. 70–81). New York: Oxford University Press.

Cadoret, R. J., Winokur, G., Langbehn, D., Troughton, E., Yates, W. R., & Stewart, M. A. (1996). Depression spectrum disease I: The role of gene-environment interaction. *American Journal of Psychiatry, 153*(7), 892–899.

Caspi, A. (1987). Personality in the life course. *Journal of Personality and Social Psychology, 53*(6), 1203–1213.

Caspi, A., McClay, J., Moffitt, T. E., Mill, J., Martin, J., Craig, I. W., et al. (2002). Role of genotype in the cycle of violence in maltreated children. *Science, 297*, 851–854.

Caspi, A., Sugden, K., Moffitt, T. E., Taylor, A., Craig, I. W., Harrington, H., et al. (2003). Influence of life stress on depression: Moderation by a polymorphism in the 5-HTT Gene. *Science, 301*(5631), 386–389.

Champoux, M., Higley, J. D., & Suomi, S. J. (1997). Behavioral and physiological characteristics of Indian and Chinese-Indian hybrid rhesus macaque infants. *Developmental Psychobiology, 31*, 49–63.

Dale, P. S., Simonoff, E., Bishop, D. V. M., Eley, T. C., Oliver, B., Price, T. S., et al. (1998). Genetic influences on language delay in two-year-old children. *Nature Neuroscience, 1*(4), 324–328.

Deater-Deckard, K., Reiss, D., Hetherington, E. M., & Plomin, R. (1997). Dimensions and disorders of adolescent adjustment: A quantitative genetic analysis of unselected samples and selected extremes. *Journal of Child Psychiatry and Psychology and Allied Disciplines, 38*(5), 515–525.

DeFries, J. C., & Fulker, D. W. (1985). Multiple regression analysis of twin data. *Behavior Genetics, 15*, 467–473.

DeFries, J. C., & Fulker, D. W. (1988). Etiology of deviant scores versus individual differences. *Acta Genetica, 37*, 205–216.

Eaves, L. J., Silberg, J. L., Meyer, J. M., Maes, H. H., Simonoff, E., Pickles, A., et al. (1997). Genetics and developmental psychopathology: 2. The main effects of genes and environment on behavioral problems in the Virginia Twin Study of Adolescent Behavioral Development. *Journal of Child Psychiatry and Psychology and Allied Disciplines, 38*(8), 965–980.

Elkins, I. J., McGue, M., & Iacono, W. G. (1997). Genetic and environmental influences on parent-son relationships: Evidence for increasing genetic influence during adolescence. *Developmental Psychology, 33*(2), 351–363.

Frith, U. (1991). *Autism and Asperger's syndrome*. Cambridge, UK: Cambridge University Press.

Gillespie, N. A., Evans, D. M., & Martin, N. G. (2001). *Genetic simplex modeling of personality in adolescent Australian twins*. Paper presented at the Behavior Genetic Association Conference, Cambridge, UK.

Goodman, R., & Stevenson, J. (1989). A twin study of hyperactivity. II. The aetiological role of genes, family relationships and perinatal adversity. *Journal of Child Psychiatry and Psychology and Allied Disciplines, 30*, 691–709.

Grabe, H. J., Lange, M., Wolff, B., Volzke, H., Lucht, M., Freyberger, H. J., et al. (2005). Mental and physical distress is modulated by a polymorphism in the 5-HT transporter gene interacting with social stressors and chronic disease. *Molecular Psychiatry, 10,* 220–224.

Green, J., Richards, M., Murton, F., Statham, H., & Hallowell, N. (1997). Family communication and genetics: The case of hereditary breast and ovarian cancer. *Journal of Genetic Counseling, 6,* 45–60.

Heath, A. C., Eaves, L. J., & Martin, N. G. (1998). Interaction of marital status and genetic risk for symptoms of depression. *Twin Research, 1,* 119–122.

Hershberger, S. L. (1994). Genotype-environment interaction and correlation. In J. C. DeFries, R. Plomin, & D. W. Fulker (Eds.), *Nature and nurture during middle childhood* (pp. 281–294). Cambridge, UK: Blackwell.

Hettema, J. M., Neale, M. C., & Kendler, D. S. (1995). Physical similarity and the equal environments assumption in twin studies of psychiatric disorders. *Behavior Genetics, 25*(4), 327–335.

Higley, J. D., Thompson, W. T., Champoux, M., Goldman, D., Hasert, M. F., Kraemer, G. W., et al. (1993). Paternal and maternal genetic and environmental contributions to CSF monoamine metabolites in rhesus monkeys (*Macaca mulatta*). *Archives of General Psychiatry, 50,* 615–623.

Jansson, M., Gatz, M., Berg, S., Johansson, B., Malmberg, B., McClearn, G. E., et al. (2004). Gender differences in heritability of depressive symptoms in the elderly.*Psychological Medicine, 34,* 471–479.

Jenkins, J. M., Rasbash, J., & O'Connor, T. G. (2000). *Understanding the sources of differential parenting: The role of child and family level effects.* Paper presented at the Society for Research in Child Development, Minneapolis, MN.

Jensen, A. R. (1978). Genetic and behavioral effects of nonrandom mating. In R. T. Osborne, C. E. Noble, & N. Weyl (Eds.), *Human variation: The biopsychology of age, race and sex* (pp. 51–105). New York: Academic Press.

Kaufman, J., Yang, B., Douglas-Palumberi, H., Houshyar, S., Lipschitz, D., Krystal, J. H., et al. (2004). Social supports and serotonin transporter gene moderate depression in maltreated children. *Proceedings of the National Academy of Sciences, 101*(49), 17316–17321.

Kendler, K. S. (1996). Major depression and generalized anxiety disorder: Same genes, (partly) different environments—revisited. *British Journal of Psychiatry, 168*(Suppl. 30), 68–75.

Kendler, K. S. (1998). Anna-Monika-Prize paper. Major depression and the environment: A psychiatric genetic perspective. *Pharmacopsychiatry, 31*(1), 5–9.

Kendler, K. S., & Gardner, C. O. J. (1998). Twin studies of adult psychiatric and substance dependence disorders: Are they biased by differences in the environmental experiences of monozygotic and dizygotic twins in childhood and adolescence? *Psychological Medicine, 28,* 625–633.

Kendler, K. S., Gardner, C. O. J., & Prescott, C. A. (2001). Panic syndromes in a population-based sample of male and female twins. *Psychological Medicine, 31*(6), 989–1000.

Kendler, K. S., Kessler, R. C., Walters, E. E., MacLean, C., Neale, M. C., Heath, A. C., et al. (1995). Stressful life events, genetic liability, and onset of an episode of major depression in women. *American Journal of Psychiatry, 152*(6), 833–842.

Kendler, K. S., Kuhn, J. W., Vittum, J., Prescott, C. A., & Riley, B. (2005). The interaction of stressful life events and a serotonin transporter polymorphism in the prediction of episodes of major depression: A replication. *Archives of General Psychiatry, 62,* 529–535.

Kendler, K. S., Neale, M. C., Kessler, R. C., Heath, A. C., & Eaves, L. J. (1992). A population-based twin study of major depression in women: The impact of varying definitions of illness. *Archives of General Psychiatry, 49,* 257–266.

Kendler, K. S., Neale, M. C., Kessler, R. C., Heath, A. C., & Eaves, L. J. (1993). A longitudinal twin study of 1-year prevalence of major depression in women. *Archives of General Psychiatry, 50*(11), 843–852.

Kendler, K. S., & Prescott, C. A. (1999). A population-based twin study of lifetime major depression in men and women. *Archives of General Psychiatry, 56*(1), 39–44.

Kendler, K. S., Thornton, L. M., & Gardner, C. O. J. (2001). Genetic risk, number of previous depressive episodes, and stressful life events in predicting onset of major depression. *American Journal of Psychiatry, 158*(4), 582–586.

Kendler, K. S., Walters, E. E., Neale, M. C., Kessler, R. C., Heath, A. C., & Eaves, L. J. (1995). The structure of the genetic and environmental risk factors for six major psychiatric disorders in women: Phobia, generalized anxiety disorder, panic disorder, bulimia, major depression and alcoholism. *Archives of General Psychiatry, 52,* 374–383.

Kendler, K. S., Walters, E. E., Truett, K. R., Heath, A. C., Neale, M. C., Martin, N. G., et al. (1994). Sources of individual differences in depressive symptoms: Analysis of two samples of twins and their families. *American Journal of Psychiatry, 151*(11), 1605–1614.

Kessler, R. C., Kendler, K. S., Heath, A. C., Neale, M. C., & Eaves, L. J. (1992). Social support, depressed mood, and adjustment to stress: A genetic epidemiologic investigation. *Journal of Personality and Social Psychology, 62*(2), 257–272.

Kessler, R. C., Kendler, K. S., Heath, A. C., Neale, M. C., & Eaves, L. J. (1994). Perceived support and adjustment to stress in a general population sample of female twins. *Psychological Medicine, 24*(2), 317–334.

Kessler, R. C., McGonagle, K. A., Zhao, S., Nelson, C. B., Hughes, M., Eshleman, S., et al. (1994). Lifetime and 12-month prevalence of DSM-III-R disorder in the United States: Results from the National Comorbidity Survey. *Archives of General Psychiatry, 51,* 8–19.

Kessler, R. C., Nelson, C. B., McGonagle, K. A., Liu, J., Swartz, M., & Blazer, D. G. (1996). Comorbidity of DSM-III-R major depressive disorder in the general population: Results from the US National Comorbidity Survey. *British Journal of Psychiatry, 168*(Suppl. 30), 17–30.

Kety, S. S. (1987). The significance of genetic factors in the etiology of schizophrenia: Results from the nations study of adoptees in Denmark. *Journal of Psychiatric Research, 21,* 423–430.

Kruesi, M. J. (1989). Cruelty to animals and CSF 5-HIAA. *Psychiatry Research, 28,* 115–116.

Kruesi, M. J., Rapoport, J. L., Hamburder, S., Hibbs, E., Potter, W. Z., Lenane, M., et al. (1990). Cerebrospinal fluid monoamine metabolites, aggression, and impulsivity in disruptive behavior disorders of children and adolescents. *Archives of General Psychiatry, 47*, 419–426.

Linnoila, M., Virkkunen, M., Scheinin, M., Nuutila, A., Rimon, R., & Goodwin, F. K. (1983). Low cerebrospinal fluid 5-hydroxindoleacetic acid concentration differentiates impulsive from nonimpulsive violent behavior. *Life Sciences, 33*, 2609–2614.

Lykken, D. T., & Tellegen, A. (1993). Is human mating adventitious or the result of lawful choice? A twin study of mate selection. *Journal of Personality and Social Psychology, 65*(1), 56–68.

Mann, J. J., Arango, V., & Underwood, M. E. (1990). Serotonin and suicidal behavior. *Annals of the New York Academy of Science, 600*, 476–485.

Marchand, J. F., & Hock, E. (1998). The relation of problem behaviors in preschool children to depressive symptoms in mothers and fathers. *Journal of Genetic Psychology, 159*(3), 353–366.

McCartney, K., Harris, J. M., & Bernieri, F. (1990). Growing up and growing apart: A developmental meta-analysis of twin studies. *Psychological Bulletin, 107*, 226–237.

Mehlman, P. T., Higley, J. D., Faucher, I., Lilly, A. A., Taub, D. M., Vickers, J. H., et al. (1994). Low cerebrospinal fluid 5-hydroxindoleacetic acid concentrations are correlated with severe aggression and reduced impulse control in free-ranging primates. *American Journal of Psychiatry, 151*, 1485–1491.

Neale, M. C., & Cardon, L. R. (1992). *Methodology for genetic studies of twins and families*. Boston: Kluwer Academic.

Neiderhiser, J. M. (2002). *The Young Adult Sibling Study: An introduction.* Paper presented at the Behavior Genetics Association, Keystone, CO.

Niederhofer, H., & Reiter, A. (2000). Maternal stress during pregnancy, its objectivation by ultrasound observation of fetal intrauterine movements and child's temperament at 6 months and 6 years of age: A pilot study. *Psychological Reports, 86*(2), 526–528.

Nolen-Hoeksema, S. (2000). The role of rumination in depressive disorders and mixed anxiety/depressive symptoms. *Journal of Abnormal Psychology, 109*, 504–511.

O'Connor, T. G., Deater-Deckard, K., Fulker, D. W., Rutter, M., & Plomin, R. (1998). Genotype-environment correlations in late childhood and early adolescence: Antisocial behavior problems and coercive parenting. *Developmental Psychology, 34*(5), 970–981.

Patterson, G. R., DeBaryshe, B. D., & Ramsey, E. (1989). A developmental perspective on antisocial behavior. *American Psychologist, 44*, 329–335.

Plomin, R., & Daniels, D. (1987). Why are children in the same family so different from one another? *Behavioral and Brain Science, 14*, 373–427.

Plomin, R., & DeFries, J. C. (1985). *Origins of individual differences in infancy: The Colorado Adoption Project*. Orlando, FL: Academic Press.

Plomin, R., DeFries, J. C., & Fulker, D. W. (1988). *Nature and nurture during infancy and early childhood*. New York: Cambridge University Press.

Plomin, R., DeFries, J. C., & Loehlin, J. C. (1977). Genotype-environment interaction and correlation in the analysis of human behavior. *Psychological Bulletin, 84*(2), 309–322.

Plomin, R., DeFries, J. C., McClearn, G. E., & Rutter, M. (1997). *Behavioral genetics* (3rd ed.). New York: W.H. Freeman.

Plomin, R., Lichtenstein, P., Pedersen, N. L., McClearn, G. E., & Nesselroade, J. R. (1990). Genetic influence on life events during the last half of the lifespan. *Psychology and Aging, 5*(1), 25–30.

Prescott, C. A., Aggen, S., & Kendler, K. S. (1999). Sex differences in the sources of genetic liability to alcohol abuse and dependence in a population-based sample of US twins. *Alcoholism: Clinical and Experimental Research, 23*(7), 1136–1144.

Price, R. A., & Vandenberg, S. G. (1980). Spouse similarity in American and Swedish couples. *Behavior Genetics, 10*, 59–71.

Purcell, S. (2001). *Gene-by-gene interaction in twin and sib-pair analysis.* Paper presented at the Behavior Genetic Association Conference, Cambridge, UK.

Radke-Yarrow, M., Cummings, E. M., Kuczynski, L., & Chapman, M. (1985). Patterns of attachment in two- and three-year-olds in normal families and families with parental depression. *Child Development, 56*(4), 884–893.

Reiss, D., Neiderhiser, J. M., Hetherington, E. M., & Plomin, R. (2000). *The relationship code: Deciphering genetic and social influences on adolescent development.* Cambridge, MA: Harvard University Press.

Reiss, D., Pedersen, N. L., Cederblad, M., Lichtenstein, P., Hansson, K., Neiderhiser, J. M., et al. (2001a). Genetic probes of three theories of maternal adjustment: I. Recent evidence and a model. *Family Process, 40*(3), 247–259.

Reiss, D., Pedersen, N. L., Cederblad, M., Lichtenstein, P., Hansson, K., Neiderhiser, J. M., et al. (2001b). Genetic probes of three theories of maternal adjustment: II. Genetic and environmental influences. *Family Process, 40*(3), 261–272.

Rende, R., Plomin, R., Reiss, D., & Hetherington, E. M. (1993). Genetic and environmental influences on depressive symptomatology in adolescence: Individual differences and extreme scores. *Journal of Child Psychiatry and Psychology and Allied Disciplines, 34*(8), 1387–1398.

Roberts, R. D., & Kendler, K. S. (1999). Neuroticism and self-esteem as indices of the vulnerability to major depression in women. *Psychological Medicine, 29*, 1101–1109.

Rowe, D. C. (1981). Environmental and genetic influences on dimensions of perceived parenting: A twin study. *Developmental Psychology, 17*, 203–208.

Rowe, D. C. (1983). A biometrical analysis of perceptions of family environment: A study of twins and singleton sibling kinships. *Child Development, 54*, 416–423.

Rowe, D. C., Jacobson, K. C., & Van den Oord, E. J. (1999). Genetic and environmental influences on vocabulary IQ: Parental education as a moderator. *Child Development, 70*(5), 1150–1162.

Scarr, S. (1992). Developmental theories for the 1990's: Development and individual differences. *Child Development, 63*, 1–19.

Scarr, S., & McCartney, K. (1983). How people make their own environments: A theory of genotype-environment effects. *Child Development, 54,* 424–435.

Silberg, J. L., & Rutter, M. (2002). Nature-nurture interplay in the risks associated with parental depression. In S. H. Goodman & I. H. Gotlib (Eds.), *Children of depressed parents: Mechanisms of risk and implications for treatment* (pp. 13–36). Washington, DC: American Psychological Association.

Simons, R. L., Lin, K.-H., Gordon, L. C., Conger, R. D., & Lorenz, F. O. (1999). Explaining the higher incidence of adjustment problems among children of divorce compared with those in two-parent families. *Journal of Marriage and the Family, 61*(4), 1020–1033.

Spotts, E. L., Lichtenstein, P., Hansson, K., Neiderhiser, J. M., Pedersen, N. L., Cederblad, M., et al. (2005). Personality and marital satisfaction: A behavioral genetic analysis. *European Journal of Personality, 19*(3), 205–227.

Spotts, E. L., & Neiderhiser, J. M. (2003). The developmental trajectory of genotype-environment correlation: The increasing role of the individual in selecting environments. In S. Petrill, R. Plomin, J. C. DeFries, & J. K. Hewitt (Eds.), *Nature, nurture, and the transition to adolescence* (pp. 295–309). New York: Oxford University Press.

Spotts, E. L., Neiderhiser, J. M., Ganiban, J., Reiss, D., Lichtenstein, P., Hansson, K., et al. (2004). Accounting for depressive symptoms in women: A twin study of associations with interpersonal relationships. *Journal of Affective Disorders, 82*(1), 101–111.

Spotts, E. L., Neiderhiser, J. M., Towers, H., Hansson, K., Lichtenstein, P., Pedersen, N. L., et al. (2004). Genetic and environmental influences on marital relationships. *Journal of Family Psychology, 18*(1), 107–119.

Suomi, S. J. (2000). A biobehavioral perspective on developmental psychopathology: Excessive aggression and serotonergic dysfunction in monkeys. In A. J. Sameroff, M. Lewis, & S. M. Miller (Eds.), *Handbook of developmental psychopathology* (2nd ed., pp. 237–256). New York: Kluwer Academic/Plenum.

Tienari, P., Wynne, L. C., Moring, J., Lahti, I., Naarala, M., Sorri, A., et al. (1994). The Finnish adoptive family study of schizophrenia: Implications for family research. *British Journal of Psychiatry, 23*(Suppl. 164), 20–26.

Towers, H. (2005). *Marriages of twin sisters are different: Associations with husbank's characteristics and the family environment.* Unpublished manuscript, George Washington University.

Tsuang, M., Stone, W. S., & Faraone, S. V. (2001). Genes, environment and schizophrenia. *British Journal of Psychiatry, 178*(Suppl. 40), s18–s24.

Turkheimer, E., Haley, A., Waldron, M., D'Onofrio, B., & Gottesman, I. (2003). Socioeconomic status modifies heritability of IQ in young children. *Psychological Science, 14*(6), 623–628.

Vandenberg, S. G. (1972). Assortative mating, or who marries whom? *Behavior Genetics, 2,* 127–157.

Whitbeck, L. B., Hoyt, D. R., Simons, R. L., Conger, R. D., Elder, G. H., Lorenz, F. O., et al. (1992). Intergenerational continuity of parental rejection and depressed affect. *Journal of Personality and Social Psychology, 63*(6), 1036–1045.

Winokur, G. (1991). *Mania and depression: A classification of syndrome and disease.* Baltimore: Johns Hopkins University Press.

Wittchen, H. U. (1996). What is comorbidity—fact or artifact? *British Journal of Psychiatry, 168*(Suppl. 30), 7–8.

PART III

APPLICATIONS TO SPECIFIC GENETIC CONDITIONS

Chapter 8

Neurodegenerative Genetic Conditions

The Example of Huntington Disease

Janet K. Williams and Susan Sobel

THE RECOGNITION THAT A DISORDER LEADING TO DEMENTIA IS INHERited was reported by Dr. George Huntington in 1872 when he described a mother and daughter with hereditary chorea (Rushton, 1994). Huntington disease (HD), a progressive neurodegenerative disorder, not only robs the individual of healthy cognitive, mental, and motor function but also creates multiple challenges for the family. One is the recognition that because the inheritance is autosomal dominant, each offspring of a person with HD is at a 50% risk to inherit the gene mutation. Unlike other neurodegenerative conditions such as Alzheimer disease, whose genetic components are not all yet clearly identified, the specific genetic mutation for HD was identified in 1993.

Identification of the gene location and discovery of the gene mutation for HD led to the development of presymptomatic testing techniques for persons at risk for HD. These tests would allow at-risk persons to learn if they have the gene mutation and thus are likely to develop HD sometime in their adult years. This knowledge has not yet led to the discovery of new treatments or new strategies to slow, alter, or stop the progression of the disease (Myers, 2005; Rosenblatt, Ranen, Nance, & Paulsen, 1999). The experiences of persons who have considered or completed presymptomatic testing for HD provide important insights into family issues associated with discovery of genetic information for a familial neurodegenerative disorder.

DESCRIPTION OF HD

HD affects approximately 1 in 20,000 people in the United States. Most people have onset of symptoms during adulthood; approximately 10% of persons have onset of symptoms prior to age 20, and another 10% have onset after age 60 (Rosenblatt et al., 1999). HD is characterized by chorea, or involuntary movement of the arms and legs; and dementia, or progressive deterioration in cognition. Motor symptoms also include impairment of voluntary movements. Difficulty in speaking, swallowing, maintaining balance, and falls are common manifestations. Loss of cognitive function is reflected in loss of speed and flexibility in mental activities that progress to more global impairments in thinking and reasoning (Rosenblatt et al., 1999). People with HD lose their abilities to process information and use this information to make judgments. Depression, behavior changes, and personality symptoms cluster around the time of onset. While depression is the most common psychiatric disorder in HD, mania or obsessive-compulsive disorders are also typical findings. As the disease progresses to the final stage of the illness, some people may receive terminal care in their home, while others will require the services of a nursing home. Although medications may help control symptoms, there is currently no way to stop the progression of the disease. In general, people live 10–15 years after the time of diagnosis and die from complications most commonly caused by dysphagia, or choking, and subsequent aspiration pneumonia (Dubinsky, R., et al., 2004; Jorde, Carey, Bamshad, & White, 1999).

Genetics of HD

The location of the gene for HD was identified in 1983, making this disease one of the first autosomal dominant inherited disorders for which presymptomatic testing through linkage analysis was possible (Gussella et al., 1983). In 1993, the specific mutation was identified. This is an unstable trinucleotide (CAG) repeat in the *IT15* gene located on the short arm of chromosome 4 (Huntington's Disease Collaborative Research Group, 1993). Persons who are found to have an expanded trinucleotide repeat in the *IT15* gene of 40 trinucleotide units or more are expected to develop HD. In general, the higher the number of repeats, the earlier the age of onset (Andrew, Goldberg, & Hayden, 1997). Trinucleotide repeats that are less than 27 are within the normal range. Case studies of individuals with 36–39 repeats report that some of these persons develop HD symptoms, while others do not (Rubinsztein et al., 1996). Repeats in the intermediate range of 27–35 repeats have been found to be unstable during meiosis and are at risk to expand to a disease allele when passed on to offspring (Myers, 2005; Nance, 1996). This means that persons with 27–35 repeats are not likely to have HD themselves, but when the gene is passed on to their offspring, the size of the repeat may expand, and the offspring could have a gene mutation that is larger and could be in the abnormal range.

PRESYMPTOMATIC TESTING FOR HD

Shortly after the identification of the location of the HD gene, genetic testing protocols for HD were developed to integrate this new technology into clinical practice. Guidelines were developed to ensure that patients make a decision about testing based on informed consent and undergo mandatory counseling before testing. Testing for HD is restricted to people over 18 years of age, except when a pregnancy is involved (Went et al., 1994). The protocol for HD presymptomatic testing includes a minimum of three face-to-face visits in which a neurological examination is performed, informed consent issues are addressed, and discussion of the impact of normal or abnormal results is completed. The testing team generally includes physicians, advanced practice genetic nurses (nurses with a master's degree who have completed graduate-level genetics course work and clinical training), genetic counselors, and mental health professionals. Results are reported in a face-to-face visit with the genetic testing team. The protocol also recommends that a support person accompany the individual seeking testing throughout the presymptomatic testing process. This is consistent with the guidelines established by representatives of the International Huntington Association and the World Federation of Neurology Research Group on Huntington's Chorea, in which the companion is identified as a spouse, partner, family member, friend, social worker, or any person who has the confidence of the participant (Went et al., 1994).

Reasons for Seeking Testing

The majority of studies of individuals participating in presymptomatic testing for mutations in the gene causing HD have focused on the at-risk person. Reduction of uncertainty about one's future is one of the primary reasons participants give for wanting a gene test (Meissen, Mastromaurao, Kiely, McNamara, & Myers, 1991; Williams, Schutte, Evers, & Forcucci, 1999). Reasons given by those who seek testing include a need to end the uncertainty of not knowing the future, to have information on which to base a decision to marry or have children, and to make plans for the future. As Kessler (1994) points out, the ostensible reasons may not cover the actual psychological ones. It is hard to imagine how to prepare for information that is so monumental. With the exception of couples who want to decide on family planning, stated reasons seem to be "ephemeral fantasies" (p. 164). The desire to know the future with respect to this disease goes beyond what can be articulated. Perhaps for people whose family life has been characterized by anything but control, knowing one's state with respect to HD is expected to provide a sense of control, illusory as that may be. Approximately 10–15% of at-risk adults complete presymptomatic HD testing, which is much lower than originally predicted (Clarke & Flinter, 1996). One reason may be that those who complete testing may believe they can cope with the results, in contrast to those who avoid testing because they fear they cannot cope with the information (Codori, Hanson, & Brandt, 1994).

Testing Outcomes

Because of the depressive component of the illness, there has been concern for the potential for suicide after confirmation of presence of a gene mutation in a neurodegenerative disease for which there is no effective treatment. The range of HD deaths reported to result from suicide is 0.5–12.7%, being four to five times the 1.0–1.5% suicide rate for the general U.S. population. A review of worldwide experience of HD testing centers reported that 26 (0.57%) of 4,527 tested persons either had committed suicide or had made a suicide attempt (Almqvist et al., 1999).

Negative psychosocial outcomes have been reported both in those who are found to have the gene mutation and in those who are not. Individuals with mutations in the HD disease range have reported emotional numbness, sadness, depression, anxiety, and anger (Codori & Brandt, 1994; Decruyenaere et al., 1996). Some persons with a mutation in the HD gene may employ a denial type of coping strategy (DudokdeWit et al., 1998). A longitudinal study, assessing the psychological effects of presymptomatic testing over a 7–10 year period, reported that pessimism in persons with the gene mutation and in their partners increased as they approached the age of onset (Timman, Roos, Maat-Kievit, & Tibben, 2004). Emotional distress is also reported in some persons with no gene mutation. Approximately 10% of those with a decreased risk, based on linkage studies conducted prior to the identification of the specific gene mutation, experience psychological difficulties in coping with their new status 2–12 months after learning the outcome (Huggins et al., 1992). Some who receive normal test results report feeling guilty, as if they have betrayed their families. Other difficulties include disappointment that the test did not resolve prior problems, such as failed attempts to change poor eating, exercise habits, or marital difficulties (Codori & Brandt,

1994; van't Spijker & ten Kroode, 1997; Wahlin et al., 1997). In addition, those who receive normal test results have described difficulties in adjusting their own expectations for future health, planning for financial security, and redefining their relationships to other family members whose risk status is not known (Williams, Schutte, Evers, & Holkup, 2000).

Some information has been reported regarding the psychological consequences of presymptomatic HD genetic information on family members. Presymptomatic testing for HD has been shown to have an impact on a marriage, but partners of people with HD gene mutations are frequently not tended to by professionals, researchers, or the social network (Kessler, 1993). One study of attitudes and expectations of people requesting presymptomatic HD testing noted that the main reason partners gave for requesting testing was planning for the future, but this was less likely to be mentioned by the probands (Tibben et al., 1993). A pretest interview assessment of psychological distress of partners revealed that partners of participants at risk for HD reported significantly higher levels of intrusive thoughts and avoidance of thinking about HD than partners of people at risk for hereditary cancer conditions (DudokdeWit et al., 1997). These authors also note that the burden of HD on partners is considerable, especially when they have children.

In their study of persons at risk for HD, Codori and Brandt (1994) noted that while the majority of persons tested report no impact on marriages, some relationships sustain positive or negative changes after testing. Huggins et al. (1992) reported an undesired loss of anticipated caregiver responsibilities by some persons whose spouses received a lower risk. A 3-year study of 37 partners reported significant differences between partners of those with the gene mutation and those without the gene mutation on measures of intrusive thoughts, avoidance of thinking about HD, and hopelessness (Tibben, Timman, Bannink, & Duivenvoorden, 1997). In a review of HD presymptomatic testing studies, Tibben, Veger-van der Vlis, and Niermeijer (1990) reported that partners of persons with the HD gene mutation had more problems with the test results than did the persons themselves, especially immediately after completion of test results. This was consistent with increased distress found in partners of people with increased risk when compared to those with a decreased risk (Quaid & Wesson, 1995). Results of studies that report effects of presymptomatic HD testing on spouses and marriages are affected by the designs of the studies as well as the measures used.

Persons who serve as support persons during presymptomatic HD testing have reported inconsistencies between expectations for immediate test results and the presymptomatic testing protocol. Furthermore, these support persons also perceived the relevance of the proband's test result for their own future. While all support persons in this study perceived their role as an important one, for some it was difficult to provide support to the person being tested, and this experience was most intense for at-risk offspring (Williams, Schutte, Holkup, Evers, & Muilenburg, 2000).

IMPACT OF HD INFORMATION
WITHIN FAMILIES

Some individuals who choose to be tested have done so in response to a recent diagnosis of HD in a relative, while others knew about HD for years and are relieved that a test finally became available. Reasons that people may not have known that HD was in their family include misdiagnosis in older generations, keeping the diagnosis a secret not shared with offspring, placement in orphanages or foster care without knowledge of the disease in the biological family, or true absence of a family history of HD (Almqvist, 2001).

Family Perceptions of Risk

When testing was on the horizon, investigators and members of families in which HD was present began to urge health professionals to consider the importance of treating presymptomatic testing as a family matter (Chapman, 1992; Hayes, 1992; A. Wexler, 1996; N. Wexler, 1979). To some extent, functioning in families with a history of members afflicted with HD resembles the dynamics of families with a chronically or terminally ill member. Illness often results in a change in family members' roles. It can result in overprotection, not only of the ill member but also of other members (Rolland, 1997). In response to anticipated loss, families may prematurely exclude the ill member from the family by diminishing his or her responsibilities or denying the presence of the illness altogether. Life cycle expectations for all members may be altered by the illness; normative goals may be delayed or, conversely, pursued in haste. Families with serious illness may not discuss it, hoping not to "make things worse" (Reiss & Kramer, 1986). Communication, both affect and content, may be restricted.

With chronic and terminal illness, the family's beliefs, particularly the family identity, may also be affected. Family identity develops over time and is based on the family's experiences and their cultural context. It defines the characteristics of the family, particularly the ways in which the family deals with adversity and unexpected events, the conditions for membership, and the obligations of members to one another. When beliefs about identity and membership are challenged by illness, a family's sense of cohesion is affected (Sobel & Cowan, 2000a, p. 51).

In addition to characteristic family responses to chronic illness, inherited disease affects family function in other specific ways. There is a search for symptoms both within the individual and among family members. A process called preselection takes place whereby one off-spring among others of an affected parent is designated as the one to have it. The preselection of this member is based on idiosyncratic rather than medical data, such as who among the offspring most physically resembles the affected parent. It also may be based on gender. This is a collective but unconscious coping strategy that binds the family's anxiety to ward off the multiple uncertainties of each member (Kessler, 1988).

Each family member also develops a subjective risk assessment. Witnessing the disease in close relatives increases members' subjective assessment of risk for having the illness. Although the mathematical risk of 50% for each offspring is simple to grasp in ordinary circumstances, a more psychological math prevails among members of families with HD. Many families translate this information into a conviction that tells each of its members something like, "If you have it, I don't."

In families with inherited disease, familial communication patterns are complex. Family communication patterns may not encourage discussion, so only partial information concerning the disease is passed on from parents to children (Fanos & Johnson, 1995). These factors can greatly affect the impact of the presymptomatic test on the individual and the family, and sometimes have greater influence over the exact nature of the impact than the specific results of the test.

The very existence of the presymptomatic test affects family functioning. It forces individuals to make a choice where none existed before. This choice is often construed in moral terms, thereby impacting a family's sense of the loyalty of its members (Sobel & Cowan, 2000a, 2003, p. 49). Three areas of family functioning have been found to be affected by the presymptomatic testing of an asymptomatic individual with HD: family membership, family communication patterns, and role changes in response to caregiving concerns. These categories are, of course, related and interactive. The following information derives from two qualitative studies that sought the families' perspective on the impact that presymptomatic testing had on them (Sobel & Cowan, 2000a, 2000b, 2003; Williams, Schutte, Evers, et al., 2000).

Impact of Genetic Information on Family Membership

This category encompasses systemic changes that are reflected both in the family structure and in its belief systems after presymptomatic testing for HD. Structural changes include disconnections and additions. Some people in committed relationships who received a normal test result went on to marry and to have a family. A few people with a normal result, however, divorced. One said, "I left my family. I wanted out of my marriage. I wasn't thinking straight. . . . I just knew that when I got that result, especially that [normal] result, it was like this new found life or something. I just needed to go" (Sobel & Cowan, 2000a, p. 52). In other cases, people who learned they had the gene mutation either ended their relationships or chose not to marry. A husband of a woman who tested positive for the presence of the gene mutation left her and their two children, saying, "I don't want to waste love and energy on a dead-end project" (Sobel & Cowan, 2000a, p. 52). Some families interviewed reported that members who tested positive for the gene mutation committed suicide or made attempts. Some parents who learned their offspring had the gene mutation were consumed with guilt that they had not informed their children (Sobel & Cowan, 2003, p. 50).

Other types of disconnections and reconnections were pervasive throughout the family system, affecting beliefs and reflecting changes in relationships among sibs, between parents and offspring, and between nuclear and extended family members. Primary among these kinds of changes was a loss of membership for the asymptomatic person who did not have the gene mutation. For families who were aware of their HD history, it had become part of their identity. When a person in this type of family learned he or she did not have the mutation, the bond with relatives was broken. Such people not only experienced survivor guilt but also simultaneously felt a loss of membership in their families. One woman whose two sisters tested positive said, when she found she did not have the gene mutation, "I don't want to be left out of the family because I'm not sick. My sisters are special people now. . . . I had been part of this very elite group of people who may be very ill, and it was like a claim to fame. You're special because you may be dying" (Sobel & Cowan, 2000a, p. 53). She felt that the testing had destroyed the family forever. She also held an erroneous but not uncommon assumption of people at risk, that is, the belief that if one has it the rest of the family will be spared. On an individual level, some people who assumed they had the mutated gene became depressed when they learned that they did not. They no longer had the excuse of HD to explain failures they might have had in the past, and they were suddenly left to confront a future without a plan (Sobel & Cowan, 2003, p. 50).

Disconnections in families also occurred for other reasons. Some who did not have the gene mutation wanted to be cut off from their painful past. They expunged all past family stories from their repertory, leaving their children without a history. One person with a normal HD gene reported her discomfort when attending a family event: "My aunt died the day after I got my results. When I went to the funeral, and her son who has it was there, who I related to really easily before, because I figured I was going to be in the same boat . . . well, it was harder for me to feel the same empathy" (Williams, Schutte, Evers, et al., 2000, p. 264). Disconnections also occurred when relatives of those tested chose not to deal with HD and avoided family gatherings and all discussion of testing. This difference among family members' coping style can lead to bitterness and conflict.

For other families, testing brought reconciliation. Frequently, families with a history of HD also have a history of conflict, alcohol and drug abuse, and secrets (Murberg, Price, & Jatali, 1988). Testing provided some families with an opportunity to reconnect and resolve the issues of the past. Said a son whose mother tested positive, "I feel a lot more need to make sure I stay in connection with her, stay in reach. It's a lot different. I want to make sure that I have good memories" (Sobel & Cowan, 2000a, p. 53). It makes a considerable difference in a family's response if the test results of offspring are the same or different. For those families in which the results were the same for all, affiliation allowed some to reconcile past difficulties. For those whose results differed, increasing conflict generally followed. For example, one woman with normal gene test results said, "I had a very difficult time telling my cousin's wife because he just recently went to a nursing home with HD. She started crying and said, 'I wish you people that get the negative results would understand that we are absolutely ecstatic for you that you don't have to go through what we've gone through.' . . . But, there are other people that have been almost jealous. These are the ones that I regret telling" (Williams, Schutte, Evers, et al., 2000, p. 264).

Impact of Gene Test Results on Communication

In many families, for different reasons, there was little or no discussion of HD. Parents did not pass the information on to offspring out of need to protect them, or out of a sense of shame because HD had previously been misdiagnosed as alcoholism and dementia. One woman spoke of HD as an ancient curse, a blot that made her feel unworthy. She kept it a secret from her children for 32 years. The presence of this secret had affected her parenting. Her children saw her as irascible and overprotective. When her test indicated she was normal, she was faced with the need to explain the presence of HD in the family and the reasons she had kept it from her children, one of whom was now a parent of two small children. Initially, her disclosure increased the tumult, but it eventually began to repair her relationships and enabled her to reconnect with her affected brother, whose symptoms had previously been too personally threatening for her to witness (Sobel & Cowan, 2000a, p. 54; 2000b, p. 242).

In other families with poor communication, testing intensified family problems. Said one woman about testing, "It has been like putting the family chemistry on a Bunsen burner. You know, what was going to pop at some point has popped earlier, with greater intensity. But this [HD] is a focus" (Sobel & Cowan, 2000a, p. 54). Occasionally, within families, members split over the issue of communication patterns. Some members wanted to maintain their previous pattern of silence and others chose to confront the issues. When families were operating with two different styles, small fractures became crevasses in the face of testing. In other families in which there had been poor communication about HD as well as other problems, testing opened up discussion about a broad range of issues.

Gene Information and Role Changes

Caregiving issues in families with inherited diseases stretch beyond the immediate situation. Memories of relatives affected in the past intertwine with fears of an indefinite future with an undetermined number of family members to be afflicted. "The test didn't matter in some ways," said a woman who learned she was normal, "because it's always going to be in my family. . . . It's [HD] always going to be part of my life" (Sobel and Cowan, 2000a, p. 54). Role changes as a consequence of testing included immediate changes in role for a few, but for others, the anticipation of caregiving roles in the future increased stress on current marital and family relationships. For a few who did not have the gene mutation, relatives and parents were able to let go of their adult offspring and allow them to proceed with their developmental milestones leading to marriage and family. But even normal results required finding a new equilibrium. Said a husband, "It certainly changes your perspective on your partner. . . . I had committed to this person, but only 50% of me had made a long-term commitment. That was my defense mechanism for coping with it—that I was going to have more than one adventure in life. Something has happened now that's dramatic enough within the relationship that it does take the relationship to a new level" (Sobel & Cowan, 2000a, p. 55).

Others found a new role for themselves that extended beyond their own immediate family. Altruistic intentions were expressed by some who felt they had escaped a future in which they could develop HD. One woman said, "And I have this overwhelming feeling that OK, I don't have it so I have to help the ones that do have it. I have to work harder at finding a place that's going to take them (patients with HD), at educating the public, educating the medical staff, and that kind of thing. I don't have the money to donate millions of dollars to research projects; I'm not smart enough to find the answer myself, you know, to find the cure. But I feel like I have to do my part now, because I was chosen as one not to have it, that's my job" (Williams, Schutte, Evers, et al., 2000, p. 265).

Some who tested positive for the gene mutation immediately lost their roles. "I used to be the one that every one would come to and talk to. . . . And now people would take that role away from me" (Sobel & Cowan, 2000a, p. 55). This woman's younger sister, the "baby" of the family, was overwhelmed with what she saw as her new position in the family. "I suddenly feel very responsible for my parents. . . . What hit me was I'm going to watch my whole family die" (Sobel & Cowan, 2000a, p. 55). Another woman who did not have the gene mutation became her affected mother's guardian and arranged for her father to divorce and marry someone else so that he could get on with his life.

Driving these changes in the families was the sense of loss and grief that accompanied the process of testing. Given the nature of the test, the primary loss incurred by testing was the loss of uncertainty concerning one's genetic status. "If we hadn't been tested, we wouldn't be in this mess now," was one response (Sobel & Cowan, 2003, p. 50). For others, the information led to relief and closure for the immediate family. When members received normal gene results, they and their unaffected relatives lost the preoccupation with impending illness and the need to search for symptoms. The knowledge that other relatives were at risk dampened their relief. The loss of anticipation of HD also led to grieving for opportunities not taken because of the prior assumption that they would be sick. They lost the bond with other family members when their relatives tested positive for the gene mutation. Some lost rescue fantasies, shared by their families, that their status of having the defective gene would protect other members from carrying it. For some who did not have the gene mutation as well as for some who did, the sense of loss facilitated delayed grief reactions for the previously unmourned deaths of other relatives from HD. One man, age 38, who had taken care of his affected father to the end, explained his negative reaction when found he did not have the mutation: "I was more sad and concerned that my father had it. I felt bad by him. I'm thinking, 'Great for me. I'm negative.' But I'm thinking about him more. He was not so lucky" (Sobel & Cowan, 2000b, p. 241).

It was however, not only deaths that were mourned, but also births. Parents who gave birth around the time of testing positive mourned for their children because they would not be around to parent them. Families grieved for those who received positive test results in advance of the onset of symptoms. "You look at my sister. She's no different than 5 minutes before, and all of a sudden, she's dying. I guess we all started grieving immediately. It was like living the next 15 years in those 5 minutes" (Sobel & Cowan, 2003, pp. 52–53). When a member tested positive for the gene mutation, relatives experienced a loss of a future that ordinarily would have involved the expected growth and transitions associated with the normal life cycle. Said one wife, "Whenever my husband and I look at an older couple, we go, 'That's not going to be us' " (Sobel & Cowan, 2003, p. 50). Another woman explained that because her sisters had the gene mutation, they would never be able to pay back their parents for their care as most adult children expect to do. "At some point, you as child will probably have to take care of your parents . . . and you will give them back some of what they've given you. And that's been taken away. My sisters will never have that chance" (Sobel & Cowan, 2003, p. 50). Parents who tested positive lost the unconditional universal hope that their children would grow up to lead healthy lives, lives better than their own, and had to confront the status of their children being at risk. Above all, what was lost for those families when a member received a positive result was a sense of meaning. Their belief system was shattered.

These families' loss and grief is disenfranchised (Sobel & Cowan, 2003). Presymptomatic testing exists in a larger social context in which society at large presently lacks information and understanding because it is such a new experience. There is little support for families' experiences with testing. This results in increased isolation of families who must deal with the impact of testing. This isolation makes families prone to conflict because there is nowhere to turn for affirmation. "People at church brushed it off with, 'God will provide a miracle.' They weren't allowing me to face reality" (Sobel & Cowan, 2003, p. 52).

Adjustment to the impact of testing for families can frequently be a long process. Three to five years after the event, families still struggled to absorb the information. They were still reconstructing their relationships in the aftermath of test results. This had been for most a crisis without a name, and consequently families felt inhibited from seeking psychological services that were appropriate and deserved. Although HD support groups exist, many people who have tested positive but are not yet symptomatic find these groups frightening. There had been no forum for families in which to tell their story and consequently there was much unfinished business for them. Members who had not been included in the initial decision for testing in many instances needed and wanted to be included. Individuals' past positions on testing needed to be explained and understood, for example, why they withheld information from other members, why they consulted with those they did, why there appeared to be a lack of response or concern on their part or others', why they kept secrets. To maintain connections, families also needed to respect members' different ways of adjusting to the problems of HD. Families struggled with answers to the questions, "What is family?" and "What are the obligations members have to each other?" Finally, families needed to find meaning that sustained them and gave them a sense of mastery in the face of adversity (Sobel & Cowan, 2000a, 2000b, 2003).

IMPLICATIONS FOR HEALTH
CARE OF FAMILIES

Until recently, medicine recognized two types of people: the well and the unwell. Genetic testing of asymptomatic people at risk for inherited disease has created a third category: the apparently well, those who are not yet ill but who know they will be. When those in this third category discover they have an inherited illness for which there is as yet no cure or even palliative measures, they are in an unimaginable state of limbo (Sobel & Cowan, 2003).

The ethical principles guiding health care, that is, the right to privacy and confidentiality of the individual and the expectation that the individual is the patient, need to be reconsidered. When dealing with inherited diseases, the family is the patient. This may be more obvious when dealing with inherited illnesses for which there are cures or for which early surveillance and detection would make a difference in the outcome. In these situations, sharing knowledge with other family members may save lives; it is clear that it is the duty of the health care provider to encourage the patient to exchange information. In conditions such as HD, for which early detection does not affect the outcome, we believe involving family members in the decision for testing and the sharing of results is critical to improving future coping. Given the lack of general understanding of the impact of testing and the ensuing feelings of loss and grief, physicians and health care professionals need to be available to validate a family's loss and provide support.

Health care professionals who treat and advise people at risk for inherited illnesses need to be aware of the psychological consequences of testing for the individual and the family. The consequences are not benign, even with a result that clears an individual from the prospect of becoming sick. As the test for HD becomes more available, more centers may offer testing. Many health care workers may have little experience

244

Applications to Specific Genetic Conditions

with HD or the presymptomatic test. It is important to work within the protocol as established for HD testing centers. Caution must be exercised in recommending presymptomatic testing, particularly for diseases for which there is no cure and palliative measures are limited. The risks are that patients may be coerced into testing by family and physicians on the premise that more information is better, and their right not to know may be disqualified or overridden.

Ethical dilemmas arise when information about one family member discloses information about another, such as in the testing of identical twins or children of parents at risk for HD (Smith et al., 1998). In families with HD, the need of one member to know must be balanced against the other's right not to know. Although the health care provider does not make the decision about presymptomatic HD testing, he or she needs to define the context and terms to facilitate the person's thinking process. These situations call for the involvement of family members in the decision for testing so that, when possible, the basis for the presymptomatic HD testing decision and the weighting of needs are understood in advance of the outcome. As a person who had presymptomatic HD testing said, "You can't take this one back. Someone should have said, 'This (the testing) will change everything, not only for you, but for your family forever' " (Sobel & Cowan, 2000a, p. 56).

REFERENCES

Almqvist, E., Bloch, M., Brinkman, R., Crauford, D., & Hayden, M. on behalf of the international Huntington disease collaborative group. (1999). A worldwide assessment of the frequency of suicide, suicide attempts, or psychiatric hospitalization after predictive testing for Huntington disease. *American Journal of Human Genetics, 64,* 1293–1304.

Almqvist, E. W., Elterman, D. S., MacLeod, P. M. & Hayden, M. R. (2001). High incidence rate and absent family histories in one quarter of patients newly diagnosed with Huntington disease in British Columbia. *Clinical Genetics, 60,* 198–205.

Andrew, S., Goldberg, Y., & Hayden, M. (1997). Rethinking genotype and phenotype correlations in polyglutamine expansion disorders. *Human Molecular Genetics, 6,* 2005–2010.

Chapman, M. A. (1992). Invited editorial: Canadian experience with predictive testing for Huntington disease: Lessons for genetic testing centers and policy makers. *American Journal of Medical Genetics, 42,* 491–498.

Clarke, A., & Flinter, F. (1996). The genetic testing of children: A clinical perspective. In T. Marteau & M. Richards (Eds.), *The troubled helix: Social and psychological implications of the new human genetics* (pp. 164–176). Cambridge, UK: Cambridge University Press.

Codori, A., & Brandt, J. (1994). Psychological costs and benefits of predictive test-ing for Huntington disease. *American Journal of Medical Genetics, 54*, 174–184.

Codori, A., Hanson, R., & Brandt, J. (1994). Self-selection in predictive testing for Huntington's disease. *American Journal of Medical Genetics, 54*, 167–173.

Decruyenaere, M., Evers-Kiebooms, G., Googaerts, A. Cassiman, J., Clooster-mans, T., Demyttenaere, K., et al. (1996). Prediction of psychological func-tioning one year after the predictive test for Huntington's disease and impact of the test result on reproductive decision making. *Journal of Med-ical Genetics, 33*, 737–743.

Dubinsky, R., and the Huntington Disease Peer Workgroup Members. (2004). *Lifting the veil of Huntington's Disease.* Robert Wood Johnson Foundation, University of Montana.

DudokdeWit, A., Tibben, A., Duivenvoorden, H., Frets, P., Zoeteweij, M., Losekoot, M., et al. (1997). Psychological distress in applicants for predic-tive DNA testing for autosomal dominant, heritable, late onset disorders. *Journal of Medical Genetics, 34*, 382–390.

DudokdeWit, A., Tibben, A., Duivenvoorden, H., Niermeijer, M., Passchier, J., Trijsburg, R., et al. (1998). Distress in individuals facing predictive DNA testing for autosomal dominant late-onset disorders: Comparing question-naire results with in-depth interviews. *American Journal of Medical Genetics, 75*, 62–74.

Fanos, J., & Johnson, J. (1995). Barriers to carrier testing for adult cystic fibrosis sibs: The importance of not knowing. *American Journal of Medical Genetics, 59*, 81–91. Gusella, J., Wexler, N., Conneally, P., Naylor, S., Anderson, M., Tanzi, R., et al. (1983). A polymorphic DNA marker genetically linked to Huntington disease. *Nature, 306*, 234–239.

Hayes, C. V. (1992). Genetic testing for Huntington's disease: A family issue. *New England Journal of Medicine, 12*, 1448–1451.

Huggins, M., Bloch, M., Wiggins, S., Adam, S., Suchowersky, O., Trew, M., et al. (1992). Predictive testing for Huntington disease in Canada: Adverse ef-fects and unexpected results in those receiving a decreased risk. *American Journal of Medical Genetics, 42*, 508–515.

Huntington's Disease Collaborative Research Group. (1993). A novel gene con-taining a trinucleotide repeat that is expanded and unstable in Hunting-ton's disease chromosomes. *Cell, 72*, 971–983.

Jorde, L., Carey, J., Bamshad, M., & White, R. (1999). *Medical genetics* (2nd ed.). St. Louis: Mosby.

Kessler, S. (1988). Invited essay on the psychological aspect of genetic testing V. Preselection: A family coping mechanism. *American Journal of Medical Genetics, 31*, 617–621.

Kessler, S. (1993). Forgotten person in the Huntington family. *American Journal of Medical Genetics, 48*, 145–150.

Meissen, G., Mastromauro, C., Kiely, D., McNamara, D., & Myers, R. (1991). Understanding the decision to take the predictive test for Huntington dis-ease. *American Journal of Medical Genetics, 39*, 404–410.

Murburg, M. M., Price, L. H., & Jatali, B. (1988). Huntington disease: Therapy strategies. *Family Systems Medicine, 6*(3), 290–303.

Myers, R. H. (2005). Huntington's disease genetics. *Neuro Rx®: The Journal of the American Society for Experimental NeuroTherapeutics, 1*, 255–262,

Nance, M. A. (1996) Invited editorial, "Huntington disease—another chapter rewritten." *American Journal of Human Genetics, 59*, 1–6.

Quaid, K., & Wesson, M. (1995). Exploration of the effects of predictive testing for Huntington disease on intimate relationships. *American Journal of Medical Genetics, 57*, 46–51.

Reiss, D., & Kramer, N. (1986). Family process, chronic illness, and death. *Archives of General Psychiatry, 43*, 795–804.

Rolland, J. (1997). Commentary. The meaning of disability and suffering: Sociopolitical and ethical concerns. *Family Process, 36*(4), 437–440.

Rosenblatt, A., Ranen, N., Nance, M., & Paulsen, J. (1999). *A physician's guide to the management of Huntington's disease* (2nd ed.). New York: Huntington's Disease Society of America.

Rubinsztein, D., Leggo, J., Coles, R., Almqvist, E., Biancalana, V., Cassiman, J., et al. (1996). Phenotypic characterization of individuals with 30–40 CAG repeats in the Huntington disease (HD) gene reveals HD cases with 36 repeats and apparently normal elderly individuals with 36–39 repeats. *American Journal of Human Genetics, 59*, 15–22.

Rushton, A. (194). *Genetics and medicine in the United States, 1800 to 1992.* Baltimore, MD: Johns Hopkins University Press.

Smith, D. H., Quaid, K. A., Dworkin, R. B., Gramelspacher, G. P., Granbois, J. A., & Vance, G. H. (1998). *Early warning: Cases and ethical guidance for presymptomatic testing in genetic diseases.* Bloomington: Indiana University Press.

Sobel, S., & Cowan, D. B. (2000a). Impact of genetic testing for Huntington disease on the family as a system. *American Journal of Medical Genetics, 90*(1), 49–59.

Sobel, S., & Cowan, D. B. (2000b). The process of family reconstruction after DNA testing for Huntington disease. *Journal of Genetic Counseling, 9*(3), 237–253.

Sobel, S., & Cowan, D. B. (2003). Ambiguous loss and disenfranchised grief: The impact of predictive testing on the family as a system. *Family Process, 42*(1), 31–46.

Tibben, A., Frets, P., van de Kamp, J., Niermeijer, M., Veger-van der Vlis, M., Roos, R., et al. (1993). Presymptomatic DNA-testing for Huntington disease: Pretest attitudes and expectations of applicants and their partners in the Dutch program. *American Journal of Medical Genetics (Neuropsychiatric Genetics), 48*, 10–16.

Tibben, A., Timman, R., Bannink, E., & Duivenvoorden, H. (1997). Three-year follow-up after presymptomatic testing for Huntington's disease in tested individuals and partners. *Health Psychology, 16*, 20–35.

Tibben, A., Veger-van der Vlis, M., & Niermeijer, M. (1990). Testing for Huntington's disease with support for all parties. *Lancet, 335*, 553.

Timman, R., Roos, R., Maat-Kievit, A., & Tibben, A. (2004). Adverse effects of predictive testing for Huntington disease underestimated: Long-term effects 7–10 years after the test. *Health Psychology, 23*(2), 189–197.

van't Spijker, A., & ten Kroode, H. (1997). Psychological aspects of genetic counselling: A review of the experience with Huntington's disease. *Patient Education and Counselling, 32*, 33–40.

Wahlin, T.-B., Lundin, A., Backman, L., Almqvist, E., Haegermark, A., Winblad, B., et al. (1997). Reactions to predictive testing in Huntington disease: Case reports of coping with a new genetic status. *American Journal of Medical Genetics, 73,* 356–365.

Went, L., Boholm, J., Cassiman, J., Craufurd, D., Falke, A., Farmer-Little, C., et al. (1994). Guidelines for the molecular genetics predictive test in Huntington's disease. *Journal of Medical Genetics, 31,* 555–559.

Wexler, A. (1996). Genetic testing of families with hereditary diseases. *Journal of the American Medical Association, 276,* 1139–1140.

Wexler, N. (1979). Genetic "Russian roulette": The experience of being at risk for Huntington disease. In S. Kessler (Ed.), *Genetic counseling: Psychological dimensions* (pp. 199–220). New York: Academic Press.

Williams, J. K., Schutte, D. L., Evers, C., & Forcucci, C. (1999). Adults seeking presymptomatic gene testing for Huntington disease. *Image: Journal of Nursing Scholarship, 31*(2), 109–114.

Williams, J. K., Schutte, D. L., Evers, C., & Holkup, P. A. (2000). Redefinition: Coping with normal results from presymptomatic gene testing for neurodegenerative disorders. *Research in Nursing and Health, 23,* 260–269.

Williams, J. K., Schutte, D. L., Holkup, P. A., Evers, C., & Muilenburg, A. (2000). Psychosocial impact of predictive testing for Huntington disease on support persons. *Neuropsychiatric Genetics, American Journal of Medical Genetics, 96*(3): 353–359.

Chapter 9

Cystic Fibrosis

Psychosocial Consequences of Genetic Testing in Screening Programs

Carolyn Constantin and Audrey Tluczek

CYSTIC FIBROSIS (CF) IS A COMMON, LIFE-SHORTENING, GENETIC DISEASE that occurs most frequently in Caucasians of European descent, but has been found with varying incidence in most ethnic and racial groups. It is an autosomal recessive genetic disease that affects the exocrine glands throughout the body and causes dysfunction and damage in multiple systems. The disorder is characterized by chronic lung disease and pancreatic insufficiency. Despite advances in treatment, there is still no cure for CF; however, survival rates have improved since the early 1990s (Kulich, Rosenfeld, Goss, & Wilmott, 2003). The median survival age for individuals with CF is approximately 35 years (Cystic Fibrosis Foundation, 2005).

The gene associated with the disease was identified in 1989 (Kerem et al., 1989; Riordan et al., 1989). Since then, over 1,400 mutations in the CF gene have been reported (Cystic Fibrosis Mutation Database, 2005), and screening tests have been established to identify individuals with the disease and couples at risk for having affected children. Implementation of these screening tests has been the subject of considerable clinical research and public debate.

This chapter provides an overview of CF and the process of translating genetic research into clinical practice through population-based

The findings and conclusions in this chapter are those of the authors and do not necessarily represent the views of the Centers for Disease Control and Prevention.

carrier screening and newborn screening programs in the United States and other countries. CF screening serves as an excellent model to highlight the technical and psychosocial issues related to genetic screening programs. Psychosocial issues for individuals and families related to the use of genetic testing in CF screening are emphasized, and current issues involving CF screening are discussed with recommendations for future investigation.

GENETICS OF CF

Due to the autosomal recessive nature of this genetic disorder, both parents must carry a mutation in the CF gene for a child to be affected. If both parents carry a CF gene mutation, there is a 25% risk of having a child affected by CF with each pregnancy. In addition, there is a 50% risk of having a child who has one CF mutation (e.g., a carrier). Furthermore, there is a 25% chance of having a child who does not have CF and does not carry a mutation.

The gene associated with CF, the cystic fibrosis transmembrane conductance regulator (*CFTR*) gene, is on chromosome 7 (Kerem et al., 1989; Riordan et al., 1989; Rommens et al., 1989). The most common mutation associated with CF is delF508, which has also been described as ΔF508 or delta F508. This mutation results in the deletion of a phenylalanine residue at codon 508 in the *CFTR* protein. A codon is the nucleotide triplet in messenger RNA that specifies which amino acid will be inserted in the polypeptide chain that folds into the specific protein during translation. This deletion results in an abnormal protein, leading to severe reduction in *CFTR* function. The classic CF phenotype includes increased sweat chloride, recurrent respiratory infection with bronchiectasis, and pancreatic insufficiency (Welsh, Ramsey, Accurso, & Cutting, 2001). Additional health challenges for adults with CF include CF-related diabetes, osteoporosis, and male infertility.

Clinical Considerations

The *CFTR* gene codes for a chloride channel protein found in the membranes of cells that line passageways of the lungs, liver, pancreas, intestines, reproductive tract, and skin. The *CFTR* protein controls the flow of salt and water in and out of cells. Altered protein function results in reduced flow of water and buildup of thick secretions, which can obstruct passageways in various organs. Clinical manifestations vary widely, and attempts to predict the severity of clinical outcomes based on genotypic analysis have proven largely unsuccessful. In some cases, individuals with "classic CF" symptoms do not have identifiable mutations, and people with identical mutations can present very different clinical pictures (i.e., variable expression) (McKone, Emerson, Edwards, & Aitken, 2003). In general, individuals with two copies of the delF508 mutation have more severe disease than those with only one copy of delF508 and a different mutation, or those with two other mutations. McKone and colleagues (2003) described distinct genetic subgroups that are associated with mild clinical manifestations and low mortality; however, providing clinical prognosis based on genotype is generally considered unreliable.

POPULATION-BASED CARRIER SCREENING FOR CYSTIC FIBROSIS

DNA-based molecular testing for CF became possible after the *CFTR* gene was identified in 1989; however, population-based carrier testing was not recommended until 2001. Guidelines for implementing CF screening in routine practice were developed for practitioners and laboratories by a joint committee consisting of the American College of Medical Genetics and American College of Obstetricians and Gynecologists (2001), and the National Human Genome Research Institute. Grody and colleagues (2001) outlined recommendations for which mutations should be included in carrier testing for CF and how results should be reported. Population-based carrier screening for CF was initiated following distribution of these guidelines.

Lessons Learned From Implementing Population-Based Carrier Screening for CF

A number of unexpected issues arose following initiation of population-based carrier screening for CF. For example, there were issues involving complex or inaccurate interpretations of test results, variability in laboratory compliance with existing guidelines, and unnecessary interventions based upon misunderstanding or miscommunication of test results.

Genetic test results are interpreted within the context of an individual's situation. In CF screening, it is important to interpret test results based on an individual's personal and family history as well as their ethnic and racial background. Since over 1,400 mutations have been identified in the *CFTR* gene (Cystic Fibrosis Mutation Database, 2005), it is impractical to test for every mutation. Thus, the American College of Medical Genetics recommended that only mutations with a frequency greater than 0.1% in the general population should be included in the screening test (Grody et al., 2001). This resulted in 25 mutations on the original test panel. Since the frequency of CF mutations varies in different ethnic groups, the test panel used to screen for CF mutations is more effective in certain populations. The panel is most useful in detecting mutations for the populations at highest risk, that is, non-Hispanic Caucasians of European ancestry and Ashkenazi Jews (see Table 9.1). When the prevalence is lower in a population, a negative test result is not as informative as it is in the populations at highest risk. Detection rates can be improved for individuals in different ethnic and racial groups if more mutations are tested using expanded test panels (Heim, Sugarman, & Allitto, 2001); however, effectively communicating risk becomes more complicated (Gates, 2004).

Another issue that emerged is that one of the mutations (I148T) originally included in the screening panel does not cause classic CF. It appears that another mutation near the I148T mutation (i.e., 3199del6) is actually associated with CF, and therefore, I148T is being dropped from the recommended panel (Watson et al., 2004). It is uncertain how many individuals were informed that they are CF carriers based on this misunderstanding. It is also uncertain how many people who screened positive for the I148T mutation are positive for the disease-associated 3199del6 mutation. Although evidence is lacking, it is likely that needless interventions related to further screening or diagnostic

Table 9.1 Cystic Fibrosis: Incidence, Carrier Frequency, and Detection Rates Using ACMG Recommended Core Panel

ETHNICITY/RACE	INCIDENCE/ BIRTH PREVALENCE (APPROX.)	CARRIER FREQ.	DETECTION RATE FOR CARRIER (ORIGINAL PANEL OF 25 MUTATIONS)	# COUPLES NEEDED TO SCREEN TO DETECT AN AFFECTED FETUS
Ashkenazi Jewish Caucasian	1:2,270	1:24	94%	2,600
Non-Hispanic Caucasian	1:2,500	1:25	88%	3,200
Hispanic Caucasian	1:13,500	1:58	72%	26,120
African American	1:15,100	1:61	65%	36,040
Asian American	1:35,100	1:94	49%	129,600

Note. From Palomaki, G. E., FitzSimmons, S. C., & Haddow, J. E. (2004). Clinical sensitivity of prenatal screening for cystic fibrosis via *CFTR* carrier testing in the United States panethnic population. *Genetics in Medicine, 6*(5), 405–414.

procedures were undertaken related to this misinterpretation. Unfortunately, there is no structure in place to contact these individuals and the psychosocial implications of this error remain unknown.

Another issue related to interpreting test results involved the R117H mutation. In some cases following a positive test result, further testing for another *CFTR* mutation is necessary to determine the clinical implications of the original finding, a procedure known as reflex testing. R117H is a mutation included in the standard recommended panel for CF screening. However, the clinical presentation varies depending on the presence and position of another mutation. There are variants (i.e., 5T/7T/9T) in the *CFTR* gene that modify the expression of the R117H mutation. Therefore, a positive finding of an R117H mutation requires further testing for 5T/7T/9T variants to determine clinical significance. Currently, laboratory policies and practices vary on reflex testing, and some laboratories will only do reflex testing when a provider orders it. Confusion arose when some laboratories included 5T genotyping in the first-tier mutation panel and reported the findings in test results (Watson et al., 2002). The 5T variant is a very common polymorphism, found in approximately 5% of the general population, and two copies of the 5T variant (homozygosity) have been associated with congenital bilateral absence of the vas deferens (CBAVD). Some laboratories reported the presence of the 5T variant alone, which is not justified, and caused confusion for providers interpreting test results (Watson et al., 2002). The implications of this confusion over interpretations of test results are not known.

PSYCHOSOCIAL IMPLICATIONS OF POPULATION-BASED CF CARRIER SCREENING

To date, the majority of psychosocial research related to CF carrier screening programs has focused on key variables described in Chapter 3. These variables include knowledge, decision making, satisfaction, and anxiety related to testing. Overall, research findings indicate that negative psychological consequences related to carrier screening for CF appear to be minimal (Callanan, Cheuvront, & Sorenson, 1999; Gordon, Walpole, Zubrick, & Bower, 2003; Henneman, Poppelaars, & ten Kate, 2002; Lerman, Tercyak, Crolye, & Hamann, 2002; Witt et al., 1996). Less is known about potential stigmatizing effects of carrying a CF mutation and gender differences related to CF carrier screening.

Knowledge and Anxiety Related
to CF Carrier Screening

It is clear that an individual's knowledge related to CF and the screening process can be improved by providing information in a variety of formats. Retention of this knowledge is poor, however, regardless of the educational method used (Axworthy, Brock, Bobrow, & Marteau, 1996; Clausen, Brandt, Schwartz, & Skovby, 1996a, 1996b; Gordon et al., 2003; Levenkron, Loader, & Rowley, 1997; Loader et al., 1996). However, certain groups of individuals demonstrate better retention. Individuals who screen positive as CF carriers demonstrate better retention (Clausen et al., 1996a; Gordon et al., 2003), and women who intend to have more children are more likely to correctly understand the meaning of a negative test result (Mennie, Axworthy, Liston, & Brock, 1997).

Imprecise recall and misunderstanding test results is a common finding in the literature (Gordon et al., 2003; Grody et al., 1997; Hartley et al., 1997; Loader et al., 1996). This finding raises concern about the impact of false reassurance and the potential for individuals to make uninformed decisions. For example, in a follow-up questionnaire 18 months after CF screening, Gordon and colleagues (2003) found that approximately 30% of 353 individuals had the misconception that a negative result meant that a person was definitely not a carrier. In addition, over half of the participants who were not tested or tested negative believed that a positive result meant that a person is very likely to be a carrier, but not definitely. Although most carriers understood correctly that they were definitely carriers, 11 thought that they were only very likely to have a CF mutation. Gordon and colleagues (2003) provided potential explanations for inaccurate recall of information including (a) memory loss with time, (b) cognitive processing that retains the underlying meaning without complex details or uncertainty, and (c) the psychological inclination to process and recall threatening personal information in a manner that minimizes risk and anxiety.

Prolonged anxiety does not appear to be a significant problem with CF screening. Increased levels of anxiety following a positive CF screening test are consistently reported in the literature; however, they are transient and decrease upon learning that the partner is negative (Gordon et al., 2003; Green, Hewison, Bekker, Bryant, & Cuckle, 2004; Grody et al., 1997; Mennie et al., 1992; Mennie, Gilfillan, Compton, Liston, & Brock, 1993). Mennie and colleagues (1993) reported the duration of this transient anxiety to be approximately 4 days while waiting for the results for the partner. Residual anxiety following a positive screening test after receiving negative results for the partner does not appear to be a significant problem.

Decision Making and Satisfaction
With Carrier Screening

In general, acceptance of CF screening is high among pregnant couples regardless of how the information is presented (Hartley et al., 1997; Loader et al., 1996; Witt et al., 1996). Screening individuals prior to pregnancy can offer advantages; however, acceptance of carrier screening in the general population is generally low unless there is a strong motivating factor, such as the presence of a known risk (Gordon et al., 2003). Some women report having difficulty refusing CF screening (Clausen et al., 1996a; Hans, Brandt, Schwartz, & Skovby, 1996; Hartley et al., 1997). This finding suggests that pregnant women may experience pressure to accept testing. Hartley and colleagues (1997) reported that 2% (6/377) of women who underwent CF screening felt that they could not refuse the test. In addition, 16% (59/377) of women accepted CF screening based on the belief that all tests in pregnancy were important and not because of the disease. Further research evaluating psychosocial pressures to accept testing during pregnancy is warranted.

The decision to accept or reject CF screening appears to be related to the intended use of the result. The main reason women or couples give for refusing the test is their opposition to terminating the pregnancy (Loader et al., 1996; Mennie et al., 1993). Other reasons for refusing the test include a very low perceived risk of having a child with CF, partner disapproval or nonparticipation, cost of testing, and high levels of anxiety that would be generated through screening (Loader et al., 1996; Mennie et al., 1993; Sturm & Ormond, 2004). Reasons given for accepting screening during pregnancy include reassurance that the child does not have CF, to be prepared in case their child is affected, and to avoid having a child with CF (Loader et al., 1996; Sturm & Ormond, 2004). In addition, women who accept carrier screening for CF are more willing to accept pregnancy termination as an option than those refusing testing (Levenkron et al., 1997; Loader et al., 1996).

Overall, most women appear to be satisfied with their choice regarding testing and state that they made the right decision (Hartley et al., 1997; Michie, Smith, McClennan, & Marteau, 1997; Witt et al., 1996). However, Clausen and colleagues (1996b) reported that 8% of 109 women identified as CF carriers later doubted their decision to accept testing, and 5% regretted their decision. The authors did not provide the reasons given for regret by these women. Hartley and colleagues (1997) reported that 2% (6/379) of women screened for a CF mutation felt they had made the wrong decision to be tested. Of the six women, three stated they needed more time than allotted to make their decision, one woman had reservations about testing during pregnancy but agreed in order to help research, and two reported feeling more anxious than normal while waiting for the results.

Reproductive Decisions

A number of studies address reproductive decisions related to CF in both carrier screening and newborn screening (Clausen et al., 1996b; Denayer, Welkenhuysen, Evers-Keibooms, Cassiman, & Van den Berghe, 1997; Henneman et al., 2001; Levenkron et al., 1997). Couples learn of their carrier status either through carrier screening or by having an affected child. From the literature, it is often difficult to separate how learning one's carrier status through screening programs impacts reproductive choices independently from those who have an affected child.

Clausen and colleagues (1996a) found that 79% (96/122) of women identified as CF carriers, who had a partner that tested negative, reported that they would not change their reproductive plans based on the results of screening. Although there are reports of women identified as carriers who stated they would consider changing their reproductive plans or who were unsure of their decisions, overall research findings suggest that knowing one's CF carrier status through screening programs does not affect one's decision of whether to have children (Clausen et al., 1996a, 1996b; Denayer et al., 1997). Henneman, Kooij, Bouman, & ten Kate (2002) interviewed couples where both were identified as CF carriers. In this qualitative study, four out of seven reported having great difficulty in deciding whether to have more children and felt it was difficult to make a decision regarding prenatal diagnosis. In addition, one of these couples reported a decision to have fewer children than originally planned. Reproductive decisions based on knowing one's carrier status after having an affected child are discussed later.

Stigmatization and Gender Differences

There is evidence that CF carrier status can influence self-perception and perception of others (Axworthy et al., 1996; Evers-Keibooms, Denayer, Welkenhuysen, Cassiman, & Van den Berghe, 1994; Gordon et al., 2003; Henneman, Kooij, et al., 2002; Marteau, Dundas, & Axworthy, 1997). Studies focusing on stigmatization related to CF carrier status are limited in number, subjects, and research methodology. In addition, the results are conflicting. Evers-Keibooms and colleagues (1994) reported a slight potential for self-stigmatization and social stigmatization related to being a CF carrier. One year following disclosure of test results, Denayer and colleagues reported on the same cohort of subjects and found no significant effect on individuals' self-concept

(Denayer, Welkenhuysen, Evers-Keibooms, Cassiman, & Van den Berghe, 1996). Participants in this study had a positive family history for CF, and generalization to population-based screening may be inappropriate. Gordon and colleagues (2003) reported that individuals identified as carriers do not have a poor perception of their current health and do not report different levels of guilt, shame, ability and activity than noncarriers. In a small qualitative study, Henneman, Kooij, et al. (2002) reported varying reactions of seven couples identified as CF carriers related to sharing information with family and friends. Reactions include delaying disclosure to family and friends, feeling unsupported after disclosure, and experience with trying to assign blame to one side of the family for passing on the gene. In contrast, Clausen and colleagues (1996a, 1996b) reported that individuals "freely" shared carrier results with family and friends.

Gender differences in response to CF carrier screening have been reported (Bekker et al., 1993; Marteau et al., 1997; Newman, Sorenson, DeVellis, & Cheuvront, 2002; Watson, Mayall, Lamb, Chapple, & Williamson, 1992). In population-based screening programs, women are approximately twice as likely as men to accept offers of free CF screening (Bekker et al., 1993; Watson et al., 1992). It has also been reported that women identified as CF carriers describe themselves in a more negative way than male carriers (Evers-Keibooms et al., 1994). In a secondary analysis, Newman and colleagues (2002) observed that men were more likely to assume that they were CF carriers than women and that their child would more likely be a carrier also. However, they found that women were more anxious prior to testing than men. The number of male participants is generally small in these studies, and additional research directed specifically at gender differences is needed to explore these relationships.

NEWBORN SCREENING FOR CF

Since the 1960s, newborn screening programs have been used as a preventative public health program to identify disorders in newborns that can affect their long-term health. These programs detect genetic or metabolic disorders in presymptomatic neonates to facilitate early intervention and thus prevent infant morbidity and mortality (Allen & Farrell, 1996). In the United States, each state selects which disorders to include in their newborn screening panel and therefore, states vary in the number of disorders screened from 4 to 41 disorders (National Newborn Screening and Genetics Resource Center, 2006). Table 9.2 outlines the original criteria for the inclusion of a disorder in newborn screening.

Table 9.2 World Health Organization (WHO) Criteria for Newborn Screening

1. The condition is a significant public health problem.

2. Effective treatment is available.

3. Facilities to diagnose and treat individuals with the condition are available.

4. The condition has a latent or pre-symptomatic phase.

5. A sensitive and reliable screening test is available.

6. The screening test is acceptable to the population.

7. The natural history of the condition is understood.

8. There is a policy regarding whom to treat.

9. Screening is cost effective relative to the cost of care.

10. Case finding can be a continuous process.

Note. From Wilson, J. M. G., & Jungner, G. (1968). *Principles and practice of screening for disease.* Public Health Papers, 34 (pp. 26–27). Geneva: World Health Organization. Available at http://whqlibdoc.who.int/php/WHO_PHP_34.pdf

The first newborn CF screening program in the United States was initiated in Colorado in 1982, followed by Wisconsin in 1985 and Wyoming in 1988. As of January 2006, 16 states offer CF newborn screening. The status of state programs can change rapidly, however, and up-to-date information about newborn screening programs can be obtained from the National Newborn Screening and Genetics Resource Center (2006).

Current protocols for CF newborn screening programs vary among the different states, yet generally a two-tiered testing is used. The first step begins with the immunoreactive trypsinogen test (IRT) performed on the dried blood spot obtained from all infants at 24 to 48 hours of age. Trypsinogen is produced in the pancreas and elevated in newborns with CF and some carriers. An elevated IRT (positive result) must be followed by confirmatory testing. Some state laboratories repeat the IRT test, while other laboratories use DNA testing. The specific IRT value warranting further testing and the number of mutations tested varies among the programs (Grosse et al., 2004). The next step involves notifying the infant's primary care provider, who refers the patient with abnormal findings for a diagnostic sweat test. When sweat test results are questionable (i.e., borderline results), further genetic testing may be recommended. Figure 9.1 illustrates the algorithm used by most states that conduct newborn CF screening.

Evidence of clinical benefit from early detection is one of the original criteria for including a disorder in newborn screening. Whether early interventions for newborns with CF provide clear clinical benefit is the

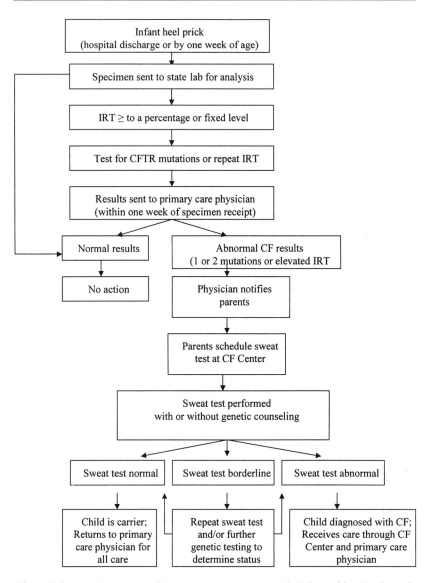

Figure 9.1 Newborn cystic fibrosis screening protocol. Adapted by A. Tluczek from Wisconsin Newborn Screening Protocol for cystic fibrosis.

subject of ongoing scientific scrutiny and heated debate (Wagener, Farrell, & Corey, 2001). A statement by the Centers for Disease Control and Prevention found newborn screening for CF to be justified and recommended that states consider newborn screening for CF (Grosse et al., 2004). While most arguments focus on the physiological outcomes of infants with CF, it is important to consider psychological benefits and risks to infants with false positive results as well as those diagnosed with CF.

PSYCHOSOCIAL ISSUES RELATED TO CF NEWBORN SCREENING

The pivotal psychosocial issues regarding newborn screening for CF seem to revolve around the controversy over whether there is sufficient evidence that the benefits outweigh the risks. The following discussion examines the research divided by the issues associated with families who have a child with CF and those related to families who have infants with false-positive screening results.

Families With Children Diagnosed With CF

Parental Distress Related to Delayed Diagnosis

Anecdotal reports of parental distress related to a delayed diagnosis and treatment for their chronically ill child are common. Children often have unnecessary invasive procedures and hospitalizations, while parents feel helpless, frustrated, angry, and mistrust the medical community (Kharrazi & Kharrazi, 2005; McCollum & Gibson, 1970). The Wisconsin randomized clinical trial of newborn screening showed that parents in the conventionally diagnosed control group had "emotionally charged" reactions to their child's delayed diagnosis (Tluczek et al., 1991). Most parents reported feelings of anxiety, sadness, and shock related to the news that their child might have CF. Other thematic results showed that parents felt misled and distressed for having missed opportunities to provide their child early treatment and to make more informed reproductive decisions. Data from researchers in the Netherlands (Merelle et al., 2003) found that parents of infants diagnosed with CF before 3 months of age reported having fewer medical visits, greater frequency of correct initial diagnosis, greater confidence in health providers, and feeling more hopeful about their child's future as compared with parents of infants diagnosed after 3 months of age. The results of these studies suggest that newborn CF screening and diagnosis may reduce parental distress and enhance patient-provider relationships.

Parents' Decisions About Genetic Testing and Reproductive Choices

Newborn CF screening and diagnosis can provide parents an opportunity to receive genetic counseling, obtain prenatal testing, make informed reproductive choices, and consider family planning alternatives. A study of Wisconsin families showed that newborn screening for CF did not significantly affect parents' reproductive decisions (Mischler et al., 1998). Of the couples in the study, 95% (95/100) correctly understood their risk of conceiving another child with CF. In couples for which the affected child was their firstborn, the majority (70%, 23/33) had conceived other children one year after the diagnosis. There were 3 children who were affected with CF out of 43 subsequent pregnancies, all of which were carried to term. In addition, of the families who had not had another child, only 22% (5/23) had obtained prenatal testing. A similar study conducted in France found that more individuals used prenatal diagnosis compared to those in the Wisconsin study. Over a 10-year period of newborn CF screening, 34% (39/114) of the French couples who had a child with CF detected by screening underwent prenatal diagnosis with subsequent pregnancies (Scotet et al., 2000). A research team in Colorado (Helton, Harmon, Robinson, & Accurso, 1991) surveyed 62 parents of infants diagnosed with CF through newborn screening and 32 parents of infants conventionally diagnosed with CF. A minority of parents from each group (6% screened group and 17% conventional group) viewed reproductive decision making as an advantage for newborn screening. Most reported that they would not consider termination of a pregnancy for CF and one third of the screened group had conceived another pregnancy at a follow-up assessment. More recently, an Australian study (Dudding, Wilcken, Burgess, Hambly, & Turner, 2000) showed that most (66%, 35/53) families who had a child diagnosed with CF through newborn screening used prenatal diagnosis, and the majority (69%, 24/35) terminated or said that they would have terminated a subsequent pregnancy with an affected fetus. While prenatal testing and pregnancy termination may be an option as a result of genetic knowledge gained from DNA testing in newborn screening for CF, cultural factors (such as beliefs, values, religious affiliations, and economic conditions) may affect parents' decisions about using these options.

In an ongoing study in Wisconsin, 10 families have shared their experiences about parenting their affected children during the first year of life. These parents described the first 6 months as an "emotional rollercoaster"; however, 12 months after the diagnosis, parents tended to view their child as healthy, active, and flourishing developmentally. One parent summed up the sentiments of many parents at this stage by stating that "this first year was not as bad as I expected." In addition, several couples for whom the affected child was their firstborn stated that they were considering having another child. These parents fully understood their risk of having another child with CF. It seems that the health of their affected child was an important factor in parents' decisions about future pregnancies.

Impact on the Parent-Infant Relationship

Infant mental health research has established a strong link between the quality of a child's relationship with his or her parents and the child's social, emotional, cognitive, and behavioral development (Clark, Tluczek, & Gallagher, 2004; Zeanah, Larrieu, Heller, & Valliere, 2000). Disturbances in this relationship have been associated with developmental psychopathology throughout a child's life span (van der Broom, 2004).

Several factors potentially pose risks to the quality of parent-infant relationships consequent to a neonatal CF diagnosis. First, research (Quittner, DiGirolamo, Michael, & Eigen, 1992; Tluczek et al., 1991) shows that having a young child diagnosed with a life-threatening illness like CF is a highly emotionally charged experience for mothers and fathers, whose distress may include psychological or somatic symptoms. Second, mental health research (O'Hara, 1997) suggests that women may be at an increased risk for depressive symptoms during the first few months postpartum. Receiving the news that one has an infant with a potentially fatal illness during a psychologically vulnerable time in a woman's life may significantly increase psychological symptoms. This could limit her emotional availability and capacity to bond with her infant. Third, at the time of CF diagnosis, when parents may feel overwhelmed with the normal tasks of caring for a newborn, they are given additional responsibilities of addressing the special needs of a child with CF. These high care needs may lead parents to focus on health-related tasks rather than connecting with their infant on an emotional level.

Several reports raise questions about the impact of a CF diagnosis in the newborn on the parent-infant relationship; however, the data remain inconclusive, suggesting that other child or parent factors may also influence the quality of the relationship. A research team in Toronto reported that toddlers who were diagnosed with CF in early infancy had higher rates of insecure mother-infant attachments than children diagnosed with CF later in infancy (Fischer-Fay, Goldberg, Simmons, & Levison, 1988). However, the infants in this study were diagnosed based upon their symptoms, not through newborn screening. Infants with more severe symptoms are likely to be identified earlier than those with less severe disease. Therefore, it is possible that the insecure parent-infant relationships in this study were a consequence of the infant health status rather than timing of diagnosis. Another study in New South Wales (Bolan & Thompson, 1990) showed mixed findings of risks and benefits to the parent-infant relationship for infants diagnosed with CF through newborn screening. The results showed that mothers of screened, symptomatic infants with CF reported lower rates of fostering dependency in their children than mothers of screened, asymptomatic infants with CF and mothers of nonscreened infants with CF diagnosed conventionally. The authors concluded that newborn screening did not increase the mothers' tendency to overprotect their infants. However, this study also noted that the mothers in the screened asymptomatic group reported significantly more intrusiveness in their parenting than the other two groups. Furthermore, a delayed diagnosis was not associated with increased maternal anxiety or other overprotective behaviors such as "excluding external influence over the child" or "wanting to know the child's thoughts." Thus, the New South Wales study showed mixed findings of risks and benefits to the parent-infant relationship for infants diagnosed with CF through newborn screening.

Parents of infants diagnosed with CF through the newborn screening program in Colorado were asked about their perceptions of how the neonatal diagnosis affected their parenting (Helton et al., 1991). All of the 62 parents reportedly maintained the same disciplinary approaches for their children with CF as they would for a child without CF. About one third of the parents described themselves as "overprotective" of their affected child and two thirds tended to be highly vigilant of their affected child's physical health. About one quarter of parents noted improved family relationships. These parents recognized the potentially shortened life span of the affected child and reprioritized their lives so that they could spend more time together as a family and offer their children enriching experiences early in life. Thus, research assessing the impact of a neonatal CF diagnosis on the parent-child relationship remains inconclusive, suggesting that other child or parent factors may also influence the quality of the relationship.

Parents' Attitudes About CF Newborn Screening

Overall, most parents favor newborn screening for CF. Merelle and colleagues (2003) found that 98% of 75 parents of a child with CF supported newborn screening for CF. Their reasons included reducing parental distress associated with delayed diagnosis, implementing early treatment for affected children, preventing unnecessary diagnostic tests, and decreasing the number of hospitalizations. Another study (Helton et al., 1991) showed that 100% of the parents of infants diagnosed with CF traditionally as well as the parents of infants diagnosed through newborn screening supported newborn CF screening. Parents cited the following advantages: preventing disease progression, avoiding misdiagnosis, minimizing parental distress related to a prolonged diagnostic process, decreasing parental guilt due to not noticing a symptom early, and enhancing parents' sense of efficacy in promoting the affected child's health. Ciske and colleagues (2001) reported that 85% of 138 parents with infants who had false-positive CF screens answered "yes" when asked if they think that newborn screening for CF should be done.

Impact of Newborn Screening and Diagnosis on Cognitive Functioning

The Wisconsin randomized clinical trial found an association between nutritional status and cognitive functioning that favored the children diagnosed with CF through newborn screening compared to those diagnosed conventionally (Koscik et al., 2004). Children diagnosed conventionally who had low alpha-tocopherol (vitamin E) levels at diagnosis had significantly lower cognitive scores. While these findings may be considered physiological in nature, the consequences of impaired cognitive functioning may have profound long-term psychosocial implications affecting the child's academic performance, career aspirations, self-esteem, and social status. More research is needed to examine the aforementioned psychosocial issues.

Families With Children Identified as Heterozygote CF Carriers

Parents' Emotional Distress and Confusion About Results

Adverse psychosocial effects associated with newborn screening programs have been a concern since their inception. Parental confusion and anxiety associated with early phases of newborn screening programs have been reported for many disorders (Bergman & Stamm, 1967; Bodegard, Fyro, & Larsson, 1990; Hampton, Anderson, Lavizzo, & Bergman, 1974; Johnson, 2001; Rothenberg & Sills, 1968; Waisbren et al., 2003). Negative consequences generally have been attributed to insufficient information about the screening process and confusion about test results (Sorenson, Levy, Mangione, & Sepe, 1984).

When newborn screening for CF was first implemented in Wisconsin, parents of infants with false-positive screening results were found to have knowledge deficits about the overall newborn screening program, confusion about test results, and short-term emotional distress

(Tluczek et al., 1992). A survey of parents whose infants had false positive CF screens showed that 88% of 138 parents understood that their
child was a CF carrier but 15% were unsure about whether being a CF
carrier could cause illness and about 22% felt anxious about their
child's carrier status (Ciske et al., 2001). During the time between first
learning about the abnormal screening results and the diagnostic
sweat test, strong emotional responses included feelings of shock, anxiety, denial, and anger. Parents also described a sense of hypervigilance
associated with closely monitoring their child for signs of CF. A recent
investigation found that many parents (68% of mothers and 32% of fathers) experienced significant levels of depressive symptoms during
this waiting period (Tluczek, Koscik, Farrell, & Rock, 2005). Little is
known about how the parents' emotional state at the time of their infant's sweat test impacts their acquisition, assimilation, or retention of
the information they receive from the genetic counseling.

Parents' Reproductive Decisions

Much less is known about the reproductive decision making of parents
with infants whose screening results were false positive as compared
to families with children diagnosed with CF. Genetic counseling in the
context of false positive CF results appears to have only a modest effect
on parents' reproductive decisions. The Wisconsin group (Mischler
et al., 1998) found that parents (17%, 10/58) who received genetic
counseling associated with false positive CF screen from the IRT/DNA
method were more likely to report changing their future reproductive
plans as compared with parents (4%, 4/100) whose infants had false
positive CF screen from IRT method and no genetic counseling. A randomized trial of genetic counseling versus no counseling in New York
showed that parents who received genetic counseling at the time of
their infant's sweat test appointment were significantly more likely to
have subsequent genetic testing than parents who received no genetic
counseling (Lagoe, Labella, Arnold, & Rowley, 2005).

Stigma and Discrimination

Although potential stigmatization and discrimination have been cited
as ethical considerations in the debate about newborn screening for CF
(Farrell & Farrell, 2003; Fost, 2003; Wilfond & Rothenberg, 2002), there
are limited reports documenting the presence of such issues as a result
of newborn screening for CF. One study showed that a minority (18%)
of individuals identified as CF carriers reported having difficulties

obtaining life insurance due to their genetic status (Low, King, & Wilkie, 1998). In an extensive review of the literature, Krumm (2002) cited several examples of genetic discrimination regarding employment (Krumm, 2002). However, no documentation of discrimination resulting from newborn screening was found. Clearly, more research is needed to determine whether and to what extent such risks are associated with genetic screening programs.

Limitations of Research

Most studies used a cross-sectional design that only captured one moment in time. The sample sizes were generally small. Data were primarily based upon parental report rather than objective observational methods, and some used nonstandardized instruments. No prospective longitudinal studies to date have documented the effects of newborn screening on the parents, the child, and the parent-child relationship. Most research focuses upon the experiences of families of infants diagnosed with CF, and scant data are available concerning the psychosocial impact of newborn screening on the families with false positive results.

SUMMARY AND CONCLUSION

Since the discovery of the CF gene in 1989, population-based screening for the disorder has been implemented for two different populations: individuals at risk for having a child with CF and newborns. The process of translating genetic technology into the clinical practice of population-based screening for CF has raised concerns over many psychosocial issues as well as emphasizing technical difficulties inherent with this rapidly advancing field.

Population-Based Carrier Screening

Overall, documented negative psychological consequences related to carrier screening for CF appear to be minimal. The literature indicates that patients who undergo CF carrier testing are at risk for misunderstanding test results and poor retention of information. Therefore, individuals may lack sufficient knowledge to make truly informed reproductive decisions. It remains unclear what specific knowledge about genetics, the disease of CF, or the benefits and risk of carrier screening are required for individuals to make informed decisions about carrier screening. While rates for CF carrier testing during pregnancy are high, the rate in the general population remains relatively low. The research also raises questions about whether pregnant women experience pressure to accept genetic testing. In addition, further investigation is warranted in the area of stigmatization issues and gender differences.

Newborn Screening

Benefits of newborn CF screening and diagnosis include preventing unnecessary diagnostic tests in affected children, thereby decreasing their parents' distress and enhancing parents' confidence in the medical community. Mounting evidence confirms that newborn CF screening offers nutritional benefits, improved pulmonary outcomes, reduced morbidity, and lower infant mortality. Parental confusion regarding false positive test results and related emotional distress has been associated with the initial implementation of CF screening programs. The waiting period between notification of abnormal screening results and diagnostic testing is extremely distressing for parents, with many reporting depressive symptoms during this wait. The short-term benefits and risks to the parent-infant relationship for infants diagnosed with CF through newborn screening are mixed, and little is known about false positive children. However, most parents whose infants have CF (diagnosed through screening or conventionally) as well as parents of infants with false positive results are in favor of newborn screening for CF.

While the use of DNA testing in newborn screening also affords couples an opportunity for prenatal testing, very few U.S. families choose this option and many have another child. Choices made by couples in the United States are not necessarily mirrored by couples in other countries. The availability of newborn CF screening and diagnosis is likely to produce increased numbers of children with "atypical" CF presentations and children known to be carriers. We need to examine the long-term social, psychological, and behavioral sequelae for these individuals and their families.

As genetic technologies continue to advance, the number of population-based genetic screening programs, like those for CF, will continue to expand and become standard clinical practice. The success of such programs will rely heavily upon effective approaches to counseling families. It is critical that evidence-based models of care address the psychosocial implications as well as the technical, financial, ethical, and legal aspects of screening programs.

REFERENCES

Allen, D. B., & Farrell, P. M. (1996). Newborn screening: Principles and practice. *Advances in Pediatrics, 43,* 231–270.

American College of Obstetricians and Gynecologists and American College of Medical Genetics. (2001). *Preconception and prenatal carrier screening for cystic fibrosis: Clinical and laboratory guidelines.* Washington, DC: American College of Obstetricians and Gynecologists.

American Society of Human Genetics. (1992). Statement of the American Society of Human Genetics on cystic fibrosis carrier screening. *American Journal of Human Genetics, 51,* 1443–1444.

Axworthy, D., Brock, D. J. H., Bobrow, M., & Marteau, T. M. (1996). Psychological impact of population-based carrier testing for cystic fibrosis: 3-year follow-up. *Lancet, 347*(9013), 1443–1446.

Baroni, M. A., Anderson, Y. E., & Mischler, E. (1997). Cystic fibrosis newborn screening: Impact of early screening results on parenting stress. *Pediatric Nursing, 23*(2), 143–151.

Bekker, H. L., Modell, M., Denniss, G., Silver, A., Mathew, C., Bobrow, M., et al. (1993). Uptake of cystic fibrosis testing in primary care: Supply push or demand pull? *British Medical Journal, 306,* 1584–1586.

Bergman, A. B., & Stamm, S. J. (1967). The morbidity of cardiac nondisease in school children. *New England Journal of Medicine, 276,* 1008–1013.

Bodegard, G., Fyro, K., & Larsson, A. (1990). Psychological reactions in 102 families with a newborn who has a falsely positive screening test for congenital hypothyroidism. *Acta Paediatrica Scandinavica, 304*(Suppl.), 1–21.

Bolan, C., & Thompson, N. L. (1990). Effects of newborn screening of cystic fibrosis on reported maternal behavior. *Archives of Disease in Childhood, 65,* 1240–1244.

Callanan, N. P., Cheuvront, B. J., & Sorenson, J. R. (1999). CF carrier testing in a high risk population: Anxiety, risk perceptions, and reproductive plans of carrier by "non-carrier" couples. *Genetics in Medicine, 1*(7), 323–327.

Ciske, D. J., Haavisto, A., Laxova, A., Zeng, L., Rock, M. J., & Farrell, P. M. (2001). Genetic counseling and neonatal screening for cystic fibrosis: An assessment of the communication process. *Pediatrics, 107,* 699–705.

Clark, R., Tluczek, A., & Gallagher, K. C. (2004). Assessment of parent-child early relational disturbances. In R. Del Carmen & A. Carter (Eds.), *Assessment of mental health disorders in infants and toddlers* (pp. 25–60). Oxford, UK: Oxford University Press.

Clausen, C. H., Brandt, N. J., Schwartz, M., & Skovby, F. (1996a). Psychological and social impact of carrier screening for cystic fibrosis among pregnant women—a pilot study. *Clinical Genetics, 49*(4), 200–205.

Clausen, C. H., Brandt, N. J., Schwartz, M., & Skovby, F. (1996b). Psychological impact of carrier screening for cystic fibrosis among pregnant women. *European Journal of Human Genetics, 4*(2), 120–123.

Cystic Fibrosis Foundation. (2005). *Median age of survival for people with CF increased to 35.1 years in 2004.* Retrieved July 6, 2005 from http://www.cff.org/home/

Cystic Fibrosis Mutation Database. (2005, November 21). Retrieved January 25, 2006, from http://www.genet.sickkids.on.ca/cftr/

Dankert-Roelse, J. E., te Meerman, G. J., Know, K., & ten Kate, L. P. (1987). Effect of screening for cystic fibrosis on the influence of genetic counseling. *Clinical Genetics, 32,* 271–275.

Denayer, L., Welkenhuysen, M., Evers-Keibooms, G., Cassiman, J. J., & Van den Berghe, H. (1996). The CF carrier status is not associated with a diminished self-concept or increased anxiety: Results of psychometric testing after at least 1 year. *Clinical Genetics, 49*(5), 232–236.

Denayer, L., Welkenhuysen, M., Evers-Keibooms, G., Cassiman, J. J., & Van den Berghe, H. (1997). Risk perception after CF carrier testing and impact of the test result on reproductive decision making. *American Journal of Medical Genetics, 69,* 422–428.

Dudding, T., Wilcken, B., Burgess, B., Hambly, J., & Turner, G. (2000). Reproductive decisions after neonatal screening identifies cystic fibrosis. *Archives of Disease in Childhood: Fetal and Neonatal Edition, 82,* F124–F127.

Edenborough, F. P. (2001). Women with cystic fibrosis and their potential for reproduction. *Thorax, 56,* 649–655.

Evers-Keibooms, G., Denayer, L., Welkenhuysen, M., Cassiman, J. J., & Van den Berghe, H. (1994). A stigmatizing effect of the carrier status for cystic fibrosis? *Clinical Genetics, 46,* 336–343.

Farrell, M. H., & Farrell, P. M. (2003). Newborn screening for cystic fibrosis: Ensuring more good than harm. *Journal of Pediatrics, 143*(6), 707–712.

Farrell, P. M., Kosorok, M. R., Laxova, A., Shen, G., Koscik, R., Bruns, T., et al. (1997). Nutritional benefits of neonatal screening for cystic fibrosis. Wisconsin Cystic Fibrosis Neonatal Screening Study Group. *New England Journal of Medicine, 337,* 963–969.

Feetham, S. L. (1999). Families and the genetic revolution: Implications for primary health care, education, and research. *Family Systems in Health, 17*(1), 27–44.

Fischer-Fay, A., Goldberg, S., Simmons, R., & Levison, H. (1988). Chronic illness and infant-mother attachment: Cystic fibrosis. *Journal of Developmental and Behavioral Pediatrics, 9,* 266–270.

Fost, N. (2003). *Routine newborn screening for cystic fibrosis: Potential risks.* Paper presented at the Newborn Screening for Cystic Fibrosis Conference, Atlanta, Georgia.

Gates, E. A. (2004). Communicating risk in prenatal genetic testing. *Journal of Midwifery and Women's Health, 49,* 220–227.

Godard, B., ten Kate, L. P., Evers-Keibooms, G., & Ayme, S. (2003). Population genetic screening programs: Principles, techniques, practices, and policies. *European Journal of Human Genetics, 11*(Suppl. 2), S49–S87.

Gordon, C., Walpole, I., Zubrick, S. R., & Bower, C. (2003). Population screening for cystic fibrosis: Knowledge and emotional consequences 18 months later. *American Journal of Medical Genetics, 120A*(2), 199–208.

Goss, C. H., Rubenfeld, G. D., Otto, K., & Aitken, M. L. (2003). The effect of pregnancy on survival in women with cystic fibrosis. *Chest, 124*(4), 1460–1468.

Green, J. M., Hewison, J., Bekker, H. L., Bryant, L. D., & Cuckle, H. S. (2004). Psychosocial aspects of genetic screening of pregnancy women and newborns: A systematic review. *Health Technology Assessment, 8*(33), 1–109.

Grody, W. W., Cutting, G. R., Klinger, K. W., Richards, C. S., Watson, M. S., & Desnick, R. J. (2001). Laboratory standards and guidelines for population-based cystic fibrosis carrier screening. *Genetics in Medicine, 3*(2), 149–154.

Grody, W. W., Dunkel-Schetter, C., Tatsugawa, Z. H., Fox, M. A., Fang, C. Y., Cantor, R. M., et al. (1997). PCR-based screening for cystic fibrosis carrier mutations in an ethnically diverse pregnant population. *American Journal of Human Genetics, 60*(4), 935–947.

Grosse, S. D., Boyle, C. A., Botkin, J. R., Comeau, A. M., Kharrazi, M., Rosenfeld, M., et al. (2004). Newborn screening for cystic fibrosis: Evaluation of benefits and risks and recommendations for State Newborn Screening Programs. *MMWR: Morbidity and Mortality Weekly Report, 53*(RR13), 1–36.

Hampton, M. L., Anderson, J., Lavizzo, B. S., & Bergman, A. B. (1974). Sickle cell "nondisease." *American Journal of Diseases in Children, 128*, 58–61.

Hans, C., Brandt, N. J., Schwartz, M., & Skovby, F. (1996). Psychological and social impact of carrier screening for cystic fibrosis among pregnant woman—a pilot study. *Clinical Genetics, 49*, 200–205.

Harris, H., Scotcher, D., Hartley, N. E., Wallace, A., Craufurd, D., & Harris, R. (1996). Pilot study of the acceptability of cystic fibrosis carrier testing during routine antenatal consultations in general practice. *British Journal of General Practitioners, 46*, 225–227.

Hartley, N. E., Scotcher, D., Harris, H., Williamson, P., Wallace, A., Craufurd, D., et al. (1997). The uptake and acceptability to patients of cystic fibrosis carrier testing offered in pregnancy by the GP. *Journal of Medical Genetics, 34*, 459–464.

Heim, R. A., Sugarman, E. A., & Allitto, B. A. (2001). Improved detection of cystic fibrosis mutations in the heterogeneous U. S. population using an expanded, pan-ethnic mutation panel. *Genetics in Medicine, 3*(3), 168–176.

Helton, J. L., Harmon, R. J., Robinson, N., & Accurso, F. J. (1991). Parental attitudes toward newborn screening for cystic fibrosis. *Pediatric Pulmonology Supplement, 7*, 23–28.

Henneman, L., Bramsen, I., van Os, T., Reuling, I., Heyerman, H., van der Laag, J., et al. (2001). Attitudes towards reproductive issues and carrier testing among adult patients and parent of children with cystic fibrosis (CF). *Prenatal Diagnosis, 21*, 1–9.

Henneman, L., Kooij, L., Bouman, K., & ten Kate, L. P. (2002). Personal experiences of cystic fibrosis (CF) carrier couples prospectively identified in CF families. *American Journal of Medical Genetics, 110*, 324–331.

Henneman, L., Poppelaars, F. A. M., & ten Kate, L. P. (2002). Evaluation of cystic fibrosis carrier screening programs according to genetic screening criteria. *Genetics in Medicine, 4*(4), 241–249.

Johnson, S. B. (2001). Screening programs to identify children at risk for diabetes mellitus: Psychological impact on children and parents. *Journal of Pediatric Endocrinology and Metabolism, 14,* 653–659.

Kent, N. E., & Farquharson, D. F. (1993). Cystic fibrosis and pregnancy. *Canadian Medical Association Journal, 149*(6), 809–813.

Kerem, B.-S., Rommens, J. M., Buchanan, J. A., Markiewicz, D., Cox, T. K., Chakravarti, A., et al. (1989). Identification of the cystic fibrosis gene: Genetic analysis. *Science, 245,* 1073–1080.

Kharrazi, M., & Kharrazi, L. D. (2005). Delayed diagnosis of cystic fibrosis and the family perspective. *Journal of Pediatrics, 147*(3 Suppl.), S21–25.

Koscik, R. L., Farrell, P. M., Kosorok, M. R., Zaremba, K. M., Laxova, A., Lai, H.-C., et al. (2004). Cognitive function of children with cystic fibrosis: Deleterious effect of early malnutrition. *Pediatrics, 113*(6), 1549–1557.

Krumm, J. (2002). Genetic discrimination: Why Congress must ban genetic testing in the workplace. *Journal of Legal Medicine, 23*(4), 491–521.

Kulich, M., Rosenfeld, M., Goss, C. H., & Wilmott, R. (2003). Improved survival among young patients with cystic fibrosis. *Journal of Pediatrics, 142*(6), 631–636.

Lagoe, E., Labella, S., Arnold, G., & Rowley, P. T. (2005). Cyctic fibrosis newborn screening: A pilot study to maximize carrier screening. *Genetic Testing, 9*(3), 255–260.

Lerman, C., Tercyak, K. P., Crolye, R. T., & Hamann, H. (2002). Genetic testing: Psychological aspects and implications. *Journal of Consulting and Clinical Psychology, 70*(3), 784–797.

Levenkron, J. C., Loader, S., & Rowley, P. T. (1997). Carrier screening for cystic fibrosis: Test acceptance and one year follow-up. *American Journal of Medical Genetics, 73,* 378–386.

Livingstone, J., Axton, R. A., Gilfillan, A., Mennie, M., Compton, M., Liston, W. A., et al. (1994). Antenatal screening for cystic fibrosis: A trial of the couple model. *British Medical Journal, 308*(6942), 1459–1462.

Loader, S., Caldwell, P., Kozyra, A., Levenkron, J. C., Boehm, C. D., Kazazian, H. H. J., et al. (1996). Cystic fibrosis carrier population screening the primary care setting. *American Journal of Human Genetics, 59,* 234–247.

Low, L., King, S., & Wilkie, T. (1998). Genetic discrimination in life insurance: Empirical evidence from a cross sectional survey of genetic support groups in the United Kingdom. *British Medical Journal, 12,* 1632–1635.

Marteau, T. M., Dundas, R., & Axworthy, D. (1997). Long-term cognitive and emotional impact of genetic testing for carriers of cystic fibrosis: The effects of test result and gender. *Health Psychology, 16*(1), 51–62.

McCollum, A. T., & Gibson, L. E. (1970). Family adaptation to the child with cystic fibrosis. *Journal of Pediatrics, 77*(4), 571–578.

McKone, E. F., Emerson, S. S., Edwards, K. L., & Aitken, M. L. (2003). Effect of genotype on phenotype and mortality in cystic fibrosis: A retrospective cohort study. *Lancet, 361,* 1671–1676.

Mennie, M. E., Axworthy, D., Liston, W. A., & Brock, D. J. (1997). Prenatal screening for cystic fibrosis carriers: Does the method of testing affect the longer-term understanding and reproductive behavior of women? *Prenatal Diagnosis, 17*(9), 853–860.

Mennie, M. E., Gilfillan, A., Compton, M., Curtis, L., Liston, W. A., Pullen, I., et al. (1992). Prenatal screening for cystic fibrosis. *Lancet, 340*(8813), 209–210.

Mennie, M. E., Gilfillan, A., Compton, M., Liston, W. A., & Brock, D. J. (1993). Prenatal cystic fibrosis carrier screening: Factors in a woman's decision to decline testing. *Prenatal Diagnosis, 13*(9), 807–814.

Merelle, M. E., Huisman, J., Alderden-van der Vecht, A., Taat, F., Bezemer, D., Griffioen, R. W., et al. (2003). Early versus late diagnosis: Psychological impact on parents of children with cystic fibrosis. *Pediatrics, 111*(2), 346–350.

Michie, S., Smith, D., McClennan, A., & Marteau, T. M. (1997). Patient decision making: An evaluation of two different methods of presenting information about a screening test. *British Journal of Health Psychology, 2,* 317–326.

Mischler, E. H., Wilfond, B. S., Fost, N., Laxova, A., Reiser, C., Sauer, C. M., et al. (1998). Cystic fibrosis newborn screening: Impact on reproductive behavior and implications for genetic counseling. *Pediatrics, 102*(1), 44–52.

National Institutes of Health. (1997). *NIH Consensus Statement. Genetic Testing for Cystic Fibrosis April, 1997.* Retrieved January 25, 2006, from http://consensus.nih.gov/cons/106/106_intro.htm

National Newborn Screening and Genetics Resource Center. (2006, January 10). *Current newborn screening (NBS) conditions by state.* Retrieved January 25, 2006, from http://genes-r-us.uthscsa.edu/

Newman, J. E., Sorenson, J. R., DeVellis, B. M., & Cheuvront, B. (2002). Gender differences in psychosocial reactions to cystic fibrosis carrier testing. *American Journal of Medical Genetics, 113,* 151–157.

O'Hara, M. W. (1997). The nature of postpartum depressive disorders. In P. J. Cooper & L. Murray (Eds.), *Postpartum depression and child development* (pp. 3–31). New York: Guilford.

Palomaki, G. E., FitzSimmons, S. C., & Haddow, J. E. (2004). Clinical sensitivity of prenatal screening for cystic fibrosis via CFTR carrier testing in the United States panethnic population. *Genetics in Medicine, 6*(5), 405–414.

Quittner, A. L., DiGirolamo, A. M., Michael, M., & Eigen, H. (1992). Parental response to CF: A contextual analysis of the diagnostic phase. *Journal of Pediatric Psychology, 17,* 683–704.

Riordan, J. R., Rommens, J. M., Kerem, B.-S., Alon, N., Rozmahel, R., Grzelczak, A., et al. (1989). Identification of the cystic fibrosis gene: Cloning and characterization of complementary DNA. *Science, 245,* 1066–1073.

Rommens, J. M., Iannzzi, M. C., Kerem, B.-S., Drumm, M. L., Melmer, G., Dean, M., et al. (1989). Identification of the cystic fibrosis gene: Chromosome walking and jumping. *Science, 245,* 1059–1065.

Rosenstein, B. J., & Cutting, G. (1998). The diagnosis of cystic fibrosis: A consensus statement. Cystic Fibrosis Foundation Consensus Panel. *Journal of Pediatrics, 132*(4), 589–595.

Rothenberg, M. B., & Sills, E. M. (1968). The PKU anxiety syndrome. *Journal of American Academy of Child Psychiatry, 7,* 689–692.

Scotet, V., de Braekeleer, M., Roussey, M., Rault, G., Parent, P., Dagorne, M., et al. (2000). Neonatal screening for cystic fibrosis in Brittany, France: Assessment of 10 years' experience and impact on prenatal diagnosis. *Lancet, 356*, 789–794.

Sorenson, J. R., Levy, H. L., Mangione, T. W., & Sepe, S. J. (1984). Parental response to repeat testing of infants with "false positive" results in a newborn screening program. *Pediatrics, 73*(2), 183–187.

Sturm, E. L., & Ormond, K. E. (2004). Adjunct prenatal testing: Patient decisions regarding ethnic carrier screening and fluorescence in situ hybridization. *Journal of Genetic Counseling, 13*(1), 45–63.

Tluczek, A., Koscik, R. L., Farrell, P. M., & Rock, M. J. (2005). Psychosocial risk associated with newborn screening for cystic fibrosis: Parents' experience while awaiting the sweat test appointment. *Pediatrics, 115*(6), 1692–1703.

Tluczek, A., Micschler, E. H., Bowers, B., Peterson, N. M., Morris, M. E., Farrell, P. M., et al. (1991). Psychological impact of false-positive results when screening for cystic fibrosis. *Pediatric Pulmonary Supplement, 7*, 29–37.

Tluczek, A., Mischler, E. H., Farrell, P. M., Fost, N., Peterson, N. M., Carey, P., et al. (1992). Parents' knowledge of neonatal screening and response to false-positive cystic fibrosis testing. *Developmental and Behavioral Pediatrics, 13*(3), 181–186.

van der Broom, D. (2004). First attachments: Theory and research. In G. Bremner & A. Fogel (Eds.), *Blackwell handbook of infant development* (pp. 296–325). Malden, MA: Blackwell.

Wagener, J. S., Farrell, P. M., & Corey, M. (2001). A debate on why my state (province) should or should not conduct newborn screening for cystic fibrosis. *Pediatric Pulmonology, 32*, 385–396.

Waisbren, S. E., Albers, S., Amato, S., Ampola, M., Brewster, T. G., Demmer, L., et al. (2003). Effect of expanded newborn screening for biochemical genetic disorders on child outcomes and parental stress. *Journal of the American Medical Association, 290*(19), 2564–2572.

Waters, D. L., Wilcken, B., Irwing, L., Van Asperen, P., Mellis, C., Simpson, J. M., et al. (1999). Clinical outcomes of newborn screening for cystic fibrosis. *Archives of Disease in Childhood Fetal and Neonatal Edition, 80*(1), F1–7.

Watson, E. K., Mayall, E. S., Lamb, J., Chapple, J., & Williamson, R. (1992). Psychological and social consequences of community carrier screening for cystic fibrosis. *Lancet, 340*, 217–220.

Watson, M. S., Cutting, G. R., Desnick, R. J., Driscoll, D. A., Klinger, K., Mennuti, M., et al. (2004). Cystic fibrosis population carrier screening: 2004 revision of American College of Medical Genetics mutation panel. *Genetics in Medicine, 6*(5), 387–391.

Watson, M. S., Desnick, R. J., Grody, W. W., Mennuti, M. T., Popovich, B. W., & Richards, C. S. (2002). Cystic fibrosis carrier screening: Issues in implementation. *Genetics in Medicine, 4*, 407–409.

Welsh, M., Ramsey, B., Accurso, R., & Cutting, G. (2001). Cystic fibrosis. In C. R. Sciver, A. L. Beaudet, W. S. Sly, & D. Valle (Eds.), *The metabolic and molecular basis of inherited disease* (8th ed., pp. 5121–5188). New York: McGraw-Hill.

Wheeler, P. G., Smith, R., Dorkin, H., Parad, R. B., Comeau, A. M., & Bianchi, D. W. (2001). Genetic counseling after implementation of statewide cystic fibrosis newborn screening: Two years experience in one medical center. *Genetics in Medicine, 3*(6), 411–415.

Wilcken, B., & Chalmers, G. (1985). Reduced morbidity in patients with cystic fibrosis detected by neonatal screening. *Lancet, 2*, 1319–1321.

Wilfond, B. S., & Rothenberg, L. S. (2002). Ethical issues in cystic fibrosis newborn screening: From data to public health policy. *Current Opinion in Pulmonary Medicine, 8*, 529–534.

Witt, D. R., Schaefer, C., Hallam, P., Wi, S., Blumberg, B., Fishbach, A., et al. (1996). Cystic fibrosis heterozygote screening in 5,161 pregnant women. *American Journal of Human Genetics, 58*(4), 823–835.

Zeanah, C. H., Larrieu, J. A., Heller, S. S., & Valliere, J. (2000). Parent-infant relationship assessment. In C. H. J. Zeanah (Ed.), *Handbook of infant mental health* (2nd ed., pp. 222–235). New York: Guilford.

Chapter 10

Psychosocial Processes in Genetic Risk Assessment for Breast Cancer

*Suzanne M. Miller, Mary B. Daly, Kerry A. Sherman,
Linda Fleisher, Joanne S. Buzaglo, Laura Stanton,
Andrew K. Godwin, and John Scarpato*

IN 2001, THE FIRST DRAFT OF THE SEQUENCE OF THE HUMAN GENOME WAS published (Collins & Guttmacher, 2001), spawning a new generation of research focused on understanding the impact of the genome on the predisposition for many diseases, especially cancer. During the last decade, tremendous effort has been devoted to understanding how these genes function in increasing the risk of cancer, and how their interaction with other genes may be altered by the presence of a mutation. However, it is not just the basic science questions that need further exploration, but also the psychosocial impact of this new knowledge on those who have genetic abnormalities (Emery, 2001).

Perhaps the most well-studied area of cancer genetics is breast cancer and the implications of these extraordinary discoveries for screening, detection, and management strategies. Breast cancer is the most common nonskin cancer and the second leading cause of cancer-related death in women. It is estimated that 269,740 individuals are diagnosed with breast cancer (both invasive and in situ) each year (American Cancer Society, 2005, p. 9). The current estimate is that inherited forms of breast cancer through genetic mutations account for about 5% to 10% of breast cancer cases (Easton, Ford, & Bishop, 1995). With the advancements in early diagnosis and new treatment regimens, more than 90% of breast cancers are now diagnosed at localized and regional stages, for which 5-year survival rates are 98% and 80%, respectively (American Cancer Society, 2005, p. 11). In addition to genetic mutations, the risk factors for breast cancer include increasing age, previous history of breast cancer, family history, and reproductive and menstrual history (National Cancer Center, 2006, p. 6).

To comprehensively address the needs of women and their spouses or partners and extended family at increased risk, psychosocial researchers and practitioners need to have a foundational knowledge of breast cancer genetics and prevention, including available risk reduction options. It is also important for them to understand women's knowledge about their risk, as well as the psychological sequelae that result from the complex decisions and options faced by at-risk individuals. This chapter provides an overview of the current state of the science in breast cancer genetics and available approaches to risk assessment and management, with an emphasis on the psychosocial impact of this emerging technology on women and their families. It concludes with recommendations to improve current research and practice in this area.

GENETIC FACTORS IN BREAST CANCER

Alterations in the *BRCA1* or *BRCA2* genes characterize part of the hereditary breast and ovarian cancer syndrome. This syndrome is indicated in families with breast cancer diagnoses at young ages, male breast cancer, ovarian cancer, or multiple family members who have been diagnosed with breast and ovarian cancers (Daly, 1999). The *BRCA1* gene, located on chromosome 17, was identified in the 1990s, followed by the identification of *BRCA2* on chromosome 13 (Narod et al., 1991; Wooster et al., 1994). *BRCA1* and *BRCA2* mutations are inherited in an autosomal dominant fashion.

These genes have been shown to function in tumor suppression and DNA repair, although they have also been implicated in other activities within the cell cycle (Chang & Elledge, 2001; Venkitaraman, 2002; Welcsh & King, 2001). Three alterations in these genes are most commonly found in women of Ashkenazi Jewish heritage: 185delAG and 5382insC on the *BRCA1* gene, and 6174delT on the *BRCA2* gene, with recent research on Ashkenazi Jewish women unselected for age or family history indicating that up to 41% of those women with ovarian cancer may carry alterations in these genes (Moslehi et al., 2000).

BRCA1/2 mutations confer between 60% and 85% lifetime risk of developing breast cancer (Nathanson, Wooster, & Weber, 2001), and 10% to 40% lifetime risk for ovarian cancer (Antoniou et al., 2003). Indeed, women with a *BRCA1/2* mutation are approximately 3 to 6 times more likely to develop breast cancer, and 9 to 35 times more likely to develop ovarian cancer, than women without *BRCA1/2* alterations. However, *BRCA1/2* mutations do not account for the total number of hereditary breast cancer cases. Breast cancer is also a component of the rare Li-Fraumeni syndrome, in which germline mutations of the *953* gene on chromosome 17p have been documented (Bell et al., 1995; Garber et al., 1991), and Cowden's syndrome, associated with germline mutation in PTEN, a protein tyrosine phosphatase with homology to tensin, located on chromosome 10q23 (Lynch, Ostermeyer, et al., 1997). In addition, it appears likely that multiple genes are involved in the causation of the remaining hereditary breast cancer cases (Antoniou, Pharoah, McMullan, Day, & Ponder, 2001; Antoniou et al., 2002; Narod et al., 1995).

CURRENT APPROACHES TO GENETIC RISK ASSESSMENT FOR BREAST CANCER

The discovery and identification of the *BRCA1* and *BRCA2* genes has led to the implementation of breast cancer familial risk assessment programs. These risk assessment programs generally entail cancer risk education, personal pedigree feedback, genetic testing for putative hereditary cases, and individualized screening recommendations. Women with strong familial breast cancer patterns or women concerned about their inherited risk often participate in risk assessment programs to determine if they are eligible for genetic testing. The key goals of genetic susceptibility testing are to identify families who may benefit from available preventive strategies and to facilitate decisions about long-term medical management.

This benefit applies both to women who have already been affected with breast cancer, as well as to unaffected individuals in these families. Women who have already been diagnosed with breast cancer and are subsequently found to be *BRCA1/2* carriers can consider various prophylactic strategies to reduce their risk of ovarian cancer and to lower their risk of a second breast cancer. For unaffected women, genetic risk feedback can help clarify their cancer risk status, reduce medical uncertainty, and facilitate informed health care decision making. Most notably, in the case of positive mutational findings, unaffected women can begin to consider such options as surgical and chemotherapeutic prophylaxis, as well as more intensive surveillance regimens. Genetic testing also provides valuable personal information to unaffected women, in that they can better plan for the future in terms of childbearing, career, retirement, or other individual and family life cycle decisions.

There are four potential outcomes of genetic testing for cancer-predisposing gene mutations:

1. Positive: a carrier of a "known" cancer-predisposing gene mutation
2. Negative: not a carrier of a known cancer-predisposing gene mutation positively identified in another family member
3. Indeterminate: not a carrier of a known cancer-predisposing gene mutation, and the carrier status of other family members is negative/unknown
4. Inconclusive: a carrier of a gene mutation that currently has no known significance

Few women receive a true negative test result; many women test indeterminate. In our current work, over 70% receive an indeterminate finding (Daly, 1999). Some indeterminate findings can be clarified into true negatives, but only upon testing of further family members. Adding to the complexity is the fact that the penetrance of *BRCA1/2* mutations is incomplete (Easton et al., 1995). Therefore, individuals who test positive do not necessarily develop breast or ovarian cancer, and those who test negative may still be at high risk for breast or ovarian cancer based on other factors (e.g., environmental factors).

Women need to be aware of the meaning of a positive, negative, or indeterminate result, for them personally and for their families. The clinical utility of a genetic test result rests on the fact that knowing one's test results can allow for an informed evaluation of the risks and benefits of existing medical strategies to facilitate screening or risk reduction. However, the limitations of current genetic testing approaches, as well as available management strategies, present at-risk individuals with numerous challenges regarding the decision about whether to undergo testing. Individuals who are candidates for *BRCA1/2* testing also need to consider the implications that their own participation in genetic risk assessment may have for their family members.

RISK REDUCTION AND MEDICAL
MANAGEMENT APPROACHES

The question of what is appropriate breast cancer screening has been a subject of debate. Specific screening recommendations currently exist for women with positive and negative test results. The current recommendation is that carriers of a *BRCA1/2* alteration undergo mammography before age 40, from as young as 25 to 35 years of age, or 10 years below the age of the youngest breast cancer diagnosis in the family (Brekelmans et al., 2001; Dershaw, 2000). The current recommendation also includes magnetic resonance imaging for routine screening for these individuals (Stoutjesdijk et al., 2001; Trecate et al., 2003). The receipt of a true negative finding can obviate the need for enhanced surveillance practices (Botkin et al., 1996). However, for women with indeterminate or inconclusive results, surveillance recommendations are less clear-cut, and are primarily based on the individual's family history (Daly, 1999).

In addition to early detection methods of breast cancer surveillance, currently several preventive options are available for BRCA1/2 carriers, including chemoprevention (i.e., tamoxifen), oral contraceptives, and prophylactic surgery. However, the efficacy of the different preventive options varies, and in some cases is unclear.

Chemoprevention

Given that breast cancer can be associated with reproductive hormones (estrogen and progesterone), chemopreventive agents generally involve hormone-based interventions. Tamoxifen is useful in those cases where women test node positive for estrogen and has been widely used for breast cancer treatment (Osborne, 1998). Its use as a chemopreventive agent has also been assessed. Evidence for the preventive utility of ta-moxifen emerged during clinical trials testing the use of tamoxifen as an adjuvant chemotherapy agent in women affected with breast cancer (Fisher, Sass, Palekar, Fisher, & Wolmark, 1989; Powles et al., 1989, 1998; Veronesi et al., 1998). The evidence for the efficacy of tamoxifen as a pri-mary chemopreventive agent has been established by the National Sur-gical Adjuvant Breast and Bowel Project P1 chemoprevention trial, showing a clear risk reduction benefit for breast cancer among women who received 5 years of tamoxifen (Fisher et al., 1998). A meta-analysis of effects from three tamoxifen chemoprevention trials suggests that tamoxifen may provide a 40% reduction in breast cancer incidence (Cuzick, 2000). The benefit was confined to estrogen-sensitive tumors. Among women identified as BRCA1/2 carriers, case control evidence suggests that tamoxifen reduces the likelihood of breast cancer by ap-proximately 50% (Narod et al., 2000), although there is some indication that tamoxifen may be more effective for BRCA2 carriers than for BRCA1 carriers (King et al., 2001). The use of tamoxifen has been associ-ated with side effects, including hot flashes and increased risk for thromboembolic events, stroke, and endometrial cancer. The long-term effects of tamoxifen on overall health are the subject of ongoing multi-center clinical trials (Eeles & Powles, 2000).

In light of the limitations of tamoxifen, several new drugs are cur-rently under investigation as alternative chemopreventive agents for breast cancer. Raloxifene, a commonly prescribed medication for the reduction of osteoporosis, appears to reduce breast cancer risk in postmenopausal women, and with fewer side effects than those associated with tamoxifen. In addition to raloxifene, aromatase inhibitors (which act by reducing estrogen level by inhibiting the enzyme aromatase) may be even more appropriate for chemopreventive use among postmenopausal women. However, until further clinical trial evidence comes to light, tamoxifen remains the only FDA-approved chemopreventive drug.

The benefit of oral contraceptive use for ovarian cancer risk reduction is equally unclear (Ozols et al., 2003). Oral contraceptive use has been reported to reduce the risk of ovarian cancer 20% after 3 years, and up to 60% after 6 years for BRCA1/2 carriers (Narod et al., 1998). However, Modan et al. (2001) found no decrease in ovarian cancer risk with oral contraceptive use among carriers of the three common BRCA1/2 alterations found in the Ashkenazi Jewish population.

Prophylactic Surgery

Bilateral prophylactic mastectomy appears to reduce the risk for breast cancer in BRCA1/2 carriers up to 90% (Hartmann et al., 2001; Meijers-Heijboer et al., 2001; Rebbeck et al., 2004). This reduced risk is similar to that found in noncarriers. The currently preferred preventive procedure is total mastectomy involving the surgical removal of all breast tissue, including nipple removal, with or without reconstruction (Chlebowski, 2002). Given the irreversibility of this surgery, it is incumbent upon the high-risk woman to carefully consider the risks and benefits of this option before making a final decision.

Bilateral prophylactic oophorectomy provides up to a 50% reduction in risk for breast cancer for women with alterations in the BRCA1 gene (Rebbeck, 2000). In addition, bilateral oophorectomy significantly lowers, but does not fully eliminate, the level of ovarian cancer risk (Eisen, Rebbeck, Wood, & Weber, 2000). Several cases of peritoneal cancers resembling ovarian cancer have been reported in women who have undergone prophylactic oophorectomy. In addition, the medical complications of prophylactic oophorectomy caused by premature menopause (notably vasomotor instability, hot flashes, osteoporosis, and cardiovascular disease) are important factors for a woman to consider before opting for this procedure.

On balance, the use of chemopreventive agents for women at high risk for breast cancer appears to be most indicated for individuals who are postmenopausal and estrogen receptor positive. To date, no chemopreventive agents have been approved for risk reduction for ovarian cancer. In terms of surgical options, both total mastectomy and bilateral oophorectomy offer significant risk reduction for breast and ovarian cancer, particularly among genetic mutation carriers. All of the available preventive options carry certain risks that must be carefully weighed against the potential benefits. In particular, since there is no one prescribed course of action for any given genetic test outcome, high-risk individuals need to consider the potential psychological, personal, and couples and family relationship consequences of each option when deciding whether to elect or forego prophylactic options (Botkin et al., 1996).

PSYCHOSOCIAL ISSUES FOR WOMEN AT INHERITED RISK OF BREAST CANCER

High-risk women are confronted with a dilemma about whether to undergo genetic testing to learn if they, and possibly their family members, are likely to develop breast or ovarian cancer, or alternatively to avoid this prospect altogether (Shoda et al., 1998). The uncertainty of genetic test results and the multiplicity of risk management approaches underscore the complexity of the decisions that need to be made among high-risk women who are considering *BRCA1/2* testing. Given the probabilistic outcomes and range of available options, the risk information to be conveyed is future oriented, highly uncertain, potentially psychologically disruptive, and has implications for the family as well as for the individual (Blackhall, Murphy, Frank, Michel, & Azen, 1995; Daly et al., 2001; Lehmann, Weeks, Klar, Biener, & Garber, 2000; Miller & Schnoll, 2000; Shoda et al., 1998).

In the absence of clear medical benefits of knowing one's genetic risk, the decision to undergo genetic testing is often based on short-term goals (e.g., uncertainty reduction upon learning the results) and potential long-term psychological and personal consequences (e.g., whether or not to undergo prophylactic surgery in the case of positive test results; Botkin et al., 1996; Shoda et al., 1998). Women must therefore realistically anticipate how they would feel if confronted with any one of the four possible testing outcomes, and plan for coping with the medical, emotional, and behavioral consequences of their chosen course of action.

The following scenario highlights the uncertainty and challenges faced by women who undergo genetic counseling and testing.

Mary and her sister Jennifer came to the family resource center for genetic testing together, as they were concerned about the high rates of breast and ovarian cancer in their family. Mary had no children, while Jennifer had two girls. Their mother, a cancer survivor, had already been found to be positive for the BRCA1 genetic mutation. Upon testing, Mary and Jennifer's results were different: Mary, like her mother, was a mutation carrier, but Jennifer was a true negative. As a result, Mary was referred for evaluation in a chemoprevention study and encouraged to increase her mammography schedule, while Jennifer was not a candidate for increased prevention and surveillance options. Jennifer felt greatly relieved about her status, especially given the fact that she had good news to report to her daughters. Mary, on the other hand, had important information to factor into her childbearing decisions: each of her children would run a 50% chance of carrying the BRCA1 gene.

Given these uncertainties and life-altering decisions, the purpose of genetic risk counseling is to facilitate decision making over the course of the genetic testing process, by providing information, addressing uncertainty, assisting with the weighing of the pros and cons of different options, and maximizing adjustment. The six major goals of genetic risk counseling are as follows:

1. Comprehension of genetic risk information to enable an adaptive decision and to determine whether family history suggests an inherited pattern
2. Effective decision making regarding whether to undergo genetic testing
3. Adjustment and minimization of the negative impact of genetic testing
4. Adherence to surveillance recommendations
5. Follow-up decision making regarding prevention options
6. Communication of test results to family members

Although the basic goals of genetic counseling remain the same for all women, the impact and interpretation of the information provided, as well as the decision-making process, are highly personal. Therefore, the process needs to be individualized and tailored to the individual's cognitive, social, and affective profile (Miller et al., 2004; Miller, Roussi, et al., 2005).

Cognitive-Social Theoretical Approach to the Correlates and Consequences of Genetic Risk for Breast Cancer

A full understanding of the ways in which individuals (or families) make decisions about *BRCA1/2* testing requires knowledge of the disease factors that confront them, as well as how they dynamically process the feedback they receive. The cognitive-social approach (see Chapter 3) provides an integrative theoretical framework that enables the conceptualization of the types of factors that undermine or facilitate initial decision making related to genetic testing, as well as the subsequent execution of these decisions. This framework is also relevant to decision making about new options that emerge as the individual progresses through the counseling process, such as whether or not to engage in certain preventive and surveillance options.

According to the cognitive-social health information processing (C-SHIP) model (Miller, Fang, Manne, Engstrom, & Daly, 1999; Miller, Shoda, & Hurley, 1996), individuals differ in how they cognitively and affectively process and respond to cancer risk-related information. This model focuses particularly on delineating the psychosocial dynamics that influence individual differences in reactions to health threats, such as hereditary risk feedback. It is a direct application to health-protective behavior of a more general cognitive-affective system theory of individual differences (Mischel & Shoda, 1995) and draws on recent theorizing to provide a cumulative, unifying conceptual framework for behavioral medicine (e.g., Ajzen & Madden, 1986; Bandura, 1986; Becker, 1974; Carver & Scheier, 1986; Carver, Scheier, & Weintraub, 1989).

According to the C-SHIP model, the impact of any health-related information will depend, in part, on how it is encoded (interpreted) by the individual, and the expectancies and beliefs, affects and emotions, and values and goals that become activated during cognitive-affective processing. These components, in turn, interact in predictable ways to determine both the self-regulatory control strategies and competencies the individual or family draws on to generate action plans, and the coping responses that are executed for dealing with the health threat over time. For example, one individual with a BRCA1/2 mutation and a high perceived risk for breast cancer might decide to undergo prophylactic mastectomy in order to avoid the health-related anxiety and worry triggered by adhering to frequent anxiety-inducing surveillance procedures that only serve to remind her about her high-risk status.

In contrast, another individual with the same genetic test result and similarly heightened risk perceptions might postpone prophylactic surgery because her immediate life goal is to start a family in the near future and to breast-feed her children. In addition, this individual may view frequent screening as a way to reduce, rather than increase, ongoing anxiety and uncertainty. Yet still another individual with the identical objective and subjective risk levels might delay making a definitive decision about surgery because of her understanding of the incomplete penetrance of BRCA1/2 (i.e., she may never get breast cancer), and consider frequent screening as an available option for addressing her high-risk status in the short term (Patenaude, 2004; Patenaude, Guttmacher, & Collins, 2002).

A key feature of the cognitive-social model is the distinction between high monitoring and low monitoring ("blunting") attentional styles or behavioral "signatures" (Miller, 1995). High monitoring individuals are generally characterized by an excessive focus on health threats, a greater desire for voluminous health-related information, greater factual knowledge about the health threat, and less satisfaction with the amount and certainty of information available to them. Low monitoring individuals, in contrast, tend to minimize and tune out health-related threats, adopting a strategy of distraction. High and low monitors display unique cognitive-emotional patterns when presented with health-related threats, such as the possibility of testing positive for the *BRCA1/2* genetic mutation: High monitors tend to be characterized by heightened risk perceptions and greater risk-related distress, but are also more vigilant for, and attentive to, prevention and management strategies that they can adopt (Miller et al., 1999; Miller, Fang, Diefenbach, & Bales, 2001).

In addition to individual difference factors, genetic risk feedback impacts on the family as an integrated unit. Since the biological implications of genetic risk for breast cancer extend beyond the at-risk individual, there is need to consider the interplay of coping process dynamics across family members. Although little research is available in this area, the ways in which individuals react to the news that they are *BRCA1/2* carriers are likely to be determined by such factors as their developmental phase within the family (e.g., young mother vs. grandparent), the family's multigenerational history of coping with breast and ovarian cancer, and family belief systems (including influences of culture, ethnicity, and gender), particularly the meaning of the illness to family members (see Chapter 2; Rolland, 1994). The potential impact of genetic risk feedback on the family highlights the importance of routine inclusion of couples and family consultations both pre- and posttesting and over the long-term adaptation phase to genetic risk information. These consultations can identify families at high risk for dysfunctional coping and adaptation that could benefit from family therapy.

Psychosocial Impact and Issues Across the Continuum of Risk Counseling and Genetic Testing

The ultimate goal of risk counseling is to facilitate informed decision making along the risk counseling continuum, from learning about one's potential risk to communication of test results to family members, and to help individuals make decisions that are consistent with their own personal values and goals at each step of the process (Miller et al., 1999; Mulley & Sepucha, 2002). In this section, we discuss the current state of the science on the psychosocial impact of each of the phases of risk counseling and genetic testing.

Comprehension of Genetic Risk Information for Informed Genetic Testing Decisions

An understanding of genetic risk and the nature of genetic mutations is a necessary component of the decision-making process for individuals contemplating genetic testing. Individuals not only need to be aware of the potential limitations and benefits of genetic testing but also need to be able to consider the likely personal impact of receiving this information (Lerman & Croyle, 1994). As a first step in the process of informed decision making, women need to understand if they are at increased risk, as well as to determine the extent to which that risk is potentially related to a genetic mutation.

Knowledge and Perception of Breast Cancer and Breast Cancer Risk. The concept of risk perception is intimately related to knowledge levels and has received considerable focus in the literature on breast cancer risk (Miller et al., 2004). In general, there is a tendency for women to overestimate their risk for inherited breast cancer and to misunderstand the limitations of available genetic testing options (Inglehart, Nelson, & Zou, 1998). In particular, it is often difficult for individuals to accurately process the difference between being at high risk due to their age or familial patterns versus being at high risk because of a genetic mutation. For example, two distinctive hallmarks of inherited disease are early onset of disease and having a first-degree relative with breast cancer. National guidelines, available through the National Comprehensive Cancer Network (2006; see Figure 10.1), have been developed to assist providers and patients in understanding the hallmarks of inherited breast cancer, the decisions required at each stage of the counseling process, and the variety of inherited patterns of breast and ovarian cancer that exist.

Knowledge about breast cancer risk factors, symptoms, and curability of breast cancer tends to be greater than knowledge about genetic risk for breast cancer (Evers-Kiebooms, Welkenhuysen, Claes, Decruyenaere, & Denayer, 2000). Despite having greater knowledge about genetic risk than average-risk women (Hailey, Carter, & Burnett, 2000; Donovan & Tucker, 2000), women at familial risk for breast cancer display a high need for additional information about their own personal risk for developing the disease, as well as a desire for information

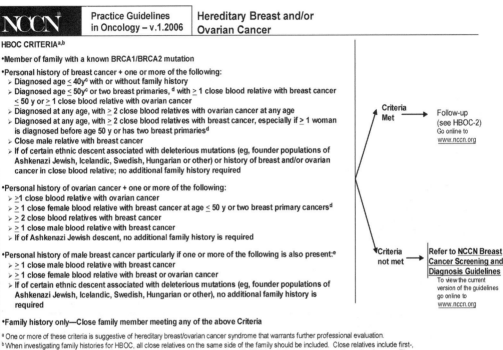

Figure 10.1 National Comprehensive Cancer Network Practice Guidelines in Oncology for hereditary breast or ovarian cancer. Reproduced with permission from the The NCCN Practice Guidelines in Oncology–v.1.2006. *The Complete Library of NCCN Clinical Practice Guidelines in Oncology* [CD-ROM]. Jenkinstown, Pennsylvania. © National Comprehensive Cancer Network, December 2005. To view the most recent and complete version of the guidelines, go online to www.nccn.org

about breast cancer prevention and detection strategies (Audrain et al., 1998; Bluman et al., 1999; Chalmers & Breen, 1995; Chalmers, Thomson, & Degner, 1996; Donovan & Tucker, 2000; Hallowell, Murton, Statman, Green, & Richards, 1997; Hopwood, 2000; Kash et al., 2000; Kinney et al., 2001; Stacey, DeGrasse, & Johnston, 2002; Tessaro, Borstelmann, Regan, Rimer, & Winer, 1997; Wonderlick & Fine, 1997).

Women of higher educational status exhibit greater breast cancer genetics knowledge and awareness of genetic testing (Armstrong, Weber, Ubel, Guerra, & Schwartz, 2002; Meischke, Bowen, & Kuniyuki, 2001).

Also, using the Internet as a source of information has been associated with greater awareness of genetic testing (Meischke et al., 2001), which is also likely to be related to educational status.

Patterns of Risk Perception. Prior to genetic risk counseling, at-risk women tend to inaccurately estimate their risk for breast cancer, when compared with objective risk estimates based on their own pedigrees (Lynch et al., 1999) and population-based norms (Smith et al., 1996). Most individuals with some family history of cancer, including those at low to moderate risk, overestimate their personal cancer risk, although in some cases women underestimate their cancer risk (Croyle & Lerman, 1999; Cull et al., 1999; Lerman, Kash, & Stefanek, 1994; Woloshin, Schwartz, Black, & Welch, 1999). There is some evidence that high-risk individuals overestimate personal risk more than average-risk individuals do (Hailey et al., 2000; Hopwood et al., 1998). Other work, however, has found that both risk groups overestimate to the same extent (Smith et al., 1996). Educational interventions that address the individual's cognitive and affective processing of their breast cancer risk have been shown to improve the appropriate use of risk counseling and genetic testing programs, with women at high risk more likely than those at average risk to obtain genetic counseling and testing (Green et al., 2005; Miller, Fleisher, et al., 2005; Schwartz, Tercyak, Peshkin, & Valdimarsdottir, 2005).

Interestingly, while women with a family history of breast cancer display better overall health behaviors than the general population (Emmons et al., 2000), they also tend to underestimate their risk of other diseases (e.g., heart disease, colon cancer; Erblich, Bovbjerg, Norman, Valdimarsdottir, & Montgomery, 2000), suggesting that a focus on the more salient health risk of breast cancer may lead to downplaying other important health risks. On balance, this pattern may compromise the overall health status of the individual.

In addition to the interaction between perceived risk and knowledge levels, women's perceptions of their risk for breast cancer appear to be influenced by the effects of expectancy and emotional factors (Hopwood, 2000). In one study, older age, higher trait anxiety, and an external locus of health control were linked to risk overestimation prior to genetic counseling (Cull et al., 1999). High levels of breast cancer worry and psychological distress have also been linked with overestimation of breast cancer risk (Cull, Fry, Rush, & Steel, 2001; Hopwood, Shenton, Lalloo, Evans, & Howell, 2001).

The interaction between risk-related cognitions and affect is exemplified in the findings of a study that examined predictors of psychological distress among women at increased risk for ovarian cancer (Schwartz, Lerman, Miller, Daly, & Masny, 1995). Individuals with a high monitoring attentional style (i.e., individuals with a tendency to scan for and focus on health threat information) displayed high perceived risk for ovarian cancer. High perceived risk, in turn, was related to greater intrusive thoughts about the cancer threat, which led to greater psychological distress (Schwartz et al., 1995; see also Fang et al., 2003; Rees & Bath, 2000). In addition, over time, high monitors tend to acquire more knowledge about their breast cancer risk status, but this knowledge has a double-edged sword: It is also linked to increasingly heightened risk perceptions over time (Miller, Fleisher, et al., 2005).

Cultural Factors. Cultural differences in awareness of breast cancer genetics are important but not well-studied. Across the spectrum of risk, African American women consistently display lower knowledge about breast and ovarian cancer genetics than white women (Armstrong et al., 2002; Donovan & Tucker, 2000; Kinney et al., 2001; Royak-Schaler et al., 2002). Indeed, despite their objective risk, African American women with a family history of breast cancer appear to be no more knowledgeable about breast cancer than women with no family history (Donovan & Tucker, 2000; Powell, 1994; Royak-Schaler et al., 2002). However, younger and better-educated African American women have increased knowledge about genetic risk factors (Donovan & Tucker, 2000; Kash et al., 2000; Royak-Schaler et al., 2002). Moreover, among African American women, religious values and beliefs impact breast screening behaviors, with high-risk women with a low "God" locus of control (i.e., a lower belief in God's control over health outcomes) being more likely to adhere to recommended screening behaviors (Kinney, Emery, Dudley, & Croyle, 2002).

In conclusion, there are inconsistencies in women's knowledge of genetic risk of breast cancer and their assessment of their own risk status, which is influenced by a variety of factors, including educational status, family history, and cultural or ethnic background. Since psychosocial factors influence the individual's knowledge and perceived risk levels, they need to be addressed as an integral part of genetic risk counseling. The process by which individual perceptions of breast cancer risk develop and the role of specific cognitive and affective factors in forming these risk perceptions appear to be important; however, these patterns are just beginning to be identified.

Cognitive-Affective Factors Influencing Decision Making in Genetic Testing

There are two steps in the initial decision-making process: first to decide whether to participate in genetic counseling (i.e., pedigree analysis and education), and second to decide whether to participate in genetic testing (i.e., genetic sequencing of blood samples and test result feedback and counseling). The decision to test is often the catalyst for more decisions (Wang, Gonzalez, & Merajver, 2004). Here we discuss the background and cognitive-affective factors that impact on the beginning steps in the decision-making process.

Background Factors. Demographic, as well as psychosocial, factors influence levels of interest in undergoing genetic risk assessment, as well as uptake of these services. Younger age and higher levels of formal education are associated with greater interest in counseling and testing (Armstrong et al., 2002; Geller et al., 1999; Hagoel et al., 2000; Jacobsen et al., 1997; Lodder et al., 2003). In terms of the impact of objective familial risk, some studies have found a positive relationship with interest in genetic testing (e.g., Armstrong et al., 2000; Brandt, Hartmann, Ali, Tucci, & Gilman, 2002; Chaliki et al., 1995; Lerman, Narod, et al., 1996; Lipkus, Iden, Terrenoire, & Feaganes, 1999), some an inverse relationship (Andrykowski, Lightner, Studts, & Munn, 1997; Armstrong et al., 2002), while still others find no association (Jacobsen., Valdimarsdottir, Brown, & Offit, 1997). In terms of actual uptake, having family members with breast cancer is a significant predictor of testing uptake, but mainly when studies are conducted in research settings (e.g., Lerman, Narod, et al., 1996). In general, approximately 80% of respondents with family histories of breast or ovarian cancer report being highly interested in undergoing testing (Berth, Balck, & Dinkel, 2003; Streuwing, Lerman, Kase, Giambarresi, & Tucker, 1995). However, only about 50% of high-risk women participating in research studies ultimately opt to be tested (Biesecker et al., 2000; Botkin et al., 2003).

In community-based clinical settings, family history does not appear to be a significant factor influencing decision making (Lee, Bernhardt, & Helzlsouer, 2002). The inconsistency in these findings suggests that the motivation to participate in a research study offering genetic testing may differ from the motivation to undergo genetic testing in a community-based setting. Among reasons why women who are candidates for genetic testing decide not to participate include the uncertainty of the test result, anticipated psychological distress, concerns about the impact of testing on family stress, health insurance concerns, and limited management options (Hadley et al., 2003; Lerman et al., 1999; Lerman, Narod, et al., 1996; Lerman & Shields, 2004).

Risk-Related Knowledge and Perceptions. Greater levels of risk-related knowledge are associated with increased interest in risk assessment programs, including among African American women (Armstrong et al., 2002; Gwyn, Vernon, & Conoley, 2003; Lerman, Narod, et al., 1996; Thompson et al., 2002). Inflated perceptions of breast cancer risk have also been associated with greater interest in genetic testing (Durfy, Bowen, McTiernan, Sporleder, & Burke, 1999; Jacobsen et al., 1997; Lerman, Daly, Masny, & Balshem, 1994; Struewing et al., 1995) and greater uptake of risk assessment services (Geller, Doksum, Bernhardt, & Metz, 1999; Schwartz et al., 2000), even among women at low to moderate risk (Helmes, Bowen, & Bengel, 2002). Similarly, perceived likelihood of being a gene carrier is positively associated with interest in testing (Bluman et al., 2003; Lerman et al., 1994). Indeed, decision making about genetic testing is more strongly influenced by perceptions of one's own personal risk of breast cancer than by an understanding of the limitations of genetic testing (Croyle & Lerman, 1999).

Perceived Benefits. Individual beliefs about the benefits of genetic testing are associated with interest and uptake. Greater endorsement of the benefits of risk assessment (e.g., providing cancer risk information for family members, learning about cancer risk, and obtaining help in deciding about prophylactic options) and reporting a positive decisional balance (i.e., more pros of genetic testing than cons) are associated with greater interest and participation in genetic testing (Armstrong et al., 2000; Cappelli et al., 1999; Helmes et al., 2002; Jacobsen et al., 1997; Lerman, Narod, et al., 1996; Lerman, Seay, Balsham, & Audrain, 1995; Thompson et al., 2002).

Values and Goals: Familial and Social Concerns and Worries. The value placed on family and the need to know one's genetic status for the sake of one's children plays an important role in decision making for *BRCA1/2* testing (Foster et al., 2002; Hallowell et al., 2002; Lerman, Seay, et al., 1995; Loader, Levenkron, & Rowley, 1998; Lynch, Lemon, et al., 1997). In turn, greater family cohesion and greater optimism predict greater uptake of genetic testing (Biesecker et al., 2000). However, anticipated difficulties in disclosing information to kin, anticipation of the emotional impact of test result disclosure to kin, and concerns about time commitment are significant barriers to the uptake of *BRCA1/2* testing participation (Geer, Ropka, Cohn, Jones, & Miesfeldt, 2001; Hallowell et al., 2002).

Anticipation of stigmatization and guilt regarding the carrier status of relatives, and fear of life insurance and job discrimination, are also associated with decreased participation in genetic counseling services, whereas lower family-related guilt is associated with increased testing participation (Armstrong et al., 2000, 2003; Thompson et al., 2002). Testing participants generally anticipate reactions of depression and anxiety if they are found to be carriers, and guilt and worry if the test is found to be negative (Lerman, Marshall, et al., 1996; Lerman, Seay, et al., 1995). Monitoring attentional style has also been found to influence predisclosure responses to genetic testing: High monitors are more likely to anticipate that genetic testing will have a negative psychological impact on them (Lerman, Daly, et al., 1994), to experience higher levels of anxiety in anticipation of the test result (Tercyak et al., 2001; Wardle, 1995), and to manifest greater mood disturbance after counseling (Lerman, Daly, et al., 1994; Lerman, Schwartz, et al., 1996). Nonetheless, high monitors are more likely to desire genetic testing (Roberts, 2000) and to believe that they should be able to obtain such testing, even if the physician does not recommend it (Benkendorf et al., 1997).

High-risk women who anticipate that they will experience high levels of distress in response to participation in genetic testing services are less likely to participate in testing (Lodder et al., 2003) and are less likely to obtain their test results following the donation of blood for testing (Coyne et al., 2002). The modality employed to recruit for genetic counseling services appears to influence willingness to participate in these services and has an impact on negative affect. At-risk women recruited through media sources experience greater cancer worry compared with women recruited through personal recommendation from an affected relative and, in turn, are less likely to participate in genetic counseling in a research setting (Bowen et al., 1999).

Among newly diagnosed breast cancer patients with a family history consistent with hereditary breast cancer, knowledge of *BRCA* mutation status has been found to influence early stage breast cancer treatment decisions (Schwartz et al., 2004). Women with breast cancer tended to opt for genetic testing at the time of diagnosis, in particular, women who had not yet reached a decision about definitive local treatment (Schwartz et al., 2004). Over three quarters (76%) of women offered rapid genetic testing results at the time of diagnosis decided to undergo genetic testing. Physician recommendation for genetic testing and indecisions about definitive local treatment were found to be associated with undergoing testing. Delay in the availability of genetic test results and low levels of anxiety were associated with the decision to proceed with treatment before receiving the results. These findings suggest that if affected women are offered timely genetic counseling and testing, they can use this information to help them make important treatment decisions.

Self-Regulatory Processes. The ability to cope with and manage the threat of breast cancer places demands on the at-risk individual that require ongoing self-regulatory strategies, particularly in terms of one's ability to plan for and effectively execute desired decisions. Individuals who view genetic testing as necessary for making long-term management decisions about their breast cancer risk are more likely to participate in genetic testing (Brandt et al., 2002; Hallowell et al., 2002; Loader et al., 1998). In contrast, individuals who do not believe that there are medical protocols to reduce long-term breast cancer risk, and who are reluctant to undergo prophylactic surgery, are less likely to undergo genetic testing (Lodder et al., 2003). Further, women who decline genetic testing and who experience high levels of cancer-related stress at the time of decision making have been found to develop greater depression over time (Lerman et al., 1998), suggesting that affect and coping may need to be addressed to facilitate a high-quality decision.

Cultural Issues. Cultural values (i.e., ethnic identity and religious affiliation) are also influential in determining attitudes to genetic testing. Ashkenazi Jewish women are more likely to undergo genetic testing than the general population (Armstrong et al., 2000; Lee et al., 2002). On the other hand, African American women are less likely than Caucasian women to participate in genetic testing (Bernhardt, 1997). However, African American women with a family history of (Kinney et al., 2001), and greater knowledge about, breast cancer genetics demonstrate increased interest in, and uptake of, genetic testing (Thompson et al., 2002). In addition, increased perceived risk for breast cancer is linked with greater interest in genetic testing among African American women (Kinney et al., 2001; Lipkus et al., 1999), as are higher levels of cancer-specific worry and anxiety (Brandt et al., 2002; Durfy et al., 1999; Helmes et al., 2002; Lerman, Schwartz, et al., 1997; Thompson et al., 2002). Fatalistic beliefs about cancer and future temporal orientation are associated with increased uptake of genetic testing among African American women at high risk; however, rates of genetic test acceptance are lower among those with heightened perceptions of familial interdependence (Hughes, Fasay, LaSalle, & Finch, 2003).

As is the case in the general population, the desire to obtain information for the sake of one's children and other family members is a factor motivating interest in testing among both Ashkenazi Jewish (Lehmann, Weeks, Klar, & Garber, 2002; Phillips et al., 2000) and African American populations (Thompson et al., 2002). African American women hold more positive beliefs about the benefits of testing and fewer concerns about the limitations of testing than white women, despite their decreased participation in risk assessment services (Hughes et al., 1997). Among Ashkenazi Jewish women, high levels of religious identity and less need for social support (Bowen, Bourcier, Press, Lewis, & Burke, 2004; Bowen, Singal, Eng, Crystal, & Burke, 2003) are associated with decreased interest in genetic testing. On the other hand, high levels of cultural identity among these women are associated with high intention to undergo testing (Bowen et al., 2003).

In summary, the genetic testing decision is determined by a constellation of background, psychosocial, and cultural factors. Ashkenazi Jewish women are most likely, and African American women least likely, to participate in genetic testing. Cognitive-emotional reasons for not participating in testing are similar among Ashkenazi Jewish, African American, and white women. In addition, religious values play a role in influencing genetic testing decisions.

The Impact of Genetic Counseling and Testing on Posttesting Adjustment

It is important to distinguish between the impact of genetic counseling, which entails pedigree analysis and education, and that of genetic testing, which entails genetic sequencing of blood samples. Breast cancer risk counseling has generally been provided through individualized counseling. However, computer-based (Green et al., 2004, 2005) and video-based (Axilbund, Hamby, Thompson, Olsen, & Griffin, 2005) education may be effective and time-efficient methods of providing genetics education in a way that complements the role of counseling, in particular with respect to addressing the cognitive or emotional aspects of genetic risk. The increased inclusion of routine pre- and posttesting family consultation and psychoeducation also hold enormous potential benefit for patients.

Effects of Genetic Counseling on Knowledge of Breast Cancer Risk and Interest in Genetic Testing. Participation in genetic counseling, with its focus on genetic risk education and pedigree assessment, is associated with short-term improvements in breast cancer genetics knowledge (Cull et al., 1999; DiCastro et al., 2002; Lerman, Biesecker, et al., 1997). The increase in knowledge is most apparent among carriers compared with noncarriers, and least apparent among women receiving inconclusive results (Claes et al., 2003). Further, the use of computer-based educational aids leads to significant increases in genetics knowledge, and they are perceived by at-risk women as useful tools in that they avoid embarrassment, make efficient use of time, and provide a clear explanation of genetics (Green, Biesecker, McInerney, Mauger, & Fost, 2001). In comparison, individualized counseling approaches are perceived as most useful in addressing personal concerns and minimizing anxiety and fears (Green et al., 2001).

Among white and Ashkenazi Jewish women at increased risk, levels of interest in genetic testing after genetic counseling either remain unchanged (Lerman, Biesecker, et al., 1997) or decline (Bowen, Burke, Yasui, McTiernan, & McLeran, 2002; Green et al., 2001; Schwartz et al., 2001). Following genetic counseling, a decline in interest among these women is related to a corresponding increase in an awareness of the risks and limitations of genetic testing (Schwartz et al., 2001). In contrast, among African American women, genetic education and counseling leads to increased interest in undergoing testing as well as marginal reductions in distress (Lerman et al., 1999).

Risk Perceptions. Breast cancer status interacts with genetic counseling in its impact on risk perceptions: Among unaffected women, counseling decreases the perceived likelihood of being a carrier, but increases perceptions of risk and breast cancer-related concerns (Bish et al., 2002). Immediately following genetic counseling, accuracy of risk comprehension and risk estimates improves in both affected and unaffected individuals, but nonetheless remains inaccurate when compared with objective risk status (Burke et al., 2000; Butow, Lobb, Meiser, Barratt, & Tucker, 2003; Cull et al., 1999; Hopwood et al., 1998). Accuracy was found to improve at 12-month follow-up in one study (Meiser et al., 2001), and another study reported sustained improvement in accuracy over time (Evans et al., 1994). Women with high baseline cancer risk-related intrusion show no improvement in risk comprehension following breast cancer risk counseling, suggesting that high levels of distress can interfere with effective cognitive processing of risk status (Lerman, Lustbader, et al., 1995).

Affective Impact. The greatest distress among women about to undergo genetic counseling is among those who are younger, nonwhite, and have lower perceptions of control over developing breast cancer (Audrain et al., 1997, 1998). Breast cancer worry and anxiety generally decrease following genetic counseling, but mainly for women at low and moderate risk, and women with improved accuracy of perceived breast cancer risk (Bish et al., 2002; Burke et al., 2000; Cull et al., 1999; Hopwood et al., 1998; Lerman, Schwartz, et al., 1996; Meiser et al., 2001). Indeed, perceptions of stress related to genetic testing concerns have been found to be significantly higher among individuals who received positive *BRCA1/2* test results (Halbert et al., 2004). Follow-up depression at 9 and 12 months postcounseling is associated with heightened perceived risk at baseline and low baseline levels of optimistic expectancy (Ritvo et al., 2000). Some evidence suggests that genetic counseling leads to no change overall in general psychological distress (Bish et al., 2002; Reichelt, Heimdal, Moller, & Dahl, 2004; Claes et al., 2005). However, a meta-analysis of 12 studies found significant decreases in general anxiety and improvements in accuracy of risk estimates following genetic counseling (Meiser & Halliday, 2002).

A randomized trial comparing individualized breast cancer risk counseling with a general health control found that the risk counseling group had less breast cancer-specific distress at 3 months postintervention (Lerman, Lustbader, et al., 1995; Lerman, Schwartz, et al., 1996). However, high monitors in both conditions had increases in general distress, suggesting that monitoring attentional style may exert an influence on postcounseling adjustment that needs to be specifically addressed (Lerman, Schwartz, et al., 1996). Inconsistencies in findings related to the emotional impact of having donated blood for genetic testing may be attributed to the fact that nonspecific measures are often used (e.g., general measures of anxiety and depression), rather than measures specific to the genetic testing context. The Multidimensional Impact of Cancer Risk Assessment, an instrument designed to assess psychological distress in the genetic testing context, may address this limitation (Cella et al., 2002).

Over the long term (i.e., 24 months), postcounseling women experience a heightened sensitivity to breast cancer cues, reflecting a more "monitoring" approach to their risk status. To cope with this increased sense of vulnerability, they tend to engage in coping strategies such as focusing on the present, reassessing priorities in life, positive thinking, adopting a healthy lifestyle, and increasing their breast cancer surveillance (Appleton, Fry, Rees, Rush, & Cull, 2000). However, a large, multicenter study reported decreased use of clinical breast examination 12 months postcounseling among women with a family history of breast cancer (Meiser et al., 2001), suggesting that some women cope by blunting and avoidance of breast cancer cues. Levels of distress among carriers are also dependent upon the specific response of partners to their spouse's positive mutation status, with distress among carrier spouses being highest among those with nonsupportive and anxious partners (Wylie, Smith, & Botkin, 2003).

Genetic Testing and Disclosure of Genetic Test Results. Overall, there appears to be satisfaction with the testing process itself, with women generally expressing no particular regrets with the decision to undergo testing (Pieterse et al., 2005; Wood, Mullineaux, Rahm, Fairclough, & Wenzel, 2000). However, the extensive time needed to wait for the results of testing, a period varying from 2 or 3 months to beyond a year, can be a source of dissatisfaction.

Increased distress during the waiting period is related to lower optimism, increased anticipation of problems, greater awareness of consequences of positive mutation, and personal and family cancer diagnoses

(Hamann, Somers, Smith, Inslicht, & Baum, 2005; Lodder et al., 1999). Reduced distress is related to the use of effective self-regulatory strategies to minimize the emotional impact of a potentially unfavorable test outcome (Lodder et al., 1999). Distress among genetic testing participants (and their partners) decreases over time while waiting for test results (usually 12 months), but increases again in the weeks immediately before disclosure of results (Broadstock, Michie, Gray, Mackay, & Marteau, 2000; Lodder et al., 1999).

Psychological outcomes after disclosure of genetic testing results vary depending on a number of factors (e.g., the particular testing results; whether the tested woman is affected with cancer or not; the time point following disclosure of testing results; and the genetic status of family members, among others (Meisner, 2005). Short-term (i.e., 1 month) general anxiety declines for carriers and noncarriers, but genetic risk-specific distress, depression, and breast cancer concern are greater for carriers than for noncarriers (Bonadona et al., 2002; Croyle, Achilles, & Lerman, 1997; Lerman et al., 1998; Wood et al., 2000). The most sustained distress is apparent among carriers who are either unaffected (Croyle et al., 1997) or who are recently diagnosed with breast cancer (Meisner, 2005; van Roosmalen et al., 2004a; Wood et al., 2000). Women receiving an inconclusive test result report a range of emotional reactions, including emotional relief, sadness, anger, and guilt (Lynch, Lemon, et al., 1997), and there is evidence that these women misconstrue the meaning of the result as a definitive confirmation that a mutation is not present within the family (Hallowell et al., 2002).

Affected mutation carriers frequently experience higher levels of anger and psychological distress than was anticipated prior to results disclosure (Dorval et al., 2000). Moreover, the genetic status of other family members impacts the way in which testing results are received. Noncarriers who have had a sister recently identified as a carrier experience higher posttest depression than other noncarriers (Lodder et al., 2001). Among female carriers, distress is greatest among those who are either tested first or whose siblings are noncarriers (Smith, West, Croyle, & Botkin, 1999).

The long-term (i.e., 6 months postdisclosure and beyond) impact of genetic testing mirrors the short-term effects. Mutation carriers experience greater anxiety-associated symptoms (e.g., sleeplessness, bad mood) and breast cancer worry than noncarriers, up to 2 years postdisclosure (DiCastro et al., 2002). While affected women show no change in distress or perceived risk following the disclosure of test results, unaffected women show a psychological benefit (i.e., decreased distress from knowing that they are not carriers; Schwartz et al., 2002). One study showed a decrease in anxiety and depression among both carriers and noncarriers 6 months and 1 year posttesting, followed by an increase 1 to 5 years following testing (Meisner, 2005; van Oostrom et al., 2003). Little is known about the longer-term effects of genetic testing, with few studies assessing the impact beyond 12 months. For individual carriers and their families living with increased risk of future illness, the longitudinal life cycle challenges are important areas for future research (see Chapter 5).

Posttesting Screening Adherence and Decision Making About Prevention Options

Screening. Prior to genetic risk assessment, mammography rates among high-risk women are directly related to age, family income, and the number of affected relatives with breast cancer, while ovarian cancer screening rates are related to having an affected relative with ovarian cancer (Isaacs et al., 2002). In general, genetic testing appears to have a facilitatory effect on screening behaviors, particularly for carriers and women over 50 years of age (Botkin et al., 2003; Lerman et al., 2000; Metcalfe et al., 2000; Peshkin et al., 2002; Plon, Peterson, Friedman, & Richards, 2000; Scheuer et al., 2002). Receipt of a positive result following genetic testing predicts increased utilization of screening procedures for ovarian cancer, including the CA125 blood test and transvaginal ultrasound (Schwartz et al., 2003). Additional predictors for ovarian screening are increased perceived risk for ovarian cancer and heightened anxiety. Following participation in genetic testing, older age and increased cancer worry increase mammography surveillance (Diefenbach, Miller, & Daly, 1999).

Risk Management. In addition to increased surveillance measures, prophylactic surgery is an option for women identified as high risk, particularly those found to be mutation carriers. The surgical morbidity of prophylactic mastectomy and oophorectomy is low, but the postsurgical and psychosocial complications may be significant, including premature menopause, decreases in perceived sexual attractiveness, self-consciousness about appearance, and feelings of decreased femininity (Lloyd et al., 2000; Lodder et al., 2002). Following genetic counseling, rates of prophylactic surgery are relatively high, with one study finding more than half of carriers choosing prophylactic surgery (Botkin et al., 2003; Morris, Johnson, Krasikov, Allen, & Dorsey, 2001). In another study, 27% of mutation carriers, 5% of patients with uninformative results, and 2% of noncarriers received prophylactic oophorectomy within the year following testing (Schwartz et al., 2003). Among carriers, acceptance rates of prophylactic oophorectomy are greater than for prophylactic mastectomy (Botkin et al., 2003; Scheuer et al., 2002), probably due to the "unseen" and less public nature of the surgery for oophorectomy. Younger, more educated women, those with a more extensive family history of breast or ovarian cancer, and those experiencing higher distress are more likely to opt for prophylactic mastectomy (Lodder et al., 2002; Metcalfe et al., 2000; Scheuer et al., 2002). Women declining prophylactic mastectomy are more likely to believe in the utility of screening as a management regimen and have lower proneness to anxiety than acceptors, who are more likely to adopt a fatalistic view of developing breast cancer (Hatcher, Fallowfield, & A'Hern, 2001).

Older women and those already affected with breast cancer are more likely to opt for prophylactic oophorectomy (Miller, Roussi, et al., 2005). Women are also more likely to opt for prophylactic oophorectomy if they feel more vulnerable to cancer, believe that surgery will prevent cancer, and are more worried about developing cancer (Miller et al., 1999). Reduction of anxiety and uncertainty, greater perceived risk of developing ovarian cancer, and greater perceived benefits of surgery are strongly associated with the desire for prophylactic oophorectomy among high-risk women (Fang et al., 2003; Fry, Rush, Busby-Earle, & Cull, 2001; Hurley et al., 2001). In a prospective study, objective risk, perceived risk, and cancer worry were the strongest predictors of prophylactic oophorectomy among women who underwent genetic testing for *BRCA1/BRCA2* mutations (Schwartz et al., 2003). These findings are consistent with studies in which affective factors, such as cancer worry and anxiety, were found to be the strongest predictors of intention to undergo prophylactic mastectomy (Stefanek, Enger, Benkendort, Flamm Honig, & Lerman, 1999; Van Dijk et al., 2003).

A new area of research that has emerged evaluates the impact of presurgical genetic counseling and *BRCA1/2* testing among newly diagnosed women with a family history consistent with hereditary breast cancer on subsequent surgical treatment decision making (Schwartz et al., 2004; Schwartz, Peshkin, et al., 2005). In a study of women offered free genetic risk assessment who had not yet received surgical treatment and had a family history of breast cancer, close to half (48%) who were found to carry a *BRCA1/2* mutation chose bilateral mastectomy as their definitive breast cancer surgery (Schwartz, Peshkin, et al., 2005). In comparison, only 24% of patients in whom no mutations were found, and 4% of women who declined genetic testing, opted for bilateral mastectomy, suggesting that the receipt of a positive genetic testing result increases the likelihood that patients will choose prophylactic surgery. Taken together, these data indicate that presurgery *BRCA1/2* testing for high-risk patients can influence patient treatment decision making.

From 6 to 18 months postsurgery, women electing to undergo pro-phylactic mastectomy experience significant decreases in psychologi-cal morbidity but no differences in sexual discomfort or degree of sexual pleasure compared with decliners (Hatcher et al., 2001; Lodder et al., 2002). The long-term effects (i.e., mean time since surgery, 14.5 years) of prophylactic surgery are promising, with women reporting decreased breast cancer worry, and no change in, or favorable effects on, emotional stability, level of stress, self-esteem, and sexual relation-ships (Frost et al., 2000). Unfortunately, little is known about rates of couple dysfunction (e.g., separation, divorce) in these situations.

A growing need is to develop more effective psychosocial interven-tions to help individuals anticipate and prepare for the results of gene-tic testing, so that they can fully process and optimally act on the results they receive (Wang et al., 2004). According to the cognitive-social model (Miller et al., 1996, 1999), the types of cognitions and affects that are activated when an individual undergoes a health challenge like *BRCA1/2* genetic counseling are relatively stable. Further, the cognitive-emotional responses that are primed predict, in turn, the individual's protective intentions and actions. In a study of women undergoing *BRCA1/2* ge-netic testing, counseling was "enhanced" to explicitly help women ac-tivate and "pre-live" the cognitive-affective reactions they were likely to experience upon receiving their genetic testing results (Miller, Roussi, et al., 2005). The goal was to enable genetic testing participants to better self-assess and systematically plan for the different potential test result scenarios. Through the use of a role-play format, the coun-selor helped individuals to realistically enact their reactions to each of the potential testing outcomes. Compared with standard genetic coun-seling, enhanced counseling led to a greater reduction of avoidant ideation after disclosure of test results, indicating more complete pro-cessing of genetic risk feedback. Further, individuals who received counseling were also more likely to seek out information about, and to ultimately undergo, preventive surgery. Another study of women un-dergoing *BRCA1/2* testing found that providing a decision aid consist-ing of a brochure and a video on the physical, emotional, and social consequences of different posttesting screening and preventive sur-gery options increased intentions to have preventive surgery com-pared with standard counseling alone (van Roosmalen et al., 2004b).

Communication of Test Results to Family Members

A notable challenge facing individuals opting to participate in genetic testing is the question of how best to include family consultations with spouses or partners and other relatives, both pre- and posttesting, as well as how to communicate test results to family members, and to which family members (Croyle & Lerman, 1999). Genetic testing participants are more likely to share test results with family members than with coworkers and insurers (Smith, Zick, Mayer, & Botkin, 2002). Gene carriers are more likely to disclose information about test results than noncarriers (Hughes et al., 2002; Wagner Costalas et al., 2003) and are also more likely than noncarriers to disclose to insurers (Smith et al., 2002). The nature of the test result influences the difficulty and distress associated with the communication process, with carriers more likely to have difficulty understanding (Hallowell et al., 2002; Wagner Costalas et al., 2003) and emotionally processing the results (Daly et al., 1997). Gene carriers are more likely to disclose to female relatives and less likely to disclose to young children (Hughes et al., 2002). However, individuals experiencing distress prior to participating in *BRCA1/2* testing are more likely to disclose test results to children (Tercyak et al., 2001).

Willingness to disclose genetic test results is also influenced by the nature of familial relationships. Women participating in risk assessment have high intentions to share, and actually share, risk information with at least one relative, typically female (Green & Frost, 1997; Julian-Reynier, Sobol, Sevilla, Nogues, & Bourret, 2000; Wagner Costalas et al., 2003). Men who are at risk of being a gene mutation carrier are frequently excluded from family conversations about breast cancer (McAllister, Evans, Ormiston, & Daly, 1998). At-risk women also have at least one first-degree or second-degree relative with whom they do not intend to share risk information, particularly where family rifts and large age differences between siblings exist (Green & Frost, 1997; Hughes et al., 2002). In these situations, family consultations and intervention are particularly important to avert serious complications that can result from keeping familial genetic risk information secret, including relational cutoffs and future unanticipated guilt reactions, if other uninformed family members develop breast or ovarian cancer. Also, couples may disagree regarding if and when to inform potentially at-risk children.

Receiving negative results (i.e., no mutation is found) is more likely to be associated with survivor guilt and with difficulties adjusting expectations based on "good" news (Wagner et al., 2000). Disclosure of testing feedback to distant family members is particularly difficult; such disclosure is more likely when the result is conclusive (i.e., definite positive or negative) and when there are a greater number of deceased affected relatives (Claes et al., 2003). For carriers, the reasons for disclosure are related to a need to obtain emotional support and advice about medical decisions (Hughes et al., 2002).

Certain barriers have been found to hinder the effective communication of genetic risk information. Lack of preparation, knowledge, and confidence in their communication skills have been cited by women undergoing cancer risk counseling as barriers to communication of genetic risk information to their families (Daly et al., 2001). Further, some families exhibit a need to maintain positively framed communications between family members, which leads to the use of restricted and avoidant communication patterns between at-risk mothers and their daughters (Grossman, 2002). The transmission of results to distant relatives is a particular challenge to carriers and inconclusives alike (Bonadona et al., 2002; Claes et al., 2003).

RECOMMENDATIONS FOR RESEARCH AND PRACTICE

The sequence of decision making, from understanding inherited risk to the choice of preventive measures for those with positive test results, is fraught with uncertainty, compounded by the myriad psychosocial implications of each subsequent decisional step in the risk assessment process (Table 10.1). Women who have an inherited susceptibility to breast cancer face a number of challenges that require detailed, accurate information, as well as support from health providers in order to ensure informed decision making that is consistent with their values and goals (Mulley & Sepucha, 2002). Overall, awareness of the risks of genetic testing is limited. Further, decision making about genetic testing is more strongly influenced by perceptions of personal cancer risk and less by perceptions of the limitations of genetic testing. Strikingly, misconceptions of personal risk of cancer tend to be fairly resistant to standard education and counseling approaches.

Psychological distress and coping processes also interact with, and importantly influence, the processing of risk information and subsequent decision making in genetic testing (Schwartz, Peshkin, et al., 2005). Negative affect, in particular anxiety and cancer worry, have been found to impact decision making with respect to genetic testing (Schwartz, Peshkin, et al., 2005) and medical management following test results (Schwartz et al., 2003). Finally, family influences play an important role in risk awareness, genetic testing decisions, and outcomes. This person-family interplay underscores the importance of initial family consultations to understand risk perception in the larger family context and to delineate family processes regarding decision making.

To improve patient-provider communication, women need to understand the meaning of a test result for them personally, but at the same time they also need to be able to thoughtfully weigh their personal values and needs, in the context of the constellation of their risk

Table 10.1   Overview of Psychosocial Factors in Breast Cancer Genetic Risk

Comprehension of genetic risk	Individuals at high genetic risk often display inaccuracies in knowledge and risk perceptions, especially related to anxiety and cultural factors.
Decision to undergo *BRCA1/2* testing	Uptake of testing is lower than interest in testing and is related to such psychosocial factors as risk perceptions, knowledge, expectations of the benefits and emotional consequences of testing, and relevance of testing to life goals.
Impact of *BRCA1/2* testing	Genetic counseling/testing generally reduces distress, but certain testing outcomes (e.g., positive carrier status) can contribute to sustained distress.
Participation in surveillance/ prevention regimens	Screening surveillance is generally high among individuals who have been tested; uptake of preventive surgery is high among certain subgroups (e.g., *BRCA1/2* carriers). Key predictors of uptake of prophylactic surgery are cancer worry, anxiety, and objective and perceived risk.
Communication of test results of family	Family concerns are a major reason to undergo genetic testing, but willingness to share genetic test results is influenced by family relationships and *BRCA1/2* carrier status.

perceptions, affective response, and self-regulatory coping responses. Unfortunately, few studies have systematically or comprehensively addressed how the individual's distinctive profile of cognitive-affective characteristics influence decisions for *BRCA1/2* testing and medical management, particularly after the genetic testing decision has been made (e.g., Schwartz, Peshkin, Tercyak, Taylor, & Valdimarsdottir, 2005). At the clinical level, providers need to be knowledgeable about breast cancer genetics and medical approaches to breast cancer risk management, but also need to develop the skills to elicit and respond to the individual's psychosocial issues, especially those related to negative affect, that are presented. Programs to address both knowledge and skills should be made available to clinicians in training, as well as to those providers already in practice. Continuing education programs have been developed through various comprehensive cancer centers and the Oncology Nursing Society.

The ultimate goal of genetic risk counseling is to facilitate informed decision making at each point in the process, from identifying inherited susceptibility to disclosure of results to family members. From the research perspective, we need to design and evaluate more effective messages and interventions to address misconceptions about inherited risk and to correct individuals' exaggerated (or minimized) perspectives about their own risk. For those individuals who are at high risk due to family history, we need to explore how to best facilitate participation in genetic risk counseling programs, and include appropriate pre- and posttesting couples and family consultations, so that women and their family members can fully process the meaning of potential test results and the potential implications for preventive options. For women who decide to participate in genetic testing, cancer worry and anxiety can be addressed through cognitive-behavioral techniques that can help them to anticipate their emotional reactions to testing and aid in their decision making about the long-term management of their cancer risk status (Miller, Roussi, et al., 2005). In particular, counseling techniques such as pre-living and role-plays can prepare them for the psychological impact of further decisions based on different test results (Miller, Roussi, et al., 2005). While the emotional consequences of undergoing genetic risk assessment are often transient (Cullen, Schwartz, Lawrence, Selby, & Mandelblatt, 2004), the impact of decisions following receipt of genetic testing results is often enduring. For women who have already undergone genetic testing and received positive results, interventions are needed to address psychological distress, and should be especially designed to facilitate medical decision making (Burke et al., 1997; Halbert et al., 2004).

Future research is necessary to evaluate the extent to which patient decisions are consonant with their values and goals, as well as to evaluate the long-term implications of making testing or management decisions that are discordant with values and goals (Schwartz et al., 2004). Greater focus is needed to understand the psychosocial mechanisms underlying beneficial effects, whether it be reduction in cancer-related worry or greater concordance between values, goals, and decisions (Schwartz et al., 2004). Moreover, efforts are needed to identify strategies to recruit and target the specific needs of minorities who may be eligible for genetic risk assessment (Hughes et al., 2004; Miller et al., 2004).

In further studies, it will also be important to determine more precisely the types of support and guidance that individuals and families require about what preventive and surveillance options to pursue. For example, this support can initially be provided by health care personnel, and then supplemented with information provided through educational and counseling media and by timely use of medical and family therapists (see Chapter 6). Perhaps one of the most challenging but unaddressed issues is whether, and how, to include key family members in the pre- and posttesting process and how to communicate breast cancer genetic test results to family members. Future research is needed to examine how practitioners can better prepare individuals to more fully understand, explain, and orient their relatives to potential test results. Education and training in communications skills may be necessary to address the lack of confidence individuals feel in communicating genetic risk information. Future research should assist in identifying effective methods to teach these critical communication skills.

As new discoveries are made in our understanding of genetics and breast cancer, so too will new psychosocial approaches and techniques need to be developed to assist individuals in understanding the science, make informed decisions, and cope with the psychosocial issues that need to be addressed.

Acknowledgments: This work was supported in part by National Cancer Institute Grants R01 CA104979 and P30 CA006927; National Human Genome Institute Grant R01 HG01766; Department of Defense Grants DAMD17-01-1-0238, DAMD17-02-1-0382, and W81XWH-06-1-0099; American Cancer Society Grant TURSG-02-227-01-PBP; and PA Department of Health Grant SAP#4100026777. We are indebted to Margaret Atchison and Stephen LaMonica for their technical assistance; we also acknowledge the resources and services of the Fox Chase Behavioral Research Core Facility, including the contributions of Pagona Roussi, Mary Ropka, and Catharine Wang.

REFERENCES

Ajzen, I., & Madden, T. J. (1986). Prediction of goal-directed behavior: Attitudes, intentions, and perceived behavioral control. *Journal of Experimental Social Psychology, 22*(5), 453–474.

American Cancer Society (2005). *Cancer facts and figures 2005.* Retrieved January 17, 2006, from http://www.cancer.org/downloads/STT/CAFF_finalPWSecured.pdf

Andrykowski, M. A., Lightner, R., Studts, J. L., & Munn, R. K. (1997). Hereditary cancer risk notification and testing: How interested is the general population? *Journal of Clinical Oncology, 15,* 2139–2148.

Antoniou, A. C., Pharoah, P. D., McMullan, G., Day, N. E., & Ponder, B. A. (2001). Evidence for further breast cancer susceptibility genes in addition to BRCA1 and BRCA2 in a population-based study. *Genetic Epidemiology, 21*(1), 1–18.

Antoniou, A. C., Pharoah, P. D., McMullan, G., Day, N. E., Stratton, M. R., Peto, J., et al. (2002). A comprehensive model for familial breast cancer incorporating BRCA1, BRCA2 and other genes. *British Journal of Cancer, 86*(1), 76–83.

Antoniou, A. C., Pharoah, P. D., Narod, S., Risch, A., Eyfjord, E., Hopper, J. L., et al. (2003). Average risks of breast and ovarian cancer associated with *BRCA1* or *BRCA2* mutations detected in case series unselected for family history: A combined analysis of 22 studies. *American Journal of Human Genetics, 72,* 1117–1130.

Appleton, S., Fry, A., Rees, G., Rush, R., & Cull, A. (2000). Psychosocial effects of living with an increased risk of breast cancer: An exploratory study using telephone focus groups. *Psychooncology, 9,* 511–521.

Armstrong, K., Calzone, K., Stopfer, J., Fitzgerald, G., Coyne, J., & Weber, B. (2000). Factors associated with decisions about clinical BRCA1/2 testing. *Cancer Epidemiology, Biomarkers, and Prevention, 9,* 1251–1254.

Armstrong, K., Weber, B., FitzGerald, G., Hershey, J. C., Pauly, M. V., Lemaire, J., et al. (2003). Life insurance and breast cancer risk assessment: Adverse selection, genetic testing decisions, and discrimination. *American Journal of Medical Genetics, 120A*(3), 359–364.

Armstrong, K., Weber, B., Ubel, P. A., Guerra, C., & Schwartz, J. S. (2002). Interest in BRCA1/2 testing in a primary care population. *Preventive Medicine, 34*(6), 590–595.

Audrain, J., Rimer, B., Cella, D., Garber, J., Peshkin, B. N., Ellis, J., et al. (1998). Genetic counseling and testing for breast-ovarian cancer susceptibility: What do women want? *Journal of Clinical Oncology, 16,* 1333–1338.

Audrain, J., Schwartz, M. D., Lerman, C., Hughes, C., Peshkin, B. N., & Biesecker, B. (1997). Psychological distress in women seeking genetic counseling for breast-ovarian cancer risk: The contributions of personality and appraisal. *Annals of Behavioral Medicine, 19*(4), 370–377.

Axilbund, J. E., Hamby, L. A., Thompson, D. B., Olsen, S. J., & Griffin, C. A. (2005). Assessment of the use and feasibility of video to supplement the genetic counseling process: A cancer genetic counseling perspective. *Journal of Genetic Counseling, 14*(3), 235–243.

Bandura, A. (1986). *Social foundations of thought and action: A social cognitive theory.* Upper Saddle River, NJ: Prentice-Hall.

Becker, D. (1974). The conditional life [French]. *Evolution Psychiatrique, 39,* 537–556.

Bell, D. W., Varley, J. M., Szydlo, T. E., Kang, D. H., Wahrer, D. C., Shannon, K. E., et al. (1999). Heterozygous germ line hCHK2 mutations in Li-Fraumeni syndrome. *Science, 286,* 2528–2531.

Benkendorf, J. L., Reutenauer, J. E., Hughes, C. A., Eads, N., Willison, J., Powers, M., et al. (1997). Patients' attitudes about autonomy and confidentiality in genetic testing for breast-ovarian cancer susceptibility. *American Journal of Medical Genetics, 73*(3), 296–303.

Bernhardt, B. A. (1997). Empirical evidence that genetic counseling is directive: Where do we go from here? *American Journal of Human Genetics, 60*(1), 17–20.

Berth, H., Balck, F., & Dinkel, A. (2003). Possibilities and limitations of genetic testing. Results of a survey in the general population and in medical students. *Zeitschrift fur Medizinische Psychologie, 12*(4), 177–185.

Biesecker, B. B., Ishibe, N., Hadley, D. W., Giambarresi, T. R., Kase, R. G., Lerman, C., et al. (2000). Psychosocial factors predicting BRCA1/BRCA2 testing decisions in members of hereditary breast and ovarian cancer families. *American Journal of Medical Genetics, 93*(4), 257–263.

Bish, A., Sutton, S., Jacobs, C., Levene, S., Ramirez, A., & Hodgson, S. (2002). No news is (not necessarily) good news: Impact of preliminary results for BRCA1 mutation searches. *Genetic Medicine, 4*(5), 353–358.

Blackhall, L. J., Murphy, S. T., Frank, G., Michel, V., & Azen, S. (1995). Ethnicity and attitudes toward patient autonomy. *Journal of the American Medical Association, 274,* 820–825.

Bluman, L. G., Rimer, B. K., Berry, D. A., Borstelmann, N., Iglehart, J. D., Regan, et al. (1999). Attitudes, knowledge, and risk perceptions of women with breast and/or ovarian cancer considering testing for BRCA1 and BRCA2. *Journal of Clinical Oncology, 17*(3), 1040–1046.

Bluman, L. G., Rimer, B. K., Regan, S. K., Lancaster, J., Clark, S., Borstelmann, N., et al. (2003). Attitudes, knowledge, risk perceptions and decision-making among women with breast and/or ovarian cancer considering testing for BRCA1 and BRCA2 and their spouses. *Psychooncology, 12*(5), 410–427.

Bonadona, V., Saltel, P., Desseigne, F., Mignotte, H., Saurin, J. C., Wang, Q., et al. (2002). Cancer patients who experienced diagnostic genetic testing for cancer susceptibility: Reactions and behavior after the disclosure of a positive test result. *Cancer Epidemiology Biomarkers Preview, 11,* 97–104.

Botkin, J., Croyle, R., Smith, K., Baty, B., Lerman, C., Goldgar, D., et al. (1996). A model protocol for evaluating the behavioral and psychosocial effects of BRCA1 testing. *Journal of the National Cancer Institute, 88*(13), 872–882.

Botkin, J. R., Smith, K. R., Croyle, R. T., Baty B. J., Wylie, J. E., Dutson, D., et al. (2003). Genetic testing for a BRCA1 mutation: Prophylactic surgery and screening behavior in women 2 years post testing. *American Journal of Medical Genetics, Part A, 118*(3), 201–209.

Bowen, D. J., Bourcier, E., Press, N., Lewis, F. M., & Burke, W. (2004). Effects of individual and family functioning on interest in genetic testing. *Community Genetics, 7*(1), 25–32.

Bowen, D. J., Burke, W., Yasui, Y., McTiernan, A., & McLeran, D. (2002). Effects of risk counseling on interest in breast cancer genetic testing for lower risk women. *Genetic Medicine, 4*(5), 359–365.

Bowen, D. J., McTiernan, A., Burke, W., Powers, D., Pruski, J., Durfy, S., et al. (1999). Participation in breast cancer risk counseling among women with a family history. *Cancer Epidemiology, Biomarkers and Prevention, 8*(7), 581–585.

Bowen, D. J., Singal, R., Eng, E., Crystal, S., & Burke, W. (2003). Jewish identity and intentions to obtain breast cancer screening. *Cultural Diversity and Ethnic Minority Psychology, 9*(1), 79–87.

Brandt, R., Hartmann, E., Ali, Z., Tucci, R., & Gilman, P. (2002). Motivations and concerns of women considering genetic testing for breast cancer: A comparison between affected and at-risk probands. *Genetic Testing, 6*(3), 203–205.

Brekelmans, C. T. M., Seynaeve, C., Bartels, C. C. M., Tilanus-Linthorst, M. M. A., Meijers-Heijboer, E. J., Crepin, C. M. G., et al. (2001). Effectiveness of breast cancer surveillance in BRCA1/2 gene mutation carriers and women with high familial risk. *Journal of Clinical Oncology, 19*(4), 924–930.

Broadstock, M., Michie, S., Gray, J., Mackay, J., & Marteau, T. M. (2000). The psychological consequences of offering mutation searching in the family for those at risk of hereditary breast and ovarian cancer—a pilot study. *Psychooncology, 9,* 537–548.

Burke, W., Culver, J. O., Bowen, D., Lowry, D., Durfy, S., McTiernan, A., et al. (2000). Genetic counseling for women with an intermediate family history of breast cancer. *American Journal of Medical Genetics, 90*(5), 361–368.

Burke, W., Daly, M., Garber, J., Botkin, J., Kahn, M. J., Lynch, P., et al. (1997). Recommendations for follow-up care of individuals with an inherited predisposition to cancer: II. BRCA1 and BRCA2. Cancer Genetics Studies Consortium. *Journal of the American Cancer Society, 277*(12), 997–1003.

Butow, P. N., Lobb, E. A., Meiser, B., Barratt, A., & Tucker, K. M. (2003). Psychological outcomes and risk perception after genetic testing and counseling in breast cancer: A systematic review. *Medical Journal of Austria, 178,* 77–81.

Cappelli, M., Surh, L., Humphreys, L., Verma, S., Logan, D., Hunter, A., et al. (1999). Psychological and social determinants of women's decisions to undergo genetic counseling and testing for breast cancer. *Clinical Genetics, 55,* 419–430.

Carver, C. S., & Scheier, M. F. (1986). Self and the control of behavior. In L. M. Hartman & K. R. Blankstein (Eds.), *Perception of self in emotional disorder and psychotherapy* (pp. 5–35). New York: Plenum Press.

Carver, C., Scheier, M., & Weintraub, J. (1989). Assessing coping strategies: A theoretically based approach. *Journal of Personality and Social Psychology, 56,* 267–283.

Cella, D., Hughes, C., Peterman, A., Chang, C. H., Peshkin, B. N., Schwartz, M. D., et al. (2002). A brief assessment of concerns associated with genetic testing for cancer: The Multidimensional Impact of Cancer Risk Assessment (MICRA) questionnaire. *Health Psychology, 21*(6), 564–572.

Chaliki, H., Loader, S., Levenkron, J. C., Logan-Young, W., Hall, W. J., & Rowley, P. T. (1995). Women's receptivity to testing for a genetic susceptibility to breast cancer. *American Journal of Public Health, 85*(8), 1133–1135.

Chalmers, J. W., & Breen, D. (1995). Positive predictive value of tests for breast disease. *British Medical Journal, 310,* 331.

Chalmers, K., Thomson, K., & Degner, L. F. (1996). Information, support, and communication needs of women with a family history of breast cancer. *Cancer Nursing, 19*(3), 204–213.

Chang, J., & Elledge, R. M. (2001). Clinical management of women with genomic BRCA1 and BRCA2 mutations. *Breast Cancer Research and Treatment, 69*(2), 101–113.

Chlebowski, R. T. (2002). Breast cancer risk reduction: Strategies for women at increased risk. *Annual Review of Medicine, 53,* 519–540.

Claes, E., Evers-Kiebooms, G., Boogaerts, A., Decruyenaere, M., Denayer, L., & Legius, E. (2003). Communication with close and distant relatives in the context of genetic testing for hereditary breast and ovarian cancer in cancer patients. *American Journal of Medical Genetics, 116A*(1), 11–19.

Claes, E., Evers-Kiebooms, G., Denayer, L., Decruyenaere, M., Boogaerts, A., Philippe, K., et al. (2005). Predictive genetic testing for hereditary breast and ovarian cancer: Psychological distress and illness representations 1 year following disclosure. *Journal of Genetic Counseling, 14*(5), 349–363.

Collins, F. S., & Guttmacher, A. E. (2001). Genetics moves into the medical mainstream. *Journal of the American Medical Association, 286,* 2322–2324.

Coyne, J. C., Kruus, L., Kagee, A., Thompson, R., Palmer, S., & Kruus, L. (2002). Benign mental health consequences of screening for mutations of BRCA1/BRCA2. *American Journal of Medical Genetics, 107*(4), 346–349.

Croyle, R. T., Achilles, J. S., & Lerman, C. (1997). Psychologic aspects of cancer genetic testing: A research update for clinicians. *Cancer, 80*(3 Suppl.), 569–575.

Croyle, R. T., & Lerman, C. (1999). Risk communication in genetic testing for cancer susceptibility. *Journal of the National Cancer Institute Monograph, 25,* 59–66.

Cull, A., Anderson, E. D., Campbell, S., Mackay, J., Smyth, E., & Steel, M. (1999). The impact of genetic counseling about breast cancer risk on women's risk perceptions and levels of distress. *British Journal of Cancer, 79*(3–4), 501–508.

Cull, A., Fry, A., Rush, R., & Steel, C. M. (2001). Cancer risk perceptions and distress among women attending a familial ovarian cancer clinic. *British Journal of Cancer, 84*(5), 594–599.

Cullen, J., Schwartz, M. D., Lawrence, W. F., Selby, J. V., & Mandelblatt, J. S. (2004). Short-term impact of cancer prevention and screening activities on quality of life. *Journal of Clinical Oncology, 22*(5), 943–952.

Cuzick, J. (2000). Future possibilities in the prevention of breast cancer: Breast cancer prevention trials. *Breast Cancer Research, 2*(4), 258–263.

Daly, M. (1999). People not statistics. *Nursing Standard, 13*(34), 22–23.

Daly, M. B., Barsevick, A., Miller, S. M., Buckman, R., Costalas, J., Montgomery, et al. (2001). Communicating genetic test results to the family: A six-step, skills-building strategy. *Family Community Health, 24*(3),13–26.

Daly, M. B., Itzen, M., Costalas, J. W., & Balshem, A. (1997, December). *The communication of BRCA1 and BRCA2 test results to at-risk relatives.* Presented at the 20th Annual San Antonio Breast Cancer Symposium, San Antonio, CA.

Dershaw, D. D. (2000). Mammographic screening of the high-risk woman. *American Journal of Surgery, 180*(4), 288–289.

DiCastro, M., Frydman, M., Friedman, I., Shiri-Sverdlov, R., Papa, M. Z., Goldman, B., et al. (2002). Genetic counseling in hereditary breast/ovarian cancer in Israel: Psychosocial impact and retention of genetic information. *American Journal of Medical Genetics, 111*(2), 147–151.

Diefenbach, M. A., Miller, S. M., & Daly, M. B. (1999). Specific worry about breast cancer predicts mammography use in women at risk for breast and ovarian cancer. *Health Psychology, 18*(5), 532–536.

Donovan, K. A., & Tucker, D. C. (2000). Knowledge about genetic risk for breast cancer and perceptions of genetic testing in a sociodemographically diverse sample. *Journal of Behavioral Medicine, 23*(1), 15–36.

Dorval, M., Patenaude, A. F., Schneide, K. A., Kieffer, S. A., DiGianni, L., Kalkbrenner, K. J., et al. (2000). Anticipated versus actual emotional reactions to disclosure of results of genetic tests for cancer susceptibility: Findings from p53 and BRCA1 testing programs. *Journal of Clinical Oncology, 18*, 2135–2142.

Durfy, S. J., Bowen, D. J., McTiernan, A., Sporleder, J., & Burke, W. (1999). Attitudes and interest in genetic testing for breast and ovarian cancer susceptibility in diverse groups of women in western Washington. *Cancer Epidemiology, Biomarkers and Prevention, 8*, 369–375.

Easton, D. F., Ford, D., & Bishop, D. T. (1995). Breast and ovarian cancer incidence in BRCA1-mutation carriers. Breast Cancer Linkage Consortium. *American Journal of Human Genetics, 56*(1), 265–271.

Eeles, R. A., & Powles, T. J. (2000). Chemoprevention options for BRCA1 and BRCA2 mutation carriers. *Journal of Clinical Oncology, 18*(21), 93S–99S.

Eisen, A., Rebbeck, T. R., Wood, W. C., & Weber, B. L. (2000). Prophylactic surgery in women with a hereditary predisposition to breast and ovarian cancer. *Journal of Clinical Oncology, 18*(9), 1980–1995.

Emery, J. (2001). In informed choice in genetic testing a different breed of informed decision-making? A discussion paper. *Health Expectations, 4*(2), 81–86.

Emmons, K. M., Kalkbrenner, K. J., Klar, N., Light, T., Schneider, K. A., & Garber, J. E. (2000). Behavioral risk factors among women presenting for genetic testing. *Cancer Epidemiology, Biomarkers and Prevention, 9*, 89–94.

Erblich, J., Bovbjerg, D. H., Norman, C., Valdimarsdottir, H. B., & Montgomery, G. H. (2000). It won't happen to me: Lower perception of heart disease risk among women with family histories of breast cancer. *Preventive Medicine, 6*, 714–721.

Evans, D. G., Fentiman, I. S., McPherson, K., Asbury, D., Ponder, B. A., & Howell, A. (1994). Familial breast cancer. *British Medical Journal, 308*, 183–187.

Evers-Kiebooms, G., Welkenhuysen, M., Claes, E., Decruyenaere, M., & Denayer, L. (2000). The psychological complexity of predictive testing for late onset neurogenetic diseases and hereditary cancers: Implications for multidisciplinary counseling and for genetic education. *Social Science and Medicine, 51*(6), 831–841.

Fang, C. Y., Miller, S. M., Malick, J., Babb, J., Hurley, K. E., Engstrom, P. F., et al. (2003). Psychosocial correlates of intention to undergo prophylactic oophorectomy among women with a family history of ovarian cancer. *Preventive Medicine, 37*(5), 424–431.

Fisher, B., Costantino, J. P., Wickerham, D. L., Redmond, C. K., Kavanah, M., Cronin, W. M., et al. (1998). Tamoxifen for prevention of breast cancer: Report of the National Surgical Adjuvant Breast and Bowel Project P-1 study. *Journal of the National Cancer Institute, 90*, 1371–1388.

Fisher, E. R., Sass, R., Palekar, A., Fisher, B., & Wolmark, N. (1989). Dukes' classification revisited: Findings from the National Surgical Adjuvant Breast and Bowel projects (Protocol R-01). *Cancer, 64*(11), 2354–2360.

Foster, C., Evans, D. G., Eeles, R., Eccles, D., Ashley, S., Brooks, L., et al. (2002). Predictive testing for BRCA1/2: Attributes, risk perception, and management in a multi-center clinical cohort. *British Journal of Cancer, 86*, 1209–1216.

Frost, M. H., Schaid, D. J., Sellers, T. A., Slezak, J. M., Arnold, P. G., Woods, J. E., et al. (2000). Long-term satisfaction and psychological and social function following bilateral prophylactic mastectomy. *Journal of the American Medical Association, 284,* 319–324.

Fry, A., Rush, R., Busby-Earle, C., & Cull, A. (2001). Deciding about prophylactic oophorectomy: What is important to women at increased risk of ovarian cancer? *Preventive Medicine, 33,* 578–585.

Garber, G. E., Goldstein, A. M., Kantor, A. F., Dreyfus, M. G., Fraumeni, J. F., & Li, F. P. (1991). Follow-up study of twenty-four families with Li-Fraumeni syndrome. *Cancer Research, 51,* 6094–6097.

Geer, K. P., Ropka, M. E., Cohn, W. F., Jones, S. M., & Miesfeldt, S. (2001). Factors influencing patients' decisions to decline cancer genetic counseling services. *Journal of Genetic Counseling, 10*(1), 25–40.

Geller, G., Doksum, T., Bernhardt, B. A., & Metz, S. A. (1999). Participation in breast cancer susceptibility testing protocols: Influence of recruitment source, altruism, and family involvement on women's decisions. *Cancer Epidemiology, Biomarkers, and Prevention, 8*(4, Pt. 2), 377–383.

Green, M. J., Biesecker, B. B., McInerney, A. M., Mauger, D., & Fost, N. (2001). An interactive computer program can effectively educate patients about genetic testing for breast cancer susceptibility. *American Journal of Medical Genetics, 103*(1), 16–23.

Green, M. J., & Frost, N. (1997). Who should provide genetic education prior to gene testing? Computers and other methods for improving patient understanding. *Genetic Testing, 1*(2), 131–136.

Green, M. J., Peterson, S. K., Baker, M. W., Friedman, L. C., Harper, G. R., Rubinstein, W. S., et al. (2005). Use of an educational computer program before genetic counseling for breast cancer susceptibility: Effects on duration and content of counseling sessions. *Genetic Medicine, 7*(4), 221–229.

Green, M. J., Peterson S. K., Baker, M. W., Harper, G. R., Friedman, L. C., Rubinstein, W. S., et al. (2004). Effect of a computer-based decision aid on knowledge, perceptions, and intentions about genetic testing for breast cancer susceptibility: A randomized controlled trial. *Journal of the American Medical Association, 292,* 442–452.

Grossman, D. (2002). Prognostic disclosure. *Annals of Internal Medicine, 137*(5, Pt. 1), 368–369.

Gwyn, K., Vernon, S. W., & Conoley, P. M. (2003). Intention to pursue genetic testing for breast cancer among women due for mammography screening. *Cancer Epidemiology, Biomarkers and Prevention, 12,* 96–102.

Hadley, D. W., Jenkins, J., Dimond, E., Nakahara, K., Grogan, L., Liewehr, D. J., et al. (2003). Genetic counseling and testing in families with hereditary nonpolyposis colorectal cancer. *Archives of Internal Medicine, 163*(5), 573–582.

Hagoel, L., Dishon, S., Almog, R., Silman, Z., Bisland-Becktell, S., & Rennert, G. (2000). Proband family uptake of familial-genetic counseling. *Psychooncology, 9*(6), 522–527.

Hailey, B. J., Carter, C. L., & Burnett, D. R. (2000). Breast cancer attitudes, knowledge, and screening behavior in women with and without a family history of breast cancer. *Health Care for Women International, 21,* 701–715.

Halbert, C. H., Schwartz, M. D., Wenzel, L., Narod, S., Peshkin, B. N., Cella, D., et al. (2004). Predictors of cognitive appraisals following *BRCA1* and *BRCA2* mutations. *Journal of Behavioral Medicine, 27*(4), 373–392.

Hallowell, N., Foster, C., Ardern-Jones, A., Eeles, R., Murday, V., & Watson, M. (2002). Genetic testing for women previously diagnosed with breast/ovarian cancer: Examining the impact of BRCA1 and BRCA2 mutation searching. *Genetic Testing, 6*(2), 79–87.

Hallowell, N., Murton, F., Statman, H., Green, J. M., & Richards, M. P. (1997). Women's need for the information before attending genetic counseling for familial breast or ovarian cancer: A questionnaire, interview and observational study. *British Medical Journal, 314,* 281–283.

Hamann, H. A., Somers, T. J., Smith, A. W., Inslicht, S. S., & Baum, A. (2005). Posttraumatic stress associated with cancer history and *BRCA1/2* genetic testing. *Psychosomatic Medicine, 67,* 766–772.

Hartmann, L. C., Sellers, T. A., Schaid, D. J., Frank, T. S., Soderberg, C. L., Sitta, D. L., et al. (2001). Efficacy of bilateral prophylactic mastectomy in BRCA1 and BRCA2 gene mutation carriers. *Journal of the National Cancer Institute, 93,* 1586–1587.

Hatcher, M. B., Fallowfield, L., & A'Hern, R. (2001). The psychosocial impact of bilateral prophylactic mastectomy: Prospective study using questionnaires and semistructured interviews. *British Medical Journal, 322,* 76.

Helmes, A. W., Bowen, D. J., & Bengel, J. (2002). Patient preferences of decision-making in the context of genetic testing for breast cancer risk. *Genetics in Medicine, 4*(3), 150–157.

Hopwood, P. (2000). Breast cancer risk perception: What do we know and understand? *Breast Cancer Research, 2*(6), 387–391.

Hopwood, P., Keeling, F., Long, A., Pool, C., Evans, G., & Howell, A. (1998). Psychological support needs for women at high genetic risk of breast cancer: Some preliminary indicators. *Psychooncology, 7*(5), 402–412.

Hopwood, P., Shenton, A., Lalloo, F., Evans, D. G., & Howell, A. (2001). Risk perception and cancer worry: An exploratory study of the impact of genetic risk counseling in women with a family history of breast cancer. *Journal of Medical Genetics, 38*(2), 139.

Hughes, C., Cella, D., Peterman, A., Chang, C. H., Peshkin, B. N., Schwartz, M. D., et al. (2002). A brief assessment of concerns associated with genetic testing for cancer: The Multidimensional Impact of Cancer Risk Assessment (MICRA) questionnaire. *Health Psychology, 21,* 564–572.

Hughes, C., Fasaye, G., LaSalle, V. H., & Finch, C. (2003). Sociocultural influences on participation in genetic risk assessment and testing among African American women. *Patient Education and Counseling, 51,* 107–114.

Hughes, C., Gomez-Caminero, A., Benkendorf, J., Kerner, J., Isaacs, C., Barter, J., et al. (1997). Ethnic differences in knowledge and attitudes about BRCA1 testing in women at increased risk. *Patient Education and Counseling, 32,* 51–62.

Hughes, C., Lerman, C., Schwartz, M., Peshkin, B. N., Wenzel, L., Narod, S., et al. (2002). All in the family: Evaluation of the process and content of sisters' communication about BRCA1 and BRCA2 genetic test results. *American Journal of Medical Genetics, 107*(2), 143–150.

Hughes, C., Peterson, S. K., Ramirez, A., Gallion, K. J., McDonald, P. G., Skinner, C. S., et al. (2004). Minority recruitment in hereditary breast cancer research. *Cancer Epidemiology, Biomarkers, and Prevention, 13*(7), 1146–1155.

Hurley, J., Franco, S., Gomez-Fernandez, C., Reis, I., Velez, P., Doliny, P., et al. (2001). Breast cancer and human immunodeficiency virus: A report of 20 cases. *Clinical Breast Cancer, 2*(3), 215–220.

Inglehart, J. A., Nelson, P. C., & Zou, Y. (1998). Mapper: An intelligent restriction mapping tool. *Bioinformatics, 14*(2), 101–111.

Isaacs, C., Peshkin, B. N., Schwartz, M., Demarco, T. A., Main, D., & Lerman, C. (2002). Breast and ovarian cancer screening practices in healthy women with a strong family history of breast or ovarian cancer. *Breast Cancer Research and Treatment, 71*(2), 103–112.

Jacobsen, P. B., Valdimarsdottir, H. B., Brown, K. L., & Offit, K. (1997). Decision-making about genetic testing among women at familial risk for breast cancer. *Psychosomatic Medicine, 59,* 459–466.

Julian-Reynier, C., Sobol, H., Sevilla, C., Nogues, C., & Bourret, P. (2000). Uptake of hereditary breast/ovarian cancer genetic testing in a French national sample of BRCA1 families. The French Cancer Genetic Network. *Psychooncology, 9*(6), 504–510.

Kash, K. M., Ortega-Verdejo, K., Dabney, M. K., Holland, J. C., Miller, D. G., & Osborne, M. P. (2000) Psychosocial aspects of cancer genetics: Women at high risk for breast and ovarian cancer. *Seminars in Surgical Oncology, 18,* 333–338.

King, M. C., Wieand, S., Hale, K., Lee, M., Walsh, T., Owens, K., et al. (2001). Tamoxifen and breast cancer incidence among women with inherited mutations in BRCA1 and BRCA2. *Journal of the American Medical Association, 286,* 2251–2256.

Kinney, A. Y., Croyle, R. T., Dudley, W. N., Bailey, C. A., Pelias, M. K., & Neuhausen, S. L. (2001). Knowledge, attitudes, and interest in breast-ovarian cancer gene testing: A survey of a large African-American kindred with a BRCA1 mutation. *Preventive Medicine, 33*(6), 543–551.

Kinney, A. Y., Emery, G., Dudley, W. N., & Croyle, R. T. (2002). Screening behaviors among African American women at high risk for breast cancer: Do beliefs about god matter? *Oncology Nursing Forum, 29*(5), 835–843.

Lee, S. C., Bernhardt, B. A., & Helzlsouer, K. J. (2002). Utilization of BRCA1/2 genetic testing in the clinical setting: Report from a single institution. *Cancer, 94*(6), 1876–1885.

Lehmann, L. S., Weeks, J. C., Klar, N., Biener, L., & Garber, J. E. (2000). Disclosure of familial genetic information: Perceptions of the duty to inform. *American Journal of Medicine, 109,* 705–711.

Lehmann, L. S., Weeks, J. C., Klar, N., & Garber, J. E. (2002). A population-based study of Ashkenazi Jewish women's attitudes toward genetic discrimination and BRCA1/2 testing. *Genetic Medicine, 4*(5), 346–352.

Lerman, C., Biesecker, B., Benkendorf, J. L., Kerner, J., Gomez-Caminero, A., Hughes, C., et al. (1997). Controlled trial of pretest education approaches to enhance informed decision-making for BRCA1 gene testing. *Journal of the National Cancer Institute, 89*(2), 148–157.

Lerman, C., & Croyle, R. (1994). Psychological issues in genetic testing for breast cancer susceptibility. *Archives of Internal Medicine, 154*(6), 609–616.

Lerman, C., Daly, M., Masny, A., & Balshem, A. (1994). Attitudes about genetic testing for breast-ovarian cancer susceptibility. *Journal of Clinical Oncology, 12*(4), 843–850.

Lerman, C., Hughes, C., Benkendorf, J. L., Biesecker, B., Kerner, J., Willison, J., et al. (1999). Racial differences in testing motivation and psychological distress following retest education for BRCA1 gene testing. *Cancer Epidemiology, Biomarkers and Prevention, 8*, 361–367.

Lerman, C., Hughes, C., Croyle, R. T., Main, D., Durham, C., Snyder, C., et al. (2000). Prophylactic surgery decisions and surveillance practices one year following BRCA1/2 testing. *Preventive Medicine, 31*(1), 75–80.

Lerman, C., Hughes, C., Lemon, S. J., Main, D., Snyder, C., Durham, C., et al. (1998). What you don't know can hurt you: Adverse psychologic effects in members of BRCA1-linked and BRCA2-linked families who decline genetic testing. *Journal of Clinical Oncology, 16*(5), 1650–1654.

Lerman, C., Kash, K., & Stefanek, M. (1994). Younger women at increased risk for breast cancer: Perceived risk, psychological well-being, and surveillance behavior. *Journal of the National Cancer Institute Monographs, 16*, 171–176.

Lerman, C., Lustbader, E., Rimer, B., Daly, M., Miller, S., Sands, C., et al. (1995). Effects of individualized breast cancer risk counseling: A randomized trial. *Journal of the National Cancer Institute, 87*(4), 286–292.

Lerman, C., Marshall, J., Audrain, J., & Gomez-Caminero, A. (1996). Genetic testing for colon cancer susceptibility: Anticipated reactions of patients and challenges to providers. *International Journal of Cancer, 69*(1), 58–61.

Lerman, C., Narod, S., Schulman, K., Hughes, C., Gomez-Caminero, A., Bonney, G., et al. (1996). BRCA1 testing in families with hereditary breast-ovarian cancer: A prospective study of patient decision making and outcomes. *Journal of the American Medical Association, 275*, 1885–1892.

Lerman, C., Schwartz, M. D., Lin, T. H., Hughes, C., Narod, S., & Lynch, H. T. (1997). The influence of psychological distress on use of genetic testing for cancer risk. *Journal of Consulting Clinical Psychology, 65*(3), 414–420.

Lerman, C., Schwartz, M. D., Miller, S. M., Daly, M., Sands, C., & Rimer, B. K. (1996). A randomized trial of breast cancer risk counseling: Interacting effects of counseling, educational level, and coping style. *Health Psychology, 15*(2), 75–83.

Lerman, C., Seay, J., Balsham, A., & Audrain, J. (1995). Interest in genetic testing among first-degree relatives of breast cancer patients. *American Journal of Medical Genetics, 57*(3), 385–392.

Lerman, C., & Shields, A. E. (2004). Genetic testing for cancer susceptibility: The promise and the pitfalls. *Nature Reviews Cancer, 4*(3), 235–241.

Lipkus, I. M., Iden, D., Terrenoire, J., & Feaganes, J. R. (1999). Relationships among breast cancer concern, risk perceptions, and interest in genetic testing for breast cancer susceptibility among African-American women with and without a family history of breast cancer. *Cancer Epidemiology, Biomarkers, and Prevention, 8*(6), 533–539.

Lloyd, S. M., Watson, M., Oaker, G., Sacks, N., Querci della Rovere, U., & Gui, G. (2000). Understanding the experience of prophylactic bilateral mastectomy: A qualitative study of ten women. *Psychooncology, 9*(6), 473–485.

Loader, S., Levenkron, J. C., & Rowley, P. T. (1998). Genetic testing for breast-ovarian cancer susceptibility: A regional trial. *Genetic Testing, 2*(4), 305–313.

Lodder, L., Frets, P. G., Trijsburg, R. W., Klijn, J. G., Seynaeve, C., Tilanus, M. M., et al. (2003). Attitudes and distress levels in women at risk to carry a BRCA1/BRCA2 gene mutation who decline genetic testing. *American Journal of Medical Genetics, 119A*(3), 266–272.

Lodder, L. N., Frets, P. G., Trijsburg, R. W., Meijers-Heijboer, E. J., Klijn, J. G., Duivenvoorden, H. J., et al. (1999). Presymptomatic testing for BRCA1 and BRCA2: How distressing are the pre-test weeks? Rotterdam/Leiden Genetics Working Group. *Journal of Medical Genetics, 36*, 906–913.

Lodder, L., Frets, P. G., Trijsburg, R. W., Meijers-Heijboer, E. J., Klijn, J. G., Duivenvoorden, H. J., et al. (2001). Psychological impact of receiving a BRCA1/BRCA2 test result. *American Journal of Medical Genetics, 98*(1), 15–24.

Lodder, L. N., Frets, P. G., Trijsburg, R. W., Meijers-Heijboer, E. J., Klijn, J. G., Seynaeve, C., et al. (2002). One year follow-up of women opting for presymptomatic testing for BRCA1 and BRCA2: Emotional impact of the test outcome and decisions on risk management (surveillance or prophylactic surgery). *Breast Cancer Research and Treatment, 73*(2), 197–112.

Lynch, E. D., Ostermeyer, E. A., Lee, M. K., Arena, J. F., Ji, H., Swisshelm, K., et al. (1997). Inherited mutations in PTEN that are associated with breast cancer, cowden disease, and juvenile polyposis. *American Journal of Human Genetics, 61*(6), 1254–1260.

Lynch, H. T., Lemon, S. J., Durham, C., Tinley, S. T., Connolly, C., Lynch, J. F., et al. (1997). A descriptive study of BRCA1 testing and reactions to disclosure of test results. *Cancer, 79*, 2219–2228.

Lynch, H. T., Watson, P., Tinley, S., Snyder, C., Durham, C., Lynch, J., et al. (1999). An update on DNA-based BRCA1/BRCA2 genetic counseling in hereditary breast cancer. *Cancer Genetics and Cytogenetics, 109*, 91–98.

McAllister, M. F., Evans, D. G., Ormiston, W., & Daly, P. (1998). Men in breast cancer families: A preliminary qualitative study of awareness and experience. *Journal of Medical Genetics, 35*(9), 739–744.

Meijers-Heijboer, H., Van Geel, B., Van Putten, W. L., Henzen-Logmans, S. C., Seynaeve, C., Menke-Pluymers, M. B., et al. (2001). Breast cancer after prophylactic bilateral mastectomy in women with a BRCA1 or BRCA2 mutation. *New England Journal of Medicine, 345*(3), 159–164.

Meischke, H., Bowen, D., & Kuniyuki, A. (2001). Awareness of genetic testing for breast cancer risk among women with a family history of breast cancer: Effect of women's information sources on their awareness. *Cancer Detection and Prevention, 25*(4), 319–327.

Meiser, B., Butow, P. N., Barratt, A. L., Schnieden, V., Gattas, M., Kirk, J., et al. (2001). Psychological Impact Collaborative Group. Long-term outcomes of genetic counseling in women at increased risk of developing hereditary breast cancer. *Patient Education and Counseling, 44*(3), 215–225.

Meiser, B., & Halliday, J. L. (2002). What is the impact of genetic counseling in women at increased risk of developing hereditary breast cancer? A meta-analytic review. *Social Science and Medicine, 54*, 1463–1470.

Meisner, B. (2005). Psychological impact of genetic testing for cancer susceptibility: An update of the literature. *Psychooncology, 14*, 1060–1074.

Metcalfe, K. A., Liede, A., Hoodfar, E., Scott, A., Foulkes, W. D., & Narod, S. A. (2000). An evaluation of needs of female BRCA1 and BRCA2 carriers undergoing genetic counseling. *Journal of Medical Genetics, 37*(11), 866–874.

Miller, S. M. (1995). Monitoring versus blunting styles of coping with cancer influence the information patients want and need about their disease: Implications for cancer screening and management. *Cancer, 76*, 167–177.

Miller, S. M., Bowen, D. J., Campbell, M. K., Diefenbach, M. A., Gritz, E. R., Jacobsen, P. B., et al. (2004). Current research promises and challenges in behavioral oncology: Report from the American Society of Preventive Oncology Annual Meeting. *Cancer Epidemiology, Biomarkers and Prevention, 13*, 171–180.

Miller, S. M., Fang, C. Y., Diefenbach, M. A., & Bales, C. (2001). Tailoring psychosocial interventions to the individual's health information processing style: The influence of monitoring versus blunting in cancer risk and disease. In A. Baum & B. Anderson (Eds.), *Psychosocial interventions in cancer* (pp. 343–362). Washington, DC: American Psychological Association.

Miller, S. M., Fang, C. Y., Manne, S. L., Engstrom, P. F., & Daly, M. B. (1999). Decision making about prophylactic oophorectomy among at-risk women: Psychological influences and implications. *Gynecologic Oncology, 75*(3), 406–412.

Miller, S. M., Fleisher, L., Roussi, P., Buzaglo, J. S., Schnoll, R., Slater, E., et al. (2005). Facilitating informed decision making about breast cancer risk and genetic counseling among women calling the NCI's Cancer Information Service. *Journal of Health Communications, 10*(Suppl. 1), 119–136.

Miller, S. M., Roussi, P., Daly, M. B., Buzaglo, J. S., Sherman, K. A., Godwin, A. K., et al. (2005). Enhanced counseling for women undergoing BRCA1/2 testing: Impact on subsequent decision making about risk prevention behaviors. *Health Education and Behavior, 32*(5), 654–667.

Miller, S. M., & Schnoll, R. A. (2000). Coping with stress: Examples from the cancer context. In J. M. M. Lewis (Ed.), *Handbook of emotions* (pp. 538–557). New York: Plenum Press.

Miller, S., Shoda, Y., & Hurley, K. (1996). Applying cognitive-social theory to health protective behavior: Breast self-examination in cancer screening. *Psychological Bulletin, 119*, 70–94.

Mischel, W., & Shoda, Y. (1995). A cognitive-affective system theory of personality: Reconceptualizing situations, dispositions, dynamics, and invariance in personality structure. *Psychological Bulletin, 102*, 246–268.

Modan, B., Hartage, P., Hirsh-Yechezkel, G., Chetrit, A., Lubin, F., Beller, U., et al. (2001). National Israel Ovarian Cancer Study Group. Parity, oral contraceptives, and the risk of ovarian cancer among carriers and noncarriers of a BRCA1 or BRCA2 mutation. *New England Journal of Medicine, 345*(4), 235–240.

Morris, K. T., Johnson, N., Krasikov, N., Allen, M., & Dorsey, P. (2001). Genetic counseling impacts decision for prophylactic surgery for patients perceived to be at high risk for breast cancer. *American Journal of Surgery, 181*(5), 431–433.

Moslehi, R., Chu, W., Karlan, B., Fishman, D., Risch, H., Fields, A., et al. (2000). BRCA1 and BRCA2 mutation analysis of 208 Ashkenazi Jewish women with ovarian cancer. *American Journal of Human Genetics, 66*, 1259–1272.

Mulley, A. G., & Sepucha, K. (2002). Making good decisions about breast cancer chemoprevention. *Annals of Internal Medicine, 137*(1), 52–54.

Narod, S. A., Brunet, J. S., Ghadirian, P., Robson, M., Heimdal, K., Neuhausen, S. L., et al. (2000). Hereditary Breast Cancer Clinical Study Group. Tamoxifen and risk of contralateral breast cancer in BRCA1 and BRCA2 mutation carriers: A case-control study. *Lancet, 356*, 1876–1881.

Narod, S. A., Feunteun, J., Lynch, H. T., Watson, P., Conway, T., Lynch, J., et al. (1991). Familial breast-ovarian cancer: Locus on chromosome 17q12-q23. *Lancet, 338*, 82–83.

Narod, S., Ford, D., Devilee, P., Barkardottir, R. B., Eyfjord, J., Lenoir, G., et al. (1995). Genetic heterogeneity of breast-ovarian cancer revisited. Breast Cancer Linkage Consortium. *American Journal of Human Genetics, 4*, 957–958.

Narod, S. A., Risch, H., Moslehi, R., Dorum, A., Neuhausen, S., Olsson, H., et al. (1998). Oral contraceptives and the risk of hereditary ovarian cancer. Hereditary Ovarian Cancer Clinical Study Group. *New England Journal of Medicine, 339*, 424–428.

Nathanson, K. L., Wooster, R., & Weber, B. L. (2001). Breast cancer genetics: What we know and what we need. *Nature Medicine, 7*(5), 552–556.

National Cancer Center. (2006). *What you need to know about breast cancer, risk factors.* Retrieved January 6, 2006, from http://www.cancer.gov/cancertopics/wyntk/breast/page4

National Comprehensive Cancer Center Network. (2006). NCCN 1.2006, *Genetic/familial high-risk assessment: Breast and ovarian guidelines.* Retrieved January 6, 2006, from http://www.nccn.org/professionals/physician_gls/PDF/genetics_screening.pdf

Osborne, C. K. (1998). Steroid hormone receptors in breast cancer management. *Breast Cancer Research and Treatment, 51*(3), 227–238.

Ozols, R. F., Daly, M. B., Klein-Szanto, A., Hamilton, T. C., Bast, R. C. Jr., & Brewer, M. A. (2003). Specific keynote: Chemoprevention of ovarian cancer: The journey begins. *Gynecological Oncology, 88*(1, Pt. 2), S59–S66; discussion S67–S70.

Patenaude, A. F. (2004). *Genetic testing for cancer: Psychological approaches for helping patients and families.* Washington, DC: American Psychological Association.

Patenaude, A. F., Guttmacher, A. E., & Collins, F. S. (2002). Genetic testing and psychology. *American Psychologist, 57*(4), 271–282.

Peshkin, B. N., Schwartz, M. D., Isaacs, C., Hughes, C., Main, D., & Lerman, C. (2002). Utilization of breast cancer screening in a clinically based sample of women after BRCA1/2 testing. *Cancer Epidemiology Biomarkers Preview, 11*, 1115–1118.

Phillips, K. A., Warner, E., Meschino, W. S., Hunter, J., Abdolell, M., Glendon, G., et al. (2000). Perceptions of Ashkenazi Jewish breast cancer patients on genetic testing for mutations in BRCA1 and BRCA2. *Clinical Genetics, 57*, 376–383.

Pieterse, A. H., Ausems, M. G., Van Dulmen, A. M., Beemer, F. A., & Bensing, J. M. (2005). Initial cancer genetic counseling consultation: Change in counselees' cognitions and anxiety, and association with addressing their needs and preferences. *American Journal of Medical Genetics A, 137*(1), 27–35.

Plon, S. E., Peterson, L. E., Friedman, L. C., & Richards, C. S. (2000). Mammography behavior after receiving a negative BRCA1 mutation test result in the Ashkenazim: A community-based study. *Genetic Medicine, 2*(6), 307–311.

Powell, D. R. (1994). Social and psychological aspects of breast cancer in African-American women. *Annals of the New York Academy of the Sciences, 736*, 131–139.

Powles, T. J., Bourne, T., Athanasiou, S., Chang, J., Grubock, K., Ashley, S., et al. (1998). The effects of norethisterone on endometrial abnormalities identified by transvaginal ultrasound screening of healthy post-menopausal women on tamoxifen or placebo. *British Journal of Cancer, 78*(2), 272–275.

Powles, T. J., Hardy, J. R., Ashley, S. E., Cosgrove, D., Davey, J. B., Dowsett, M., et al. (1989). Chemoprevention of breast cancer. *Breast Cancer Research and Treatment, 14*(1), 23–31.

Rebbeck, T. R. (2000). Prophylactic oophorectomy in BRCA1 and BRCA2 mutation carriers. *Journal of Clinical Oncology, 18*(21 Suppl.), 100S–103S.

Rebbeck, T. R., Friebel, T., Lynch, H. T., Neuhausen, S. L., van't Veer, L., Garber, G., et al. (2004). Bilateral prophylactic mastectomy reduces breast cancer risk in BRCA1 and BRCA2 mutation carriers. The PROSE Study Group. *Journal of Clinical Oncology, 22*(6), 1055–1062.

Rees, C. E., & Bath, P. A. (2000). Exploring the information flow: Partners of women with breast cancer, patients, and healthcare professionals. *Oncology Nursing Forum, 8*, 1267–1275.

Reichelt, J. G., Heimdal, K., Moller, P., & Dahl, A. A. (2004). BRCA1 testing with definitive results: A prospective study of psychological distress in a large clinic-based sample. *Family Cancer, 3*(1), 21–28.

Ritvo, P., Robinson, G., Irvine, J., Brown, L., Matthew, A., Murphy, K. J., et al. (2000). Psychological adjustment to familial genetic risk assessment: Differences in two longitudinal samples. *Patient Education and Counseling, 40*(2), 163–172.

Roberts, J. S. (2000). Anticipating response to predictive genetic testing for Alzheimer's disease: A survey of first-degree relatives. *Gerontologist, 40*(1), 43–52.

Rolland, J. S. (1994) *Families, illness, and disability: An integrative treatment model.* New York: Basic Books.

Royak-Schaler, R., Klabunde, D. N., Green, W. F., Lannin, D. R., DeVellis, B., Wilson, K. R., et al. (2002). Communicating breast cancer risk: Patient perceptions of provider discussions. *Medscape Women's Health, 7*(2), 2.

Scheuer, L., Kauff, N., Robson, M., Kelly, B., Barakat, R., Satagopan, J., et al. (2002). Outcome of preventive surgery and screening for breast and ovarian cancer in *BRCA* mutation carriers. *Journal of Clinical Oncology, 20,* 1260–1268.

Schwartz, M. D., Benkendorf, J., Lerman, C., Isaacs, C., Ryan-Robertson, A., & Johnson, L. (2001). Impact of educational print materials on knowledge, attitudes, and interest in BRCA1/BRCA2: Testing among Ashkenazi Jewish women. *Cancer, 92,* 932–940.

Schwartz, M. D., Hughes, C., Roth, J., Main, D., Peshkin, B. N., Isaacs, C., et al. (2000). Spiritual faith and genetic testing decisions among high-risk breast cancer probands. *Cancer Epidemiology, Biomarkers and Prevention, 9,* 381–385.

Schwartz, M. D., Kaufman, E., Peshkin, B. N., Isaacs, C., Hughes, C., DeMarco, T., et al. (2003). Bilateral prophylactic oophorectomy and ovarian cancer screening following *BRCA1/BRCA2* mutation testing. *Journal of Clinical Oncology, 21,* 4034–4041.

Schwartz, M. D., Lerman, C., Brogan, B., Peshkin, B. N., Halbert, C. H., DeMarco, T., et al. (2004). Impact of *BRCA1/BRCA2* counseling and testing on newly diagnosed breast cancer patients. *Journal of Clinical Oncology, 22,* 1823–1829.

Schwartz, M. D., Lerman, C., Miller, S. M., Daly, M., & Masny, A. (1995). Coping disposition, perceived risk, and psychological distress among women at increased risk for ovarian cancer. *Health Psychology, 14*(3), 232–235.

Schwartz, M. D., Peshkin, B. N., Hughes, C., Main, D., Isaacs, C., & Lerman, C. (2002). Impact of *BRCA1/BRCA2* mutation testing on psychologic distress in a clinic-based sample. *Journal of Clinical Oncology, 20*(2), 514–520.

Schwartz, M. D., Peshkin, B. N., Tercyak, K. P., Taylor, K. L., & Valdimarsdottir, H. (2005). Decision making and decision support for hereditary breast-ovarian cancer susceptibility. *Health Psychology, 24*(4), S78-S84.

Schwartz, M. D., Tercyak, K. P., Peshkin, B. N., & Valdimarsdottir, H. (2005). Can a computer-based system be used to educate women on genetic testing for breast cancer susceptibility? *Nature Clinical Practice Oncology, 2*(1), 24–25.

Shoda, Y., Mischel, W., Miller, S., Diefenbach, M., Daly, M., & Engstrom, P. (1998). Psychological interventions and genetic testing: Facilitating informed decisions about BRCA1/2 cancer susceptibility. *Journal of Clinical Psychology in Medical Settings, 5,* 3–17.

Smith, B. L., Gadd, M. A., Lawler, C., MacDonald, D. J., Grudberg, S. C., Chi, F. S., et al. (1996). Perception of breast cancer risk among women in breast center and primary care settings: Correlation with age and family history of breast cancer. *Surgery, 120*(2), 297–303.

Smith, K. R., West, J. A., Croyle, R. T., & Botkin, J. R. (1999). Familial context of genetic testing for cancer susceptibility: Moderating effect of siblings' test results on psychological distress one to two weeks after BRCA1 mutation testing. *Cancer Epidemiology Biomarkers Preview, 8,* 385–392.

Smith, K. R., Zick, C. D., Mayer, R. N., & Botkin, J. R. (2002). Voluntary disclosure of BRCA1 mutation test results. *Genetic Testing, 6*(2), 89–92.

Stacey, D., DeGrasse, C., & Johnston, L. (2002). Addressing the support needs of women at high risk for breast cancer: Evidence-based care by advanced practice nurses. *Oncology Nursing Forum, 29*(6), E77–E84.

Stefanek, M., Enger, C., Benkendort, J., Flamm Honig, S., & Lerman, C. (1999). Bilateral prophylactic mastectomy: A vignette study. *Preventive Medicine, 29,* 216–221.

Stoutjesdijk, M. J., Boetes, C., Jager, G. J., Beex, L., Bult, P., Hendriks, J., et al. (2001). Magnetic resonance imaging and mammography in women with a hereditary risk of breast cancer. *Journal of the National Cancer Institute, 93,* 1095–1102.

Streuwing, J. P., Lerman, C., Kase, R. G., Giambarresi, T. R., & Tucker, M. A. (1995). Anticipated uptake and impact of genetic testing in hereditary breast and ovarian cancer families. *Cancer Epidemiology, Biomarkers, and Prevention, 4*(2), 169–173.

Tercyak, K. P., Lerman, C., Peshkin, B. N., Hughes, C., Main, D., & Isaacs, C. (2001). Effects of coping style and BRCA1 and BRCA2 test results on anxiety among women participating in genetic counseling and testing for breast and ovarian cancer risk. *Health Psychology, 20,* 217–222.

Tessaro, I., Borstelmann, N., Regan, K., Rimer, B. K., & Winer, E. (1997). Genetic testing for susceptibility to breast cancer: Findings from women's focus groups. *Journal of Women's Health, 6*(3), 317–327.

Thompson, H. S., Valdimarsdottir, H. B., Duteau-Buck, C., Guevarra, J., Bovbjerg, D. H., Richmond-Avellaneda, C., et al. (2002). Psychosocial predictors of BRCA counseling and testing decisions among urban African-American women. *Cancer Epidemiology, Biomarkers and Prevention, 11,* 1579–1585.

Trecate, G., Verhnaghi, D., Bergonzi, S., De Simone, T., Fengoni, E., Costa, C., et al. (2003). Breast MRI screening in patients with increased familial and/or genetic risk for breast cancer: A preliminary experience. *Tumori, 89,* 125–131.

Van Dijk, S., Otten, W., Zoeteweij, M. W., Timmermans, D. R., van Asperen, C. J., Breuning, M. H., et al. (2003). Genetic counseling and the intention to undergo prophylactic mastectomy: Effects of breast cancer risk assessment. *British Journal of Cancer, 88,* 1675–1681.

van Oostrom I., Meijers-Heijboer, H., Lodder, L. N., Duivenvoorden, H. J., van Gool, A. R., Seynaeve, C., et al. (2003). Long-term psychological impact of carrying a BRCA1/2 mutation and prophylactic surgery: A 5-year follow-up study. *Journal of Clinical Oncology, 21*(2), 3867–3874.

van Roosmalen, M. S., Stalmeier, P. F., Verhoef, L. C., Hoekstra-Weebers, J. E., Oosterwijk, J. C., Hoogerbrugge, N., et al. (2004a). Impact of BRCA1/2 testing and disclosure of a positive test result on women affected and unaffected with breast or ovarian cancer. *American Journal of Medical Genetics, 124A*(4), 346–355.

van Roosmalen, M. S., Stalmeier, P. F., Verhoef, L. C., Hoekstra-Weebers, J. E., Oosterwijk, J. C., Hoogerbrugge, N., et al. (2004b). Randomised trial of a decision aid and its timing for women being tested for a BRCA1/2 mutation. *British Journal of Cancer, 90*(2), 333–342.

Venkitaraman, A. R. (2002). Cancer susceptibility and the functions of BRCA1 and BRCA2. *Cell, 108*(2), 171–182.

Veronesi, A., Pizzichetta, M. A., Ferlante, M. A., Zottar, M., Magri, M. D., Crivellari, D., et al. (1998). Tamoxifen as adjuvant after surgery for breast cancer and tamoxifen or placebo as chemoprevention in healthy women: Different compliance with treatment. *Tumori, 84*(3), 372–375.

Wagner, T. M., Moslinger, R., Langbauer, G., Ahner, R., Fleischmann, E., Auterith, A., et al. (2000). Attitude towards prophylactic surgery and effects of genetic counseling in families with BRCA mutations. Austrian Hereditary Breast and Ovarian Cancer Group. *British Journal of Cancer, 82*, 1249–1253.

Wagner Costalas, J., Itzen, M., Malick, J., Babb, J. S., Bove, B., Godwin, A. K., et al. (2003). Communication of BRCA1 and BRCA2 results to at-risk relatives: A cancer risk assessment program's experience. *American Journal of Medical Genetics, 119C*, 11–18.

Wang, C., Gonzalez, R., & Merajver, S. D. (2004). Assessment of genetic testing and related counseling services: Current research and future directions. *Social Science and Medicine, 58*, 1427–1442.

Wardle, J. (1995). The assessment of obesity: Theoretical background and practical advice. *Behavior Research and Therapy, 33*(1), 107–117.

Welcsh, P. L., & King, M. C. (2001). BRCA1 and BRCA2 and the genetics of breast and ovarian cancer. *Human Molecular Genetics, 10*(7), 705–713.

Woloshin, S., Schwartz, L. M., Black, W. C., & Welch, H. G. (1999). Women's perceptions of breast cancer risk: How you ask matters. *Medical Decision Making, 19*(3), 221–229.

Wonderlick, A. L., & Fine, B. A. (1997). Knowledge of breast cancer genetics among patients and first-degree relatives of affected individuals. *Journal of Genetic Counseling, 6*(2), 111–130.

Wood, M. E., Mullineaux, L., Rahm, A. K., Fairclough, D., & Wenzel, L. (2000). Impact of BRCA1 testing on women with cancer: A pilot study. *Genetic Testing, 4*(3), 265–272.

Wooster, R., Neuhausen, S. L., Mangion, J., Quirk, Y., Ford, D., Collins, N., et al. (1994). Localization of a breast cancer susceptibility gene, BRCA2, to chromosome 13q12–13. *Science, 265*, 2088–2090.

Wylie, J. E., Smith, K. R., & Botkin, J. R. (2003). Effects of spouses on distress experienced by BRCA1 mutation carriers over time. *American Journal of Medical Genetics, 119C*(1), 35–44.

Chapter 11

Genetic and Family-Related Issues Within a Complex Disease Model

Colorectal Cancer

Neal J. Meropol, Joanne S. Buzaglo,
Suzanne M. Miller, Hetal R. Sheth, Beth J. Stearman,
and Laura Stanton

COLORECTAL CANCER (CRC) IS THE SECOND LEADING CAUSE OF CANCER death in the United States, occurring approximately equally in men and women. An estimated 56,730 mortalities occurred in 2004, accounting for about 10% of all cancer deaths. Most colon cancers are diagnosed between the ages of 60 and 75, and almost 25% of patients have distant metastases at the time of diagnosis. Another 40% have regional disease involving the surrounding lymph nodes, increasing the risk for subsequent development of metastatic disease. CRC can present anywhere in the large intestine including the cecum, ascending colon, transverse colon, descending colon, sigmoid colon, and rectum. The American Cancer Society (2004) estimated that 146,940 new cases would be diagnosed in the United States in 2004, including 106,370 cases of colon cancer and 40,570 cases of rectal cancer (Jemal et al., 2004). While mortality rates have declined over the past 20 years, reflecting increases in screening and use of adjuvant therapy, CRC continues to account for a large number of cancer deaths.

Most (65–85%) colorectal cancers are "sporadic," with no family history. "Familial" colorectal cancers account for 10–20% of cases, and occur in individuals who have one or more relatives with colorectal cancer, but who do not fit a clear high-risk pattern. Sporadic and familial CRC usually arises in late adulthood and is essentially a preventable cancer if screening procedures such as fecal occult blood testing and colonoscopy are employed appropriately. These cancers are likely caused by a combination of environmental, behavioral, and low-penetrant genetic factors. In contrast, approximately 5% of CRC are "hereditary," representing syndromes in which genetic susceptibility is the primary risk factor. These syndromes are caused by mutated cancer susceptibility genes being passed on from parent to child. This passage of altered genes is what constitutes high-risk families, that is, those families in which individuals are at an increased risk for CRC development at an early age.

The two most important heritable syndromes of CRC are: hereditary nonpolyposis colorectal cancer (HNPCC) and familial adenomatous polyposis (FAP). Since these syndromes are caused by germ line mutations, such that an abnormal gene is present in every cell of the individual's body, individuals with a family history of CRC can be tested for either of these syndromes by a blood test, even in the absence of the disease. If an individual is found to be carrying a germ line mutation for either HNPCC or FAP, the person is termed a *carrier*. Carriers may or may not be affected or symptomatic. Nevertheless, even if they are not, they will be at high risk for CRC due to an inherited predisposition. If a germ line mutation is found in a parent, that mutation has a 50% chance of being passed on to his or her children. Each of the first-degree relatives (FDRs) of carriers has a 50% chance of having the same mutation found in his or her family member. For the most part, the genetic change is inherited from parent to child. However, sometimes spontaneous or new mutations occur for the first time in the individual. FAP is one of the diseases that are characterized by a relatively high frequency (~25–30%) of spontaneous germ line mutations. Once an individual has the mutation, he or she can pass it on to his or her children and to subsequent generations. In such cases, the affected individual can pass the risk of cancer to his or her children, even though those children's grandparents were not at increased risk for the disease.

HEREDITARY SYNDROMES

CRC may be the most common form of hereditary cancer and is therefore a frequent reason for asymptomatic individuals to request genetic evaluation (Kinney, DeVellis, Skrzynia, & Millikan, 2001). As noted above, the two most common forms of inherited CRC are HNPCC and FAP. Approximately 5% of all CRC cases occur in patients with HNPCC, and approximately 1% occur in patients with FAP (American

Medical Association, 2001; Salovaara et al., 2000). In each of these syndromes, multiple primary tumors and early-age onset of CRC are characteristic features. Both are inherited in an autosomal dominant pattern. Therefore, families with these syndromes may have many family members with cancer across several generations. Germ line mutations can be present in unaffected individuals as well. This is due to incomplete penetrance of cancer among carriers. Nevertheless, such carriers can pass the syndrome to their offspring. Many individuals seek genetic evaluation to find an explanation for the CRC in their families in order to determine their risk for CRC.

Hereditary Nonpolyposis Colorectal Cancer

HNPCC is an inherited syndrome characterized by CRC and extra-colonic cancers (usually of the endometrium, biliary tree, stomach, ovaries, and renal pelvis). HNPCC-related CRCs are often multiple and are found in the right side of the colon at an early age. Muir-Torre syndrome is a variant of HNPCC that exhibits sebaceous gland tumors such as sebaceous adenomas or keratocanthomas. Germ line mutations of genes responsible for DNA mismatch repair cause HNPCC. Two of these genes (*MLH1* and *MSH2*) account for the majority (approximately 90%) of HNPCC cases, and genetic testing for mutation of these genes is commercially available. In situations where HNPCC is suspected, the first step in the genetic evaluation is frequently a test for microsatellite instability (MSI), which can be conducted on a resected tumor sample. Microsatellites are genomic regions where short DNA sequences are repeated (Lynch & de la Chapelle, 2003). In patients with HNPCC, these sequences are not replicated properly, usually because of abnormal MLH1 or MSH2 proteins. This finding in the tumors of patients with HNPCC is called MSI. MSI is found in more than 90% of HNPCC-related CRC, as compared to only 15% of sporadic CRCs (American Medical Association, 2001). Thus, MSI analysis can function as a screening test, which in combination with family history and other criteria can indicate further referral for genetic testing (germ line mutation analysis). Whereas MSI is performed on a colon tumor, mutation analysis (or genetic testing) is performed on a blood sample. Since MSI is present in 15% of sporadic cases of CRC, however, the use of this test as a screen for hereditary CRC may create false concern. Sometimes an additional screening test may be done in conjunction with or instead of MSI. This test, known as immunohistochemistry (IHC) and also done on tumor tissue, screens for the presence or absence of proteins commonly implicated in HNPCC (e.g., MLH1 and MSH2). If one of these proteins is absent by IHC staining, it can direct genetic testing to that specific gene.

In families where there are at least three cases of colorectal cancer among first-degree relatives across two generations, with at least one case occurring at a young age (less than 50 years of age), the risk of HNPCC is high enough to forgo screening with MSI or IHC testing, and proceed directly to genetic testing (germ line mutation anaysis). In any case, if genetic testing is pursued and a germ line mutation is found, the individual's risk of CRC increases to more than 70% before the age of 70 (as compared to the general population risk of less than 5%); further, these findings confer an additional increased risk of other HNPCC-associated cancers. For example, mutations in these genes are associated with a 40% to 60% risk of endometrial cancer before age 70, and with a 50% risk of a second cancer within 15 years of initial diagnosis.

The diagnosis of HNPCC is often characterized by confusion and uncertainty.

Cathy did not feel at particular risk for CRC, given that many of her family members who had died of cancer had other types of cancer. In fact, she felt more concerned about endometrial and ovarian cancer, since she resembled her grandmother, and she had been told that her grandmother had died of cancer in her "female" organs. As a result, she was an aggressive consumer of ovarian cancer information, but not equivalently aware of CRC. Upon genetic consultation, she was made aware that her family history was most suggestive of HNPCC. She also learned that even though she took after her grandmother, this did not necessarily mean that she was destined to develop the same cancer found in her grandmother. Cathy was dismayed to learn that her genetic test results could be uninformative if no genetic alteration is detected. Specifically, if a mutation is not identified in the family that meets clinical criteria for HNPCC, the existence of a germ line mutation in a gene for which testing is not available cannot be ruled out.

In clinical practice, HNPCC testing often does not generate clear-cut decisions, as testing is not always conclusive. Without an identified mutation in the family, genetic testing results may or may not be informative. HNPCC genetic testing is most informative if an affected family member is tested first. Once the familial mutation is known, genotyping of at-risk relatives for the specific mutation is highly accurate, technically easy, and economical, resulting in vitually 100% sensitivity and 100% specificity. If a given family member is found to be positive for the familial mutation, he or she can undergo more vigilant screening to reduce mortality from the disease.

The benefit of genetic testing for HNPCC is that test results can facilitate the identification of individuals who are candidates for more aggressive screening. For example, one set of guidelines recommends that people with an HNPCC mutation begin annual CRC screening with colonoscopy between the ages of 20 and 25, and consider beginning endometrial screening between the ages of 30 and 35 (American Medical Association, 2001). Genetic testing also provides the opportunity to explore surgical interventions, such as prophylactic colectomy, with individuals identified as mutation carriers who do not have cancer. In HNPCC, surgical interventions (prophylactic colectomy) may be considered for mutation carriers who have had adenomas at an early age or for those who are unwilling or unable to undergo periodic surveillance. In women identified as mutation carriers for HNPCC, prophylactic total abdominal hysterectomy-bilateral salpingo-oophorectomy may be considered because of the associated heightened risk for ovarian and endometrial cancer. It should be noted that whereas the utility of CRC screening with colonoscopy is proven for mutation carriers, the benefit of screening for uterine and other cancers is uncertain. In an individual with newly diagnosed cancer in the context of HNPCC, the more extensive surgical approach (total vs. partial colectomy) will often be selected given the high risk of subsequent metachronous primary CRC.

Familial Adenomatous Polyposis

FAP is characterized by the early development of hundreds to thousands of precancerous colonic (and occasionally extracolonic) polyps, with almost certain progression to colon cancer if prophylactic colectomy is not performed. By 15 years of age, at least 50% of FAP patients develop adenomas, and 95% will develop adenomas by age 35. FAP is caused by a germ line mutation in the *APC* tumor suppressor gene. As noted above, there is a de novo abnormality in 25–30% of affected individuals, meaning that many patients with FAP have no family history of the disease. If prophylactic removal of the colon and rectum is not performed, 100% of patients with FAP will develop colorectal cancer, with the average age at diagnosis ranging from 34–43 years. Variations of FAP include attenuated FAP (characterized by fewer polyps) and Gardner's syndrome (characterized by polyps and colorectal cancers that develop at a young age as well as benign tumors of the skin, connective tissues, and bones). Studies have demonstrated that these related syndromes arise from mutations in the *APC* gene. Another syndrome (known as Turcot's syndrome) involves CRC and medulloblastomas. This syndrome is sometimes (approximately 65% of cases) associated with mutations in the *APC* gene. Moreover, a recently defined autosomal recessive syndrome related to *MYH* gene mutation may also account for some cases of attenuated FAP (Sampson et al., 2003).

Genetic testing is now available for persons at high risk for FAP and attenuated FAP. Commercially available genotyping for FAP in at-risk individuals has a reported sensitivity of approximately 90%, identifying an *APC* gene mutation or rearrangement in approximately 90% of clinically diagnosed FAP individuals. When used appropriately, the *APC* gene test can confirm the clinical diagnosis of FAP at the molecular level, determine the necessity of aggressive screening and surveillance for at-risk relatives, and aid in surgical management and family planning decisions (Cromwell et al., 1998). In general, screening of individuals at risk for FAP begins with sigmoidoscopy by age 10–12. Clinically, the identification of FAP by either genetic testing or clinical presentation is a strong indication for prophylactic surgery.

An individual or family receiving a FAP diagnosis is confronted with devastating news. As an adolescent-onset disease, FAP presents challenging treatment decisions, in particular the possibility of major surgery, at a time when the individual's psychosocial focus is usually short-term and characterized by a sense of invulnerability. Most FAP diagnoses result from screening family members of known FAP cases, the development of cancer, or gastrointestinal bleeding. In most FAP families, many relatives have already died of the disease, such that at the time of a new diagnosis there is typically an existing focus on the disease burden. In the remaining families, an individual is undergoing treatment as the genetic testing is underway.

Dennis had been aware that early CRC ran in his father's family, and so presented for colonoscopy at age 28 (as soon as insurance coverage permitted), in hopes of establishing a baseline normal colonoscopy. The diagnostic procedure instead revealed multiple adenomatous polyps, and immediate prophylactic surgery was advised. Genetic testing confirmed an APC mutation. As Dennis recovered from colectomy, his extended family underwent genetic testing. While on the surface the family was grateful, it was clear that family members were actually wrestling with intense feelings. Dennis's mother, who was widowed by his father's CRC, was dealing with both her grief for a son with drastic surgery and potentially reduced life expectancy, and reactivated memories of his father's death. As mutation-positive and mutation-negative relatives continued to be identified, she did not feel that her present and past problems were being honored properly by family members focused on their own futures in the form of FAP genetic testing. One sister became a clearinghouse for FAP information, and the tension between another sibling who wanted her children tested prior to adolescence and the family members who felt she was acting in error was nearly unbearable.

This case illustrates how a diagnosis such as FAP, and the accompanying surgery, can dramatically threaten family adjustment. Colectomy is a major surgery that can, at worst, leave the patient with an exterior ostomy appliance to catch fecal waste. Such drastic surgical intervention and outcomes can negatively impact crucial identity formation that occurs during late adolescence, typically the time at which the prophylactic surgery is recommended. If surgery is delayed until later, the psychosocial challenges for the individual then center on marriage and family planning. Clearly, a diagnosis of FAP, or either positive or (uncertain) results from FAP genetic testing, will affect both marriage and family planning by casting doubt upon the affected individual's future.

For families that already have children, a FAP diagnosis signifies a poignant burden. In the case of a new mutation in the child, the unaffected parents may feel confused, overwhelmed, and angry about sudden changes in the dynamics and progression of family life. Families can become destabilized by the struggle to comprehend the risk to nonsymptomatic children, and by the difficulty of resolving concerns associated with genetic testing of children and any accompanying surgical recommendation.

Relative to adult-onset hereditary cancers, genetic testing is not recommended for minors because of the concern that a full understanding of medical and psychosocial ramifications is not developed until adulthood. However, because FAP is an early-onset disease, genetic testing is presently offered to children with affected parents. The testing is offered not because of possible treatment interventions at an early age but because of the burden of surveillance. Cases of CRC development prior to age 20 are rare, so current recommendations do not include prophylactic colon surgery for young children. However, in the absence of genetic information, the children of FAP parents would have to undergo frequent screening sigmoidoscopies. Negative results of FAP testing in children would eliminate the cost and discomfort of these procedures. Studies conducted before the clinical availability of FAP testing showed that the majority of parents favored the procedure in early childhood (Friedl, Caspari, Piechaczek, & Propping, 1991), or even at birth (Whitelaw, Northover, & Hodgson, 1996). Some studies have shown that children, as a group, do not exhibit clinically significant distress over the first year after genetic testing (Michie, Bobrow, & Marteau, 2001). Further research is needed to identify the optimal timing of disclosure and the appropriate framing of cancer genetic risk information to children, particularly given the potentially negative perception of children who carry a FAP mutation by their peers (Petersen & Boyd, 1995).

GENETIC TESTING FOR HEREDITARY
SYNDROMES

As reviewed elsewhere in this volume, genetic testing necessitates appropriate genetic counseling and informed consent. A careful and thorough family history must be taken, including a three-generation pedigree of all relatives who have developed cancer or polyps, the location of the disease, and the age at diagnosis for each individual. A pedigree is similar to a genogram, but it focuses on the pattern of a genetic susceptibility in a family. The pedigree is a useful tool in risk assessment to identify the hereditary cancer syndrome, determine the appropriate genetic test, and determine who is the best candidate to pursue genetic testing.

Pedigree analysis and genetic testing can be facilitated by a genetic counselor. Genetic counselors have training in medical and cancer genetics as well as psychosocial issues. Since these cancer syndromes have implications for the individual and family, testing can cause a great deal of anxiety and distress, especially if the individual has not been adequately counseled about the implications of genetic testing. It is vital that the patient be carefully informed of all available options and be allowed to develop a unique point of view in the light of the disease threat. During a genetic counseling session, the counselor can clearly explain the risk, benefits, limitations, and potential results of genetic testing. One limitation of genetic testing is that the results may not be clear-cut, especially if a mutation has not been identified in the family. If no mutation is detected after genetic analysis, there may be many reasons for that "indeterminate" or uninformative negative result. Accordingly, it is prudent to reserve use of the term *negative* for cases in which there is a known familial mutation for which the individual tested negative. Some individuals do not pursue genetic testing because they feel that its limitations outweigh its benefits. Others feel that the potential benefit of giving family members the opportunity to be proactive about their health in the light of information provided by genetic testing offsets its limitations.

Another potential implication of genetic testing is that individuals receiving negative test results may not fully appreciate the risk of developing sporadic CRC and may feel a false sense of security. Additional concerns include the identification of a variant of unknown significance in which the genetic change found has not been fully understood in terms of whether it confers cancer risk, a circumstance that can cause distress to the client. Finally, in rare cases, nonpaternity may be deduced from the results of testing. For all these reasons, genetic testing should be done in the context of genetic counseling, and the individual should assume full responsibility for the final decision as to whether to proceed with genetic testing.

Risk identification through genetic testing can open the door for the beneficial use of chemopreventive agents in CRC syndrome carriers (Hawk, Lubit, & Limberg, 1999). For example, evidence suggests a reduction in the number of adenomas in response to selective cyclooxygenase-2 (COX-2) inhibitors in individuals with FAP awaiting surgery. The same strategy has been suggested for HNPCC and is currently undergoing clinical trial. Calcium and folate are also being studied as potential chemopreventive agents against CRC. Availability of chemopreventive options would be seen as advantages of genetic testing.

In Cathy's case, she had always felt that she would undergo prophylactic removal of her uterus and ovaries to prevent cancer in these organs, and was quite prepared for that option. However, the possibility of colectomy was new and frightening to her, and it took her some time to realize that surgery did not guarantee 100% freedom from cancer. In patients with a mutation known to cause FAP or in patients with clear polyposis, surgery is generally recommended as soon as the patient's level of maturity will permit, but as Cathy's case illustrates, individuals can be ready for one type of preventive surgery and not be ready for another type. It also illustrates that risk perception and subsequent medical management are strongly influenced by availability. Availability is the term used to describe how Cathy's family experience with cancer strongly colors her risk perception for certain types of cancer and, ultimately, her comfort with certain risk reduction strategies.

FAMILY ISSUES IN COLORECTAL CANCER

Research on interpersonal and familial effects of varying levels of disease risk and status is in its infancy, but some findings exist within the CRC domain. First, genetic testing intentions and uptake often are correlated with concern for children and other family members in CRC, as in other cancer contexts (Esplen et al., 2001; Hadley et al., 2003; Lerman et al., 1999; Lerman, Marshall, Audrain, & Gomez-Caminero, 1996; Lynch et al., 1997). Second, there are indications that greater family support and greater need for social support tend to be associated with increased interest in testing (Audrain-McGovern, Hughes, & Patterson, 2003; Glanz, Grove, Lerman, Gotay, & Le Marchand, 1999; Lerman et al., 1996; Petersen et al., 1999). How these factors connect with other individual characteristics on either a state or trait level is not well delineated at the present time. Decisions on how to communicate genetic testing results to family members may cause additional stress on individuals who must cope with genetic testing feedback (Daly et al., 2001). A recent study cited both family functioning and individual characterstics influence a client's satisfaction with hereditary breast and ovarian cancer genetic testing and counseling (Tercyak, DeMarco, Mars, & Peshkin, 2004).

Future CRC-specific research must incorporate family factors into research more directly to aid in the development of more effective screening and interventions. It will be important to distinguish family factors by mutation status. It is likely, for example, that individuals testing positive will be very concerned about the risk to their children, but that individuals who test negative in the context of a high-risk family may feel guilty that they will not bear the same disease burden as some of their siblings. While screening for CRC is recommended to begin at age 50 for people of average risk, for those at a heightened risk of developing CRC because of a family history, adopting appropriate screening behavior becomes even more essential. Genetic counselors and physicians must be aware of the many complex factors that contribute to intentions to undergo and adhere to CRC screening regimens. At-risk individuals, usually FDRs of CRC patients, confront both psychological and nonpsychological concerns in grappling with the decision to seek genetic testing or screening (Manne et al., 2002). Some of these concerns include physician recommendations, family input, perceived costs and benefits of screening, and closeness to the affected family member.

Taking these in sum provides strong indication for the need to consider the entire familial context when advising genetic testing to a patient or patient's relative. Often a patient relies on an extensive network of kinship ties, ranging from blood relatives to close friends, to make decisions about treatment or testing (Koehly et al., 2003). In this respect, the individual is part of a greater system (Allmond, Buckman, & Gofman, 1979). Therefore, an individual's relationship with others in the system weaves a fine fabric of family functioning. Each person in the system may have a defined role (e.g., ambassador or first utilizer). Depending on an individual's defined role within the system, his or her experience with genetic testing may serve as a model for the rest of the family (DudokdeWit et al., 1997). The various dynamics that arise from these relationships can impact a person's willingness to engage in screening and genetic testing and subsequently to divulge the results of the testing (Bowen, Ludman, Press, Vu, & Burke, 2003; Wilson et al., 2004).

To properly implement efforts to increase screening behaviors, all outside mediating factors must be considered. Multiple factors come together to form associational webs whereby it is not just physician input that influences the decision to pursue genetic testing, but physician input mediated by perceived benefit (Manne et al., 2003). Persons who perceive a strong association between health benefit and screening are more likely to engage in those protective behaviors. This cognitive linkage, along with the degree of closeness with affected family members, may determine intentions to undergo CRC-related preventive procedures. While closeness with an affected sibling may well contribute to increased desire for genetic testing (Manne et al., 2002), unaffected siblings are not likely to seek any screening unless they perceive health benefits as a result of that behavior (Manne et al., 2003). Other potential mediating cognitive-affective influences include perceived susceptibility to disease, potential severity of the disease upon diagnosis, perceived risk of testing and screening, and overall cancer-related distress. The weight each of these dimensions will carry will vary from person to person, and additional research is needed to further delineate the causal interactions.

TWO THEORETICAL APPROACHES: DISEASE TYPOLOGY AND COGNITIVE-AFFECTIVE-SOCIAL PROCESSES IN CRC GENETIC RISK

Given the importance of screening and early detection of the hereditary syndromes of CRC, it is important to understand any pertinent disease characteristics as well as individual or familial cognitive-affective processes that underlie (or undermine) effective adherence to screening recommendations. There are two specific theoretical frameworks that help to conceptualize research on the various barriers to genetic colorectal cancer screening, prevention, and control: the disease typology model (see Chapter 2), and the cognitive-social approach (see Chapter 3).

The disease typology model emphasizes disease characteristics such as time of onset, typical course, degree of impairment, and whether or not treatment is available. This model asserts that different disease characteristics pose unique threats even though the diseases may be similar. For example, both rheumatoid arthritis (RA) and FAP are genetically transmitted diseases with early adulthood onset. However, RA is relatively manageable, with relatively good treatment options, and no reduction in longevity. Moreover, the penetrance of RA is not complete; only some family members get it, and the severity of each individual's disease varies. FAP, however, is characterized by poor treatment options, dramatically compromised longevity if left untreated, and 100% penetrance; if you have the genetic mutation, you will get the disease.

Clearly, then, RA and FAP represent two distinct disease threats. HN-PCC is intermediate in its threat; the disease is not 100% penetrant, even if the specific family mutation is known, and unlike FAP, prophylactic surgery is not an established recommendation for all patients. In some ways, this lack of clarity relative to HNPCC can be as upsetting as the finality of FAP genetic findings. The decision to undergo a colectomy to manage HNPCC hinges upon not only medical considerations but also an individual's current and lifetime values and goals. Clearly, a full understanding of the challenge of any disease requires an understanding of both disease factors and individual dynamics.

As reviewed earlier in this volume, the cognitive-social model emphasizes individual differences in reactions to a health threat. This model directly applies a general cognitive-affective system theory of individual differences to health-protective behavior (e.g., Miller, 1995; Miller & Diefenbach, 1998; Miller, Shoda, & Hurley, 1996) and draws on recent theorizing to provide a cumulative, unifying conceptual framework for behavioral medicine (e.g., Ajzen & Madden, 1986; Bandura, 1986; Scheier & Carver, 1985). According to this model, the impact of any health-related information will depend, in part, on how it is encoded (interpreted) and the subsequent activation of expectancies, beliefs, affects, goals, and values in response to the health threat. Activated cognitive-affective components interact to determine the specific self-regulatory control strategies, plans, and competencies used by the individual or family to generate plans and coping responses: for example, adhering to necessary screening procedures depending on particular genetic risk status, or communicating with family members. For example, one individual with an HNPCC mutation might decide to undergo prophylactic colectomy in order to avoid the anxiety triggered by frequently required surveillance procedures. Another individual with the same genetic finding might postpone prophylactic surgery because of the value she places on bodily integrity. A third individual might delay all action, understanding the incomplete penetrance in HNPCC and the effectiveness of frequent colonoscopic screening. Such differences highlight the need for a theoretical framework that emphasizes not only specific disease components but also individual and familial differences in knowledge, distress, encoding, and coping style.

Health-Relevant Expectancies and Beliefs

Health-related expectancies include potential outcomes of a CRC diagnosis, obtaining effective medical care, self-influence of health outcomes, and self-efficacy (e.g., one's confidence in one's ability to adhere to recommended CRC screening regimens in light of heightened genetic risk). Across a wide range of disease models, beliefs in the benefits of screening and any follow-up interventions are consistently associated with better screening histories and increased intentions to screen; for example, in a worksite survey of Caucasian men with no history of CRC, the intention to undergo direct, nongenetic CRC screening was associated with past screening participation, belief in the benefits of screening, perceived self-efficacy, and belief in the efficacy of the surgical removal of polyps and subsequent biopsy, as well as higher perceived CRC risk (Myers, Vernon, Tilley, Lu, & Watts, 1998). Increased levels of fatalism (the belief that one does not have control over one's fate; Powe & Weinrich, 1999), and the low expectation of screening utility (Rawl, Menon, Champion, Foster, & Skinner, 2000) have been documented to be associated with poor rates of direct CRC screening adherence and may well pertain to genetic risk evaluation as well.

Knowledge

There is a high degree of interaction between an individual's beliefs and knowledge. Given a conviction that CRC is incurable, for example, provision of any additional knowledge would be unproductive. Conversely, lacking any knowledge about genetic CRC screening availability would also preclude any existing beliefs about the efficacy of early, presymptomatic intervention. In the CRC literature, inaccurate beliefs and misconceptions are often linked with a lack of knowledge (Codori, Petersen, Miglioretti, & Boyd, 2001; Weitzman, Zapka, Estabrook, & Goins, 2001; Wolf et al., 2001). Many individuals lack accurate information about the genetic aspects of colorectal cancer, including risk factors, and hence are unable to make informed decisions about undergoing enhanced screening and genetic testing (Kinney et al., 2000). A number of factors may contribute to this lack of knowledge and awareness. First, advances in genetic understanding of heritable syndromes are relatively recent. Second, little attention has been given to the dissemination of CRC genetic risk factors, such as family history. Finally, the majority of individuals do not understand the genetic syndromes of CRC—their incidence, course, screening, prevention, or treatment options (Beeker, Kraft, Goldman, & Jorgensen, 2001; Morgan, Roufeil, Kaushik, & Bassett, 1998; Schapira et al., 1993). This lack of CRC-related knowledge can hinder the ability to process risk or make informed decisions about health-protective behaviors and ultimately may serve as a barrier to screening and desire for genetic testing (Beeker, Kraft, Southwell, & Jorgensen, 2000; Hart, Barone, & Mayberry, 1997; Smith et al., 2001; Wolf et al., 2001). In the context of colorectal cancer, as well as other cancers, awareness of increased risk does not necessarily translate directly into action (Kinney et al., 2001; Lipkus et al., 1999).

Two additional factors may help explain why people are ill-informed about hereditary CRC. First, in the general population, men and women are largely unaware of the risk factors for even sporadic CRC—a much more common disease than the genetic forms of CRC. Very few know that risk for the disease increases with age, for example, or that CRC can be present without the expression of symptoms (Beeker et al., 2000). If individuals are uninformed about the most common form of CRC, it would be unrealistic to expect sufficient awareness of the more uncommon hereditary forms. Evidence indicates that even doctors' knowledge of hereditary forms of CRC is inadequate. A New York State survey of practicing adult gastroenterologists reported that only 52% of the sample that responded to the questionnaire was aware of genetic tests for FAP, and only 34% were aware of genetic tests for HNPCC (Batra, Valdimarsdottir, McGovern, Itzkowitz, & Brown, 2002). Clearly, there is a need for physician education regarding the availability and importance of CRC genetic screening.

Perceived Risk

Cancer-relevant encodings refer to strategies and constructs with respect to self and situations regarding health risks and vulnerabilities. Examples include perceived vulnerability of having genetic syndromes of CRC and likelihood of intergenerational transmission. Evidence from general population studies indicating that accurate knowledge can influence desires for genetic testing suggests the need for increased dissemination of information about CRC risk factors. Although individuals tend to expect their primary care physicians to provide information about their relative risk and medical options, primary care physicians as well as specialists are not appropriately informed regarding the optimal care for genetically at-risk patients to successfully carry out this task (Batra et al., 2002).

Among individuals with a family history of CRC, some research suggests that perceived risk correlates with increased demand for cancer susceptibility testing (Glanz et al., 1999; Lerman et al., 1996; Petersen et al., 1999). For example, increased perceived risk was a significant predictor of test uptake, along with greater perceived confidence in the ability to cope with unfavorable genetic information, more frequent cancer thoughts, and having had at least one colonoscopy (Codori et al., 1999). Among those who thought about getting CRC more often, the probability of testing increased as perceived risk increased to 50% likelihood of getting CRC. In contrast, among those who never or rarely thought about getting CRC, risk perception was unrelated to testing decision (Codori et al., 1999).

Additional support for the influence of risk perception is provided by a study of both breast cancer and CRC FDRs (Daly et al., 2003). In this 399-subject study, elevated risk perception was frequently reported. Interestingly, in the 84 CRC FDRs as well as in the breast cancer FDRs, elevated risk perception was closely correlated with increased cancer-related distress, which in turn was related to a history of smoking, but not with uptake of preventive breast or colon cancer screening behavior. In a separate study of individuals (both diagnosed and non-diagnosed) presenting for genetic testing at a CRC risk assessment program, increased perception of absolute CRC risk (0–100%), CRC risk compared to others the same age, and increased certainty about developing CRC were all associated with higher scores on measures of state and trait anxiety, cancer-related distress, and depressive symptoms (Meropol et al., 2003).

Risk-Related Affect: Distress

Genetic testing can have a negative impact, particularly when results indicate positive mutational status (Tercyak et al., 2004). In one study of the personal repercussions of disclosure of carrier status of a cancer-predisposing mutation for hereditary breast, ovarian, or nonpolyposis colorectal cancers, some patients spontaneously complained of negative feelings ranging from no longer feeling cured by their treatment (this question was only pertinent for survivors) to unhappiness or worry, either for themselves or for their children, 1 month after result disclosure (Bonadona et al., 2002).

Two studies have examined the emotional outcomes of undergoing genetic testing for CRC. A Finnish study used a prospective follow-up questionnaire focusing on general anxiety, fear of cancer and death, satisfaction with life, and attitudes toward the future in the course of a predictive genetic testing protocol for HNPCC (Aktan-Collan, Haukkala, Mecklin, Uutela, & Kaariainen, 2001). At every measurement, the mutation-positive individuals were more afraid of cancer than those who were mutation-negative; however, in both groups, fear of cancer decreased significantly from baseline to after disclosure. The mutation-positive individuals were more anxious than their counterparts immediately after the test disclosure, but this difference disappeared at the follow-ups. In other variables (e.g., satisfaction with life), differences between the groups defined by mutation status or by changes with time were not detected. These findings suggest fear of cancer diminishes over time and that no long-term harmful emotional impact occurs from genetic testing at 1-year follow-up.

A more recent study examined the impact of HNPCC genetic test results on depression, anxiety, genetic testing-specific distress, cancer worries, quality of life, and perceived risk among cancer-affected and unaffected participants (Gritz et al., 2005). While HNPCC genetic testing does not result in long-term adverse psychological outcomes, mutation carriers with no prior personal cancer history can experience increased distress during the time immediately following disclosure of test results. Further, higher levels of baseline mood disturbance and lower quality of life predicted significantly higher levels of depression, state anxiety, and genetic testing-specific distress, and lower quality of life regardless of mutation status. Individuals are motivated to participate in genetic testing for CRC to relieve their concerns about themselves and their family members (Madlensky, Esplen, & Goel, 2004; Vernon et al., 1999); however, they can sometimes experience potential adverse psychological effects associated with testing (Kinney et al., 2001). Taken together, while genetic testing for CRC may not typically engender long-lasting emotional consequences, specific subsets of individuals undergoing genetic testing, in particular carriers of a genetic mutation and those with higher levels of distress prior to genetic testing, can be at risk for both short- and long-term increased distress with regard to their CRC cancer risk (Gritz et al., 1999, 2005; Vernon et al., 1997).

Goals and Values: Interest in Genetic Testing

As in most disease models, hypothetical interest in genetic counseling and testing for hereditary CRC is notably higher in the general population than in high-risk families. Random-digit dial surveys of adult residents of Utah (Croyle & Lerman, 1993; Smith & Croyle, 1995), and Ontario, Canada (Graham et al., 1998) indicate that over 80% of respondents endorsed at least some interest in genetic testing for hereditary CRC, and 40–47% indicated they would be very interested. Notably, in the Canadian study, interest in testing declined by 20% (from 87% to 67%) when respondents were informed that only 1% of the population is estimated to carry a CRC mutation.

When high-risk families are studied, interest ranges more widely: from 26% to 70%. In one study of FDRs recruited from a tumor registry for hereditary CRC, only 26% reported definite intentions to have testing, less than half indicated they probably intended to be tested, and only 46% indicated an interest in genetic counseling (Glanz et al., 1999). In another, earlier study of FDRs of patients undergoing CRC treatment (Lerman, Marshall, et al., 1996), 51% indicated that they definitely intended to undergo genetic testing. In that study, more than 80% of the pool endorsed each of the following reasons for testing as being important: to find out if more screening tests are needed, to know if children are at risk, to be reassured, and to plan for the future. A majority (60%) identified insurance concerns as important reasons not to seek testing, although current HIPPA laws offer some protection against insurance discrimination for predisposed individuals. A third study of FDRs recruited from a cancer registry found that 70% said they would have testing if it were free (Petersen et al., 1999). Across these studies, perceived risk of CRC and worry about developing cancer were independently associated with increased desire for testing. Other correlates included higher education, greater family support, preference for independent decision making, female gender, and Caucasian ethnicity.

The cause of variation in these findings is unclear at the present time. There is an indication that the barrier is not common to all genetic testing that confers increased CRC risk, but specific to the CRC genetic diseases: one recent report from a CRC risk assessment clinic population directly compared the uptake of HNPCC genetic testing with testing for the APC I1307K mutation, which may be associated with increased CRC risk among Ashkenazi Jews. Specifically, 85% who were offered APC I1307K testing actually underwent testing, but only 14% of those offered HNPCC testing accepted that option (Johnson et al., 2000). Whether this finding is replicable and the possible reasons for the observed discordance are currently unknown, but are likely population-dependent (i.e., ethnicity in this case).

CONCLUSION

Increasing understanding of the genetic influences on CRC risk will surely impact the diagnosis, prognosis, and treatment of the disease. Moreover, this knowledge may lead to more effective cancer control through the use of genetics to quantify individual cancer risk (Olopade & Pichert, 2001) or the design of environmental guidelines and tailored prevention strategies for those especially susceptible to genetically transmitted CRC. The genetic syndromes of CRC can be thought of as a representative model for a disease with multiple genetic pathways and presentations, highlighting psychological issues of disease risk adjustment, genetic testing uptake, and management adherence. Further research is needed to illuminate how best to invite all genetically at-risk individuals to participate in informed disease management. There is limited research on family communication and effects within CRC kinships, which might provide ways to conceptualize interventions to facilitate effective communication, adjustment, and decision making across the family continuum. Educating family members and spouses about strengthening positive emotional support and reducing critical behavior can result in more effective coping and less emotional distress around testing for genetic risk (Manne, Pape, Taylor, & Dougherty, 1999). Within the context of increased knowledge and familial support, strategies for risk management, with or without testing uptake, can be developed that echo the individual and family values and goals.

While the current status of research regarding individual and family genetic testing for CRC risk assessment suggests a framework for integrating research findings into tailored psychosocial interventions to optimize genetic knowledge, testing, and preventive strategies in the CRC domain, there continue to be many unknowns. Efforts should be undertaken to design tailored messages to match behavioral signatures for distinct subtypes of CRC cancer risk. Further, research should be designed to discern at which point in the reaction chain the individual is most receptive to intervention (e.g., pre- or postgenetic testing). Finally, it will be important to follow individuals across the continuum of care to ascertain the long-term impact of CRC risk on adjustment, adherence, and the influence of specific components of psychosocial interventions over time.

Acknowledgments: This chapter was supported in part by the Fox Chase Cancer Center Behavioral Research Core Facility NCI grant P30 CA006927. Further, this chapter was supported, in part, under a grant with the Pennsylvania Department of Health. The Department specifically disclaims responsibility for any analyses, interpretations, or conclusions. We are indebted to Margie Atchison, Caroline Ridgway, and John Scarpato for their technical assistance.

REFERENCES

Ajzen, I., & Madden, T. J. (1986). Prediction of goal-directed behavior: Attitudes, intentions, and perceived behavioral control. *Journal of Experimental Social Psychology, 22*, 453–474.

Aktan-Collan, K., Haukkala, A., Mecklin, J. P., Uutela, A., & Kaariainen, H. (2001). Psychological consequences of predictive genetic testing for hereditary non-polyposis colorectal cancer (HNPCC): A prospective follow-up study. *International Journal of Cancer, 93*, 608–611.

Allmond, B. W., Buckman,W., & Gofman, H. F. (1979). *The family is the patient.* St. Louis, MO: C.V. Mosby.

American Cancer Society. (2004). *Statistics for 2004.* Retrieved February 8, 2004, from Web site: http://www.cancer.org/docroot/STT/stt_0.asp

American Medical Association. (2001). *Identifying and managing risk for heredi-tary nonpolyposis colorectal cancer and endometrial cancer (HNPCC)* [Brochure]. Chicago: Author.

Audrain-McGovern, J., Hughes, C., & Patterson, F. (2003). Effecting behavior change: Awareness of family history. *American Journal of Preventive Medicine, 24,* 183–189.

Bandura, A. (1986). *Social foundations of thought and action: A social cognitive theory.* Englewood Cliffs, NJ: Prentice-Hall.

Batra, S., Valdimarsdottir, H., McGovern, M., Itzkowitz, S., & Brown, K. (2002). Awareness of genetic testing for colorectal cancer predisposition among specialists in gastroenterology. *American Journal of Gastroenterology, 97,* 729–733.

Beeker, C., Kraft, J. M., Goldman, R., & Jorgensen, C. (2001). Strategies for in-creasing colorectal cancer screening among African Americans. *Journal of Psychosocial Oncology, 19,* 113–132.

Beeker, C., Kraft, J. M., Southwell, B. G., & Jorgensen, C. M. (2000). Colorec-tal cancer screening in older men and women: qualitative research find-ings and implications for intervention. *Journal of Community Health, 25,* 263–278.

Bonadona, V., Saltel, P., Desseigne, F., Mignotte, H., Saurin, J. C., Wang, Q., et al. (2002). Cancer patients who experienced diagnostic genetic testing for cancer susceptibility: Reactions and behavior after the disclosure of a positive test result. *Cancer Epidemiology, Biomarkers, and Prevention, 11,* 97–104.

Bowen, D. J., Ludman, E., Press, N., Vu, T., & Burke, W. (2003). Achieving util-ity with family history. *American Journal of Preventive Medicine, 24,* 177–181.

Codori, A. M., Petersen, G. M., Miglioretti, D. L., & Boyd, P. (2001). Health be-liefs and endoscopic screening for colorectal cancer: Potential for cancer prevention. *Preventive Medicine, 33,* 128–136.

Codori, A. M., Petersen, G. M., Miglioretti, D. L., Larkin, E. K., Bushey, M. T., Young, C., et al. (1999). Attitudes toward colon cancer gene testing: Factors predicting test uptake. *Cancer Epidemiology, Biomarkers, and Prevention, 8,* 345–351.

Cromwell, D. M., Moore, R. D., Brensinger, J. D., Petersen, G. M., Bass, E. B., & Giardiello, F. M. (1998). Cost analysis of alternative approaches to colorectal screening in familial adenomatous polyposis. *Gastroenterology, 114,* 893–901.

Croyle, R. T., & Lerman, C. (1993). Interest in genetic testing for colon cancer susceptibility: Cognitive and emotional correlates. *Preventive Medicine, 22,* 284–292.

Daly, M. B., Barsevick, A., Miller, S. M., Buckman, R., Costalas, J., Montgomery, et al. (2001). Communicating genetic test results to the family: A six-step, skills-building strategy. *Family and Community Health, 24,* 13–26.

Daly, M. B., Ross, B. S., Babb, J. S., Balshem, A. M., Malick, J. D., Manne, S., et al. (2003, June). *The association of risk perception with distress and health be-haviors among individuals with a family history of cancer.* Paper presented at the Annual Meeting of the American Society of Clinical Oncology, Chicago, Illinois.

DudokdeWit, A. C., Tibben, A., Frets, P. G., Meijers-Heijboer, E. J., Devilee, P., Klijn, J. G. M., et al. (1997). BRCA1 in the family. *American Journal of Medical Genetics, 71*, 63–71.

Esplen, M. J., Madlensky, L., Butler, K., McKinnon, W., Bapat, B., Wong, J., et al. (2001). Motivations and psychosocial impact of genetic testing for HNPCC. *American Journal of Medical Genetics, 103*, 9–15.

Friedl, W., Caspari, R., Piechaczek, B., & Propping, P. (1991). Reliability of presymptomatic test for adenomatous polyposis-coli. *Lancet, 337*(8750), 1172–1172.

Glanz, K., Grove, J., Lerman, C., Gotay, C., & Le Marchand, L. (1999). Correlates of intentions to obtain genetic counseling and colorectal cancer gene testing among at-risk relatives from three ethnic groups. *Cancer Epidemiology, Biomarkers, and Prevention, 8*, 329–336.

Graham, I. D., Logan, D. M., Hughes-Benzie, R., Evans, W. K., Perras, H., McAuley, L. M., et al. (1998). How interested is the public in genetic testing for colon cancer susceptibility? Report of a cross-sectional population survey. *Cancer Prevention and Control, 2*, 167–172.

Gritz, E. R., Peterson, S. K., Vernon, S. W., Marani, S. K., Baile, W. F., Watts, B. G., et al. (2005). Psychological impact of genetic testing for hereditary nonpolyposis colorectal cancer. *Journal of Clinical Oncology, 23*, 1902–1910.

Gritz, E. R., Vernon, S. W., Peterson, S. K., Baile, W. F., Marani, S. K., Amos, C. I., et al. (1999). Distress in the cancer patient and its association with genetic testing and counseling for hereditary non-polyposis colon cancer. *Cancer Research, Therapy, and Control, 8*, 35–49.

Hadley, D. W., Jenkins, J., Dimond, E., Nakahara, K., Grogan, L., Liewehr, D. J., et al. (2003). Genetic counseling and testing in families with hereditary nonpolyposis colorectal cancer. *Archives of Internal Medicine, 163*, 573–582.

Hart, A. R., Barone, T. L., & Mayberry, J. F. (1997). Increasing compliance with colorectal cancer screening: The development of effective health education. *Health Education Research, 12*, 171–180.

Hawk, E., Lubet, R., & Limburg, P. (1999). Chemoprevention in hereditary colorectal cancer syndromes. *Cancer, 86*(11 Suppl.), 2551–2563.

Jemal, A., Tiwari, R. C., Murray, T. Ghafoor, A., Samuels, A., Ward, E., et al. (2004) Cancer statistics. *CA Cancer Journal for Clinicians, 54*(1), 8–29.

Johnson, K. A., Rosenblum-Vos, L., Petersen, G. M., Brensinger, J. D., Giardiello, F. M., & Griffin, C. A. (2000). Response to genetic counseling and testing for the APC I1307K mutation. *American Journal of Medical Genetics, 91*, 207–211.

Kinney, A. Y., Choi, Y. A., DeVellis, B., Kobetz, E., Millikan, R. C., & Sandler, R. S. (2000). Interest in genetic testing among first-degree relatives of colorectal cancer patients. *American Journal of Preventive Medicine, 18*, 249–252.

Kinney, A. Y., DeVellis, B. M., Skrzynia, C., & Millikan, R. (2001). Genetic testing for colorectal carcinoma susceptibility: Focus group responses of individuals with colorectal carcinoma and first-degree relatives. *Cancer, 91*, 57–65.

Koehly, L. M., Peterson, S. K., Watts, B. G., Kempf, K. K., Vernon, S. W., & Gritz, E. R. (2003). A social network analysis of communication about hereditary nonpolyposis colorectal cancer genetic testing and family functioning. *Cancer Epidemiology, Biomarkers, and Prevention, 12,* 304–313.

Lerman, C., Hughes, C., Trock, B. J., Myers, R. E., Main, D., Bonney, A., et al. (1999). Genetic testing in families with hereditary nonpolyposis colon cancer. *Journal of the American Medical Association, 281,* 1618–1622.

Lerman, C., Marshall, J., Audrain, J., & Gomez-Caminero, A. (1996). Genetic testing for colon cancer susceptibility: Anticipated reactions of patients and challenges to providers. *International Journal of Cancer, 20,* 58–61.

Lipkus, I. M., Crawford, Y., Fenn, K., Biradavolu, M., Binder, R. A., Marcus, A., et al. (1999). Testing different formats for communicating colorectal cancer risk. *Journal of Health Communication, 4,* 311–324.

Lynch, H., & de la Chapelle, A. (2003). Hereditary colorectal cancer. *New England Journal of Medicine, 348*(10), 919–932.

Lynch, H. T., Lemon, S. J., Karr, B., Franklin, B., Lynch, J. F., Watson, P., et al. (1997). Etiology, natural history, management and molecular genetics of hereditary nonpolyposis colorectal cancer (Lynch syndromes): Genetic counseling implications. *Cancer Epidemiology, Biomarkers, and Prevention, 6,* 987–991.

Madlensky, L., Esplen, M. J., & Goel, V. (2004). Reasons given by relatives of colorectal cancer patients for not undergoing screening. *Preventive Medicine, 39,* 643–648.

Manne, S., Markowitz, A., Winawer, S., Guillem, J., Meropol, N. J., Haller, D., et al. (2003). Understanding intention to undergo colonoscopy among intermediate-risk siblings of colorectal cancer patients: A test of a mediational model. *Preventive Medicine, 36,* 71–84.

Manne, S., Markowitz, A., Winawer, S., Meropol, N. J., Haller, D., Rakowski, W., et al. (2002). Correlates of colorectal cancer screening compliance and stage of adoption among siblings of individuals with early onset colorectal cancer. *Health Psychology, 21,* 3–15.

Manne, S. L., Pape, S. J., Taylor, K. L., & Dougherty, J. (1999). Spouse support, coping, and mood among individuals with cancer. *Annals of Behavioral Medicine, 21,* 111–121.

Meropol, N., Ross, B., Babb, J., Balshem, A., Manne, S., Parlanti, A., et al. (2003, March). *Risk perceptions and quality of life among individuals at increased risk of colorectal cancer.* Paper presented at the annual meeting of the American Society of Preventive Oncology, Philadelphia, PA.

Michie, S., Bobrow, M., & Marteau, T. M. (2001). Predictive genetic testing in children and adults: A study of emotional impact. *Journal of Medical Genetics, 38,* 519–526.

Miller, S. M. (1995). Monitoring versus blunting styles of coping with cancer influence the information patients want and need about their disease: Implications for cancer screening and management. *Cancer, 76,* 167–177.

Miller, S. M., & Diefenbach, M. A. (1998). The Cognitive-Social Health Information-Processing (C-SHIP) model: A theoretical framework for research in behavioral oncology. In D. S. Krantz & A. Baum (Eds.), *Technology and methods in behavioral medicine* (pp. 219–244). Mahwah, NJ: Lawrence Erlbaum.

Miller, S. M., Shoda, Y., & Hurley, K. (1996). Applying cognitive-social theory to health-protective behavior: Breast self-examination in cancer screening. *Psychological Bulletin, 119,* 70–94.

Morgan, J., Roufeil, L., Kaushik, S., & Bassett, M. (1998). Influence of coping style and precolonoscopy information on pain and anxiety of colonoscopy. *Gastrointestinal Endoscopy, 48,* 119–127.

Myers, R. E., Vernon, S. W., Tilley, B. C., Lu, M., & Watts, B. G. (1998). Intention to screen for colorectal cancer among white male employees. *Preventive Medicine, 27,* 279–287.

Olopade, O. I., & Pichert, G. (2001). Cancer genetics in oncology practice. *Annals of Oncology, 12,* 895–908.

Petersen, G. M., & Boyd, P. A. (1995). Gene tests and counseling for colorectal cancer risk: Lessons from familial polyposis. *Journal of the National Cancer Institute Monographs, 17,* 67–71.

Petersen, G. M., Larkin, E., Codori, A. M., Wang, C. Y., Booker, S. V., Bacon, J., et al. (1999). Attitudes toward colon cancer gene testing: Survey of relatives of colon cancer patients. *Cancer Epidemiology, Biomarkers, and Prevention, 8,* 337–344.

Powe, B. D., & Weinrich, S. (1999). An intervention to decrease cancer fatalism among rural elders. *Oncology Nursing Forum, 26,* 583–588.

Rawl, S. M., Menon U., Champion, V. L., Foster, J. L., & Skinner, C. S. (2000). Colorectal cancer screening beliefs: Focus groups with first-degree relatives. *Cancer Practice, 8,* 32–37.

Salovaara, R., Loukola, A., Kristo, P., Kaariainen, H., Ahtola, H., Eskelinen, M., et al. (2000). Population-based molecular detection of hereditary nonpolyposis colorectal cancer. *Journal of Clinical Oncology, 18,* 193–200.

Sampson, J. R., Dolwani, S., Jones, S., Eccles, D., Ellis, A., Evans, D. G., et al. (2003). Autosomal recessive colorectal adenomatous polyposis due to inherited mutations of MYH. *Lancet, 362*(9377), 39–41.

Schapira, D. V., Pamies, R. J., Kumar, N. B., Herold, A. H., Van Durme, D. J., Woodward, L. J., et al. (1993). Cancer screening: Knowledge, recommendations, and practices of physicians. *Cancer, 71,* 839–843.

Scheier, M. F., & Carver, C. S. (1985). Optimism, coping, and health: Assessment and implications of generalized outcome expectancies. *Health Psychology, 4,* 219–247.

Smith, K. R., & Croyle, R. T. (1995). Attitudes toward genetic testing for colon cancer risk. *American Journal of Public Health, 85,* 1435–1438.

Smith, R. A., von Eschenbach, A. C., Wender, R., Levin, B., Byers, T., Rothenberger, D., et al. (2001). American Cancer Society guidelines for the early detection of cancer: Update of early detection guidelines for prostate, colorectal, and endometrial cancers; also: Update 2001—testing for early lung cancer detection. *CA: A Cancer Journal for Clinicians, 51,* 38–80.

Tercyak, K., DeMarco, T., Mars, B., & Peshkin, B. (2004). Women's satisfaction with genetic counseling for hereditary breast-ovarian cancer: Psychological aspects. *American Journal of Medical Genetics, 131A,* 36–41.

Vernon, S. W., Gritz, E. R., Peterson, S. K., Amos, C. I., Perz, C. A., Baile, W. F., et al. (1997). Correlates of psychologic distress in colorectal cancer patients undergoing genetic testing for hereditary colon cancer. *Health Psychology,* *16,* 73–86.

Vernon, S. W., Gritz, E. R., Peterson, S. K., Perz, C. A., Marani, S., Amos, C. I., et al. (1999). Intention to learn results of genetic testing for hereditary colon cancer. *Cancer Epidemiology, Biomarkers and Prevention, 8,* 353–360.

Weitzman, E. R., Zapka, J., Estabrook, B., & Goins, K. V. (2001). Risk and reluctance: Understanding impediments to colorectal cancer screening. *Preventive Medicine, 32,* 502–513.

Whitelaw, S., Northover, J. M., & Hodgson, S. V. (1996). Attitudes to predictive DNA testing in familial adenomatous polyposis. *Journal of Medical Genetics, 33,* 540–543.

Wilson, B., Forrest, K., van Teijlingen, E., McKee, L., Haites, N., Matthews, E., et al. (2004). Family communication about genetic risk: The little that is known. *Community Genetics, 7,* 15–24.

Wolf, R. L., Zybert, P., Brouse, C. H., Neugut, A. I., Shea, S., Gibson G., et al. (2001). Knowledge, beliefs, and barriers relevant to colorectal cancer screening in an urban population: A pilot study. *Family and Community Health, 24,* 34–47.

Chapter 12

Lung Cancer Susceptibility
Implications for Smoking and Behavior Change

Kenneth P. Tercyak, Lisa S. Cox, and Peter G. Shields

IT HAS BEEN WELL ESTABLISHED THAT CIGARETTE SMOKING IS THE LEADING preventable cause of disease and death in the United States and a leading indicator of health worldwide. That is because smoking is a significant risk factor for heart disease, stroke, lung and other cancers, and chronic lung diseases. These and other tobacco-related illnesses result in over 430,000 deaths annually, with direct medical costs in excess of $50 billion (U.S. Department of Health and Human Services [USD-HHS], 2000). Unfortunately, no segment of the population is safe from smoking's harms, including children, families living in poverty, and every racial and ethnic group. Thus, preventing and reducing tobacco use is a major public health initiative, and efforts to control tobacco use must reach out across individual, familial, and societal levels.

To successfully control tobacco use in this manner, it is necessary to have as complete an understanding as possible of its etiology so that effective prevention and treatment programs can be implemented. Fortunately, decades of research on the biological, psychological, and social aspects of smoking and other forms of tobacco use have advanced our understanding of this complex problem. Perhaps the most striking recent advances are those that stem from a biobehavioral perspective, which seeks to integrate knowledge across each of the three above-mentioned aspects. This includes work on genetic biomarkers of lung cancer susceptibility as well as genes related to smoking behavior.

Researchers have speculated that some, though not all, of an individual's smoking behavior can be attributed to genetic factors (see Marteau & Lerman, 2001, for review). In addition, a proportion of tobacco smokers who go on to develop lung cancer may also be at increased risk to do so due to common genetic variants (polymorphisms; Amos, Xu, & Spitz, 1999). However, the influence of these different susceptibility pathways on a complex behavioral trait such as smoking, or on a complex biological process such as oncogenesis, is relatively limited and is largely determined by their interaction with environmental influences. In light of the ambiguous clinical interpretation of these and other risk-conferring biomarkers, communicating genetic risk information to individual patients and their families in a manner that is understandable and meaningful, without evoking excessive worry or fear, is a formidable challenge (Marteau, 1999). Thus, the relative safety and efficacy of incorporating biomarker feedback into health behavior change programs is currently being explored in research settings (see McClure, 2002, for review).

On the one hand, basic research into genetic biomarkers offers an unprecedented opportunity to deepen our understanding of why some individuals are more prone to smoke or to develop lung cancer whereas others are not. On the other hand, this research also carries with it important ethical, psychosocial, and behavioral challenges associated with bringing safe and effective lung cancer and smoking gene susceptibility testing into clinical practice. Translational research that seeks to integrate these opportunities will help to prepare us for a time when such testing becomes a basic component in the detection, management, and understanding of tobacco-related illness risks.

In light of our emerging genetic knowledge, this chapter begins by presenting an overview of the problem of smoking in the United States, including ways to define, identify, and measure smoking behavior, and discusses smoking's consequences for individuals and families. Next, we review a conceptual model for understanding the biobehavioral basis of tobacco use, genetic biomarkers of lung cancer susceptibility, other smoking-related biomarkers, and genes associated with smoking behavior. We also review the function of genetic susceptibility testing in cancer prevention and control, the ethical issues associated with such testing, theoretical models that can guide the incorporation of biomarker feedback about lung cancer and smoking susceptibility into clinical practice, and the results of clinical trials designed to test the efficacy of such approaches on altering smoking behavior. Finally, we discuss the future implications of lung cancer and smoking gene susceptibility testing for smoking and behavior change at the individual, familial, and societal level, including ways in which physicians, nurses, and other health professionals can prevent and treat tobacco use among children, adults, and their family members.

EPIDEMIOLOGY OF TOBACCO USE

Smoking Behavior and Nicotine Dependence

Nicotine is a psychoactive substance, the primary pharmacological ingredient in tobacco, and the chemical that causes nicotine dependence (USDHHS, 1988). Nicotine from cigarette smoking is carried in the vapor phase and on tar droplets to the lungs and is then readily absorbed (McDonald & Olson, 1994). After nicotine is absorbed in the lungs, blood nicotine levels increase rapidly. In an adult smoker, nicotine is metabolized quickly and distributed into almost all tissue. Inhaled smoke results in liberal nicotine concentration that is delivered to the brain and provides immediate drug reinforcement and perceived drug effects (Henningfield & Keenan, 1993).

Cigarette smoking produces repeated, brief, highly concentrated doses of nicotine. Frequent exposure to nicotine results in tolerance to its toxic effects (e.g., dizziness and nausea) and an experience of rewarding effects that may include pleasure, arousal, improved task performance, decreased feelings of anxiety and depression, and decreased hunger (Benowitz, 1992). The reinforcing properties of nicotine appear to be related to its simultaneous actions on many types of neurons and its effects on the release of dopamine, norepinephrine, and serotonin (USDHHS, 1988).

In contrast, smoking abstinence produces nicotine withdrawal that may cause considerable distress to the individual (Hughes & Hatsukami, 1986). Withdrawal from nicotine is often characterized by physiological, affective, and behavioral changes including irritability, anxiety, depression, impatience, restlessness, difficulty concentrating, nocturnal awakening, decreased heart rate, and hunger (Hughes, Higgins, & Bickel, 1994). Because withdrawal is due specifically to nicotine deprivation, nicotine replacement can be used during the course of treatment to effectively decrease most of its symptoms (Fiore, Smith, Jorenby, & Baker, 1994; Gross & Stitzer, 1989).

Nicotine dependence can be defined as the compulsive use of nicotine resulting in physiological, cognitive, and behavioral changes (American Psychiatric Association [APA], 1994). The clinical conceptualization of nicotine dependence is outlined in the fourth edition of the *Diagnostic and Statistical Manual of Mental Disorders* (*DSM-IV*; APA, 1994) and emphasizes the role of tolerance development and nicotine withdrawal. Common features of nicotine dependence include: (a) the smoker's desire or unsuccessful effort to reduce the amount of tobacco used; (b) a significant amount of time spent obtaining and using tobacco; (c) adjustment of social, recreational, or occupational activities in order to adapt to tobacco use; and (d) the continued use of tobacco despite the presence of medical or social problems related to tobacco.

Nonsmokers may be exposed to tobacco smoke as well, along with its negative consequences. Secondhand smoke or environmental tobacco smoke contains more than 4,000 chemicals including over 40 known carcinogens and is related to lung cancer, nasal and sinus cancer, cardiovascular disease, pulmonary disease, and sudden infant death syndrome (U.S. Environmental Protection Agency [USEPA], 1992). Secondhand smoke is classified as a Class A carcinogen, meaning there is no safe level of exposure.

Prevalence of Smoking and Nicotine Dependence in the United States

Approximately one in every four adults is a current cigarette smoker (American Cancer Society [ACS], 2002). National data indicate that men are more likely to smoke (26%) than women (22%; CDC, 2001). Smoking prevalence varies across racial and ethnic groups, with the highest rates in American Indians and Alaska Natives (41%), intermediate rates among whites (26%) and African Americans (27%), and lowest among Hispanics (19%) and Asians and Pacific Islanders (15%; CDC, 2001; USDHHS, 1998). Other sociodemographic factors relate to smoking as well. For example, smoking prevalence varies in relation to education level, with college graduates demonstrating lower rates of smoking (11%) than adults without a high school education (38%; CDC, 2001; National Center for Health Statistics, 2001). In addition, higher rates of smoking are found in persons living in poverty, among active military personnel, and individuals who are separated or divorced (see Giovino, Henningfield, Tomar, Escobedo, & Slade, 1995, for review).

According to the 1994 *Report of the Surgeon General*, smokers commonly report their age of first cigarette use as 14.5 years (USDHHS, 1994). Among daily smokers, 89% started smoking by 18 years of age, and almost 37% had tried their first cigarette before the age of 14. According to the 1997 Youth Risk Behavior Survey, over 70% of high school students had ever tried smoking, and 35.8% went on to smoke daily. Of those daily smokers, 73% had tried to stop smoking, but only 13.5% were successful. National youth data collected in 1999 showed that white (39%) and Hispanic (33%) students were more likely to have smoked in the past month than African American students (20%), while white students (20%) were more likely to report frequent smoking than either Hispanic (10%) or African American (7%) students (CDC, 2000).

Among smokers, nicotine dependence ranges from 51% to 90% (Giovino et al., 1995). Among those trying even a single cigarette, 33%

to 50% will become nicotine dependent (USDHHS, 1994). Estimates of dependence prevalence and rates of transition from use to dependence are similar across tobacco, cocaine, and heroin (Anthony, Warner, & Kessler, 1994; Woody, Cottler, & Cacciola, 1993). Rates of nicotine dependence are higher among females than males and among whites than members of ethnic and racial minority groups, and are lowest among older adults (Kandel & Chen, 2000). Despite smoking at lower rates (e.g., fewer cigarettes per day), adolescents show similar rates of nicotine dependence compared to adults (Kandel & Chen, 2000). Differences in rates of nicotine dependence across groups may be related to potential differences in sensitivity to nicotine (Kandel & Chen, 2000) and differences in nicotine metabolism (Benowitz & Jacob, 2000), which could contribute to differences in the reinforcing value of nicotine administered through smoking.

Measurement of Smoking and Nicotine Dependence

Smoking may be assessed using biochemical (e.g., expired air carbon monoxide, assessment of nicotine or cotinine levels) or self-report measures. It should be noted that considerable interindividual variability exists in the metabolism of nicotine (Benowitz & Jacob, 2000; Benowitz, Jacob, & Perez-Stable, 1996; Benowitz, Zevin, & Jacob, 1997). Self-reported smoking status is generally considered highly accurate (Velicer, Prochaska, Rossi, & Snow, 1992). Interestingly, findings suggest that true rates of smoking are likely to be closer to self-reported rates than to biochemically confirmed rates (Ockene et al., 1992). Estimated lifetime smoking is frequently reported by multiplying the rate of smoking (packs per day; one pack contains 20 cigarettes) by years of smoking to calculate number of pack years of smoking. Assessment of smoking history commonly includes age of first cigarette, age of regular use, rates of smoking over time, type and brand of tobacco used, number of stop attempts, and length of abstinence.

Reliable self-report measures of nicotine dependence have been developed for use in clinical and research settings. The Diagnostic Interview Schedule (DIS-IV) is a reliable structured interview used to assess the diagnosis of nicotine dependence as defined within the *DSM-IV* (APA, 1994). The DIS-IV includes detailed assessment of smoking history (current usage, age at initiation, cigarettes per day) and evaluates physiological, cognitive, and behavioral features of nicotine dependence, including evidence of nicotine tolerance, withdrawal, and compulsive drug use behavior. The Fagerström Tolerance Questionnaire (FTQ; Fagerström, 1978) is a short self-administered measure of physiological dependence (e.g., high rates of smoking and smoking after awakening to avoid withdrawal) and behavioral features (e.g., difficulty refraining from smoking). The Fagerström Test for Nicotine Dependence (FTND) is also a short self-administered measure, and an abbreviated version of the FTQ (Heatherton, Kozlowski, Frecker, & Fagerström, 1991; Payne, Smith, McCracken, McSherry, & Anthony, 1994). The FTND has been correlated with biochemical measures of nicotine dependence including exhaled air carbon monoxide (CO), salivary cotinine, and salivary nicotine (Heatherton et al., 1991).

Impact of Smoking on Personal and Family Health and Well-Being

Cigarette smoking is the most preventable cause of morbidity and mortality in men and women, accounting for one in five deaths in the United States (CDC, 1994; McGinnis & Foege, 1993). Tobacco use accounts for at least 30% of all cancer deaths, including cancer of the lung, mouth, larynx, pharynx, esophagus, pancreas, uterine cervix, kidney, and bladder (ACS, 2002). Smoking also dramatically increases risk of developing serious illnesses such as chronic obstructive pulmonary disease, coronary heart disease, peripheral artery disease, and stroke (USDHHS, 1990).

Smoking is responsible for over 87% of lung cancers (USDHHS, 1989). In 2002, cancer of the lung or bronchus accounted for an estimated 169,400 new cancer cases (13% of cancer diagnoses) and 154,900 deaths (28% of all cancer deaths; ACS, 2002). Lung cancer mortality rates are 12 times higher for current female smokers and 22 times higher for current male smokers than for lifelong never smokers (USDHHS, 1989). Further, about 3,000 nonsmoking adults die of lung cancer each year as a result of exposure to secondhand smoke (USEPA, 1992). For individuals with cancer, continued smoking can lead to increased risk for tumor progression, the development of a second primary cancer, and poorer survival (Johnson et al., 1986; Johnston-Early et al., 1980; Kawahara et al., 1998; Richardson et al., 1993; Silverman, Gorsky, & Greenspan, 1983; Stevens, Gardner, Parkin, & Johnson, 1983).

Multiple health benefits are associated with stopping smoking. Within hours of stopping smoking, blood pressure and heart rate decrease, and reduced levels of CO result in increased oxygen transport and availability (USDHHS, 1990). Within days of stopping smoking, individuals experience improvements in smell, taste, circulation, and breathing. Within months of stopping smoking, improvements to the immune system and metabolic system, increased energy, and decreased shortness of breath may be experienced (USDHHS, 1990). Stopping smoking is also associated with increased quality of life including improved energy level, sleep adequacy, cognitive functioning, psychological well-being, and self-esteem (Stewart, King, Killen, & Ritter, 1995).

Smoking behavior is significant within the family. Smoking is more common among youths who have at least one smoking parent (Tyas & Pederson, 1998), while youths whose parents stop smoking or object to smoking are less likely to use tobacco (Distefan, Gilpin, Choi, & Pierce, 1998; Farkas, Distefan, Choi, Gilpin, & Pierce, 1999; Flay et al., 1994). Moreover, parental smoking increases childhood risk for illnesses including respiratory tract infections and asthma (USEPA, 1992). Within the family, smoking can be resistant to change. Smokers are more likely than nonsmokers to choose spouses who smoke (Sutton, 1980), and spousal smoking is associated with smoking relapse for individuals who are trying to stop smoking (Dale et al., 1997). Furthermore, spousal smoking has been associated with decreased cancer screening among women (Clark, Rakowski, & Ehrich, 2000). In contrast, spousal concern about the effects of smoking on health, objection to smoking, and smoking abstinence may promote cessation by the smoking spouse (Dale et al., 1997; Hanson, Isacsson, Janzon, & Lindell, 1990; West, McEwen, Bolling, & Owen, 2001).

Attention to eliminating smoking within the family is a central step in promoting family health. Poignantly, family members of patients with lung cancer are more likely to smoke than the general population (McDuffie, 1991). Moreover, there is evidence that family members of individuals with lung cancer are at greater risk of developing cancer themselves (Ooi, Elston, Chen, Bailey-Wilson, & Rothschild, 1986). Evidence that lung cancer may be the result of a gene-environment interaction (Sellers et al., 1990) suggests that reducing environmental tobacco smoke within the family is of particular importance. Indeed, cancer patients report that having family members stop smoking strongly supports their own cessation (Knudsen, Schulman, van den Hoek, & Fowler, 1985). Furthermore, cancer patients express interest in helping other family members stop smoking (Schilling et al., 1997).

UNDERSTANDING SMOKING FROM A
BIOBEHAVIORAL PERSPECTIVE

In light of the national toll associated with tobacco use, a large number of local, state, and federal agencies are working to reduce the prevalence of smoking. Among these is the National Cancer Institute (NCI) at the National Institutes of Health and its tobacco-related research programs.

Recently, the NCI created the Tobacco Research Implementation Group (TRIG) and charged it with establishing the institute's tobacco-related cancer research priorities (TRIG, 1998). Guiding these priorities was the biobehavioral model of nicotine addiction and tobacco-related cancers. As noted by TRIG, this model provides a framework for conceptualizing the broad spectrum of tobacco research factors and recognizes that tobacco use and nicotine addiction "arise from a complex interplay of social, psychological, and biological factors that interact with genetic vulnerabilities to nicotine addiction" (p. 6).

Social and Psychological Aspects

Social influences on smoking include tobacco industry marketing, exposure to family members and peers who smoke, and the portrayal of smoking in the media. Children have been found to be particularly vulnerable to these sources of influence, and social influences are believed to be responsible for a significant portion of the initiation of smoking among young people (USDHHS, 1994). Psychological influences on smoking include depression and other forms of emotional and behavioral distress, and these factors impact the development and maintenance of smoking over time for both children and adults (USD-HHS, 1994).

Based upon the biobehavioral model, a study set out to evaluate the independent effects of exposure to others who smoke and receptivity to tobacco advertising on adolescent smoking practices and the moderating influence of depression on these relationships (Tercyak, Goldman, Smith, & Audrain, 2002). Study volunteers were 1,123 high school freshmen who completed a self-report survey. Of the participants, 60% identified themselves as never smokers (i.e., never tried or experimented with smoking, even a few puffs), and 40% reported being ever smokers (i.e., ever smoked at least a partial or whole cigarette). In statistical analyses, the adjusted likelihood of ever smoking was greater for students reporting exposure to peer smoking. Further, a significant interaction was detected between receptivity to tobacco advertising and depression; specifically, adolescents with a high receptivity to tobacco advertising and clinically significant depressive symptoms were more likely to smoke than adolescents without these symptoms.

These and other data support the hypothesis that adolescents with both high advertising receptivity and depressed moods are most vulnerable to experiment with smoking. Along with behavioral, neurochemical, and physiological mediating factors, these findings represent one example of research addressing an intermediate outcome among youth that can affect the development of tobacco-related cancers in adulthood.

BIOMARKERS

Biomarkers are measurable events occurring in the human body (Grandjean, 1995) and their assays provide some measurement of exposure in tissue (e.g., the level of a tobacco constituent or an effect in exhaled air, sputum, saliva, blood, skin, urine, internal organ, or body part). Because many biomarkers have the potential to be useful to understand smoking behavior and carcinogenesis, and new technologies are bringing forth others, it is critical that any such assays undergo rigorous development and validation prior to being used in clinical settings. This section briefly reviews pertinent categories of biomarkers, with some examples.

Biomarkers of Exposure

These assays reflect the amount of tobacco smoke constituents that enter the body. While exposure can be assessed by asking smokers about the number of cigarettes smoked per day, this method only partially estimates actual exposure because it does not incorporate how efficiently a cigarette is smoked (i.e., the number of puffs taken per cigarette, the depth of inhalation, and the time for inhalation). Biomarkers of exposure include CO, cotinine, and nitrosamines. CO is the most general measure, and has some limitations: For example, it is only a marker of recent exposure, and can reflect background factors such as automobile exhaust. Cotinine is more specific to smoking but has some weaknesses as well: For example, it is quite susceptible to interindividual differences, and cannot be used to verify complete cessation in individuals who are using nicotine replacement therapy. Nitrosamines are a more complex measure that represents a direct assessment of exposure to carcinogens (Atawodi et al., 1998; Mohtashamipur, Norpoth, & Lieder, 1985).

Biomarkers of Harm

Biomarkers of potential harm can range from nonfunctional effects on cells that serve as surrogate markers for actual harm to preclinical and clinical disease. These measurements are generally limited to the research setting. It has become possible to measure background mutations in cancer-related genes of noncancerous tissues (Aguilar, Harris, Sun, Hollstein, & Cerutti, 1994; Mao et al., 1997; Sidransky, 1997). An emerging area of tumor suppressor gene silencing is the study of hypermethylation of genes in tumors. Lesions in the *p16* gene in sputum of smokers has been associated with smoking (Lerman, Shields, et al.,

1997). Biomarkers of pathobiological effect include morphological markers of preneoplastic lesions (e.g., dysplasia) or altered phenotypic expression of normal cellular functions (e.g., overexpression of the proto-oncogene Erb-B2).

Biomarkers of Susceptibility

Another general class of biomarkers relates to heritable traits and genetic susceptibility. Genes can affect how and how much one smokes, carcinogen metabolism, detoxification, DNA damage repair, and how cells die. Carcinogen metabolism and detoxification can be assessed using functional assays and the measurement of metabolites, or by determining genetic polymorphisms. There has been extensive study of genetic polymorphisms in smoking-related cancer risk (Shields, 2000). Examples include, not in order of importance, N-acetyltransferase 2 (NAT2; Brockmoller, Cascorbi, Kerb, Sachse, & Roots, 1998), glutathione-S-transferase M1 (GSTM1; Bell et al., 1993), cytochrome P450 1A1 (CYP1A1) genes (Bishop, 1987; Ishibe et al., 1997), and glutathione-S-transferase Pi (Ryberg et al., 1997). Genetic polymorphisms for DNA repair enzymes also exist (Mohrenweiser & Jones, 1998), though studies must still be completed that indicate an effect of these genetic variants on tobacco-related cancer risk.

Genetic Determinants of Smoking

Twin studies support a genetic role for smoking initiation (Carmelli, Swan, Robinette, & Fabsitz, 1992) and smoking persistence (Heath & Martin, 1993). Several converging lines of evidence point to the neurotransmitter dopamine as one possible explanation for these genetic effects. Nicotine stimulates reward mechanisms in the brain. Nicotine and nicotinic acetylcholine receptors are most closely linked to dopaminergic pathways by increasing dopamine secretion into neuronal synapses (Dani & Heinemann, 1996), and the importance of dopamine to nicotine dependence has been highlighted in several reviews (e.g., Berridge & Robinson, 1998). Nicotine not only stimulates prolonged secretion of dopamine but also desensitizes the receptor. There is strong support for the relationship of nicotine stimulation to dopamine responses. Importantly, dopamine transporter inhibits antidepressants, such as bupropion, that are now being used to treat nicotine addiction (Hurt et al., 1997). Further biochemical support comes from an autopsy study of brains from smokers and nonsmokers where the ratio of homovanillic acid (a dopamine metabolite) to dopamine was reduced in smokers (less dopamine turnover), with higher dopamine levels (Court et al., 1998). In a separate study, serial cerebral spinal fluid levels from smokers had lower concentrations of homovanillic acid compared with nonsmokers, confirming lower dopamine turnover (Geracioti et al., 1999).

It has been hypothesized that persons with higher levels of synaptic dopamine, or more stimulation of dopamine receptors, would have higher endogenous stimulation and so would have a lower reward benefit of nicotine. Thus, these individuals might be less likely to become smokers and would also have less difficulty stopping smoking. This hypothesis is consistent with current studies using genetic polymorphisms as a surrogate marker of dopaminergic activity (Lerman et al., 1999; Sabol et al., 1999), and also with literature showing that blockage of the dopamine transporter by bupropion aids smoking cessation (Hurt et al., 1997).

The dopamine D2 receptor (*DRD2*) A polymorphism has also been under study. The *DRD2* A2 allele has been associated with higher levels of postsynaptic receptors (Noble, Blum, Ritchie, Montgomery, & Sheridan, 1991), so that these persons would be hypothesized not to need the rewarding effects of nicotine. Two previous reports had demonstrated an association with smoking (Comings et al., 1996; Noble et al., 1994), though this finding is inconsistent (Singleton et al., 1998). The "at-risk" *DRD2* allele also is associated with smoking more cigarettes per day (Spitz et al., 1998). Examining the *SLC6A3* and the *DRD2* A alleles for a gene-gene interaction, there appears to be an interactive multigenic effect for these two genes, where a different combination of genes has greater predictive power for smoking risk (Lerman et al., 1999). Specifically, persons with the *SLC6A3* 9 and *DRD2* A2 alleles were half as likely to be smokers compared with persons without the *SLC6A3* 9 and *DRD2* A2 alleles. Importantly, using a different study design, Sabol and colleagues (1999) found support for the importance of *SLC6A3* in smoking cessation.

A study of smokers and nonsmokers also examined associations for a dopamine D4 receptor (*DRD4*; Lerman et al., 1998). This genetic polymorphism, which is a variable nucleotide repeat polymorphism, has been reported to affect clozapine and dopamine binding (Asghari et al., 1995; van Tol et al., 1992), although a clinical effect is not clear (Rao et al., 1994). A study by Shields and colleagues (1998) found that African Americans, but not Caucasians, with longer alleles had an increased risk of smoking and, in those persons who smoked, used a higher number of cigarettes per day. However, the small number of African Americans limited this study.

A final polymorphism of interest in the dopamine-related pathway is in dopamine beta-hydroxylase (*DBH*). The *DBH* protein is involved in the conversion of dopamine to dobutamine, which then limits the availability of this neurotransmitter for the stimulation of reward pathways. In a study of 225 smokers, persons with the 1368 GG genotype smoked few cigarettes, and the effect was greater in women and in Caucasians (McKinney et al., 2000).

ROLE OF BIOMARKERS IN LUNG CANCER AND SMOKING SUSCEPTIBILITY TESTING

Health professionals often provide education and personalized feedback to their patients about their risks of developing a number of adverse health events, including heart disease, lung cancer, or chronic lung disease. This feedback is provided in an effort to motivate patients to change the behaviors they are engaging in that contribute to these risks, such as overeating, a sedentary lifestyle, and smoking.

In the past, cancer risk estimates offered to patients have largely relied upon population-level information, such as age, gender, race, and family history, to determine an individual's level of risk. However, due to recent advances in molecular genetics, we will soon see a growing number of more sophisticated cancer risk estimation procedures that incorporate individual-level information, such as the genetic susceptibilities reviewed above.

First, this section introduces the concept of lung cancer/smoking susceptibility testing via genotyping and the ethical issues raised by such testing, and describes DNA testing's role in tobacco control. Then this section discusses, in greater detail, the theoretical rationale for incorporating susceptibility testing into stop-smoking treatment, to review three commonly studied biomarkers, and to evaluate the results of studies that incorporated biomarker feedback on smoking and behavior change.

Susceptibility Testing

An individual's susceptibility to developing lung cancer is affected by multiple genetic and environmental factors (Amos et al., 1999; Shields, 1999). This includes an individual's genotype for enzymes that are involved in the activation or detoxification of cancer-causing agents, as well as the repair of DNA damaged by smoking. In addition, genes involved in the release and reuptake of neurotransmitters such as dopamine have also been associated with smoking behavior. Thus, it will increasingly be possible to determine an individual's susceptibility to lung cancer and susceptibility to smoking via various combinations of these and other DNA susceptibility tests.

Ethical Aspects

As has been highlighted in numerous ways throughout this volume, genetic and other forms of disease susceptibility testing carry with them a host of ethical challenges. These challenges include maintaining the privacy and confidentiality of sensitive genetic information, protecting patients against unwanted disclosure of genetic information to third parties, informing patients about the potential for insurance, employment, and other forms of discrimination based upon their genetic status, and the potential for adverse psychological responses from tested individuals and their family members (Holtzman & Watson, 1998).

With regard to lung cancer/smoking gene susceptibility testing, these issues are in need of further exploration (Spitz, Wei, Li, & Wu, 1999). In one study, the provision of biomarker feedback about lung cancer susceptibility aroused higher levels of fear among smokers attempting to stop smoking, and also led them to have higher levels of psychological distress compared to smokers attempting to stop without such feedback (Lerman, Gold, et al., 1997). In light of these potential risks, it is likely that genetic and psychosocial counseling should accompany such information, as it does for other forms of cancer risk communication (Croyle & Lerman, 1999).

In addition to the risks mentioned above, it is possible that not all individuals or family members who are at increased susceptibility to lung cancer, the harms of smoking, or smoking itself are interested in participating in investigations designed to elucidate the role of genetic factors in tobacco control. This may be especially true when testing could have implications for vulnerable populations, such as children. For example, in an observational study of the natural history of smoking adoption among adolescents that included the collection of DNA markers of smoking susceptibility, the overall active parental consent rate was 54% (Audrain, Tercyak, Goldman, & Bush, 2002). An analysis of participation revealed that parents and guardians who declined to allow their teenagers to volunteer for the study had lower levels of formal education, were less likely to be Caucasian, and were less likely to report having ever experimented with smoking themselves.

Among the most frequently cited reasons parents gave for declining consent were lack of interest and confidentiality concerns. Confidentiality concerns were noted despite the inclusion of multiple project safeguards and a certificate of confidentiality issued to the study on behalf of the U.S. Department of Health and Human Services. The certificate of confidentiality is the highest level of protection offered to participants in federally funded research studies to maintain the privacy and confidentiality of their data. Though relatively few parents

singled out DNA testing per se as a primary deterrent to study participation, these data highlight some family members' attitudes toward
tobacco control efforts and about the potential use and misuse of sensitive information. These data also raise important issues about the moderating role of education level, race, and smoking among family
members and the need to account for such factors when designing and
implementing research in this area. As such, additional work on these
and other factors are necessary to elucidate family members' perceptions of the risks and benefits of participating in smoking susceptibility
testing and tobacco control programs involving a genetic component.
To the extent that these efforts are guided and informed by health behavior and health education theories, it increases the likelihood that
these efforts will produce greater change.

Theoretical Rationale for Incorporating
Susceptibility Testing into Stop-Smoking Treatment

Several theoretical models have been posited to account for changes in
patient health behavior. These models include the health belief model
(HBM), the transtheoretical model (TM), and the cognitive-social
health information processing model (C-SHIP). Below, we review each
of these frameworks, their application to smoking behavior, and the
underlying rationale for incorporating susceptibility testing into stop-
smoking treatment. Understanding these and other models of health
behavior are important in order to safely and effectively incorporate
genetic and other forms of lung cancer/smoking susceptibility testing
into clinical practice and to produce more effective change.

Health Belief Model

The HBM was first developed in the 1950s (see Strecher & Rosenstock,
1997, for review). The model is used to predict health behavior based
on one's beliefs—in particular beliefs that: (a) one is susceptible to a
health event, (b) the event is harmful, (c) steps can be taken to reduce
the risks of the event, and (d) the costs of taking steps to reduce one's
risk are outweighed by the benefits. The model also incorporates other
variables, such as environmental cues that activate readiness to change
and one's self-confidence for change.

    To date, only limited research has applied the HBM to the study of
cigarette smoking. That is because the majority of current cigarette
smokers, former cigarette smokers, and nonsmokers already perceive
the behavior of smoking as dangerous (Strecher & Rosenstock, 1997).

However, with the possibility of incorporating personal susceptibility testing for lung cancer into stop-smoking treatments, this opens up new opportunities to provide individual feedback about one's risks rather than relying on population risks only. To the extent that this feedback could strengthen beliefs about personal susceptibility, enhanced motivation and success with stopping smoking might be seen.

Transtheoretical Model

The TM was developed in the early 1980s (see Prochaska, Redding, & Evers, 1997, for review). The TM is an integrative model of behavior change that describes how individuals modify a problem behavior, such as smoking. The primary organizing construct of the TM is the stages of change, which recognizes change as a process involving progress through a series of five stages. These five stages, and their application to cigarette smoking, are as follows:

1. *Precontemplation*—smokers are not intending to stop smoking in the foreseeable future, usually measured as the next six months.
2. *Contemplation*—smokers are intending to change in the next six months.
3. *Preparation*—smokers are intending to take action in the immediate future, usually measured as intending to stop smoking in the next month.
4. *Action*—smokers have made specific overt modifications in their lifestyles within the past 6 months, such as actually stopping smoking.
5. *Maintenance*—former smokers are working to prevent relapse to smoking (Velicer, Prochaska, Fava, Norman, & Redding, 1998).

In addition to the stages of change, the TM also posits that there are processes of change that are responsible for moving patients along from one stage to the next. One process in particular that is relevant to the discussion of susceptibility testing is consciousness raising. Consciousness raising involves increasing one's awareness about the causes, consequences, and cures for smoking, and it has been positively associated with smokers' attempts to stop smoking (Schnoll et al., 2002b). Interventions that increase awareness include feedback and education—both of which are employed during genetic susceptibility testing. Like the HBM, it is possible that increasing one's awareness of personal susceptibility (rather then nonspecific susceptibility) could produce greater change.

Cognitive-Social Health Information Processing Model

The C-SHIP model was articulated by Miller, Shoda, and Hurley (1996) and is derived from a cognitive-affective system theory of personality developed by Mischel and Shoda (1995). Unlike the HBM and TM, C-SHIP focuses on the beginnings and preservation of health protective behavior by addressing how different types of individuals process information about cancer and other threats, and disease prevention and control options. C-SHIP recognizes that protective behaviors are strongly influenced by cognitive and affective factors that influence information processing, including individual differences in patients' tendencies to seek out or avoid threatening information. These factors are highly important when health professionals seek to engage their patients in gene susceptibility testing for lung cancer/smoking, as well as when health professionals and patients work together to initiate complex behaviors that are difficult to maintain over time, such as stopping smoking.

The generalizability of C-SHIP to tobacco control is currently under investigation by Schnoll and others in a randomized clinical trial (Schnoll et al., 2002a). In this study, the impact of an individualized behavioral stop-smoking treatment for cancer patients is being explored. Cancer patients were selected for study as smoking negatively impacts upon their survival time and efficacy of their treatment, and it also promotes the development of second primary cancers. Guided by C-SHIP, treatment targets cognitive and emotional variables that are considered predictive of smoking by cancer patients, such as perceived risk, self-efficacy, fatalistic beliefs, pros and cons of stopping smoking, and emotional distress. Preliminary results suggest that one's readiness to stop smoking is positively associated with increased self-efficacy, risk perceptions, and greater awareness of the benefits of stopping smoking (Schnoll et al., 2002b). Consistent with C-SHIP, these data suggest that treatments to facilitate self-efficacy and recognition of stop-smoking benefits and risk awareness, such as lung cancer/smoking gene susceptibility test result feedback, might be efficacious in promoting cessation.

Impact of Incorporating Biomarker Feedback on Smoking and Behavior Change

Some of the earliest studies that incorporated biomarker feedback to motivate smokers to stop smoking were those that relied upon CO measurements. Though CO is not a genetic susceptibility test, it is included here because it is paradigmatic of biomarker feedback used in helping patients stop smoking. For example, Risser and Belcher (1990) randomized 90 smokers seen in a general screening clinic to an education-only condition or an education plus enhanced motivational intervention condition. The enhanced condition provided immediate feedback about CO values and pulmonary functioning and symptoms. The results suggested that smokers in the enhanced condition were two times as likely to report stopping smoking, and this effect was largely attributed to the potency of the CO component.

Unfortunately, the results of CO feedback on smoking and behavior change have not been uniform, with some investigations showing little or no effect (Bauman, Bryan, Dent, & Koch, 1983; Rand, Stitzer, Bigelow, & Mead, 1989; Walker & Franzini, 1985). McBride et al. (2000) set out to evaluate if the method of communicating feedback about lung cancer susceptibility (GST) to smokers, with and without CO feedback, affected patients' perceptions of the risks and benefits of stopping smoking, and motivation to stop. The two methods of communication that were investigated in this study were telephone and in-person counseling. In general, there were few differences between the study groups, and over 50% of the 144 patients who participated interpreted their GST susceptibility results correctly. However, neither CO feedback nor counseling was associated with an increase in smokers' perceived risk of lung cancer, which has been conceptualized as a motivator for stopping smoking. As baseline levels of perceived lung cancer risk were already quite high in the sample, it is possible that little room for improvement existed. In addition to highlighting the potential feasibility of incorporating biomarker feedback into stop-smoking treatment programs, this study also points to the need for additional research on the role of CO feedback on smoking and behavior change.

Another study that assessed biomarker feedback feasibility was conducted by Ostroff and colleagues (1999). There, the researchers examined smokers' hypothetical interest in receiving biomarker testing for tobacco-related cancer susceptibility during a routine visit to a dental clinic. The majority of patients were interested such testing (83%) and understood the association between the biomarker test result and the likelihood of developing a tobacco-related cancer. Women reported greater interest in testing than men (95% vs. 81%), as did smokers with higher perceptions of their risk for developing cancer. These data highlight the potential role that dental professionals and dental clinics can play in providing personal susceptibility feedback to smokers to motivate cessation.

A pair of studies by Lerman and colleagues (Audrain et al., 1997; Lerman, Gold, et al., 1997) reported on the immediate, short-term (2 months later), and long-term (12 months later) impact of incorporating biomarkers of exposure and genetic susceptibility into smoking cessation treatment. Over 400 smokers were randomized into either a stop-smoking counseling condition only, or stop-smoking counseling and CO feedback conditions with or without *CYP* gene feedback. Immediately posttreatment, the combined counseling and CO/*CYP* feedback condition produced greater effects on smoking-related cognitions and emotions than did counseling with CO feedback, or counseling only. These findings suggest that genetic information may be more powerful in its immediate effects than other types of motivational feedback. Though this study failed to find a similarly strong impact of the combined counseling and CO/*CYP* feedback condition relative to the other two conditions on either readiness to stop smoking or actual stopping in the short or long term, it did lead to significantly more stop0smoking attempts by 12 months.

GENES, FAMILIES, AND TOBACCO
CONTROL: A LOOK AHEAD

Helping Smokers Stop Smoking

Clearly, the health risks associated with tobacco use and the multiple benefits of stopping smoking provide an ethical imperative for all health professionals to treat nicotine dependence, especially among patients with cancer and their family members. Patients with lung cancer are motivated and able to stop smoking, and report interest in receiving tobacco use treatment interventions (see Cox, Africano, Tercyak, & Taylor, 2005, for review). Resources for educating health professionals in providing nicotine dependence intervention are also available (e.g., Fiore et al., 2000; Hecht et al., 1994; Prokhorov, Hudmon, & Gritz, 1997; Schnoll & Miller, 2000).

Current recommendations for treating nicotine dependence are found in the U.S. Public Health Service Report titled *Treating Tobacco Use and Dependence: A Clinical Practice Guideline* (Fiore et al., 2000). Health care providers are instructed to assess tobacco use in all patients and to provide clinical intervention to all smokers. Current smokers interested in stopping smoking should receive counseling to develop a plan to stop smoking and obtain support, pharmacotherapy (e.g., nicotine replacement therapy: patch, gum, inhaler, and nasal spray; bupropion) to aid cessation, and scheduled for follow-up to prevent relapse. Current smokers who are not interest in stopping should be provided with a motivational intervention, including information about the personal health risks of smoking, benefits of stopping smoking, and multiple resources available to aid cessation. Former smokers should receive reinforcement for their decision to stop smoking, feedback about the benefits of stopping, and assistance with any problems that may have arisen as a result of stopping (e.g., depression and weight gain). Because there is a strong dose-response relationship between the intensity and effectiveness of intervention, more intensive interventions (extended or repeated interventions and pharmacotherapy) may be needed for individuals who have greater difficulty stopping (Fiore et al., 2000).

Future Implications

The concepts summarized throughout this chapter represent what is currently known about incorporating information about genetic susceptibility to smoking and lung cancer into tobacco control. However, it is important to keep in mind that even without the benefit of knowing any feedback about one's individual or family genetic risk, the health message remains the same: No level of exposure to tobacco smoke is considered safe.

Like any complex behavior, cigarette smoking is determined by multiple causes, and the relative influence of genes compared with environmental factors must be kept in mind. For example, among youths the development of smoking occurs in stages, beginning with experimentation and commonly resulting in regular use (USDHHS, 1994). It is clear that not all youths progress through the stages of smoking and become regular smokers; some never start, others start and then stop, and still others progress quite rapidly. Both environmental and genetic factors contribute to this process, though the relative contributions of each remain in question. Since childhood is the most likely time in life when smoking is initiated, it has been suggested that studies in pediatric genetic epidemiology hold great promise for the prevention of tobacco use (Swan, 1999). As such, we recognize this as an emerging area of study and that will likely have significant impact on the health and well-being of children and families in the years to come.

Of course, communicating risk information about personal and familial gene susceptibilities to tobacco or lung cancer remains an important direction for the future as well. Comprehensive risk counseling programs evaluating individuals and families with an eye toward tobacco-related cancers have yet to be established. In doing so, it will be necessary to have a more complete integration of health behavior goals, including stopping smoking, into standard genetic counseling protocols.

Among those who already smoke, the possibility exists that their stop-smoking treatment could be maximally effective when tailored to their needs (Velicer et al., 1993), including their genotype. Pharmacogenetics attempts to understand individual differences in response to prescription and nonprescription drugs based on gene-drug interactions (Wolf, Smith, & Smith, 2000). As applied to tobacco use, health care providers might, one day, have guidelines available to them that indicate which drugs are susceptible to these gene-based metabolic variations. When combined with DNA profiles from individual smokers, this knowledge could then be applied to optimally match stop-smoking drugs (e.g., bupropion and nicotine replacement therapy) to patients to promote cessation.

Until such time when these and other questions are fully answered, health professionals should continue to discourage tobacco use and treat nicotine dependence among all individuals and their family members, and to recognize the promise that genetic advances hold for controlling tobacco use among all segments of society.

REFERENCES

Aguilar, F., Harris, C. C., Sun, T., Hollstein, M., & Cerutti, P. (1994). Geographic variation of p53 mutational profile in nonmalignant human liver. *Science, 264,* 1317–1319.

American Cancer Society. (2002). *Cancer facts and figures—2002.* Atlanta, GA: Author.

American Psychiatric Association. (1994). *Diagnostic and statistical manual of mental disorders* (4th ed). Washington, DC: Author.

Amos, C. I., Xu, W., & Spitz, M. R. (1999). Is there a genetic basis for lung cancer susceptibility? *Recent Results in Cancer Research, 151,* 3–12.

Anthony, J. C., Warner, L. A., & Kessler, R. C. (1994). Comparative epidemiology of dependence on tobacco, alcohol, controlled substances and inhalants: Basic findings from the National Comorbidity Survey. *Experimental and Clinical Psychopharmacology, 2,* 244–268.

Asghari, V., Sanyal, S., Buchwaldt, S., Paterson, A., Jovanovic, V., & van Tol, H. H. (1995). Modulation of intracellular cyclic AMP levels by different human dopamine D4 receptor variants. *Journal of Neurochemistry, 65,* 1157–1165.

Atawodi, S. E., Lea, S., Nyberg, F., Mukeria, A., Constantinescu, V., Ahrens, W., et al. (1998). 4-Hydroxy-1-(3-pyridyl)-1-butanone-hemoglobin adducts as biomarkers of exposure to tobacco smoke: Validation of a method to be used in multicenter studies. *Cancer Epidemiology, Biomarkers and Prevention, 7,* 817–821.

Audrain, J., Boyd, N. R., Roth, J., Main, D., Caporaso, N. F., & Lerman, C. (1997). Genetic susceptibility testing in smoking-cessation treatment: One-year outcomes of a randomized trial. *Addictive Behaviors, 22,* 741–751.

Audrain, J., Tercyak, K. P., Goldman, P., & Bush, A. (2002). Recruiting adolescents into genetic studies of smoking behavior. *Cancer Epidemiology, Biomarkers and Prevention, 11,* 249–252.

Bauman, K. E., Bryan, E. S., Dent, C. W., & Koch, G. G. (1983). The influence of observing carbon monoxide level on cigarette smoking by public prenatal patients. *American Journal of Public Health, 73*, 1089–1091.

Bell, D. A., Taylor, J. A., Paulson, D. F., Robertson, C. N., Mohler, J. L., & Lucier, G. W. (1993). Genetic risk and carcinogen exposure: A common inherited defect of the carcinogen-metabolism gene glutathione S-transferase M1 (GSTM1) that increases susceptibility to bladder cancer. *Journal of the National Cancer Institute, 85*, 1159–1164.

Benowitz, N. L. (1992). Cigarette smoking and nicotine addiction. *Medical Clinics of North America, 76*, 415–437.

Benowitz, N. L., & Jacob, P. (2000). Effects of cigarette smoking and carbon monoxide on nicotine and cotinine metabolism. *Clinical Pharmacology and Therapeutics, 67*, 653–659.

Benowitz, N. L., Jacob, P., & Perez-Stable, E. (1996). CYP2D6 phenotype and the metabolism of nicotine and cotinine. *Pharmacogenetics, 6*, 239–242.

Benowitz, N. L., Zevin, S., & Jacob, P. (1997). Sources of variability in nicotine and cotinine levels with use of nicotine nasal spray, transdermal nicotine, and cigarette smoking. *British Journal of Clinical Pharmacology, 43*, 259–267.

Berridge, K. C., & Robinson, T. E. (1998). What is the role of dopamine in reward: Hedonic impact, reward learning, or incentive salience? *Brain Research. Brain Research Reviews, 28*, 309–369.

Bishop, J. M. (1987). The molecular genetics of cancer. *Science, 235*, 305–311.

Brockmoller, J., Cascorbi, I., Kerb, R., Sachse, C., & Roots, I. (1998). Polymorphisms in xenobiotic conjugation and disease predisposition. *Toxicology Letters, 102–103*, 173–183.

Carmelli, D., Swan, G. E., Robinette, D., & Fabsitz, R. (1992). Genetic influence on smoking—a study of male twins. *New England Journal of Medicine, 327*, 829–833.

Centers for Disease Control and Prevention. (1994). Cigarette smoking among adults—United States, 1993. *Morbidity and Mortality Weekly Report, 43*, 925–930.

Centers for Disease Control and Prevention. (2000). Youth Risk Behavior Surveillance—United States, 1999. *Morbidity and Mortality Weekly Report, 49*, 1–96.

Centers for Disease Control and Prevention. (2001). Cigarette smoking among adults—United States, 1999. *Morbidity and Mortality Weekly Report, 50*, 869–873.

Clark, M. A., Rakowski, W., & Ehrich, B. (2000). Breast and cervical cancer screening: Associations with personal, spouse's, and combined smoking status. *Cancer Epidemiology, Biomarkers and Prevention, 9*, 513–516.

Comings, D. E., Ferry, L., Bradshaw-Robinson, S., Burchette, R., Chiu, C., & Muhleman, D. (1996). The dopamine D2 receptor (DRD2) gene: A genetic risk factor in smoking. *Pharmacogenetics, 6*, 73–79.

Court, J. A., Lloyd, S., Thomas, N., Piggott, M. A., Marshall, E. F., Morris, C. M., et al. (1998). Dopamine and nicotinic receptor binding and the levels of dopamine and homovanillic acid in human brain related to tobacco use. *Neuroscience, 87*, 63–78.

Cox, L. S., Africano, N. L., Tercyak, K. P., & Taylor, K. L. (2003). Nicotine dependence treatment for patients with cancer. *Cancer, 98*(3), 632–644.

Croyle, R. T., & Lerman C. (1999). Risk communication in genetic testing for cancer susceptibility. *Journal of the National Cancer Institute Monographs, 25,* 59–66.

Dale, L. C., Olsen, D. A., Patten, C. A., Schroeder, D. R., Croghan, I. T., Hurt, R. D., et al. (1997). Predictors of smoking cessation among elderly smokers treated for nicotine dependence. *Tobacco Control, 6,* 181–187.

Dani, J. A., & Heinemann, S. (1996). Molecular and cellular aspects of nicotine abuse. *Neuron, 16,* 905–908.

Distefan, J. M., Gilpin, E. A., Choi, W. S., & Pierce, J. P. (1998). Parental influences predict adolescent smoking in the United States, 1989–1993. *Journal of Adolescent Health, 22,* 466–474.

Fagerström, K. O. (1978). Measuring degree of physical dependence to tobacco smoking with reference to individualization of treatment. *Addictive Behaviors, 3,* 235–241.

Farkas, A. J., Distefan, J. M., Choi, W. S., Gilpin, E. A., & Pierce, J. P. (1999). Does parental smoking cessation discourage adolescent smoking? *Preventive Medicine, 28,* 213–218.

Fiore, M. C., Bailey, W. C., Cohen, S. J., Dorfman, S. F., Goldstein, M. G., Gritz, E. R., et al. (2000). *Treating tobacco use and dependence: A clinical practice guideline.* AHRQ Publication No. 00-0032. Rockville, MD: USDHHS, Public Health Service.

Fiore, M. C., Smith, S. S., Jorenby, D. E., & Baker, T. B. (1994). The effectiveness of the nicotine patch for smoking cessation: A meta-analysis. *Journal of the American Medical Association, 271,* 1940–1947.

Flay, B. R., Hu, F. B., Siddiqui, O., Day, L. E., Hedeker, D., Petraitis, J., et al. (1994). Differential influences of parental smoking and friends' smoking on adolescent initiation and escalation of smoking. *Journal of Health and Social Behavior, 35,* 248–265.

Geracioti, T. D. Jr., West, S. A., Baker, D. G., Hill, K. K., Ekhator, N. N., Wortman, M. D., et al. (1999). Low CSF concentration of a dopamine metabolite in tobacco smokers. *American Journal of Psychiatry, 156,* 130–132.

Giovino, G. A., Henningfield, J. E., Tomar, S. L., Escobedo, L. G., & Slade, J. (1995). Epidemiology of tobacco use and dependence. *Epidemiologic Reviews, 17,* 48–65.

Grandjean, P. (1995). Biomarkers in epidemiology. *Clinical Chemistry, 41,* 1800–1803.

Gross, J., & Stitzer, M. L. (1989). Nicotine replacement: Ten-week effects on tobacco withdrawal symptoms. *Psychopharmacology (Berlin), 98,* 334–341.

Hanson, B. S., Isacsson, S. O., Janzon, L., & Lindell, S. E. (1990). Social support and quitting smoking for good. Is there an association? Results from the population study, "Men born in 1914," Malmo, Sweden. *Addictive Behaviors, 15,* 221–233.

Heath, A. C., & Martin, N. G. (1993). Genetic models for the natural history of smoking: Evidence for a genetic influence on smoking persistence. *Addictive Behaviors, 18,* 19–34.

Heatherton, T. F., Kozlowski, L. T., Frecker, R. C., & Fagerström, K. O. (1991). The Fagerström Test for Nicotine Dependence: A revision of the Fagerström Tolerance Questionnaire. *British Journal of Addiction, 86*, 1119–1127.

Hecht, J. P., Emmons, K. M., Brown, R. A., Everett, K. D., Farrell, N. C., Hitchcock P., et al. (1994). Smoking interventions for patients with cancer: Guidelines for nursing practice. *Oncology Nursing Forum, 21*, 1657–1666.

Henningfield, J. E., & Keenan, R. M. (1993). Nicotine delivery kinetics and abuse liability. *Journal of Consulting and Clinical Psychology, 61*, 743–750.

Holtzman, N. E., & Watson, M. S. (Eds.). (1998). *Promoting safe and effective genetic testing in the United States. Final Report of the Task Force on Genetic Testing.* Baltimore, MD: Johns Hopkins University Press.

Hughes, J. R., & Hatsukami, D. (1986). Signs and symptoms of tobacco withdrawal. *Archieves of General Psychiatry, 43*, 289–294.

Hughes, J. R., Higgins, S. T., & Bickel, W. K. (1994). Nicotine withdrawal versus other drug withdrawal syndromes: Similarities and dissimilarities. *Addiction, 89*, 1461–1470.

Hurt, R. D., Sachs, D. P., Glover, E. D., Offord, K. P., Johnston, J. A., Dale, L. C., et al. (1997). A comparison of sustained-release bupropion and placebo for smoking cessation. *New England Journal of Medicine, 337*, 1195–1202.

Ishibe, N., Wiencke, J. K., Zuo, Z. F., McMillan, A., Spitz, M., & Kelsey, K. T. (1997). Susceptibility to lung cancer in light smokers associated with CYP1A1 polymorphisms in Mexican- and African-Americans. *Cancer Epidemiology, Biomarkers and Prevention, 6*, 1075–1080.

Johnson, B. E., Ihde, D. C., Matthews, M. J., Bunn, P. A., Zabell, A., Makuch, R. W., et al. (1986). Non-small cell lung cancer: Major cause of late mortality in patients with small cell lung cancer. *American Journal of Medicine, 80*, 1103–1110.

Johnston-Early, A., Cohen, M. H., Minna, J. D., Paxton, L. M., Fossieck, B. E. Jr., Ihde, D. C., et al. (1980). Smoking abstinence and small cell lung cancer survival: An association. *Journal of the American Medical Association, 244*, 2175–2179.

Kandel, D. B., & Chen, K. (2000). Extent of smoking and nicotine dependence in the United States: 1991–1993. *Nicotine and Tobacco Research, 2*, 263–274.

Kawahara, M., Ushijima, S., Kamimori, T., Kodama, N., Ogawara, M., Matsui, K., et al. (1998). Second primary tumors in more than 2-year disease-free survivors of small-cell lung cancer in Japan: The role of smoking cessation. *British Journal of Cancer, 78*, 409–412.

Knudsen, N., Schulman, S., van den Hoek, J., & Fowler, R. (1985). Insights on how to quit smoking: A survey of patients with lung cancer. *Cancer Nursing, 8*, 145–150.

Lerman, C., Caporaso, N. E., Audrain, J., Main, D., Bowman, E. D., Lockshin, B., et al. (1999). Evidence suggesting the role of specific genetic factors in cigarette smoking. *Health Psychology, 18*, 14–20.

Lerman, C., Caporaso, N., Main, D., Audrain, J., Boyd, N. R., Bowman, E. D., et al. (1998). Depression and self-medication with nicotine: The modifying influence of the dopamine D4 receptor gene. *Health Psychology, 17*, 56–62.

Lerman, C., Gold, K., Audrain, J., Lin, T. H., Boyd, N. R., Orleans, C. T., et al. (1997). Incorporating biomarkers of exposure and genetic susceptibility into smoking cessation treatment: Effects on smoking-related cognitions, emotions, and behavior change. *Health Psychology, 16,* 87–99.

Lerman, C., Shields, P. G., Main, D., Audrain, J., Roth, J., Boyd, N. R., et al. (1997). Lack of association of tyrosine hydroxylase genetic polymorphism with cigarette smoking. *Pharmacogenetics, 7,* 521–524.

Mao, L., Lee, J. S., Kurie, J. M., Fan, Y. H., Lippman, S. M., Lee, J. J., et al. (1997). Clonal genetic alterations in the lungs of current and former smokers. *Journal of the National Cancer Institute, 89,* 857–862.

Marteau, T. M. (1999). Communicating genetic risk information. *British Medical Bulletin, 55,* 414–428.

Marteau, T. M., & Lerman, C. (2001). Genetic risk and behavioural change. *British Medical Journal, 322,* 1056–1059.

McBride, C. M., Halabi, S., Bepler, G., Lyna, P., McIntyre, L., Lipkus, I., et al. (2000). Maximizing the motivational impact of feedback of lung cancer susceptibility on smokers' desire to quit. *Journal of Health Communication, 5,* 229–241.

McClure, J. B. (2002). Are biomarkers useful treatment aids for promoting health behavior change? An empirical review. *American Journal of Preventive Medicine, 22,* 200–207.

McDonald, J. L., & Olson, B. L. (1994). Pharmacodynamic and pharmacokinetic properties of nicotine from cigarettes, Nicorette, and Nicoderm. *Health Values, 18,* 64–68.

McDuffie, H. H. (1991). Clustering of cancer in families of patients with primary lung cancer. *Journal of Clinical Epidemiology, 44,* 69–76.

McGinnis, J. M., & Foege, W. H. (1993). Actual causes of death in the United States. *Journal of the American Medical Association, 270,* 2207–2212.

McKinney, E. F., Walton, R. T., Yudkin, P., Fuller, A., Haldar, N. A., Mant, D., et al. (2000). Association between polymorphisms in dopamine metabolic enzymes and tobacco consumption in smokers. *Pharmacogenetics, 10,* 483–491.

Miller, S. M., Shoda, Y., & Hurley, K. (1996). Applying cognitive-social theory to health-protective behavior: Breast self-examination in cancer screening. *Psychological Bulletin, 119,* 70–94.

Mischel, W., & Shoda, Y. (1995). A cognitive-affective system theory of personality: Reconceptualizing situations, dispositions, dynamics, and invariance in personality structure. *Psychological Review, 102,* 246–268.

Mohrenweiser, H. W., & Jones, I. M. (1998). Variation in DNA repair is a factor in cancer susceptibility: A paradigm for the promises and perils of individual and population risk estimation? *Mutation Research, 400,* 15–24.

Mohtashamipur, E., Norpoth, K., & Lieder, F. (1985). Isolation of frameshift mutagens from smokers' urine: Experiences with three concentration methods. *Carcinogenesis, 6,* 783–788.

National Center for Health Statistics. (2001). *Health, United States, 2000 with urban and rural chartbook.* Hyattsville, MD: Public Health Service.

Noble, E. P., Blum, K., Ritchie, T., Montgomery, A., & Sheridan, P. J. (1991). Allelic association of the D2 dopamine receptor gene with receptor-binding characteristics in alcoholism. *Archives of General Psychiatry, 48,* 648–654.

Noble, E. P., St. Jeor, S. T., Ritchie, T., Syndulko, K., St. Jeor, S. C., Fitch, R. J., et al. (1994). D2 dopamine receptor gene and cigarette smoking: A reward gene? *Medical Hypotheses, 42*, 257–260.

Ockene, J., Kristeller, J. L., Goldberg, R., Ockene, I., Merriam, P., & Barrett, S. (1992). Smoking cessation and severity of disease: The Coronary Artery Smoking Intervention Study. *Health Psychology, 11*, 119–126.

Ooi, W. L., Elston, R. C., Chen, V. W., Bailey-Wilson, J. E., & Rothschild, H. (1986). Increased familial risk for lung cancer. *Journal of the National Cancer Institute, 76*, 217–222.

Ostroff, J. S., Hay, J. L., Primavera, L. H., Bivona, P., Cruz, G. D., & LeGeros, R. (1999). Motivating smoking cessation among dental patients: Smokers' interest in biomarker testing for susceptibility to tobacco-related cancers. *Nicotine and Tobacco Research, 1*, 347–355.

Payne, T. J., Smith, P. O., McCracken, L. M., McSherry, W. C., & Antony, M. M. (1994). Assessing nicotine dependence: A comparison of the Fagerström Tolerance Questionnaire (FTQ) with the Fagerström Test for Nicotine Dependence (FTND) in a clinical sample. *Addictive Behaviors, 19*, 307–317.

Prochaska, J. O., Redding, C. A., & Evers, K. E. (1997). The transtheoretical model and stages of change (pp. 60–84). In K. Glanz, F. M. Lewis, & B. K. Rimer (Eds.), *Health behavior and health education: Theory, research, and practice* (2nd ed., pp. 60–84). San Francisco: Jossey-Bass.

Prokhorov, A. V., Hudmon, K. S., & Gritz, E. R. (1997). Promoting smoking cessation among cancer patients: A behavioral model. *Oncology, 11*, 1807–1813.

Rand, C. S., Stitzer, M. L., Bigelow, G. E., & Mead, A. M. (1989). The effects of contingent payment and frequent workplace monitoring on smoking abstinence. *Addictive Behaviors, 14*, 121–128.

Rao, P. A., Pickar, D., Gejman, P. V., Ram, A., Gershon, E. S., & Gelernter, J. (1994). Allelic variation in the D4 dopamine receptor (DRD4) gene does not predict response to clozapine. *Archives of General Psychiatry, 51*, 912–917.

Richardson, G. E., Tucker, M. A., Venzon, D. J., Linnoila, R. I., Phelps, R., Phares, J. C., et al. (1993). Smoking cessation after successful treatment of small-cell lung cancer is associated with fewer smoking-related second primary cancers. *Annals of Internal Medicine, 119*, 383–390.

Risser, N. L., & Belcher, D. W. (1990). Adding spirometry, carbon monoxide, and pulmonary symptom results to smoking cessation counseling: A randomized trial. *Journal of General Internal Medicine, 5*, 16–22.

Ryberg, D., Skaug, V., Hewer, A., Phillips, D. H., Harries, L. W., Wolf, C. R., et al. (1997). Genotypes of glutathione transferase M1 and P1 and their significance for lung DNA adduct levels and cancer risk. *Carcinogenesis, 18*, 1285–1289.

Sabol, S. Z., Nelson, M. L., Fisher, C., Gunzerath, L., Brody, C. L., Hu, S., et al. (1999). A genetic association for cigarette smoking behavior. *Health Psychology, 18*, 7–13.

Schilling, A., Conaway, M. R., Wingate, P. J., Atkins, J. N., Berkowitz, I. M., Clamon, G. H., et al. (1997). Recruiting patients to participate in motivating their relatives to quit smoking. A cancer control study of the CALGB. *Cancer, 79*, 152–160.

Schnoll, R. A., Malstrom, M., James, C., Rothman, R. L., Miller, S. M., Ridge, J. A., et al. (2002a). Correlates of tobacco use among smokers and recent quitters diagnosed with cancer. *Patient Education and Counseling, 46,* 137–145.

Schnoll, R. A., Malstrom, M., James, C., Rothman, R. L., Miller, S. M., Ridge, J. A., et al. (2002b). Processes of change related to smoking behavior among cancer patients. *Cancer Practice, 10,* 11–19.

Schnoll, R. A., & Miller, S. M. (2000). Smoking cessation initiatives for cancer patients. *Primary Care and Cancer, 20,* 10–15.

Sellers, T. A., Bailey-Wilson, J. E., Elston, R. C., Wilson, A. F., Elston, G. Z., Ooi, W. L., et al. (1990). Evidence for mendelian inheritance in the pathogenesis of lung cancer. *Journal of the National Cancer Institute, 82,* 1272–1279.

Shields, P. G. (1999). Molecular epidemiology of lung cancer. *Annals of Oncology, 10,* S7–S11.

Shields, P. G. (2000). Epidemiology of tobacco carcinogenesis. *Current Oncology Reports, 2,* 257–262.

Shields, P. G., Lerman, C., Audrain, J., Bowman, E. D., Main, D., Boyd, N. R., et al. (1998). Dopamine D4 receptors and the risk of cigarette smoking in African-Americans and Caucasians. *Cancer Epidemiology, Biomarkers and Prevention, 7,* 453–458.

Sidransky, D. (1997). Nucleic acid-based methods for the detection of cancer. *Science, 278,* 1054–1059.

Silverman, S. Jr., Gorsky, M., & Greenspan, D. (1983). Tobacco usage in patients with head and neck carcinomas: A follow-up study on habit changes and second primary oral/oropharyngeal cancers. *Journal of the American Dental Association, 106,* 33–35.

Singleton, A. B., Thomson, J. H., Morris, C. M., Court, J. A., Lloyd, S., & Cholerton, S. (1998). Lack of association between the dopamine D2 receptor gene allele DRD2*A1 and cigarette smoking in a United Kingdom population. *Pharmacogenetics, 8,* 125–128.

Spitz, M. R., Shi, H., Yang, F., Hudmon, K. S., Jiang, H., Chamberlain, R. M., et al. (1998). Case-control study of the dopamine D2 receptor gene and smoking status in lung cancer patients. *Journal of the National Cancer Institute, 90,* 358–363.

Spitz, M. R., Wei, Q., Li, G., & Wu, X. (1999). Genetic susceptibility to tobacco carcinogenesis. *Cancer Investigation, 17,* 645–659.

Stevens, M. H., Gardner, J. W., Parkin, J. L., & Johnson, L. P. (1983). Head and neck cancer survival and life-style change. *Archives of Otolaryngology, 109,* 746–749.

Stewart, A. L., King, A. C., Killen, J. D., & Ritter, P. L. (1995). Does smoking cessation improve health-related quality-of-life? *Annals of Behavioral Medicine, 17,* 331–338.

Strecher, V. J., & Rosenstock, I. M. (1997). The health belief model (pp. 41–59). In K. Glanz, F. M. Lewis, & B. K. Rimer (Eds.), *Health behavior and health education: Theory, research, and practice* (2nd ed., pp. 41–59). San Francisco: Jossey-Bass.

Sutton, G. C. (1980). Assortative marriage for smoking habits. *Annals of Human Biology, 7,* 449–456.

Swan, G. E. (1999). Implications of genetic epidemiology for the prevention of tobacco use. *Nicotine and Tobacco Research, 1,* S49–S56.

Tercyak, K. P., Goldman, P., Smith, A., & Audrain, J. (2002). Interacting effects of depression and tobacco advertising receptivity on adolescent smoking. *Journal of Pediatric Psychology, 27,* 145–154.

Tobacco Research Implementation Group. (1998). *Tobacco research implementation plan. Priorities for tobacco research beyond the year 2000.* Bethesda, MD: National Cancer Institute, National Institute of Health.

Tyas, S. L., & Pederson, L. L. (1998). Psychosocial factors related to adolescent smoking: A critical review of the literature. *Tobacco Control, 7,* 409–420.

U.S. Department of Health and Human Services. (1988). *The health consequences of smoking. Nicotine addiction: A report of the Surgeon General, 1988.* DHHS Publication No. (CDC) 88–8406. Rockville, MD: USDHHS, Public Health Service, Centers for Disease Control, Center for Health Promotion and Education, Office on Smoking and Health.

U.S. Department of Health and Human Services. (1989). *Reducing the health consequences of smoking: 25 years of progress. A report of the Surgeon General.* Atlanta, GA: USDHHS, Public Health Service, Centers for Disease Control and Prevention, National Center for Chronic Disease Prevention and Health Promotion, Office on Smoking and Health.

U.S. Department of Health and Human Services. (1990). *The health benefits of smoking cessation: A report of the Surgeon General.* DHHS Publication No. (CDC) 90–8416. Rockville, MD: USDHHS, Public Health Service, Centers for Disease Control, Center for Chronic Disease Prevention and Health Promotion, Office on Smoking and Health.

U.S. Department of Health and Human Services. (1994). *Preventing tobacco use among young people: A report of the surgeon general.* Atlanta, GA: USDHHS, Public Health Service, Centers for Disease Control and Prevention, National Center for Chronic Disease Prevention and Health Promotion, Office on Smoking and Health.

U.S. Department of Health and Human Services. (1998). *Tobacco use among US racial/ethnic minority groups—African Americans, American Indians and Alaska Natives, Asian Americans and Pacific Islanders, and Hispanics: A report of the surgeon general.* Atlanta, GA: USDHHS, Centers for Disease Control and Prevention, National Center for Chronic Disease Prevention and Health Promotion, Office on Smoking and Health.

U.S. Department of Health and Human Services. (2000). *Healthy people 2010: Understanding and improving health* (2nd ed). Washington, DC: USDHHS.

U.S. Environmental Protection Agency. (1992). *Respiratory health effects of passive smoking: Lung cancer and other disorders.* Washington, DC: USEPA Report No. EPA/600/6-90/006F.

van Tol, H. H., Wu, C. M., Guan, H. C., Ohara, K., Bunzow, J. R., Civelli, O., et al. (1992). Multiple dopamine D4 receptor variants in the human population. *Nature, 358,* 149–152.

Velicer, W. F., Prochaska, J. O., Bellis, J. M., DiClemente, C. C., Rossi, J. S., Fava, J. L., et al. (1993). An expert system intervention for smoking cessation. *Addictive Behaviors, 18,* 269–290.

Velicer, W. F., Prochaska, J. O., Fava, J. L., Norman, G. J., & Redding, C. A. (1998). Smoking cessation and stress management: Applications of the transtheoretical model of behavior change. *Homeostatis, 38,* 216–233.

Velicer, W. F., Prochaska, J. O., Rossi, J. S., & Snow, M. G. (1992). Assessing outcome in smoking cessation studies. *Psychological Bulletin, 111,* 23–41.

Walker, W. B., & Franzini, L. R. (1985). Low-risk aversive group treatments, physiological feedback, and booster sessions for smoking cessation. *Behavior Therapy, 16,* 263–274.

West, R., McEwen, A., Bolling, K., & Owen, L. (2001). Smoking cessation and smoking patterns in the general population: A 1-year follow-up. *Addiction, 96,* 891–902.

Wolf, C. R., Smith, G., & Smith, R. L. (2000). Science, medicine, and the future: Pharmacogenetics. *British Medical Journal, 320,* 987–990.

Woody, G. E., Cottler, L. B., & Cacciola, J. (1993). Severity of dependence: Data from the DSM-IV field trials. *Addiction, 88,* 1573–1579.

Chapter 13

Genetics and Reproductive Issues
Psychosocial Issues and Prenatal Testing

Linda Hammer Burns

THE LAST HALF OF THE 20TH CENTURY SAW STUNNING ADVANCEMENTS IN reproductive medicine and genetics. The original goals of medical genetics and reproductive medicine were to maximize fertility and provide appropriate prenatal genetic testing and counseling. These goals supported those of most expectant parents to have a baby with maximum health and minimum defects. With the assistance of reproductive and genetic medicine, individuals who historically would have remained childless can now become pregnant through a variety of interventions. These techniques can also detect many genetic disorders via prenatal diagnosis and treat some of those disorders through gene therapies.

Understandably, these reproductive advances can influence consumer (and even professional) expectations, for some fostering unrealistic or misguided beliefs about feasibility, success, and applicability of any given technology. In addition, the ability of reproductive medicine and medical genetics to facilitate the conception of a healthy baby can be fraught with moral dilemmas and technological complications, triggering struggles at various levels of society from individuals to policy makers (Bonnickson, 2001; Massey, Slayden, Shapiro, & Wininger, 2001; Reame, 2000; Soules, 2001). This chapter addresses issues related to genetics and reproduction, including preconception genetic counseling and testing, prenatal genetic counseling and testing, genetically affected pregnancy and pregnancy loss, multiple pregnancies following in vitro fertilization (IVF), genetic causes of infertility, the use of assisted reproductive technologies for genetic reasons, genetic counseling and screening of potential gamete and embryo donors, and interprofessional collaboration.

GENETIC COUNSELING
AND REPRODUCTIVE ISSUES

Counselors working in reproductive medicine may be genetic counselors or mental health professionals (psychologists, family therapists, social workers, psychiatrists). Both infertility and genetic counselors provide expert advice, patient education, and act as consultants to members of the reproductive treatment team consultants. The primary goal of genetic counseling is to impart scientific information and guidance about genetic diagnoses, disorders, and heritability; genetic counseling traditionally has not involved psychotherapy. Shiloh (1996) identified the key aspects of genetic counseling as helping to identify the meanings of genetic information, patients' and families' coping with a genetic condition, recall and comprehension of information conveyed in genetic counseling, and decision making. The primary goal of infertility counselors (who are licensed mental health professionals) is the psychological evaluation and treatment as well as education and preparation of individuals and couples undergoing treatment for infertility. Four roles delineated for infertility counselors in the field of reproductive genetics are (1) providing psychological services to patients, (2) consulting with genetic counseling teams, (3) training genetic counselors, and (4) researching the psychological aspects of genetic counseling (Burns & Leroy, 1999). In a survey of Midwestern infertility clinics, 50% of the clinics stated that they employed a mental health professional, while only 22% stated that they employed a genetic counselor. However, 96% of the clinics that did not employ a genetic counselor had a genetic counselor off-site to which they commonly referred patients (Swanson, 2003).

The pedigree, much like the genogram (see Chapter 4), is used by reproductive health psychologists and infertility counselors to gather psychosocial information, evaluate family dynamics and relational patterns, and document reproductive genetic problems such as family incidence of reproductive loss (e.g., repeated miscarriage), incidence of genetic disorders (e.g., sibling with translocation), and evidence of genetic reproductive disorders (e.g., Y chromosome deletion). Genograms and pedigrees can be used by professionals to identify basic themes such as attachments, emotions, anger, gender/sexuality, and culture/religion (DeMaria, Weeks, & Hof, 1999). Eunpu (1995) developed a list of questions that assist in family assessment:

1. What is the family's expectation regarding childbearing?
2. What messages were given about the importance or role of children?

3. What messages were given about abortion and contraception?
4. Were there conflicts between family attitudes/beliefs and those of your community, cultural, or religious group?
5. What messages, myths, or beliefs were given about pregnancy loss?
6. What were the family's experiences of pregnancy loss or of childhood death?
7. What does it mean to meet your family's expectations for childbearing? (p. 122)

Eunpu also suggested that professionals use genograms or pedigrees to explore adoption, infertility, and pregnancy loss and their impact on family structure and process, the couple's desire for children, and their relationships with extended families. As much as possible, infertile couples benefit from being treated as a unit (versus individual psychotherapy). Reproductive counseling should include education to facilitate decision making regarding treatment and family-building alternatives, skill development for dealing with medical specialists, supportive counseling, stress-reduction techniques, bibliotherapy, and identification of support within the family and community, including relevant support groups for identified genetic disorders.

While typically it is a genetic counselor, nurse practitioner, or physician who identifies a genetic disorder in the process of taking a patient's family history, it is not infrequent that an infertility counselor's genogram identifies a disorder, pattern, or issue that becomes an important part of the patient's diagnosis and treatment plan (DeMaria et al., 1999). The diagnosis of a genetic disorder within the context of a reproductive event can precipitate a crisis, sometimes destabilizing individuals, families, and marriages (Leon, 1995). A couple presenting for reproductive counseling for genetic reasons may explore their feelings about raising a child affected with a known genetic disorder and address feelings of guilt, anger, and ambivalence. Decruyenaere (1997) suggested psychotherapeutic interventions for these couples to improve their acquisition and recall of information, become more aware of the psychological defenses that influence their perception of risk, and provide enough time to process complex medical information.

Family factors are often influential in the psychosocial adjustment of the infertile couple, especially if the genetic diagnosis affects other family members or has implications for the reproductive future of siblings (see Chapter 4). Negative or inaccurate beliefs about heredity, disability, and medical technologies can limit a couple's options and increase their emotional distress. Alternatively, healthy mental hygiene habits can facilitate adjustment by reinforcing effective coping skills and encouraging adaptability and emotional warmth (Enupu, 1997).

Genetic testing and counseling may be used to identify the cause of infertility for repeated miscarriage, provide information that helps couples facilitate family-building decisions, or screen potential gamete donors. Areas in which genetic and infertility counseling intertwine include the following:

1. Preconception genetic test counseling
2. Prenatal genetic counseling and testing
3. Genetically affected pregnancy or pregnancy losses
4. Genetic causes of infertility
5. Use of assisted reproductive technologies (IVF, donor, preimplantation genetic diagnosis) for genetic reasons
6. Genetic screening of potential gamete or embryo donors

PRECONCEPTION GENETIC
TEST COUNSELING

Karen and Thomas Aitkin (ages 27 and 30) had been married for 3 years. Mrs. Aitkin's father and uncle had Huntington disease. Prior to attempting pregnancy, Mr. and Mrs. Aitkin decided to pursue genetic counseling and testing in order to understand their risk of having an affected child. Both partners felt they would not proceed with a pregnancy if Mrs. Aitkin was found to have the Huntington's mutation. In fact, Mrs. Aitkin was found not to have the mutation and the couple went on to have one child. However, Mrs. Aitkin remains worried about her six siblings and their children, all of whom have chosen not to be tested.

Preconception genetic counseling of men and women who are considering pregnancy refers to their preparation and education about any definable increased risk for a fetal genetic disorder (Bernstein, Sanghvi, & Markatz, 2000). Preconception genetic counseling helps couples accomplish these tasks:

- Comprehend the medical facts, including any genetic diagnosis, probable cause of the disorder, and available management
- Appreciate the way in which heredity contributes to the disorder and the risk of occurrence or recurrence in specific relatives
- Understand the options for dealing with the risk of recurrence, including prenatal genetic diagnosis
- Make the best possible adjustment to the disorder in any affected family member

This process should be voluntary and available to all women receiving prenatal care (Van den Veyer, 2002). It is typically recommended for women over the age of 35 (due to the increased risk of Down syndrome and other age-related chromosomal problems), men over the age of 46 (due to increased unstable DNA structure affecting fertility), and patients with known familial genetic disorders. It is also recommended for patients who would benefit from education about preventable reproductive problems, such as the negative impact of alcohol, illegal and recreational drugs, and tobacco on fertility and fetal development (Haidl, Jung, & Schill, 1996; Jolly, Sebire, Harris, Robinson, & Regan, 2000) (see Table 13.1).

Preconception genetic counseling offers couples the opportunity to consider any genetic risks and plan their family accordingly, as was the case for Mr. and Mrs. Aitkin. Although her siblings preferred not to know their genetic risk or that of their children, Mrs. Aitkin did want to know. She did not want to feel responsible if her offspring were to develop Huntington's because she passed on the mutation.

PRENATAL GENETIC COUNSELING AND TESTING

Tracy and Donald Beacon (ages 38 and 35) had been married for 10 years but had been unable to conceive. They eventually conceived with infertility

Table 13.1 Indications for Genetic Counseling and Possible Prenatal Testing

Mother over 35 years of age at expected date of confinement

High or low maternal serum AFP screen

Family history of X-linked disorder in male related to mother through female family member

Member of ethnic group in which carrier screening for common disorder is available

Maternal illness

Exposure to medications or substance use

Two or more first-trimester miscarriages

Abnormal finding on ultrasound

Parental anxiety (primarily for reassurance)

Note. From Allen, J. F. (1991). A guide to genetic counseling. *Journal of the American Academy of Physician Assistants, 4,* 136. Reprinted by permission of the American Academy of Physician Assistants.

treatments and decided to undergo prenatal testing because of Mrs. Beacon's age. Blood tests were normal but the ultrasound revealed that the fetus had a very severe form of spina bifida. While Mr. and Mrs. Beacon were struggling to decide whether to terminate this wanted pregnancy, Mrs. Beacon miscarried. The couple tried to conceive for 2 years following the miscarriage, again with significant medical treatments. The couple eventually conceived naturally, much to their surprise. Mrs. Beacon again underwent prenatal testing including ultrasound, which this time revealed a normal daughter who was delivered at full term.

Prenatal genetic testing is useful when a disorder has been well defined, the prevalence of the disorder has been established, a remedy is available, screening is available and cost effective, prenatal screening is safe and simple, and the prenatal testing has low false positive rates for high detection rates (Van den Veyer, 2002). Prenatal screening measures are performed early in pregnancy for the purposes of detecting chromosomal problems and fetal anomalies related to (1) advanced maternal age, (2) family history of a genetic disease, (3) two or more unexplained miscarriages or prior children with birth defects, or (4) exposure to potentially harmful substances. Prenatal testing involves procedures ranging from blood tests to the insertion of a needle into the uterus. Noninvasive forms of prenatal testing include blood tests that assess maternal serum alpha-fetoprotein (MASAFP or simply AFP) with triple screen (measuring human chorionic gonadotropin, unconjugated estriol, and inhibin A that can date with fetal maturity) and ultrasound (also known as sonogram or sonography), which can detect some physical abnormalities. Invasive prenatal testing measures to detect genetic disorders and other fetal abnormalities include chorionic villus sampling (CVS) which samples DNA, fetoscopy (a fiber-optic scope), amniocentesis (tests amniotic fluid), late placental biopsy (late CVS), and fetal blood sampling. First-trimester testing for suspected problems at 10–12 weeks of gestation typically involves blood tests, ultrasound, and CVS. While first-trimester blood tests and ultrasounds are less physically invasive (and therefore less risky to the pregnancy), rates of false positives are high (5–10%), which may require repeat testing. CVS is typically less invasive than amniocentesis and occurs at an earlier stage of pregnancy (typically at 10–12 weeks of gestation), with comparable accuracy of amniocentesis. However, like amniocentesis, CVS carries a risk of triggering miscarriage. The most accurate and least risky prenatal testing remains amniocentesis when performed at 15–16 weeks gestation. Late placental biopsy and fetal sampling can be performed as late as 40 weeks of gestation, but involve some risks to the pregnancy, mother, and fetus.

Prenatal testing typically is not a single event but a process of a variety of procedures administered throughout the pregnancy. In addition, no single test or procedure is 100% accurate and without risks. False positives and procedural side effects can wreak emotional havoc on expectant parents. In short, prenatal testing offers potential parents information: whether distressing or reassuring, it can facilitate grieving about the death of their fetus via stillbirth or neonatal death or giving birth to a less than healthy baby. By contrast, prenatal testing can facilitate the expectant parents' attachment to their baby, for example, through ultrasound images of their "normal" baby.

The postinfertility pregnancy is a highly valued, purposeful pregnancy typically achieved after significant investment of time, money, effort, and emotion. Frequently, the prospect of postpregnancy complications at this point seems remote to expectant parents. Prenatal testing can often make the postinfertility pregnancy a tentative pregnancy in which attachment to the pregnancy and fetus is delayed, the experience of pregnancy altered, and expectations of parenthood influenced (Rothman, 1994). It can alter the experience of pregnancy (for better or worse) for many previously infertile women by both validating the existence of the baby (e.g., ultrasound, photos, confirmation of gender) and/or invalidating the baby's health (e.g., detection of fetal anomaly, absence of fetal heartbeat; Ji et al., 2005; Sandelowski, 1988).

Frequently, infertile couples are unaware of genetic risks (especially those related to age) because the focus of their attention has been on getting pregnant, not on the challenges and risks of pregnancy itself (Glazer, 1995). Even the confirmation of pregnancy after infertility is less an event than an ambiguous process in which monitoring with repeated blood tests and ultrasounds can heighten anxiety about a successful outcome. Pregnancy after infertility can involve myriad medical technologies to evaluate and manage what can be high-risk pregnancies. This was clearly the case for Mr. and Mrs. Beacon, with their first pregnancy, in which prenatal testing brought the worst possible news for them. Their focus on getting pregnant had left them unprepared for the possibility something could be wrong with their pregnancy, let alone something as dramatic as spina bifida. Their struggles with grief and decision making about terminating a wanted pregnancy were heightened by their history of infertility and the uncertainty of whether they would be able to achieve another pregnancy.

Schover, Collins, Quigley, Blankstein, and Kanoti (1998) found that the majority of couples undergoing IVF were reluctant to use prenatal testing because they intended to continue the pregnancy even if faced with severe fetal abnormalities. Of these couples, 82% found the triple blood tests acceptable, 47% planned to have amniocentesis or chorionic villi sampling, and only 6% said they would terminate an affected pregnancy. Sandelowski, Harris, and Holditch-Davis (1991) compared the experience of prenatal testing in infertile and fertile couples and found that for infertile couples, prior infertility affected prenatal decision making in that infertile couples cited a greater variety of reasons for declining amniocentesis. Advanced maternal age was the most important determining factor in their decisions to proceed with amniocentesis. These couples balanced the known value of the pregnancy with the putative value of information obtainable from amniocentesis and the risks of the procedure itself. They concluded that because infertile couples were accustomed to failed effort and loss, they were more likely to highly value the pregnancy and the baby and, as a result, were more keenly aware of how amniocentesis could either enhance or depreciate it.

Zuzkar (1987), in a review of the psychological impact of prenatal diagnosis of a fetal anomaly, found two opposing perspectives in expectant parents: prenatal diagnosis as helping emotional preparation and prenatal diagnosis as prolonging the period of emotional upset. Most parents experience a mourning process following prenatal diagnosis or birth of a disabled child, in which they grieve the loss of the expected, healthy child (Solnit & Stark, 1961). Advance knowledge of the problem may provide some measure of control and preparation for the events surrounding the birth, enhancing long-term coping and family adjustment (Allen & Mulhauser, 1995). To summarize, for many previously infertile couples, decisions to proceed with prenatal genetic testing or counseling are influenced by past infertility experiences, mourning the losses of infertility, personal identity issues, medical recommendations or indications, and willingness of either partner to acknowledge and accept a genetic problem related to their infertility (Shapiro & Djurdijnovic, 1988).

GENETICALLY AFFECTED PREGNANCY
AND PREGNANCY LOSSES

Mary and Arthur Lawrence (ages 27 and 29) had experienced two miscarriages and several years of infertility when Mrs. Lawrence became pregnant using infertility treatment. During a routine ultrasound as part of her obstetrical care, the fetus was determined to have Potter's syndrome as well as a number of other major anomalies. Potter's syndrome, also known as renal agenesis, is one of several kidney abnormalities in which the fetus's kidneys fail to develop, resulting in failure of the lungs and other organs to properly develop. It is a fatal condition in which babies are stillborn or die soon after birth. Mr. and Mrs. Lawrence decided to terminate the pregnancy, as it was clear the baby had only days to live in utero. Genetic testing later revealed that in addition to Potter's syndrome, the baby had a translocation that was later found in Mr. Lawrence and his father.

The decision to terminate their much-wanted pregnancy was difficult for Mr. and Mrs. Lawrence. Although Mrs. Lawrence would have preferred to let the pregnancy take its course, two factors influenced their decision to terminate: (1) the need for live tissue for the most accurate genetic testing and (2) the fact that continuing this pregnancy would mean time lost toward attempts to achieve another pregnancy. Time had felt like an ever-present burden to Mr. and Mrs. Lawrence, a feeling shared by many infertile couples. Now, finally pregnant with their first child, time again became a factor. If they waited for the fetus to die in utero, identifying the genetic disorder affecting their baby would be more difficult, and yet this was a piece of information that might also help them know why they were infertile and perhaps offer a solution or treatment alternative. In fact, when genetic testing revealed that a translocation in Mr. Lawrence had caused their fetus's genetic disorder, the couple pursued parenthood via donated sperm, a procedure they would not have thought necessary had they not obtained the genetic diagnosis.

This case illustrates the myriad psychological decisions and reactions following the termination of a pregnancy due to fetal anomaly. The grieving response of a couple to the termination of a wanted and/or affected pregnancy appears to be more similar to that following spontaneous miscarriages than to most lesser responses to other elective terminations (Leon, 1995; Lloyd & Laurence, 1985; Zeanah et al, 1993). They are rarely protracted or disturbed (Leon, 1995). However, Zeanah, Dailey, Rosenblatt, and Saller (1993) found poor social support predicts protracted grief. Blumberg, Golbus, and Hanson (1975) found a high rate of mild depression following termination of a pregnancy for genetic reasons. However, study participants said they would choose the same course of action in another pregnancy. Risk factors for significant psychological distress following the loss of a wanted pregnancy after infertility treatment include prior history of depression, poor social support, ambivalence or coercion about the termination, and disturbed marital relationship (Stotland, 2000).

Even when a couple is confident that termination of the pregnancy is the right decision for them, some find ending a wanted pregnancy devastating (Magyari, Wedehase, Ifft, & Callanan, 1987). Adding to the distress is the variety of decisions the couple must consider, such as termination techniques, termination facility and caregivers, autopsy, genetic testing of fetal tissue, disposal of fetal remains, and the lack of social support. Typically, both practical and psychological benefits exist for infertile couples pursuing genetic counseling following a fetal loss, even though the information uncovered may be provisional or difficult to accept (Leon, 1995). Chromosomal problems causing miscarriage or other pregnancy loss may be due to a chromosome problem in one or both parents (thereby increasing the risk of a subsequent pregnancy loss), an error in cell division ("packaging error"), or to a problem with the egg or sperm. Genetic causes of fetal loss may be sporadic, chromosomally abnormal, or recurrent. Sporadic miscarriage occurs in 12–15% of all clinically recognized pregnancies. Parental chromosome analysis has shown that at least 50% of clinically recognized pregnancy losses and 7% of all stillbirths are due to chromosomal abnormalities (Digman, 1987; Geraedts, 1996; Tho & McDonough, 1994).

Schover and colleagues (1998) found that couples undergoing IVF were significantly more likely to opt for prenatal testing if they would consider terminating a pregnancy should the fetus have a severe genetic abnormality. Roman Catholic couples tended to have more conservative attitudes about pregnancy termination than those of other religions. However, neither socioeconomic status nor whether the infertility factor was male or female were predictors of a couple's attitudes. A review of studies from 1994 to 2004 found that the vast majority of couples choose to terminate pregnancies with severe abnormalities after prenatal genetic testing and usually make the termination decision before knowing the results of genetic testing (Sjogren & Uddenberg, 1988; Wertz, 1998). Termination rates range from 73 to 90% for prenatal diagnosis of Down syndrome to 100% for prenatal detection of anencephaly or spina bifida (Robinson, Bender, & Linden, 1989), but for less severe defects, termination rates are lower (Robinson et al, 1989; Verp, Bombard, Simpson, & Elias, 1988). Similarly, a study of 53,000 pregnancies at a university hospital between 1984 and 1997 assessed the degree to which prenatal knowledge of fetal anomalies and sociodemographic characteristics impacted decision making about outcome (Schechtman, Gray, Baty, & Rothman, 2002). This study found that the severity of anomalies directly correlated with termination rates and that severity of central nervous system anomalies were most likely to lead to abortion. Older and more educated mothers were also more likely to terminate than younger, less educated mothers.

Recurrent Pregnancy Loss

Couples generally receive a formal genetic evaluation for recurrent pregnancy loss if they have had any of the following: (1) two or more miscarriages, (2) a miscarriage plus a stillbirth or malformed fetus, or (3) a defective baby (Tho & McDonough, 1994). Genetic counseling following pregnancy loss usually involves chromosome studies (karotyping) of both parents, a detailed family history, and when available, fetal tissue, photographs of the fetus, radiographic studies, fetal autopsy reports, laboratory testing, assessment of the placenta and cord, and other studies as appropriate (Curry, 1992). Assessment of the potential parents should include family history of genetic disorders, maternal and paternal age, and family history of infertility, miscarriage, and stillbirth.

Multiple Pregnancies Following IVF

Another form of pregnancy loss is the reduction of a multiple pregnancy either because there are too many fetuses to safely carry to full term or because an anomaly has been detected in one or more of the fetuses. In this circumstance, prenatal testing can provide information and guidance in decision making, helping couples determine whether they should reduce the pregnancy, if there is a fetal anomaly, and how many fetuses could safely continue with this pregnancy. In a study of genetically high-risk patients, 86% became pregnant—with a 67% multiple pregnancy rate—following the use of assisted reproduction (Brambati, Tului, Baldi, & Guercilena, 1995). CVS and karotyping were done before the pregnancies were reduced to singletons or twins either because a genetic disease was present or to reduce risk of prematurity. All babies were born at term and healthy. The rate of chromosomal disorders was higher (7.2%) in the study series than in singleton pregnancies not undergoing fetal reduction (Brambati et al., 1995). Acceptability of prenatal testing and multifetal reduction was very high (90%).

It should be noted that higher-order multiples are often an iatrogenic condition—the result of more than two to three embryos being transferred. There is a growing recognition that this practice is dangerous to mothers and infants, potentially causing miscarriage, prematurity, preeclampsia, and gestational diabetes (American Society for Reproductive Medicine [ASRM], 2003; ESHRE Task Force on Ethics and Law, 2003; Lee & Morgan, 2001). Many physicians are voluntarily working to avoid multiple pregnancies by limiting the number of embryos they are willing to transfer and by better educating their patients about the risks and dangers of a multiple pregnancy. In addition, regulatory agencies (e.g., in the United Kingdom) and legislation (e.g., in Italy) have addressed this issue by restricting the number of embryos that can be transferred during any given IVF or frozen embryo transfer (FET) cycle.

GENETIC CAUSES OF INFERTILITY

Maria and Herman Austin (ages 27 and 41) had been married a year and half when they sought medical advice regarding fertility. After a brief medical evaluation, Mr. Austin was diagnosed with Klinefelter's syndrome (the presence of an extra Y chromosome). Mr. Austin was disappointed for reproductive reasons but relieved because with testosterone replacement therapy, he felt physically better than he had in years. Mrs. Austin, who was from Bolivia and had met her husband through a "pen pal" organization, stated she was comfortable with whatever reproductive choice her husband preferred. However, it was not clear that she could clearly understand the diagnosis or the alternatives that were being presented. As a couple with limited resources, they decided on the use of donor sperm to start a family (versus IVF, other medical procedures, or adoption, which financially were not feasible for them).

In a survey of Midwestern infertility clinics, it was found that the most common genetic causes of male factor infertility were microdeletion of the Y chromosome, congenital bilateral absence of the vas deferens (CBAVD), chromosomal translocations, and Klinefelter's syndrome (Swanson, 2003). Men with Klinefelter's syndrome typically have problems with language impairment, obesity, breast enlargement, small testicles, infertility, hypogonadism, and decreased sexual libido, although testosterone replacement therapy can improve symptoms resulting from testosterone deficiency. The most common genetic causes of female factor infertility were Turner's syndrome and chromosomal translocations (Swanson, 2003; see Tables 13.2 and 13.3). Turner's syndrome is a relatively common genetic disorder affecting many body systems. It is associated with short stature, failure to mature sexually, learning difficulties, skeletal abnormalities, hearing loss, liver dysfunction, heart and kidney abnormalities, infertility, and thyroid dysfunction. In addition, there is increasing awareness of genetic and congenital anomalies after IVF, either because of genetic disorders in the parents or as a result of the procedure itself (Coutifaris, 2004).

Genetic factors—including single-gene disorders, chromosome abnormalities, or genetic disorders affecting the reproductive tract (e.g., Klinefelter's syndrome, Turner's syndrome)—have long been known as a cause of primary infertility. However, the extent of genetic causes of infertility has come to light only more recently. Genetically based

Table 13.2   Genetic Causes of Male Factor Infertility

Y chromosome microdeletion

CBAVD (congenital bilateral absence of vas deferens)

Translocation carrier

Klinefelter syndrome

Kall syndrome

Androgen insensitivity syndrome

45,X/46,XY

Kartagener syndrome

Myotonic dystrophy

Noonan syndrome

46,XX male

Note. From Swanson, A. L. (2003). *The provision of genetic counseling services for patients with a genetic cause of infertility.* Unpublished master's thesis, University of Minnesota, Minneapolis, MN.

Table 13.3   Genetic Causes of Female Factor Infertility

Turner syndrome

Translocation carrier

Inherited thrombophilia

Androgen insensitivity syndrome

Fragile X syndrome

X chromosome deletion

Other: polycystic ovary disease, endometriosis, premature ovarian failure, advanced maternal age

Note. From Swanson, A. L. (2003). *The provision of genetic counseling services for patients with a genetic cause of infertility.* Unpublished master's thesis, University of Minnesota, Minneapolis, MN.

infertility can reveal other health issues, the possibility of transmission of that genetic disorder to offspring, and the identification of a genetic disorder in other family members. Understandably, this ripple effect can have significant psychological, social, and medical consequences for infertile individuals and couples.

Recent discoveries of male factor infertility range from gonadotropin-releasing hormone deficiency to the absence of sperm (azoospermia; Dohle et al., 2002; Mak & Jarvi, 1996). Obstructive azoospermia as a cause of infertility was found in 7–15% of infertile men who had microdeletions of the Yq chromosome (Cram et al., 2000; de Vries et al., 2001). Obstructive azoospermia can now be treated by surgically removing sperm from the testes and inserting a single sperm into an oocyte via intracytoplasmic sperm injection (ICSI) as part of an IVF procedure. However, ICSI runs the risk of transmitting a possible genetic defect to a son. Cram and associates (2000) studied 99 consecutive ICSI-conceived boys. They found all of the sons inherited their father's Yq deletion. The willingness to have a genetically shared child even if it involves transmitting a genetic disorder has been demonstrated in many other studies (Levron et al., 2001).

The most common form of obstructive azoospermia occurs in about 1–2% of infertile men with CBAVD, also sometimes referred to as genital cystic fibrosis. Men with CBAVD are often asymptomatic. For those men who are identified as having CBAVD, it is recommended that the man's female partner be tested for cystic fibrosis carrier status. If both partners carry a cystic fibrosis mutation, their risk of miscarriage is 25% and their risk of having a child with cystic fibrosis is 25%. It is interesting to note that even with education about genetic risk, 71% of couples in which the man had CBAVD had no interest in receiving genetic counseling (Schover et al., 1998).

Genetic causes of infertility in women can result in recurrent pregnancy loss, gynecological malignancies, genetic disorders such as cystic fibrosis, and gynecological anomalies such as Turner's syndrome. Pregnancy losses due to genetic factors can involve a wide spectrum of abortive processes that occur at fertilization of the ovum, cleavage of the zygote, implantation of the blastocyst, or during embryonic development prior to fetal viability (Tho & McDonough, 1994). The most common cause of reproductive failure due to genetic factors in women is advanced maternal age—although women are often misinformed about this. Maternal age increases the risk of aneuploidy (an incorrect number of chromosomes as in trisomy 21 or Down syndrome and trisomy 18). In one study, Ma and colleagues (1994) found 42.7% chromosomal abnormalities evident in discarded oocytes following failed IVF cycles. Other genetic causes of female factor infertility are as noted in Table 13.3.

Although genetic causes are a small percentage of the etiology of infertility in men or women, when they occur they can be significant because the genetic cause may be a disorder that has significant health consequences, as was the case for Mr. Austin, whose Klinefelter's syndrome had been undiagnosed and untreated until he tried to conceive.

Very frequently, treatment options for couples with genetic causes of infertility involve assisted reproductive technology or donated gametes, as was the case for Mr. and Mrs. Austin.

Infertility is a multifaceted, intergenerational developmental crisis impacting familial and social relationships, marital functioning, economic well-being, and individual mental health. Assisted reproduction offers treatment options and family-building alternatives for patients who, in the past, would have remained childless. But assisted reproduction, particularly when it involves a third party, is not without consequences—financial, emotional, physical, and relational. For this reason, patient preparation and education are paramount. Pretreatment counseling is recommended or required by an increasing number of professional organizations, governments, and infertility clinics. Families and children created via these technologies are also seeking assistance in dealing with the psychosocial legacy of third-party conception. This area is a new frontier for medical and mental health professionals to provide consultation and therapy to families created under unique circumstances with unique psychosocial needs, issues, and family dynamics (Burns & Covington, 1999).

USE OF ASSISTED REPRODUCTIVE
TECHNOLOGIES FOR GENETIC REASONS

Sara and John Detroit (ages 34 and 37) had been married for 7 years and had experienced eight miscarriages, all at 8 weeks or less. Every infertility workup had failed to uncover the cause of the miscarriages. Mr. and Mrs. Detroit were referred for genetic testing and counseling, which determined that Mrs. Detroit was a carrier of a translocation so rare it had never been previously reported. As a result, it could not be determined with complete certitude that (1) the translocation was the cause of the couple's miscarriages, (2) how or if the translocation would affect any subsequent pregnancies, and (3) the impact on any offspring if pregnancy could be successfully maintained. After some grieving, the couple decided to pursue parenthood using a donated egg (oocyte). Mrs. Detroit became pregnant on the first attempt and delivered a healthy baby boy without incident.

While egg donation continues to be far more complicated than sperm donation, it is an increasingly popular alternative for women who face infertility for genetic reasons. Although Mr. and Mrs. Detroit were shocked to learn that their only reproductive alternative was a donated egg, this did give them the opportunity to have a child that was genetically linked to Mr. Detroit. Furthermore, Mrs. Detroit could feel she contributed to the birth of her child through the biological link of pregnancy. For many infertile women, donor oocyte and donor embryo pregnancies are preferred means of reproduction. Despite its growing popularity, however, oocyte donation (OD) is not universaly available, accessible, or legally allowable and remains a medically complicated and financially costly reproductive alternative for infertile couples.

Gamete Donation

The use of donated gametes is not a treatment for infertility because it means that an infertile couple is unable to have a child that is genetically related to both of them. Instead, parenthood achieved via donated gametes allows them to become parents, allowing one partner to be genetically linked to the child both partners will parent. It also allows the couple to share the pregnancy experience and, as such, control the prenatal environment. Although the use of donated sperm has been an available treatment since the late 1880s and is typically inexpensive and anonymous, there is now a push toward greater openness. The primary reasons men and women donate gametes are altruism and some financial remuneration. Questions about disclosure, especially telling the child, are important considerations for potential parents. Their unwillingness or inability to consider these issues may be an indication that they are not prepared for this form of parenthood.

Pretreatment counseling is required by legislation in Canada (Assisted Human Reproduction Act, 2004; Blyth et al., 2004); recommended by legislation in the United Kingdom and Australia, and recommended by professional guidelinesin the United States and Europe (ASRM, 2002a, b, c; ESHRE, 2002). Unlike sperm donation, which was historically anonymous and secret, oocyte donation began with sister-to-sister oocyte donation (Lessor, Reitz, Balmaceda, & Asch, 1990). Despite legislative, professional, and consumer movements promoting openness and disclosure, researchers have continued to find that the majority of gamete recipients and donors prefer anonymity and privacy (ASRM, 2004; Bertrand-Servais, Letur-Konirsch, Raoul-Duval, & Frydman, 1993; Greenfield & Klock, 2004; Khamsi, Endman, Lacanna, & Wong, 1997; Lessor et al., 1990). Nevertheless, the 20th century saw an evolution of public policy from secrecy and anonymity to openness and mandated disclosure, government-established donor registries (Assisted Human Reproduction Act, 2004; Blyth, Crawshaw, & Daniels, 2004), and the elimination of donor anonymity in various countries (e.g., United Kingdom, Canada) (Assisted Reproduction Act, 2004; HFEA, 2004) and parts of Australia. In the United States, the ethics committee of ASRM recommended that donor gamete offspring be informed of the circumstances of their conception (ASRM, 2004). Still, many couples (often influenced by cultural beliefs) pursue third-party reproduction only if it is anonymous for all parties, leading to a dramatic increase in "reproductive tourism" as patients cross national or international borders to pursue treatment that is psychosocially, economically, or legally more compatible to them (Pennings, 2004).

In a 1998 study, Schover and colleagues found that only 19% of couples at risk of transmitting a genetic disorder would consider using a donated gamete (either oocyte or sperm) to avoid transmitting their own genetic disorder to their child. In this study, 12% of the men had CBAVD; 40% of the women were over the age of 35; and 15% had another genetic disorder (e.g., Huntington disease). In a prior study, Schover and colleagues (1996) reported that the chief reason couples chose donor insemination was finances. If a couple could afford IVF/ICSI, they almost universally preferred to have a genetically shared child. Not one of the men in the study (including men with cystic fibrosis mutations) considered using donor insemination to prevent the transmission of the possible genetic anomaly to the child, nor did the men consider transmission of the genetic defect problematic.

Embryo Donation

Embryos can be created by combining donated oocytes and sperm or are the result of "extra" embryos from an IVF cycle, in which one couple chooses to donate them (in a form of prenatal adoption) to another infertile couple. Embryo donation has been an available treatment in parts of the United States, Australia, Asia, and several European countries since the 1990s, although legislation prohibits it in several countries and a majority of states in the United States (International Infertility Counseling Association, 2004). While there are hundreds of thousands of frozen embryos in storage throughout the world, there remain significant barriers to their "prenatal adoption": (1) the majority of frozen embryos do not survive the thawing process; (2) embryos must be legally relinquished by the conceiving coupled and adopted by the carrying/intended parents; and (3) it is unlikely that the embryos or their genetic parents underwent genetic screening or testing prior to conception.

Surrogacy and Gestational Carriers

Gestational carrier and surrogacy pregnancies are increasingly common reproductive alternatives for women who have no uterus due to illness (e.g., cancer) or for congenital reasons (e.g., Kuster-Rokintansky-Hauser syndrome). Couples might consider surrogacy (with the use of the surrogate's uterus and oocytes) as a means of avoiding the transmission of a genetic disorder in the mother (e.g., cystic fibrosis). Conception in surrogacy typically involves insemination. By contrast, a gestational carrier (use of the gestational carrier's uterus only) involves the creation of embryos from the prospective parents via IVF with the transfer of the resulting embryos to the uterus of the gestational carrier and, as such, is a reproductive solution for a woman with ovarian function but no uterus (e.g., Kuster-Rokitansky-Hauser syndrome). A fundamental question with surrogacy is, to whom does the child belong: the genetic mother or the carrying mother? These questions have led many countries (and some states within the United States) to legally ban or regulate these arrangements. Nevertheless, some couples continue to consider surrogacy a feasible option despite legal, psychological, and social complexities, high financial cost, and potential risks to the health of the surrogate mother and the baby. Professional guidelines exist on the preparation and education of participants in surrogacy and gestational carrier arrangements (ASRM, 2004; ESHRE, 2000).

Some forms of assisted reproduction, such as gestational carriers and surrogacy, can facilitate the transmission of a genetic disorder that was previously undetected or untransmitted. The consequences are not always predictable or foreseeable. For example, it has been reported that some women with Turner's syndrome, who used donated oocytes to conceive, died during pregnancy as a result of aortic aneurysm—due to preexisting complications from Turner's syndrome (Nagel & Tesch, 1997).

Preimplantation Genetic Diagnosis

One way to prevent pregnancies with genetic disorders is preimplantation genetic diagnosis (PGD). PGD involves the integration of three specific medical technologies: IVF, embryo assessment, and molecular genetic testing (Jones, 1996) to produce embryos from which one or two cells are biopsied and tested for a genetic disorder or disease (Harper & Wells, 1999). The unaffected embryos are then transferred to the uterus for normal gestation. When preconception genetic counseling determines that there is a genetic disorder, this technology allows couples to avoid having a child with the genetic disorder by selecting only unaffected embryos for embryo transfer.

IVF/PGD was groundbreaking technology in the early 1990s because it allows individuals with a genetic condition the opportunity to screen potential embryos before pregnancy, thereby eliminating (or at least decreasing) the need for prenatal genetic testing, pregnancy termination

(Blatt, 1996), or repeated miscarriages. It avoids some religious conflicts, personal struggles, and cultural conflicts that are common to genetic disease. However, estimates of successful "take-home baby" rates are lower than for traditional IVF for a variety of reasons, including embryo damage (Soussis et al., 1996).

The financial cost of IVF/PGD is estimated as significantly greater than regular IVF, in large part due to the additional cost of assessing the embryos for rare genetic disorders or uncommon translocations. PGD is limited to certain genetic diseases and to centers where expertise in genetic counseling, molecular genetics, and embryology coexists (ASRM Practice Committee, 2004; ASRM/SART, 2001; Thornhill et al., 2005). While a growing number of genetic disorders can be detected using PGD, further prenatal testing for other genetic disorders is often necessary and can result in the discovery of a different genetic or chromosomal disorder warranting pregnancy termination for fetal anomaly (Verlinsky et al., 2001). Moral objections to PGD are often based on the nature of the procedure (destruction of affected embryos) and potential abuses, such as the use of PGD for sex selection on the basis of parental preference.

GENETIC COUNSELING AND SCREENING OF ANONYMOUS GAMETE AND EMBRYO DONORS

Tasha and Mason Lewis (ages 30 and 31) had been married for 10 years and had three children, Alex (age 7), Andrew (age 5), and Aimee (age 2). Each child was planned and there were no problems with the conceptions, pregnancies, or deliveries. Each child was normal and healthy. Mrs. Lewis worked part-time as a hospital nurse and learned about possibly being an egg donor at work. After looking into the process and discussing it with her husband, she contacted the nearby university fertility clinic. She reasoned that she was healthy, had her ideal-size family, and wanted to help other women who were unable to have children. During the psychological interview and psychological testing, she was cooperative and forthcoming and asked appropriate and educated questions, as did her husband. Both seemed comfortable with the medical regime, the physical demands of being an egg donor, and the concomitant psychosocial issues. She had discussed being a donor with family and friends, all of whom were supportive. Her family enthusiastically helped her complete the family medical history. Mrs. Lewis preferred permanent anonymity, but would provide additional medical information in the future. She and her husband planned to tell their children about her donation some point in the future, if needed. Mrs. Lewis donated oocytes. Two pregnancies were achieved as a result of her donation—one a triplet pregnancy, though as was part of the contract, she was not informed of these outcomes.

Sperm Donor, Identified

Bob Chen (age 26) was single, had no children, and was a graduate student. He was the youngest of seven brothers who had emigrated from Taiwan with his family when he was 5. His eldest brother, Jim (age 37), was married but childless due to male factor infertility: azoospermia of unknown etiology. Jim and his wife, Susan (age 31), asked Bob to be an identified sperm donor, after discussing the plan with their parents, who were supportive. They felt that this solution would maintain ties to the family ancestors. Jim and Susan (also Chinese American) were keenly aware of the limited number of donors of Chinese heritage. After cooperating with the psychological interview and testing (as did Jim and his wife), all parties rejected genetic counseling, preferring to proceed with sperm donation as planned. Susan became pregnant during the first treatment cycle and gave birth to a healthy son. Susan and Jim went on to have a second child with the sperm that Bob had originally banked. In the meantime, Bob married and began his own family. Although everyone in the family was aware of the sperm donation arrangement, all parties agreed to not tell the children involved and keep the matter "private."

Genetic screening of donated gametes (and, less commonly, embryos) has gained increasing attention and importance, fueled in part by their increasing use and acceptance. Many consumers, justifiably, expect anonymous donors to have had a complete medical, psychological, and genetic evaluation. Some may wish to produce the "perfect child" as a replacement for the genetically shared child they were unable to have (Jones, 1996).

Genetic assessment of potential sperm or oocyte donors typically involves a family and medical history and standard questionnaire as well as psychological assessment, preparation, and education (ASRM, 2004; ESHRE, 2000; Verlinsky et al., 2001, 2004). However, sperm banks and oocyte donation programs (where available) have not historically engaged the services of genetic counselors or required karotyping of all donors because it was not considered cost effective and the number of identifiable genetic disorders was limited. However, these practices and policies are in the process of change, in part as a result of research that found that 8.2% of women with normal physical exams and histories tested positive for a major genetic abnormality (Licciardi et al., 1997). Research on the quality of semen donated to commercial sperm banks found they differ widely in terms of the percentage of motile and progressively motile sperm (Carrell et al., 2000). These findings led to recommendations that all gamete donor facilities and programs use thorough screening protocols to minimize transmission of genetic abnormalities or carrier status. This has been more feasible with the easier access and reduced cost of genetic testing and the mapping of the human genome.

The original ASRM (1993) Guidelines for Gamete Donation made a distinction between male and female gamete donors, as well as identified and anonymous donors. Both ASRM (1993, 2002a, b, c, 2003) and ESHRE (2002) guidelines recommend psychological counseling for all parties involved in oocyte donation, but does not specify counseling for sperm donation unless it is identified or intrafamilial sperm donation. This is, in part, because sperm donation is physically noninvasive and is not as physically demanding for the donor as oocyte donation. The psychological aspects of sperm donation by a man are not yet given the same weight as oocyte donation by a woman or the donation of "extra embryos" from an infertile couple's IVF cycle to another couple (a form of prenatal adoption).

Schover (1993) provided a comprehensive list of issues to be addressed in a structured clinical interview with oocyte donors, including the donor's motivation, any coercion, any history of criminal behavior, significant familial pressure or dysfunction, overall stability, and past history or current evidence of major psychopathology or chemical dependency. The following issues should be considered in evaluating identified gamete donors: future relationships with participants, future relationships with child(ren), telling the child(ren), and implications of negative outcome of treatment or conflicts regarding treatment. An ideal candidate can provide informed consent, is able and motivated to comply with treatment, and has a history of stable employment and relationships.

Donors cannot have a personal or family history of a genetic disorder. It is interesting to note that this criterion is not applicable to intrafamilial donations. In identified donations, the criterion is that the recipient couple (or individual) be informed of any genetic disorder. The ASRM Ethics Committee (2003) recommended that familial donations be prohibited that would create consanguinity, such as a sister donating to her brother's wife. Furthermore, "certain arrangements that create the impression of incest, like a brother donating sperm to his sister who is also using donated eggs, need to be evaluated carefully, even though there is no consanguinity" (p. 1559). The committee recommends counseling to patients and donors who are considering intrafamilial gamete donation. "Patients from close families willing to help them overcome their infertility are very fortunate, but, we need to take care to ensure that the plan is in the best interest of everyone involved—intended parents, donors or surrogates, and especially the children" (p. 1559).

Culturally sensitive counseling is always relevant in infertility and genetic counseling but is even more important in circumstances, as described above, when the donation is intrafamilial. While many Western countries have adopted or are moving toward elimination of donor anonymity and only identified gamete donations, in many countries and cultures that is absolutely unacceptable. Patrilineal cutures that value male bloodlines and/or religious beliefs regarding ancestors or patrilinity aften consider intrafamilial sperm donation the only acceptable form of assisted reproduction, although it is understood by all members of the family that it is a famil secret. Of particular challenge for the genetic and infertility counselor is providing culturally sensitive counseling while considering the wishes and well-being of all parties involved—including any and all offspring.

Embryo Donation

Suzy and Max Herman (ages 32 and 36) had been through several years of infertility treatment when they finally became pregnant with triplets during an IVF cycle. Only two of the eight embryos produced during the IVF cycle were transferred to Mrs. Herman, leaving six cryopreserved embryos. One of the transferred embryos split and the other implanted, resulting in triplets and a difficult pregnancy involving bed rest, hospitalization, and premature delivery. The two boys and a girl were briefly hospitalized but had no long-term problems. Although Mr. and Mrs. Herman were relieved and thrilled with their new family, they continued to feel uncomfortable about their six cyropreserved embryos. Initially, they planned to use them themselves, but as time went on, they rejected this option. They were uncomfortable destroying the embryos or donating them for research. In the end, when their children were 4 years old, they decided to donate the extra embryos to an infertile couple. After contacting an agency, they chose not to meet or maintain contact with the recipients although they wanted to know the results of the donation. All six embryos were used and a singleton pregnancy was achieved. The donating couple did not volunteer any genetic information, nor were they asked to provide genetic histories by the agency or the recipient couple.

Embryo donation is usually the result of cryopreserved embryos provided by an infertile couple who have undergone IVF. The couple donate the embryos they do not intend to use for their own purposes because they do not wish them destroyed or used for research. Most embryo donations are available through infertility programs and are anonymous. The donated embryos typically do not undergo preconception genetic screening. Donated embryos, and the children born as a result of them, may very well be affected by a genetic disorder (detectable or undetectable, anonymous or identified). To date, there are no government regulations for gamete or embryo donation practices, although practice guidelines have been developed by professional organizations (ASRM, 1993, 2002a; Boivin et al., 2001; see Table 13.4).

In a study of embryo donation in Finland, couples were given limited information about the donating couple (e.g., age, height, weight) but no genetic information (Soderstrom-Anttila, Foudila, Ripatti, & Siegberg, 2001). Of the recipients, 92% wanted information regarding medical diseases in the donor family and the donor's own children. In addition, 45% of recipients thought that they should be informed about whether ICSI had been used to create the embryos. As in other studies on disclosure and donated gametes, this study reported that two thirds of the recipient couples thought the child should be informed about his or her conception, although only 29% thought the child should receive information about the donor. The embryo donors in this study were motivated by altruism and minimal financial incentives. (Couples received a discount on their own IVF cycle.)

Gestational Carriers and Surrogates

Amanda Johnson (age 34) had lived with her husband, Rodney (age 29) for 7 years, but they had been married less than a year. Mr. Johnson was in nursing school and Mrs. Johnson worked at a bank. They were childless by choice.

Table 13.4 Guidelines for Genetic Screening of Oocyte Donors

1. The donor should be generally healthy and
   a. Not have a Mendelian disorder or major malformation
   b. Not be a carrier for a known single-gene disorder
   c. Not have or be a carrier for a multifactorial disorder
   d. Not have a major familial disorder
   e. Not have a chromosomal rearrangement
   f. Be young (males younger than 50 years, females younger than 35 years)

2. First-degree relatives of the donor should be free of
   a. Major malformations
   b. Mendelian disorders
   c. Chromosomal disorders

3. Permanent record keeping

Note. From American Society of Reproductive Medicine. (2002). Guidelines for gamete and embryo donation. *Fertility and Sterility, 77*, Suppl 5.

although they had never used birth control. Mr. Johnson did not want children. Mrs. Johnson was satisfied with this arrangement under their current circumstances, but she hoped that her husband would change his mind after he finished school. Mrs. Johnson's sister, Nancy Sauer (age 40) was married to her second husband, Howard (age 54). Mr. Sauer had been married twice previously and had one son, Lars (age 13) from his second marriage, which had ended in a conflictual divorce and protracted custody battle. After 3 years of marriage during which the couple underwent extensive infertility treatment, Mr. and Mrs. Sauer were told their only alternative for a genetically linked child was via surrogacy, perhaps with Mrs. Sauer's sister as a surrogate. Although Mrs. Johnson and her husband were cooperative and forthcoming during the psychological interview and psychological testing, it became clear that Mrs. Johnson did not want to be a surrogate for her sister. However, she did not feel she could refuse her sister and could not, in fact, think of a single circumstance in which she had ever refused her sister anything. Mrs. Johnson worried that if her husband persisted in his opposition to children, she would feel jealous of her sister and the child she had carried for her—a child that would genetically be her son or daughter. The infertility counselor worked with the Johnsons about their differences and coached Mrs. Johnson about how she might tell her sister that, as much as she loved her and would do most anything for her, she could not carry a baby for her sister when she had not herself had children yet. This couple's session was followed by a family session with both couples, in which Mrs. Johnson relayed this message to her sister. It was a painful and difficult session, but with the therapist's support all agreed that a surrogacy could not happen within the family unless all parties were fully comfortable with the process. The Sauers went on after this to adopt a child.

As a general rule, childless women are not considered appropriate candidates for surrogacy, primarily because without having experienced pregnancy, birth, and parenthood, it is probably impossible for the woman to provide informed consent. While surrogates (like donors) are expected to be free of heritable disorders, potential surrogates and carriers must also evidence mental and relationship stability, the ability to manage the relationship with the intended parents and the demands of pregnancy, and the ability to maintain boundaries in her personal life and with the intended parents. Conflicts may arise about prenatal testing, decisions about selective reduction, or sufficient support to the surrogate during pregnancy or postpartum (Braverman, 1993). More complicated are intrafamilial and identified arrangements in which one or both parties bring a relationship history, personal expectations, and sometimes differing agendas to the arrangement.

Assisted Reproduction Counseling

Assisted reproduction, as outlined here, involves donated gametes, embryos, gestational carriers, and surrogates. On the horizon are a wide array of controversial assisted reproductive technologies including deliberate conception of a fetus as a potential donor to a sibling with a known genetic disorder (i.e., savior siblings); haploidization (fertilization of an oocyte by the nucleus of another female's oocyte); sex selection for nongenetic reasons; human embryonic stem cell lines for therapeutic use through donated gametes or embryos (Kalfoglou & Gittelsohn, 2000; Lanzendorf et al., 2001; Strong, Gingrich, & Kutteh, 2000); and therapeutic cloning (reproductive somatic cell nuclear transfer; Katayama, 2001). At the same time, developments continue to emerge in reproductive genetics that provide greater opportunities for patient care and education in reproductive decision making.

Regardless of the reproductive technology employed, the standard of care is to provide all participants with adequate education, preparation, and screening. These guidelines all suggest that when a genetic disorder has been identified or reproduction is to involve donated gametes, genetic counseling and testing should be recommended and made available to all participants. However, some couples still choose to make their own arrangements without the assistance of medical, mental health, or legal professionals. Furthermore, an increasing number of participants are using the Internet to make reproductive arrangements, contributing to potential abuses.

A COLLABORATIVE APPROACH TO
REPRODUCTIVE MEDICINE

Within family practice and other health care specialties, there is a growing movement toward collaborative health care based on a multidisciplinary treatment approach to patient care that includes medical and mental health caregivers (McDaniel, Campbell, Hepworth & Lorenz, 2004). Reproductive medicine has moved in the same direction, recognizing the increasing importance of a collaborative multidisciplinary team including reproductive endocrinologists, embryologists, urologists, perinatologists, nurses, mental health professionals, genetic counselors, and other professionals working in the field (Clapp & Adamson, 1999; see also Chapter 10). Toward this end, an increasing number of caregivers have obtained cross-professional credentialing, for example, nurses, embryologists, and physicians trained as mental health professionals and social workers trained as genetic counselors. This collaborative approach emphasizes expertise and minimizes rigid professional distinctions (but not expertise) in the tradition of transdisciplinary training, allowing genetic counselors to provide more psychological support or counseling, mental health professionals to provide more genetic education and assessment, and physicians the opportunity to address both medical genetics and emotional issues within the context of comprehensive patient care (Kentenich et al., 2002).

A collaborative approach that includes genetic counselors has gained increasing acceptance with a growing number of reproductive medicine practices in the United States and Europe (Strauss, 2002). A questionnaire survey sent to members of the American College of Obstetrics and Gynecology found that 87% had access to genetic counselors: 21% of the counselors were on site, with 66% in the community (Wilkins-Haug et al., 1999). Also, 11% of the genetic counselors were available for telephone consultation. Physician knowledge of genetic risk, especially in the areas of aneuploidy and neural tube defects, was very good, but the researchers recommended greater affiliation with genetic counseling centers to facilitate specialized education and referral. Respondents cited the rapidity of changes in the field of genetic testing (e.g., the Human Genome Project) as the greatest obstacle to keeping them up-to-date on genetic information for patients.

To improve preconception health care for women, a group of obstetricians and gynecologists at a multispeciality training facility developed a curriculum on preconception health for women to be targeted for three medical specialties (internal medicine, family practice, and pediatrics) and include nurses and midwives (Freda et al., 2002). The curriculum promotes preconception health, such as teaching women about the importance of taking folic acid daily to reduce the incidence of neural tube defects, and provides information about genetic risks and disorders.

A multidisciplinary approach to reproductive care, including mental health professionals, was suggested and supported at a 1997 multidisciplinary Human Genome Project conference, the Genetic Self (McDaniel & Campbell, 1999). Professional organizations of mental health professionals in reproductive medicine began in the 1980s and include the spectrum of mental health professionals (psychology, psychiatry, family therapy, social work, psychiatric nursing). In 2004 the International Infertility Counseling Organization (IICO) was founded and became a special interest group of the International Federation of Fertility Societies with a goal to promote the provision of collaborative care of infertile patients; professional development in the field of reproductive health counseling; and the provision of culturally sensitive counseling and medical treatment to infertile patients. What began with only five infertility counseling organizations has grown to eleven worldwide in less than 2 years with the support of IICO and its educational support, guidance, and opportunities for professionals worldwide. In the United States, the

ASRM (then the American Fertility Society) granted special interest group status in 1984 to what became the Mental Health Professional Group and in 2001 to the Genetic Counselors Special Interest Group. The British Infertility Counseling Organization was established in 1988, the Australia/New Zealand Infertility Counseling Organization in 1989, and the European Society of Human Reproduction and Embryology granted special interest group status to the Psychology Special Interest Group in 1993. Each organization has promoted a multidisciplinary approach to the psychosocial needs of infertile individuals through the development of professional standards of patient care and collaboration with governing agencies.

CONCLUSION

Reproductive medicine is a complex field in which medicine, technology, psychology, and social policy combine to address unique patient needs, yielding significant professional challenges. Helping future parents to understand the genetic risks and benefits of new reproductive technologies requires a professional team that can utilize the latest scientific methods as well as particular individual, couple, and extended-family dynamics. More and more opportunities exist to build families using new technologies; a biopsychosocial approach to assessment and treatment can ensure that donors and recipients make informed decisions that optimize the chances of healthy and well-adjusted individuals and families in the future.

REFERENCES

Allen, J. S. F., & Mulhauser, L. C. (1995). Genetic counseling after abnormal prenatal diagnosis: Facilitating coping in families who continue their pregnancies. *Journal of Genetic Counseling, 4,* 251–265.

American Society for Reproductive Medicine. (1993). Guidelines for gamete donation. *Fertility and Sterility, 59*(Suppl. 1):1S–9S.

American Society for Reproductive Medicine. (2002a). Guidelines for gamete and embryo donation. *Fertility and Sterility, 77* (Suppl. 5). Retrieved June 16, 2006, from http://www.asrm.org

American Society for Reproductive Medicine. (2002b). Guidelines for oocyte donation. *Fertility and Sterility, 77* (Suppl. 5): S6–8.

American Society for Reproductive Medicine. (2002c). Guidelines for sperm donation. *Fertility and Sterility, 77* (Suppl. 5): S2–5.

American Society of Reproductive Medicine. (2003). Revised minimum standards offering assisted reproductive technology. *Fertility and Sterility, 80,* 1556–1559.

American Society for Reproductive Medicine. (2004 pending). Guidelines for gestational carriers. www.asrm.org

American Society for Reproductive Medicine Practice Committee. (2004). Preimplantation genetic disgnosis. *Fertility and Sterility, 82,* S1.

American Society for Reproductive Medicine and Society for Assisted Reproductive Technology. (2001). *Practice committee report on preimplantation genetic diagnosis.* www.asrm.org

American Society for Reproductive Medicine, Ethics Committee. (2003). Family members as gamete donors and surrogates, *Fertility and Sterility, 80,* 1556–1559.

American Society for Reproductive Medicine, Ethics Committee. (2004). Informing offspring of their conception by gamete donation. *Fertility and Sterility, 81,* 527–531.

Assisted Human Reproduction Act. (2004). Canada. March 29.

Bernstein, P. S., Sanghvi, T., & Merkatz, I. R. (2000). Improving preconception care. *Journal of Reproductive Medicine, 45,* 546–552.

Bertrand-Servais, M., Letur-Konirsch, H., Raoul-Duval, A., & Frydman, R. (1993). Psychological considerations in anonymous oocyte donation. *Human Reproduction, 8,* 878–879.

Blatt, R. J. R. (1996). Conceiving for the future: The impact of the human genome project on gamete donation. In M. M. Seibel & S. L. Crockin (Eds.), *Family building through egg and sperm donation* (pp. 285–294). Boston: Jones and Bartlett.

Blumberg, B., Golbus, M. & Hanson, K. (1975). Prenatal diagnosis: The experience of families who have children. *American Journal of Medical Genetics, 9,* 729–739.

Blyth, E., Crawshaw, M., & Daniels, K. (2004). Policy formation in gamete donation and egg sharing in the UK—a critical appraisal. *Social Science and Medicine, 59,* 2617–2626.

Boivin, J., Appleton, T. C., Baetens, P., Baron, J., Bitzer, J., Corrigan, E., et al. (2004). Guidelines for counselling in infertility: Outline version. *Human Reproduction, 16*(6), 1301–1304.

Bonnickson, A. (2001). Commentary: Unnatural deeds to breed unnatural troubles. *Fertility and Sterility, 76,* 1084–1085.

Brambati B., Tului, L., Baldi, M., & Guercilena, S. (1995). Genetic analysis prior to selective fetal reduction in multiple pregnancy: Technical aspects and clinical outcome. *Human Reproduction, 10,* 818–825.

Braverman, A. M. (1993). Surrogacy and gestational carrier programs. In D. M. Greenfeld (Ed.), *Psychological issues in infertility. Infertility and Reproductive Medicine Clinics of North America* (pp. 517–531). Philadelphia: WB Saunders.

Burns, L. H., & LeRoy, B. (1999). Infertility and genetic counseling. In L. H. Burns & S. N. Covington (Eds.), *Infertility counseling: A comprehensive guide for the clinician* (pp. 199–225). New York: Parthenon.

Carrell, D. T., Cartmill, D., Jones, K. P., Hatasaka, H. H., & Peterson, C. M. (2000). Prospective, randomized, blinded evaluation of donor sperm quality provided by seven commercial sperm banks. *Fertility and Sterility, 78,* 16–21.

Clapp, D., & Adamson, D. (1999). In L. H. Burns & S. N. Covington (Eds.), *Infertility counseling: A comprehensive guide for the clinician* (pp. 199–225). New York: Parthenon.

Coutifaris, C. (2004). Congenital and genetic abnormalities following IVF. In *Postgraduate Course 16: Genetic and congenital anomalies after IVF: A review* (pp. 38–46). Philadelphia: American Society of Reproductive Medicine.

Cram, D. S., Ma, K., Bhasin, S., Arias, J., Pandjaitan, M., Chu, B., et al. (2000). Y chromosome analysis of infertile men and their sons conceived though intracytoplasmic sperm injection: Vertical transmission of deletions and rarity of de novo deletions. *Fertility and Sterility, 74,* 909–915.

Curry, C.J.R. (1992). Pregnancy loss, stillbirth, and neonatal death: A guide for the pediatrician. In J. G. Hall (Ed.), *Medical genetics I. The Pediatric Clinics of North America* (pp. 157–92). Philadelphia: WB Saunders.

Decruyenaere, M. (1997). Risk perception and risk communication in genetic counseling. In *Course IX: The new genetics and reproductive decisions: Psychosocial and ethical issues* (pp. 113–120). Cincinnati, OH: American Society for Reproductive Medicine.

DeMaria, R., Weeks, G., & Hof, L. (1999). *Focused genograms: Intergenerational assessments of individuals, couples, and families.* Philadelphia: Brunner/Mazel.

de Vries, J. W., Repping, S., Oates, R., Carson, R., Leschot, N. J., & van der Veen, F. (2001). Absence of deleted azoospermia (DAZ) genes in spermatozoa of infertile men with somatic DAZ deletions. *Fertility and Sterility, 75,* 476–479.

Digman, P. S. (1987). Genetics and pregnancy loss: Value of counseling between pregnancies. In J. R. Woods & J. L. Esposito (Eds.), *Pregnancy loss: Medical therapeutics and practical considerations* (pp. 198–206). Baltimore, MD: Williams and Wilkins.

Dohle, G. R., Halley, D. J. J., Van Hemel, J. O., van den Ouwel, A. M., Pieters, M. H., Weber, R. F., et al. (2002). Genetic risk factors in infertile men with severe oliogozoospermia and azoospermia. *Human Reproduction, 17,* 13–16.

European Society of Human Reproduction & Embryology. Psychological Special Interest Group. (2000). *Guidelines on infertility counseling.* www.eshre.com

European Society of Human Reproduction & Embryology Task Force on Ethics and Law. (2002). Gamete and embryo donation. *Human Reproduction, 17,* 1407–1408.

European Society of Human Reproduction & Embryology Task Force on Ethics and Law. (2003). Ethical issues related to multiple pregnancies in medically assisted procreation. *Human Reproduction, 18,* 1976–1979.

Eunpu, D. L. (1995). The impact of infertility and treatment guidelines for couples therapy. *American Journal of Family Therapy, 23,* 115–128.

Eunpu, D. L. (1997). Systemically-based psychotherapeutic techniques in genetic counseling. *Journal of Genetic Counseling, 6,* 1–20.

Freda, M. C., Chazotte, C., Bernstein, P., Harrison, E., & March of Dimes Preconception Working Group (2002). Interdisciplinary development of a preconception health curriculum for four medical specialties. *Obstetrics and Gynecology, 99,* 301–306.

The Genetic Self: The Impact of the Human Genome Project on You and Your Practice. (1997). National Institutes of Health and National Human Genome Research Institute Conference. Airlie House, Airlie, VA, June 27–29.

Geraedts, J.P.M. (1996). Chromosomal anomalies and recurrent miscarriage. In S. Daya (Ed.), *Recurrent miscarriage. Infertility and Reproductive Medicine Clinics of North America* (pp. 667–688). Philadelphia: WB Saunders.

Glazer, E. (1995). Pregnancy after infertility. In *Proceedings of the eighth national conference for IVG nurse coordinators and support personnel* (pp. 25–28). Boston: Serono Symposia.

Greenfield, D. A., & Klock, S. C. (2004). Disclosure decisions among known and anonymous oocyte donation recipients. *Fertility and Sterility, 81,* 527–531.

Haidl, G., Jung, A., & Schill, W. B. (1996). Ageing and sperm function. *Human Reproduction, 11,* 558–560.

Harper, J. C., & Wells, D. (1999). Recent advances and future developments in PGD. *Prenatal Diagnosis, 19,* 1193–1199.

Human Fertizisation and Embrology Authority. (2004). The regulation of donor-assisted conception. Available at www.hfea.gov.uk/AboutHFEA/Consultations/SeedConsult.pdf.

International Infertility Counseling Association. (2004). Global perspectives in infertility counseling. Postgraduate course. Montreal, Canada, May 23.

Ji, E. K., Pretorius, D. H., Newton, R., Uyan, K., Hull, A. D., Hollenbach, K., et al. (2005). Effects of ultrasound on maternal-fetal bonding: A comparison of two- and three-dimensional imaging. *Journal of Ultrasound Obstetrics & Gynecology, 25,* 473–477.

Jolly, M., Sebire, N., Harris, J., Robinson, S., & Regan, L. (2000). The risks associated with pregnancy in women aged 35 years or older. *Human Reproduction, 15,* 2433–2437.

Jones, J. L. (1996). Advances in human genetics: Implications for infertility nursing practice. *Infertility and Reproductive Medicine Clinics of North America, 7,* 577–585.

Kalfoglou, A. L. (2000). Looking back, looking forward: The legacy of the National Advisory Board on Ethics in Reproduction (NABER). *Women's Health Issues, 10,* 92–103.

Kalfoglou, A. L., & Gittelsohn, J. (2000). A qualitative follow-up study of women's experiences with oocyte donation. *Human Reproduction, 15,* 798–805.

Katayama, A. (2001). A seminar on human cloning: Human reproductive cloning and related techniques: An overview of the legal environmental and practitioner attitudes. *Journal of Assisted Reproduction and Genetics, 18,* 442–450.

Kentenich, H., Henning, K., Himmel, W., et al. (2002). Practical therapy in sterility—A manual for gynecologists for a psychosomatic point of view. In B. Strauss (Ed.), *Involuntary childlessness: psychological assessment, counseling, and psychotherapy* (pp. 176–186). Seattle: Hogrefe and Huber.

Khamsi, F., Endman, M. W., Lacanna, I. C., & Wong, J. (1997). Some psychological aspects of oocyte donation from known donors on altruistic basis. *Fertility and Sterility, 68,* 323–327.

Lanzendorf, S. E., Boyd, C. A., Wright, D. L., Muasher, S., Oehninger, S., & Hodgen, G. D. (2001). Use of human gametes obtained from anonymous donors for the production of human embryonic stem cell lines. *Fertility and Sterility, 76,* 132–137.

Lee, R. G., & Morgan, D. (2001). *Human fertilization and embryology: Regulating the reproductive revolution.* London: Blackstone.

Leon, I. G. (1995). Pregnancy termination due to fetal anomaly: Clinical considerations. *Journal of Infant Mental Health, 16,* 112–126.

Lessor, R., Reitz, K., Balmaceda, J., & Asch, R. (1990). A survey of public attitudes toward oocyte donation between sisters. *Human Reproduction, 5,* 889–892.

Levron, J., Aviram-Goldring, A. L., Madgar I., Raviv, G., Barkai, G., & Dor, J. (2001). Sperm chromosome abnormalities in men with severe male factor infertility who are undergoing in vitro fertilization with intracytoplasmic sperm injection. *Fertility and Sterility, 76,* 479–484.

Licciardi, F., Jansen, V., Fantini, D., et al. (1997). Strict genetic screening is necessary for oocyte donors. *Journal of Assisted Reproductive Genetics, 14* (Suppl.), 49s.

Lloyd, J., & Laurence, K. (1985). Sequelae and support after termination of pregnancy for fetal malformation. *British Medical Journal, 290,* 907–909.

Ma, S., Kalousek, D. K., Yuen, B. S., Gomel, V., Katagiri, S., & Moon, Y. S. (1994). Chromosome investigation in in vitro fertilization failure. *Journal of Assisted Reproduction and Genetics, 11,* 445–451.

Magyari, P. A., Wedehase, R. D., Ifft, R. D., & Callanan, N. P. (1987). A supportive intervention protocol for couples terminating pregnancy for genetic reasons. *Birth Defects Original Articles Service, 6,* 75–83.

Mak, V., & Jarvi, K. A. (1996). The genetics of male infertility. *Journal of Urology, 156,* 1245–1257.

Massey, J. B., Slayden, S., Shapiro, D. M., & Wininger, D. (2001). Unnatural deeds do breed unnatural troubles. *Fertility and Sterility, 76,* 1083–1084.

McDaniel, S. H., & Campbell, T. L. (1999). Editorial: Genetic testing and families. *Families, Systems, and Health, 17,* 1–4.

McDaniel, S. H., Campbell, T. L., Hepworth, J., & Lorenz, A. (2004). *Family-oriented primary care* (2nd ed.). New York: Springer-Verlag.

Nagel, T. C., & Tesch, L. G. (1997). ART and high risk patients. *Fertility and Sterility, 68,* 7489.

Pennings, G. (2004). Legal hormonization and reproductive tourism in Durope. *Human Reproduction, 19,* 2689–2694.

Reame, N. (2000). Making babies in the 21st century: New strategies, old dilemmas. *Women's Health, 10,* 152–159.

Robinson, A., Bender, B., & Linden, M. (1989). Decision following the intrauterine diagnosis of sex chromosome aneuploidy. *American Journal of Medical Genetics, 34,* 552–554.

Rothman, B. K. (1994). The tentative pregnancy: Then and now. In K. H. Rothenberg & E. J. Thomson (Eds.), *Women and prenatal testing: Facing the challenges of genetic technology* (pp. 260–270). Columbus: Ohio State University Press.

Sandelowski, M. (1988). A case of conflicting paradigms: Nursing and reproductive technology. *Advances in Nursing Science, 10,* 35–45.

Sandelowksi, M., Harris, B. G., & Holditch-Davis, D. (1991). Amniocentesis in the context of infertility. *Health Care for Women International, 12,* 167–178.

Schechtman, K. B., Gray, D. L., Baty, J. D., & Rothman, S. M. (2002). Decision-making for termination of pregnancies with fetal anomalies: Analysis of 53,000 pregnancies. *Obstetrics and Gynecology, 99,* 216–222.

Schover, L. R., Thomas, A. J., Falcone, T., Attaran, M., & Goldberg, J. (1998). Attitudes about genetic risk of couples undergoing in-vitro fertilization. *Human Reproduction, 13,* 862–866.

Schover, L. R., Thomas, A. J., Miller, K. F., Falcone, T., Attaran, M., & Goldberg, J. (1996). Preferences for intracytoplasmic spesrm injection versus donor insemination in severe male factor infertility: A preliminary report. *Human Reproduction, 11,* 2461–2464.

Shapiro, C. H., & Djurdjinovic, L. (1990). Understanding our infertile genetic counseling patients. In B. A. Fine, E. L. Getting, K. Greendale, et al. (Eds.), *Strategies in genetic counseling: Reproductive genetics and new technologies* (pp. 127–131). White Plains, NY: March of Dimes Defects Foundation.

Shiloh, S. (1996). Genetic counseling: A developing area of interest for psychologists. *Professional Psychology: Research and Practice, 27,* 475–486.

Sjogren, B., & Uddenberg, N. (1988). Prenatal diagnosis and maternal attachment to the child-to-be. *Journal of Psychosomatic Obstetrics and Gynecology, 9,* 73–87.

Soderstrom-Anttila, V., Foudila, T., Ripatti, U., & Siegberg, R. (2001). Embryo donation: Outcome and attitudes among embryo donors and recipients. *Human Reproduction, 6,* 1120–1128.

Solnit, J. A., & Stark, M. H. (1961). Mourning and the birth of a defective child. *Psychoanalytic Study of the Child, 16,* 523–527.

Soules, M. R. (2001). Human reproduction cloning: Not ready for prime time. *Fertility and Sterility, 76,* 232–234.

Soussis, I., Harper, J. C., Kontogianni, E., Paraschos, T., Packham, D., Handyside, A. H., et al. (1996). Pregnancies resulting from embryos biopsied for preimplantation diagnosis of genetic disease: Biochemical and ultrasonic studies in the first trimester of pregnancy. *Journal of Assisted Reproductive Genetics, 13,* 254–265.

Stotland, N. L. (2000). Induced abortion in the United States. In N. L. Stotland & D. E. Stewart (Eds.), *Psychological aspects of women's health care: The interface between psychiatry and obstetrics and gynecology* (pp. 219–240). Washington, DC: American Psychiatric Press.

Strauss, B. (2002). The relationship of research and practice in fertility medicine. In B. Strauss (Ed.), *Involuntary childlessness: Psychological assessment, counseling, and psychotherapy* (pp. 151–169). Seattle, WA: Hogrefe and Huber.

Strong, C. (1997). Models for a psychosocial team approach to genetic counseling. In *Course IX: The new genetics and reproductive decisions: Psychosocial and ethical issues* (pp. 133–134). Cincinnati, OH: American Society for Reproductive Medicine.

Strong, C., Gingrich, J. R., & Kutteh, H. H. (2000). Ethics of postpartum sperm retrieval after death or persistent vegetative state. *Human Reproduction, 4,* 739–745.

Swanson, A. L. (2003). *A survey of Midwest infertility clinics: Current clinical practices with a genetic cause of infertility and the provision of genetic counseling services.* Unpublished doctoral dissertation, University of Minnesota, Minneapolis.

Tho, S. P. T., & McDonough, P. G. (1994). Genetics of fetal wastage, sporadic, and recurrent abortion. *Infertility and Reproductive Medicine Clinics of America, 5,* 157–176.

Thornhill, A. R., deDie-Smulders, C. E., Geraedts, J. P., Harper, J. C., Harton, G. L., Lavery, S. A., et al. (2005). ESHRE PGD Consortium 'Best practice guidelines for clinical preimplantation genetic diagnosis (PGD) and preimplantation genetic screening (PGS)'. *Human Reproduction, 20*(1), 35–48.

Van den Veyver, I. B. (2002). Prenatal genetic screening. In *Postgraduate Course 13: Genetic counseling and molecular application for the infertile couple* (pp. 33–45). Seattle, WA: American Society of Reproductive Medicine.

Verlinsky, Y., Cohen, J., Munne, S., Gianaroli, L., Simpson, J. L., Ferraretti, A. P., et al. (2004). Over a decade of experience with preimplantation genetic diagnosis: A multicenter report. *Fertility and Sterility, 82,* 292–294.

Verlinsky, Y., Rechitsky, S., Verlinsky, O., Strom, C., & Kuliev, A. (2001). Preimplantation testing for phenylketonuria. *Fertility and Sterility, 76,* 346–349.

Verp, M., Bombard, A., Simpson, J. L., & Elias, S. (1988). Parental decision following prenatal diagnosis of fetal chromosome abnormality. *American Journal Medical Genetics, 29,* 613–622.

Wertz, D. (1998). Eugenics is alive and well: A survey of genetic professionals around the world. *Science Context, 11,* 493–510.

Wilkins-Haug, L., Hill, L., Schmidt, L., Holzman, G. B., & Schulkin, J. (1999). Genetics in obstetricians' offices: A survey study. *Obstetrics and Gynecology, 93,* 642–647.

Zeanah, C. H., Dailey, J., Rosenblatt, M. J., & Saller, D. N. Jr. (1993). Do women grieve after terminating pregnancies because of fetal anomalies? A controlled investigation. *Obstetrics and Gynecology, 82,* 270–275.

Zuzkar, D. (1987). The psychological impact of prenatal diagnosis of fetal abnormality: Strategies for investigation and intervention. *Women's Health Review, 12,* 91–103.

Chapter 14

Genetic Screening for Type 1 Diabetes

Psychosocial Impact on Families

Suzanne Bennett Johnson

TYPE 1 DIABETES (T1D), ALSO KNOWN AS JUVENILE OR CHILDHOOD DIA-
betes, is one of the most common chronic diseases of childhood. In the
United States, over 200,000 children have T1D (National Institute of Diabetes and Digestive and Kidney Diseases, 2003) and the incidence is increasing worldwide (Onkamo, Vaananen, Karvonen, & Tuomilehto,
1999). There are large international differences in incidence, ranging from
0.7 cases per 100,000 in Shanghai, China, to 35.3 cases per 100,000 in Finland, one of the largest variations seen in any noncommunicable disease.
As might be expected, there are significant racial differences, with incidence greatest among Caucasians (LaPorte, Matsushima, & Chang, 1995).

Patients with T1D suffer from an autoimmune-mediated destruction of the insulin-producing beta cells in the pancreas. Destruction of
the beta cells can be slow or rapid, the latter occurring most often in
children (World Health Organization, 1999). During this time, islet cell
antibodies (ICA) are detectable in the blood of most individuals before
frank diabetes occurs. However, not everyone with ICA goes on to develop T1D (Dorman, McCarthy, O'Leary, & Koehler, 1995).

This chapter briefly reviews the genetics of T1D and discusses ethical
issues associated with genetic testing for T1D risk. It then reviews the
available literature addressing the psychosocial impact of T1D genetic
testing: cognitive, affective, and behavioral effects, as well as participant reactions to participation in genetic studies. Finally, recommendations for practice and future research are provided.

THE GENETICS OF TYPE 1
DIABETES MELLITUS

Genetics have long been presumed to play a causal role in T1D, since individuals with T1D relatives are at an increased risk for developing the disease themselves. However, most children diagnosed with T1D have no family history of the disease and the concordance rate among monozygotic twins is less than 50% (Dorman et al., 1995).

The HLA region of chromosome 6 contains genes that control the immune response, and with the discovery of the class II antigens (HLA-DR, DQ, DP), the role of HLA-DR, DQ genotypes in T1D became clearer. Approximately 95% of T1D patients have DR3 and/or DR4; a child with both DR3 and DR4 is particularly susceptible (Dorman et al., 1995). Nevertheless, very few individuals with the highest-risk HLA genotypes actually go on to develop diabetes (Carmichael et al., 2003). It appears that certain HLA genotypes place an individual at increased risk for T1D, but other factors determine whether the at-risk individual goes on to develop the disease. A variety of environmental triggers have been proposed, including both viral and nutritional exposures. However, currently the cause of T1D remains unknown. The presence of gene-environment interactions may explain the observed weak effects of candidate environmental agents and genes on T1D risk. Without accounting for these interactions, the true effect of either the environmental agent or gene may be underestimated. Consequently, the National Institutes of Health has initiated an international multisite natural history study, The Environmental Determinants of Diabetes in the Young (TEDDY), which will identify genetically at-risk infants at birth and follow them over time, collecting detailed information on diet, illness, and other environmental exposures (http://www.teddystudy.org).

THE ETHICS OF GENETIC TESTS
FOR T1D RISK

Currently, there is no known effective method to prevent T1D in at-risk individuals. Consequently, genetic screening for T1D risk raises a number of ethical issues. Genetic screening for T1D risk is particularly controversial because those screened are usually infants or children. Infants and young children do not have the cognitive capability to make the decision to be genetically screened for T1D risk; their parents make this decision for them. Parents who decide to screen the child and learn the child is at increased risk face the added burden of explaining this to the child when the child becomes older.

The situation is further complicated by the poor predictive power of genetic tests for T1D risk. Most children with increased genetic risk will never develop diabetes. The parent, and certainly the child, may have considerable difficulty understanding what "increased risk" associated with certain genotypes actually means. The absence of an effective prevention strategy may also cause unnecessary distress, including worry about an unpredictable, uncontrollable impending disease. Concerns about possible insurance discrimination have also been raised; an individual's at-risk genotype might be viewed as evidence of a preexisting condition, warranting denial of insurance coverage.

Some believe that genetic testing for T1D should not be conducted at all. Others have argued that genetic test results should not be disclosed to participating families or that only families with T1D should be permitted to participate. Most agree that if genetic testing is conducted, it should be limited to carefully monitored research studies with the utmost care taken to protect the privacy of test results (American Academy of Pediatrics, 2001; Johnson, 2001; Ross, 2003; Roth, 2001; Weber, 1997). Those who conduct genetic testing studies for T1D risk cogently argue that understanding the natural history of T1D is a necessary precursor to successful disease prevention. Only by identifying genetically at-risk infants and children and following them, searching for environmental triggers, are we likely to develop a successful disease prevention strategy (Schatz, Krischer, & She, 2002).

PSYCHOSOCIAL IMPACT OF GENETIC TESTS FOR T1D RISK

A number of excellent investigators worldwide have begun studies of infants and children at risk for T1D. These include PANDA in north Florida and Georgia (Carmichael et al., 2003), DAISY in Colorado (Yu et al., 1999), DEWIT in Washington State (Wion et al., 2003), DIPP in Finland (Hoppu et al., 2004), BABYDIAB in Germany (Hummel, Ziegler, & Roth, 2004), and DiPiS in Sweden (Lernmark et al., 2004). In these studies, thousands of infants are screened at birth to identify those at risk for T1D. At-risk infants are then followed for signs of autoimmune disease, such as ICA, and developing diabetes. We are only beginning to understand the psychosocial ramifications of study participation. Most studies of psychosocial impact have focused on mothers of at-risk children, examining the mother's cognitive understanding of the child's risk, her emotional response, and how she and other family members cope with the news. Fewer studies have examined possible behavior changes in response to the news that the child is at risk for T1D. As child participants identified through newborn genetic screening programs grow older, studies on the impact of genetic testing on their psychosocial growth and development will be conducted. Similarly, as this research area matures, more sophisticated studies of parent-child interactions will emerge.

To date, this literature is primarily one that assesses parental cognitive understanding of genetic test results and possible harm associated with the decision to have a child genetically tested for T1D risk. Although there may be benefits to this type of genetic testing, in the absence of a successful means to prevent T1D in at-risk children, issues of possible harm have remained paramount.

Cognitive Impact: Understanding T1D Risk

There are only a few published studies examining individuals' perception of T1D risk. Hendrieckx, DeSmer, Kristoffersen, and Bradley (2002) asked over 400 adolescent and adult siblings and offspring of people with T1D to rate their own risk for developing diabetes, compared to other people their own age, on a 5-point scale ranging from much lower to much higher. The participants had been screened for ICA but were uninformed about the results. They appeared to be well aware of their increased T1D risk, scoring a mean of 3.5 on the 5-point scale. Actual lifetime risk of T1D in first-degree relatives varies across countries but is estimated at 2–5% among siblings and offspring in the United States (Dorman et al., 1995). Although this risk is clearly higher than the risk in the general population, more than 90% of first-degree relatives never develop T1D. The participants in the Hendrieckx et al. (2002) study were accurate in describing themselves as at increased risk compared to the general population. However, the 5-point rating scale did not permit an assessment of the participants' perceived actual lifetime risk for T1D.

Lernmark et al. (2004) asked over 12,000 parents of infants genetically screened for T1D risk to estimate their child's risk of diabetes by selecting one of four answers: no risk, don't know; small risk, or great risk. Parents did not know their child's genetic test results. The majority (63%) of parents from the general population selected the "no risk" or "don't know" categories. In contrast, parents of infants with a first-degree diabetic relative were far more likely to select the "small risk" (63%) or "great risk" (15%) categories. Parents of infants with a first-degree diabetic relative appeared to be well aware of the child's increased risk, even in the absence of genetic test results. However, this study, like the Hendrieckx et al. (2002) study, did not assess parental perceptions of the child's actual risk.

Johnson and Tercyak (1995) studied 64 children and adults who had tested positive for ICA, indicating autoimmune destruction of the pancreatic beta cells had begun. A structured interview was conducted approximately 1 week after ICA test result notification. Participants were reinterviewed approximately 4 months later. On each occasion, participants selected one of four risk categories: will never get diabetes; don't know; will get diabetes a long time from now; or will get diabetes soon. Initially, most participants selected the "don't know" category. However, by 4 months more than 40% of the ICA+ participants were selecting the "will never get diabetes" category. This study suggested that for many individuals, diabetes risk perception may change over time toward a more self-protective, low or no-risk assessment.

Risk Perception Accuracy

A simple rating of relative risk does not permit an assessment of the accuracy of the participants' risk perceptions. To do so would require a standard method of risk information communication followed by a careful assessment of the participant's risk perception. As part of PANDA, we initiated a procedure that used standard language to inform mothers of their infant's genetic test results. Only mothers of genetically at-risk infants were contacted by telephone, and the child's risk was explained using a script that provided both a label (e.g., high risk) and a numerical estimate (e.g., out of 100 babies with the same genetic markers as your baby, 10 will go on to develop diabetes). Mothers were then subsequently recontacted by telephone and asked to recall their child's risk. If they provided an inaccurate label or numerical estimate, they were read a list of risk categories and asked to select the category that best described the child's risk. The mother's response was then compared to the child's actual risk and was categorized as don't know, accurate, underestimate, or overestimate (Carmichael et al., 2003). Mothers were interviewed approximately 1 month, 4 months, and 1 year after risk notification and their risk perception accuracy assessed on each occasion. We have used this approach to study two cohorts, an initial sample of 435 women and a second sample of 190 women. The results for the 1-month, 4-month, and 1-year interviews for both cohorts are provided in Table 14.1. At 1 month, approximately 75% of mothers were accurate about their baby's risk for T1D. However, risk perception accuracy decreased over time; the number of mothers underestimating risk increased. In contrast, overestimation of risk was relatively rare and did not change much over time.

Table 14.1 Risk Perception Accuracy Over Time for Two Cohorts of Mothers With Infants at Risk for T1D (%)

RISK PERCEPTION	COHORT 1 ($n = 435$)			COHORT 2 ($n = 190$)		
	1 MONTH	4 MONTHS	1 YEAR	1 MONTH	4 MONTHS	1 YEAR
Accurate	73	62	49	78	69	48
Underestimate	13	24	35	12	19	34
Overestimate	3	3	2	1	2	2
Don't know	10	11	14	9	10	16

Predictors of Risk Perception Accuracy

Using both cohorts, we have begun to examine predictors of risk perception accuracy. In Cohort 1, we found that initial accuracy was predicted by time, maternal education, and ethnic/minority status; mothers were more likely to be accurate if they were educated, white, and had very recently been informed of their baby's diabetes risk. Although accuracy declined over time, it declined most sharply for mothers of infants in the highest-risk group. Since an increase in underestimation of risk explained this decline, we examined predictors of underestimation. Mothers who reported little anxiety about the child's diabetes risk and whose child had no diabetic relative were more likely to underestimate the child's risk for T1D (Carmichael et al., 2003).

In Cohort 2, we began to explore whether other psychological factors might predict risk perception accuracy. Since postpartum depression occurs in one out of eight women postdelivery (Wisner, Parry, & Piontek, 2002), we thought this might be one important variable for consideration, in addition to maternal anxiety. We found that anxiety and depression had an inverse relationship to risk perception accuracy. Mothers with high anxiety and low depression were more likely to be accurate, while mothers with low anxiety and high depression were more likely to underestimate the baby's risk for T1D (Hood, 2003; Johnson, 2004).

We also used Cohort 2 to explore whether information seeking was an important predictor of risk perception accuracy and whether sending a letter restating the information given to the mother by telephone might improve risk perception accuracy. Our hypotheses were confirmed: Information seekers tended to be more accurate, and sending a letter home did improve risk perception accuracy (Carmichael, 2003; Johnson, 2004).

Our findings to date suggest that risk perception accuracy is a dynamic concept, with many mothers underestimating their infant's risk as time passes. Both demographic and psychological factors seem important to risk perception accuracy and to the tendency to underestimate risk over time. Educated mothers from the majority culture who are information seekers tend to be more accurate. Maternal depression is associated with risk underestimation, while maternal worry and anxiety about the child's risk are associated with greater risk perception accuracy. A simple intervention—sending a letter home restating the child's risk for T1D—appears to improve risk perception accuracy.

Emotional Impact: Anxiety, Worry, and Depression

Most studies that have examined the emotional impact of prediabetes risk assessment have focused on anxiety or worry and have used the state component of the State-Trait Anxiety Inventory (STAI) or the State-Trait Anxiety Inventory for Children (Speilberger, 1973, 1983; Speilberger, Gorsuch, & Lushene, 1970). Only more recently have investigators begun to expand their assessments to include depression (Hood et al., 2005).

Anxiety and Distress

Early studies assessed anxiety or worry in ICA+ children, adults, or their family members, documenting elevated levels of anxiety and distress upon learning of an individual's increased T1D risk. Negative emotional reactions appeared to dissipate over time, although parents of ICA+ children often reported continued distress (Galatzer et al., 2001; Johnson, 2001; Johnson, Riley, Hansen, & Nurick, 1990; Johnson & Tercyak, 1995). All of these studies assessed anxiety or distress post-ICA+ test notification, comparing results to available normative data. Hummel et al. (2004) took a different approach, conducting STAI assessments before and after parents were notified of ICA test results. All children tested for ICA were offspring of T1D parents. Consequently, the parent respondent in this study either had T1D or was married to someone with T1D. Consistent with prior studies, parents who were told their child was ICA+ exhibited an increase in STAI scores, while parents who were told their child was ICA– showed a decline in STAI scores. The highest anxiety scores were reported by mothers of ICA+ children after notification of the child's positive test result. Whether or not the parent had T1D did not appear to affect the results.

Johnson, Baughcum, Carmichael, She, and Schatz (2004) examined STAI scores in mothers of infants genetically screened for T1D risk.

Only mothers of genetically at-risk infants were assessed. Although STAI scores after genetic test results notification were not as high as those seen in samples of mothers with ICA+ children, the decline in STAI scores over time was replicated (see Table 14.2). Further, mothers of children in the highest genetic risk category responded with more elevated STAI scores (42.7 ± 11.1), comparable to those seen in fathers of ICA+ children after ICA test result notification (43.8 ± 8.1; see Table 14.2).

Using a pre-post design similar to that of Hummel et al. (2004), Yu et al. (1999) examined parenting stress 5–7 weeks postpartum in a sample of 88 mothers who agreed to have their infants genetically screened for T1D risk. Parenting stress was assessed again 4–5 months after mothers had been given their infant's genetic test results. At that time, mothers of high-risk and low-risk infants reported similar, normative levels of parenting stress. These findings are consistent with those of other studies that report a decline in parental anxiety and distress over time (Galatzer et al., 2001; Johnson & Tercyak, 1995).

Neither the Johnson et al. (2004) or Yu et al. (1999) studies examined the emotional impact of genetic screening on fathers. Lernmark et al. (2004) addressed this issue in a large sample of mothers and fathers whose infants were genetically screened for T1D risk. However, none of the parents had been informed of the child's genetic test result. Nevertheless, mothers reported greater worry about the child developing a chronic or serious disease than fathers. This was particularly the case among mothers of infants with a first-degree T1D relative; 42% of these mothers reported they were worried or very worried in response to this question. These findings are consistent with Hummel et al.'s (2004) study of parents of children tested for ICA; fathers consistently scored lower on the STAI than mothers both before and after learning the ICA test results (see Table 14.2).

Predictors of Anxiety and Distress

Studies from our laboratory (Carmichael, 2003; Hood, 2003; Johnson et al., 2004) and the Lernmark et al. (2004) study have sufficient samples sizes to begin to explore predictors of anxiety and distress. This issue is important because most studies show considerable variability across individuals in how they respond to news of increased T1D risk (see Table 14.2).

In the Lernmark et al. (2004) sample, parents had their children genetically tested for T1D risk but were uninformed of the test results. As mentioned previously, mothers were generally more worried about the child developing a serious illness in the future than fathers. For both mothers and fathers, those who were less educated, immigrants,

Table 14.2   Comparison Group State STAI Scores and Parents' State STAI Scores of ICA+, ICA–, and Genetically at-Risk Children Assessed at Different Times Pre- and Postresults

	PRETEST	POSTTEST	4 MONTHS POSTTEST	1 YEAR POSTTEST
Mothers of ICA+ children				
Johnson & Tercyak, 1995 ($n = 33$)		55.4 ± 14.4	38.7 ± 8.7	
Hummel et al., 2004 ($n = 25$)	42.5 ± 10.4	51.3 ± 13.1		
Fathers of ICA+ children				
Hummel et al., 2004 ($n = 25$)	39.4 ± 7.6	43.8 ± 8.1		
Mothers of ICA-children				
Hummel et al., 2004 ($n = 224$)	39.7 ± 10.3	37.1 ± 10.3		
Fathers of ICA-children				
Hummel et al., 2004 ($n = 189$)	37.8 ± 8.9	35.9 ± 8.1		
Mothers of genetically at-risk children				
Johnson et al., 2004 ($n = 433$) Cohort 1		37.0 ± 13.5	30.9 ± 11.0	28.1 ± 9.5
Carmichael, 2003 ($n = 190$) Cohort 2		36.1 ± 10.5	31.6 ± 10.5	29.8 ± 8.8
Comparison groups				
Pregnant women undergoing amniocentesis Tercyak et al., 2001 ($n = 100$)	44.9 ± 11.0			
Pregnant women Marteau & Bekker, 1992 ($n = 200$)	37.6 ± 11.0			
Working women Speilberger, 1983 ($n = 210$)	36.2 ± 11.0			

younger, had less knowledge about diabetes, and believed the child to be at greater risk for T1D reported greater worry. In addition, single mothers with T1D in the family, who were dissatisfied with the information they received as part of the study, reported greater worry.

In the Johnson et al. (2004) sample, STAI scores were obtained from mothers of infants identified as at risk for T1D by genetic screening. Compared to a normative sample, STAI scores were significantly elevated in women who were Hispanic, had a high school education or less, overestimated the child's risk, or whose infant was in the extremely high-risk category. STAI scores were reassessed 4 months and 1 year after risk notification. As expected, STAI scores declined over time. However, single mothers, those who overestimated the child's risk, and mothers whose infants were female or who had a first-degree T1D relative failed to exhibit such rapid decline in STAI scores.

Preferred coping style in response to information that you or your child is at risk for T1D may also be an important determinant of anxiety and distress. There is some evidence that ICA+ children who use wishful thinking and avoidance coping strategies remain more anxious about their ICA+ status months after being notified of their increased risk (Johnson & Tercyak, 1995). In this study, few participants blamed themselves for their own or their child's ICA+ status. However, ICA+ adults and mothers of ICA+ children who did engage in self-blame also reported greater anxiety about their own or their child's increased T1D risk. Among mothers of at-risk infants identified through genetic screening, wishful thinking has been associated with elevated STAI scores (Hood, 2003). In contrast, mothers with high levels of dispositional optimism tended to report lower levels of anxiety in response to the infant's increased risk (Carmichael, 2003).

Taken together, these studies suggest that demographic factors, risk perception, and preferred coping style are important determinants of parental anxiety and worry about the child's risk for developing T1D.

Depression

Hood et al. (2005) assessed current depression (using the Center for Epidemiological Studies–Depression [CES-D] scale; Radloff, 1977), history of major depression (using the Structured Clinical Interview for DSM-IV Axis 1 disorders [SCID-I]; First, Spitzer, Gibbon, & Williams, 1997) and history of postpartum depression (using the Edinburgh Postnatal Depression Scale [EPDS]; Cox, Holden, & Sagorsky, 1987) in a sample of 192 mothers of PANDA infants at risk for T1D. Approximately 12% were above the cutoff for depression on the CES-D, 18% reported a history of major depression, and 13% were above the cutoff on the EPDS.

There was no evidence of elevated depression scores compared to normative samples.

Predictors of Depression

Although Hood and colleagues (2005) did not find elevated depression scores for their sample of mothers of genetically at-risk infants, there was considerable variability in CES-D scores. Uneducated mothers, minority mothers, and those with a history of postpartum depression were more likely to have elevated CES-D scores when they were initially assessed approximately 1 month after the mother was informed of her child's increased T1D risk. As mentioned previously, higher CES-D scores were associated with poorer risk perception accuracy and a tendency to underestimate the baby's risk (Hood, 2003).

Preferred coping style also seemed to play a role in depression scores assessed 4 months after the mother was informed of her child's increased T1D risk. Controlling for initial CES-D scores and history of postpartum depression, mothers who used wishful thinking coping strategies and blamed themselves for the child's increased T1D risk were more likely to have higher CES-D scores 4 months after receiving their child's genetic test results.

The small literature available to date suggests that newborn screening for T1D risk does not appear to result in significant levels of depression for most mothers of at-risk children. However, some mothers—those who are uneducated and from minority cultures, who have a history of postpartum depression, and who use wishful thinking coping strategies or blame themselves for the child's T1D risk— may be particularly vulnerable. These women may experience significant depressive symptoms that warrant monitoring and possible intervention.

Behavioral Impact: Surveillance and Prevention Efforts

There have been a number of reports of increased surveillance of children perceived to be at increased risk for T1D. Lucidarme, Domingues-Muriel, Castro, Czernichow, and Levy-Marchal (1998) reported that 80% of 131 parents of diabetic children reported home blood glucose testing of unaffected siblings; in most cases, they never reported this type of surveillance to the child's physician. A substantial minority of these parents (40%) also reported that if a screening program identified an unaffected sibling as at risk for T1D, they would change their behavior toward that child. Hendrieckx et al. (2002) questioned over 400 adolescent and adult first-degree relatives of patients with T1D; all had been screened for ICA but none had received their ICA test results. However, 79% stated they would make behavioral changes if their test results indicated they were ICA+. Of these, most would change their diet (87%); increased exercise (30%), medical surveillance (20%), and home blood glucose testing (9%) were also reported.

While Lucidarme et al. (1998) and Hendrieckx et al (2002) examined intentions for behavior change in individuals tested for ICA before the results were known, Johnson and Tercyak (1995) interviewed a small sample of ICA+ children and adults who were well aware of their ICA+ status. Over half of the children and a quarter of the ICA+ adults reported making behavior changes in response to their ICA+ status. The most common changes reported were in diet and exercise.

Baughcum et al. (2005) attempted to comprehensively address possible behavior change in families of 192 children identified as at risk for T1D through newborn screening. Approximately two thirds of mothers interviewed reported doing something to try and prevent diabetes in the child. Among those reporting behavior changes, monitoring behaviors (e.g., watching for signs of diabetes, checking blood glucose; 59%) were most common, followed by modifications in the child's diet (34%) and physical activity (14%). Potentially harmful prevention behaviors (e.g., limiting contact with other children; delaying immunizations; giving medications, including insulin) were rare.

Predictors of Behavior Change

Several studies have linked anxiety or worry about getting diabetes with behavior change in populations tested for ICA (Hendrieckx et al., 2002; Johnson & Tercyak, 1995). Among mothers of children identified as at increased risk through newborn genetic screening, those who reported increased surveillance or efforts to prevent T1D in the child were more anxious, perceived the child as at higher risk, used certain coping styles (information seeking, problem-focused coping, seeking social support, wishful thinking), and were more likely to have an infant with a first-degree diabetic relative (Baughcum et al., 2005).

Currently, it is not possible to prevent T1D. Nevertheless, it appears that many at-risk individuals and parents of at-risk children report engaging in increased medical surveillance and a variety of other behaviors they believe may prevent the disease. Fortunately, it appears that most of these behaviors are directed at increased surveillance or promoting a healthier lifestyle. Nevertheless, the implications of these efforts for natural history studies and prevention trials are considerable. Often these behaviors go undetected by study investigators (Johnson, 2002). Although environmental triggers are presumed important to diabetes onset in at-risk children, scientists have yet to identify which environmental events are critical to disease onset. Certainly, diet and exercise could play a role. Unless carefully monitored, families' spontaneous prevention behaviors could threaten the internal validity of any natural history study or prevention trial.

Reactions to Study Participation:
Satisfaction and Burden

Studies that identify individuals at risk for T1D, through genetic or ICA testing, usually hope to monitor these at-risk individuals over long periods of time for early signs of T1D or hope to enroll them in a prevention trial. These studies can be very demanding for both the at-risk individual and family members. A few studies have attempted to examine participant satisfaction with natural history studies of T1D and experimental prevention trials.

Lucidarme et al. (1998) reported that more than 90% of parents of T1D children wanted the unaffected siblings screened for T1D risk; however, only 52% would agree to have their child participate in an experimental prevention trial. A qualitative study by Gustafsson Stolt, Liss, Svensson, and Ludvigsson (2002) suggested that most of the 21 Swedish mothers interviewed had a favorable view of pediatric screening programs for disease risk. However, among those who declined to have their child screened, many cited concerns about putting the child through frequent blood tests. Similar results were reported by Hummel et al. (2004), who obtained questionnaire data from parents who had their offspring tested for ICA; one or both parents had T1D. More than 95% of parents reported wanting to know the child's risk status. This declined somewhat for those parents who learned the child was ICA+ (87% reported wanting to know the child's risk status post–ICA testing; 100% wanted to know before testing). Most parents viewed the child's blood withdrawal as a burden for the child but not for themselves. However, post–blood draw, more parents viewed it as a personal burden. This was particularly the case for parents of children who tested ICA+. Johnson and Tercyak's (1995) study of ICA+ children, adults, and family members noted that 96% of the adult participants were glad they participated in the study, but 10% of the children stated they wished they had not joined the study, citing concerns about the blood withdrawals.

Lernmark et al. (2004) reported that 32% of parents whose infants were genetically screened for T1D risk felt reassured by having the child participate in the study; 89% reported they were satisfied with the information given about the project. However, none of these parents knew the results of the child's genetic tests at the time they completed the study questionnaires. Those who were dissatisfied with the information given were more likely to be worried about the child's future health status. In a study of 190 mothers informed of their infant's increased T1D risk, 61% reported receiving the right amount of information; 38% felt they did not get enough (Carmichael, 2003). This study also reported the interesting finding that parental satisfaction with the information received was associated with underestimating the child's actual risk.

The preliminary findings to date suggest that most parents have a favorable attitude toward genetic screening for T1D risk. Difficulties seem to arise once the genetic testing results are known. If the child is found to have no increased risk, the parent is usually relieved. For those whose child's test results suggest increased T1D risk, the picture becomes more complex, particularly since these families are encouraged to participate in long-term surveillance studies or prevention trials. The burden of repeated blood draws and worry about the child is mixed with the reassurance increased surveillance can provide. For those who agree to enter experimental prevention trials, the demands of the study protocol can be considerable. Yet many remain optimistic that the experimental intervention will succeed (Johnson, 2002; Tercyak, Johnson, & Schatz, 1998).

RECOMMENDATIONS FOR PRACTICE
AND FUTURE RESEARCH

We have made great strides in our understanding of the genetics underlying T1D risk. We understand the autoimmune nature of this disease and with a simple blood test, we can identify individuals whose pancreatic beta cells are being destroyed prior to disease onset. Yet most of those with the highest-risk genotypes never go on to develop T1D. The etiology of this disease is complex and is presumed to involve one or more environmental triggers in genetically at-risk individuals. However, we have yet to identify those triggers, although a number of candidates have been suggested (e.g., diet and viral exposures); a multisite international trial (TEDDY) is underway to elucidate the genetic-environmental interactions that may underlie T1D.

Currently, we are unable to prevent T1D in at-risk individuals. All prevention trials to date have failed. Consequently, genetic screening for T1D risk is not recommended as part of clinical practice since no successful disease prevention strategy can be offered.

Genetic screening for T1D risk does continue as part of research strategies to understand the natural history of this disease and find a cure. Individuals who wish to participate in these protocols need to understand the advantages and disadvantages of participating in studies of this type (see Table 14.3). Disadvantages include the burden any parent must carry in making the decision to have a child genetically tested when there is no known method to prevent the disease in those determined to be at risk. Not only is the child unable to make this decision, but the parent faces the additional task of explaining to the child his or her increased risk status when the child is older. To further complicate the situation, high-risk genetic test results have poor predictive power. Although most genetically at-risk children will never develop T1D, the parent and child may feel they are living with an unpredictable, uncontrollable threat to the child's well-being. Clearly this could cause considerable distress, although studies suggest that this distress dissipates over time.

Advantages of genetic testing include the relief associated with low-risk genetic test results, a finding experienced by the majority of parents who decide to have a child tested. Possible early detection of T1D in genetically at-risk children who are being closely followed may

Table 14.3 Advantages and Disadvantages of Participating in Genetic Studies of Infants and Children Tested for T1D Risk

ADVANTAGES	DISADVANTAGES
Possible relief associated with low-risk genetic test results	Child is unable to make the decision to be tested
Possible early detection of T1D in genetically at-risk children	Parent may need to explain high-risk results to the child when the child is older
Increased access to possible prevention trials	Possible distress associated with high-risk genetic test results in parents or child
Opportunity to contribute to science and the possible prevention of T1D	Poor predictive power of high-risk genetic test results
	No currently available prevention
	Demanding nature of natural history studies

provide a sense of security for many parents. Certainly those who have children with at-risk genotypes will be the first to be offered participation in future T1D prevention trials. For many, the opportunity to contribute to science and possibly find a cure for this complex disease justifies the distress and demands of research participation. We are forever indebted to the many individuals and families who willingly participate in research of this type; without them we will never understand the natural history of this disease, an understanding that is essential to the development of a successful prevention strategy. Certainly we owe these children and families privacy of any test results and careful attention to their psychological needs and concerns.

We need to develop better ways to successfully communicate disease risk, a complex concept in T1D and for the health literature at large. We need to identify those who are particularly vulnerable to the stress of learning that they, or their child, are at risk for a life-threatening disease like T1D. Although many cope with this news with great resilience, we need to recognize some do not. Mechanisms must be in place to ensure that those in need can easily access appropriate counseling resources. Research protocols must include more than the biology and genetics of T1D; they must assess the cognitive, emotional, and behavioral impact of their procedures.

REFERENCES

American Academy of Pediatrics. (2001). Ethical issues with genetic testing in pediatrics. *Pediatrics, 107,* 1451–1455.

Baughcum, A., Johnson, S. B., Carmichael, S., Lewin, A., She, J.-X., & Schatz, D. (2005). Maternal efforts to prevent type 1 diabetes in at-risk children. *Diabetes Care, 28*(4), 916–921.

Carmichael, S. (2003). *Newborn genetic screening for type I diabetes: Factors affecting maternal risk perception, anxiety and study participation.* Unpublished doctoral dissertation, University of Florida.

Carmichael, S., Johnson, S. B., Baughcum, A., North, K., Hopkins, D., Dukes, M., et al. (2003). Prospective assessment of newborns of diabetes autoimmunity (PANDA): Maternal understanding of infant diabetes risk. *Genetics in Medicine, 5,* 77–83.

Cox, J., Holden, J., & Sagorsky, R. (1987). Detection of postnatal depression: Development of the Edinburgh Postnatal Depression Scale. *British Journal of Psychiatry, 150,* 782–786.

Dorman, J., McCarthy, B., O'Leary, L., & Koehler, A. (1995). Risk factors for insulin-dependent diabetes. National Diabetes Data Group. In *Diabetes in America* (2nd ed.). NIH Publication No. 95-1468. Bethesda, MD: National

Institutes of Health. Retrieved from http://www.niddk.nih.gov/health/diabetes/dia/

First, M., Spitzer, R., Gibbon, M., & Williams, J. (1997). *Structured clinical interview for DSM-IV axis I disorders*. Washington, DC: American Psychiatric Press.

Galatzer, A., Green, E., Ofan, R., Benzaquen, H., Yosefsberg, Z., Weintrob, N., et al. (2001). Psychological impact of islet cell antibody screening. *Journal of Pediatric Endocrinology and Metabolism, 14*, 675–679.

Gustafsson Stolt, U., Liss, P.-E., Svensson, T., & Ludvigsson, J. (2002). Attitudes to bioethical issues: A case study of a screening project. *Social Science and Medicine, 54*, 1333–1344.

Hendrieckx, C., De Smer, F., Kristoffersen, I., & Bradley, C. (2002). Risk assessment for developing type 1 diabetes: Intentions of behavioural changes prior to risk notification. *Diabetes/Metabolism Research and Reviews, 18*, 36–42.

Hood, K. (2003). *Maternal response to newborn genetic screening for type 1 diabetes: The role of depression*. Unpublished doctoral dissertation, University of Florida.

Hood, K., Johnson, S. B., Carmichael, S., Laffel, L., She, J., & Schatz, D. (2005). Depressive symptoms in mothers of infants identified as genetically at risk for type 1 diabetes. *Diabetes Care, 28*, 1898–1903.

Hoppu, S., Ronkainen, M., Kimpimäki, T., Erkkilä, S., Korhonen, S., Ilonen, J., et al. (2004). Insulin autoantibody isotypes during the prediabetic process in children with increased genetic risk for type1 diabetes: The Finnish Type 1 Diabetes Prediction and Prevention Study. *Pediatric Research, 54*, 236–242.

Hummel, M., Ziegler, A., & Roth, R. (2004). Psychological impact of childhood islet autoantibody testing in families participating in the BABYDIAB study. *Diabetic Medicine, 21*, 324–328.

Johnson, S. B. (2001). Screening programs to identify children at risk for diabetes mellitus: Psychological impact on children and parents. *Journal of Pediatric Endocrinology and Metabolism, 14*, 653–660.

Johnson, S. B. (2002, May). *Participant experiences in the DPT-1: Preliminary results*. Paper presented to the NIH Type 1 TrialNet Study Group, Bethesda, MD.

Johnson, S. B. (2004). *Type 1 risk perception*. Invited presentation, annual meeting of the American Diabetes Association, Orlando, Florida.

Johnson, S. B., Baughcum, A., Carmichael, S., She, J.-X., & Schatz, D. (2004). Maternal anxiety associated with newborn genetic screening for type 1 diabetes. *Diabetes Care, 27*, 392–397.

Johnson, S. B., Riley, W., Hansen, C., & Nurick, M. (1990). The psychological impact of islet cell antibody (ICA) screening: Preliminary results. *Diabetes Care, 13*, 93–97.

Johnson, S. B., & Tercyak, K. (1995). Psychological impact of islet cell antibody screening for IDDM on children, adults, and their family members. *Diabetes Care, 18*, 1370–1372.

LaPorte, R., Matsushima, M., & Chang, Y. (1995). Prevalence and incidence of insulin dependent diabetes. National Diabetes Data Group. *Diabetes in*

America (2nd ed.). NIH Publication No. 95-1468. Bethesda, MD: National Institutes of Health. Retrieved from http://www.niddk.nih.gov/health/diabetes/dia/

Lernmark, B., Elding-Larsson, H., Hansson, G., Lindberg, B., Lynch, K., & Sjoblad, S. (2004). Parent responses to participation in genetic screening for diabetes risk. *Pediatric Diabetes, 5,* 174–181.

Lucidarme, N., Domingues-Muriel, E., Castro, D., Czernichow, P., & Levy-Marchal, C. (1998). Appraisal and implications of predictive testing for insulin-dependent diabetes mellitus. *Diabetes and Metabolism, 24,* 550–553.

Marteau, R., & Bekker, H. (1992). The development of a six-item short-form of the state scale of the Spielberger State-Trait Anxiety Inventory (STAI). *British Journal of Clinical Psychology, 31,* 301–306.

National Institute of Diabetes and Digestive and Kidney Diseases. (2003). *National Diabetes Statistics fact sheet: General information and national estimates on diabetes in the United States.* Bethesda, MD: U.S. Department of Health and Human Services, National Institutes of Health.

Onkamo, P., Vaananen, S., Karvonen, M., & Tuomilehto, J. (1999). Worldwide increase in incidence of type I diabetes—the analysis of the data on published incidence trends. *Diabetologia, 42,* 1395–1403.

Radloff, L. (1977). The CES-D scale: A self-report depression scale for research in the general population. *Applied Psychological Measurement, 1,* 385–401.

Ross, L. F. (2003). Minimizing risks: The ethics of predictive diabetes mellitus screening research in newborns. *Archives of Pediatric and Adolescent Medicine, 157,* 89–95.

Roth, R. (2001). Psychological and ethical aspects of prevention trials. *Journal of Pediatric Endocrinology and Metabolism, 14,* 669–674.

Schatz, D. A., Krischer, J., & She, J.-X. (2002). To screen or not to screen for pre-type 1 diabetes? *Hormone Research, 57*(Suppl. 1), 12–17.

Speilberger, C. (1973). *Test manual for the State-Trait Anxiety Inventory for Children.* Palo Alto, CA: Consulting Psychologists Press.

Speilberger, C. (1983). *Manual for the State-Trait Anxiety Inventory STAI (Form Y).* Palo Alto, CA: Consulting Psychologists Press.

Speilberger, C., Gorsuch, R., & Lushene, R. (1970). *Test manual for the State-Trait Anxiety Inventory.* Palo Alto, CA: Consulting Psychologists Press.

Tercyak, K., Johnson, S. B., Roberts, S., & Cruz, A. (2001). Psychological response to prenatal genetic counseling and amniocentesis. *Patient Education and Counseling, 43,* 73–84.

Tercyak, K., Johnson, S. B., & Schatz, D. (1998). Patient and family reflections on the use of subcutaneous insulin to prevent diabetes: A retrospective evaluation from a pilot prevention trial. *Journal of Diabetes and Its Complications, 12,* 279–286.

Weber, B. R. R. (1997). Psychological aspects in diabetes prevention trials. *Annals of Medicine, 29,* 461–467.

Wion, E., Brantley, M., Stevens, J., Gallinger, S., Peng, H., Glass, M., et al. (2003). Population-wide infant screening for HLA-based type 1 diabetes risk via dried blood spots from the public health infrastructure. *Annals of the New York Academy of Science, 1005,* 400–403.

Wisner, K., Parry, B., & Piontek, C. (2002). Postpartum depression. *New England Journal of Medicine, 347*, 194–199.

World Health Organization. (1999). *Definition, diagnosis and classification of diabetes mellitus and its complications.* Geneva: Department of Noncommunicable Disease Surveillance, World Health Organization. Retrieved from http://www.staff.ncl.ac.uk/philip.home/who dmc.htm#Heading

Yu, M., Norris, J., Mitchell, C., Butler-Simon, Groschek, M., Follansbee, D., et al. (1999). Impact of maternal parenting stress of receipt of genetic information regarding risk of diabetes in newborn infants. *American Journal of Medical Genetics, 86*, 219–226.

Chapter 15

Inherited Cardiovascular Diseases
M. Dominique Ashen

NUMEROUS INHERITED CONDITIONS AND PREDISPOSITIONS FALL UNDER the umbrella of inherited cardiovascular disease. Familial cardiovascular conditions range from arrhythmias and structural abnormalities of the heart to those that contribute to coronary artery disease (CAD), such as hyperlipidemia, hypertension, abnormal blood clotting disorders, endothelial dysfunction, and inflammation. Familial hypertrophic cardiomyopathy (FHCM) is an inherited structural or electrical abnormality of the heart and is the leading cause of sudden cardiac death in individuals under the age of 35. FHCM typically follows a single-gene autosomal dominant model of inheritance with some known and unknown environmental and genetic modifiers (Maron et al., 2003). To a limited extent, individuals diagnosed with FHCM can modify their risk for sudden cardiac death or slow the development of congestive heart failure through both medical and behavioral interventions. CAD, by comparison, is characterized by the development of atherosclerotic plaque in coronary vessels. Plaque instability and clot formation can lead to cardiac events such as myocardial infarction (MI), stroke, or sudden cardiac death. CAD typically follows a multigene, multifactorial pattern of inheritance. However, since environmental and behavioral factors play a large role in the development of CAD, an individual diagnosed with CAD can reduce the risk of cardiac events and death through medication and lifestyle interventions, even in the background of an inherited predisposition.

In this new era of genetic and genomic discovery and technology, information about heritability as well as genetic mechanisms underlying cardiovascular conditions is increasingly available to individuals and their families. The meaning of a diagnosis of FHCM or CAD and the process of adjustment for the individual and family can vary greatly, based in part on the inherited and environmental factors that determine the development and outcome of each condition. This information has psychosocial implications that affect medical and behavioral interventions that, at some level, influence personal choice. The consequences of personal choice regarding treatment decisions and behavior modification carry high stakes in terms of the potential to reduce the risk of sudden cardiac death for both FHCM and CAD. Thus, the psychosocial implications for these two diagnoses in the individual and family can be far reaching.

The purpose of this chapter is to discuss behavioral, psychological, and social responses of individuals and their families to the heritable or genetic information they receive during risk assessment and risk modification of FHCM and CAD. The difference in pattern of inheritance for these two diseases provides an interesting backdrop to compare and contrast the way individuals and their families respond to this type of information. The specific objectives of this chapter are (1) to provide a basis for understanding the genetics of FHCM and CAD and (2) to increase clinician awareness and understanding of the range of behavioral, psychological, and social responses in order to optimize strategies for risk assessment and management and thus, reduction of cardiac events and sudden death.

FAMILIAL HYPERTROPHIC CARDIOMYOPATHY

A cardiomyopathy is a disease of the heart muscle. Each of the three main types of cardiomyopathy (dilated, hypertrophic, and restrictive) has a characteristic pattern of heart damage. In hypertrophic cardiomyopathy, the left ventricle becomes thickened and stiff. The distribution of muscle thickening within the septum and left ventricular wall varies, leading to several subtype classifications. The hypertrophied muscle often leads to impairment of systolic and diastolic function. Microscopically, the hypertrophied heart muscle exhibits an abnormal array of muscle fibrosis, resulting in electrical abnormalities or arrhythmias that can lead to sudden cardiac death. Over time, an individual with hypertrophic cardiomyopathy typically develops congestive heart failure. While some individuals develop hypertrophic cardiomyopathy secondary to a known cause, such as long-standing high blood pressure or CAD as in ischemic hypertrophic cardiomyopathy, others develop FHCM.

FHCM is a genetically heterogeneous condition that is usually inherited as an autosomal dominant condition with variable expressivity and variable penetrance (Maron et al., 2003). It is estimated that approximately 1 in 500 individuals carries a mutation that is associated with FHCM (Maron et al., 1995). Mutations have been identified in nine genes that encode for sarcomeric proteins, that are involved in the contractile function of cardiac muscle, and one additional gene that encodes for a subunit of protein kinase-A. Across these 10 different genes, over 100 mutations have been identified in individuals from families with FHCM, the majority of which have been identified in sarcomeric genes encoding beta-myosin heavy chain (about 35%), myosin binding protein-C (about 15%), and troponin T (about 15%; Richard et al., 2003; Spirito, Seidman, McKenna, & Maron, 1997). With the variable expressivities and penetrance of these primary mutations, researchers believe that there are yet undiscovered genetic or environmental modifiers. This reported variance in the location of the mutations on the sarcomere is manifested in the different phenotype or expression and difference in age and mortality.

FHCM is the most common cause of sudden cardiac death in the young, particularly competitive athletes. Several mutations in the beta-myosin heavy chain gene have been associated with a high incidence of sudden cardiac death, particularly Arg403Gln (24 cases in 85 patients) and Arg719Gln (22 cases in 61 patients), or a low-incidence benign course of sudden cardiac death, Leu908Val (2 cases in 46 patients; Marian, 1995). The identification and characterization of mutations associated with increased incidence of sudden cardiac death provides the opportunity to provide prophylactic therapeutic interventions.

The diagnostic criteria for FHCM include an unexplained left ventricular wall thickness greater than 13 mm in the absence of chamber dilation, systemic hypertension (blood pressure above 160/100) and aortic stenosis with a mean gradient greater than or equal to 20 mm Hg. Hypertrophic cardiomyopathy is thought to be familial (FHCM) when (1) two or more individuals in one family are diagnosed with unexplained hypertrophic cardiomyopathy or (2) one individual is diagnosed with unexplained hypertrophic cardiomyopathy and one of their first-degree relatives (i.e., mother, father, sister, brother, or child) had an unexplained sudden death under the age of 35.

FHCM Risk Assessment and Risk Modification

In determining whether a new diagnosis of hypertrophic cardiomyopathy is inherited, it is important to assess medical history of the individual and family. A family medical history questionnaire and pedigree design and analysis provide a starting point for the clinician. However, a genogram, which plots the biological relationships and psychosocial issues in the family, may be more helpful to the clinician's understanding of individual dynamics as well as individual–family dynamics (Olsen, Dudley-Brown, & McMullen, 2004; see Chapter 4).

Screening of additional family members is also an important part of FHCM assessment and evaluation. The current American College of Cardiology clinical guidelines recommend that all first-degree relatives (both adults and children) of an individual with hypertrophic cardiomyopathy obtain a baseline echocardiogram and electrocardiogram (ECG) to evaluate for signs of the condition (Maron et al., 2003). Although hypertrophy may not always be present in individuals who have inherited a genetic mutation for FHCM, echocardiogram and electrocardiogram screening for individuals in families where there is a diagnosis of hypertrophic cardiomyopathy remains the best way to achieve early diagnosis and management. As hypertrophic cardiomyopathy is known to exhibit incomplete phenotypic penetrance and delayed, late-onset left ventricular hypertrophy well into adulthood, it is recommended that, regardless of age, all first-degree family members of anyone with unexplained hypertrophic cardiomyopathy undergo serial echocardiography (every 3–5 years) past adolescence and into midlife (Maron et al., 2003; Maron, Seidman, & Seidman, 2004). It is recommended that any individual from a family with known FHCM who experiences syncope, shortness of breath, chest pain, or heart palpitations undergo screening regardless of whether or not they are a first-degree relative.

While the clinician's assessment of an individual's personal and family medical history remains the primary basis for diagnosis of FHCM, clinical genetic testing for FHCM is currently available in the United States (Harvard Medical School, n.d.). The mutations that can be identified are those most commonly associated with hypertrophic cardiomyopathy as well as those which infer a higher risk of sudden cardiac death (Table 15.1). However, genetic testing is expensive and is often not covered by insurance. There are also issues of confidentiality and fear of discrimination that must be addressed (Secretary's Advisory Council on Genetics, Health and Society, 2004). It is important to keep in mind that as the potential to measure genetic contribution to this disease becomes increasingly available, the genetic heterogeneity of the condition combined with the probable existence of additional unknown genetic and environmental modifiers may complicate how a positive genetic test result may be interpreted for a given individual (Charron et al., 2002; Marian & Roberts, 2003).

Medical treatment for FHCM focuses on reduction of septal hypertrophy, prevention of sudden cardiac death, and management of heart

Table 15.1 Clinical Genetic Testing for FHCM

GENE	NAME	OMIM#	LOCUS
HCM-A			
MYH7	Myosin, heavy chain 7	160760	14q12
MYBPC3	Myosin-binding protein c, cardiac	600958	11p11.2
TNNT2	Troponin t2, cardiac	191045	1q32
TNNI3	Troponin i, cardiac	191044	19q13.4
TPM1	Tropomyosin 1	191010	15q22.1
HCM-B			
ACTC	Actin, alpha, cardiac muscle	102540	15q14
MYL2	Myosin regulatory light chain	160781	12q23-q24.3
MYL3	Myosin essential light chain, cardiac	160790	3p

Note. From Harvard Medical School, Partners Healthcare Center for Genetics and Genomics, n.d. *Hypertrophic cardiomyopathy genetic test.* Retrieved from http://www .hpcgg.org/LMM/comment/HCM%20Info%20Sheet.htm

failure. Treatment options include lifestyle modifications (including exercise limitations, pharmacological interventions, surgery or alcohol ablation, the placement of a pacing device and heart transplant (Maron et al., 2003; Spirito et al., 1997). Risk factor modification for FHCM focuses on reducing individual risk of sudden cardiac death and slowing or preventing progression to heart failure.

CORONARY ARTERY DISEASE

Diseases of the cardiovascular system remain the leading cause of illness and death in the United States today. Single-gene mutations, chromosomal defects, and multigene and environmental factors as well as their interaction may underlie the complexity of cardiovascular diseases (Lashley, 1999). CAD, a type of cardiovascular disease, is characterized by progression from a healthy vasculature to subclinical atherosclerosis to clinical atherosclerosis to either myocardial infarction (MI), stroke, or death involving a complex multifactorial interaction. Scheuner (2003), in an extensive review of genetic factors underlying CAD, outlines multiple CAD candidate genes that code for enzymes, receptors, and ligands that drive biochemical processes underlying the complex process of atherosclerosis (Figure 15.1, left). These include genes involved in lipid metabolism, inflammatory response, endothelial function, platelet function, fibrinolysis, homocysteine metabolism, insulin sensitivity, and blood pressure regulation. Environmental risk factors, including dietary intake

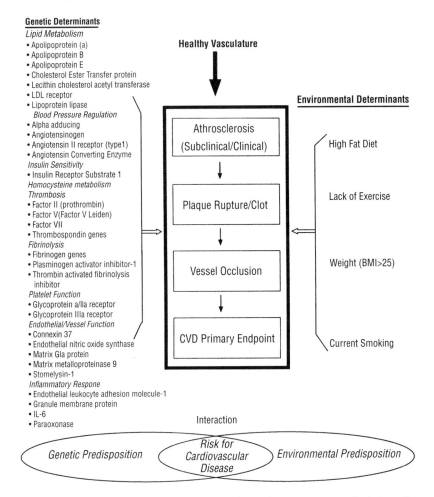

Figure 15.1 Genetic and environmental predispopsition underlying the development of coronary artery disease. Adapted from Scheuner (2003) and Stephens & Humphries (2003).

of saturated fats, sedentary lifestyle, obesity, and cigarette smoking, which are driven by individual behavioral choices, also impact the development of CAD (Figure 15.1, right). They contribute as causal risk factors (those directly linked to increased risk of CAD, such as smoking) and predisposing risk factors (those that intensify the effect of causal risk factors, such as diet, inactivity, and obesity). At the molecular level, these environmental risk factors may modify the function of gene products. The overlap in genetic determinants and environmental determinants, which represents the interaction of an individual's genetic makeup (non-modifiable) and environmental factors (modifiable), underlies the development of CAD in individuals with high genetic risk (Stephens & Humphries, 2003; Figure 15.1, bottom).

CAD Risk Assessment and Risk Modification

Evaluation of risk for CAD includes a family history, physical exam, and assessment of lifestyle, lipid and nonlipid risk factors as well as atherosclerotic plaque burden (Cobb, Kraus, Root, & Allen, 2003; Expert Panel on Detection, 2001; Grundy et al., 2004; Linton & Fazio, 2003). Elevated blood pressure (above 140/90) directly contributes to increased risk of CAD (Chobanian et al., 2003; Kannel, 2000). Obesity (body mass index above 30), physical inactivity, consumption of a diet high in saturated fat, and cigarette smoking are lifestyle risk factors that increase an individual's risk for CAD (Ascherio et al., 1994; National Institutes of Health, 1998; Powell, Thompson, Caspersen, & Kendrick, 1987; Waters et al., 1996; Wilson, D'Agostino, Sullivan, Parise, & Kannel, 2002). Lifestyle risk factors are considered direct targets for risk reduction intervention through therapeutic behavioral changes including weight loss, regular exercise, a low-fat, low-cholesterol diet, and cigarette smoking cessation. Weight loss and a regular aerobic exercise program also contribute to normalization of blood pressure (Chobanian et al., 2003). Emerging lipid risk factors (elevated triglycerides, non-HDL cholesterol, lipoprotein (a), apolipoprotein B, and an increased number of small dense LDL cholesterol particles) and nonlipid risk factors (elevated homocysteine and C-reactive protein) are also associated with increased risk for CAD (Expert Panel on Detection, 2001; Grundy et al., 2004). Evaluation of these biochemical markers during risk assessment contributes incrementally to the individual assessment of CAD risk. Finally, since atherosclerosis may be actively progressing years before the presence of ischemic symptoms, MI, stroke, or death, assessment of the preclinical atherosclerotic process will enhance risk assessment. Technologies currently used to assess preclinical vascular disease include ankle/brachial index, electron beam coronary calcification scoring, carotid ultrasound, brachial artery flow-mediated dilation, and MRI or CT imaging (Cobb et al., 2003).

One of the most important components of risk factor assessment in a multigene, multifactorial disorder such as CAD is assessment of family history (Guttmacher, Collins, & Carmona, 2004). A positive family history of premature CAD, defined as MI, stroke, or death in a first-degree male relative under 55 years old or a first-degree female relative under 65 years old, increases an individual's risk for development of

CAD (Barrett-Connor & Khaw, 1984). Recently, a sibling history of subclinical coronary atherosclerosis has been shown to be more strongly associated with risk for CAD than a parental history (Nasir et al., 2004). A history of premature CAD in any first-degree relative may reflect genetic predisposition via a complex interaction of multiple genes with environmental factors or environmental factors operating on a susceptible genetic background.

Family history of CAD is generally assessed through questions about premature MI, stroke, or death as well as hypertension and dyslipidemia. A pedigree analysis can be helpful in elucidating a pattern of heredity for monogenetic cardiovascular disorders, such as familial hypercholesterolemia (Li, Chen, & Chen, 2003), as well as an extended family history of MI, stroke, or death. A pedigree analysis in combination with a genogram, however, can aid the clinician in evaluating individual and individual-family psychosocial issues and focusing attention on those most at risk for CAD (Rogers & Rohrbaugh, 1991; Wimbush & Peters, 2000).

Together, physical exam and assessment of lifestyle, lipid and nonlipid risk factors, as well as preclinical vascular disease contribute incrementally to overall risk assessment for a disease that represents the expression of multiple interacting genetic and environmental risk factors. The multifactorial genetic nature of CAD promotes a level of uncertainty for individuals and their families as to the contribution of genes and their interaction with environmental factors resulting in expression of clinical disease in each individual. While genetic factors cannot be altered to reduce risk for CAD, modifications in lifestyle and lipid and nonlipid risk factors, which can influence gene expression, reduce an individual's risk for developing CAD (Expert Panel on Detection, 2001). Thus, the current primary focus in CAD risk modification combines medication management and a multipronged approach to changes in lifestyle, including the combination of dietary changes, development of a regular exercise program, weight loss, and cigarette smoking cessation.

Gerling, Soloman, and Bryer-Ash (2003) evaluated the advantages and disadvantages of DNA, mRNA, and protein screening for disease prediction in general. In applying their model to CAD specifically, the power to identify specific genes, mRNA, and proteins underlying this complex disease will confer the ability to detect early CAD, predict future CAD, and develop preliminary interventions to prevent clinical outcomes from CAD (MI, stroke, or death). However, while there are protein markers (such as lipoproteins, CRP, and homocysteine) that are linked to increased risk of developing CAD, there is a lack of clinically useful DNA markers.

IMPLICATIONS FOR INDIVIDUALS
AND FAMILIES

Information about the influence of genetics in both FHCM and CAD is becoming readily available to individuals and their families (see http://www.genome.gov/). While there is evidence for specific inherited genetic mutations underlying FHCM, which typically follows a single-gene autosomal dominant model of inheritance, clinical genetic testing is limited and financially prohibitive for many families. For CAD, which typically follows a multigene, multifactorial pattern of inheritance, there is a lack of definitive, clinically useful genetic markers. Gene-environment interactions further complicate the understanding of the genetic mechanisms underlying these complex cardiovascular diseases. Genetics influences the development and progression of these diseases, but the specific genetic mechanisms and their interaction with environmental factors are not clearly understood. This provides a level of uncertainty for individuals and families about the role of genetics in their disease process. There are multiple psychosocial implications for individuals and their families with a diagnosis of heritable cardiovascular conditions such as FHCM and CAD. The following is a discussion of some of the psychosocial implications that arise during the process of risk assessment and the development of risk modification strategies for FHCM and CAD.

Family History

Family health history is a window into the role that inheritance plays in disease. Individual and family risk assessment for both FHCM and CAD relies on the results of clinical evaluation and screening interpreted within the context of a family health history. However, lack of knowledge and lack of communication between family members about illness in past generations may result in a relative lack of knowledge about family health history. Often there is no defined reason for the death of a relative other than "heart trouble," and individuals must retrieve further information about the symptoms and circumstances surrounding a relative's illness or death. Depending on the dynamics that already exist in the family, the process of obtaining a family history and the family history itself can be perceived by the individual and family in either a negative or positive light.

The task of obtaining family medical history may bring up unresolved emotions for individuals and their families (Weil, 2000). The individual requesting details of the family health history may be perceived with suspicion and distrust by relatives who question the motivation behind their inquiry into something that may have never been discussed. In addition, family members may respond to the request for information with resistance and denial as a result of not wanting to consider that they themselves may be at risk for developing a similar cardiac condition. This can be particularly applicable to the risk assessment process for FHCM, where individuals may refuse to take part for fear that they too may have the genes that confer susceptibility for developing FHCM.

In addition, the place individuals hold in the family and the way they are perceived by the family may affect the family's response to their search for a familial explanation for their illness and their request for family health history. For example, an individual who is overweight, inactive, smokes, and has a poor diet may find it difficult to convince family members of a heritable component for a diagnosis of CAD that may extend to other family members. This can be frustrating and disappointing to an individual who is attempting to deal with a new diagnosis and place it in the context of the family.

There is the potential for individuals and their families to experience guilt or anger in the process of obtaining family health history. For example, parents and other family members may search for an explanation for the sudden death of an adolescent or young adult diagnosed on autopsy with hypertrophic cardiomyopathy, one of the leading causes of sudden death in individuals under the age of 35. This can extend to feelings of guilt and thoughts of what could have been done to prevent an individual's death as well as what could have been done to prevent the death of other family members. Should assessment of their family health history reveal information that may have provided an earlier diagnosis in the family and thus potentially prevented the death of the child or other family member, the emotional impact of blame, guilt, or anger on intrafamilial relationships could prove devastating (Kessler, Kessler, & Ward, 1984; Targum, 1981).

On the other hand, a complete and accurate family health history may prove beneficial to both the individual and the family members (Guttmacher et al., 2004). For example, an individual may have a family history of CAD in which every male, through several generations on either the maternal or paternal side, has died at an early age of an MI. A significant family history of this nature can, in many cases, motivate an individual to obtain CAD risk assessment and development of risk modification strategies so that they do not follow in the same path. Obtaining an accurate family history can also initiate action that extends to future generations. Often individuals at risk for FHCM and CAD use family history to take actions that minimize risk for the youngest members of their families. Overall, relatives may appreciate that someone is taking the familial nature of a disease seriously and look forward to learning what they could do to prevent the disease or sudden death that may be viewed as inevitable in their family.

Effective Communication

When there is a possibility of an inherited cardiovascular condition that carries with it the risk of sudden cardiac death, effective communication of this risk and modifications to minimize this risk are essential. Time spent communicating with the patient about his or her risk for disease has been shown to be positively correlated with a patient's adjustment to and quality of life with a disease diagnosis (Cox, O'Donoghue, McKenna, & Steptoe, 1997). Often after being diagnosed with FHCM or CAD, an individual may say, "What do I do now?" It is critical at this point for the provider to clearly communicate the basis for the disease and outline the management strategies that best reduce risk of disease progression and cardiac events. Providing the "big picture" to help answer this question and put the disease process in perspective will allow patients the ability to make changes that are important in reducing their risk for a cardiac event.

Since there is a basis for heritability in both FHCM and CAD, it is also important that clinicians extend their communication of risk assessment and risk modification to the family. Often family dynamics create barriers to communication about risk and modification of risk for disease. Identifying barriers to communication and providing anticipatory guidelines to facilitate communication to overcome these barriers can normalize the process of communication within a family unit.

It may be difficult for a patient to communicate with his or her family the need to make adjustments in the daily schedule in order to incorporate a specific risk management strategy, especially if his or her role provides major financial or emotional support to the family. For example, an individual who has two jobs and is the primary financial supporter of the family may find it difficult to communicate with his spouse the need to cut back on work in order to make time for changes in lifestyle, especially if the marriage is unstable or they are financially unstable. In another example, the individual whose role is to maintain the house, care for the children, and prepare meals may find it difficult to communicate with her family the need for others to assist her in her duties so that she can incorporate the needed risk management strategy into her daily schedule. Fear of reprisal and imbalance of normal family functioning may result in hesitancy or complete avoidance of communication between family members.

Including family members in the discussion of risk assessment and risk management may assist them in understanding the reasons underlying specific risk management strategies and their potential role as family members in incorporating these strategies into daily life. In short, interfamily communication may strengthen the family's abilities to work as a unit. Thus, for FHCM, CAD, or numerous other inherited cardiovascular diseases, the importance of effective communication to drive risk factor modification and disease management cannot be understated.

Attributing Meaning to an Illness

Individuals and family members usually carry with them a belief system through which they understand and attribute meaning to their illness or a relative's illness or death (Rolland, 1994; Weil, 2000; Chapter 2). The variable contribution of genetic and environmental factors to the expression of FHCM or CAD in an individual, however, complicates the meaning that an individual places on risk assessment and risk modification. For example, an individual with a good lifestyle (body mass index under 25, regular physical exercise, and a low-fat, low-cholesterol diet) but a high coronary plaque burden may find it difficult to accept that he or she may have a genetic predisposition for CAD despite these excellent lifestyle choices. In accepting the fact that there is a genetic component to their disease, individuals may feel they have no control over the course of the disease. This can be a daunting feeling, especially for those with a family history of multiple individuals dying at an early age of a heritable cardiovascular disease. For both FHCM and CAD, this is an important time for clinicians to stress the therapeutic goal of developing management strategies (through medication management and lifestyle modification) to prevent progression of disease and reduce risk for cardiac events.

Gender issues can also affect the meaning an individual attributes to illness, not only in the risk assessment process but also in the risk management process. For instance, while CAD is considered predominantly a disease of males, it is also the number one cause of death in women. However, few women perceive CAD as a significant threat of death (Sparks & Frazier, 2002). Providing information about the heritable nature of the disease and the relative risk to both genders is important in dispelling the view that one gender has a greater genetic predisposition than the other. In addition, gender differences may affect the way men and women cope with a disease diagnosis, find or respond to support from other family members or those external to the family, and actually recover from a cardiac event (Kristofferzon, Lofmark, & Carlsson, 2003). Understanding traditional gender role patterns and daily time commitments, gender-specific needs, and gender-specific psychosocial support systems will influence the way a provider develops strategies for communicating risk. It may also affect the choice of strategies to minimize progression of the disease and risk for a cardiac event.

An individual's life stage also contributes to the meaning he or she attributes to disease. For instance, a young, healthy individual diagnosed with FHCM or CAD may perceive sudden death as a remote possibility compared with an older individual with multiple morbidities or one who has experienced a cardiac event in the past. Diagnosis of FHCM or CAD may also thrust a younger adult patient into a more mature life stage, with more responsibility and decision making, for which the patient is unprepared (Rancour, 2002).

The overlap between an individual's life stage and the family's life stage further complicates the meaning attributed to disease. For instance, a young adult diagnosed with FHCM or CAD who has a significant family history of sudden cardiac death at an early age and is the parent of a newborn may view the diagnosis with more anxiety than an individual whose children are grown and living independently. In this case, the responsibility an individual acknowledges for dependents can play a significant role in the way the individual attributes meaning to the disease and his or her level of motivation to reduce risk of death from that disease. Knowledge of developmental stages through the life cycle for both individuals and families can alert the clinician to emerging problems that require lifecycle-specific psychosocial support that can reduce or avert emotional stress.

The Individual and Change

In working with individuals to develop risk modification strategies, clinicians must take into account factors that motivate change or act as barriers to change (Smith, 1998). The health belief model (Becker, 1993; Becker & Maiman, 1975; Clark et al., 1992; Janz & Becker, 1984) can be readily applied to understanding the likelihood that a person will take the preventive action required to reduce the risk for cardiac events and sudden death. In the context of FHCM and CAD, a person must first recognize a familial link for heart disease in order to perceive a personal risk. The perceived threat or seriousness of the disease is then influenced by demographic (age, sex, race, ethnicity), sociopsychological (personality, social class, peer pressure) and other variables (media, advice from health care professionals and others, and the illness of a family member). Together, these underlie an individual's perception of the barriers to and benefits of taking preventive action and thus, the likelihood that a person will initiate and maintain adherence to preventive strategies developed to reduce risk. In a test of the health belief model for susceptibility to CAD, perceptions of severity of CAD, knowledge of risk factors of CAD, and general health motivation together explained 76% of the variance in CAD preventive behaviors (Ali, 2002).

There are multiple examples of how demographic, psychosocial, and other variables affect the likelihood that an individual will take the preventive action required to reduce the risk for cardiac events and sudden death. One example relates to the influence of the media. News about new discoveries in disease etiology, the development of new drugs, results from recent clinical trials, and positive or adverse effects from specific treatments can have a dramatic influence on the way individuals perceive the threat or seriousness of an illness and the way in which they respond. For example, information from the latest clinical trials investigating optimal LDL-C levels with statins (Cannon et al., 2004; Nissen et al., 2004), readily available through the Web, newspapers, journals, magazines, and TV and radio news, motivated many individuals to gain information about optimizing their statin medication in order to lower their risk for morbidity and mortality from CAD.

Personal Choice

Risk modification strategies for both FHCM and CAD require a level of personal choice and decision making. Some individuals may more readily make and accept personal choices that are required to modify lifestyle than others. Limitation of strenuous physical activity is one focus for the prevention of sudden cardiac death in individuals with a diagnosis of FHCM. While this modification may prove relatively easy to accomplish for one individual, it may be devastating for another. For instance, the apparently healthy college athlete who has been diagnosed with FHCM based on familial screening may find it difficult to understand his or her risk for sudden cardiac death. If the individual's sense of identity is tied to athletic competition, having to consider the decision to stop participation could lead to feelings of anger and blame toward those in the family that brought him or her to the screening process (Targum, 1981). In addition, pressure from other family members to limit physical activity could actually lead to a rebellious and opposite action and thus contribute to an increased risk for sudden cardiac death.

CAD, by comparison, focuses on the development of a regular exercise program as a risk management strategy. For many individuals, this modification involves a personal choice to accommodate a regular aerobic exercise program. This can be influenced by socioeconomic factors or the physical inability to exercise. For instance, time constraints, especially for those that are the primary financial support for the family or the primary caregiver for children or elderly parents, as well as lack of access to exercise equipment or facilities, can provide barriers to development of a regular exercise program. An environmental factor is unsafe neighborhoods for walking and play. Individuals with arthritis, congenital abnormalities, and fear of falling related to age or medical disabilities may also find it difficult to develop a regular exercise program important in CAD risk reduction.

Risk modification strategies for individuals with FHCM and CAD also rely heavily on medication management. Personal choice in taking medication can be affected by cost, lack of insurance coverage, lack of knowledge about drug function, the inability to link drug use with risk reduction, and medication side effects. For example, without regular lipid analyses to reinforce the link between the use of a medication and reduction in cholesterol, an individual may discontinue use of lipid-lowering medication. For example, the public press on the side effects of some CAD-related medications may result in persons stopping the medication without contacting their health care provider. This is especially true if they link side effects to the use of their medication. By comparison, home blood pressure monitoring may actually reinforce the use of blood pressure lowering medications by allowing individuals to regularly link lower blood pressure with use of their medication.

The Immediate Family

The family is a dynamic system under constant change that strives for a balance between family members' needs and expectations. Sometimes disease or information on risk can cause an imbalance in this system, with family dysfunction acting as a hindrance to obtaining a new balance. Within the context of an inherited cardiovascular disease, normal emotions and tensions between generations related to life cycle patterns may escalate, creating barriers to change within the family. Dysfunction resulting from marital difficulties, caretaker duties for young children or elderly parents, death of a family member, or loss of employment are just a few examples of forces that may result in not only lowering the priority an individual gives to personal risk management goals but also lessening support from family members for these goals. Thus, early assessment of family functioning is essential in order to plan and implement interventions that promote family coping (Marsden & Dracup, 1991).

Both the risk assessment and risk modification processes for FHCM and CAD can be positively and negatively influenced by family dynamics. Communicating risk for a disease as well as strategies for minimizing this risk can function as a springboard to educate family members about risk of disease and death and strategies to reduce this risk. Families, in turn, can act in a positive way to support changes an individual must undertake to reduce risk. For instance, fear of the loss of a loved one to MI, stroke, or sudden cardiac death can result in motivation of family members to change food purchasing habits, eating patterns, and exercise patterns with the goal of promoting the individual's health as well as the health of the family. Recognizing the heritable nature of the disease may also influence the positive health practices individuals extend to maintain their children's health.

Family members of an individual diagnosed with FHCM and CAD may also seek risk reduction interventions for themselves. When an individual is diagnosed with FHCM or CAD, other members of the family, sometimes many family members, may come into the clinic for risk assessment and the development of strategies to reduce risk. Thus, multiple generations can be positively affected by the diagnosis of FHCM or CAD.

However, disease can also act as a burden to the family system. For instance, individuals with FHCM and CAD often require multiple medications. As these medications can be expensive, this can be a drain on family finances, especially if insurance coverage is suboptimal. In addition, family members are often involved in the process of obtaining, organizing, and dispensing medication, which can be overwhelming and stressful for family members on a long-term, day-to-day basis. In another example, an individual with congestive heart failure, as a result of FHCM, may be required to monitor his or her weight and modify the amount of medication taken in response to that daily weight. Family members are often involved in this time-consuming process. In fact, individuals and their spouses found this to be one of the most stressful aspects of managing hypertrophic cardiomyopathy (Cox et al., 1997).

Dietary restrictions required in FHCM and CAD risk modification can also be challenging for families. Often it is difficult to incorporate individual dietary requirements that differ substantially from those of the family, whether it involves modification of sodium and fluid levels for FHCM or saturated fats and sodium for CAD. This can affect family economics (what is purchased) and patterns of eating out as well as family cultural norms (what types of food are eaten and how families share meals).

The Social Family

In addition to the immediate family, the individual with FHCM or CAD functions within a social family. The social family includes those with whom they work, worship, and go to school. These environments provide a specific context in which individuals modify their behavior. Individuals can receive tremendous support from their social families in terms of encouragement, regular activity, and hope that are important in offsetting stressors (such as depression, anxiety, anger, apathy, and despair) and motivating change (Kobayashi & Shibuya, 2004). When the social family is absent, in full or in part, individuals may experience these stressors, which in turn may impair their motivation for change.

Returning to work can be a very positive influence. The desire to work and the social aspects of work were identified as important issues for women with CAD and FHCM (Wingate, Loscalzo, & Hozdic, 2003). Returning to work, however, can also be a source of stress, especially for individuals who find that their physical ability is impaired (an individual with a manual labor job after bypass surgery) or they are required to significantly curtail their physical activity on the job (an individual diagnosed with FHCM). This can result in a significant loss of identity and purpose for an individual as well as dramatically affecting financial stability.

For a young individual, the school family offers identity and support. However, there are potential peer influences that may make it difficult to initiate or adhere to a risk modification strategy that reduces risk of sudden cardiac death. For a young individual diagnosed with FHCM, curtailing or stopping a school sport may be difficult, especially if the individual has always participated in sports. However, there can also be support from team members as well as coaches to keep an individual involved in a less physical way.

Genetic Testing

There are multiple psychosocial issues surrounding genetic testing that impact the individual as well as the family. Knowing the specific genetic basis of a disease can lead to the perception that the cause for and consequences of the disease are uncontrollable. This can have a negative impact on an individual's motivation to change and, thus, the reduction of risk for that disease.

Genetic testing can also impact the family. Multiple questions arise as to how individuals communicate results from genetic testing to family members, how family members respond to this information, and the positive and negative influences of the family in response to an individual's decisions made in response to this information. Individuals diagnosed with a genetic disease may share genetic testing information with at-risk individuals and persuade them to seek testing (Peterson et al., 2003). While it may be more difficult and distressing to communicate test results to family members than to those outside the family, individuals may feel that it is their responsibility, not that of clinicians or genetic counselors, to inform family members (Plantinga et al., 2003). As noted in this chapter, information about the heritability of a disease, particularly specific information about mutations obtained through genetic testing, can have both a positive and negative influence on family members. Genetic counselors play an important role in identifying communication and coping strategies within families and developing strategies by which family members can take an active role in learning about their risk for a heritable disease.

CONCLUSION

Despite limited utilization of genotyping in the clinic, clinicians are able to provide information about what is believed to be the hereditary and nonhereditary components of FHCM and CAD to individuals and families. Knowledge that both nonmodifiable hereditary factors and modifiable risk factors contribute to a disease process highlights the need to integrate the knowledge of individual and family dynamics for the purpose of risk assessment and modification. This forces clinicians to expand their vision of the individual to a vision of the family.

The entire process of risk assessment and development of risk modification strategies can be extremely time consuming, especially when the process of inquiry brings up unresolved emotional issues. As part of a multidisciplinary team, genetic counselors, nurse practitioners, physician's assistants, and physicians knowledgeable about the psychosocial aspects of communicating and educating individuals and families about an inherited condition and trained to help them work through and cope with issues and emotions are uniquely able to impart this information compared with primary care settings that are disease oriented and time limited.

REFERENCES

Ali, N. S. (2002). Prediction of coronary heart disease preventive behaviors in women: A test of the health belief model. *Women's Health, 35,* 83–96.

Ascherio, A., Hennekens, C. H., Buring, J. E., Master, C., Stampfer, M. J., & Willett, W. C. (1994). Trans-fatty acids intake and risk of myocardial infarction. *Circulation, 89*(1), 94–101.

Barrett-Connor, E., & Khaw, K. (1984). Family history of heart attack as an independent predictor of death due to cardiovascular disease. *Circulation, 69,* 1065–1069.

Becker, M. H. (1993). A medical sociologist looks at health promotion. *Journal of Health and Social Behavior, 34*(1), 1–6.

Becker, M., & Maiman, L. (1975). Sociobehavioral determinants of compliance with health and medical recommendations. *Medical Care, 13*, 12.

Cannon, C. P., Braunwald, E., McCabe, C. H., Rader, D. J., Rouleau, J. L., Belder, R., et al. (2004). Intensive versus moderate lipid lowering with statins after acute coronary syndromes. *New England Journal of Medicine, 350*, 1495–1504.

Charron, P., Heron, D., Gargiulo, M., Richard, P., Dubourg, O., Desnos, M., et al. (2002). Genetic testing and genetic counseling in hypertrophic cardiomyopathy: The French experience. *Journal of Medical Genetics, 39*, 741–746.

Chobanian, A. V., Bakris, G. L., Black, H. R., Cushman, W. C., Green, L. A., Izzo, J. L. Jr., et al. (2003). The seventh report of the Joint National Committee on Prevention, Detection, Evaluation, and Treatment of High Blood Pressure: The JNC 7 report. *Journal of the American Medical Association, 289*(19), 2560–2571.

Clark, N. M., Janz, N. K., Becker, M. H., Schork, M. A., Wheeler, J., Liang, J., et al. (1992). Impact of self-management education on the functional health status of older adults with heart disease. *Gerontologist, 32*(4), 438–443.

Cobb, F. R., Kraus, W. E., Root, M., & Allen, J. D. 2003. Assessing risk for coronary heart disease: Beyond Framingham. *American Heart Journal, 146*(4), 572–580.

Cox, S., O'Donoghue, A., McKenna, W., & Steptoe, A. (1997). Health related quality of life and psychological wellbeing in patients with hypertrophic cardiomyopathy. *Heart, 78*, 182–187.

Expert Panel on Detection Evaluation and Treatment of High Blood Cholesterol in Adults. (2001). Executive summary of the third report of the National Cholesterol Education Program (NCEP) Expert Panel on Detection, Evaluation, and Treatment of High Blood Cholesterol in Adults (Adult Treatment Panel III). *Journal of the American Medical Association, 285*, 2486–2497.

Gerling, I. C., Soloman, S. S., & Bryer-Ash, M. (2003). Genomes, transcriptomes and proteomes. *Archives of Internal Medicine, 163*, 190–198.

Grundy, S. M., Cleeman, J. I., Merz, C. N., Brewer, H. B. Jr., Clark, L. T., Hunninghake, D. B., et al. (2004). Implications of recent clinical trials for the National Cholesterol Education Program Adult Treatment Panel III guidelines. *Circulation, 110*, 227–239.

Guttmacher, A. E., Collins, F., & Carmona, R. H. (2004). The family history—more important than ever. *New England Journal of Medicine, 351*, 2333–2336.

Harvard Medical School–Partners Healthcare Center for Genetics and Genomics. (n.d.). *Hypertrophic cardiomyopathy genetic test.* Retrieved from http://www.hpcgg.org/LMM/comment/HCM%20Info%20Sheet.htm

Janz, N. K., & Becker, M. H. (1984). The health belief model: A decade later. *Health Education Quarterly, 11*(1), 1–47.

Kannel, W. B. (2000). Elevated systolic blood pressure as a cardiovascular risk factor. *American Journal of Cardiology, 285*(2), 251–255.

Kessler, S., Kessler, H., & Ward, P. (1994). Psychological aspects of genetic counseling. III. Management of guilt and shame. *American Journal of Medical Genetics, 17*, 673–697.

Kobayashi, H., & Shibuya, M. (2004). Psychological stress reaction and psychological stressors in women with ischemic heart disease under follow-up treatment on an outpatient basis. *Journal of Japan Academy of Nursing Science, 23*, 31–40.

Kristofferzon, M., Lofmark, R., & Carlsson, M. (2003). Myocardial infarction: Gender differences in coping and social support. *Journal of Advanced Nursing, 44*, 360.

Lashley, F. R. (1999). Genetic testing, screening and counseling issues in cardiovascular disease. *Journal of Cardiovascular Nursing, 13*(4), 110–126.

Li, J. J., Chen, M. Z., & Chen, X. (2003). A pedigree analysis of familial hypercholesterolemia in monozygote twin brothers. *Angiology, 54*(6), 711–713.

Linton, M. F., & Fazio, S. (2003). A practical approach to risk assessment to prevent coronary artery disease and its complications. *American Journal of Cardiology, 92*(Suppl.), 19i–26i.

Marian, A. (1995). Sudden cardiac death in patients with hypertrophic cardiomyopathy: From bench to bedside with an emphasis on genetic markers. *Clinical Cardiology, 18*, 189–198.

Marian, A. J., & Roberts, R. (2003). To screen or not is not the question—it is when and how to screen. *Circulation, 107*(17), 2171–2174.

Maron, B. J., Seidman, J. G., & Seidman, C. E. (2004). Proposal for contemporary screening strategies in families with hypertrophic cardiomyopathy. *Journal of the American College of Cardiology, 44*(11), 2125–2132.

Maron, B., McKenna, W. J., Danielson, G. K., Kappenberger, L. J., Kuhn, H. J., Seidman, C. E., et al. (2003). American College of Cardiology/European Society of Cardiology clinical expert consensus document on hypertrophic cardiomyopathy. *Journal of the American College of Cardiology, 42*, 1687–1713.

Maron, B. J., Gardin, J. M., Flack, J. M., Gidding, S. S., Kurosaki, T. T., & Bild, D. E. (1995). Prevalence of hypertrophic cardiomyopathy in a general population of young adults: Echocardiographic analysis of 4111 subjects in the CARDIA Study. *Circulation, 92*, 785–789.

Marsden, C., & Dracup, K. (1991). Different perspectives: The effect of heart disease on patients and spouses. *AACN Clinical Issues in Critical Care Nursing, 2*, 285–292.

Nasir, K., Michos, E. D., Rumberger, J. A., Braunstein, J. B., Post, W. S., Budoff, M. J., et al. (2004). Coronary artery calcification and family history of premature coronary heart disease: Sibling history is more strongly associated than parental history. *Circulation, 110*(15), 2150–2156.

National Institutes of Health. (1998). Clinical guidelines on the identification, evaluation and treatment of overweight and obesity in adults: The evidence report. *Obesity Research, 6*(Suppl. 2), 51s–209s.

Nissen, S. E., Tuzcu, E. M., Schoenhagen, P., Brown, B. G., Ganz, P., Vogel, R. A., et al. (2004). Effect of intensive compared with moderate lipid-lowering therapy on progression of coronary atherosclerosis: A randomized controlled trial. *Journal of the American Medical Association, 291*, 1071–1080.

Olsen, S., Dudley-Brown, S., & McMullen, P. (2004). Case for blending pedigrees, genograms and ecomaps: Nursing's contribution to the "big picture." *Nursing Health Science, 6*(4), 295–308.

Peterson, S. K., Watts, B. G., Koehly, L. M., Vernon, S. W., Baile, W. F., Koklmann, W. K., et al. (2003). How families communicate about HNPCC genetic testing: Findings from a qualitative study. *American Journal of Medical Genetics, 119*(1), 78–86.

Plantinga, L., Natowicz, M. R., Kass, N. E., Hull, S. C., Gostin, L. O., & Faden, R. R. (2003). Disclosure, confidentiality and families: Experiences and attitudes of those with genetic versus nongenetic medical conditions. *American Journal of Medical Genetics 119*(1), 51–59.

Powell, K. E., Thompson, P. D., Caspersen, C. J., & Kendrick, J. S. (1987). Physical activity and the incidence of coronary heart disease. *Annual Review of Public Health, 8*, 253–287.

Rancour, P. (2002). Catapulting through life stages: When younger adults are diagnosed with life threatening illnesses. *Journal of Psychosocial Nursing and Mental Health Services, 40*, 32–37.

Richard, P., et al. (2003). Hypertrophic cardiomyopathy: Distribution of disease genes, spectrum of mutations, and implications for a molecular diagnosis strategy. *Circulation, 107*, 2227–2232.

Rogers, J. C., & Rohrbaugh, M. (1991). The SAGE-PAGE trial: Do family genograms make a difference? *Journal of the American Board of Family Practitioners, 4*(5), 319–326.

Rolland, J. (1994). *Families, illness and disability: An integrative treatment model.* New York: Basic Books.

Scheuner, M. T. (2003). Genetic evaluation for coronary artery disease. *Genetic Medicine, 5*(4), 269–285.

Secretary's Advisory Council on Genetics, Health and Society. (2004). *Perspectives on genetic discrimination.* Retrieved from http://www4.od.nih.gov/oba/SACGHS/meetings/October2004/SACGHSOct2004postmeeting.htm

Smith, A. (1998). Patient education. In D. Baker, J. Scheuette, & W. Uhlman (Eds.), *A guide to genetic counseling* (pp. 99–121). New York: Wiley-Liss.

Sparks, E. A., & Frazier, L. Q. (2002). Heritable cardiovascular disease in women. *Journal of Obstetrics, Gynecology and Neonatal Nursing, 31*, 217–228.

Spirito, P., Seidman, C., McKenna, W., & Maron, B. (1997). The management of hypertrophic cardiomyopathy. *New England Journal of Medicine, 337*, 775–785.

Stephens, J. W., & Humphries, S. E. (2003). The molecular genetics of cardiovascular disease: Clinical implications. *Journal of Internal Medicine, 253*, 120–127.

Targum, S. (1981). Psychotherapeutic considerations in genetic counseling. *American Journal of Medical Genetics, 8*, 281–289.

Waters, D., Lesperance, J., Gladstone, P., et al. (1996). Effects of cigarette smoking on the angiographic evolution of coronary atherosclerosis: A Canadian Coronary Atherosclerosis Intervention Trial (CCAIT) substudy. CCAIT Study Group. *Circulation, 94*, 614–621.

Weil, J. (2000). *Psychosocial genetic counseling.* New York: Oxford University Press.

Wilson, P. W., D'Agostino, R. B., Sullivan, L., Parise, H., & Kannel, W. B. (2002). Overweight and obesity as determinants of cardiovascular risk: The Framingham experience. *Archives of Internal Medicine, 162*, 1867–1872.

Wimbush, F. B., & Peters, R. M. (2000). Identification of cardiovascular risk: Use of a cardiovascular specific genogram. *Public Health Nursing, 17*(3), 148–154.

Wingate, S., Loscalzo, F., & Hozdic, T. (2003). Perceptions of activity and vocational status in women with cardiac illness. *Progress in Cardiovascular Nursing, 18*, 127–133.

Chapter 16

Genetics and Family Relationships in Schizophrenia and the Schizophrenia Spectrum Disorders

Pekka Tienari, Lyman C. Wynne, and Karl-Erik Wahlberg

MAJOR FEATURES OF THE BROAD FIELD OF BEHAVIORAL GENETICS HAVE been cogently discussed in Chapter 7 by Spotts, Towers, and Reiss. In the more specific domain of schizophrenia, research has tended either to emphasize genetic contributions and ignore or dismiss the psychosocial environment or, contrariwise, to make claims for the psychosocial environment without giving credence to genetics. In this chapter, we briefly provide an overview of this controversy and summarize recent integrative findings from the Finnish Adoptive Family Study of Schizophrenia.

A major source of difficulty in sorting out the origins of this condition began with uncertainty and historical inconsistency about diagnoses and boundaries of the clinical phenotypes that have been selected for study. Emil Kraepelin (1896) brought together the disorders of catatonia, paranoia, and hebephrenia into the large rubric of "dementia praecox," beginning in adolescence or early adulthood. Kraepelin described a poor-prognosis malady that he sweepingly differentiated from manic-depressive psychosis. Eugen Bleuler (1911/1950) placed less emphasis upon prognosis as he introduced "fundamental symptoms" for the renamed "group of schizophrenias." This richly but vaguely defined concept of heterogeneity under an overarching syndrome extended to his observation that the symptoms could also be found in a "latent" nonpsychotic form.

In the first systematic family study of schizophrenia, Rüdin (1916) found that siblings of schizophrenic patients had elevated rates of both "schizophrenia" and other potentially related psychotic disorders. However, neither he nor subsequent investigators of familial aggregation have found a classical Mendelian pattern for any of the variably defined diagnoses of schizophrenia. The primary consensus has been that the familial transmission of schizophrenia could not be explained by a single major genetic locus (Riley & Kendler, 2005). For several decades, twin and family studies, with varying degrees of methodological sophistication, strongly supported the conclusion that schizophrenia does aggregate in families. Nevertheless, during the 1950s and early 1960s, disputes raged about the key essential features of schizophrenia and about the possibility that schizophrenia runs in families for environmental instead of, or as well as, genetic reasons.

THE CONCEPT OF THE SCHIZOPHRENIA
SPECTRUM

Then, at the 1967 landmark Puerto Rico schizophrenia conference, Rosenthal and Kety (1968) reported Danish adoption data that convinced most researchers that genetics indeed contribute to schizophrenia and that this genetic effect extends to Bleuler's revived concept of nonpsychotic latent schizophrenia. Kety, Rosenthal, Wender, and Schulsinger (1968) asserted that there is a polygenic "*spectrum* of disorders having some features in common with schizophrenia but varying considerably in intensity" (p. 359). At that time, there was no consensus about the diagnostic components or criteria of this spectrum. In addition, Kety and colleagues acknowledged that their Danish adoption study was "not designed to evaluate the importance of a large number of environmental factors" (p. 359). Thus, there was a lot of room for debate and new research about what is transmitted, and how it is transmitted, in families. In turn, the answers to these questions would have major implications for the identification of persons at risk and for treatment and possible prevention of schizophrenic illness (Wahlberg & Wynne, 2001).

The formulation of the spectrum concept came at a time when there was widespread consternation among psychiatrists, especially researchers, over evidence that psychiatric diagnosis was wildly unreliable, even for the major psychoses of schizophrenia and manic-depressive disorder, especially between the United States and Great Britain (Gurland, Fleiss, & Cooper, 1970; Kramer, 1969). These concerns raised large question marks about the boundaries for the diagnostic complexity of the schizophrenia spectrum. From the 1960s to the 1980s, there was a concerted attempt to define all psychiatric diagnoses categorically and operationally as presumptive entities. (In the 1980 version of the *Diagnostic and Statistical Manual of Mental Disorders* [*DSM-III*; American Psychiatric Association, 1980] the effort to define criteria for the intermediate diagnosis of schizoaffective disorder failed; this category was listed with the statement that no consensus could be reached about criteria.)

Gradually, in genetic-epidemiological studies, certain categories of personality disorders and nonschizophrenic psychotic disorders were selected for the schizophrenia spectrum because they were found with statistically greater frequencies in the biological relatives of schizophrenic patients than in relatives of matched control probands. The category most commonly accepted as belonging with schizophrenia in the spectrum has been schizotypal personality disorder, partly expressed in nonpsychotic personality traits of oddness, suspiciousness, and social isolation, partly in neuropsychological deficits, and partly in features shared with several nonschizophrenic psychotic illnesses (Riley & Kendler, 2005).

These findings, in which diverse, multiple contributions to clinical heterogeneity within the putative schizophrenia spectrum are expected, have been explored further by Kendler, Neale, and Walsh (1995) using a multiple-threshold model. They hypothesized that the heterogeneous disorders in the spectrum are influenced by the same underlying liability or vulnerability. Evaluating the spectrum concept in Ireland, they arranged hierarchically five disorders (or subgroups of disorders)— schizophrenia, schizoaffective disorder, schizotypal/paranoid personality disorder, other nonaffective psychoses, and psychotic affective illness. Kendler, Karkowski, and Walsh (1998) have also used latent class analysis to assess the "relatively complex typology" of familial vulnerability to psychotic syndromes.

SAMPLE SELECTION IN THE FINNISH
ADOPTION STUDY

The Finnish Adoptive Family Study of Schizophrenia has compared adoptees at high versus low genetic risk for schizophrenia spectrum disorders and, in the same sample, compared adoptees in dysfunctional versus "healthy" rearing families. This design permits study of genetic and rearing-family contributions to spectrum illness separately and, for the first time in schizophrenia research, the joint effect or interaction of genetics (G) and rearing-family environment (E).

Sample selection began in 1969 with review of hospital records for all women who had been in Finnish psychiatric hospitals on January 1, 1960, or were admitted subsequently through 1979. A national epidemiological sample of 19,447 women who had been diagnosed at least once with a schizophrenic or paranoid psychosis was identified. This list was checked manually in every census and parish register in the country to find those schizophrenic/paranoid women who had adopted away one or more offspring. After exclusions for reasons such as adoption by a relative, a sample of 190 index adoptees remained. They and their adoptive families were matched demographically with 192 control adoptive families and offspring who had been adopted away by diagnostically unscreened biological control mothers. Research diagnoses using *DSM-III-R* (American Psychiatric Association, 1987) criteria were obtained for all available biological and adoptive parents and adoptees through personal interviews and through review of hospital records and registers. Longitudinal follow-up of adoptees by new interviewers has taken place for as much as 21 years after initial evaluation. Full details about the selection procedures have been reported (Tienari et al., 1987, 2000, 2003).

THE GENETIC BOUNDARY OF
SCHIZOPHRENIA AND THE
SCHIZOPHRENIA SPECTRUM

Before considering the interplay of genetics and rearing-family environment, we examined the question of how closely diagnoses of index and control offspring corresponded to the diagnoses of their biological, adopting-away mothers. First, can a phenotypic genetic boundary be drawn around the starting point of narrowly defined typical schizophrenia in the index biological mothers (Tienari et al., 2003)? In adoptees whose biological mothers had typical schizophrenia, the mean lifetime, age-corrected morbid risk for narrowly defined schizophrenia was 5.34% ($SE = 1.97\%$), compared to 1.74% ($SE = 1.00\%$) for low-risk adoptees, a marginally nonsignificant difference ($p = 0.063$). In contrast, in adoptees whose biological mothers had broad schizophrenia spectrum disorders, the mean age-corrected morbid risk was 22.46% ($SE = 3.56\%$) compared to 4.36% ($SE = 1.51\%$), a highly significant difference ($p < 0.001$). Schizotypal personality disorder, not typical schizophrenia, was the only specific disorder found significantly more often in adoptees with biological mothers diagnosed as typical schizophrenics (2.9%) compared to adoptees with nonspectrum biological mothers (0%).

Including 53 adoptees who had biological mothers in the broad schizophrenia spectrum beyond typical schizophrenia, the total of 190 index adoptees defined as at genetic high risk (HR) were compared with the 192 low-risk (LR) adoptees. The difference between these broadly defined HR adoptees and the LR adoptees was significant ($p < 0.001$) for schizophrenia, schizotypal personality disorder, and non-schizophrenic nonaffective psychoses (collectively but not for the specific component disorders). The data did not support inclusion in the spectrum of paranoid or avoidant personality disorders nor affective disorders with psychotic features. Thus, the Finnish adoption study findings supported the genetic hypothesis for a broad spectrum of disorders but without a sharply defined outer boundary. This finding becomes conceptually and empirically relevant when we go on to consider joint effects with the rearing environment.

POSSIBLE INTERACTION OF GENETICS AND REARING FAMILY ENVIRONMENT

The adoption design that was best suited for fulfilling our dual purpose of studying both genetics and rearing family environment was an extension of the approach used by Rosenthal and colleagues (1968) in Denmark. They had tested the genetic hypothesis by comparing adopted-away offspring of psychotic versus control proband parents but left open the possibility, implemented in the Finnish Study, of additionally observing, testing, diagnosing, and comparing the adoptive rearing parents of these offspring. Thereby, both the genetic effect from the biological parents and the environmental relationship of the adoptive parents and offspring could separately and jointly be assessed.

The selection and implementation of methods for evaluating adoptive family relationships was complicated. In predicting longitudinally to the outcome of adoptees, we have explored the use of three primary alternative sets of adoptive parent/family data. These data sets have been evaluated both as independent environmental predictors of adoptee outcome and, jointly with genetic liability, as possible contributors to genotype-environmental interaction. The adoptive parent/family data sets that have been used are (1) global family ratings (GFR) from tape-recorded interviews in the adoptive family homes (Wynne et al., in press-a); (2) more specific family ratings, the Oulu Family Rating Scales (OPAS), based upon home observations and tape recordings (Tienari et al., 2005); and (3) Communication Deviance (CD) measures of the adoptive parents, independently scored from tape-recorded Rorschach protocols (Wahlberg et al., 1997). In addition to predicting diagnostic outcomes of the adoptees (Wahlberg et al., 2004), the CD of the adoptive parents has been used to predict subsyndromal thought disorder of the adoptees, using the Index of Primitive Thought (Wahlberg et al., 1997) and the Thought Disorder Index (Wahlberg et al., 2000).

Global Family Ratings

As a more direct measure of the adoptive family environment, we used the GFR of the adoptive families (available for an N of 333 families). The raters were experienced clinicians who usually spent 14–16 hours in the family homes, observing and tape recording interviews and tests with the family conjointly, with the parental pair, and with each individual family member. The biological mothers were separately diagnosed from personal interviews whenever possible and from hospital and clinic records. After a median longitudinal interval of 12 years, adoptees were individually rediagnosed by interviewers who were blind to the diagnoses of the biological parents. The procedures of data collection, the reliability of the measures used, and the criteria for each of the five levels of the GFR have been reported in detail (Wynne et al., in press-a).

Very briefly, the criteria for these five GFR levels were as follows:

1. Healthy: needs and routines satisfactorily change with circumstances and development
2. Mildly disturbed: diffficulties resolved without major complaints or symptoms
3. Moderately disturbed: episodes of clearly dysfunctional, unsatisfying relationships, but not pervasively
4. Rigid, constricted: marked, unresolved difficulty moving through developmental transitions
5. Severely chaotic: openly conflictual, disruptive affect and communication (for a more complete description of criteria, see Wynne et al., in press-a)

The goal of this substudy was to use these GFRs as an environmental measure predictive of outcome for adoptees at low versus high genetic risk. A reference group of 70 adoptees at genetic low risk had been reared in adoptive families rated as "healthy" at GFR levels of 1 or 2. Their birth (biological) mothers had no lifetime diagnosis of a spectrum disorder. The prevalence of broad-spectrum diagnoses in these adoptees was minimal (2.9%). When rearing family dysfunction was severe (at GFR levels of 4 or 5), low genetic risk seemed to have a protective effect, with adoptee disorders only slightly more frequent than in the reference group. Conversely, when genetic risk was high, healthy family rearing appeared to have a protective effect against high genetic risk of the adoptees. In sharp contrast, when both broad genetic risk and rearing family dysfunction were high, 40% of the adoptees developed a spectrum disorder ($p < 0.001$)—clear evidence of genotype × environment interaction.

Specific Family Rating Scales (OPAS)

Complementary to GFR, 33 scales from a variety of sources were selected for ratings of specific aspects (OPAS) of adoptive family functioning (Tienari et al., 2004, 2005), each defined operationally for five levels from "healthy" to "severely dysfunctional." Some of the scales, borrowed from family researchers such as Beavers and Hampson (1990), had generalized applicability for the study of family relationships, for example, Nonacknowledgement and Manifest Anxiety. Other scales were constructed to tap concepts that have been hypothesized as especially relevant to families with schizophrenic members, for example, Narrow Range of Affect and Disrupted Communication. Extensive pilot testing and statistical evaluations of the ratings were carried out to examine interrater reliability and raters' consensual understanding of the items. The family interviewers rated families both from personal observation and from tape recordings of one another's interviews.

Finally, 9 scales were deleted as psychometrically unsatisfactory, and the remaining 24 were factor analyzed into three groups, labeled as critical/conflictual, constricted, and boundary problems (Tienari et al., 2004). Of 303 adoptive families with OPAS ratings, 145 had adoptees who were at genetic high risk (HR) and 158 at genetic low risk (LR). Only in the adoptees at genetic HR was there a significant association between the OPAS family ratings and adoptee diagnoses of schizophrenia spectrum disorder. Using a logistic regression model, both genotype (from birth mothers) and environment (with OPAS ratings) have statistically significant main effects.

However, when the genotype-environment interaction term was added, the model improved ($p = 0.018$ using the log likelihood ratio test). In the presence of interaction between G and E, the adjusted odds ratio was clearly nonsignificant in the LR group but very highly significant in the HR group (odds ratio 10.0, 95% CI. 3.26–30.69). Longitudinally, this finding of significant (G × E) interaction was sustained in the followup of HR adoptees who initially had a nonspectrum diagnosis or no diagnosis (Tienari et al., 2004).

Both with GFR and the more specific OPAS ratings, these measures of disordered family relationships were a more significant predictor of a reared offspring's outcome than were the psychiatric diagnoses of the adoptive parents (Wynne et al., in press-a). The findings confirm similar earlier conclusions of Wynne, Singer, Bartko, and Toohey (1977) and the more recent findings of Johnson et al. (2001) that disordered parenting was a more important predictor of the child's psychiatric diagnosis than was parental psychiatric diagnosis.

Communication Deviance in Adoptive Parents

A third method of assessing functioning of adoptive parents is Communication Deviance (CD), primarily measured in the Finnish study using tape-recorded and blindly scored Rorschach protocols (Wahlberg et al., 1997). CD is language production that is ambiguous and hard for a listener to follow. In this study, 42 categories of CD have been scored and evaluated as predictors of three indices of adoptee functioning: the subsyndromal Index of Primitive Thought (IPT; Watkins & Stauffacher, 1952), the subsyndromal Thought Disorder Index (TDI; Johnston & Holzman, 1979), and syndromal psychiatric disorders (Wahlberg et al., 2004).

Using the odds ratios and risk differences for high scores on the IPT of adoptees, the CD of the adoptive parents had no influence on the IPT of the adoptees stratified at low genetic risk, but did have a strong effect with adoptees at high genetic risk. That is, there was a strong interaction effect for the combination of adoptive parents' CD and adoptees' genetic risk in predicting the IPT measure of thinking disorder in the adoptees. In this same report (Wahlberg et al., 1997), the hypothesis was tested that oddities of the adoptees might disturb the rearing parents enough so that their communication patterns were modified. That is, perhaps the direction of environmental effect is from genetically at-risk adoptees to adoptive parents. However, this hypothesis was not supported: CD of adoptive parents who had reared offspring at genetic HR ($n = 58$) was no different from CD of adoptive parents who had reared genetic LR adoptees ($n = 96$).

In another report using adoptive parent CD as a predictor of adoptee thinking disorder, we used the TDI, instead of the IPT, as the measure of adoptee thinking under conditions of high versus low genetic risk and high versus low CD of adoptive parents (Wahlberg et al., 2000). The most clear-cut finding in a logistic regression analysis focused on the TDI subscale for Idiosyncratic (Peculiar) Verbalization. The odds ratio that adoptive parent CD would explain high scores on this scale was significantly higher ($p = 0.03$) for adoptees at genetic HR than for those at genetic LR. It is striking that this same form of thought disorder was found by Shenton, Solovay, Holzman, Coleman, and Gale (1989) to be the only factor that differentiated biological relatives of psychotic patients.

Family Vignettes

Complementary to the quantitative data summarized here, we have also presented a qualitative series of family vignettes as a small effort to help readers feel the distinctions that have been made between families (Wynne et al., in press-b). Two examples of these vignettes are inserted with the recommendation that they be recognized as merely illustrations of the considerable diversity to be found in the actual clinical material.

Vignette of a Healthy Family

Family #80 was interviewed in June 1979 in their countryside village home. The father, age 53, was a foreman in a small local firm and the mother, age 54, was a nursemaid taking care of three to four small children at her own home. Their adoptive offspring was a 17-year-old girl, soon to begin her education as a dental nurse in Helsinki, far from home (because she speaks Swedish and the only Swedish-speaking school for this training is in Helsinki).

The family was cooperative in helping organize the interview and test procedures during the visit, during which they politely offered the interviewer coffee and a meal. During the visit, all three expressed themselves positively and freely—not playfully, but able to see the humorous side of things and able to accept or modify occasional views that were divergent.

The parents vividly recalled how, after 14 years of frustrated infertility, their life had gained new meaning when the adoptee had been placed with them after 7 months in an orphans' home, where the baby had been taken directly from the birth clinic. The parents said that although they had been satisfied with each other before the baby's arrival, until then they had not been so accustomed to show their love openly. Now the parents were somewhat sad but accepting that their daughter would be moving to Helsinki, but she had promised to come back quite often. The parents said that they were proud that their daughter had the courage to move to the capital without knowing anybody there; she would live in the rooming house belonging to the school. Just before our meeting, she had become engaged to a local boy. Both parents said that he was well known to them, that they liked him, and hoped that he would become their son-in-law.

None of the family members had had troublesome psychiatric symptoms, but some had had mild somatic symptoms with their "stomachs" and minor allergies. Each family member had individual activities—the daughter in sports, the father in hunting, and the mother in a ladies club. They said, with wry humor, that none of them was willing to be "on stage."

Global Family Rating. Level 1, "healthy" on a five-point scale (Wynne et al., in press-a).

OPAS Family Rating Scales. All scales were rated 1 or 2, in the normal range (Wahlberg et al., 1997).

Comment. The question could be raised whether this family showed moderate generational enmeshment, one of the OPAS scales. However, within the cultural context of this family, such an assessment seems inappropriate.

Diagnoses. From personal interviews, neither adoptive parent was given a psychiatric diagnosis. In the Finnish health registers, there was no record that the adoptee's biological mother had ever been diagnosed as having had a psychiatric disorder, but the biological father had been registered for alcohol use. The adoptee was not given a diagnosis upon interview initially at age 17, nor when interviewed at age 32 by a new diagnostician, nor by register records when she was 39.

Rorschach Measures. Individual Rorschach protocols, independently scored from tape recordings, were consistent with the clinical assessment. Both adoptive parents had low CD scores, and the adoptee had a low TDI (Wahlberg et al., 2000).

Vignette of a Rigid, Constricted Family (#90)

In June 1978, the parents were interviewed separately from their adoptive daughter, K, age 18, because they were living separately at that time. The adoption had taken place after only a short period of deliberation when the parents were nearly 50 years old. The adoptive parents shared highly rigid religious beliefs, with strict moral standards. However, apart from their formal religious activities, their emotional life took place in parallel with little interaction. They expressed few feelings, positive or negative, directly to each other. However, without the possibility of conflict being mentioned by the interviewer, the parents repeatedly claimed that they had never quarreled and that child rearing had gone well. Both in the interview with the couple and in their description of their history, it became apparent that they have had many disagreements but with the emotional intensity blurred or denied. The atmosphere of the family could be described as pseudomutual (Wynne, Ryckoff, Day, & Hirsch, 1958).

The parents stated that their strong religious convictions kept them separated from their neighbors. They said that they had had to block K's relationships with her peers during her childhood. At the same time, they had worried that K was alone so much.

Later, as the parents became weakened with musculoskeletal pain, it was difficult for them to continue running their small farm. Although it would have been economically possible for them to move, they felt duty-bound by their religious beliefs, in which physical work was strongly emphasized. In accord with this precept, they expected K to work on the farm. When she was not motivated to do so, they accused her of causing their somatic symptoms. When K reached puberty, the parents felt her sexuality was "sinful" and they were sure she would become a "bad woman" unless they strictly controlled her activities. This further served to isolate the family from their environment, in which they saw evil everywhere.

Although the adoptive parents had no knowledge about K's biological parents, they openly blamed her "badness" on her heredity, in addition to blaming the irreligious community in which they lived.

At age 15, K's schoolwork deteriorated, and the school arranged for her to be sent to a child guidance clinic. However, the parents rejected the clinic because of fears that the girl would be somehow encouraged to have too much sexual freedom. K nevertheless continued to have contact with the clinic social worker, who supported K when she abruptly announced that she did not wish to return home. She obtained residence and a job as an aide in a home for the aged, and, thereafter, both parents and daughter refused to see each other.

In joint interviews with the parental couple, their communication was stiff and constricted, although unambiguous and highly rational. They exhibited no overt anxiety. All three family members have had numerous muscular and joint pains. There seemed to be little empathy between the parents and K and, in a sense, they have emotionally abandoned each other.

Global Family Rating. Level 4 (rigid, constricted).

OPAS Ratings. This family received ratings of 3 and 4 on most OPAS scales, except scales for rigid family environment and invariant parent-parent conflict.

Diagnoses. Adoptive mother: dysthymia. Adoptive father: anxiety disorder not otherwise specified. Adoptee's biological mother: schizophrenia.

The biological father was not found. Adoptee: initially, oppositional defiant disorder during adolescence, with low IQ and learning difficulties; at follow-up when she was 31 years old, schizotypal personality disorder.

Comment. Speculatively, it is possible that the daughter may have been protected from typical schizophrenia by the clarity of her conflict with her parents and by her positive extrafamilial experience with her teacher and other adults after age 15. However, with a schizophrenic biological mother and with a quite severe degree of dysfunctional earlier rearing experience, this adoptee's schizotypal outcome seems strikingly expectable.

COMMENTS AND IMPLICATIONS

About 40 years, ago the diathesis (vulnerability)/stress (stressor) model for broadly defined schizophrenia became widely accepted as a conceptual framework for research and clinical practice (e.g., Rosenthal, 1963). *Diathesis* was usually understood to imply genetics or a biological base. *Vulnerability* could include genetics and/or presymptomatic effects of environmental factors that have increased liability for illness. *Stress* and *stressors* could either be acute precipitating factors in the environment or chronic or recurring environmental conditions that would increase vulnerability. These broad terms were seldom operationally defined, partly because there was little agreement about the criteria for clinical phenotypes that could be identified as the outcome of the putative diathesis and stressors. Gradually, these terms have been used less often than the concepts from behavioral genetics that have somewhat more explicit referents in statistical and conceptual models, namely, genetics (G) and environment (E).

On the whole, schizophrenia research has not participated fully in the advances of behavioral genetics that have been applied to various other behavioral dimensions and neuropsychiatric disorders. Since the 1970s and 1980s, diagnostic systems such as the Research Diagnostic Criteria (Spitzer, Endicott, & Robbins, 1975) and the *DSM-III* (1980) and *DSM-III-R* (1987) have been formulated with interview procedures and diagnostic criteria that have greatly improved diagnostic reliability, if not always validity. However, earlier psychiatric records, which it has been important to review for older patients, did not use these criteria. It has been necessary, as in the Finnish adoption study, to rediagnose subjects for sample selection and the study of course of illness (Tienari et al., 2000). Actually, in schizophrenia studies, the older hospital records describing psychotic patients usually have been more adequate and accessible for research purposes than older records for patients with personality and nonpsychotic disorders.

The concept of a schizophrenia spectrum has been generally accepted since it was labeled by Kety et al. (1968). However, definition of the outer part of the spectrum has not been refined in many family studies that have arbitrarily limited the spectrum to schizophrenia and schizotypal personality disorders, sometimes with only one or two other disorders added. The Finnish study has contributed to defining the scope of the spectrum by using the adoption design to specify a full range of disorders related to proband birth mothers (Tienari et al., 2000).

Another approach to the spectrum concept has been the study of neuropsychological measures of genetic vulnerability. Here we refer to measures such as the Continued Performance Test (Nuechterlein et al., 1992), the Span of Apprehension Test (Asarnow, Granholm, & Sherman, 1991), and the Smooth Pursuit Eye Movement Test (Holzman, Proctor, & Hughes, 1973). Such measures (which have been included, not yet reported, in the procedures of the Finnish adoption study) can be expected to provide a link between genotype and symptomatic/diagnostic status.

On the biological environmental side, extensive studies have been carried out attempting to link obstetrical complications (McNeil & Kaij, 1978) and maternal influenza during midpregnancy (Brown et al., 2004), to later schizophrenia. Whether or not these putative precursors constitute distinctive subsets of schizophrenic heterogeneity remains to be confirmed. The fetal environment figures prominently in epigenetic aspects of neurodevelopmental theories of schizophrenia (Weinberger, 1987). We have proposed that psychosocial factors, including the family rearing environment, may also contribute epigenetically to gene expression later on (Wynne, 1968). These various factors underscore what has been called a multifactorial formulation of schizophrenia spectrum disorders, with both genetic and environmental influences (Rutter, 2004).

During the past decade, a considerable number of studies have used genetic linkage analysis in an attempt to identify specific susceptibility genes for schizophrenia and variably defined spectrum disorders (Faraone et al., 1998). Much of this work was contradictory and inconclusive, especially when confronting multiple genes of small effect. Nervertheless, a current view seems to be emerging that 4–6 specific susceptibility genes are noteworthy (Riley & Kendler, 2005).

Another complexity in the analysis of genetic and environmental effects arises because a substantial portion of the genetic influence comes about indirectly, through either exposure or sensitivity to the environment, operating through dimensional attributes such as temperament rather than by acting on any disorder as such (Rutter & Silberg, 2002). The processes by which genes lead to certain protein products are merely the starting point on a complicated biological path that finally leads to diverse forms of behavior and pathology (Rutter, 2004).

Conceptually, the Finnish study provides explicit evidence for two points that are expected by most schizophrenia researchers but are resisted because they make our task more difficult. First, defined clinically and phenotypically, the genetic boundary of "schizophrenia" falls along a broad continuum (or continua) and cannot be delimited as a neat genetic entity. Second, there appear to be significant contributions to the expressed disorder from the psychosocial domain, probably through reciprocal transactions between individual persons and their environment, including but not restricted to family relationships.

The approach to genotype-environment interaction in the Finnish study has been previously defined by Kendler and Eaves (1986) as genetic control of sensitivity to the environment or environmental control of genetic expression. Similarly, Gottesman and Bertelsen (1989) have proposed that schizophrenic genotypes may remain unexpressed until released by some kind of environmental stressor. These formulations appear to be compatible with the Finnish study findings of significant genotype-environment interaction.

On this path to disorder or health, an emerging research endeavor involves the clinical assessment of prodromal signs and symptoms signaling the impending onset of schizophrenia (Wahlberg & Wynne, 2001). At least three programs are exploring preventive research in which psychosocial support and carefully monitored neuroleptic medications are made available (Falloon, 1992; McFarlane, 2001; McGorry & Kulkarni, 1994). Such approaches are compatible with the findings summarized here: Either healthy genes or a healthy environment can be protective against the development of serious mental illness. Educational and supportive programs may be helpful in contributing to such protection. More problematic is the ethics of prescribing medications with potent side effects when the term *prodromal* implies, sometimes mistakenly, a relentless emergence of illness.

The possible relevance of these findings to genetic counseling with persons at risk for schizophrenia has not been explored, so far as we are aware. Our current view is that it would be inappropriate and unnecessary to advise against reproduction by persons who have a first-degree relative with schizophrenia. The actual low degree of liability, together with the possibility of supportive, healthy rearing should be quietly reassuring to professionals and families alike. Persons who are worried about the risks for themselves when one or more relatives have had schizophrenia do deserve careful, supportive attention from professionals who are qualified to assess liability from any source and to evaluate prodromal symptoms if they should emerge.

Acknowledgments: Partial funding was provided by grant MH 39663 from the National Insitute of Mental Health, the Scottish Rite Schizophrenia Research Program, the National Research Board in Finland, and the Signe och Ane Gyllenberg Foundation.

REFERENCES

American Psychiatric Association. (1980). *Diagnostic and statistical manual of mental disorders* (3rd ed.). Washington, DC: Author.

American Psychiatric Association. (1987). *Diagnostic and statistical manual of mental disorders* (3rd ed., rev.). Washington, DC: Author.

Asarnow, R. F., Granholm, E., & Sherman, T. (1991). Span of apprehension in schizophrenia. In S. R. Steinhauer, J. H. Gruzelier, & J. Zubin (Eds.), *Handbook of schizophrenia, vol. 5: Neuropsychology, psychophysiology, and information processing* (pp. 335–370). Amsterdam: Elsevier.

Beavers, W. R., & Hampson, B. (1990). *Successful families: Assessment and intervention.* New York: Norton.

Bleuler, E. (1950). *Dementia praecox or the group of schizophrenias.* Trans. J. Zinkin. New York: International Universities Press. (Original work published 1911)

Brown, A., Begg, M. D., Gravenstein, S., Schaefer, C. A., Wyatt, R. J., Bresnahan, M., et al. (2004). Serologic evidence of prenatal influenza in the etiology of schizophrenia. *Archives of General Psychiatry, 61,* 774–780.

Falloon, I. R. H. (1992). Early intervention for first episodes of schizophrenia: A preliminary exploration. *Psychiatry, 55,* 4–15.

Faraone, S. V., Matise, T., Svracik, D., Pepple, J., Malaspina, D., Suarez, B., et al. (1981). Genome scan of European-American schizophrenia pedigrees: Results of the NIMH Genetics Initiative and Millenium Consortium. *American Journal of Medical Genetics, 81,* 290–295.

Gottesman, I. I., & Bertelsen, A. (1989). Confirming unexpressed genotypes for schizophrenia: Risks in the offspring of Fischer's Danish identical and fraternal discordant twins. *Archives of General Psychiatry, 46,* 867–872.

Gurland, B. J., Fleiss, J. L., & Cooper, J. E. (1970). Cross-national study of the diagnosis of mental disorders: Hospital diagnoses and hospital patients in New York and London. *Comprehensive Psychiatry, 11,* 18–25.

Holzman, P. S., Proctor, L. R., & Hughes, D. W. (1973). Eye-tracking patterns in schizophrenia. *Science, 181,* 179–181.

Johnson, J. G., Cohen, P., Kasen, S., et al. (2001). Association of maladaptive parental behavior with psychiatric disorder among parents and their offspring. *Archives of General Psychiatry, 58,* 453–460.

Johnston, M. H., & Holzman, P. S. (1979). *Assessing schizophrenic thinking.* San Francisco: Jossey-Bass.

Kendler, K. S., & Eaves, L. J. (1986). Models for the joint effect of genotype and environment on liability to psychiatric illness. *American Journal of Psychiatry, 143,* 279–289.

Kendler, K. S., Karkowski, L. M., & Walsh, D. (1998). The structure of psychosis: Latent class analysis of probands from the Roscommon Family Study. *Archives of General Psychiatry, 55,* 492–499.

Kendler, K. S., Myers, J. M., O'Neill, et al. (2000). Clinical features of schizophrenia and linkage to chromosomes 5q, 6p, 8p, and 10p in the Irish study of high-density schizophrenia families. *American Journal of Psychiatry, 157,* 402–408.

Kendler, K. S., Neale, M. C., & Walsh, D. (1995). Evaluating the spectrum concept of schizophrenia in the Roscommon Family Study. *American Journal of Psychiatry, 152,* 749–754.

Kety, S. S., Rosenthal, D., Wender, P. H., & Schulsinger, F. (1968). The types and prevalence of mental illness in the biological and adoptive families of adopted schizophrenics. In D. Rosenthal & S. S. Kety (Eds.), *The transmission of schizophrenia* (pp. 345–362). Oxford, UK: Pergamon Press.

Kraepelin, E. (1896). *Psychiatrie* (5th ed.). Leipzig: Johann Ambrosius Barth.

Kramer, M. (1969). Cross-national study of diagnosis of the mental disorders: Origin of the problem. *American Journal of Psychiatry, 125* (Suppl. 10), 1.

McFarlane, W. R. (2001). Family-based treatment in prodromal and first episode psychosis. In T. Miller et al. (Eds.), *Early intervention in psychotic disorders* (pp. 197–230). Netherlands: Kluwer.

McGorry, P. D., & Kulkarni, J. (1994). Prevention and preventively oriented clinical care in psychiatric disorders. *Australian Journal of Neuropsychopharmacology, 7,* 62–69.

McNeil, T. F., & Kaij, L. (1978). Obstetric factors in the development of schizophrenia: Complications in the births of preschizophrenics and in reproduction by schizophrenic parents. In L. C. Wynne, R. L. Cromwell, & S. Matthysse (Eds.), *The nature of schizophrenia: New approaches to research and treatment* (pp. 401–429). New York: Wiley.

Nuechterlein, K. H., Dawson, M. E., Gitlin, M., Ventura, J., Goldstein, M. J., Snyder, K. S., et al. (1992). Developmental processes in schizophrenic disorders: Longitudinal studies of vulnerability and stress. *Schizophrenia Bulletin, 18,* 387–425.

Riley, B. P., & Kendler, K. S. (2005). Schizophrenia: Genetics. In B. J. Sadock & V. A. Sadock (Eds.), *Kaplan and Sadock's comprehensive textbook of psychiatry* (8th ed., vol. 1, pp. 1354–1371). Philadelphia: Lippincott Williams and Wilkins.

Rosenthal, D. (Ed.). (1963). *The Genain quadruplets.* New York: Basic Books.

Rosenthal, D, & Kety, S. S. (Eds.). (1968). *The transmission of schizophrenia.* Oxford, UK: Pergamon Press.

Rosenthal, D., Wender, P. H., Kety, S. S., Schulsinger, F., Welner, J., & Ostergaard, L. (1968). Schizophrenics' offspring reared in adoptive homes. In D. Rosenthal & S. S. Kety (Eds.), *The transmission of schizophrenia* (pp. 377–391). Oxford, UK: Pergamon Press.

Rüdin, E. (1916). *Zur Vererbung und Neuentstehung der Dementia Praecox.* Berlin: Springer Verlag OHG.

Rutter, M. (2004). Pathways of genetic influences on psychopathology. *European Review, 12*, 19–33.

Rutter, M., & Silberg, J. (2002). Gene-environment interplay in relation to emotional and behavioral disturbance. *Annual Review of Psychology, 53*, 463–490.

Shenton, M. E., Solovay, M. R., Holzman, P. S., Coleman, M., & Gale, H. G. (1989), Thought disorder in the relatives of psychotic patients. *Archives of General Psychiatry, 46*, 897–901.

Spitzer, R. L., Endicott, J., & Robins, E. (1975). *Research diagnostic criteria (RDC) for a selected group of functional disorders.* New York: Biometrics Research, New York State Psychiatric Institute.

Tienari, P., Sorri, A., Lahti, I., Naarala, M., Wahlberg, K.-E., et al. (1987). Genetic and psychosocial factors in schizophrenia: The Finnish Adoptive Family Study. *Schizophrenia Bulletin, 13*, 477–484.

Tienari, P., Wynne, L. C., Läksy, K., Moring, J., Nieminen, P., Sorri, A., et al. (2003). Genetic boundaries of the schizophrenia spectrum: Evidence from the Finnish Adoptive Family Study of Schizophrenia. *American Journal of Psychiatry, 160*, 1587–1594.

Tienari, P., Wynne, L. C., Moring, J., Läksy, K., Nieminen, P., Sorri, A., et al. (2000). Finnish Adoptive Family Study: Sample selection and adoptee DSM-III-R diagnoses. *Acta Psychiatrica Scandinavica, 101*, 433–443.

Tienari, P., Wynne, L. C., Sorri, A., Lahti, I., Läksy, K., Moring, J., et al. (2004). Genotype-environment interaction in schizophrenia-spectrum disorder: Long-term follow-up study of Finnish adoptees. *British Journal of Psychiatry, 184*, 216–224.

Tienari, P., Wynne, L. C., Sorri, A., Lahti, I., Moring, J., Nieminen, P., et al. (2005). Observing relationships in Finnish adoptive families: Oulu Family Rating Scale. *Nordic Journal of Psychiatry, 59*, 256–263.

Wahlberg, K.-E., & Wynne, L. C. (2001). Possibilities for prevention of schizophrenia. *International Journal of Mental Health, 30*, 91–103.

Wahlberg, K.-E., Wynne, L. C., Hakko, H., Läksy, K., Moring, J., Miettunen, J., et al. (2004). Interaction of genetic risk and adoptive parent Communication Deviance: Longitudinal prediction of adoptee psychiatric disorders. *Psychological Medicine, 34*, 1531–1541.

Wahlberg, K.-E., Wynne, L. C., Oja, H., Keskitalo, P., Anais-Tanner, H., Koistinen, P., et al. (2000). Thought Disorder Index of Finnish adoptees and Communication Deviance of their adoptive parents. *Psychological Medicine, 30*, 127–136.

Wahlberg, K.-E., Wynne, L. C., Oja, H., Keskitalo, P., Pykaslainen, L., Lahti, I., et al. (1997). Gene-environment interaction in vulnerability to schizophrenia: Findings from the Finnish Adoptive Family Study of Schizophrenia. *American Journal of Psychiatry, 154*, 355–362.

Watkins, J. G., & Stauffacher, J. C. (1952). An index of pathological thinking in the Rorschach. *Journal of Projective Techniques, 16*, 276–286.

Weinberger, D. R. (1987). Implications of normal brain development for the pathogenesis of schizophrenia. *Archives of General Psychiatry, 44*, 660–669.

Wynne, L. C. (1968). Methodologic and conceptual issues in the study of schizophrenics and their families. In D. Rosenthal & S. S. Kety (Eds.), *The transmission of schizophrenia* (pp. 185–199). Oxford, UK: Pergamon Press.

Wynne, L. C., Ryckoff, I., Day, J., & Hirsch, S. (1958). Pseudo-mutuality in the family relations of schizophrenics. *Psychiatry*, 205–220.

Wynne, L. C., Singer, M. T., Bartko, J. J., & Toohey, M. L. (1977). Schizophrenics and their families: Research on parental communication. In J. M. Tanner (Ed.), *Developments in psychiatric research*. London: Hodder & Stoughton.

Wynne, L. C., Tienari, P., Nieminen, P., Sorri, A., Lahti, I., Moring, J., et al. (in press-a). Genotype-environment interaction in the schizophrenia spectrum: Genetic liability and Global Family Ratings in the Finnish Adoption Study. *Family Process*.

Wynne, L. C., Tienari, P., Sorri, A., Lahti, I., Moring, J., & Wahlberg, K-E. (in press-b). Genotype-environment interaction in the schizophrenia spectrum: Qualitative observations. *Family Process*.

PART IV

ETHICAL, LEGAL, POLICY, AND PROFESSIONAL ISSUES

Chapter 17

Ethical Issues in Reproductive Genetics

Kelly Ormond and Lainie Friedman Ross

REPRODUCTIVE GENETICS IS A RELATIVELY NEW FIELD OF MEDICINE IN which individuals and couples are counseled and potentially offered genetic testing for their reproductive risks of having a child with a genetic condition. Such genetic counseling and testing can be provided either preconception or prenatally (during a pregnancy). In this chapter, we explore the various stages at which reproductive genetic counseling and testing can occur, the options they provide, and their ethical and social implications for the individual and family, specifically related to aspects of abortion and disability rights. Finally, we conclude by considering some of the special issues related to prenatal testing for adult-onset conditions.

PRECONCEPTION AND PRENATAL GENETIC COUNSELING AND TESTING

An individual or couple may seek or be referred for reproductive genetic counseling because of known risk factors within one's family or ethnic group, or because one is at high risk for other reasons such as maternal age (associated with a higher rate of chromosome anomalies) or maternal illnesses (e.g., maternal diabetes is associated with various birth defects, including spina bifida and congenital heart disease). Some of the conditions that can be detected through prenatal diagnosis are not "genetic" in the strict sense, and prenatal testing is broader than simply the detection of genetic conditions. We will, however, focus our discussion on those conditions that are known to be primarily genetic in origin.

Individuals and couples may not be aware that they carry certain gene mutations that may affect the health or well-being of their fetus. For example, individuals who are carriers of autosomal recessive or X-linked gene mutations (e.g., sickle-cell anemia, cystic fibrosis, hemophilia) are virtually always asymptomatic, as are men and women who carry a balanced chromosome translocation (a rearrangement of genetic material on the chromosomes that preserves the number and amount of chromosomal material). Additionally, many couples are offered genetic screening for a variety of conditions that are more common in their ethnic communities (e.g., sickle-cell anemia in African American populations, cystic fibrosis [CF] in Caucasian populations, and Tay-Sachs in Ashkenazi Jewish populations). In most cases, there is no family history of the condition, and even if there is, an individual may not be aware of it or understand why it is important. For a couple who is already pregnant at the time they learn of genetic risk factors, this new awareness can be anxiety provoking, require rapid decision making, and put a substantial amount of stress on the couple. Additionally, family relationships may be transformed when couples who have recently learned of their own genetic risk consider sharing that information with other family members who may also be at risk.

Reproductive genetic counseling can help individuals and couples determine their personal risk for having a child with a genetic condition. This risk may be as high as 100% (e.g., the risk that a couple who both have sickle-cell anemia will pass the disease on to their child) or lower than 1% (e.g., the risk that a woman under 40 years old will give birth to a child with a chromosome abnormality such as Down syndrome). For known Mendelian genetic conditions, objective risks can be provided based on the known mode of inheritance, but knowing the probability of inheriting a gene mutation does not necessarily tell one how severe the condition will be ("variable expression"), or whether it will present at all ("variable penetrance"); these issues are particularly salient for conditions where symptoms present in adulthood. Additionally, data suggest that people individualize statistical risk based on their own experiences (including employment; e.g., see Roggenbuck, Olson, Sellers, & Ludowese, 2000) and the framing of the material (e.g., see Tversky & Kahneman, 1981). Even within a couple or family unit, an objective risk assessment may have different subjective perceptions (Beeson & Bolbus, 1985; Sorenson & Wertz, 1986). For these reasons, genetic counseling can offer individuals and couples information about the wide-ranging possibilities that they may face if they do conceive a child with such a genetic endowment, and the resources to make decisions based on their personal values.

Joe and Mary Smith have been married for four years. At their first obstetrical visit, Mary is offered CF carrier testing as recommended by the American College of Obstetrics and Gynecology (2001). She accepts, and when she is found to be a carrier, the obstetrician briefly explains that CF is the most common autosomal recessive condition in Caucasians and that it is associated with lung and intestinal problems and a shortened life expectancy. The obstetrician explains that the fetus is at risk only if Joe is also a carrier, and Joe voluntarily undergoes testing. He, too, is found to be a carrier. The obstetrician refers them for genetic counseling.

Reproductive genetic counseling may occur prior to a conception or at various points during a pregnancy. Clearly, preconception genetic counseling offers individuals and couples the greatest number of options if they are found to be at increased genetic risk. First, they may choose not to have children at all, or not to have genetically related children, and either to adopt or to have children with different partners (including the use of donated gametes) to minimize their risks. Alternatively, they may choose to procreate and take their chances, or to procreate and undergo prenatal testing either prior to implantation (preimplantation genetic diagnosis) or during pregnancy (via amniocentesis or chorionic villus sampling, CVS).

Individuals obtaining genetic counseling during a pregnancy are limited to deciding to undergo prenatal diagnosis through ultrasound, maternal serum screening, or invasive measures such as amniocentesis or CVS, or to continue the pregnancy with an awareness of the genetic risk. Invasive prenatal diagnostic procedures, including amniocentesis and CVS, are available to women at increased risk of specific conditions (e.g., chromosomal anomalies) and allow sampling of fetal chromosomal and DNA material for various genetic tests, most often those conditions with onset in infancy or childhood. With both amniocentesis and CVS, the fetal cells are routinely cultured and examined for number and structure (called *karyotyping*). While specific DNA-based genetic tests can be performed for couples at risk for Mendelian genetic conditions where a known mutation can be detected, these prenatal tests do not routinely or automatically test for all genetic diseases, and therefore normal results do not guarantee a healthy child. Additionally, since amniocentesis and CVS are invasive tests, they carry an increased risk for fetal complications, specifically miscarriage (between 1 in 100 to 1 in 300, depending on the procedure and the provider's experience). Because of these risks, invasive prenatal testing is offered more restrictively than noninvasive testing. Indications for such testing currently include: (1) maternal age greater than 35 years; (2) individuals with a family history of a genetic condition for which testing is available; (3) a prior screening test (e.g., ultrasound or maternal serum screening) that suggests an increased likelihood of fetal abnormality; and (4) extreme parental anxiety. Depending on the results of prenatal testing, some may choose pregnancy termination.

When deciding whether or not to have prenatal diagnosis, prospective parents must not only consider whether they desire genetic information about their future child, but they must also consider their perception of the risk for genetic disease and how their perception of risk fits with the actual risk for the condition and whether treatment and preventive steps exist to alter the likelihood of disease onset and the expected course (see Chapter 2). The parents need to think about the perceived burden associated with having an affected child, what level of risk (e.g., miscarriage of a healthy fetus) they are willing to take in order to obtain information regarding specific genetic diseases, and the degree of certainty that testing will provide. For example, a couple might weigh the potentially beneficial and highly accurate information that invasive prenatal diagnosis can provide against the increased risk of miscarriage that is associated with these procedures.

The Smiths meet the genetic counselor when Mary is 15 weeks pregnant. The counselor needs to help them decide whether to undergo an amniocentesis for CF, since the fetus has a 25% chance of having inherited the condition. Neither Joe nor Mary has ever known anyone who had been diagnosed with CF, and they discuss the clinical features, variability of symptoms, and potential treatments with the genetic counselor. The genetic counselor offers to connect them with some of her patients who have CF, including parents of a young child with CF, and an adult with CF who has recently undergone a lung transplant. After spending a week learning more about CF, the couple decides that while uncertain about whether they would terminate an affected pregnancy "so far along into the pregnancy," they do want to undergo genetic testing. They are nervous about the risks to their fetus, but feel that waiting the remainder of the pregnancy without knowing whether a child will be affected would create too much anxiety for their current coping resources. If the fetus is found to carry two CF mutations, they will weigh their perception of raising a child with CF against the increasing gestational age of the fetus.

The Smiths' decision is complicated by the fact that they learn about their CF status when pregnant, and that they only meet the genetic counselor when they have already begun the second trimester of pregnancy. Studies show that the timing of counseling and when testing is offered or performed can influence which options are available and whether or not individuals and couples choose to avail themselves of these various options (Bekker et al., 1993). For example, a couple at risk of having a child affected with Tay-Sachs may not feel comfortable undergoing prenatal diagnosis at 18–20 weeks gestation, or may not consider pregnancy termination of an affected child in the late second trimester, whereas they may have considered it as an option if information had been available at 10–14 weeks gestation. Or a couple who presents for genetic counseling at 10 weeks of gestation may have to weigh the earlier timing of CVS (and subsequent ability to undergo a prenatal diagnostic procedure, and perhaps abortion, before a pregnancy is disclosed to others and before significant emotional bonding has occurred with the fetus) against its slightly increased risk of miscarriage as compared to amniocentesis.

In the future, evolving genetic technologies may allow noninvasive genetic testing of the fetus in early pregnancy through the detection of fetal cells in maternal blood samples. Finally, for those who seek genetic testing and are willing to undergo in vitro fertilization, preimplantation genetic diagnosis allows for testing the embryo prior to implantation. This minimizes the risk of fetal harm and avoids the need for women to choose whether to continue an in utero pregnancy.

Regardless of when and how it is performed, prenatal diagnosis offers potential benefits. First, one must always remember that prenatal diagnosis most frequently results in normal or reassuring results, rather than the diagnosis of an abnormality, and the reduction of uncertainty provides significant emotional benefit for most parents. For those faced with a fetal abnormality, the potential benefit is that the knowledge may increase their options, including the decision whether to continue or to terminate the pregnancy. For those parents who continue the pregnancy, prenatal diagnosis can provide knowledge that allows increased emotional preparation, education regarding the specific condition and its medical treatments, increased medical preparation at the time of delivery, and, in some cases, the rare option for treatment in utero (e.g., in utero surgery or transfusion). For some parents, the experience may result in a wanted child with special needs; others may choose to plan to relinquish the child for a special needs adoption.

The Smiths decide to undergo amniocentesis for CF, and the fetus is found to carry two CF mutations. The couple is informed by the genetic counselor that the child would have CF, and that the severity of the condition cannot be specifically provided. A detailed description of the condition and its range of clinical features are provided, and the couple is provided with the options of pregnancy termination or continuing the pregnancy. In order to assist the couple in making decisions, the couple speaks with physicians who care for children and adults with CF, and contacts parents who have children with CF and individuals who themselves have CF. After learning more about the condition, the couple decides to continue the pregnancy to term. Having several months to incorporate the knowledge of the diagnosis both individually and as a family, and to share the news with relatives and friends, the couple are able to enjoy and celebrate the birth of a much-wanted child. The genetic counselor suggests a consultation with a medical family therapist to discuss further the common psychosocial challenges for families raising a child with CF.

ETHICS AND PRENATAL DIAGNOSIS

Alternatively, when some couples like the Smiths learn that the fetus carries two CF mutations, they may decide, after counseling and after conversations with health care providers and affected families, to terminate the pregnancy. They make this decision based on their own belief about the potential challenges that a future child with CF would face, both medically and socially. The counselor gives them information regarding abortion services and encourages them to mobilize support resources, including the family and friends whom they feel comfortable sharing this information with. They also encourage the couple to attend a pregnancy loss support group specifically for families having undergone difficult decisions such as this one.

This version of the case raises the oft-asked question regarding the mission or goal of prenatal diagnosis because of the high percentage of abnormal prenatal diagnoses that do result in pregnancy termination (Mansfield, Hopfer, & Marteau, 1999). Many critics are concerned that the sole purpose of a prenatal diagnostic program is a "search and destroy" mission for fetuses with anomalies, a modern day eugenics program, if you will. As a result, many obstetrics and genetics professionals struggle over how to offer prenatal diagnosis and discuss fetal abnormalities in ways that are nondirective, and avoid the suggestion of eugenics (Bernhardt, 1997). The task is made harder in that we have the means to test for and diagnose a large number of disabilities, yet at present we have very few therapeutic options. There are some preventive measures; for example, the use of preconception folate supplementation to minimize the occurrence of neural tube defects, and the avoidance of alcohol and other teratogens during pregnancy. For many conditions, however, the only way to prevent the disability is to selectively terminate the fetus, giving rise to the objection that prenatal diagnosis encourages the individual or couple to focus on a part rather than the whole of an individual (see below).

In this light, some have tried to resolve the concern by developing policy proposals regarding which tests should be available. At minimum, such a policy decision would consider the following factors: (1) medical severity and age of onset of the condition, (2) availability of treatment, (3) prevalence of the condition, (4) the timing that testing is offered, (5) sensitivity of the available testing, and (6) economic factors, including cost-benefit ratios (Botkin, 1997, 2000). Such an assessment, however, raises further questions, including: (1) Who should decide what are good reasons for making prenatal testing available? (2) Who should decide whether or not a particular individual or couple undergoes such testing? (3) How can these tests be offered in such a way as to respect autonomy but at the same time avoid making a societal statement regarding individuals with and without particular traits?

Currently the default has been to leave reproductive decisions to the woman or couple independently, in the context of a specific pregnancy and social situation, but it must be acknowledged that the default is a decision with moral undertones. The mere availability of prenatal testing has widespread implications and poses difficult questions to the individual prospective parents, their extended family and wider social circle, and society at large regarding our attitudes toward disability and difference, and our attitudes regarding abortion. To these ethical issues we now turn.

Abortion

A discussion of prenatal diagnosis must address the ethical issues related to abortion. Abortion, in and of itself, remains an ethically controversial issue, and the debate is often filled with rhetoric. Abortion is either spontaneous (e.g., miscarriage), or medically induced by surgical or medical means. Even the language used to discuss abortion is controversial, as various positions often use different words to strengthen their case. For example, those who are against abortion refer to abortion as "murder," whereas those who support a woman's right to have an abortion use the language of "termination." Despite its controversy, statistics suggest that surgical abortion is one of the most common surgical procedures in the United States (MacIsaac & Darney, 2000), and health care professionals who provide these services recognize that women elect to undergo an abortion for a variety of social, economic, and medical indications, including fetal anomalies.

The ethical aspects of abortion are well described in the literature (some classic references include Mahowald, 1993; Noonan, 1970; Sherwin, 1992; Thompson, 1971) and are only briefly summarized here. The debate over the morality of abortion centers primarily on the issue of the moral status of the fetus, and whether the fetus is a person. The concept of personhood is a technical concept to be distinguished from being human. While all acknowledge that a fetus conceived by two human beings is human, not all will agree on whether it is a person. For some, all humans are persons and it is the criterion of humanness that endows personhood; others argue that persons have certain characteristics or potentials such as the ability to have relationships, to have a concept of self, or to have the capacity to become independent (Noonan, 1970). Still others utilize a theory of fetal "ensoulment," which may or may not be based on religious undertones, or the notion of quickening (a woman's sensation of fetal movement) or fetal viability, as ways to determine fetal personhood.

One's belief in the personhood of a fetus often corresponds with one's stance with regard to abortion. The most conservative view (e.g., that of Catholic theologians) is that the fetus is a person from the moment of conception, invested with the same rights and protections as any sentient being; therefore, its destruction is equivalent to murder. At the other end of the spectrum is the view that until the moment of birth (or in its radical form, even for some period after birth; Singer, 1993), the fetus/infant is not a person and has less moral status than a competent adult. Most individuals subscribe to an intermediate view: although the fetus may not have the same moral status as a competent adult, the fetus has developing personhood, and at some point in a pregnancy, the moral status of the fetus gives it a right to life. The right is prima facie and not absolute, and must be weighed against the competing rights to privacy and self-determination of the pregnant woman, a being with full moral status. Legally, the courts often ascribe to this intermediate view, and define the beginning of the third trimester, or 24 weeks gestation, which was previously the lower limit on fetal viability, as the stage at which the fetus's right to life may outweigh the woman's rights (*Planned Parenthood of Southeastern Pennsylvania v. Casey*, 1992; *Roe v. Wade*, 1973).

According to reproductive technology case law, the woman's right to bodily integrity means that her decision trumps her male partner's interest in becoming or not becoming a parent (*Planned Parenthood of Central Missouri v. Danforth*, 1976; *Thornburgh v. ACOG et al.*, 1982). Specific case determinations exist in the context of the disposition of embryos created by in vitro fertilization (*A.Z. v. B.Z.*, 2000; *Davis v. Davis*, 1992). These kinds of ethical and legal issues point to the critical implications for couples and families and a vital reason why consultation with a medical family therapist is essential in these situations. This can help couples clarify a healthy decision-making process and avert severely dysfunctional family crises in the aftermath.

Disability

Many members of the disability community, even those who consider themselves to be pro-choice regarding abortion, have been critical of prenatal diagnosis. They articulate four major concerns (Parens & Asch, 2000). First, they claim that the major problem with having a disability is not the disability per se, but the discrimination that individuals with disabilities and their families face. The counterclaim is that while the problems faced by the disabled community are worsened by discrimination, it is not the case that all problems of disability are socially constructed. For example, the inability to see or to hear is not inherently neutral.

A second concern of disability advocates is that prenatal diagnosis will decrease the number of individuals with congenital disability, leading to decreased social tolerance of those with disabilities, both congenital and acquired. In the last two decades, major strides have been made in providing legal protections to persons with disabilities, including passage and enforcement of the Americans with Disabilities Act (1992). Yet, despite the implementation of this act in the past decade, individuals with disabilities continue to report discrimination in employment (Olnoy & Kennedy, 2001) and other life areas (Stothers, 2000).

A third argument against prenatal diagnosis is that it reinforces the medical model of disability, making it a problem to be solved, and thereby denying its social construction. The medical model of disability focuses on the "abnormal" medical aspects of a condition, such as the inability to walk related to spina bifida, and ignores other aspects of the person. This argument concludes that individuals and couples who choose to undergo prenatal diagnosis and to abort an affected child who was otherwise wanted are being influenced by the medical model as they focus on a part rather than the whole of an individual.

A fourth critique of prenatal diagnosis suggests that in terminating a pregnancy affected with a disability, parents are making a mistaken decision that the child will not fulfill the parental dreams of a successful life. The disability rights community raises concern about what it means if future parents are only willing to accept their dreams for a perfect child. Data suggests that individuals with disability (of various types) consistently report a higher quality of life than was predicted for them by nondisabled individuals (Gerhart, Kozoil-McLain, Lowenstein, & Whiteneck, 1994], and individuals with disability do not significantly differ from nondisabled individuals on quality of life assessments or other measures of life satisfaction (Cameron, Titus, Kostin, & Kostin, 1973; Stensman, 1985). Disability activists fear that prospective parents receive biased information from both health care providers and society and that they are not aware that many individuals with disabilities enjoy full lives as functioning members of society.

The counterarguments to the third and fourth critiques are multiple. First, one can agree that raising a child with disabilities can be very rewarding, but this does not necessarily mean that it is a mistake to try and avoid disabilities. Pregnant women are given folic acid and encouraged not to use drugs in order to prevent disability. Prenatal screening and abortion or embryo selection are another means to prevent disability. Some argue that folic acid supplements and drug avoidance, as two methods of disability prevention, are different because they promote healthy development, while abortion and embryo selection end the potential life of a fetus or embryo based frequently on one trait. But if abortion is morally permissible—and many members of the disability rights movement are pro-choice—then one could argue that abortion should be permissible to avoid undesirable outcomes. Many individuals do not desire disability if given the choice. Second, the wish to avoid having a child with disabilities does not imply that if a child should be disabled in some manner, that he or she will be unwanted, rejected, or loved less. It is not inconsistent to say that it is preferable, all things considered, to want children who are healthy with full capacities, and yet to love and cherish all of one's children, regardless of their abilities and disabilities.

Third, those who reject the disability critique do not do so to intentionally harm those with disabilities. It is not inconsistent to prefer healthy children with full capacities and yet seek to minimize discrimination toward individuals with disabilities, support policies that allow those with disabilities to maximize their potentials, and support programs that help those with disabilities to overcome their disabilities. For most individuals, decisions about prenatal diagnosis and selective abortion are made within a family unit and are based not only on one's views toward a specific disability, but also on one's personal and parental goals and the goals of the family as a whole. Therefore, one can argue that no underlying message about disability is necessarily intended in these decisions. And yet, whether one can truly separate the personal from the social is not so clear-cut. Barbara Katz Rothman (1984) has shown that there is always a social context to our "personal" decision making, including the societal pressure put on individuals to take advantage of medical technology, financial pressures, and a perception of social discrimination and difficulty obtaining accessible services for individuals with disabilities. Therefore, we must consider how societal views on disability shape personal decisions in pregnancy.

In summary, critiques of prenatal diagnosis from disability advocates suggest that prenatal diagnosis expresses discriminatory (if not eugenic) views against people who carry the trait being screened for, that prenatal diagnosis currently reinforces the medical model of disability rather than supporting a social construct of disability, and that decisions about selective abortion of a fetus with a disability are frequently based on inaccurate or biased information. The counterarguments are that prenatal diagnosis empowers women and couples with the ability to prevent some disabilities, to make choices about what challenges they are willing to undergo as parents, and that these decisions are personal and in no way reflect a negative or discriminatory attitude toward the disability community.

PRENATAL DIAGNOSIS AND REPRODUCTIVE DECISION MAKING

The central feature of reproductive genetic counseling is its emphasis on informed consent and informed decision making. An informed choice is one that (1) is made with adequate and relevant information, (2) is consistent with the decision maker's values, and (3) is implemented freely (Lidz, Appelbaum, & Meisel, 1988). A primary role of health care providers in this setting is to encourage families to discuss their personal values in the context of the current situation and to facilitate decisions about undergoing genetic testing, and the potential abortion of an affected fetus, based on those values. Who constitutes the family and which of the members need to be included in discussions is a critical issue (see Chapters 4 and 6). Genetic counselors often ascribe to a "nondirective" approach. Based on the concept that the professional cannot entirely know the entire decision making context of the family, this approach stresses that the health care professional should strive for neutrality in presenting health and social information regarding the condition of interest. It does not, however, mean that the genetic counselor takes on a passive role in the process, but rather that the counselor can encourage the family to ask challenging questions regarding their own personal values and consider how each option may impact their lives and relationships as a couple, immediate family, and extended family.

Hypothetical scenarios are often used with individuals and couples to help them consider and discuss (between themselves and with the health care professional) their values and beliefs regarding their goals as individuals, as potential parents, and as a family, in addition to what they can offer children of various abilities and disabilities. Couples are not bound by their pretesting decisions. Anecdotally, many couples change their mind regarding their previous decisions, both in choosing to continue an affected pregnancy to term or choosing to terminate a pregnancy that the couple previously planned to continue to term regardless of outcome. Most of the research in this area focuses on the impact of pretest information and education; we need more studies on the decision making after an abnormal diagnosis and the ways that information and emotional support affect such decisions (Marteau & Dormandy, 2001).

Several complex factors complicate decision making in the reproductive genetics setting. The information communicated is, by definition, value laden in content, in context, and in the manner in which it is communicated. For example, significant differences in the number and types of positive, neutral, and negative statements can be found in the various pamphlets about CF designed for prenatal versus pediatric use (Loeben, Wilfond, & Marteau, 1998). Studies demonstrate both informational biases and differences in pregnancy decisions based on the type of health care provider giving information, particularly after an ambiguous abnormal prenatal diagnosis (Abramsky, Hall, Levitan, & Marteau, 2001; Holmes-Siedle, Ryynanen, & Lindenbaum, 1987; Marteau, Drake, & Bobrow, 1994; Robinson, Bender, & Linden, 1989). Specifically, prospective parents who were counseled by professionals with training in clinical genetics (geneticist or genetic counselor) were significantly less likely to terminate a pregnancy affected with Klinefelter syndrome than those parents who spoke with other health care professionals, such as obstetricians. More research is needed to address the underlying reasons for this difference, but may include different health professional disciplines' level of directiveness about outcomes (including the amount of positive versus negative information given), and health care providers' general views toward the condition that are impacted by the degree of current awareness and personal experience. While the explicit content of prenatal discussions is critical, equally important is the tone and perspective that is subtly communicated. The data show wide variability in the overall tone in which such information is given (Bernhardt, 1997; Bernhardt et al., 1998; Michie, Bender, & Linden, 1997). Clearly, all counseling has inherent biases: the order in which topics are discussed, the amount of time spent on each topic, and the tone used to discuss various issues. Ideally, individuals and couples are given realistic and nonjudgmental descriptions of conditions, and providing information is separated from the decision-making process. Health care professionals should be aware of any biases that may impact their work with clients and circumstances where disclosing them may be beneficial.

Not only is genetic risk information communicated with biases; it is also interpreted subjectively. For example, individuals evaluate risks differently based on how the information is framed. Not only do verbal descriptors (e.g., low, moderate, high) impact perceptions differently than numerical expressions (Shiloh & Sagi, 1989), but the use of percentages versus fractions (Grimes & Snively, 1999; Kessler & Levine, 1987) and the relative comparison to other risk factors (e.g., comparison to baseline population risks) also play a role in subjective interpretation of risk (Shiloh & Sagi, 1989). For example, an individual presented with a 90% chance of a healthy child may perceive a lower risk than one presented with a 10% (or a 1 in 10) chance of an affected child. An individual's own multigenerational experience with the disorder in question also can alter perception of the objective risk information. For example, does the individual have a family member or friend who has the condition or had it in previous generations? How well or poorly did that individual and the family cope with the condition? A history of individual or family dysfunction in the context of the same or another illness would likely increase fears, just as legacies of resilience in the face of adversity can empower families (Rolland, 1994; see Chapter 5). An individual whose family member (or self) was mildly affected by a specific condition or underwent successful treatment may view the risk to a fetus as having minimal impact on the family, while an individual whose experience involved more morbidity or mortality could view the impact as high.

It is also true that the medical prognosis is often uncertain even when the diagnosis is clear. For example, while an amniocentesis clearly diagnoses Down syndrome, it does not tell the prospective parents (1) the child's predicted IQ (which ranges from mild to moderate-severe mental retardation); (2) whether the child will have concomitant health problems found more frequently in children with Down syndrome (including congenital heart disease or leukemia); or (3) whether the child will ultimately be able to hold a job and live semi-independently. Hypothetically, if people underwent testing for conditions that develop in late childhood or adulthood, this would be even more complex. For example, variable expression and penetrance mutations, such as diagnosis of a *BRCA1* mutation, confers added risk of breast and ovarian cancer, but the diagnosis of the mutation does not tell when, or even if, the individual will ultimately develop breast or ovarian cancer, nor whether preventive measures would prevent disease or how that individual might respond to treatment if ultimately diagnosed with cancer. It is difficult to communicate the range and likelihood of various potential prognoses clearly, and prospective parents may receive biased information as a result. In addition, the uncertainty generated by a range of prognoses (even when narrow) complicates the health care provider's responsibility to provide full information, and complicates parental decision making by adding more abstraction to an already abstract situation.

The timing of the information at various stages of pregnancy means that decisions about pregnancy continuation versus termination must often be made quickly, particularly given the limitations as to when women can obtain pregnancy termination, both legally and logistically. This pressure is compounded by the fact that individuals and couples are often in a state of shock and denial, and may not be able to appreciate fully the complexities of the medical information. Rapid decisions may be made at a time when anxiety may overshadow reasonable consideration of all options (Shiloh, 1996).

Prenatal diagnosis and subsequent decision making occur in a social context rather than a vacuum. The decisions made by the couple will impact each partner, the couple's relationship, and also the broader family (including current and future children, and other relatives) and society at large. Each partner may have different goals and values and each may differ in their desire for control, information-seeking styles, and health locus of control (Shiloh, 1996). An inability to resolve such differences can lead to ongoing stress, guilt, and blame, and adversely affect their relationship with each other and with the prospective child. In some situations, disagreements between partners or between family members can lead to not being fully truthful about pregnancy-related decisions. For example, some individuals may inform family members that a pregnancy loss occurred, rather than disclosing a selective abortion for an affected fetus. This may be particularly true if there exists a family member affected by the specific condition, who may personalize selective abortion as a statement of the member's worth to himself or herself, to the family, and to society at large. Such decisions, whether or not revealed, can dysfunctionally alter family relationships. This underscores the importance of prevention-oriented couple and family consultations with a medical family therapist to help families achieve a decision that considers the impact on other parts of the family system.

Finally, whether or not individual decisions are made with a thought toward the broader social impact on the disability community, the availability of prenatal testing and its use in diagnosing disability supports social policies that separate individuals with disabilities from those without disabilities.

ADDITIONAL ISSUES RAISED BY PRENATAL
TESTING FOR ADULT-ONSET CONDITIONS

If one accepts that prenatal genetic testing is morally acceptable given the disability community arguments and abortion issues discussed above, there is still the question of whether it is morally acceptable to offer prenatal testing for a condition that will not become symptomatic until adulthood. Adult-onset genetic conditions are more likely to vary in their penetrance, in part because most have complex genetic causes with polygenic and environmental influences. For example, while Huntington disease is an autosomal dominant disorder with close to 100% penetrance over the lifetime, the age of onset is variable even within families. Other adult-onset conditions, such as colon cancer, cardiovascular disease, or breast cancer, are inherited in a Mendelian fashion only in a minority of cases. Even when these genes are mutated, the chance that a mutation will cause symptoms and disease ranges significantly (perhaps as much as from 10 to 80%), often based on the specific mutation present in the family.

It is unclear to what degree treatments or cures may be developed in the intervening time between the birth and adulthood of a potentially affected individual. Is it morally acceptable for prospective parents to make such prenatal decisions based on information that will likely change significantly during the childhood of their offspring? Also, as in pediatric genetic testing, there is concern that parental knowledge of the prospective child's genotype may lead to discrimination both within and outside of the family (see Chapter 18). For example, if a child is known to have inherited a significantly increased risk for psychiatric illness, parents may blame the child's genes for bad behavior (perhaps inappropriately) and may adopt a view of genetic determinism. This bias may affect the child's resources within the family (e.g., money for college, time spent with the child, etc.), and can also potentially lead to discrimination if the child's medical records document the predisposition. Many genetics organizations advocate against prenatal genetic testing for adult-onset conditions for exactly these reasons.

Despite these concerns, some individuals and families with adult-onset conditions that can be identified by a single gene mutation do express interest in prenatal genetic diagnosis.[1] Research has assessed both the actual and hypothetical uptake of prenatal diagnostic testing for a variety of adult-onset and variable-onset conditions (ranging from neurodegenerative conditions, vision loss conditions such as retinitis pigmentosa, and physical degeneration conditions such as Alport syndrome). For example, Simpson et al. (2002) reported on 305 prenatal exclusion diagnostic tests performed for Huntington disease in several European countries over a 5-year period. In all, 131 affected fetuses were discovered (43% of at-risk pregnancies). Eight of these pregnancies were continued. The authors note that the number of prenatal tests was less than 10% of the number of predictive tests in a comparable period, which is highly indicative of low prenatal uptake in those known to carry the mutation (Simpson et al., 2002). On a hypothetical basis, Lima et al. (2001) surveyed affected and at-risk individuals regarding Machado-Joseph disease (a progressive adult-onset neurodegenerative condition). Of the 78 respondents, 77.8% reported that they would make use of prenatal diagnosis, and of these, 36.1% would terminate a pregnancy with a positive result. Of 53 patients with Alport syndrome (an X-linked kidney disorder) and their relatives, 43% felt positively toward spending research dollars on prenatal diagnosis, and 28% felt that termination of an affected male fetus was appropriate (Pajari, Koskimies, Muhonen, & Kaariainen, 1999). In contrast, Trippitelli, Jamison, Folstein, Bartko, and DePaulo (1998) documented that 43.9% of patients and spouses of patients with bipolar disorder, a psychiatric condition, were interested in prenatal genetic diagnosis although they reported that they would probably or definitely not consider pregnancy termination (55% and 65% of patients and spouses respectively). Jones, Scourfield, McCandless, and Craddock (2002) demonstrated slightly less positive views toward prenatal genetic diagnosis of bipolar disease, such that 29% of patients and 13% of psychiatrists surveyed expressed positive views toward prenatal testing. Lodder et al. (2000) surveyed carriers and noncarriers of BRCA1/2 mutations, and found that only non–mutation carriers would consider pregnancy termination of a female (14%) or male (10%) carrier of a BRCA1/2 mutation. Finally, of note is a study by Milner, Han, and Petty (1999) that asked hypothetically whether participants would support prenatal diagnosis for 16 neurological/psychiatric disorders and personality traits. This study found strong support (>60–81%) for prenatal diagnosis for all conditions, with some slight influence of gender, professional training, and the potential availability of curative treatment.

In combination, these data suggest that there is currently moderate interest in prenatal diagnosis for genetic conditions of adult onset (at least on a hypothetical basis), and that there is less interest in pregnancy termination of affected fetuses. But the data vary considerably based on the likely severity of the condition, whether treatments exist that can help prevent onset or alter progression, and current knowledge about the likelihood that a specific mutation will lead to symptomatic disease (see Chapter 2). Also, one must also remember that many hypothetical studies of interest in genetic testing have demonstrated higher hypothetical interest than was documented when tests became available. The following case illustrates this point.

A couple presents for prenatal genetic counseling when the pregnancy is at 12 weeks gestation. The husband has recently learned that his mother, who was diagnosed with breast cancer at age 35 and ovarian cancer at age 63, was recently diagnosed as carrying a BRCA1 mutation. The man reports understanding that this means that he has a 50% chance of also carrying the mutation, and if so there is a 50% chance that his offspring will inherit the condition. His wife, whose best friend recently died of breast cancer, is quite interested in testing the fetus and considering pregnancy termination if a fetus is affected. She expresses that breast cancer is a "terrible disease for the entire family," and that it should be prevented if at all possible. The husband feels differently and is frustrated at having to make these decisions during a pregnancy. He expresses that his mother did well after her diagnosis of breast cancer, and that his sister is currently in treatment for breast cancer at age 40. He also reports that the oncologist had explained to the family that not everyone who carries a BRCA1 mutation will develop breast cancer, and that screening and treatment are usually not begun until after age 18. He is not sure that he would do anything differently in a pregnancy if he knew a future daughter would inherit the BRCA1 mutation, and wonders if he might treat a daughter differently if he knew she was at increased risk.

The genetic counselor validates the feelings expressed by both members of the couple and asks if they have discussed their personal responses to breast cancer in the past. They have not and are encouraged to spend some time at home considering the various ways that prenatal genetic testing might impact their own perception of a child and their family relationships, including their relationship with their other daughter. They are also reminded that in general the genetic service providers do not endorse prenatal or childhood testing for adult-onset disorders that are potentially treatable (American Society of Human Genetics Board of Directors and Amereican College of Medical Genetics Board of Directors, 1995), and the reasons for such recommendations are discussed. The couple calls the genetic counselor back a week later, and they say that based on their discussions, they have agreed that pursuing testing at this time is not in the best interest of the family. In situations like this, it is useful to make a referral to a family therapist if the couple encounters difficulties with decision making or relationship problems before or after the prenatal testing decision.

CONCLUSION

The ultimate goal in prenatal diagnosis and counseling should be to move toward educating and empowering patients to make informed reproductive decisions. To achieve this goal, health care providers must inform their patients of all available options at each stage of prenatal care in a nondirective, easily understood manner, and then respect their patients' informed decisions. To be capable of this approach, many health care providers will need to learn more about, and clarify, their own personal views and biases toward various types of illnesses and disabilities in order to be able to assist patients in clarifying theirs. Reproductive genetics increases the range of procreative options for individuals and couples; its accessibility and acceptability has ethical and social ramifications that go far beyond them. Informed decision making needs to take all of these factors into account.

NOTE

1. Readers should note that the conditions described as testable during pregnancy include a wide range of genetic conditions that are fully penetrant (such that testing a pregnancy or unaffected individual would be considered predictive testing) and conditions where a genetic mutation does not guarantee development of the condition (such that testing a pregnancy or unaffected individual would be considered predispositional testing). While these testing scenarios pose different issues, the dearth of data in this area makes it difficult to summarize the range of findings available. The reader should consider the penetrance and severity of each condition when interpreting the following studies, and also to recognize that respondents to hypothetical scenarios may also have misinterpreted the degree of information that would be obtained in an actual prenatal testing situation.

REFERENCES

Abramsky, L., Hall, S., Levitan, J., & Marteau, T. M. (2001). What parents are told after prenatal diagnosis of a sex chromosome abnormality: Interview and questionnaire study. *British Medical Journal, 322,* 463–466.

American College of Obstetricians and Gynecologists and American College of Medical Genetics. (2001). *Preconception and prenatal carrier screening for cystic fibrosis: Clinical and laboratory guidelines* (pp. 1–33). Washington, DC: ACOG.

American Society of Human Genetics Board of Directors and The American College of Medical Genetics Board of Directors. (1995). Points to consider: Ethical legal, and psychosocial implications of genetic testing in children and adolescents. *American Journal of Human Genetics, 57,* 1233–1241.

A.Z. v. B.Z., 725 N.E.2d 1051 (Mass. 2000).

Beeson, D., & Bolbus, M. S. (1985). Decision making: Whether or not to have prenatal diagnosis and abortion for X-linked conditions. *American Journal of Medical Genetics, 20,* 107–114.

Bekker, H., Modell, M., Denniss, G., Silver, A., Mathew, C., Bobrow, M., et al. (1993). Uptake of cystic fibrosis testing in primary care: Supply push or demand pull? *British Medical Journal, 306,* 1584–1586.

Bernhardt, B. A. (1997). Empirical evidence that genetic counseling is directive: Where do we go from here? *American Journal of Human Genetics, 60*(1), 17–20.

Bernhardt, B. A., Geller, G., Doksum, T., Larson, S. M., Roter, D., & Holtzman, N. A. (1998). Prenatal genetic testing: Content of discussions between obstetric providers and pregnant women. *Obstetrics and Gynecology, 91*(5, Pt. 1), 648–655.

Botkin, J. R. (1997). Fetal privacy and confidentiality. *Hastings Center Report* 35(5), 32–39.

Botkin, J. R. (2000). Line drawing: Developing professional standards for prenatal diagnostic services. In E. Parens & A. Asch (Eds.), *Prenatal testing and disability rights* (pp. 288–307). Washington, DC: Georgetown University Press.

Cameron, P., Titus, D. G., Kostin, J., & Kostin, M. (1973). The life satisfaction of non-normal persons. *Journal of Consulting and Clinical Psychology, 41,* 207–214.

Davis v. Davis, 842 S.W.2d 588. (Tenn. 1992).

Gerhardt, K. A., Kozoil-McLain, J., Lowenstein, S. R., & Whiteneck, G. G. (1994). Quality of life following spinal cord injury: Knowledge and attitudes of emergency care providers. *Annals of Emergency Medicine, 23,* 807–812.

Grimes, D. A., & Snively, G. R. (1999). Patients' understanding of medical risks: Implications for genetic counselling. *Obstetrics and Gynecology, 93,* 910–914.

Holmes-Siedle, M., Ryynanen, M., & Lindenbaum, R. H. (1987). Parental decisions regarding termination of pregnancy following prenatal detection of sex chromosome abnormality. *Prenatal Diagnosis, 7*(4), 239–244.

Jones, I., Scourfield, J., McCandless, F., & Craddock, N. (2002). Attitudes towards future testing for bipolar disorder susceptibility genes: A preliminary investigation. *Journal of Affective Disorders, 71*(1–3), 189–193.

Katz Rothman, B. (1984). The meanings of choice in reproductive technology. In R. Arditti, R. Duelli-Klein, & S. Minden (Eds.), *Test tube women* (pp. 23–33). New York: Pandora Press.

Kessler, S., & Levine, E. K. (1987). Psychological aspects of genetic counselling IV. The subjective assessment of probability. *American Journal of Medical Genetics, 28,* 361–370.

Lidz, C. W., Appelbaum, P. S., & Meisel, A. (1988). Two models of implementing informed consent. *Archives of Internal Medicine, 148,* 1385–1389.

Lima, M., Kay, T., Vasconcelos, J., Mota-Vieira, L., Gonzalez, C., Peixoto, A., et al. (2001). Disease knowledge and attitudes toward predictive testing and prenatal diagnosis in families with Machado-Joseph disease from the Azores Islands (Portugal). *Community Genetics, 4*(1), 36–42.

Lodder, L. N., Frets, P. G., Trijsburg, R. W., Meijers-Heijboer, E. J., Klijn, J. G., & Niermeijer, M. F. (2000). Attitudes towards termination of pregnancy in subjects who underwent presymptomatic testing for the BRCA1/BRCA2 gene mutation in the Netherlands. *Journal of Medical Genetics, 37*(11), 883–884.

Loeben, G. L., Marteau, T. M., & Wilfond, B. S. (1998). Mixed messages: Presentation of information in cystic fibrosis-screening pamphlets. *American Journal of Human Genetics, 63*(4), 1181–1189.

MacIsaac, L., & Darney, P. (2000). Early surgical abortion: An alternative to and backup for medical abortion. *American Journal of Obstetrics and Gynecology, 193*(2, Suppl.), S76–S83.

Mahowald, M. B. (1993). *Women and children in health care: An unequal majority.* New York: Oxford University Press.

Mansfield, C., Hopfer, S., & Marteau, T. M. (1999). Termination rates after prenatal diagnosis of Down syndrome, spina bifida, anencephly, and Turner and Klinefelter syndromes: A systematic literature review. European

Concerted Action: DADA (Decision-making After the Diagnosis of a Fetal Abnormality). *Prenatal Diagnosis, 19*(9), 808–812.

Marteau, T., Drake, H., & Bobrow, M. (1994). Counseling following diagnosis of a fetal abnormality: The differing approaches of obstetricians, clinical geneticist and genetic nurses. *Journal of Medical Genetics, 31*, 864–867.

Marteau, T. M., & Dormandy, E. (2001). Facilitating informed choice in prenatal testing: How well are we doing? *American Journal of Medical Genetics, 106*(3), 185–190.

Michie, S.,Bender, B. G., & Linden, T. M. (1997). Nondirectiveness in genetic counseling: An empirical study. *American Journal of Human Genetics, 60*(1), 40–47.

Milner, K. K., Han, T., & Petty, E. M. (1999). Support for the availability of prenatal testing for neurological and psychiatric conditions in the psychiatric community. *Genetic Testing, 3*(3), 279–286.

Noonan, J. T. (1970). An almost absolute value in history. In J. T. Noonan (Ed.), *The morality of abortion: Legal and historical perspectives* (pp. 51–59). Cambridge, MA: Harvard University Press.

Olney, M. F., & Kennedy, J. (2001). National estimates of vocational service utilization and job placement rates for adults with mental retardation. *Mental Retardation, 39*(1), 32–39.

Pajari, H., Koskimies, O., Muhonen, T., & Kaariainen, H. (1999). The burden of genetic disease and attitudes towards gene testing in Alport syndrome. *Pediatric Nephrology, 13*(6), 471–476.

Parens, E., & Asch, A. (Ed.). (2000). *Prenatal testing and disability rights.* Washington, DC: Georgetown University Press.

Planned Parenthood of Central Missouri v. Danforth, 428 U.S. 52 (1976) Supreme Court of the United States (July 1, 1976).

Planned Parenthood of Southeastern Pennsylvania v. Casey, 60 USLW (U.S. Law Week) 4795 (June 30, 1992).

Robinson, A., Bender, B. G., & Linden, M. G. (1989). Decisions following the intrauterine diagnosis of sex chromosome aneuploidy. *American Journal of Medical Genetics, 34*(4), 552–554.

Roe v. Wade, 410 U.S. 113 (1973).

Roggenbuck, J., Olson, J. E., Sellers, T. A., & Ludowese, C. (2000). Perception of genetic risk among genetic counselors. *Journal of Genetic Counseling, 9*(1), 47–59.

Rolland, J. (1994). *Families, illness, and disability: An integrative treatment model.* New York: Basic Books.

Sherwin, S. (1992). Abortion. In S. Sherwin (Ed.), *No longer patient: Feminist ethics and health care* (pp. 99–116). Philadelphia: Temple University Press.

Shiloh, S. (1996). Decision-making in the context of genetic risk. In T. M. Marteau & M. Richards (Eds.), *The troubled helix: Social and psychological implications of the new human genetics* (pp. 82–103). Cambridge, UK: Cambridge University Press.

Shiloh, S., & Sagi, M. (1989). Effect of framing on the perception of genetic recurrence risks. *American Journal of Medical Genetics, 33*, 130–135.

Simpson, S. A., Zoeteweij, M. W., Nys, K., Harper, P., Durr, A., Jacopini, G., et al. (2002). Prenatal testing for Huntington's disease: A European collaborative study. *European Journal of Human Genetics, 10*(11), 689–693.

Singer, P. (1993). *Practical ethics* (2nd ed.). Cambridge, UK: Cambridge University Press.

Sorenson, J. R., & Wertz, D. C. (1986). Couple agreement before and after genetic counseling. *American Journal of Medical Genetics, 25,* 549–555.

Stensman, R. (1985). Severely mobility-disabled people assess the quality of their lives. *Scandinavian Journal of Rehabilitative Medicine, 17,* 87–89.

Stothers, W. G. (2000). After 10 years, the ADA is changing the landscape of America. Retrieved from http://www.accessiblesociety.org/topics/ada/ada10thannivoped.htm

Thompson, J. J. (1971). A defense of abortion. *Philosophy and Public Affairs, 1*(1), 47–66.

Thornburg v. ACOG et al. (1982) 106 S.Ct. 2169.

Trippitelli, C. L., Jamison, K. R., Folstein, M. F., Bartko, J. J., & DePaulo, J. R. (1998). Pilot study on patients' and spouses' attitudes toward potential genetic testing for bipolar disorder. *American Journal of Psychiatry, 55*(7), 899–904.

Tversky, A., & Kahneman, D. (1981). The framing of decisions and the psychology of choice. *Science, 211*(4481), 453–458.

Chapter 18

Ethical Issues in Pediatric Genetics

Lainie Friedman Ross and Norman Fost

CLINICAL GENETICS IS AN INTEGRAL PART OF PEDIATRICS. GENETIC DIS-
eases are common in childhood: as many as 53 per 1,000 children and
young adults can be expected to have diseases with an important genetic component, and this number increases to 79 per 1,000 if all congenital anomalies are included (Baird, Anderson, Newcombe, & Lowry,
1988). While prenatal testing and selective abortion may decrease the
number of children born with some genetic conditions (particularly for
children with Down syndrome; Mansfield, Hopfer, & Marteau, 1999;
Verloes et al., 2001), the impact is likely to be small for the near future in
the United States because of (1) the lack of access to, and availability of,
prenatal testing for many women; (2) the lack of fetal gene therapies;
(3) the risks of fetal therapies generally; and (4) the moral unacceptabil-
ity of elective termination for some women and families (Singer, 1993).

Despite the importance of genetics to child health, newborn screening for some rare treatable genetic diseases is the only aspect of genetics that has been incorporated into routine pediatric practice (American
Academy of Pediatrics, 1996), but the Human Genome Project will
undoubtedly accelerate the "geneticization" of pediatrics (Touchette,
Holtzman, Davis, & Feetham, 1997) for diagnostic, preventive, and
therapeutic purposes (Burke, 2003; Cote & Gagel, 2003; Dewar & Hall,
2003; Khoury, McCabe, & McCabe, 2003). In preparation, it is worth examining the social and ethical implications of genetic testing in childhood for the children, adolescents, and their families. In this chapter,
we consider the ethical and psychosocial issues raised by genetic testing
(1) for diagnostic purposes, (2) in newborn screening programs, (3) to
predict adult-onset conditions, (4) to predict childhood-onset conditions,
and (5) to determine carrier status.

DIAGNOSTIC GENETIC TESTING

When an individual patient has an identifiable symptom or specific risk factor that is best diagnosed via genetic testing, the use of genetic testing to confirm a clinical diagnosis is similar to using other diagnostic medical tests. The differential diagnosis of a child born with weak muscle tone and a large tongue include both the genetic condition of Down syndrome and the (usually) nongenetic condition of hypothyroidism; the former is tested by chromosomal analysis, the latter by endocrine function. The differential diagnosis of a child who has failure to thrive and chronic recurrent upper respiratory infections includes both cystic fibrosis (CF), an autosomal recessive genetic condition, and AIDS, a nongenetic condition. In the symptomatic child, CF can be diagnosed by measuring sweat chloride or by genetic mutational analysis, whereas HIV may be determined by Western blot or polymerase chain reaction (PCR) testing (the latter test being a genetic test used to diagnose a nongenetic disorder). None of these tests is medically controversial in a symptomatic child when performed postnatally to provide appropriate clinical services for the affected child and family, provided that adequate consent is obtained.

NEWBORN SREENING

Current newborn screening programs in the United States seek to diagnose children with medical conditions for which early treatment can reduce morbidity and mortality. Although states have different panels of tests, the most common tests are for phenylketonuria (PKU), hypothyroidism, hemoglobinopathies (including sickle-cell disease), congenital adrenal hyperplasia, and galactosemia (American Academy of Pediatrics, 2000). Each of these conditions is an autosomal recessive genetic condition (except hypothyroidism), meaning that an affected child typically has two asymptomatic parents who carry this recessive allele, and the affected child is homozygous recessive (received two recessive alleles, one from each parent). Each of these conditions meets the criteria for universal screening: Each represents an important health problem for which there is an accepted cost-effective treatment that, if begun early, can prevent many if not all of the negative sequellae of the condition (National Screening Commission, n.d.; Wilson & Jungner, 1968). The screening test is simple and cheap and the follow-up testing is highly accurate.

Scientific and technological advances now make it possible to test newborns for dozens of medical conditions using the same Guthrie cards used for PKU testing (Report of a Workgroup, 2001). This is tempting for four reasons. First, the newborn period is the most efficient time to screen an entire cohort of individuals. Second, newborns are already tested for a variety of conditions and so additional testing can be easily incorporated into standard practice. Third, tandem mass spectrometry, developed in the 1990s, can be used to screen for a large number of medical conditions (genetic and nongenetic) quickly and cheaply. Fourth, children who have abnormal screens can be followed longitudinally such that physicians and researchers can learn the natural history of these conditions, their prevalence, and what factors either exacerbate or minimize their expression.

Yet there are reasons to proceed with caution (Botkin et al., 2006; Holtzman, 1989). Many families will react adversely to abnormal genetic screening tests, even if follow-up studies are normal (Mischler et al., 1998; Rothenberg & Sills, 1968; Sorenson, Levy, Mangione, & Sepe, 1984) or if the condition is mild (Levy-Lahad & Zimran, 1997). Soon after implementation of mandatory newborn screening for PKU, Rothenberg and Sills identified a syndrome that they named the PKU anxiety syndrome, by which they referred to "parents who persist in their belief that their babies are or will become mentally retarded despite repeat negative tests and considerable reassurance and support from physicians" (Rothenberg & Sills, 1968, p. 691). More than a decade later, Sorenson et al. (1984) found that more than one third of parents whose infants had abnormal metabolic screens were still concerned about the health of their infant despite normal follow-up. More recently, Mischler et al. (1998) surveyed parents of children who had false positive newborn screening tests for CF. One year later, 3–8% did not understand that their child did not have CF, and 10% reported that they thought about the results once a week or more. Of these parents, 17% said the experience had changed their feelings about having more children. One should also be cautious because some of these children, once labeled, will be treated in ways that can harm their interests by outside institutions including insurers, schools, and employers. Given the familial implications of genetic tests, we must understand their impact on the extended family, who may be labeled by blood ties. Billings et al. (1992) mailed "an advertisement to solicit cases" to 1,119 professionals working in the fields of clinical genetics, genetic counseling, disability medicine, pediatrics, and social services in New England to solicit cases of possible genetic discrimination. They received 42 responses and excluded 13 as not meeting their criteria. The 29 responses described 41 separate incidents of possible discrimination, including 32 incidents involving insurance and 7 involving employment. Incidents involved asymptomatic or mildly ill persons as well as those who were at risk because of affected family members.

Finally, one should be cautious because often we will not know whether current therapies are necessary or effective, in part, because we do not know how many children with these conditions would have remained asymptomatic or done well regardless of treatment (NIH Technology Assessment Panel on Gaucher Disease, 1996; Schilling et al., 2002; Wilcken, Wiley, Hammond, & Carpenter, 2003), particularly for conditions that do not express themselves in the newborn period.

Despite these calls for caution, there are also concerns about fairness, given the wide disparities between the states in the number of conditions included in their newborn screening programs. The Advisory Committee on Heritable Disorders and Genetic Diseases in Newborns and Children was created in February 2004 to examine these issues. They have endorsed the report by the American College of Medical Genetics (ACMG)/Health Resources and Services Administration (HRSA) (2004), which recommends that all states screen for 29 core conditions and 25 secondary conditions (Advisory Committee on Heritable Disorders and Genetic Diseases in Newborns and Children Meeting Minutes, 2005). The recommendations have been criticized by geneticists, health economists, and ethicists (Botkin et al., 2006; Natowicz, 2005), and stand in sharp contrast with the recommendations of the Health Technology Assessment Programme of the National Health Service of the United Kingdom (Pandor, Eastham, Beverley, Chilcott, & Paisley, 2004) and the Human Genetics Society of Australasia (2004). Both of these groups have recently developed lists of conditions to be included in a national newborn screening program, and their lists are notably shorter than the list recommended by the ACMG/HRSA.

In all 50 states, it is mandatory to at least offer newborn screening, but only 2 states require parental permission (American Academy of Pediatrics, 2000). The major benefit of mandatory screening is to ensure that all children are screened in order to treat quickly and accurately those who are affected (true positives) and to reassure those who do not have the disease (true negatives). The major danger of mandatory screening is that historically the tests have become institutionalized prior to an adequate understanding of what the test can and cannot do (Acuff & Faden, 1991; National Research Council, 1975; Reilly, 1977). Consider, for example, the history of PKU screening. In 1963, Massachusetts adopted a mandatory screening program even though a collaborative project to study the effects of dietary restriction on the physical, cognitive, and psychosocial development of affected children did not begin until 1967 (American Academy of Pediatrics, 1982). Many other states implemented mandatory PKU statutes before it was realized that there were children with elevated levels of phenylalanine who would not respond to a phenylalanine-restricted diet, or that there were some benign causes of elevated levels of phenylalanine that did not require treatment (National Research Council, 1975). The result was that some healthy children were placed on diets that led to iatrogenic retardation, and in some cases severe malnutrition and death (Holtzman, 1970).

The major arguments against requiring parental consent for new-born screening are that the process is time consuming and that even when consent is sought, the consent is perfunctory and not informed (Statham, Green, & Snowdon, 1993). Some also argue that consent is unnecessary because refusal for such clearly beneficial tests would constitute neglect. That consent is perfunctory does not argue against the need for consent, but rather is a criticism of the professionals who are not fulfilling their role in the consent process. The observation that refusal of standard treatment may constitute neglect notwithstanding, a charge of neglect does not eliminate the need for consent. Consent is generally required for all medical treatment, including standard care. A charge of neglect merely transfers the responsibility for consent to someone else, usually a court-appointed guardian. Whether or not re-fusal of newborn testing rises to the standards for reportable neglect is a separate question, given the low probability of harm if a newborn is not tested for a set of disorders that are collectively uncommon.

There are several arguments in favor of taking parental consent seri-ously. First, informed consent is a basic principle for all medical care. Consent serves as a symbol of respect for the patient and family, which is important given that families are the primary source of child rearing, and given that families, and not the state, will bear the greatest costs if an affected child is not screened and diagnosis is delayed. Second, procuring parental consent serves a valuable educational role. If con-sent is meaningful, it must be informed, which requires education—about both the purpose and limitations of screening. This education may increase the likelihood that parents follow up on abnormal screen-ing results. Knowledge of negative test results also may be reassuring to parents, particularly those with personal knowledge of the condi-tions being tested. And finally, consent is particularly important if newborn screening is expanded to conditions that have a later onset or that are not treatable, as there will be many families who will not want to know this information.

Consider two examples of newborn screening programs that have expanded to include conditions that present beyond infancy. One is a pilot study in Wales that began in the 1990s to screen newborn males for Duchenne muscular dystrophy (DMD; Bradley, Parsons, & Clarke, 1993), a progressive untreatable neuromuscular condition that presents in boys around 4–6 years and leads to serious disability and death in young adulthood. The potential benefits of early diagnosis are for family planning decisions—both logistical (e.g., a house with or without stairs) and reproductive. Early diagnosis also avoids diagnostic delays (Bushby, Hill, & Steele, 1999; Firth, 1983; Mohamed, Appleton, & Nicolaides, 2000), but it also risks interfering with parent-child bonding and adversely impacting child rearing. The "vulnerable child syndrome" refers to children with diagnoses of serious disorders who are treated differently by their parents because of the label, in a way that is harmful to the child's development (Green & Solnit, 1964).

A second example is the alpha-1-antitrypsin deficiency (alpha-1) screening program begun in Sweden in the 1970s. Alpha-1 causes chronic obstructive lung disease in young adults and presents earlier and more severely in those who smoke and are exposed to passive smoke. Thus, newborn screening was begun to educate parents of affected children not to smoke and to encourage parents and physicians to share these facts with the children as they matured (Thelin, McNeil, Aspegren-Jansson, & Sveger, 1985c). Sweden disbanded the program after five years because of the psychological stress it had caused in some families who had tested positive (McNeil, Thelin, Aspegren-Jansson, Sveger, & Harty, 1985). Follow-up data found increased smoking by fathers of affected children (Thelin et al., 1985c) and negative long-term effects in the mental and physical health of the mother (McNeil, Harty, Thelin, Aspegren-Jansson, & Sveger, 1986; Sveger, Thelin, & McNeil, 1999; Thelin, McNeil, Aspegren-Jansson, & Sveger, 1985b); in mother-child but not father-child interactions (McNeil et al., 1986); in parents' long-term emotional adjustment to their children's alpha-1 status (McNeil, Thelin, Aspegren-Jansson, & Sveger, 1985); and in the parents' view of their children's health (McNeil, Thelin, Aspegren-Jansson, & Sveger, 1985), although this improved over time (Thelin, McNeil, Aspegren-Jansson, & Sveger, 1985a). However, more recent data show the affected probands understand the risks of smoke exposure (Sveger, Thelin, & McNeil, 1997). In 1997, the World Health Organization came out in support of neonatal screening for alpha-1 (Memoranda, 1997), although in Sweden there is still debate as to whether it may be better to wait until preadolescence (Sveger & Thelin, 2000). In retrospect, the alpha-1 researchers realize that some of the stress might have been avoided if the parents had been informed about the testing and given the opportunity to consent or refuse testing, which was not the case when alpha-1 testing was incorporated into universal screening programs in the 1970s (Sveger & Thelin, 2000).

Both DMD and alpha-1 tests in the newborn period are examples of predictive genetic testing, testing children for conditions that will not manifest immediately. Most predictive genetic testing services are offered to adults for life planning (to determine the need and frequency of screening for certain forms of breast or colon cancer, or to define one's risk for dementia) and reproductive planning (both carrier testing and prenatal testing), but predictive genetic testing in pediatrics is possible and desired by many parents (Wertz, 1994). It is very controversial and challenges us to examine the goals of genetic testing and the responsibilities of parents in making medical decisions on behalf of and even with their children. This controversy is the focus of the next two sections.

PREDICTIVE GENETIC TESTING FOR ADULT-ONSET CONDITIONS

Predictive genetic testing encompasses a wide range of genetic tests. It includes both presymptomatic genetic testing, wherein the gene confers virtual certainty that the individual will have the condition (e.g., DMD), and predispositional genetic testing, wherein the gene confers increased susceptibility ranging from 10–90% penetrance (e.g., diabetes mellitus type I and inherited breast cancer [BRCA1], respectively). It includes predictive genetic testing for diseases that manifest themselves in early childhood (retinoblastoma, a form of eye cancer), midchildhood (DMD), adolescence (familial adenomatous polyposi [FAP], a form of colon cancer that presents in adolescents and young adults), and adulthood (BRCA1). It includes predictive genetic testing for conditions that have wide variability in disease severity (alpha-1) and those that have a predictable course (DMD).

Most of the focus on the ethical issues in predictive genetic testing of children and adolescents has been on parental requests for testing their children for conditions that present in adulthood for which no treatments exist in childhood (hence these recommendations may not apply to alpha-1, for which there are clinical recommendations that the child not smoke and not be exposed to secondhand smoke). There has been wide consensus by many professional groups that such predictive genetic testing for adult-onset conditions should be deferred until adulthood because children should be able to decide for themselves whether they want this information when they reach maturity (American Academy of Pediatrics, 2001; American Society of Human Genetics/American College of Medical Genetics [ASHG/ACMG], 1995; Working Party of the Clinical Genetics Society, 1994). Consider, for example, the conclusion of the Working Party of the Clinical Genetics Society (1994) of the U.K.: "the working party believes that predictive testing for an adult onset disorder should generally not be undertaken if the child is healthy and there are no medical interventions established as useful that can be offered in the event of a positive test result" (p. 785). The Genetics Interest Group (GIG), the U.K. umbrella organization for parent advocacy groups, supported this conclusion (Dalby, 1995).

The ASHG and the ACMG (1995) were more willing to consider that predictive genetic testing goes beyond clinical benefit and must address psychosocial benefits and risks in their report, "Points to Consider: Ethical, Legal and Psychosocial Implications of Genetic Testing in Children and Adolescents." In the section titled "The Impact of Potential Benefits and Harms on Decisions About Testing," the report stated, "If the medical or psychosocial benefits of a genetic test will not accrue until adulthood, as in the case of carrier status or adult-onset diseases, genetic testing generally should be deferred" (p. 1233).

However, the report was less clear on who should decide, the families or the health care providers, when the balance of benefits and harms is uncertain. In the section quoted above, the report suggested that when harms and benefits were uncertain, "the provider should respect the decision of competent adolescents and their families" (p. 1233), while in another part of the report, the authors conclude:

> Until more information is available regarding the risks and benefits of genetic testing, the provider's guiding principle continues to be primum non nocere—first do no harm. Thus, when faced with uncertainty, the provider may be obligated to avoid the possibility of harm, rather than to provide unclear benefits. There may be rebuttable presumption to defer testing unless the risk/benefit ratio is favorable. (p. 1238)

Despite the ambivalence of these statements, the data suggest that many parents want to test their children (Hamann et al., 2000; Patenaude, Basilil, Fairclough, & Li, 1996; Wertz, 2002).

What are the potential psychosocial risks and benefits? One potential psychosocial risk is the possibility of stigmatization associated with genetic abnormality, even in the absence of phenotypic abnormality (Billings et al., 1992). A second risk is the potential for inhibiting parent-child bonding or other disruptions in normal family relationships due to guilt on the part of parents or on behalf of the unaffected siblings (so-called survivor guilt). There is also the potential for a variation of the vulnerable child syndrome and modification of parental expectations (often subconsciously; ASHG/ACMG, 1995; Working Party of the Clinical Genetics Society, 1994).

The potential psychosocial benefits include the following: (1) family uncertainty about the future can be reduced; (2) planning for the future can be more practical, and (3) parental expectations for the child's future can be more "realistic" (ASHG/ACMG, 1995; Working Party of the Clinical Genetics Society, 1994). Note that these benefits accrue primarily to the parents. Whether advance planning actually benefits the child is an empirical question for which there is little data, and which would be difficult to predict in a specific case (Michie, 1996). These issues are further complicated by the long time lag between genetic diagnosis and the onset of symptoms.

One reason parents may want to test their children for adult-onset conditions is to ensure that their children, as adults, seek appropriate medical care. Although one can argue that parents discharge their responsibilities by advising the child of the pros and cons of testing and that final authority should reside with the child as an adult, the counterargument must also be considered. Those at risk for inherited cancers are often at risk during young adulthood, a time when many believe themselves to be invulnerable. While parents cannot force their adult children to seek appropriate medical care, if they know that their child is at risk, they may try to inculcate the need for such a practice in later adolescence and adulthood. Just because the parent is no longer legally empowered to consent for their adult children's medical care does not mean that they interpret their responsibility as fully discharged.

In some cases, it may be the adolescent and not the parent who wants to know whether or not he or she carries a familial genetic predisposition for an adult-onset condition. Both the working party and the ASHG/ACMG concluded that "mature" adolescents should be allowed to consent to genetic testing (ASHG/ACMG, 1995; Working Party of the Clinical Genetics Society, 1994). While the U.K. policy was clear that mature adolescents could consent legally without parental consent, the U.S. document was less clear. The recent statement on genetic testing of children by the American Academy of Pediatrics Committee on Bioethics (2001) did not clarify whether the adolescent's consent alone was legally adequate, although in other documents the committee has concluded that the mature adolescent's consent is morally adequate (American Academy of Pediatrics, 1995). Unfortunately, there is no consensus on how to decide whether an adolescent is mature. At a minimum, it requires that the adolescent is capable of appreciating the nature and importance of the decision for which he or she consents. Unfortunately, there is no objective standard to make this determination, and the evaluation depends on the subjective determination of the health care providers.

There may be some valid moral and pragmatic arguments why predictive genetic testing should be deferred until adulthood or should involve the adolescent's parents. First, it may be that the adolescent is requesting genetic test for a condition for which the parent has chosen not to learn his or her own status. As such, genetic testing of the adolescent would give the teenager information about his or her parent that the parent does not know and does not want to know (Ross, 2000). Parents have several arguments to support this position. First, they have a right to privacy about their genetic makeup. Depending on the genetic test, unexpected findings may be uncovered, including misattributed paternity. Second, the fear of discrimination is widespread, and a positive test in only one family member can put the whole family at risk for discrimination, an issue that may be less pertinent to an adolescent who is not responsible for procuring health and life insurance. Third, parents may decide that prohibiting gene testing of their children may prevent intrafamilial dissension between those who test positive and those who test negative. Although this may eventually happen if the siblings get tested as young adults, the fact is that, at least in the United States, approximately half of 18- to 24-year-olds do not live with their parents (Fields & Casper, 2000), and that may alleviate some of the risk for tension (Ross, 2000).

Whether it is the parent or the adolescent who seeks testing, a preventive family counseling evaluation and intervention, when appropriate, may be crucial in identifying high-risk families and helping them with these complex issues.

PREDICTIVE GENETIC TESTING FOR DISEASES THAT PRESENT IN CHILDHOOD

Despite the focus on predictive genetic testing, professional statements fail to address the parental interest in predictive genetic testing of newborns for diseases that present later in childhood. For example, there is often interest in testing newborns for CF or newborn males for DMD, when symptoms may not appear for months or years respectively, despite lack of clinical benefit with early diagnosis. The medical benefits of early diagnosis for either condition are uncertain at best. There is evidence that children with CF who are diagnosed in the newborn period by genetic testing are likely to be taller and heavier for at least part of their childhood, compared with affected children diagnosed by clinical symptoms (Dankert-Roelse & te Meerman, 1995; Farrell et al., 1997, 2001), but is not clear whether this surrogate measure is associated with improved mortality or quality of life (Murray, Cuckle, Taylor, Littlewood, & Hewison, 1999). Other studies have shown a correlation between nutritional status and pulmonary function (Dankert-Roelse & te Meerman, 1995; Waters et al., 1999), but this has not yet been demonstrated in the only prospective randomized trial of newborn genetic diagnosis of CF (Waters et al., 1999). Newborn diagnosis also avoids delay in diagnosis. Historical data from Australia in the 1980s show that the time from presentation to diagnosis in CF was 2.6 years (Wilcken, Towns, & Mellis, 1983), and 1.3 years in France in the 1990s (Siret et al., 2003). The data from Wisconsin show that 20% of children not diagnosed in the newborn period were still not diagnosed by 4 years of age (Farrell, 2000), and the delay may be greater in girls (Lai, Kosorok, Laxova, Makholm, & Farrell, 2002). In DMD, data show that there is over a 2-year delay between the time a parent first notices symptoms and when a diagnosis is made (Bushby et al., 1999; Firth, 1983; Mohamed et al., 2000). Many express anger and frustration regarding the delay and the medical odyssey to obtain a diagnosis and support newborn screening (Bradley et al., 1993; Helton, Harmon, Robinson, & Accurso, 1991).

To date, there are scant empirical data about the psychosocial benefits and risks of newborn screening for CF and DMD, although they are currently being studied in Wisconsin (CF), Colorado (CF), and Wales (DMD). The risk to the child may be that the family treats the child as vulnerable even before symptoms develop, and that the family may be unable to get proper health insurance because of a preexisting condition. Early diagnosis may benefit the family in making more realistic lifestyle decisions (e.g., a house in a rural area without access to emergency medical services versus a more urban location for families with a child with CF; a house with stairs versus a ranch for families with a child with DMD).

There are also potential reproductive benefits of such screening. In newborn screening for both CF and DMD, many families may not be aware of their own reproductive risks. In the former, both parents may be carriers and may not have or know of a clinically affected relative; in the latter, women are silent carriers because this is an X-linked disease. Contrast such predictive genetic testing with predictive genetic testing in families with a known risk for a genetic disease such as FAP (an autosomal dominant form of early-onset colon cancer) in which preventive measures are not needed for a decade. Here the main benefits are for family planning and for psychological relief from ambiguity. There may also be specific benefits to the child in that learning one's risk status in adolescence may be more difficult than learning this information at a younger age. However, early diagnosis may be harmful to intrafamilial relationships and place the child and family at risk of social discrimination. Unfortunately, no empirical data exist.

Michie, McDonald, Bobrow, McKeown, and Marteau (1996) described a single case of the parents of two daughters, aged 2 and 4, who were tested for the gene for FAP, and who were interviewed before testing, afterward, and 15 months later. The parents offered seven reasons for wanting testing: (1) the technology was available and accurate; (2) to avoid the worry of uncertainty; (3) the ability to support children by providing information; (4) to avoid the children's resentment that the parents had not forewarned them; (5) to help the family prepare for the future; (6) to encourage vigilance about screening; and (7) because they have a right, as parents, to decide. One child tested positive; the other negative. The parents stated that they did not treat the children differently and had no regrets. Unfortunately, as Michie and Marteau (1996) noted, this is one of the few empirical examples that have been reported (Codori, Petersen, Boyd, Brandt, & Giardiello, 1996; Michie, S., Bobrow, M., & Marteau, 2001; Grosfeld, Beemer, Lips, Hendriks, & ten Kroode, 2000).

Given the lack of empirical data, should parents be allowed to test their infants for conditions that will not present until later in childhood? Although there may not be clinical benefits, there are potential psychosocial risks and benefits that should not be underestimated. In many ways, the medical benefit of genetic testing in pediatrics is the simple question. Equally important and more difficult to know is the impact of testing, both immediate and long-term, on the child and family. Some would argue that all requests for genetic tests that do not offer obvious and immediate medical benefit should be refused. However, such a blanket prohibition assumes that the psychosocial benefits do not outweigh the risks (Cohen, 1998; Robertson & Savulescu, 2001; Ross, 2002). It is conceivable that the psychosocial benefits of a test, even a test that has little or no medical benefit for the child, may be critically important for a particular family's well-being. We believe that pediatricians and other health care providers offering services to children and their families need to work with families to ensure that they understand what the test can and cannot do, and to ensure that the family has considered all potential consequences and repercussions that such information may have on the individual child as well as on the family unit. In most cases, clinicians will be able to convince parents to defer genetic testing when it offers no medical benefit to the child. But if they are unsuccessful, clinicians will need to decide whether or not to accept that the parents may know what is in the child's best interest, or refer the child and family elsewhere. Studies show that there are health care providers willing to respect wide parental discretion (Wertz & Reilly, 1997; Working Party of the Clinical Genetics Society, 1994).

CARRIER TESTING

Carriers of recessive genes (and female carriers of X-linked conditions) are usually asymptomatic and unaware that they carry particular genes. For most recessive genetic traits, being a carrier confers no known medical morbidity or benefit. As such, tests to identify carrier status are not intended to provide a medical benefit to the patient, but serve to provide information that may be important for reproductive decisions.

Carrier testing is most often done in the prenatal setting. Sometimes, however, carrier status is determined incidentally. For example, children with a quantifiable amount of hemoglobin S on newborn screening in the United States are generally brought back for retesting. Hemoglobin electrophoresis determines whether they are homozygous for hemoglobin S (sickle-cell anemia) or whether they are heterozygous (carriers for sickle-cell anemia). Similarly, in the Wisconsin newborn screening program for CF, molecular testing results in the unintended diagnosis of heterozygote children, and parents are offered counseling and testing to rule out the possibility that both might be carriers and at risk for having a homozygous child in a future pregnancy.

But sometimes parents request to test their children for carrier status electively. Often the interest is prompted by the diagnosis of a sibling or other relative with the disease (Balfour-Lynn, Madge, & Dinwiddie, 1995). The professional consensus is against testing children for carrier status. The main arguments for refusing a parental request for carrier state testing are these: (1) it takes away the child's right not to know as an adult; (2) it fails to respect the child's right to confidential reproductive knowledge; (3) it may adversely affect the child's self-concept; and (4) it may expose the child to unwarranted genetic discrimination. There is also concern that parental misunderstanding of test results will lead to treating the child who is a carrier as an ill or potentially ill child (Hampton, Anderson, Lavizzo, & Bergman, 1974). The arguments in favor of honoring the parents' requests are that being informed of carrier status in childhood may make it easier to accept that status and incorporate it into one's personal identity (Fanos, 1997) and that parents, not the health care providers, are in a better position to decide if the benefits of knowledge outweigh the risks for a particular child (Dalby, 1995). In addition, knowledge of one's carrier status does not force one to use or act upon this knowledge in one's reproductive planning.

The advocacy group GIG offered several case examples in which early disclosure might be beneficial. It considered a child whose sibling has Duchenne muscular dystrophy or whose older sister had given birth to a baby boy with fragile X or whose cousins had CF. It considered that the child might be worried about his or her own health or about his or her reproductive risks, and it criticized the Clinical Genetics Society, which seemed to prefer answers with a "worry about it later" slant (Dalby, 1995). Rather, GIG noted that placing the interests of the child at the fore may require testing in childhood. It argued that the concerns of treating a child differently because of carrier status and of being given misinformation are unsubstantiated.

We support a policy that discourages testing of young children for carrier status, but we do not seek a blanket prohibition because, as GIG has explained, this information may be important for some families.

CONCLUSION

For parents to interpret the risks and benefits of a particular genetic test, they need to understand the differences between genetic testing in a child who is symptomatic, genetic testing for the presence of a virtually 100% penetrant gene that has not yet expressed itself, and genetic testing to determine increased susceptibility to a particular disease. They need to understand that testing may (1) uncover disease risk for conditions for which treatments and preventions may or may not exist; (2) uncover information that only has relevance in the reproductive context; and (3) yield results of varying predictive value.

The first step in helping parents to calculate the risks and benefits is to delineate the possible medical benefits and risks, if any, of genetic testing. The next step is to consider the psychosocial benefits and risks for the child and the family. Families need to explore all of the possible implications and repercussions of testing for both the child and the family as a unit. Genetic testing is complicated because knowledge about one family member may have significant impact on other family members. This is further complicated in pediatrics because the decisions may have life-long repercussions for the individual who did not personally consent to this testing. Further research on the psychosocial impact of genetic testing of children is needed to ensure that policies and practices meet the needs of children as children and as future adults, and as members of families, communities, and society at large.

REFERENCES

Acuff, K. L., & Faden, R. R. (1991). A history of prenatal and newborn screening programs: Lessons for the future. In R. R. Faden G. Geller, & M. Powers (Eds.), *AIDS, women and the next generation* (pp. 59–93). New York: Oxford University Press.

Advisory Committee on Heritable Disorders and Genetic Diseases in Newborns and Children. (2005). Minutes from the January 14–15, 2005 meeting. Retrieved January 14, 2006 from http://www.mchb.hrsa.gov/programs/genetics/committee/3rdmeeting.htm

American Academy of Pediatrics, Committee on Bioethics. (1995). Informed consent, parental permission, and assent in pediatric practice. *Pediatrics, 95*, 314–317.

American Academy of Pediatrics, Committee on Bioethics. (2001). Ethical issues with genetic testing in pediatrics. *Pediatrics, 107*, 1451–1455.

American Academy of Pediatrics, Committee on Genetics. (1982). New issues in newborn screening for phenylketonuria and congenital hypothyroidism. *Pediatrics, 69*, 104–106.

American Academy of Pediatrics, Committee on Genetics. (1996). Newborn screening fact sheet. *Pediatrics, 98*, 473–501.

American Academy of Pediatrics, Newborn Screening Task Force. (2000). Serving the family from birth to the medical home. Newborn screening: A blueprint for the future. A call for a national agenda on state newborn screening programs. *Pediatrics, 106*(Suppl.), 389–422.

American College of Medical Genetics (ACMG) / Health Resources and Services Administration (HRSA). (2004). Newborn screening: Toward a uniform screening panel and system. Retrieved January 14, 2006 from ftp://ftp.hrsa.gov/mchb/genetics/screeningdraftforcomment.pdf

American Society of Human Genetics/American College of Medical Genetics. (1995). Points to consider: Ethical, legal, and psychosocial implications of genetic testing in children and adolescents. *American Journal of Human Genetics, 57*, 1233–1241.

Baird, P. A., Anderson, T. W., Newcombe, H. B., & Lowry, R. B. (1988). Genetic disorders in children and young adults: A population study. *American Journal of Human Genetics, 42*, 677–693.

Balfour-Lynn, I., Madge, S., & Dinwiddie, R. (1995). Testing carrier status in siblings of patients with cystic fibrosis. *Archives of Diseases of Childhood, 72*, 167–168.

Billings, P. R., Kohn, M. A., de Cuevas, M., Beckwith, J., Alper, J. S., & Natowicz, M. R. (1992). Discrimination as a consequence of genetic testing. *American Journal of Human Genetics, 50*, 476–482.

Botkin, J. R., Clayton, E. W., Fost, N. C., Burke, W., Murray, T. H., Baily, M.A., et al. (2006). Newborn screening technology: Proceed with caution. *Pediatrics, 117*, 1793–1799.

Bradley, D. M., Parsons, E. P., & Clarke, A. J. (1993). Experience with screening newborns for Duchenne muscular dystrophy in Wales. *British Medical Journal, 306*, 357–360.

Burke, W. (2003). Genomics as a probe for disease biology. *New England Journal of Medicine, 349*, 969–974.

Bushby, K. M. D., Hill, A., & Steele, J. G. (1999). Failure of early diagnosis in symptomatic Duchenne muscular dystrophy. *Lancet, 353*, 557–558.

Codori, A.-M., Petersen, G. M., Boyd, P. A., Brandt, J., & Giardiello, F. M. (1996). Genetic testing for cancer in children: Short-term psychological effect. *Archives of Pediatrics and Adolescent Medicine, 150*, 1131–1138.

Cohen, C. B. (1998). Wrestling with the future: Should we test children for adult-onset genetic conditions. *Kennedy Institute of Ethics Journal, 8,* 111–130.

Cote, G. J., & Gagel, R. F. (2003). Lessons learned from the management of a rare genetic cancer. *New England Journal of Medicine, 349,* 1566–1568.

Dalby, S. (1995). GIG [Genetic Interest Group] response to the UK Clinical Genetics Society report "The genetic testing of children." *Journal of Medical Genetics, 32,* 490–492.

Dankert-Roelse, J. E., & te Meerman, G. J. (1995). Long term prognosis of patients with cystic fibrosis in relation to early detection by neonatal screening and treatment in a cystic fibrosis centre. *Thorax, 50,* 712–718.

Dewar, J. C., & Hall, I. P. (2003). Personalized prescribing for asthma—is pharmacogenetics the answer? *Journal of Pharmacy and Pharmacology, 55,* 279–289.

Fanos, J. H. (1997). Developmental tasks of childhood and adolescence: Implications for genetic testing. *American Journal of Medical Genetics, 71,* 22–28.

Farrell, P. M. (2000). Improving the health of patients with cystic fibrosis through newborn screening. Wisconsin Cystic Fibrosis Neonatal Screening Study Group. *Advances in Pediatrics, 47,* 79–115.

Farrell, P. M., Kosorok, M. R., Laxova, A., et al. (1997). Nutritional benefits of neonatal screening for cystic fibrosis. *New England Journal of Medicine, 337,* 963–969.

Farrell, P. M., Kosorok, M. R., Rock, M. J., et al. (2001). Early diagnosis of cystic fibrosis through neonatal screening prevents severe malnutrition and improves long-term growth. *Pediatrics, 107,* 1–13.

Fields, J., & Casper, L. (2001, June). *Current population reports: America's families and living arrangements 2000.* Retrieved October 11, 2002, from http://www.census.gov/prod/2001pubs/p20-537.pdf

Firth, M. A. (1983). Diagnosis of Duchenne muscular dystrophy: Experiences of parents of sufferers. *British Medical Journal, 286,* 700–701.

Green, M., & Solnit, A. J. (1964). Reactions to the threatened loss of a child: A vulnerable child syndrome. *Pediatrics, 34,* 58–66.

Grosfeld, F. J. M., Beemer, F. A., Lips, C. J. M., Hendriks, K. S. W. H., & ten Kroode, H. F. J. (2000). Parents' responses to disclosure of genetic test results of their children. *American Journal of Medical Genetics, 94,* 316–323.

Hamann, H. A., Croyle, R. T., Venne, V. L., Baty, B. J., Smith, K. R., & Botkin, J. R. (2000). Attitudes toward the genetic testing of children among adults in a Utah-based kindred tested for a BRCA1 mutation. *American Journal of Medical Genetics, 92,* 25–32.

Hampton, M. L., Anderson, J., Lavizzo, B. S., & Bergman, A. B. (1974). Sickle cell "nondisease": A potentially serious public health problem. *American Journal of Diseases of Children, 128,* 58–61.

Helton, J. L., Harmon, R. J., Robinson, N., & Accurso, F. J. (1991). Parental attitudes toward newborn screening for cystic fibrosis. *Pediatric Pulmonology Supplement, 7,* 23–28.

Holtzman, N. (1970). Dietary treatment of inborn errors of metabolism. *Annual Review of Medicine, 21,* 335–356.

Holtzman, N. A. (1989). *Proceed with caution*. Baltimore: Johns Hopkins University Press.

Human Genetics Society of Australasia (HGSA). HGSA Policy Statement 2004. HGSA/Royal College of Australasian Physicians (RCAP) Newborn Screening Joint Subcommittee. (2004). Newborn blood-spot screening. Retrieved January 20, 2006 from http://www.hgsa.com.au/Word/HGSA policyStatementNewbornScreening0204-18.03.04.doc

Khoury, M. J., McCabe, L. L., & McCabe, E. R. (2003). Population screening in the age of genomic medicine. *New England Journal of Medicine, 348,* 50–58.

Lai, H. C., Kosorok, M. R., Laxova, A., Makholm, L. M., & Farrell, P. M. (2002). Delayed diagnosis of US females with cystic fibrosis. *American Journal of Epidemiology, 156,* 165–173.

Levy-Lahad, E., & Zimran, A. (1997). Gaucher's disease: Genetic counselling and population screening. *Bailliere's Clinical Haematology, 10,* 779–792.

Mansfield, C., Hopfer, S., & Marteau, T. M. on behalf of European Concerted Action: DADA (Decision-Making After the Diagnosis of a Fetal Abnormality). (1999). Termination rates after prenatal diagnosis of Down syndrome, spina bifida, anencephaly, and Turner and Klinefelter syndromes: A systematic literature review. *Prenatal Diagnosis, 19,* 808–812.

McNeil, T. F., Harty, B., Thelin, T., Aspegren-Jansson, E., & Sveger, T. (1986). Identifying children at high somatic risk: Long-term effects on mother-child interaction. *Acta Psychiatrica Scandinavica, 74,* 555–562.

McNeil, T. F., Thelin, T., Aspegren-Jansson, E., & Sveger, T. (1985). Identifying children at high somatic risk: Possible effects on the parents' views of the child's health and parents' relationship to the pediatric health services. *Acta Psychiatrica Scandinavica, 72,* 491–497.

McNeil, T. F., Thelin, T., Aspegren-Jansson, E., Sveger, T., & Harty, B. (1985). Psychological factors in cost-benefit analysis of somatic prevention. A study of the psychological effects of neonatal screening for alpha 1-antitrypsin deficiency. *Acta Paediatrica Scandinavica, 74,* 427–432.

Memoranda: Alpha$_1$-antitrypsin deficiency: Memorandum from a WHO meeting. (1997). *Bulletin of the World Health Organization, 75,* 397–415.

Michie, S. (1996). Predictive genetic testing in children: Paternalism or empiricism. In T. Marteau & M. Richards (Eds.), *The troubled helix: Social and psychological implications of the new genetics* (pp. 177–183). Cambridge, UK: Cambridge University Press.

Michie, S., Bobrow, M., & Marteau, T. M. on behalf of the FAP Collaborative Research Group. (2001). Predictive genetic testing in children and adults: A study of emotional impact. *Journal of Medical Genetics, 38,* 519–526.

Michie, S., & Marteau, T. M. (1996). Predictive genetic testing in children: The need for psychological research. *British Journal of Health Psychology, 1,* 3–14.

Michie, S., McDonald, V., Bobrow, M., McKeown, C., & Marteau, T. (1996) Parents' responses to predictive genetic testing in their children: Report of a single case study. *Journal of Medical Genetics, 33,* 313–318.

Mischler, E. H., Wilfond, B. S., Fost, N., et al. (1998). Cystic fibrosis newborn screening: Impact on reproductive behavior and implications for genetic counseling. *Pediatrics, 102*, 44–52.

Mohamed, K., Appleton, R., & Nicolaides, P. (2000). Delayed diagnosis of Duchenne muscular dystrophy. *European Journal of Paediatric Neurology, 4*, 219–223.

Murray, J., Cuckle, H., Taylor, G., Littlewood, J., & Hewison, J. (1999). Screening for cystic fibrosis. *Health Technology Assessment, 3*(8).

National Research Council, Committee for the Study of Inborn Errors of Metabolism. (1975). *Genetic screening: Programs, principles, and research.* Washington, DC: National Academy of Sciences.

National Screening Commission. (n.d.). *The criteria for appraising the viability, effectiveness and appropriateness of a screening programme.* Retrieved from http://www.doh.gov.uk/nsc/pdfs/.PDF

Natowicz, M. (2005). Newborn Screening—Setting Evidence-Based Policy for Protection. *New England Journal of Medicine, 353*, 867–870.

NIH Technology Assessment Panel on Gaucher Disease. (1996). Gaucher disease: Current issues in diagnosis and treatment. *Journal of the American Medical Association, 275*, 548–553.

Pandor, A., Eastham, J., Beverley, C., Chilcott, J., & Paisley, S. (2004). Clinical effectiveness and cost-effectiveness of neonatal screening for inborn errors of metabolism using tandem mass spectrometry: A systematic review. *Health Technology Assessment, 8*(12).

Patenaude, A. F., Basilil, L., Fairclough, D. L., & Li, F. P. (1996). Attitudes of 47 mothers of pediatric oncology patients towards genetic testing for cancer predisposition. *Journal of Clinical Oncology, 14*, 415–421.

Reilly, P. (1977). *Genetics, law and social policy.* Cambridge, MA: Harvard University Press.

Report of a Workgroup. (2001). Using tandem mass spectrometry for metabolic disease screening among newborns. *MMWR: Morbidity and Mortality Weekly Report, 50*(RR03), 1–22.

Robertson, S., & Savulescu, J. (2001). Is there a case in favour of predictive genetic testing in young children? *Bioethics, 15*, 26–49.

Ross, L. F. (2000). Genetic testing of adolescents: Is it in their best interest? *Archives of Pediatrics and Adolescent Medicine, 154*, 850–851.

Ross, L. F. (2002). Predictive genetic testing for conditions that present in childhood. *Kennedy Institute of Ethics Journal, 12*, 225–244.

Rothenberg, M. B., & Sills, E. M. (1968). Iatrogenesis: The PKU anxiety syndrome. *Journal of the American Academy of Child Psychiatry, 7*, 689–692.

Schilling, F. H., Spix, C., Berthold, F., Erttmann, R., Fehse, N., Hero, B., et al. (2002). Neuroblastoma screening at one year of age. *New England Journal of Medicine, 346*, 1047–1053.

Singer, E. (1993). Public attitudes toward fetal diagnosis and the termination of life. *Social Indicators Research, 28*, 117–136.

Siret, D., Betraudeau, G., Branger, B., Dabadie, A., Dagorne, M., David, V., et al. (2003). Comparing the clinical evolution of cystic fibrosis screened neonatally to that of cystic fibrosis diagnosed from clinical symptoms: A

10-year retrospective study in a French region. *Pediatric Pulmonology, 35,* 342–349.

Sorenson, J. R., Levy, H. L., Mangione, T. W., & Sepe, S. J. (1984). Parental response to repeat testing of infants with "false-positive" results in a newborn screening program. *Pediatrics, 73,* 183–187.

Statham, H., Green, J., & Snowdon, C. (1993). Mother's consent to screening newborn babies for disease. *British Medical Journal, 306,* 858–859.

Sveger, T., & Thelin, T. (2000). A future for neonatal alpha 1-antitrypsin screening? *Acta Paediatrica, 89,* 259–261.

Sveger, T., Thelin, T., & McNeil, T. H. (1997). Young adults with $alpha_1$-antitrypsin deficiency identified neonatally: their health, knowledge about and adaptation to the high-risk condition. *Acta Paediatrica, 86,* 37–40.

Sveger, T., Thelin, T., & McNeil, T. F. (1999). Neonatal alpha1-antitrypsin screening: Parents' views and reactions 20 years after the identification of the deficiency state. *Acta Paediatrica, 88,* 315–318.

Thelin, T., McNeil, T. F., Aspegren-Jansson, E., & Sveger, T. (1985a). Identifying children at high somatic risk: Parents' long-term emotional adjustment to their children's alpha-antitrypsin deficiency. *Acta Psychiatrica Scandinavica, 72,* 323–330.

Thelin, T., McNeil, T. F., Aspegren-Jansson, E., & Sveger, T. (1985b). Identifying children at high somatic risk: Possible long-term effects on the parents' view of their own health and current life situation. *Acta Psychiatrica Scandinavica, 71,* 644–653.

Thelin, T., McNeil, T. F., Aspegren-Jansson, E., & Sveger, T. (1985c). Psychologic consequences of neonatal screening for $Alpha_1$ antitrypsin deficiency. *Acta Paediatrica Scandinavica, 74,* 787–793.

Touchette, N., Holtzman, N. A., Davis, J. G., & Feetham, S. (1997). *Toward the 21st century: Incorporating genetics into primary health care.* New York: Cold Spring Harbor Press.

Verloes, A., Gillerot, Y., Maldergem, L. V., et al. (2001). Major decrease in the incidence of trisomy 21 at birth in south Belgium: Mass impact of triple test? *European Journal of Human Genetics, 9,* 1–4.

Waters, D. L., Wilcken, B., Irwing, L., et al. (1999). Clinical outcomes of newborn screening for cystic fibrosis. *Archives of Disease in Childhood: Fetal and Neonatal Edition, 80:* F1–7.

Wertz, D. C. (1994). Patients' ethical views on genetic privacy, disclosure to relatives, and testing children [abstract]. *American Journal of Human Genetics, 55,* 295a.

Wertz, D. (2002). Testing children and adolescents. In J. Burley & J. Harris (Eds.), *A companion to genetics* (pp. 92–113). Walden, MA: Blackwell.

Wertz, D. C., & Reilly, P. R. (1997). Laboratory policies and practices for the genetic testing of children: A survey of the helix network. *American Journal of Human Genetics, 61,* 1163–1168.

Wilcken, B., Towns, S. J., & Mellis, C. M. (1983). Diagnostic delay in cystic fibrosis: Lessons from newborn screening. *Archives of Disease in Childhood, 58,* 863–866.

Wilcken, B., Wiley, V., Hammond, J., & Carpenter, K. (2003). Screening newborns for inborn errors of metabolism by tandem mass spectrometry. *New England Journal of Medicine, 348,* 2304–2312.

Wilson, J. M., & Jungner, G. (1968). *Principles and practice of screening for disease.* Public Health Papers 34. Geneva: World Health Organization.

Working Party of the Clinical Genetics Society (UK). (1994). The genetic testing of children. *Journal of Medical Genetics, 31,* 785–797.

Chapter 19

Genetic Testing

Legal and Policy Issues for Individuals and Their Families

Jean McEwen

THE GENETIC TESTING OF ADULTS TO PREDICT THEIR FUTURE HEALTH raises many policy issues, and sometimes legal issues, for individuals, their families, and society. Many of these stem from the notion of genetic exceptionalism—the idea that genetic information is somehow unique, or at least sufficiently different from other types of medical information, so that it requires special and sometimes different treatment in both policy and law (Annas, 1999). The notion of genetic exceptionalism, in turn, derives from the fact that genetic information has certain unique features; it may, for example, implicate the interests of multiple family members, including reproductive interests (Green & Mathew, 1998). The notion of genetic exceptionalism also derives from the fact that genetic information has an especially well-documented history of misuse (Reilly, 2000). While proponents of genetic exceptionalism have come under considerable criticism in the recent academic literature (Gostin & Hodge, 1999; Lemmens, 2000), this approach has generally been accepted in the legislatures and the courts, where genetic testing and genetic information are sometimes treated differently from nongenetic medical data.

The primary focus of this chapter is on genetic testing expressly undertaken for predictive purposes, because this type of testing raises perhaps the most vexing policy and legal issues. By 2010, it is expected that predictive genetic tests will be available for as many as a dozen common conditions, allowing individuals who wish to know this information to learn their individual risk status and take steps to reduce it where preventive strategies are available (Collins & McKusick, 2001). Currently, predictive genetic testing of adults falls into two main categories: presymptomatic testing to determine whether an individual is presymptomatic for a highly penetrant genetic disorder, typically caused by a single gene (e.g., Huntington disease); and predispositional testing to determine whether an individual has an increased susceptibility to an incompletely penetrant genetic disorder in which environmental factors, and sometimes multiple genes, play a role (e.g., heart disease, type 2 diabetes, cancer). Another type of predictive genetic testing, which many expect to become standard practice by 2020, is pharmacogenomics testing to predict individual response to particular medications (Roses, 2000).

Some, but not all, predictive genetic testing can also be classified as genetic screening: a search in a wider population for individuals with a particular genotype. Population-based genetic screening raises many of the same issues as predictive genetic testing in clinical contexts, but it involves additional public health and policy issues as well (Clarke, 1995). The focus of this chapter, however, is primarily on those legal and policy issues most likely to arise from genetic testing of individuals and families in the routine practice of clinical medicine, since these are the issues likely to be of greatest concern in the arena of family therapy.[1]

GENETIC PRIVACY, CONFIDENTIALITY, AND INFORMED CONSENT

At the level of the individual, genetic testing raises issues relating to privacy and confidentiality—both of which, in turn, are embodied in the legal doctrine of informed consent. Privacy, in a legal sense, can be defined as the limited access to a person, the right to be let alone, and the right to keep certain information from being disclosed to other individuals (Rothstein, 1998). Confidentiality, by contrast, is the right of an individual to prevent the redisclosure of certain sensitive information that was originally disclosed in the confines of a confidential relationship (Rothstein, 1998). The requirement of informed consent, in the context of genetic testing, is designed to ensure that the individual being offered testing understands the risks and benefits of the test and can make a free and voluntary choice whether to have it (Holtzman & Watson, 1997).

The concept of privacy incorporates four categories of concern: (1) informational privacy concerns about access to personal information;

(2) physical privacy concerns about access to persons and personal spaces; (3) decisional privacy concerns about governmental and other third-party interference with personal choices; and (4) proprietary privacy concerns about the appropriation of one's unique DNA (conceived of as a repository of valuable human "personality" owned by each individual as a form of private property; Allen, 1997). In practice, the term *genetic privacy* is most often used to denote privacy of the informational type, which in turn incorporates the right of confidentiality. For example, the Genetic Privacy Act, a model statute drafted in the early 1990s that served as an initial model for legislation in a number of states, was designed primarily to safeguard informational privacy, although it also incorporated some notions of proprietary privacy (Annas, Glantz, & Roche, 1995b; see also Annas, Glantz, & Roche, 1995a).

Concerns about genetic privacy extend far beyond mere informational privacy, however, and the doctrine of informed consent is intended to safeguard the full range of these concerns. For example, taking a biological sample for genetic testing without first obtaining the voluntary consent of the individual would constitute unwanted physical contact. Such unwanted contact would compromise that person's interests in bodily integrity and security, constituting an invasion of physical privacy (Allen, 1997).

The informed consent doctrine also helps protect individuals' interests in decisional privacy. Genetic testing, after all, can usually be performed with quite painless and minimally invasive procedures (e.g., needle sticks, cheek swabs). The nature of the information provided by the testing, however, can be quite powerful, calling into question for some the very way in which they define themselves and relate to others. Learning that one is (or is not) at increased risk for certain types of genetic or genetically influenced disorders (e.g., Huntington disease, hereditary breast cancer, schizophrenia) can for some people lead to considerable anxiety, depression, and loss of self-esteem. Should one's genetic risk status be learned by others—within or outside the family—stigmatization or discrimination may occur. Individuals thus have a right to choose whether to have information of this type generated, and cannot be coerced or subtly pressured into having a genetic test. It is, in fact, respect for autonomous decision making and the concept of decisional privacy that primarily underlie the norm of nondirectiveness in the contemporary practice of genetic counseling.

The doctrine of informed consent also protects the fourth type of privacy—propriety privacy (Allen, 1997; see also Andrews, 1986; Barrad, 1993). In *Moore v. Regents of University of California* (1991), a California court, while rejecting a patient's argument that commercial development of cell lines derived from his excised cells amounted to theft, recognized that patients have a right to information about their physicians' economic and research interests. Proprietary privacy issues are most often raised in discussions of the rights surrounding the use of stored tissue samples and the information learned from individuals or families with genetic disorders in the research context (Marshall, 2000). The model Genetic Privacy Act (which, as noted, has been influential in some state legislatures) sought to address this issue by expressly placing ownership of DNA in the individual from whom samples are derived (Annas et al., 1995b). Similarly, principles established by the American Society of Human Genetics' Ad Hoc Committee on DNA Technology assigned ownership and property rights of DNA deposited in databanks to the depositor or donor (American Society of Human Genetics, 1988).

The National Institutes of Health-Department of Energy Task Force on Genetic Testing, in its 1997 report, strongly advocated obtaining written informed consent for all genetic tests done in the clinical context. The task force recommended that health care providers describe, for each test offered, the purpose of the test, the likelihood that it will give a correct prediction, the implications of the test results, the options, and the benefits and risks of the process (Holtzman & Watson, 1997). However, whether this recommendation will become the standard of practice remains uncertain; as the number of available genetic tests proliferates, it will become impractical to require written informed consent for every one—especially in the setting of managed care. Genetic testing in the future also will increasingly involve tests to determine genetic risk for more common, complex disorders (e.g., asthma, hypertension, cancer, depression)—disorders in which many genetic variants operate together and with environmental factors to confer disease risk (Collins & Guttmacher, 2001). Tests for such disorders will be notably difficult to interpret and explain because many people who carry a disease-associated variant will never develop the disorder in question. This will make obtaining meaningful informed consent an even more challenging prospect.

DISCLOSURE OF GENETIC INFORMATION WITHIN FAMILIES

Like the doctrine of informed consent, the doctrine of patient confidentiality is complicated in the context of genetic testing because genetic information is inherently familial. That is, information about an individual also, by its nature, reveals genetic risk information about that person's biological relatives. As a very straightforward example, knowing that someone is a carrier for cystic fibrosis (CF)—an autosomal recessive disorder—means that if that person's partner or spouse is also a carrier, there is a one-in-four chance with each pregnancy that the child will be affected. It also means that the person's siblings may be carriers of the CF gene and thus also at risk of having affected children should their partner or spouse be a carrier. For this reason, the family members of a person who has tested positive as a CF carrier may have a strong interest in knowing such information, both for disease prevention and reproductive decision making (Suter, 1993). Some of the most difficult legal and policy issues in genetic testing thus arise in clarifying when physicians, genetic counselors, or health care providers have a privilege—or even an ethical or legal duty—to disclose to a patient's relatives otherwise presumptively confidential genetic information of this type.[2]

The federal Privacy Rule, a comprehensive set of regulations issued by the U.S. Department of Health and Human Services in 2003 to implement the requirements of the Health Insurance Portability and Accountability Act of 1996 (HIPAA), provides that protected health information (defined in HIPAA to include genetic information) may be disclosed if the provider believes it is "necessary to prevent or lessen a serious and imminent threat to a person or the public" when such disclosure is made to someone the provider believes can prevent or lessen the threat (Standards for Privacy of Individually Identifiable Health Information, 2003). Just what circumstances would constitute such a "serious and imminent threat" in the specific context of genetic information remains unclear, but it seems likely that disclosure would be justified only in exceptional circumstances. The situation may be further complicated, however, depending on whether the provider has a direct relationship with both the patient who does not want the information disclosed and another family member who may have an interest in the information.

Under the standard set out by the President's Commission for the Study of Ethical Problems in Medicine and Biomedical and Behavioral Research and subsequently endorsed by the Institute of Medicine (President's Commission for the Study of Ethical Problems, 1983; Institute of Medicine, 1994), overriding patient confidentiality to warn a patient's relative of genetic risk is ethically justifiable only when the patient refuses to communicate information despite reasonable attempts to persuade him or her to do so, when failure to give that information has a high probability of resulting in imminent, serious, and irreversible harm to the relative, and when communication of the information will enable the relative to avert the harm.

The American Society of Human Genetics, which has also endorsed this general standard, has further taken the position that health care professionals have a duty to inform the patient, both prior to the testing and again upon refusal to communicate results, of the implications of the genetic test results and the potential risks to family members (American Society of Human Genetics, 1998). If the patient still declines to share the information, the provider generally should not take it upon himself or herself to do so, except in exceptional cases. If left with the impression that the provider will inform relatives when the person considering testing does not want them informed, some people will decline testing; this would have the effect of denying information not only to the relative but also to the person offered testing.

Applying these professional standards in practice has proven challenging, however, and controversy persists regarding the relative weight to be accorded to individual privacy interests and a patient's family members' asserted right to know. Health care providers themselves appear to be divided, often making it difficult to determine the prevailing legal standard of care (Andrews, 1997). In general, however, the more common the disorder, the more indeterminate the genetic test result, and the less likely having knowledge of the result would (for most people) affect reproductive decision making, the less likely the provider will be able to cite a justification for breaching confidentiality. Thus, a provider may arguably be allowed to warn, over the objection of a husband who tests positive for the gene for Huntington disease, his wife of childbearing age. However, that provider would be much less justified in disclosing to a spouse a test result that suggested only a 20% increased genetic risk for hypertension in the spouse and an even less certain risk in their future offspring.

Further complicating the analysis of whether a health care provider has a privilege to breach patient confidentiality to warn relatives of genetic risk is the fact that some commentators have argued for, and some courts have suggested, the possible existence of an affirmative duty to do so. Advocates of such a duty draw an analogy to the mandatory reporting and contact tracing requirements in the infectious disease context (Shaw, 1977). The arguments for a duty to disclose in the genetics context are much weaker than in the infectious disease context, however, because genetic risk factors are not transmitted to others in the same way infectious diseases are; the mode of transmission is "vertical" rather than "horizontal." Moreover, the role of the state in preventing genetic disorders (and in preventing the birth of children with such disorders) is far less clear-cut than its public health role in preventing the spread of infectious disease.

Advocates of a legal duty to disclose to relatives in cases where patients refuse to divulge pertinent genetic risk information also analogize to the line of cases, beginning with *Tarasoff v. Regents of California*

(1976), in which courts have found a duty on the part of psychothera-
pists to disclose their patients' threats of serious harm to identified
third parties (Burnett, 1999; Deftos, 1997). However, this approach has
been criticized as too ambiguous in its description of the boundaries of
legitimate disclosure (Merz, Cho, & Sankar, 1998). The applicability of
the *Tarasoff* reasoning to the genetics context also is flawed in that genetics cases generally do not involve imminent harm or threats delivered
by one person to another (Suter, 1993).

To date, only two courts have explicitly addressed the question of
the disclosure obligations of health care providers in the specific context of clinical genetics. In *Pate v. Threlkel* (1995), a Florida state court
held that a physician may have a legal duty to warn a patient of a genetic disorder (there, hereditary medullary thyroid cancer) when that
disorder has potential health ramifications for the patient's relatives.
However, the court stated that this duty could be satisfied merely by
warning the patient of the genetic nature of the disorder; the patient
could then ordinarily be expected to pass on the warning to the relevant family members. The *Pate* court stated that to require a physician
affirmatively to seek out and warn various members of the patient's
family will often be difficult or impractical and could place too heavy a
burden on the physician.

In *Safer v. Estate of Pack* (1996), a New Jersey state court recognized
an even more expansive duty to warn. That case involved a woman
whose father had been treated for multiple polyposis over a 7-year period, until his death from colorectal cancer at age 45. The woman, who
learned of her father's medical history only after she herself was diagnosed with colorectal cancer many years later, filed suit against her father's physician, claiming that had she been apprised of the facts
relevant to her own genetic risk, she might have had the benefits of
earlier examination, monitoring, detection, and treatment.

The court stated that it could see "no impediment, legal or otherwise, to recognizing a physician's duty to warn those known to be at
risk of avoidable harm from a genetically transmissible condition,"
reasoning that in terms of foreseeability, there was "no essential difference between the type of genetic threat at issue [t]here and the menace
of infection, contagion or a threat of physical harm." The court went a
step further than the *Threlkel* court, stating that the duty owed was not
only to the patient himself but also extends beyond the interests of a
patient to members of the patient's immediate family who may be adversely affected by a breach of that duty.

The *Safer* court did not decide precisely how the physician's duty is
to be discharged, except to require that "reasonable steps be taken to
assure that the information reaches those likely to be affected or is

made available for their benefit." The court also acknowledged that an overly broad and general application of the duty might lead to confusion, conflict, or unfairness. It also acknowledged that conflicts requiring further judicial resolution may sometimes arise between the physician's duty to warn and fidelity to an expressed preference of the patient that nothing be said to family members.

It is too early to know whether either the relatively limited duty to warn recognized in *Threlkel* or the more expansive duty recognized in *Safer* signal the beginning of a trend toward expanding the legal liability of health care professionals toward the relatives of patients in the clinical genetic testing context. Both cases may be limited to their facts, and neither is binding on courts in other jurisdictions. In addition, the Privacy Rule promulgated pursuant to HIPAA, which, as noted, establishes what appears to be a fairly high threshold for disclosure of protected health information, may discourage further judicial recognition or expansion of a duty to warn.

A model of patient care has been proposed, called the *family covenant*, that would articulate the roles of the physician, patient, and the family prior to genetic testing, as the participants consensually define them (Doukas & Berg, 2001). The initial agreement would define the boundaries of autonomy and benefit for all participating family members. The clinician or health professional would then serve as a facilitator in the relationship, working with all parties in resolving potential conflicts over access to genetic information. While some commentators have been supportive of this family covenant model (Bartels, 2001), others have criticized it as an inefficient use of already overburdened medical and counseling professionals and as requiring too great an upfront commitment of time and energy to appeal to most families (Stock, 2001).

UNEXPECTED FINDINGS

Misattributed Paternity

A particularly thorny disclosure issue that has plagued geneticists for years is how to handle unexpected findings uncovered in the course of genetic testing—such as the finding of misattributed paternity when multiple members of a family are being tested (Lucassen & Parker, 2001). Genetic risk estimates are based on the assumption that the biological relationships assumed to exist among family members are accurate. An individual's misunderstanding about his or her biological relationship to other family members can thus confound the clinical determination of whether he or she is at increased risk for getting (or

passing on) a genetic disorder—with ramifications for health and reproductive planning.

Various strategies have been suggested to deal with this situation—
all with some ethical and legal limitations. The approach recommended
by the President's Commission is for the health care provider frankly to
disclose the finding (President's Commission for the Study of Ethical
Problems, 1983). This approach, however, may elevate principles of individual autonomy over allegiance to the integrity of the family unit. It
also ignores the very real risk in some cases that serious psychological
or even physical harm may result from such a disclosure.

A second approach is for the provider to skirt the issue, engage in
some form of partial disclosure, or outright misrepresent the truth if
asked by a man whether he is indeed the biological father. This approach seems reasonable where a genuine and serious risk of harm to
the woman or family appears likely if the information were to be disclosed. However, it carries legal risks, as well as potential ethical risks
should it influence an individual or the couple to make decisions about
their future health or reproduction based on erroneous information
(Reilly, 1993).

A third strategy—the approach recommended by the Institute of
Medicine (1994)—is to tell only the mother and leave with her the
choice of what to do with the information. This approach, while intu-
itively appealing, seems difficult to reconcile with the notion that the
ethical and legal obligations of the provider in the situation where
multiple family members are being tested run equally to all family
members (Ross, 1996).

An emerging approach to this problem is to address the issue before
the testing takes place, as part of the informed consent process. While
this approach has obvious advantages, it also has limitations, given the
practical realities of the setting in which genetic testing typically takes
place. For example, the very inclusion of the subject of paternity
among the subjects treated in an informed consent document may provoke anxiety on the part of a woman who for the first time realizes that
the issue of misattributed paternity could surface if she proceeds with
the testing, leaving her confused about how to back out discreetly from
a test in which she had initially expressed interest (Biesecker, 1997).
The complexity of these issues suggests the importance of the role of
family therapist consultants in cases of this type.

Pleitropic Genetic Tests

Another issue arises from the increasing availability of pleitropic genetic
tests, which are tests to determine increased genetic risk for one disorder

that may simultaneously (and perhaps unexpectedly) provide information about another. A classic example is testing for the *APOE4* genetic variant, now known to be associated with increased risk not only for heart disease, but also for early-onset Alzheimer disease. Should patients undergoing *APOE4* testing to inform genetic assessment of heart disease risk be informed of their increased genetic risk for Alzheimer disease, if they are found to have the *APOE4* variant? What about in cases where the relationship between the two disorders is not known at the time of the testing, but only becomes apparent later? Does a provider have an ethical or legal duty to go back to the patient and tell him or her of the later finding? Or would doing so amount to giving the patient information he or she would prefer not to know, perhaps even exposing the provider to liability for such disclosure? Some commentators have concluded that as an ethical matter, all information should be disclosed (Wachbroit, 1998). Nevertheless, disclosing unwanted information may create unnecessary psychological distress and could in some cases be viewed as a breach of informed consent. Unfortunately, there are no clear answers to these questions from the standpoint of legal liability, because such questions for the most part have not yet reached the courts.

ACCESS TO AND USE OF GENETIC INFORMATION BY THIRD PARTIES OUTSIDE THE FAMILY

As predictive genetic testing becomes a part of routine health care, questions will increasingly arise regarding rights of access to and use of genetic information by third parties outside the family. Genetic test information, if placed in the "wrong hands" and misused, can lead to stigmatization of or discrimination against those who are tested and also, in some cases, their entire families or even larger racial or ethnic groups—as occurred in the 1960s with sickle-cell anemia testing in African Americans (Markel, 1992). The fear of being stigmatized or discriminated against may lead some people to refuse genetic testing even when it could be beneficial (Rothstein, 1992a). It also may lead them to withhold information, provide inaccurate information, engage in "physician-hopping" to avoid establishing a comprehensive medical record, pay out of pocket for care covered by insurance, or avoid care altogether (Gostin, Hodge, & Calvo, 2001).

Few rigorous empirical studies have been conducted that document the actual extent of genetic discrimination in the United States (Hall, 1999). The studies to date have been based principally on anecdotal evidence and may reflect some self-selection bias (Billings et al., 1992; Lapham, Kozma, & Weiss, 1996). In addition, the studies do not always clearly distinguish between discrimination against individuals who are merely at genetic risk for having a particular disorder in the future ("true" genetic discrimination) and discrimination against those who are already ill (discrimination to be sure, but treatment no different from that experienced by many individuals with nongenetic disorders).

Nevertheless, some instances of true genetic discrimination based solely on risk status have occurred, and the incidence of this type of discrimination may increase in the future as more tests become available for assessing individual disease risk. In some cases, even mere perceptions of the risk of genetic discrimination may have adverse effects, as patients engage in self-protective behavior designed to shield themselves from the risk of misuse of their genetic data.

Insurance

Much of the discourse to date in the legal and policymaking arenas has been on genetic discrimination in the context of health insurance (Brockett & Tankersley, 1997; Rothenberg, 1995). The concern is that in the absence of legal protections against genetic discrimination in health insurance, insurers will simply turn away high-risk individuals or deny coverage for medical costs associated with the very condition for which the individual is most in need of coverage. In addition, in cases where a known family history of a particular disorder exists (e.g., Huntington disease), it may be unfair to force individuals into the choice between having to undergo a genetic test (and risk learning information they do not want to know) and being able to obtain coverage at affordable rates (Kass, 1997).

Nevertheless, assessment of risk is at the very foundation of the U.S. insurance industry, making it quite rational for insurance companies to seek access to (and use) individual genetic information in an effort to avoid "adverse selection" of applicants (Epstein, 1994; Nowlan, 2002). For example, suppose that an otherwise healthy young man, currently without health insurance, learns unexpectedly, as a result of participating in a research study, that he carries a genetic variant associated with a markedly increased risk of early-onset prostate cancer. From the standpoint of a health insurer, it would be unfair for this person to obtain health insurance at standard rates without revealing this information, since he has a high likelihood of developing early-onset prostate cancer and thus incurring higher-than-average medical costs that the insurer will have to pay. These costs would be spread among all other subscribers, increasing everybody's premiums.

Genetic discrimination can also occur in other types of insurance, such as life, disability, mortgage, and long-term care insurance, where the risks of adverse selection are arguably even greater. People found to be at increased genetic risk for developing various types of cancers or Alzheimer disease, for example, may find it hard to obtain these types of coverages just at the time when the need for them becomes most apparent. Because life, disability, mortgage, and long-term care insurance are generally considered less essential than health insurance, this problem has not generated as much public discussion, but discrimination based on predictive genetic test results in these areas can have serious practical ramifications for individuals and families (Rothstein, 2001; Zick, Smith, Mayer, & Botkin, 2000).

In the life insurance context, for example, the number of individuals at significant risk for being denied coverage based on the results of predictive genetic testing is not yet large, because only a small number of tests have been developed with sufficient predictive power to be of interest to life insurers. Moreover, the available tests that do have high predictive power tend to be those for late-onset Mendelian (single-gene) disorders (e.g., Huntington disease), which by their nature are relatively rare. This situation may change, however, as tests become available to assess individual genetic risk for more common, complex disorders (e.g., cancer, heart disease, hypertension, diabetes). Not only do such disorders tend to affect large numbers of people, they also generally are influenced by many environmental factors. Should a life insurer be permitted to deny coverage or charge increased premiums to an individual who has genetic variants that merely confer a moderately increased risk for one of these disorders? This and similar questions will raise difficult policy issues regarding the appropriate balance between fairness and actuarial justification.

As the baby boom generation ages and as limitations on Medicaid financing expand, long-term care insurers can also be expected increasingly to show interest in using genetic tests (e.g., tests for susceptibility to Alzheimer disease or other dementias) to determine individuals' eligibility for coverage. Here again it remains unclear how the law will evolve to balance the competing interests of the parties, especially as improved predictive tests become available.

Employment

Considerable discussion has also centered on the risks of genetic discrimination in employment (Rothstein, 1992b). Employers concerned about controlling escalating health care costs or limiting absenteeism are understandably interested in identifying those who are at increased risk for premature illness; those in workplaces with potentially hazardous substances may also wish to identify those with heightened susceptibility to their effects. For example, in *Norman-Bloodsaw v. Lawrence Berkeley National Labs,* a class action lawsuit, black employees of a laboratory research center that received funding from the U.S. Department of Energy alleged that their employer had tested them for the sickle-cell gene without their knowledge or consent (1998). A federal appeals court ruled that federal and state constitutional guarantees of privacy prohibited this testing. In 2001, the U.S. Equal Employment Opportunity Commission (EEOC) brought a challenge to Burlington Northern Santa Fe Railway's policy of requiring employees who had filed claims for work-related carpal tunnel syndrome to provide blood samples for a genetic test for chromosome 17 deletion (claimed to cause carpal tunnel syndrome in rare cases). Burlington Northern's genetic testing program was carried out without the knowledge or consent of its employees, and at least one worker was threatened with termination for failing to submit a blood sample for testing (U.S. Equal Employment Opportunity Commission, 2001). The lawsuit was quickly settled in favor of the employees; Burlington Northern was prohibited from requiring the tests, from analyzing any blood previously obtained, and from retaliating against any workers who opposed the testing. However, neither the *Lawrence Berkeley* nor *Burlington Northern* cases dealt with the question of whether an employer should be able to access genetic information already contained in a worker's medical records—a situation that occurs much more frequently and that may present considerable privacy risks.

Legal Evidence

Genetic information can also be expected increasingly to be used as evidence in the courts, in a variety of civil cases (Rothstein, 1994–1995). For example, genetic test results may be used to establish causation (or lack of causation) in toxic torts cases (Weiss, 1999). They may also be used to help estimate probable life expectancy and associated future earnings when assessing the measure of damages in personal injury or medical malpractice cases (Rothstein, 1996). In custody and adoption cases, genetic testing may be used in an effort to assess fitness to serve as a parent, since an individual who carries a gene for a disorder associated with early morbidity or mortality may be considered less suitable as a parent than one who does not. This has already occurred in at least one case, where a judge, at the instigation of a husband seeking to terminate his wife's parental rights in a divorce proceeding, ordered the wife, who had a family history of Huntington disease, to be tested to see whether she carried the Huntington gene. The woman, who did not wish to be tested, simply disappeared and was no longer able to see her children (Andrews, 1997).

Law Enforcement

Genetic information will also be of interest to law enforcement officials—especially if tests become available that purport to predict the propensity of individuals to addictive or aggressive behavior. The U.S. Supreme Court has already held that predictions of future criminal conduct may be considered as a factor in deciding whether to grant bail and in setting the amount (*United States v. Salerno*, 1987). Likewise, in determining whether to grant or deny parole, parole boards are given broad discretion and may rely on a wide range of considerations (*Greenholtz v. Inmates of Nebraska Penal and Correctional Complex*, 1979). Law enforcement officials thus will have considerable incentives to use genetic information when making decisions in these areas—despite the highly indeterminate nature and dubious validity of such information.

Education

Educational institutions will also have an interest in accessing and using genetic test results (Rothstein, 1997). Elementary schools, for example, may seek genetic test results to identify children at risk for learning disabilities. While this could be useful in some cases, it could also lead to the placement of some children in preordained educational tracks before they have had a chance to demonstrate their ability or motivation, making low expectations a self-fulfilling prophecy. Genetic information could also be used to determine which individuals should have preferential access to higher education or professional training. Again, while these types of cases have not yet frequently occurred, they could become commonplace in the future, and it is not yet clear how many of these issues will be handled as a matter of policy or of law.

EXISTING LEGAL PROTECTIONS

Two types of legal protections are available to ensure against the misuse of genetic information (including genetic test results) by third parties outside the family: (1) laws that prohibit discrimination based on genetic data; and (2) laws that limit the extent to which third parties may obtain access to the data in the first place. Currently, no comprehensive federal law exists that either specifically prohibits genetic discrimination or that uniquely guarantees the privacy of genetic information. However, a number of generally relevant laws exist at both the federal and state levels.

In the context of health insurance, at the federal level, HIPAA (1996) affords some limited protection against discrimination against individuals based on their genetic makeup. HIPAA prohibits excluding an individual from group insurance coverage because of a past or present medical condition. Genetic information is included as part of the definition of a medical condition. HIPAA also forbids insurance companies from charging one person within a group higher premiums than other "similarly situated" individuals in the same group. It limits exclusions in group health plans for preexisting conditions to 12 months, and prohibits such exclusions if the individual has been previously covered for that condition for 12 months or more. HIPAA also states explicitly that genetic information in the absence of a current diagnosis of illness shall not be considered a preexisting condition.

In 2003, Standards for Privacy of Individually Identifiable Health Information (the so-called Privacy Rule) went into effect to implement the requirements of HIPAA. The Privacy Rule for the first time places strict federal limits on the circumstances in which covered entities (defined to include health plans, health care clearinghouses, and health care providers) may use or disclose protected health information. As further discussed below, however, some uncertainty exists about the likely practical effect of these regulations, particularly with regard to some of the unique issues raised by genetic data.

Most states have now enacted legislation designed to conform to the general mandate of HIPAA; in addition, some states have enacted laws specifically designed to limit access to genetic information. Genetic-specific privacy legislation in a number of states now expressly requires informed consent of the individual for genetic testing or for any third party to acquire, retain, or disclose genetic information; several states go further and define genetic information as personal property (Gostin et al., 2001). In addition, as of June 2005, 43 states had enacted laws that either strictly prohibit genetic discrimination in the underwriting of health insurance policies or contain more limited protections (National Human Genome Research Institute, 2003a). Some of these laws apply to both individual and group policies, while others apply only to group policies (National Conference of State Legislatures, 2005). Several states have also enacted laws that regulate in varying degrees the use of genetic information by life, disability, and long-term care insurers (Gostin et al., 2001).

Also as of May 1, 2003, 31 states had passed laws specifically designed to prevent genetic discrimination in the context of employment

(National Human Genome Research Institute, 2003b). The scope of these laws varies widely; all prohibit discrimination based on the results of genetic tests; many extend the protections to inherited characteristics; and some include test results of family members, family history, and information about genetic testing such as the receipt of genetic services.

At the federal level, the Americans with Disabilities Act of 1990 (ADA) prohibits employers from discriminating against individuals with disabilities when making hiring decisions or in the terms and conditions of employment (ADA, 2001). The ADA is written in general rather than genetic-specific terms, but has been interpreted by the EEOC (1995) to prohibit discrimination against an individual based on genetic predisposition.

In 2000, an Executive Order was issued that bars genetic discrimination in the federal workplace (Executive Order No. 13,145, 2000). It prohibits federal government agencies from obtaining genetic information from employees or job applicants and from using genetic information in hiring and promotion decisions. "Genetic information" is defined in the Executive Order to include information about an individual's genetic tests, information about the genetic tests of an individual's family members, and information about the occurrence of a disease, medical condition, or disorder in family members of the individual.

LIMITATIONS OF EXISTING LAWS

Despite the array of existing federal and state laws just described, significant legal loopholes continue to exist. In the area of health insurance, for example, at the federal level, HIPAA (1996) generally applies only to employer-based and commercially issued group health plans; it does not protect private individuals who seek health insurance in the open market, who in most cases can be charged higher premiums based on their genetic makeup even if they are currently healthy. It also does not limit the collection of genetic information by insurers, prohibit insurers from requiring an individual to take a genetic test, or prohibit the disclosure by insurers of genetic information. These statutory limitations are also reflected in the Privacy Rule implemented in 2003 pursuant to HIPAA (Standards for Privacy of Individually Identifiable Health Information, 2003). Thus, for example, the insurance arm of an employer that provides insurance coverage for its employees would not be covered by the Privacy Rule, and one can easily imagine the situation in which genetic information contained in the medical records of a company's enrollees finds its way into the hands of a human resources department. If the employer happens to be a bank or a mortgage company, such information could also make its way into the company's lending department—in most cases without legal impediment.

Moreover, no federal laws have been enacted that relate specifically to access to or use of genetic information by life, disability, mortgage, or long-term care insurers. Indeed, it is routine for such entities to make an individual's consent to release any medical records that might contain such data a quid pro quo for benefit eligibility.

In the employment area, the actual extent of protection against genetic discrimination provided by the ADA similarly remains far from complete. The ADA applies only to employers with 15 or more employees, authorizes unlimited preemployment medical examinations and inquiries (thus permitting employers access to medical records with genetic information), and does not unambiguously apply to unaffected carriers of recessive and X-linked disorders (ADA, 2001). The EEOC's interpretation that the ADA should be read to prohibit discrimination based on genetic predisposition is not binding on courts and has not yet been tested in the U.S. Supreme Court.

Recent U.S. Supreme Court cases have engendered additional uncertainty about the interpretation of the ADA in the context of workplace-based genetic discrimination. In *Bragdon v. Abbott* (1998), the Court ruled that an asymptomatic HIV-positive woman was "disabled" within the meaning of the ADA because she was impaired in carrying out the major life activity of reproduction (since any child produced could carry the HIV infection). By this reasoning, it could be argued that an asymptomatic individual carrying a genetic marker for a disease should also be considered disabled, since that person's offspring could likewise carry the genetic marker and, if the gene were dominant, would probably also develop the disorder.

On the other hand, in *Sutton v. United Airlines, Inc.* (1999), the Court suggested that there may be a legal distinction between those with treatable and untreatable genetic disorders: The former may not be covered under the ADA if their disability could somehow be ameliorated through medical treatment. Further case law will be required to more definitively resolve this and other issues regarding the applicability of the ADA in the specific context of genetic testing.

The 2000 Executive Order explicitly barring genetic discrimination in federal employment reaches only a limited number of employees (Executive Order No. 13,145, 2000); Congress has not yet passed a federal genetic nondiscrimination law for private sector employment. In addition, the Executive Order is merely a statement of administrative policy and creates no legally enforceable rights for federal workers. Likewise, at the state level, the various genetic-specific statutes enacted to safeguard against genetic discrimination in the workplace afford only limited legal protection. These laws typically prohibit discrimination based on genetic information but as a practical matter have little effect on employer access to genetic data. Employees are routinely asked to consent to the release of medical records, which may include genetic information, as a condition of obtaining employment. Employers can also routinely gain access to sensitive genetic information through the examination of health insurance claims.

Most existing state genetic privacy laws also provide only limited protection in this regard. These laws prohibit only the unauthorized collection, retention, or disclosure of genetic information; they do nothing to address the myriad situations that arise every day in which individuals are asked to consent to the release of genetic and other medical information as a condition of obtaining employment—or for that matter insurance or other benefits.

Given the gaps in existing law, interest in comprehensive genetic-specific privacy and genetic discrimination legislation remains high at both the federal and state level. At the federal level, two genetic-specific bills were introduced in the 109th Congress (S. 306, 2005; H.R. 1227, 2005). However, it remains unclear at this writing how this legislation will ultimately fare. At the state level, numerous bills regarding genetic discrimination in insurance and/or employment (some to establish new protections and others to modify or clarify existing statutes) are pending in the legislatures (National Human Genome Research Institute, 2005).

However, as earlier mentioned, the notion that genetic information is so unique that it requires special protections, different from that accorded to other types of medical data, has been increasingly questioned in recent years (Gostin & Hodge, 1999; Ross, 2001). Critics of the "genetic exceptionalism" approach argue, with considerable persuasiveness, that (1) the distinction between "genetic" and "nongenetic" information has become increasingly murky; (2) it is generally impossible as a practical matter to segregate genetic from nongenetic information, even if the two could be distinguished; (3) it is unfair to accord greater legal protection to information termed *genetic* than to other types of information that may be equally or more sensitive; and (4) treating genetic information differently may tend only further to stigmatize individuals with genetic disorders and thus prove self-defeating (Murray, 1997). In recognition of these features, some state lawmakers have begun to incorporate their genetic protections into broader health privacy or antidiscrimination laws (Gostin et al., 2001). Whether a similar shift in focus will occur on the federal level is not yet known.

As our understanding of genetics becomes more sophisticated, it is indeed becoming increasingly difficult to distinguish genetic from nongenetic information. The ideas that have infused the debates about law and policy in this area will need to be continually reassessed to ensure that they remain congruent with current scientific developments. Only in this way can the competing interests involved in this highly complex arena be balanced appropriately.

CONCLUSION

Predictive genetic testing for adult-onset genetic conditions raises many policy and legal challenges for individuals and their families—as well as for the health care professionals who interact with them. Among these are issues relating to privacy, confidentiality, and informed consent, and issues relating to the disclosure of genetic information within families. At the broader societal level, predictive genetic testing also raises concerns about who should have access to genetic information and how, if at all, various institutions should be able to use it. A number of federal and state legal protections have been enacted in an effort to safeguard the privacy of genetic information and limit the ability of some entities—principally insurers and employers—to discriminate against individuals based on genetic status, but the reach and effectiveness of these laws varies considerably.

While the policy issues raised by predictive genetic testing are in some respects not that different from the issues raised by other types of medical testing, or by the proliferation of other health information more generally, predictive genetic testing does involve certain unique features. In the future, as more genetic tests become available to assess individual susceptibility to common, complex conditions, resolution of these issues in the broader health care and societal contexts will become increasingly challenging for those who are charged with fashioning sound public policy and law.

NOTES

1. This chapter does not discuss the legal or policy implications of forensic genetic testing (DNA-based testing conducted solely for the purposes of establishing identification—such as for criminal justice purposes or for establishing parentage or other family relationships in various legal contexts). However, it should be noted that forensic DNA testing is now routinely used in child support enforcement cases, in settling estates, in determining immigration status, and in establishing entitlement to certain public benefits (see McEwen, 2001). Although DNA tests to establish paternity or filiation do not typically have

direct health implications, they can have ramifications for relationships among family members (see Litovsky & Schultz, 1988). Forensic DNA testing done for criminal justice purposes (and by the military) has fewer direct implications for families, but raises legal and policy issues that may also be of general interest to the reader (see Asplen, 1999; *Mayfield v. Dalton*, 1995; National Research Council, 1992).

2. Discussion of the legal and ethical duties of family members to each other regarding the disclosure of genetic information is beyond the scope of this chapter (for a discussion of these issues, see Andrews, 1997; Rhodes, 1998).

REFERENCES

Allen, A. L. (1997). Genetic privacy: Emerging concepts and values. In M. A. Rothstein (Ed.), *Genetic secrets: Protecting privacy and confidentiality in the genetic era* (pp. 31–59). New Haven: Yale University Press.

American Society of Human Genetics, Ad Hoc Committee on DNA Technology. (1988). DNA banking and DNA analysis: Points to consider. *American Journal of Human Genetics, 42,* 781.

American Society of Human Genetics, Social Issues Committee, Subcommittee on Family Disclosures. (1998). Professional disclosure of familial genetic information. *American Journal of Human Genetics, 62*(2), 474.

Americans with Disabilities Act (ADA), 42 U.S.C., Sections 12101-213 (2001).

Andrews, L. B. (1997). Body science. *ABA Journal, 83,* 44.

Andrews, L. B. (1997). Gen-etiquette: Genetic information, family relationships, and adoption. In M. A. Rothstein (Ed.), *Genetic secrets: Protecting privacy and confidentiality in the genetic era* (pp. 255–280). New Haven, CT: Yale University Press.

Andrews, L. B. (1986). My body, my property. *Hastings Center Report, 16,* 28.

Annas, G. (1999). Genetic privacy: There ought to be a law. *Texas Review of Law and Politics, 4,* 9.

Annas, G. J., Glantz, L. H., & Roche, P. A. (1995a). Drafting the Genetic Privacy Act: Science, policy and practical considerations. *Journal of Law, Medicine, and Ethics, 23,* 360.

Annas, G. J., Glantz, L. H., & Roche, P. A. (1995b). *The Genetic Privacy Act and Commentary.* Boston: Boston University School of Public Health.

Asplen, C. H. (1999). From crime scene to courtroom: Integrating DNA technology into the criminal justice system. *Judicature, 83*(Nov.–Dec.), 144.

Barrad, C. V. (1993). Genetic information and property theory. *Northwestern University Law Review, 87,* 1037.

Bartels, D. M. (2001). Family covenants and confidentiality. *American Journal of Bioethics, 1*(3), 15.

Biesecker, B. B. (1997). Privacy in genetic counseling. In M. A. Rothstein (Ed.), *Genetic secrets: Protecting privacy and confidentiality in the genetic era* (pp. 108–125). New Haven, CT: Yale University Press.

Billings, P. R., Kohn, M. A., deCuevas, M., Beckwith, J., Alper, J. S., & Natowicz, M. R. (1992). Discrimination as a consequence of genetic testing. *American Journal of Human Genetics, 50*(3), 476.

Bragdon v. Abbott, 524 U.S. 624 (1998).

Brockett, P. L., & Tankersley, E. S. (1997). The genetics revolution, economics, ethics, and insurance. *Journal of Business Ethics, 16,* 1661.

Burnett, J. W. (1999). A physician's duty to warn a patient's relatives of a patient's genetically inheritable disease. *Houston Law Review, 36,* 559.

Clarke, A. (1995). Population screening for genetic susceptibility to disease. *British Medical Journal, 311*(6996), 35.

Collins, F. S., & Guttmacher, A. E. (2001). Genetics moves into the medical mainstream. *Journal of the American Medical Association, 286,* 2322.

Collins, F. S., & McKusick, V. A. (2001). Implications of the Human Genome Project for medical science. *Journal of the American Medical Association, 285,* 540.

Deftos, L. J. (1997). Genomic torts: The law of the future—the duty of physicians to disclose the presence of a genetic disease to the relatives of the patients with the disease. *University of San Francisco Law Review, 35,* 105.

Doukas, D. J., & Berg, J. W. (2001). The family covenant and genetic testing. *American Journal of Bioethics, 1*(3), 2.

Epstein, R. A. (1994). The legal regulation of genetic discrimination: Old responses to new technology. *Boston University Law Review, 74*(1), 1.

Equal Employment Opportunity Commission. (1995). *EEOC Compliance Manual,* Vol. 2, EEOC Order No. 915.002.

Executive Order No. 13,145, 65 *Federal Register* 6,877 (2000).

Gostin, L. O., & Hodge, J. G. Jr. (1999). Genetic privacy and the law: An end to genetics exceptionalism. *Jurimetrics Journal, 40,* 21.

Gostin, L. O., Hodge, J. G., & Calvo, C. M. (2001). *Genetics policy and law: A report for policymakers* (p. 12). Washington, DC: National Conference of State Legislatures.

Green, R. M., & Thomas, M. (1998). DNA: Five distinguishing features for policy analysis. *Harvard Journal of Law and Technology, 11,* 571.

Greenholtz v. Inmates of Nebraska Penal and Correctional Complex, 442 U.S. 1 (1979).

Hall, M. A. (1999). Legal rules and industry norms: The impact of laws restricting health insurers' use of genetic information. *Jurimetrics, 40,* 93.

Health Insurance Portability and Accountability Act of 1996 (HIPAA), Pub. L. No. 104-191, 110 Stat. 1936 (enacted Aug. 21, 1996).

Holtzman, N. A., & Watson, M. S. (Eds.). (1997, September). *Promoting safe and effective genetic testing in the United States.* Final Report of the Task Force on Genetic Testing. Baltimore, MD: Johns Hopkins University Press.

H.R. 1910, Genetic Nondiscrimination in Health Insurance and Employment Act (Rep. Louise Slaughter) (2003).

Institute of Medicine, Division of Health Sciences Policy, Committee on Assessing Genetic Risks. (1994). *Assessing genetic risks: Implications for health and social policy.* Washington, DC: National Academy Press.

Kass, N. E. (1997). The implications of genetic testing for health and life insurance. In M. A. Rothstein (Ed.), *Genetic secrets: Protecting privacy and confidentiality in the genetic era* (p. 301). New Haven, CT: Yale University Press.

Lapham, E. V., Kozma, C. & Weiss, J. O. (1996). Genetic discrimination: Perspectives of consumers. *Science, 274,* 621.

Lemmens, T. (2000). Selective justice, genetic discrimination, and insurance: Should we single out genes in our laws? *McGill Law Journal, 45,* 347.

Litovsky, A. Z., & Schultz, K. (1988). Scientific evidence of paternity: A survey of statutes. *Jurimetrics, 39,* 79.

Lucassen, J., & Parker, M. (2001). Revealing false paternity: Some ethical considerations. *Lancet, 357,* 1033.

Markel, H. (1992). The stigma of disease: Implications of genetic screening. *American Journal of Medicine, 93*(2), 209.

Marshall, E. (2000). Genetic testing—families sue hospital, scientist for control of canavan gene. *Science, 290,* 1062.

Mayfield v. Dalton, 901 F. Supp. 300 (D. Haw. 1995).

McEwen, J. E. (2001). Genetic information, ethics, and information relating to biological parenthood. In T. H. Murray & M. J. Mehlman (Eds.), *Encyclopedia of ethical, legal and policy issues in biotechnology* (pp. 356–364). New York: Wiley.

Merz, J. F., Cho, M. K., & Sankar, P. L. (1998). Familial disclosure in defiance of nonconsent. *American Journal of Human Genetics, 63,* 898.

Moore v. Regents of University of California, 793 P.2d 479 (Cal. 1989), cert. denied, 499 U.S. 936 (1991).

Murray, T. H. (1997). Genetic exceptionalism and 'future diaries': Is genetic information different from other medical information? In M. A. Rothstein (Ed.), *Genetic secrets: Protecting privacy and confidentiality in the genetic era* (pp. 60–73). New Haven, CT: Yale University Press.

National Conference of State Legislatures. (2005, June). State genetic nondiscrimination in health insurance. Retrieved from http://www.ncsl.org/programs/health/genetics/ndishlth.html

National Human Genome Research Institute. (2003a). Genetic information and health insurance enacted state legislation. Retrieved from http://www.genome.gov/10002338

National Human Genome Research Institute. (2003b). Genetic information and the workplace enacted state legislation. Retrieved from http://www.genome.gov/10002339

National Human Genome Research Institute, Policy and Legislation Database. Retrieved from http://www.genome.gov/PolicyEthics/LegDatabase/pubsearch.cfm.

National Research Council, Commission on Life Sciences, Board on Biology, Committee on DNA Technology in Forensic Science. (1992). *DNA technology in forensic science.* Washington, DC: National Academy Press.

Norman-Bloodsaw v. Lawrence Berkeley National Laboratories, No. C96-16526, 135 F.3d 1260 (9th Cir. 1998).

Nowlan, W. (2002). A rational view of insurance and genetic discrimination. *Science, 297,* 195.

Pate v. Threlkel, 640 So.2d 183 (Fla. 1995).

President's Commission for the Study of Ethical Problems in Medicine and Biomedical and Behavioral Research. (1983). *Genetic screening and counseling.* Washington, DC: U.S. Government Printing Office.

Reilly, P. R. (2000). Eugenics, ethics, sterilization laws. In T. H. Murray & M. J. Mehlman (Eds.), *Encyclopedia of ethical, legal, and policy issues in biotechnology* (p. 210). New York: Wiley.

Reilly, P. R. (1993). Public policy and legal issues raised by advances in genetic screening and testing. *Suffolk University Law Review, 27*, 1327.

Rhodes, R. (1998). Genetic links, family ties, and social bonds: Rights and responsibilities in the face of genetic knowledge. *Journal of Medicine and Philosophy, 23*(1), 10.

Roses, A. D. (2000). Pharmacogenetics and the practice of medicine. *Nature, 405*, 857.

Ross, L. F. (1996). Disclosing misattributed paternity. *Bioethics, 10*(2), 114.

Ross, L. F. (2001). Genetic exceptionalism vs. paradigm shift: Lessons from HIV. *Journal of Law and Medical Ethics, 29*(2), 141.

Rothenberg, K. H. (1995). Genetic information and health insurance: State legislative approaches. *Journal of Law, Medicine and Ethics, 23*(4), 312.

Rothstein, L. A. (1997). Genetic information in schools. In M. A. Rothstein (Ed.). *Genetic secrets: Protecting privacy and confidentiality in the genetic era* (pp. 317–331). New Haven, CT: Yale University Press.

Rothstein, M. A. (1992a). Discrimination based on genetic information. *Jurimetrics, 33*(1), 13.

Rothstein, M. A. (1992b). Genetic discrimination in employment and the Americans with Disabilities Act. *Houston Law Review, 29*(1), 23.

Rothstein, M. A. (1994–1995). The use of genetic information for nonmedical purposes. *Journal of Law and Health, 9*(1), 109.

Rothstein, M. A. (1996). Preventing the discovery of plaintiff genetic profiles by defendants seeking to limit damages in personal injury litigation. *Indiana Law Journal, 71*, 876.

Rothstein, M. A. (1998). Genetic privacy and confidentiality: Why they are so hard to protect? *Journal of Law, Medicine, and Ethics, 26*, 198.

Rothstein, M. A. (2001). Predictive testing for Alzheimer's disease in long-term care insurance. *Georgia Law Review, 35*, 707.

S. 16, Equal Rights and Equal Dignity for Americans Act of 2003 (Sen. Tom Daschle). (2003).

S. 1053, Genetic Information Nondiscrimination Act of 2003 (Sen. Olympia Snowe). (passed by the U.S. Senate, Oct. 14, 2003).

Safer v. Estate of Pack, 677 A.2d 1188 (N.J. 1996).

Shaw, M. W. (1977). Confidentiality and privacy: Implications for genetic screening. *Progress in Clinical Biological Research, 18*, 305.

Standards for Privacy of Individually Identifiable Health Information, 45 CFR Part 160 and Part 164, Subparts A and E (2003).

Stock, G. (2001). The family covenant: A flawed response to the dilemmas of genetic testing. *American Journal of Bioethics, 1*(3), 17.

Suter, S. M. (1993). Whose genes are these anyway? Familial conflicts over access to genetic information. *Michigan Law Review, 91*, 1854.

Sutton v. United Airlines Inc., 527 U.S. 461 (1999).

Tarasoff v. Regents of University of California, 551 P.2d 334 (Cal. 1976).

United States v. Salerno, 481 U.S. 739 (1987).

U.S. Equal Employment Opportunity Commission. (2001, April 18). EEOC settles ADA suit against BNSF for genetic bias. EEOC press release.

Wachbroit, R. (1998). The question not asked: The challenge of pleiotropic genetic tests. *Kennedy Institute of Ethics Journal, 8*(2), 131.

Weiss, R. B. (1999). The use of genetic information in the courtroom. *Wake Forest Law Review, 34*, 889.

Zick, C. D., Smith, K. R., Mayer, R. N., & Botkin, J. R. (2000). Genetic testing, adverse selection, and the demand for life insurance. *American Journal of Medical Genetics, 93*, 29.

Chapter 20

Professional Collaboration to Assess and Care for Genetic Disorders

Susan H. McDaniel, June Peters, and Louise Acheson

As discussed in previous chapters, the management of genetic disorders begins with a suspicion, prompted by family history or current symptomatology, and may progress to testing or diagnosis and treatment. Many health professionals participate at each stage of this process. The most effective and comprehensive approach for the care of people with genetic disorders and their families involves collaboration among an interdisciplinary genetic health care team that includes primary care physicians and nurse practitioners; geneticists; genetic counselors; specialists, such as surgeons, diabetologists, and pulmonologists; and family-oriented mental health professionals and clergy.

While describing typical roles for these professionals on the genetic health care team, we want to emphasize that in practice the roles can be quite fluid, based on professional availability and talent. Rural family physicians typically will play a more substantial role in genetic screening or diagnosis than those practicing in a city. Geneticists working with a genetic counselor or a genetic nurse may function as a unit; without a genetic counselor, the geneticist may take that role or make use of a nurse, social worker, or other mental health professional. Many genetic counselors now work in specialty settings such as cancer centers or perinatal groups with physicians of varying specialties but without a clinical geneticist on the premises. Regardless, each professional brings the perspective and training of his or her profession to the working of the team; the precise role definitions in any given situation or setting will be defined by functional ability and professional availability.

Figure 20.1 is a flow chart that describes how a patient with the suspicion of a genetic disorder might encounter health professionals, from a continuity relationship with a primary care clinician, mental health professional, or clergy, to periodic contact with a geneticist, genetic counselor, and medical or surgical specialist or subspecialist. The bidirectional arrows between professionals indicate the importance of communication and collaboration for optimal team functioning. Initial responsibility for activating the team can fall to any member of the team, but mostly likely the primary care provider. The first referral will likely depend on which symptom is first presented to the primary care clinician. If, for example, the patient is having a hematologic crisis, the first referral would be to a hematology subspecialist. If the hematologist suspects a hereditary syndrome, the next referral could be to the genetic specialists. Or, if the initial symptom is anxiety, the first referral might be to a psychiatrist or psychologist. If a subsequent evaluation implicated a hereditary condition, then referral to the genetic specialists would follow. Within a patient and across family members, symptoms and concerns are likely to recur periodically, with varying presentations, so that the genetic health care team may be activated and reactivated by different professionals at different points in time,

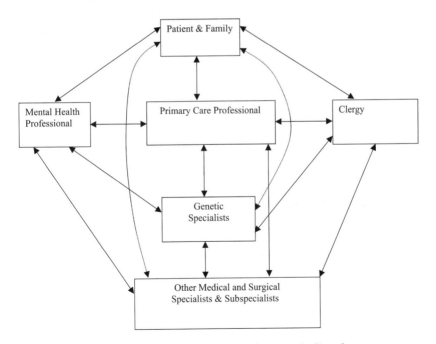

Figure 20.1   The health care team for genetic disorders.

making clear communication across the team essential for continuity and comprehensive care.

This chapter describes the genetic health care team, including each professional's role and function. We illustrate these roles and collaboration with a case example. We conclude with a discussion of education, training, and interprofessional collaboration for the genetic health care team, including the barriers that can impede collaboration. We begin with primary care clinicians, who have a continuity relationship with patients and families that often precedes diagnosis of a genetic condition and lasts beyond the crisis of initially identifying a problem.

PRIMARY CARE PROFESSIONALS

Primary care clinicians often have both longitudinal and contextual knowledge of a patient and family that is directly relevant to identifying and discussing genetic information (Hayflick & Eiff, 1998). Those who care for family members as well as the identified patient are especially well positioned to provide a family-based approach to managing genetic risk. Genograms and other devices to record family relationships and intergenerational patterns of events are part of the training of family physicians and family nurse practitioners (Carter & McGoldrick, 1998; McGoldrick, Gerson, & Shellenberger, 1999). However, they are used selectively by most primary care clinicians (Medalie, Zyzanski, Langa, & Stange, 1998; Acheson, Wiesner, Zyzanski, Goodwin, & Stange, 2000). Until the late 1990s, family history in family medicine more often focused on understanding family psychosocial issues than on elucidating patterns of disease inheritance (Like, Rogers, & McGoldrick, 1988; Rogers, 1994; Rogers, Rohrbaugh, & McGoldrick, 1992). Today, with renewed emphasis on genetic aspects of disease, primary care clinicians are in a unique position to combine medical history with longitudinal, psychosocial knowledge of the family (Daly et al., 1999; Guttmacher, Collins, & Carmona, 2004; Martin & Wilikovsky, 2004; Rich et al., 2004).

A major role of primary care is to identify risk for genetically related conditions in the family (Whelan et al., 2004; Worthen, 1999). Clinicians may recognize familial or genetic risk in several ways. Family medical history may reveal clustering of related diseases in the family. Congenital anomalies or early fetal loss may be noted (Falk & Robin, 2004). The presence of an unusual condition, or exceptionally early onset of a common disease, can signal inherited susceptibility. A known genetic condition diagnosed in a relative, or membership in an ethnic group with increased carrier frequency of particular recessive mutations, can be indications for genetic assessment (Emery, Watson, Rose, & Ander-mann, 1999). In addition, screening for genetic risk factors is an integral part of providing prenatal care or preconception counseling (Emery & Hayflick, 2001).

Primary care clinicians are often involved in the early stages of iden-tifying who may benefit from genetic assessment, helping patients and families to decide when it is appropriate to pursue genetic information and preparing them for consultation (Martin & Wilikovsky, 2004). As with other referrals and tests, the choice of whether and when to pur-sue genetic information will depend on an assessment of the value of this genetic information for the care of the individual (Burke, Acheson, et al., 2002; Burke, Atkins, et al., 2002; Evans, Skrzynia, & Burke, 2001). For genetically related conditions, however, patient and clinician may also be concerned about the value of the information for the care of relatives (McDaniel, Campbell, Hepworth, & Lorenz, 2005). Family physicians and nurse practitioners may help families decide on the timing of genetic testing that may be done once in a lifetime for a par-ticular disorder. They also may be aware of the patient's experiences, such as the caretaker burden, stigma regarding an illness, or prema-ture death of family members, that can have an impact on the indi-vidual's response to genetic diagnosis or familial disease (Walter, Emery, Braithwaite, & Marteau, 2004). This knowledge may lead the primary care clinician to refer the patient and family to a family ther-apist to help with decision making and communication regarding ge-netic testing.

Primary care clinicians collaborate with many consultants in the care of individuals with known genetically related conditions and their relatives (Hayflick & Eiff, 1998). They may be the most likely coordina-tors for the larger genetic health care team and can provide an invalu-able medical and psychosocial perspective to increase the success of specialists who have more focused tasks. Prenatal diagnosis, expanded newborn screening for congenital disorders, and the transition from care by pediatric specialists to adult primary care are all situations in which collaboration is essential (McCandless, 2004; Tyler & Edman, 2004). After the process of genetic diagnosis, the primary care clinician needs basic information from geneticists and other specialists about the diagnosis, management, and available support resources for con-tinuing care (Acheson & Wiesner, 2004).

Finally, primary care involves a longitudinal perspective, in which the clinician often provides care in the nonsymptomatic phase, the di-agnosis or testing and posttesting phases, and the long-term adapta-tion phase, as well as any symptomatic or treatment phases (Rolland & Williams, 2005; see Chapter 2). Genetic information (the family history, for example) takes on new meaning and sometimes more urgency, as diseases progress, family members are newly diagnosed, and patients enter new phases of the life cycle. Primary care clinicians need to respond to the differing impact of genetic conditions over a lifespan (Tyler & Edman, 2004), to the development of new knowledge, and to the recurring needs to communicate the implications to relatives at risk. Portable, private, and enduring records of families' genetic information are becoming essential (Acheson & Wiesner, 2004; Rich et al., 2004).

THE WILSON FAMILY AND THEIR PRIMARY CARE CLINICIAN

Amy Wilson[1] is a 43-year-old married white woman with three children, ages 14, 11, and 3 (Figure 20.2). Amy is well educated with an upper-middle-class lifestyle, including exercise and good nutrition. John Wilson is an administrator at a college; Amy is a homemaker. She had a number of seemingly unrelated medical conditions beginning at 7 years of age, including migraine headaches, anemia and other hematologic problems, gallstones, bronchitis, and asthma. After her mother, with whom she was close, died about 5 years ago from "blood problems," Amy became edgy and somewhat depressed when her own medical problems flared. Depressed

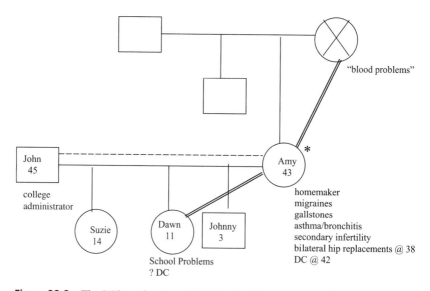

Figure 20.2 The Wilson family, with inherited bone marrow failure syndrome (dyskeratosis congenita, DC).

feelings occurred again when she had secondary infertility of unknown cause while trying to conceive a third child. When Amy reported feeling distant from her husband, John, Dr. A referred the couple to a family therapist (Dr. M) at that time. Amy's last child was born with the help of in-vitro fertilization (IVF) with donor eggs.

Dr. A, the family's primary care physician, found treating Amy a challenge. She watched as Amy and John became more distant as a couple while Amy's medical problems mounted. She saw Amy, like many good mothers, as trying hard to protect her children from any negative events. It was as if Amy was protecting herself from further pain by protecting her children. John became increasingly frustrated by Amy's medical problems and attended fewer and fewer doctor visits. He told Dr. A that he alternated between feeling scared about all that befell his wife, and feeling that she made too much of her symptoms.

In the meantime, Dr. A became increasingly worried about Amy's anemia and progressive bone marrow failure. She referred Amy to a hematologist, Dr. H, for evaluation and stabilization of her symptoms. Dr. H then became suspicious of a genetic condition and recommended that Dr. A refer Amy to a geneticist.

In this case, the primary care clinician managed various long-term symptoms without a unifying diagnosis. Serious medical conditions in the patient's mother, for example anemia, then leukemia and pulmonary fibrosis, were not initially recognized as potentially related to a heritable disorder. However, unusual symptoms or a pattern of illness in a family may prompt referral to a geneticist. Dr. A is aware that if an uncommon condition is diagnosed by the genetic specialty team, she will need to become educated about the condition along with the patients and families. With rare conditions, if there is limited knowledge of the natural history of the illness, she knows that the family will still live with uncertainty and the need for vigilance even after diagnosis and treatment. She also knows that, if strategies for treating the disease or preventing its complications are unproven, the pros and cons of identifying the genetic alteration through genetic testing in children and other family members need to be carefully considered. Genetic information may be harmful if no definitive treatment is available (American Society of Clinical Oncology, 2003). It is not recommended to test healthy minor children unless it is necessary for their current health care (American Academy of Pediatricians, 2001; American Society of Human Genetics [ASHG], 1995). Patients may consult with their primary care clinicians, as well as genetic counselors, when making decisions about testing minor children and disclosing to other at-risk family members.

GENETICISTS AND GENETIC COUNSELORS

The genetic specialty team provides genetic counseling and diagnosis to patients such as Amy and her family. The ASHG proposed a definition of genetic counseling in 1975 that has since been widely adopted:

> Genetic counseling is a communication process which deals with the human problems associated with the occurrence or risk of occurrence of a genetic disorder in a family. This process involves an attempt by one or more appropriately trained persons to help the individual or family to: 1) comprehend the medical facts including the diagnosis, probable course of the disorder, and the available management; 2) appreciate the way that heredity contributes to the disorder and the risk of recurrence in specified relatives; 3) understand the alternatives for dealing with the risk of recurrence; 4) choose a course of action which seems to them appropriate in view of their risk, their family goals, and their ethical and religious standards and act in accordance with that decision, and 5) to make the best possible adjustment to the disorder in an affected family member and/or to the risk of recurrence of that disorder. (p. 240)

This definition reflects the genetic counseling process, which is based on the delivery of scientific information as part of an interpersonal interaction that respects client autonomy while recognizing the importance of the family. Genetic counseling has expanded from an early pediatric emphasis—newborn screening, prenatal diagnosis, and care of children with birth defects and hereditary conditions—to now include adult areas of practice such as inherited cancers, neurogenetic disease, psychiatric illness, and cardiovascular problems. Further, clients have become more culturally diverse and biomedical technology detects more conditions. Despite these changes, certain philosophical underpinnings of genetic counseling remain, such as voluntary utilization of services, equal access, informed consent through client education, complete disclosure, nondirective counseling where a clear medical indication for a particular choice is not known, attention to psychosocial and affective dimensions in counseling, and client confidentiality to the greatest extent possible (Walker, 1998).

Providers of components of genetic counseling include a variety of genetic health professionals. Those certified by the American Board of Medical Genetics include the clinical geneticist (MD or OD), PhD medical geneticist, and several specialty geneticists who provide clinical services with any one of a variety of doctoral degrees, including clinical cytogeneticist, clinical biochemical geneticist and clinical molecular geneticist (MD, DDS, DMD, DO, PhD, or DSC), genetic counselor (MS, MA, MPH, or PhD), genetic nurse (RN or bacculaureate-prepared RN), and the genetics advance practice nurse (MS, MSN, or PhD). The diagnosis and management team should include at least one genetics professional, such as a genetic counselor, clinical geneticist, or genetics nurse clinician.

The first masters-prepared genetic counselors appeared in the early 1970s. At the close of 2004, there were 33 masters degree training programs in the United States, Canada, England, and Australia (National Society of Genetic Counselors [NSGC], 2006).

In the United States, the term *genetic counselors* is generally reserved for masters-prepared health professionals who have completed a curriculum in genetic counseling that is accredited by the American Board of Genetic Counseling (ABGC, 1996). Many people enter the field from a variety of disciplines, including biology, genetics, nursing, psychology, public health and social work. The specific requirements for training program accreditation are laid out on the ABGC (2003) Web site. The didactic and clinical training components of the curriculum must support development of competencies categorized into the following domains: medical genetics; communication skills; critical-thinking skills; interpersonal, counseling, and psychosocial assessment skills; and professional ethics and values. Some of the specific medical genetics tasks include constructing comprehensive family pedigrees, eliciting appropriate medical histories, aiding the medical evaluations, doing literature and genetic database searches, recognizing genetic syndromes, and interpreting and summarizing medical and family history information for patients and primary care physicians. The genetic counselor also learns to provide pretesting informed consent, to disclose genetic test results in sensitive ways, help the family adjust to the diagnosis, and provide referrals to other specialists. The training programs include a variety of hands-on clinical rotations in which students must demonstrate their competence in a variety of practice settings such as prenatal diagnosis, pediatric genetics, and cancer genetics. A 2004 survey by the National Society of Genetic Counselors documents the exponential growth of this profession from 100 in 1979 to 2181 in 2004 (Bennett et al., 2004; personal communication from NSGC office; Star/Rosen Public Relations, 2004).

Physicians may become eligible for certification in clinical genetics by the American Board of Medical Genetics or the Canadian College of Medical Genetics by completing accredited residency or fellowship programs in genetics. These physicians usually have knowledge and experience in genetic counseling as well as in research and in diagnosing and treating genetic conditions and birth defects.

Genetics nurse clinicians have their own professional society and are credentialed by the International Society of Nurses in Genetics. They have formed special interest groups within other nursing organizations such as Oncology Nurses Society. Some nurses, especially those educated earlier, have certification by the ABGC.

Genetic Risk Assessment and Counseling

A genetic consultation usually consists of a genetic evaluation and genetic counseling. The evaluation is the process of determining the presence, absence, or future likelihood of a genetic condition. The tools used are a medical history, family health and social history, physical examination, and testing. Often medical record review, dysmorphology examination, laboratory testing, clinical diagnostic studies, and other specialty consultations are needed (Petty, 1998).

Because so many issues are involved, comprehensive risk assessment and counseling benefit from a multidisciplinary approach. See Table 20.1 for the tasks that may be split among a number of different members of the genetic specialty team.

Table 20.1 Tasks of the Genetic Specialty Team

Recording individual medical history and family history

Psychosocial assessment of:

- Risk perception, motivation, beliefs, knowledge, attitudes
- Family issues, ethno-cultural background, socioeconomic status, and demographics
- Psychological status assessment, stressors, resources, and coping strategies
- Health behaviors, such as diet, exercise, use of alcohol, tobacco, other known carcinogens or teratogens, screening and prevention activities

Risk assessment including explaining concepts of risk (absolute and relative risks and odds ratios), conveying risk information effectively, determining numeric risk, for example, in the case of cancer, for the disease and for a heritable mutation in a cancer susceptibility gene

Triage of families into those considered to be at low, moderate, or high risk for having a hereditary illness

Facilitating molecular testing where appropriate

Pretest genetic counseling and informed consent involve discussing:

- The purpose of the test and who to test
- Education and general information about principles of heredity and what is known about the condition in question
- Possible results of the testing and what they mean (positive, true negative, possible false negative, variants of uncertain significance)

(continued)

Table 20.1   *(Continued)*

- The likelihood of a positive result based on statistical models and pedigree analysis as needed
- The technical aspects and accuracy of the test
- Economic considerations such as cost of the test and insurance coverage
- Any risks of genetic discrimination
- A psychosocial assessment focused on anticipated reaction to results, the timing and readiness for testing, available support, and relevant family issues
- Any confidentiality issues
- How test results will be used for medical surveillance and preventive measures
- The alternatives to genetic testing (such as ongoing surveillance without testing)
- The storage and possible reuse of genetic material for further testing or research
- Any mechanics of sample collection and shipping

Disclosure of results and posttest counseling is also a multistep process, optimally conducted during a face-to-face meeting. Disclosure involves:

- Describing the results
- Support for the emotional impact of the results
- Interpretation and significance of the test results
- Medical management
- Discussion about communication with relatives
- Planning for future medical contacts
- Connecting the patient and family with needed professional and lay resources

THE WILSON FAMILY AND THEIR GENETIC SPECIALTY TEAM

The hematologist, Dr. H, who was trying to find a reason for Amy's progressive bone marrow failure and other medical problems, recommended referring the family for evaluation by a medical geneticist, Dr. R, at a tertiary medical center.

Amy told Dr. A that she planned to go to the geneticist by herself. (When nervous, Amy tended to isolate herself.) However, with some support and encouragement from her family physician and family therapist, she eventually decided that it would be best if John attended the first visit with her. John was actually quite relieved to be given a concrete role to play in getting to the bottom of Amy's medical concerns. Dr. R and Ms. P, the genetic counselor, began building rapport and setting the frame for the visit by eliciting the couple's concerns and explaining the purpose and agenda for the visit. Ms. P took a thorough family history of all family members, requesting medical records to confirm diagnoses wherever possible in accordance with consensus genetic pedigree guidelines (Bennett et al., 1995) The pedigree at this point (Figure 20.3) suggested possible autosomal dominant inheritance of Amy's condition, if Amy's mother's hematological and pulmonary problems indeed represented a version of Amy's condition.

Dr. R took Amy's past medical and social history and review of systems. This information revealed more details that raised the likelihood of a genetic disorder—that for decades Amy had dyed her gray hair dark and worn synthetic fingernails. A careful physical examination was completed over the course of two visits. In addition, Ms. W, the clinical social worker, was called in for a consultation, as is standard in this genetics group for complex cases.

The genetic dysmorphology exam is similar to the usual physical exam but contains additional features, depending on the condition in

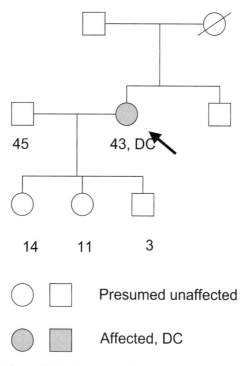

Figure 20.3   Genetic pedigree prior to testing.

question. The special elements of the dysmorphology exam are the recognition of specific major and minor developmental anomalies that may be clues to early developmental disruptions. It involves taking key measurements and recording descriptions of facial features, hands, feet, limbs, and skin, with photographic documentation of unusual features and comparison to published standards. These may lead to pattern recognition of a given syndrome (Petty, 1998), as in Amy's case.

The genetic specialty team has a number of genetic resources from which to seek information on genetic conditions based on the history, physical exam, lab, and other evaluations. These include standard genetic reference books (see Cassidy & Allanson, 2005; Emery, Rimoin, Connor, & Pyeritz, 1997; Gorlin, Cohen, & Levin, 1990; Jones, 1997; Jorde, Carey, Bamshad, & White, 2003; Scriver, Beaudet, Sly, & Balle, 2001), medical literature searches, special genetic databases, and a compendium of genetic disorders known as Online Mendelian Inheritance in Man, or OMIM (http://www.ncbi.nlm.nih.gov/omim). Another useful source is the several hundred clinical summaries on the GeneTests Web site (http://www.genetests.org/). GeneTests is a voluntary database of all known genetic tests, clinical genetic testing laboratories, and clinical summaries of selected conditions. For inherited cancer susceptibility syndromes, the main sources of online information are the evidence-based National Cancer Institute Physicians Desk Query information databases (http://cancer.gov/cancertopics/pdq/genetics).

These sources can help to determine the genetic etiology of the condition, including the possible modes of inheritance, chromosome locations of possible genes, molecular genetics, incidence, and carrier frequency. They also allow geneticists and other health care providers to develop some sense of the range of clinical features, age of onset, natural history, life span, variable expression, and gene penetrance. Finally, it is possible to learn about testing, surveillance, management, and treatment options.

For Amy, the differential diagnoses generated by the genetic specialty team included well over a dozen known syndromes of inherited bone marrow failure in combination with additional medical problems. Several of these, such as Fanconi anemia, were ruled out by the observed inheritance pattern that was probably autosomal dominant, the lack of certain clinical features such as abnormal thumbs, and key laboratory studies. The most likely diagnosis that might explain Amy's hematological and skin pigmentation changes, prematurely gray hair, and nail dystrophy was a rare condition known as dyskeratosis congenita (DC). DC is a multisystem disorder involving cutaneous abnormalities, aplastic anemia, and increased predisposition to cancer. It is most commonly inherited as an X-linked

*recessive (XLR) or autosomal dominant condition. XLR inheritance was less
likely in this case because the disease was manifest in a female.*

*Once the genetic specialty team reached a significant threshold of
suspicion regarding the diagnosis of DC, they searched for additional
information in the medical literature, hematology sources, and GeneTests.
The genetic counselor learned that just a few months prior to the
evaluation, mutations had been discovered in a gene known as TERC
(known initially as hTR) that were responsible for some cases of the
autosomal dominant form of DC. Testing was being performed at that time
on a research basis. The genetics specialty team worked with a clinical
testing laboratory to transfer the genetic test technology from a research to
a clinical laboratory so that the testing could be done under optimal
conditions. While disclosure of research results is undertaken in certain
circumstances with full disclosure of the uncertainties or weaknesses of the
research information, it is preferable to perform testing under the stringent
testing conditions of a CLIA-approved clinical genetics laboratory (CLIA
88, 1992; Markel & Yashar, 2004). The genetics specialty team conducted
pretest genetic education and counseling to ensure that Amy understood
the meaning of the testing. Amy gave verbal and written informed consent
indicating that she was well aware of the risks, benefits, and limitations of
genetic testing for DC. Then she gave a blood specimen and the genetic
testing was ordered.*

*The testing took several months to complete. After that time, Ms. P
contacted Amy to let her know that her test results were available and to
schedule the disclosure appointment. (Disclosure involves discussing the
genetic, medical, social, and emotional implications of the result.) After
confirming that Amy still wanted to know the results, Dr. R, Ms. P, and Ms.
W discussed the findings with Amy and John, showing them that Amy
carried a mutation in the TERC gene responsible for her DC. John's first
thought was of Amy; he was very caring in expressing concern for her
current and future well-being. Amy had a lot of questions, despite having
had thorough pretest counseling. (Recipients often forget key information
while in a state of shock around the time of diagnosis.) As is commonly the
case, her first concerns were for her children. The genetic team described the
genetic implications, namely that Amy probably inherited the mutation from
her mother and that the older children had a 50-50 chance of inheriting that
same mutation from her. Those who had a mutation would presumably
develop DC at some point, although there were many unknowns about the
age of onset, penetrance, expression, and full spectrum of the condition.
Amy and John were especially concerned about the middle daughter, Dawn,
because she also had a history of migraines, anemia, and asthma. During
this discussion with Ms. P, Amy acknowledged that she and John had not
discussed the IVF with Johnny or the other children, although they had been*

intending to do so. Amy felt it important to have these discussions now, with the recognition that only their older children needed to be tested. She and Ms. P agreed that the couple would take this particular concern to family therapy.

The geneticist, genetic counselor, and clinical social worker worked with Amy and John about their other concerns regarding talking with the older children about the results. For herself, Amy felt both relieved and concerned to hear that the causes of her various medical problems could be explained by an underlying genetic condition. These issues were addressed in more detail by the multidisciplinary research team.

Since being asymptomatic is no protection against having a mutation in a condition with uncertain penetrance, and prevention and early treatment are very important to outcomes, it was decided to test both older children at the same time. The clinical research team provided thorough pretest genetic counseling and informed consent with the parents and the children. The educational portion included locating and developing age-appropriate visual counseling aids to help the family comprehend and retain the complex medical and genetic information, and to prompt discussion of psychosocial issues (e.g., living with the risk information as one enters adulthood; the guilt, worry, and anger that can occur if one sibling is at risk and others are not, etc.). Once the team was satisfied that Amy and the children understood the issues, they secured consent from Amy and John, and assent of the two children. Blood was drawn from the children for genetic testing. The testing was conducted at a CLIA-certified clinical genetics laboratory with quality control appropriate to the disclosure of genetic information for use in clinical management (CLIA 88, 1992). During this time, Amy and John had several family therapy sessions with Dr. M to work out the issues about disclosing information about IVF and their son. They also had couples sessions to focus on living with Amy's risk for future illness, and dealing with family identity issues given her genetic condition.

When the family's genetic results were in, Amy and John returned to learn that Dawn also had the mutation and hence, an early diagnosis of DC (Figure 20.4). Amy was heartbroken as she thought about the implications of the diagnosis for her young daughter, with whom she felt especially close. The results added weight to the probability that Amy's mother was also affected. At this time, the team began grief counseling with Amy to begin to deal with her feelings. This process was taken to a deeper level in ongoing family therapy sessions. The team also planned with the parents for the return visit with Suzie and Dawn for the purpose of genetic disclosure, and planning for Dawn's medical evaluations.

The couple returned to Dr. R, Ms. P, and Ms. W, their original genetics specialty team, to discuss the meaning of the diagnosis and to have the session to discuss the results with Dawn and Suzie. Disclosing genetic test

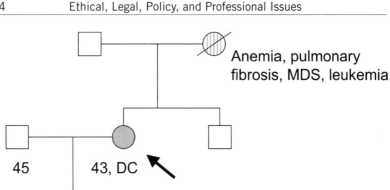

Anemia, pulmonary
fibrosis, MDS, leukemia

45   43, DC

14   11   3

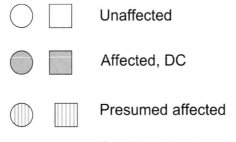

○ □   Unaffected

◐ ◼   Affected, DC

◑ ▥   Presumed affected

Figure 20.4   Genetic pedigree after testing.

results to children is a challenging undertaking for professionals and families alike. While previous cultural practices favored sheltering children from the information, today there is research leading to general agreement that the child should be told as much about the illness as his or her age allows (ASHG, 1995; NSGC, 1995; Weil, 2000, pp. 181–211).

In this case, Suzie was quite interested in science at school and Dawn demonstrated that she too had some knowledge in that she spontaneously drew a double helix when asked if she knew what DNA was. Building on this, the genetics team began to inquire about the children's awareness regarding why they were there, the purpose of the testing, and to clarify any misperceptions. They asked each child if she was interested in learning the genetic test results. Each child, with the parents, was given her particular results by the genetic counseling team. For Dawn, when she indicated that she was interested in hearing the results, the team and parents together used verbal explanations augmented by drawings, models, Internet Web sites, and other means of engaging Dawn's interest in the hereditary and medical aspects of her condition as a prelude to the medical evaluations to follow. The clinical social worker also spent time with Dawn trying to draw out her feelings. Although defended in terms of expressing feelings directly in front of the genetic team, Dawn indicated a good level of understanding and interest in participating in the process. Disclosure to Suzie followed a similar process, except that the discussion focused on the meaning of a negative test result. She was very concerned about her sister's result, which was revealed in the subsequent family meeting to discuss the implications of each result. The genetic specialty team worked to decrease parental anxiety, inform and reassure Dawn, further discuss Suzie's feelings about why she was negative and her sister positive, and describe the future evaluations for Amy and Dawn.

The effective genetic disclosure to this entire family was due to a strongly coordinated team approach and the openness and willingness of the family to deal therapeutically with each of the challenges the inherited condition presented them individually and as a family. Following disclosure, Dr. R, Ms. P, and Dr. A communicated with the family physician and the family therapist about how the disclosure session went. They also worked to coordinate Amy and Dawn's visits for annual multisystem medical evaluations, including bone marrow aspirations to track hematological changes over time. The first such exams showed that Dawn was already showing subtle signs of changes. In addition, Amy's condition required androgen therapy, a treatment that is necessary but can have side effects, such as hirsutism, virilization, liver problems, and mood changes. However, these risks seemed worthwhile to Amy and her team in the context of the benefit of stimulating hematopoiesis and thereby delaying the need for bone marrow transplantation. Given the medical complexity and the stress associated with this genetic condition, Dr. R and Ms. P also used the Genetic Alliance Web site to locate a support group for the couple as an adjunct to the family and couples therapy. Amy and John found the group invaluable in providing education about the illness, and support from those who had the experience themselves.[2]

Throughout evaluation and treatment, Dr. R and Ms. P stayed in close touch with the family's primary care physician and family therapist. Once treatment was returned to the hematologist, the primary care physician, and the family therapist, the genetic specialty team offered these professionals ongoing consultation as needed, and had several follow-up phone calls and e-mails with Amy and John to offer support and information.

MENTAL HEALTH PROFESSIONALS

Some patients go through the process of genetic screening and testing relying only on the support of their primary care clinician and genetic and medical specialists. The primary care clinician cares for their over-all, long-term health needs. The geneticist and genetic counselor take care of diagnosis, education, and early emotional adjustment. A medical specialist may treat the genetic disorder. However, many patients also seek the help of a mental health professional at some point in the process, through their primary care clinician or specialist at a cancer center, for example. Mental health professionals can play invaluable roles in each stage of the process of uncovering, managing, and treating a genetic disorder.

Mental health professionals interested in genetic disorders range from psychiatrists and psychologists to social workers, psychiatric nurses, counselors, and marriage and family therapists. There is much potential overlap in the functioning of these professionals to provide assessment, consultation, and psychotherapy. Selection of appropriate mental health professionals should be based on their skill, training, and experience dealing with patients with genetic concerns. In terms of special skills, psychiatrists can be of particular use in consulting about organic brain syndromes and psychopharmacology, psychologists in consulting about needed lifestyle changes and affective responses to diagnoses and illness, and social workers in consulting about community resources and larger systems issues. In addition to education about genetic conditions, it is useful for all mental health professionals working in this area to have a firm foundation in family systems training as a basis for understanding genetic decision making, family patterns of illness, and how genetic problems can ignite or exacerbate other relationship problems (see Chapter 4 for a summary of family systems concepts relevant to genetic concerns).

Like primary care clinicians, some mental health professionals also have a continuity relationship with an individual or family, counseling them before, during, and after diagnosis or testing. Others are consulted at focused periods in the process. Systemic consultation in the pretest phase can augment the initial genetic counseling to explore decision making in situations that are complex medically or psychosocially. Mental health professionals can provide additional support during the stressful period of testing and treatment. Soon after testing, a family therapist can provide useful consultation as patients cope with new information, work through the meaning of it for them and their family, and decide with whom and how to communicate it. In the long term, the primary care clinician provides medical follow-up, while a family-oriented mental health professional can provide psychosocial follow-up to families as they experience the challenges of genetic disorders in themselves and in new generations (see Chapter 5).

Any person can be stressed by the decision to undergo predictive testing for a disease that runs in the family, or by the decision to test a fetus for a genetic condition. But patients with a past history of mental illness—depression, anxiety, psychosis, interpersonal conflict—are especially vulnerable when coping with decisions and information regarding familial illness (Lerman, Croyle, Tercyak, & Hamann, 2002). In these cases, the inclusion of a mental health professional is essential. As with other illness challenges, testing, diagnosis, or treatment of a genetic disorder and living with genetic risk information are stressful but also offer the patient and family an opportunity to communicate in a more healthy way, to grieve old losses, and to repair and renew important relationships. The role of the mental health professional is to minimize psychosocial distress and pathology, and to encourage growth whenever possible.

THE WILSON FAMILY AND THEIR
FAMILY THERAPIST

Amy Wilson first sought the help of Dr. M, a family therapist, at the suggestion of her primary care clinician when dealing with the stress of infertility. The therapist asked that John join them as they worked through the grief the couple felt at not being able to conceive their third child. Suzie and Dawn had been born without difficulty, and the couple felt at the time that their family was complete. However, Amy loved being a homemaker and a mother. As her children became more and more involved in school and sports activities, she longed for another baby. She felt it might distract her from her medical problems and bring her and her husband closer together. Stopping all birth control, she was surprised when they didn't conceive. After several years of fertility workups, Amy and John eventually decided to use anonymous donor eggs. There was discussion about how to disclose the IVF with Suzie and Dawn, and their future child. When Amy eventually delivered their third child, they stopped their psychotherapy sessions.

When Dr. A referred Amy for genetic consultation, she returned to therapy with Dr. M, saying that she was scared about what the geneticist might find and worried about what the results might mean for their daughters. She had disclosed few of her fears to John. In addition, it turned out that Amy and John had not gotten around to talking to the children about the fact that Johnny was born with the help of assisted reproductive technologies. Only Amy's closest friends knew. Therapy focused on helping Amy and John to understand the importance of handling this information matter-of-factly. Together they made a baby book for Johnny, telling the story of how he came to be their son. With some coaching, Suzie and Dawn helped with putting the book together. Johnny was delighted with his special story, complete with many pictures. After the family discussed this process in therapy, they began to talk more about DC and the genetic issues across generations.

The DC diagnosis phase seemed to bring the couple together for the first time in years. Together, they shared their concern for Dawn. Amy then talked about her guilt in transmitting the genetic mutation to Dawn. The genetic team provided the family with information for the children to read when they had questions at home after the genetic counseling sessions. Toward the end of their time together, Amy acknowledged that Suzie had been asking questions at home about her mother's illness over the past year, and even asked if there was a chance it was contagious.

After the diagnosis was revealed, John remained worried, and Amy was grief-stricken about Dawn. Dawn herself seemed to take the news of her diagnosis in stride. Suzie was somewhat concerned about Dawn, but that seemed to recede into the background over time. Multiple family therapy sessions were spent with Amy talking about realizing that her mother also had had this condition, and what it would mean for her daughter. The therapist coached John to listen and be supportive. The focus of the sessions was on the couple's ability to communicate and support each other as they came to grips with this new reality.

In addition to the kind of consultation provided to Amy Wilson and her family, mental health professionals can also provide consultation focused on surveillance behaviors (McDaniel, 2006), psychoeducational groups for patients coping with genetic disorders (Speice, McDaniel, Rowley, & Loader, 2002), and extended family consultations in concert with geneticists and genetic counselors (McDaniel, 2005).

Another important role for a family therapist is consultation and support for the rest of the genetic health care team itself. Given the stresses and strains of their roles, this consultation can be important to the professional functioning and personal adjustment of the primary care clinicians, geneticists, genetic counselors, and specialists who deal with the difficult issues of familial illness on a daily basis. These health professionals manage their patients' anxiety and then have their own personal and family health history to deal with as well (McDaniel et al., 2005). For example, a family physician whose sister died at a young age of breast cancer came to speak to the family therapist working in her office because she felt guilty about not wanting to raise concerns about genetic risk with her patients who had a history of breast cancer in their families. She was well aware of the connection between this reluctance and her own family experience, but was unable to develop a strategy to manage her patients appropriately, until speaking about the problem with the family therapist. After the family therapist listened, empathized with, and normalized the physician's experience, the physician decided to use her nurse practitioner to raise genetic concerns with these patients. She left the discussion with the therapist saying she felt relieved, then some months later reported that she'd successfully discussed the issues with two patients herself. Somehow knowing she could rely on her nurse practitioner allowed the physician to go ahead and interact with her patients in an area about which she knew a considerable amount.

OTHER IMPORTANT MEMBERS OF THE GENETIC HEALTH CARE TEAM

As illustrated in Figure 20.1 and in Amy's case, medical specialists often play a crucial role in identifying, diagnosing, and treating genetic conditions. These specialists include physicians from such disciplines as hematology, neurology, cardiology, gastroenterology, oncology, surgery, orthopedics, rehabilitation medicine, otolaryngology, dentistry, ophthalmology, and developmental pediatrics. These professionals have a focused and crucial role in the lives of patients with genetic conditions and their families. They may be present only in one illness episode, or they may have a continuity relationship if the condition is ongoing.

In addition, for many families, priests, ministers, rabbis, imams, shamans, or other spiritual leaders play an important role as members of the team. They may have a long and deep relationship with patients and their families, and can provide important support at each stage of the illness threat, from suspicion to treatment and adaptation. There has been a long tradition of genetic counselors and pastoral counselors working together (Anderson, 2002; Baumiller, Fletcher, & Madden, 1988; Fletcher, 1983).

EDUCATION, TRAINING, AND COLLABORATION FOR THE GENETIC HEALTH CARE TEAM

The education and training of professionals on the genetic health care team includes information specific to each discipline and role, as well as common information on genetic disorders and on interprofessional collaboration. Table 20.2 lists Web sites where various professionals can obtain information and training in genetic disorders. (Listed below these are Web sites that include clinically relevant information and sites that provide education and information for the public.)

Collaboration, simply defined in the *American Heritage Dictionary* as "working together," requires a range of conceptual and clinical skills,

Table 20.2   Web Education Regarding Genetic Disorders

National Coalition for Health Professional Education in Genetics	www.nchpeg.org
Family physicians	
American Academy of Family Physicians Annual Clinical Focus (CME): Genomics 2005	http://www.aafp.org/x25023.xml
Genetics in primary care faculty development curriculum	http://genes-r-us.uthscsa.edu/resources/genetics/primary_care.htm
Geneticists	www.acmg.net
Genetic counselors	www.nsgc.org
Nurses	www.isong.org
	www.nchpeg.org
Obstetrics/gynecology	http://www.acog.org/
Pediatricians	http://www.aap.org/profed.html
Psychologists	www.apa.org/science/genetics/homepage.html
Psychiatrists	www.psych.org
Social workers	www.naswdc.org
General sites	www.genome.gov
	www.nchpeg.gov
	www.geneclinics.org
	www3.ncg.ncbi.nlm.nih.gov/omim
	genetics.faseb.org/genetics/ashg/ashgmenu.htm
Lay sites	ghr.nlm.nih.gov
	www.geneticalliance.org/index.html
	www.hhs.gov/familyhistory/download.html
National Organization of Rare Disorders	http://www.rarediseases.org/

as well as personal and relational self-awareness (McDaniel & Campbell, 1997). These core competencies include an understanding of health care and family systems and how an individual can affect the whole; good communication skills with people who have different theories, training, and language; an interest in developing partnerships with other professionals to provide comprehensive, biopsychosocial care; and a willingness to develop case-specific leadership based on the expertise most needed by a particular patient (McDaniel & Campbell, 1996). While it is held out as a goal by many health professionals, collaboration is often not a reality. The next section describes the specific barriers to collaboration encountered by those on the genetic health care team.

Barriers to Collaboration

All team members share a desire to help the patient and family deal with any genetically related health concerns. But team members have different professional training, different goals, different working styles, and different professional cultures (Acheson, 2003; McDaniel et al., 2005; Suther & Goodson, 2003).

For example, some collaborative efforts have encountered a cultural chasm between primary care clinicians and genetic specialists. Primary care clinicians typically have a longitudinal relationship with patients, understanding their psychosocial context as well as their health history, seeing them through many different kinds of diseases and problems, and referring them to specialists when the problem requires another level of care. They tend to manage ambiguity by being pragmatic in style, relational in orientation, and somewhat critical of applying specialty-based screening recommendations and diagnostic tests. Genetic specialists, on the other hand, see patients at a specific point in time for a focused problem related to a potential or actual genetic condition. They are experts on genetics and knowledgeable about the latest scientific and technological advances in their particular specialty. They believe diagnosis and information are intrinsically valuable to families coping with multiple levels of uncertainty and can lead to prevention or treatment in ways that are sometimes unforeseen. While their focus is specific and concrete, they do manage the ambiguity of the fact that testing for multifactorial genomic conditions only provides information about risk and is not predictive and that the diagnoses of single-gene testing do not provide information about how and when a disease might emerge.

To stereotype, genetic specialists would like primary care clinicians to do a better job of identifying genomic conditions and referring these families for expert genetic counseling and diagnosis. Primary care clinicians, on the other hand, would like genetic specialists to recognize that currently, genetics has a limited role in clinical care for most common illnesses, and the task of identifying the minority of patients for whom genetic assessment is indicated competes with many other clinical demands. Primary care clinicians usually do not want to suggest testing unless there are treatment options to help prevent onset or alter the disease course or outcomes (see Chapter 2). They emphasize that screening should be evidence-based, although the evidence is difficult to accumulate for rare genetic conditions (Burke et al., 2002). They also may face difficulty referring patients who fear discrimination or do not have the financial resources to seek care by genetic specialists. In addition, the nondirective model of traditional prenatal genetic counseling contrasts with the medical or shared decision-making models familiar in primary care and other medical specialties. However, as genomics expands into the realm of preventive care, geneticists and other clinicians are finding common ground by exploring situations in which the shared decision-making model makes sense for both disciplines (Burke et al., 2002; Emery, 2001; Kessler, 1997; Martin & Wilikovsky, 2004).

Mental health professionals have their own culture that is distinct from that of primary care clinicians and genetic specialists. Their goal is not usually to identify a genetic condition, but rather to focus on the patient's and family's experience of the problem, to help with decision making, difficult family communication, and the emotional responses to an actual or potential genetic condition. Family-oriented mental health professionals play an important role in helping with genetic conditions that have an inevitable effect on other family members. These family therapists (whether trained as psychologists, psychiatrists, social workers, pastoral counselors, or marriage and family therapists) may see patients before, during, and after a genetic condition is identified. They may complement the psychosocial aspects of work done by the primary care clinician or the genetic counselor, providing more time and expertise in helping with psychological and interpersonal aspects of coping with a genetic condition. Family therapists are likely to have a process-oriented, facilitative style that contrasts with the action-oriented, precise style of the primary care clinician. Some may be suspicious of biologically based new technologies and unaware of recent genetic advances. However, most are interested in a collaborative model of practice.

While there is much overlap, these differences illustrate why patients managing genetic conditions benefit from a multidisciplinary team approach. The challenge lies in the professionals understanding each other's training, goals, language, and working styles, so that communication is effective. Systems of communication—whether phone, letter, or electronic—must be clear and consistent. Primary care clinicians, specialists, and subspecialists tend to have regular contact in making and responding to referrals. Mental health professionals may not reliably communicate in this, sometimes believing that communication with other professionals is a breach of patient confidentiality. (This problem is easily dispensed with by asking for permission from the patient and family to communicate with the team as part of their coordinated treatment.) Communication can be difficult for reasons other than differing cultures and working styles. Rural practice and geographic distance create barriers to easy access to genetic specialists, requiring extra effort by primary care clinicians to communicate with genetic experts (Acheson, Stange, & Zyzanski, 2001).

Interprofessional Education and Training

Many of these barriers can be surmounted by interprofessional education and training at all levels, from beginning students to professional continuing education, from lectures and seminars to shared clinical practice. Health care and public health professional disciplines are recognizing that the new era of genetics and genomics has yielded screening, testing, and treatments that require interdisciplinary collaboration and education (Expert Panel Report on Genetics and Nursing, 2000; Jenkins et al., 2001; Lea, Feetham, & Monsen, 2002). Drawing from curricula on interprofessional collaboration (Frank, McDaniel, Bray, & Heldring, 2004; McDaniel & Campbell, 1996, 1998; McDaniel et al., 2005; National Coalition for Health Professional Education in Genetics [NCHPEG], 2004 and 2005), the following are collaborative skills important for the genetic health care team:

- To learn each other's role and professional culture
- To learn preferred modes of communication—the referral letter, the chart note, the phone call, in-person communication
- To learn to complement and rely on each other appropriately
- To learn to develop an integrated treatment plan

Significant leadership in this regard is provided by the National Coalition for Health Professional Education in Genetics (NCHPEG). NCHPEG is an organization of organizations, committed to a national effort in the United States to promote health professional education and access to information about advances in human genetics. NCHPEG members are an interdisciplinary group of leaders from more than 140 diverse health professional organizations, consumer and volunteer groups, government agencies, private industry, managed care organizations, and genetics professional societies.

The mission of NCHPEG is to promote health professional education and access to information about advances in human genetics to improve health care. NCHPEG is an important resource with goals to integrate genetics content into the knowledge base of health care professionals and students of the health professions, develop educational tools and information resources to facilitate the integration of genetics into health professional practice, and strengthen and expand the coalition's interdisciplinary community of organizations and individuals committed to coordinated genetics education for health professionals. NCHPEG work has been funded by federal agencies (the Department of Energy, the National Institutes of Health, the Health Resources and Services Administration, and the Office of Rare Diseases) and grants from nonprofit organizations (such as the Robert Wood Johnson Foundation and the Josiah Macy Jr Foundation).

Significant NCHPEG contributions include establishing competencies in genetics essential for all health professionals and focusing on the integration of genetics and genomics into practice and education for all health care professionals (Jenkins et al., 2001). A second edition of the core competencies (NCHPEG, 2005) updates the guidance to a broad range of individuals and groups as they plan educational initiatives in genetics and genetically based health care, and includes information about how the competencies have been used by diverse groups since their initial publication in 2001.

NCHPEG also has developed core principles of genetics for all health professionals that focus on basic biology related to genetics (NCHPEG, 2004). This document augments the core competencies and provides additional guidance about the content that should constitute basic instruction in genetics for those in health care. Another significant resource for all health professionals is Genetics Resources on the Web (GROW, http://www.geneticsresources.org/). The GROW goal is to optimize the use of the Web to provide health professionals and the public with high-quality information related to human genetics, with a particular focus on genetic medicine and health. Of importance is that sites found through GROW are reviewed for accuracy of information.

As reported in Chapter 1, further evidence of the recognition of the need for interdisciplinary education and collaboration is the U.S. Department of Health and Human Services' Family History Initiative (http://www.hhs.gov/familyhistory/). While this initiative to increase awareness of the significance of a person's family history is directed to the public, information regarding the initiative has been developed and disseminated to all health care and public health professionals in the

United States. Through printable forms from http://www.hhs.gov/ familyhistory, the intent is that individuals and their families may complete the profile and bring their questions to their primary care clinician (Guttmacher et al., 2004).

True interprofessional collaboration will require changing the health care infrastructure and policy stances over time. Issues such as equitable billing and reimbursement, widespread access to high-quality genetics services, building societal consensus on personally and politically sensitive issues, and protection of privacy while maintaining family medical information all need to be addressed.

A professional health care team is to the individual practitioner as a family is to the patient. In addition to complementary skills, it can provide feedback and support in caring for patients and families coping with challenging genetic conditions. Like a family, it can function well or poorly, depending on members' ability to respect each other's roles, communicate effectively, problem solve, and cope with inevitable stress. Too often, clinicians function in isolation from each other, leaving patients and families to carry information back and forth between providers and resolve differences of opinion on their own. A focus on interprofessional teams as part of health professional education and advances in the technology of communication (such as electronic medical records) may help clinicians participate in and benefit from a collaborative approach to caring for patients and families with genetic conditions.

NOTES

1. The case reported here is an amalgam of actual cases, camouflaged to protect the confidentiality of the families involved.

2. The umbrella organization that represents all genetic disorder support groups is the Genetic Alliance (www.geneticalliance.org).

REFERENCES

Acheson, L. S. (2003). Fostering applications of genetics in primary care: What will it take? *Genetics in Medicine, 5*, 63–65.

Acheson, L. S., Stange, K. C., & Zyzanski, S. J. (2001). What genetic issues do family physicians encounter? Abstract 1539. *American Journal of Human Genetics, 69*(4 Suppl.), 445.

Acheson, L., & Wiesner, G. (2004). Current and future applications of genetics in primary care medicine. *Primary Care Clinics in Office Practice, 31*, 449–460.

Acheson, L. S., Wiesner, G. L., Zyzanski, S. J., Goodwin, M. A., & Stange, K. C. (2000). Family history-taking in community family practice: Implications for genetic screening. *Genetics in Medicine, 2*, 180–185.

American Academy of Pediatrics Committee of Bioethics. (2001). Ethical issues with genetic testing in pediatrics. *Pediatrics, 107,* 1451–1455.

American Board of Genetic Counseling. (1996). *Requirements for raduate programs in genetic counseling seeking accreditation by the ABGC.* Bethesda, MD: Author.

American Board of Genetic Counseling. (2003). *Required criteria for graduate programs in genetic counseling seeking accreditation by the American Board of Genetic Counseling.* Retrieved from http://www.abgc.net/genetics/abgc/accred/acc-03/acc-01.htm

American Society of Clinical Oncology. (2003). American Society of Clinical Oncology policy statement update: Genetic testing for cancer susceptibility. *Journal of Clinical Oncology 21,* 2397–2406.

American Society of Human Genetics Ad Hoc Committee on Genetic Counseling. (1975). Genetic counseling. *American Journal of Human Genetics, 27,* 240–242.

American Society of Human Genetics Board of Directors and the American College of Medical Genetics Board of Directors. (1995). Ethical, legal, and psychosocial implications of genetic testing in children and adolescents. *American Journal of Human Genetics, 57,* 1233–1241.

Anderson, R. R. (2002). *Religious traditions and prenatal genetic counseling.* Omaha: Munroe-Meyer Institute, University of Nebraska Medical Center.

Baumiller, R. C., Fletcher, J., & Madden, L. (1988). *A workbook for pastoral care of individuals and families with special needs.* Washington, DC: National Center for Education in Maternal and Child Health, Department of Health and Human Services.

Bennett, R. L., Allain, D., Baker, D., Callanan, N., LeRoy, B., & Walker, A. P. (2004, March 6). *Genetic counselor training programs in the United States, capacities and needs: A report of the National Society of Genetic Counselors.* Abstract 31. American College of Medical Genetics Annual Clinical Meeting, Kissimee, FL.

Bennett, R. L., Steinhaus, K. A., Uhrich, S. B., et al. (1995). Recommendations for standardized human pedigree nomenclature. *American Journal of Human Genetics, 56*(3), 745–752.

Burke, W., Acheson, L., Botkin, J., Bridges, K., Davis, A., Evans, J., et al. (2002). Genetics in primary care: A USA faculty development initiative. *Community Genetics, 5,* 138–146.

Burke, W., Atkins, D., Gwinn, M., Guttmacher, A., Haddow, J., Lau, J., et al. (2002). Genetic test evaluation: Information needs of clinicians, policy makers, and the public. *American Journal of Epidemiology, 156,* 311–318.

Carter, B., & McGoldrick, M. (1998). *The expanded family life cycle: Individual, family and social perspectives* (3rd ed.). Boston: Allyn and Bacon.

Cassidy, S. B., & Allanson, J. E. (2005). *Management of genetic syndromes* (2nd ed.). Hoboken, NJ: Wiley-Liss.

Clinical Laboratory Improvement Amendments of 1988, Public Law 100-578, 42 USC 263a et seq. (1992). *Federal Register, 57*(40), 7001–7288.

Daly, M., Farmer, J., Harrop-Stein, C., Montgomery, S., Itzen, M., Costalas, J. W., et al. (1999). Exploring family relationships in cancer risk counseling using the genogram. *Cancer Epidemiology, Biomarkers and Prevention, 8,* 393–398.

Emery, A. E. H., Rimoin, D. L., Connor, J. M., & Pyeritz, R. E. (Eds.). (1997). *Principles and practice of medical genetics* (Vols. 1 & 2, 3rd ed.). New York: Churchill Livingston.

Emery, J. (2001). Is informed choice in genetic testing a different breed of informed decision making? A discussion paper. *Health Expectations, 4*, 81–86.

Emery, J., & Hayflick, S. (2001). The challenge of integrating genetic medicine into primary care. *British Medical Journal, 322*, 1027–1030.

Emery, J., Watson, E., Rose, P., & Andermann, A. (1999). A systematic review of the literature exploring the role of primary care in genetic services. *Family Practice, 16*, 426–445.

Evans, J. P., Skrzynia, C., & Burke, W. (2001). The complexities of predictive genetic testing. *British Medical Journal, 322*, 1052–1056.

Expert Panel Report on Genetics and Nursing. (2000). *Implications for education and practice*. BHP00177. Washington, DC: Health Resources and Services Administration.

Falk, M., & Robin, N. H. (2004). The primary care physician's approach to congenital anomalies. *Primary Care Clinics in Office Practice, 31*, 605–619.

Fletcher, J. C. (1983). Genetic decision making and pastoral care: Clergy involvement. Relating practice to principle. *Hospital Practice, 18*(4), 38K–38L, 38P.

Frank, R., McDaniel, S., Bray, J., & Helding, H. (2004). *Primary care psychology*. Washington, DC: American Psychological Association Publications.

Gorlin, R. J., Cohen, M. M., & Levin, L. S. (1990). *Oxford monographs on medical genetics, no. 19: Syndromes of the head and neck* (3rd ed.). New York: Oxford University Press.

Guttmacher, A. E., Collins, F. S., & Carmona, R. H. (2004). The family history— more important than ever. *New England Journal of Medicine, 351*, 2333–2336.

Hayflick, S. J., & Eiff, M. P. (1998). Role of primary care providers in the delivery of genetics services. *Community Genetics, 1*, 18–22.

Jenkins, J., Blitzer, M., Boehm, K., Feetham, S., Gettig, B., Johnson, A., et al. (2001). Recommendations of core competencies in genetics essential for all health professionals. *Genetics in Medicine, 3*(2), 155–158.

Jones, K. L. (Ed.). (1997). *Smith's recognizable patterns of human malformations* (5th ed.). Philadelphia: Saunders.

Jorde, L. B., Carey, J. C., Bamshad, M. J., & White, R. L. (2003). *Medical genetics* (3rd ed.). St. Louis, MO: Mosby.

Kessler, S. (1997). Psychological aspects of genetic counseling: XI. Nondirectiveness revisited. *American Journal of Medical Genetics, 72*, 164–171.

Lea, D. H., Feetham, S. L., & Monsen, R. B. (2002). Genomic-based health care in nursing: A bidirectional approach to bringing genetics into nursing's body of knowledge. *Genetics in Medicine, 3*(2), 155–158.

Lerman, C., Croyle, R., Tercyak, K., & Hamann, H. (2002). Genetic testing: Psychological aspects and implications. *Journal of Consulting and Clinical Psychology, 70*, 784–797.

Like, R. C., Rogers, J., & McGoldrick, M. (1988). Reading and interpreting genograms: A systematic approach. *Journal of Family Practice, 26*, 407–412.

Markel, D. S., & Yashar, B. M. (2004). The interface between the practice of medical genetics and human genetic research: What every genetic counselor needs to know. *Journal of Genetic Counseling, 13*(5), 351–368.

Martin, J. R., & Wilikovsky, A. S. (2004). Genetic counseling in primary care: Longitudinal, psychosocial issues in genetic diagnosis and counseling. *Primary Care Clinics in Office Practice, 31,* 509–524.

McCandless, S. E. (2004). A primer on expanded newborn screening by tandem mass spectrometry. *Primary Care Clinics in Office Practice, 31,* 583–604.

McDaniel, S. H. (2005). The psychotherapy of genetics. *Family Process, 44,* 25–44.

McDaniel, S. H. (2006). Does DNA determine destiny? A role for medical family therapy with genetic screening for breast cancer and other genetic illnesses. In D. R. Crane & E. S. Marshall (Eds.), *Handbook of families and health: Interdisciplinary perspectives* (pp. 396–406). Thousand Oaks, CA: Sage.

McDaniel, S., & Campbell, T. (1996). Training for collaborative family healthcare. *Families, Systems & Health, 14*(2), 147–150.

McDaniel, S., & Campbell, T. (1997). Training health professionals to collaborate. *Families, Systems & Health, 15*(4), 353–359.

McDaniel, S. H., Campbell, T. L., Hepworth, J., & Lorenz, A. (2005). Genetic screening, testing, and families. *Family-oriented primary care* (2nd ed.). New York: Springer-Verlag.

McGoldrick, M., Gerson, R., & Shellenberger, S. (1999). Genogram applications in family practice. *Genograms: Assessment and intervention* (2nd ed.). New York: Norton.

Medalie, J. H., Zyzanski, S. J., Langa, D., & Stange, K. C. (1998). The family in family practice: Is it a reality? *Journal of Family Practice, 46,* 390–396.

National Coalition for Health Professional Education in Genetics. (2004 and 2005). *NCHPEG principles of genetics for health professionals.* Retrieved from http://www.nchpeg.org/eduresources/core/coreprinciples.pdf

National Society of Genetic Counselors. (1995). Position statement. Retrieved from www.nsgc.org/bout/position.asp#adultonsetdis

National Society of Genetic Counselors. (2006). Master's level genetic counseling training programs. Retrieved from http://www.nsgc.org/Training Program.asp

Petty, E. (1998). The medical genetics evaluation. In D. L. Baker, J. L. Schuette, & W. R. Uhlmann (Eds.), *Genetic counseling* (pp. 75–98). New York: Wiley-Liss.

Rich, E., Burke, W., Heaton, C., Haga, S., Pinsky, L., Short, M. P., et al. (2004). Reconsidering the family history in primary care. *Journal of General Internal Medicine, 19,* 273–280.

Rogers, J. C. (1994). Can physicians use family genogram information to identify patients at risk of anxiety or depression? *Archives of Family Medicine, 3,* 1093–1098.

Rogers, J. C., Rohrbaugh, M., McGoldrick, M. (1992). Can experts predict health risk from family genograms? *Family Medicine, 24,* 209–215.

Rolland, J., & Williams, J. (2005). Toward a biopsychosocial model for 21st century genetics. *Family Process, 44,* 3–24.

Scriver, C. R., Beaudet, A. L., Sly, W. S., & Balle, D. (Eds.). (2001). *The metabolic and molecular bases of inherited disease* (Vols. 1–4, 8th ed.). New York: McGraw-Hill.

Speice, J., McDaniel, S. H., Rowley, P., & Loader, S. (2002). Family-oriented psychoeducation group for women found to have a BRCA mutation. *Clinical Genetics, 62,* 121–127.

Star/Rosen Public Relations. (2004). NSGC video press release. Retrieved from www.nsgc.org/video.asp

Suther, S., & Goodson, P. (2003). Barriers to the provision of genetic services by primary care physicians: A systematic review of the literature. *Genetic Medicine, 5,* 70–76.

Tyler, C., & Edman, J. (2004). Down syndrome, Turner syndrome, and Klinefelter syndrome: Primary care throughout the lifespan. *Primary Care Clinics in Office Practice, 31,* 627–648.

Walker, A. P. (1998). The practice of genetic counseling. In D. L. Baker, J. Schuette, & W. R. Uhlmann (Eds.), *A guide to genetic counseling* (pp. 1–26). New York: Wiley-Liss.

Walter, F., Emery, J., Braithwaite, D., & Marteau, T. (2004). Lay understanding of familial risk of common, chronic diseases: A systematic review and synthesis of qualitative research. *Annals of Family Medicine, 3,* 583–594.

Weil, J. (2000). *Psychosocial genetic counseling.* Oxford, UK: Oxford University Press.

Whelan, A., Ball, S., Best, L., Best, R. G., Echiverri, S. C., Ganschow, P., et al. (2004). Genetic red flags: Clues to thinking genetically in primary care practice. *Primary Care Clinics in Office Practice, 31,* 497–508.

Worthen, H. G. (1999). Inherited cancer and the primary care physician: Barriers and strategies. *Cancer, 86,* 2583–2588.

Index